THE web server BOOK

Tools & Techniques for Building
Your Own Internet Information Site

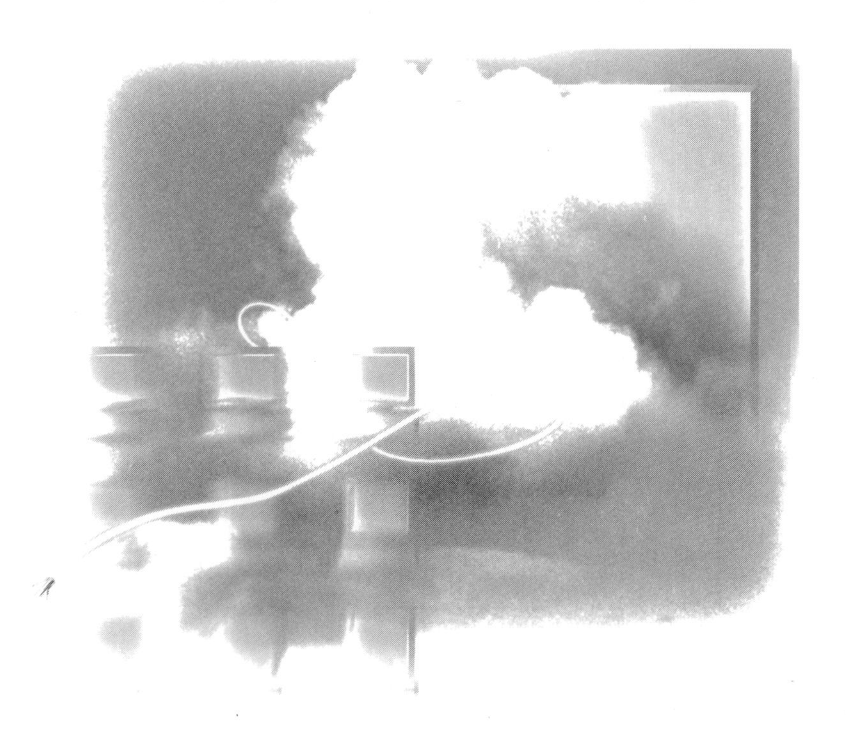

THE web server BOOK

Tools & Techniques for Building
Your Own Internet Information Site

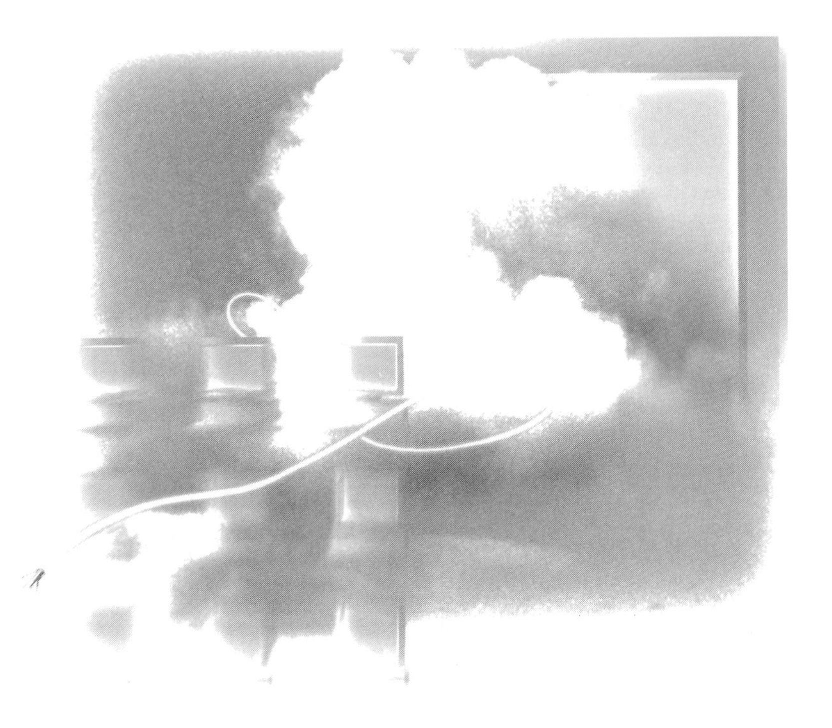

Jonathan Magid
R. Douglas Matthews
& Paul Jones

Library of Congress Cataloging-in-Publication Data
Jones, Paul. 1950-
The web server book : tools & techniques for building your own Internet information site / Paul Jones, Jonathan Magid & R. Douglas Matthews. -- 1st ed.
p. cm.
Includes bibliographical references and index.
ISBN 1-56604-234-8
1. World Wide Web (Information retrieval system) I. Magid, Jonathan. II. Matthews, R. Douglas. III. Title.
TK5105.888.J66 1995
005.75--dc20 95-8560
CIP

Book design: Marcia Webb
Cover design and illustration: Tom Draper Design
Vice President, Ventana Press: Walter R. Bruce III
Art Director: Marcia Webb
Design staff: Dawne Sherman, Brad King
Editorial Manager: Pam Richardson
Editorial staff: Angela Anderson, Jonathan Cato, Beth Snowberger
Developmental Editor: Tim C. Mattson
Project Editor: Jessica Ryan
Copy Editor: Nancy Crumpton
Print Department: Wendy Bernhardt, Dan Koeller
Production Manager: John Cotterman
Production staff: Patrick Berry, Cheri Collins, Jaimie Livingston
Index service: Dianne Bertsch, Answers Plus
Proofreader: Vicky Wells
Technical review: Matthew Saderholm

First Edition 9 8 7 6 5 4 3 2 1
Printed in the United States of America

For information about our audio products, write us at Newbridge Book Clubs, 3000 Cindel Drive, Delran, NJ 08375

Ventana Press, Inc.
P.O. Box 2468
Chapel Hill, NC 27515
919/942-0220
FAX 919/942-1140

Limits of Liability and Disclaimer of Warranty

The authors and publisher of this book have used their best efforts in preparing the book and the programs contained in it. These efforts include the development, research and testing of the theories and programs to determine their effectiveness. The authors and publisher make no warranty of any kind, expressed or implied, with regard to these programs or the documentation contained in this book.

The authors and publisher shall not be liable in the event of incidental or consequential damages in connection with, or arising out of, the furnishing, performance or use of the programs, associated instructions and/or claims of productivity gains.

Trademarks

About the Authors

Jonathan Magid has been the system administrator and a programmer for the SunSITE project at the University of North Carolina at Chapel Hill since the project's start in 1992. He is currently working on his undergraduate degree in American History and on an Honors project in poetry. He is the author of several articles about the Internet and UNIX, as well as several utilities for administrating information systems.

R. Douglas Matthews is an undergraduate at the University of North Carolina at Chapel Hill, majoring in Anthropology and Religious Studies. He has worked at SunSITE since January 1994, in WAIS, Gopher and World Wide Web development. He is involved in a Web presence provider company, Netit.com, and also teaches HTML authoring and design classes.

Paul Jones is a lecturer in the School of Journalism and Mass Communication and in the School of Information and Library Science at the University of North Carolina at Chapel Hill. He has managed SunSITE.unc.edu since its beginning in 1992.

Jones holds a BS in Computer Science from North Carolina State University and an MFA in Poetry from Warren-Wilson College. His articles and poems have appeared in over 50 literary journals including *Southern Review, Poetry, Southern Humanities Review*, and *Ironwood*. His award winning chapbook, *What the Welsh and Chinese Have In Common*, was republished in HTML after the initial publication sold out. The book can be found at http://sunsite.unc.edu/pjones/poetry/.

Acknowledgments

First and foremost, all of the authors owe David McConville a great deal of thanks. David wrote Chapter 8, "True Multimedia," in its entirety, and the sections of Chapter 13, "Future Directions" covering Virtual Reality Modeling Language and Teleconferencing. David should be seen as a full coauthor of this book, and as a very close friend to all of us. Thanks also to Chris Colomb, for his important contributions to Chapter 3, "Setting Up the Server." Chris's knowledge and expertise was invaluable in completing this chapter.

Even though he is a coauthor of this book, Paul Jones deserves thanks for work outside of writing the book itself. Paul started the SunSITE project in 1992, making all of our experiences possible and creating an environment in which an incredible amount of learning and development goes on. In a very basic way, this book could never have happened without him.

I'd like to thank Walt Bruce and Dykki Settle for suggesting that we write a book to share what we've learned while doing Web development for SunSITE. Credit also goes to my editor, Jessica Ryan, for her calm and cool in the final days, as the book continued to grow.

I'd also like to thank all the people who have worked on and with SunSITE over the years; this is your book too. Special thanks to Simon Spero for explaining the bits that didn't quite fit and for contributing a script. I'd also like to thank the developers who write the free software on which the Internet depends. Matt Welsh generously contributed the material that went into the Linux Appendices. The entire Linux and GNU community is responsible for Slackware, but Patrick Volkerding brought it all together.

Finally, I'd like to thank my family and friends for supporting me, no matter how long I spent in front of the computer. And most thanks to my favorite girl, Merry, who kept me sane.

—Jonathan Magid

Thanks to my father, to whom I am indebted for anything I have ever done or will do in the future. He has loved, taught and helped me without limits. Thanks also to Jason, Mark, Radha and especially Mary Beth—my closest friends who have supported, encouraged, challenged, helped, and most important, been patient with me.

—R. Douglas Matthews

My contribution to this book would not have been possible without the enthusiasm and imagination of all those who have worked on the UNC SunSITE project since its beginning, including Tom Snee, Darlene Fladager, Dykki Settle, Eric (Max) Leach, Terry Mancour, Beth (Icky) Lyons, Robert (Pyro) Ingram, Kevin Gamiel, Gwenn Conner, Nassib Nassir, Doug Norton, Luke Duncan, Nash Foster, Marcus Cox, Cheryl Friedman, Qin Fang, Glenn Lewis, Ahmet Taylor, Kelly Boley, Jim Fullton and most especially Judd Knott as well as the other authors of and contributors to this book, Jonathan Magid, Doug Matthews, David McConville and Chris Colomb. Life as I know it would not be possible without the support and love of Sally Greene and Tucker Jones.

—Paul Jones

Contents

Section II: Adding Content

Section III: Adding Interactivity

Section IV: Final Considerations

Section V: Appendices

Introduction

The World Wide Web has emerged as *the* hottest new information technology. This vast network of hyperlinked multimedia resources spans the globe, bringing information and entertainment to a growing population of users. With this book, you can be a part of it!

You have in your hands everything you need to use the Internet as your very own printing press. The Companion CD-ROM includes all the software you need to create a Web server on your UNIX workstation, as well as on Linux, a multitasking, UNIX-compatible operating system.

The Web Server Book will teach you how to use these tools to create a secure and professional-looking presence on the Web, including these secrets of Web-wizardry:

- How Web servers work.
- How to include sharp inline images in your Web pages.
- How to create clickable imagemaps.
- How to create interactive forms and how to write CGI scripts.
- How to embed audio and animation in your pages.

This Isn't "Just Another Internet Book"

Two years ago, the Internet didn't exist as far as the popular media was concerned. There were no books or articles detailing its wonders, nor were there slick TV spots tempting us with a networked utopia. Research universities and high-tech companies had almost exclusive access to the Internet. Even if you knew that you wanted to be wired, it was almost impossible for an individual or small organization to get access.

Today, dozens of Internet books crowd the shelves, and more that 250 Internet Service Providers (ISPs) are in the United States alone. A tremendous amount of material about the Internet is out there, and its quality ranges from carefully edited tour guides to mere conglomerations of network FAQs and text files.

Still, all these sources have one thing in common: they want to bring you, as a consumer, to this vast amount of information. What they don't do is tell you how to add to it. These guides seem to suggest that only Network Experts can run a server, and they leave you feeling that the Internet is merely a library to be searched by the patient reader.

The Internet is much more than this. It's a platform for the communication and distribution of information. Everyone has something to say or to show; it may be as personal as a photo from a vacation or as important as a business catalog, but the impulse to communicate is a basic part of human nature. This book will show you how to transform that impulse into an Internet server: your own home on the World Wide Web.

Hardware & Software Requirements

This book assumes you have a computer that runs UNIX and has a direct Internet connection. You can also use the tools and skills in this book to serve Web documents to an internal network, or off space leased on someone else's server, but if you want to run your own Internet server, you'll need

- A UNIX workstation with 32mb RAM and 1gb hard drive *or* a 486/33 with 16mb RAM and 500mb hard drive (minimum).
- A SVGA monitor, if you want to work with images.
- A sound card, if you want to work with audio (check Appendix C for Linux compatibility).
- A CD-ROM drive (check Appendix C for Linux compatibility).
- A full-time, direct Internet connection.

The process of finding an Internet service provider can be complex, and it's beyond the scope of this book. We recommend you investigate the options by talking to your local network providers. You can use your WWW client to look at this list of companies that provide Internet connectivity at http://www.yahoo.com/Business/Corporations/Internet_Access_Providers/.

After you get an Internet connection, you'll need a computer running UNIX. If you don't already have a UNIX workstation, you can use your 486 or 586 PC clone to run Linux, a free UNIX-compatible operating system. Read Appendix D, "Installing Linux," to learn how to install and configure Slackware, a popular Linux distribution.

The text of this book assumes that you have a basic understanding of UNIX, although you don't have to be a UNIX guru. If you're not familiar with UNIX, read an introductory UNIX book, such as Ventana's *Voodoo UNIX*, by Charlie Russel and Sharon Crawford. *Running Linux*, by Matt Welsh and Lar Kaufman, is an excellent introduction for Linux users.

The CD-ROM included with this book contains the source code for all the programs discussed. In addition, for most of the programs, the CD-ROM includes precompiled distributions for AIX, Iris, OSF/1, Solaris, SunOS, Linux and Ultrix. For a few of the programs discussed, precompiled distributions are not provided on the CD-ROM, but are available from the *Web Server Book Online Companion.*

What's Inside

Chapter 1, "What Is the Web," provides a brief overview of hypertext and how it's used in the World Wide Web. It explains the relationship between Web servers, browsers and URLs. This chapter also shows you the newsgroups and mailing lists you can use to keep up with the ever-changing Web.

Chapter 2, "The Basic Pieces," briefly describes the various technologies that go into the Web. It discusses the file formats that are common on the Internet, and how the Web uses MIME types to deal with them intelligently. The chapter ends with an introduction to HTML, the HyperText Markup Language, and tkHTML, a WYSIWYG HTML editor.

Chapter 3, "Setting Up the Server," compares the most popular Web server software and takes you through the process of installing and configuring version 1.4 of the popular NCSA server. For those who can't wait to start serving, it also provides a brief guide to renting space on someone else's server.

Chapter 4, "System Security," provides an introduction to this important subject. You'll learn what security precautions to take in order to minimize the risks inherent in being a pioneer on the Electronic Frontier.

Chapter 5, "Importing Documents to the Web," shows how to convert your documents from several popular word processors and desktop publishing systems to HTML.

Chapter 6, "Checking Your Work," shows you how to use multiple browsers and HTML validation utilities to ensure that your documents will look their best on every browser.

Chapter 7, "Images on the Web," is an extensive look at using graphics effectively on the Web. It covers the commonly used graphics formats and ways to improve the appearance of your inline images. It thoroughly explains advanced topics like transparency, interlacing and clickable imagemaps.

Chapter 8, "True Multimedia: Adding Audio & Animation," gives a useful introduction to employing film and sound clips in your pages. Not only does it describe the various standards, but it also gets you started creating your own multimedia files and making links to them.

Chapter 9, "Searching & Indexing," shows you how to make full-text indexes of your site and other collections of documents with freeWAIS.

Chapter 10, "Simple Forms," reveals the secrets of interactive forms. It thoroughly explains how to write a form in HTML and how to use gform, a generic forms handler, to process the data from it. This chapter also helps you set up a forms gateways for searching WAIS databases.

Chapter 11, "CGI: Advanced Forms for Programmers," covers the more advanced features of the Web. It shows you how to write CGI scripts to process forms, generate HTML on the fly, and create gateways to other Internet services.

Chapter 12, "Fitting in: Joining the Virtual Community," describes how to attract people to your server and how to keep them coming back.

Chapter 13, "Future Directions," explains the newest technologies that are shaping the future of the World Wide Web. It covers the new features of HTML version 3.0, VRML, the Virtual Reality Modeling Language, as well as real-time conferencing, HTTP-NG, electronic commerce, and other emerging Internet technologies.

Appendix A, "About the Online Companion," describes this informative tool as well as its most valuable features—the annotated software library and the Software Archive.

Appendix B, "About the Companion CD-ROM," describes the contents of the CD-ROM included with your copy of *The Web Server Book*. The Companion CD-ROM contains all the software you need to create your very own platform for interactive electronic publishing on the Internet. Not only does the CD-ROM include all the Web-related software discussed in-depth in the book, but it also includes the popular Slackware distribution of Linux, a multitasking, UNIX-compatible operating system for 386 or better PC-compatible computers.

Appendix C, "Linux Hardware Compatibility HOWTO," lists most of the hardwares supported by Linux and helps you locate any necessary drivers.

Appendix D, "Installing Linux," demonstrates how to install the Slackware Linux distribution from the CD-ROM.

Appendix E, "The Linux XFree86 HOWTO," describes how to obtain, install and configure version 3.1.1 of the XFree86 version of the X Window System (X11R6) for Linux systems. It is a step-by-step guide to configuring XFree86 on your system.

Appendix F, "Legacy Technologies: FTP & Gopher," shows you how to configure your FTP server to allow anonymous logins, and tells you why we recommend leaving Gopher strictly alone.

Also included is "References," a bibliography of online and printed references.

Command-line Conventions

This is not a book about theory. Instead, it teaches you the dozens of disparate skills you'll need to be a wizardly Webmaster. For this reason, there are many examples that you can type in at the command-line. Here's an example:

```
$ for i in *.html
> do
> echo $i
> grep -i '<TITLE>' $i
> done
```

The first line of the example begins with a dollar sign. You don't need to type the dollar-sign yourself; this is the default command-line prompt of /bin/sh, the Bourne Shell command-line interpreter. Similarly, you don't need to type the greater-than sign; it's printed by the shell when it expects more input from the keyboard to finish the command.

When a command-line is too long for a single line, you can continue it onto additional lines by appending a backslash:

```
# ls -l *.html | awk '{ size += $5 }; \
> END { print size }'
```

Once you've completed the line, the shell executes the commands.

You should note that this example printed a pound sign (also called a hash mark) for the prompt—this signifies that the command should typed in as root, or superuser.

All of the examples in this book assume you use the Bourne shell, or a shell that is backwards compatible with it, such as GNU's bash (the Bourne Again Shell), or the KornShell. I use the Bourne shell for the examples because it has a clean, unambiguous syntax, and it's available on every UNIX machine.

If you use a non-compatible shell, like the C shell, you'll either need to change to Bourne or translate the examples. None of the little shell scripts in this book are very complex, so it wouldn't be difficult. For example, the first example might look like this in C shell:

```
% foreach i (*.html)
? echo $i
? grep -i '<TITLE>' $i
? end
```

As you can see, they're not very different, and few of the examples in this book are any more complicated than this one.

To Protect & To Serve

After you begin using the Internet for distributing information, you may never want to go back to traditional media. The advantages become obvious:

- You can reach millions of people, both down the street and on the other side of the world.
- You can make updates and corrections immediately, which allows you to develop your material incrementally, making small changes without the overhead of reprinting.
- Most people use computers to compose their copy in the first place, so importing these documents to the Web is simple and convenient.
- Providing information on the Net is a two-way street. Messages don't flow only one way as they do with traditional media, but go back and forth between the client and server. This interactivity can provide the basis for dialogue between author and reader.

Companies can use this interaction to realistically evaluate the effectiveness of their advertising. Organizations and governments can use it to form virtual communities of people with similar interests and concerns. The Internet is more than a channel for reaching new audiences; it's also an opportunity to swap advice and opinions and to discover new friends and colleagues.

Of course, to discover the benefits of running a Web server you have to take the plunge and start serving. Chapter 1, "What Is the Web," is an introduction to the concept of hypertext and how it works in the World Wide Web. If you're a long-time veteran of the Web, you can skip ahead to Chapter 2, "The Basic Pieces," which explains the basic technologies that make the Web work.

SECTION I

Gathering the Pieces

1

What Is the Web?

The World Wide Web is a collection (now a massive collection) of clients and servers that support the WWW protocol, HTTP, on the Internet. At this very moment, more servers and clients all over the world are being put into use on the Web. Every online service is providing or has announced that they will soon provide WWW access. This chapter gives you a brief overview of the concepts of clients, servers and protocols used to create the World Wide Web. In the process, we will learn about the history and development of the WWW, as well as where to go to keep current.

Clients & Servers

Client, server and protocol are very simple concepts. It's harder to describe them than it is to understand them. Figure 1-1 tells it all—two ovals connected by a double-ended arrow.

A client is a program that wants something. A server is a program that provides something. A client can request things from many different servers. A server can provide things to many different clients. In general, a client usually initiates a conversation or session with a server. A server is usually an automatic program that waits for client requests. A client is usually acting at the request of a single user or at the request of a program acting as if it were a person. A protocol is the definition of the ways that clients may make requests of servers and of how servers should be expected to answer those requests. In this book, a WWW client is also called a browser.

Figure 1-1: *A simple client-server diagram.*

Common World Wide Web clients include Mosaic, Netscape and Lynx. The common servers come from CERN, NCSA and Netscape. If you have used the Web, you are already on your way to understanding the concepts of client, server and protocol. Let's take a look at the specific jobs of client and server on the Web.

On the Web, it is the client's job to

- Help you form a request (which is usually initiated when you click on a link).
- Send your request to a server.
- Inform you of the status of your request.
- Present the results of your request by properly decoding inline images, rendering HTML documents and transferring various files to their proper viewers.

A viewer is a program that can be called by your WWW client to present certain kinds of files. For example, Acrobat files are not presented by your WWW client, but by an Acrobat viewer. Sound files might be "viewed" by a program such as SoundMachine on a Macintosh when a sound file is referenced and downloaded by your WWW client.

In general, WWW clients can also make requests of servers other than Web servers including Gopher, FTP, news and mail.

As illustrated in Figure 1-2, a Web server's job is to

- Receive requests.
- Validate requests, including security screening.
- Retrieve and properly form data in response to requests, which includes pre- and post-processing of the data by means of CGI scripts and programs and marking files with the proper MIME type.
- Deliver information to the requesting client.

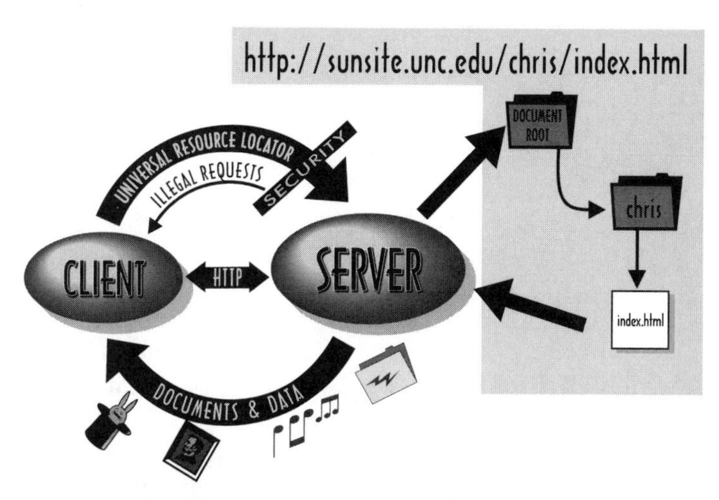

Figure 1-2: *Server tasks.*

The Web is said to have a "stateless" protocol because the server immediately forgets about the interaction after it delivers the response to the client. In a stateful protocol, the client and server would remember a good bit of information about each other and their various requests and responses.

The Web is an easily implemented protocol because a stateless protocol is light (not much essential code or resources are required). Another appealing feature of stateless protocols is that you can move quickly and easily from server to server (at the client side) or from client to client (on the server side) without much cleanup or tracking. This ability to move quickly is ideal for hypertext. (See the section on hypertext later in this same chapter for a definition of hypertext).

However, attempting to transact business in a stateless environment is pretty complex and has so far been implemented in some fairly tricky ways as protocol workarounds. Much of the arcane programming that has occurred on the Web has been in an attempt to impose state on the stateless protocol.

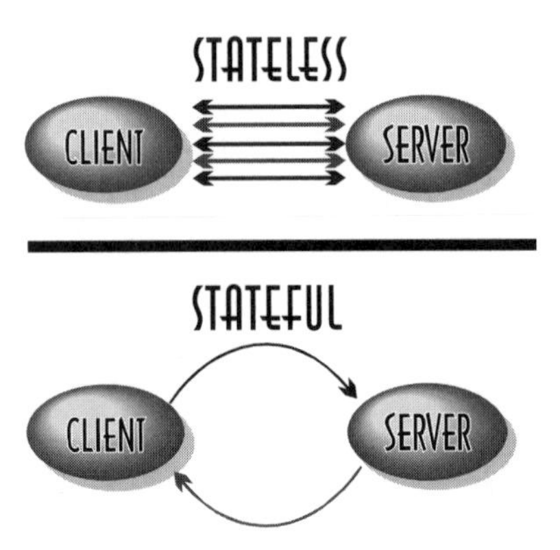

Figure 1-3: *Stateless and stateful relationships.*

The Internet and whatever is emerging from it are extremely widely distributed networks that support standard or, at least interoperable, protocols and allow for that interoperability to take place even across commercial and national domains. That is to say that no one owns the Internet or the TCP/IP protocol or the WWW. Different companies in different countries can and do create clients and servers independently, and the resulting products work together on the Web seamlessly—most of the time.

The great advantage of this approach is that the development field is fairly open, if not completely so. This means that a group of undergraduate computer science majors can create a product and, eventually, a company that competes with products designed by software engineers from the world's largest computer companies, and the product of the undergrads can win on its own merits. The use of protocols, clients and servers is also competitive and reasonably priced. This means that you may become a publisher with only a small investment, and you may compete with some of the world's largest publishers and make your product accessible to millions of people all over the world. Granted, you will have to be creative in your design, content, presentation and advertising, but the point is that for the moment, there is a new concept of freedom of the press. And finally, you can actually afford to own a press yourself.

The Information Server

At first, it sounds so simple, and in some ways, it is. This Christmas 1994 I heard of people dropping out of medical school and out of law school to start companies that would put catalogs on the Web. Oddly, the folks enthusiastically telling me about this were accountants—very careful, very particular accountants who are not often given to excitement. True, with a small investment and good old-fashioned hard work, you have an opportunity to be part of the Web, but you must also be creative.

A successful Web publisher has

- Interesting content.
- Attractive presentation.
- Swift, reliable access.
- A high level of interactivity.
- Reasonable security.
- High entertainment value.
- A dynamic presence.

In short, publishing yet another online catalog of workshirts is not enough. You have to go beyond the limits of print and conventional mail. Luckily, you can. You have the opportunity to be more than a billboard on the Information Highway, and this book will help you.

Other Things To Keep in Mind

First, despite the hype, the Information Highway is more of an Information Railroad. That is, all the tracks on which this information travels are owned by various telephone companies just as the rails on which rail freight is carried are owned and operated (for the largest part) by railroad companies; highways on the other hand are owned and operated by and for the public. When you are paying for your connection to the Internet, you are most likely paying a telephone provider either directly or indirectly. At present, you usually pay a flat rate for your connection to the Internet and your usage of that connection. The flat rate makes it easier to budget and easier to present to your bank, spouse, stockholders, board or other funding sources. But it may not always be this way. You should keep an eye on upcoming legislation regarding the regulation and allowable rates for telephone companies and for Internet service providers. In the upcoming months, even weeks, legislation will effect the price you pay for an Internet connection, the way in which you will be charged and who can supply you with such a connection.

Second, copyright law is in a state of flux, even as we write. No matter how the law changes, it will not be right or legal to publish materials to which others hold the copyright. Still, one of the main questions being asked at the moment is: what constitutes publishing, copying and holding of information in the electronic environment? Remember that in the United States, you pay a hidden royalty for every blank video and audio tape you buy and that royalty is distributed among a group of large copyright holders.

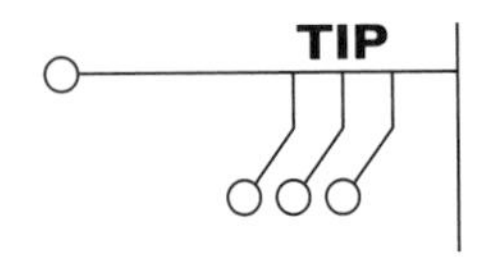

For more current and reliable discussions of copyright on the Internet, see the Coalition for Networked Information's cni-copyright discussion group archives at gopher://gopher.cni.org:70/11/cniftp/forums/cni-copyright.

Third, the content of your server may be subject to some swiftly changing laws. Recently (early March 1995), an extremely ignorant and poorly written bill was floating around the United States Senate. This bill would make server administrators completely responsible for the contents of their servers. Since the laws concerning decency, free speech, libel, privacy and fair use vary from community to community and from country to country, these areas of responsibility are difficult to determine. What's considered decent in San Francisco might not be considered decent in Tokyo, and vice versa. The questions of jurisdiction, even those concerning copyright, remain open.

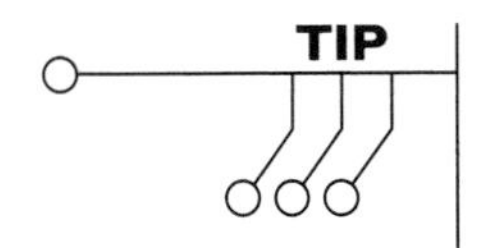

For more information on pending legislative activities in the United States, see the Electronic Frontier Foundation's Action Alerts at http://www.eff.org.

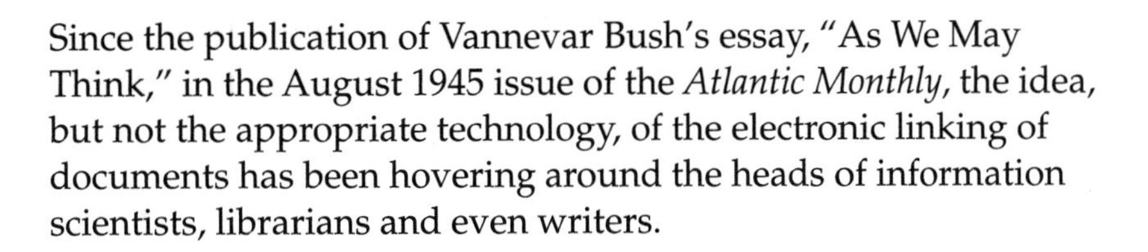

Origins of the World Wide Web

Since the publication of Vannevar Bush's essay, "As We May Think," in the August 1945 issue of the *Atlantic Monthly*, the idea, but not the appropriate technology, of the electronic linking of documents has been hovering around the heads of information scientists, librarians and even writers.

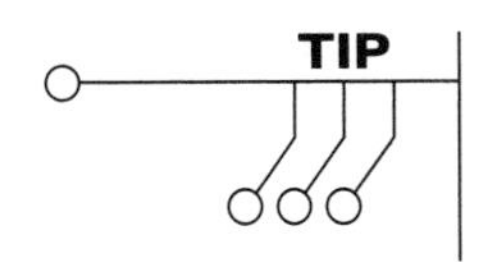

Bush's essay may be found on the WWW at http://www.csi.uottawa.ca/~dduchier/misc/vbush/as-we-may-think.html.

Writers had been anticipating the linkage of ideas long before Bush's article. Aren't footnotes no more than a primitive ink and paper hyperlink to another work? Isn't Ezra Pound's use of brief references and borrowings from other authors a more subtle version of the same thing? T. S. Eliot's "Wasteland," Robert Frost's *New Hampshire: A Poem with Grace Notes* and Vladimir Nabokov's *Pale Fire* are other literary attempts to use what could be easily defined as hypertext in a paper environment. The point is that the need for something like hypertext has been in the air for quite some time.

Yet it was Bush who associated the idea with electronic technology. Bush foresaw that the new technologies that had emerged from the war effort could be applied to expand the way we think. Although his description of the Memex with its odd recording and retrieval devices seems as antiquated as his implicit social views—all scientists are male, all secretaries and clerical help are females—Bush's fundamental idea about how we think as we organize and use information has been the basis for what we today know as the World Wide Web and hypertext.

Hypertext

The term, invented by Ted Nelson in 1965, usually means text that is not constrained to be linear. That is to say that, while parts or even all of a hypertext document may be linear, parts or all of a document may be nonlinear. Hypertext escapes the bounds of linearity by means of links or references to other texts.

Hypermedia, of which hypertext is a limited subset, is media (texts, pictures, sound, video, whatever) that links to other media in a nonlinear fashion. You could think of hypertext as the salvation for those of us with short attention spans, with cluttered desks, who are not reading one book but are about halfway through six at the same time, who consider getting lost when traveling a diversion instead of a frustration. Of course, from a negative viewpoint, you could say that hypertext is a mirror of our more or less disorderly minds, desks and lives.

The first hypertext implementations were by Douglas Engelbart, inventor of the mouse, and by Ted Nelson. Both Nelson's and Engelbart's implementations of hypertext were highly constrained by the 1960s technology and by intricate design assumptions. Both projects were also more visionary than implementable. Nelson, for example, claimed that his project, Xanadu, proposed dealing with all copyright and accounting problems. Because of this robustness, Xanadu, according to Nelson, should be used for putting the entire world's literary corpus online.

In 1987 Jeff Conklin reviewed 18 different hypertext/hypermedia implementations in an IEEE publication. Interestingly enough, only eight allowed concurrent multiple users and of those eight only four allowed graphics and supplied graphical browsers. Few, if any, implementations came close to what we were to have less than four years later.

Xanadu's History

Nelson coined the term *hypertext* in 1965 and named his project, which would implement his vision of distributed hypertext, Xanadu, in 1967. A project Xanadu group was formed in 1979 with design work completed in 1981. But by 1987, Xanadu was still noted for "a crude front end . . . which runs on Sun workstations" (Conklin 1987). In 1988, things were looking up for Nelson and Xanadu when Xanadu was bought by Autodesk and Nelson was hired to continue the project there. By late 1988, the 1981 design was implemented but was quickly put aside in favor of a "MUCH FINER design" (quote from Nelson). By August 1992, Autodesk, having already spent several million dollars on Xanadu, decided to drop the Xanadu project, leaving Nelson to shift for himself. As of this writing, Nelson's project has gone to the Far East and continues development in Australia, and Nelson is in Japan working with the Sapporo HyperLab. Like Samuel Coleridge's poem "Kubla Khan," Xanadu remains incomplete.

For the most current developments regarding Xanadu and Nelson, see http://www.aus.xanadu.com:70/0h/xanadu/.

Tim Berners-Lee, CERN & the World Wide Web

In March 1989 at the European Particle Physics Laboratory, also known as CERN, Tim Berners-Lee proposed a project that would allow scientists to easily browse fellow researchers' papers. A later phase of the proposed project would allow scientists to create new documents on their servers. Tim was strongly influenced by Ted Nelson's self-published *Literary Machines 90.1* (Nelson 1980), but unlike Nelson, he was not at all concerned about the copyright of his materials, the royalties or even tracking the usage as clients moved among servers. However grand the name, the World Wide Web was to be lean and mean. The first phase of Tim's proposed project would require three months to implement and three months for the second phase. Tim wisely noted that the second phase, which might include collaborative authoring, annotations, graphics and the like, should be considered open-ended. The proposed development team consisted of four software engineers and one programmer.

Tim's paper circulated at CERN and, after several rewrites, the project got underway in October 1990. By December 1990, a line-mode browser and a NeXTStep browser were implemented, and access was available to hypertext files, as well as to USENET newsgroups within CERN.

To support his project, Tim proposed a new language be developed for the transport and rendering of hypertext documents. This language was to be a subset of the already proven open language called Standard Generalized Markup Language or SGML. Tim's new language would be known as HyperText Markup Language or HTML.

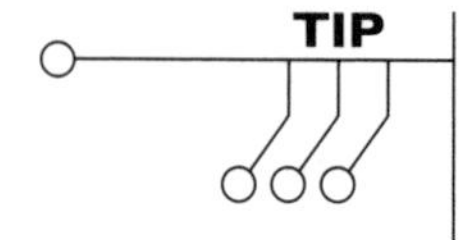

HTML will be briefly covered in the next chapter, "The Basic Pieces."

The protocol for handling HTML and other WWW documents was to be called HyperText Transfer Protocol or HTTP, which follows the Internet tradition of ending almost every protocol name with the letters *TP*. The server then is called a HyperText Transfer Protocol daemon or an HTTPD, which follows the UNIX tradition of ending the name of any independent process with the letter *d* and using that spelling of daemon. This book will deal with HTTP extensively.

HTTP uses a concept called the Uniform Resource Locator or URL (pronounced "you-are-el") to locate any available data object on the Internet or on Internet-worked hosts. The *U* in *URL* is sometimes said to stand for "Universal" and, in fact, is referred to that way in several important documents.

The basic idea behind the URL concept is that given certain information, you should be able to access any publicly available

data on any machine on the Internet. That certain information consists of the following basic pieces of a URL:

- The access protocol to be used.
- The machine on which the data resides.
- The port from which to request the data.
- The path to that data.
- The name of the file containing that data.

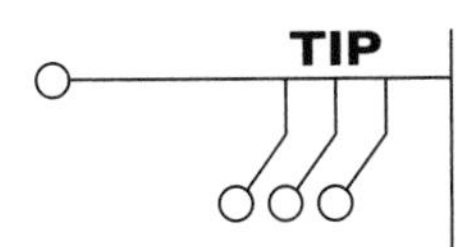

URLs will be more fully covered in the next chapter, "The Basic Pieces."

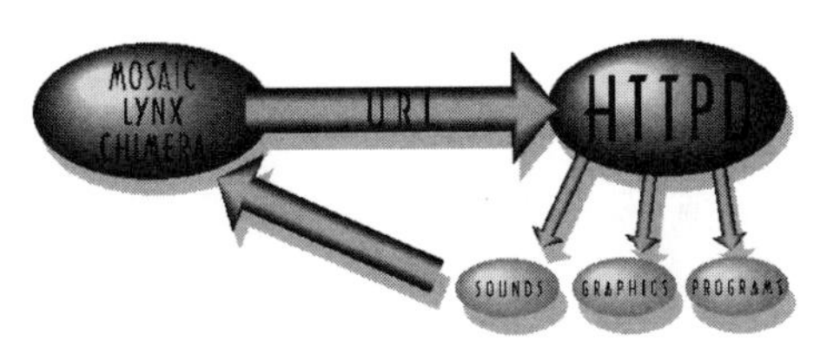

Figure 1-4: *A Uniform Resource Locator.*

The Release of WWW

During August 1991, Tim's presentation and software were announced as available from CERN in USENET newsgroups, notably alt.hypertext, comp.sys.next, comp.text.sgml and comp.mail.multi-media. The cat was now out of the bag; unfortunately the implementation of the software was most robust on an interesting, but not widely used, platform, the NeXT workstation.

Tim gave his WWW presentation at several conferences, including the Hypertext '91 conference in San Antonio, Texas, in December of that year. Among the other demonstrators at the conference were two people from Autodesk. Some have noticed that Autodesk ended their support for Xanadu not long after Tim's WWW presentation.

WWW was fully distributed throughout CERN by July 1992 and included Viola, a NeXTStep client that allowed drag-and-drop page building and linking, as well as the line-mode clients. A line-mode client is a text-only browser usually written to operate in a simulated VT-100 environment (not a real VT-100 environment since VT-100s are no longer manufactured). WWW was warmly accepted and was beginning to create a buzz on the Internet.

In January 1993, there were 50 known WWW servers in the world, including one at the University of North Carolina. Several browsers were released, including clients for the Macintosh and X Windows. When a new client was released the next month from the National Center for Supercomputing Applications (NCSA) at the University of Illinois at Urbana-Champaign, the WWW, as we now know it, began to take shape.

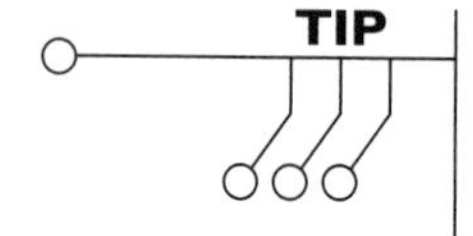

For more about CERN see http://www.cern.ch/.

NCSA Mosaic

If you are reading this, you have probably used Mosaic or one of the many WWW clients that owes a heavy debt to that program. Until the introduction of Mosaic, one of the problems with the WWW was that there were no reliable clients or browsers for some of the most common computers and operating systems. CERN had focused mostly on initial implementation, document sharing and linking. Tim and his development team were quick to meet the local demands of CERN and to meet their deadlines, which is no small matter. But CERN was quite a large NeXT shop, and they were more interested in servers, rather than clients, despite the release of their Mac and X Windows browsers, which were somewhat unreliable and clunky. NCSA, on the other hand, had experience as cross-platform client developers. Their NCSA telnet client is still widely used.

The NCSA Systems Development Group, headed by Joe Hardin, took on a project to create useful WWW browsers that would not only handle the WWW but, as Tim Berners-Lee had described, would support several other access protocols. This client was called Mosaic and was first released for X Windows in February 1993.

Later that month, Marc Andreessen posted a message to www-talk@cern.ch describing a simple extension to HTML. Marc proposed that images could be placed in the browser with a tag to be called <IMG>. What followed Marc's simple suggestion reveals a lot about the way that the WWW developed. A spirited exchange of messages ensued, including notes and points from Jim Davis, Jay Weber and Tim Berners-Lee.

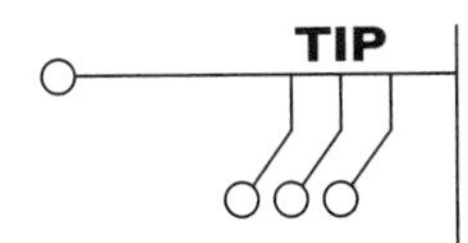

You can read it all on the WWW-talk archives at http://gummo.stanford.edu/html/hypermail/www-talk-1993q1.index.html.

For those who are believers in waiting for standards to be firm and well defined, reading this newsgroup archive should be instructive. One of the strongest arguments against implementing the <IMG> tag was that it should be incorporated in the "soon to be released" HTML version 2.0 standard. However the NCSA team decided that it needed a quicker solution and didn't wait for the standards debates to reach a consensus. As we write this book, the elements of HTML v3.0 are already being incorporated in new browsers, such as Netscape, and a debate over the relationship between standards and the speed of development is raging.

The NCSA team also gave careful consideration to the use of MIME types for identifying media formats, particularly the formats of sounds, pictures, movies and the like. Using MIME types seemed like a logical move since the Multimedia Internet Mail Extensions were already a long way toward being able to define and encode most known data types. MIME typing has the added advantage of being extendable and of having been proven to work. Even better, much of the code needed to handle MIME was already written and ready to be used by new applications—WWW clients and servers.

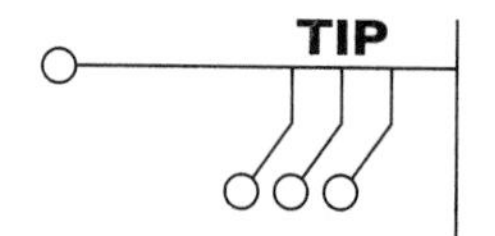

MIME types will be covered in the next chapter, "The Basic Pieces."

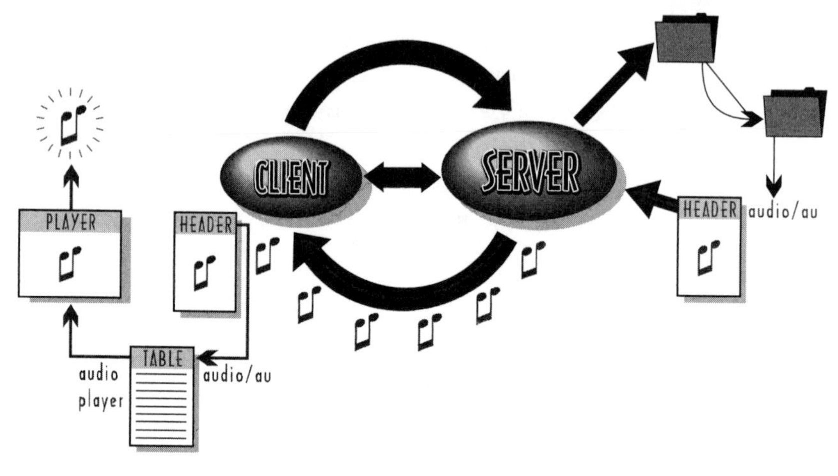

Figure 1-5: *MIME and the Web.*

With the addition of the <IMG> tag, Mosaic became truly multimedia. Suddenly, the pages of hypertext began to look a little more familiar. Instead of dryly presenting scientific and scholarly information for the benefit of other scientists and scholars, the pages included photographs of people who scientists had worked with for years but had never met. The authors of these pages had the opportunity to make their pages visually pleasing.

Until the creation of the <IMG> tag, HTML had been a very limited implementation of SGML. SGML is a language for defining the structure of a document, not necessarily its presentation. Now, you could not only have a very limited structure markup, but you had a very limited formatting language as well.

In December 1993, John Markoff wrote an article for the *New York Times* business section lauding Mosaic as the killer application of the Internet. The article included a screen shot of a Mosaic page, and everyone everywhere began to understand why being able to incorporate images into text on a widely distributed network was important. To many, the screen shot looked like a giant billboard glaring "your ad here." The WWW accounted for only 78 megabytes of Internet backbone traffic in December 1992 but for over 225,443 megabytes in December 1993. By November 1994, WWW traffic accounted for over 3,126,195 megabytes. The growth pattern was unmistakable. The number of known servers at CERN had grown to 1,500 by June 1994.

The Web had matured and was what the Internet had needed for so long; a decent graphical user interface to the anarchic, widely distributed World had arrived and been recognized.

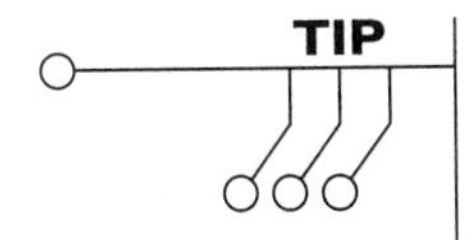

For more information about current usage statistics and general Internet developments, see the Internet Society pages at http://www.isoc.org/.

Netscape & the Browser Explosion

NCSA licensed their server technology to Spyglass, a commercial reseller, and their client software to a number of other vendors. Others realized that they, too, could write their own useful, special-purpose clients. Soon a surfeit of browsers was loose in the world, but of those, only two or three were free, including shareware or free to educational institutions and not-for-profits. While these special versions could interoperate with most WWW servers, each had some small improvement that its developers hoped would set it apart. Over 20 WWW browsers were reviewed in a recent issue of *Interactive Age*, but only a few had a measurable market share.

In March 1994, a mass migration from NCSA to Silicon Valley began. Among the first to leave was Marc Andreessen who, along with Jim Clark, formerly of Silicon Graphics, founded what was, at first, called Mosaic Communications (before NCSA's lawyers called them). By October 1994, the company, renamed Netscape Communications, had hired many of the Mosaic, WWW and Lynx developers. Netscape released its first browser and announced that it was working on a secure server to allow transactions over the Internet.

By November 1994, Netscape accounted for about 20 percent of the accesses on several large servers, and by January 1995, it accounted for 80 percent. Netscape was clearly superior to the other browsers. The Netscape developers actually implemented many of the features that were still being discussed by the HTML standards group. Andreessen, Eric Bina, Rob McCool and company replayed the drama surrounding the adoption and implementation of the <IMG> tag. While keeping a close eye on the direction in which the standards were moving and being regular participants in the USENET newsgroups that discussed WWW issues, the Netscape developers, in the interest of producing an exceptional product, are willing to push beyond the limits of a developing standard, and they have been rewarded. Of course, as of this writing, they offer their clients free to educational institutions and not-for-profits, both of which are still a large portion of the Internet.

You will notice that many servers on the Internet have a notice telling you that to fully appreciate their pages, you will need the Netscape client.

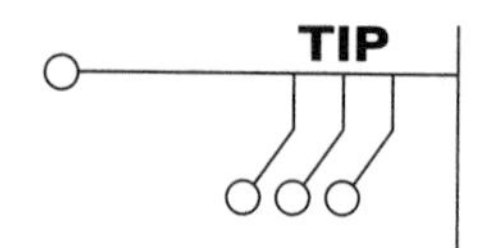

Check out Netscape's latest release and ordering information at http://www.netscape.com/.

Servers

With all this attention on browsers or clients, you might ask: what about servers? After all, this is the Server Book, is it not? To date, only two servers are widely used, one from NCSA and one from CERN. Each is an easy-to-install, well-known entity. Each has a number of famous tricks and features that we will discuss throughout the book. Neither implements any real form of security or encryption, but such features could easily be added to the servers. Servers are available for nearly every operating system including Macintosh and Microsoft Windows.

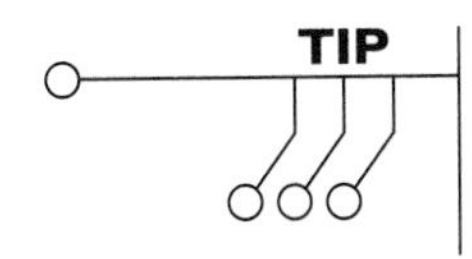

For more information on servers, see Chapter 3, "Setting Up the Server," and the W3 Consortium's server pages at http://www.w3.org/hypertext/WWW/Daemon/Overview.html.

Those serious about transacting business in a totally electronic environment should consider licensing a secure server called Netsite from Netscape or joining CommerceNet and using Enterprise Integration Technologies' Secure HTTPD. Further information on security can be found in Chapter 4, "System Security."

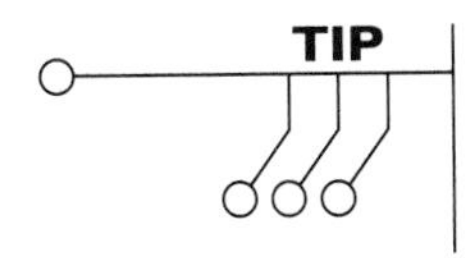

For more information on security in general, see Chapter 4, "System Security." For more on the Netsite server, see the Netscape site at http://www.netscape.com/. For more on CommerceNet and EIT's Secure HTTPD server and Secure Mosaic client, see http://www.eit.com/projects/s-http/.

Another viable server alternative for electronic commerce that's emerging is the First Virtual Holdings model, which requires no encryption and only the registration of one of your credit cards. With the First Virtual Holdings model, your authorization requests travel in MIME-encoded electronic mail. You do not need any special server but you need to add scripts, which you may get from First Virtual Holdings, to your existing server.

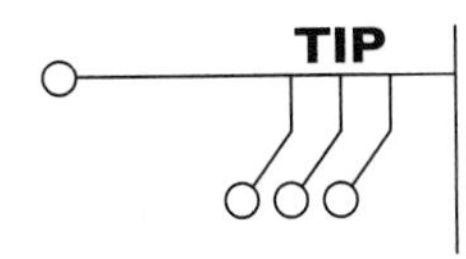

For more of the evolving details concerning First Virtual Holdings, see http://www.fv.com/.

The W3 Consortium

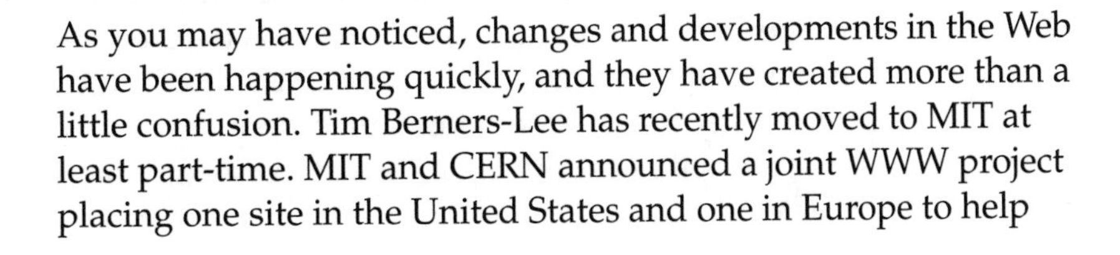

As you may have noticed, changes and developments in the Web have been happening quickly, and they have created more than a little confusion. Tim Berners-Lee has recently moved to MIT at least part-time. MIT and CERN announced a joint WWW project placing one site in the United States and one in Europe to help provide information and archives relating to WWW development. The European W3 Consortium (W3C) is run by INRA, the French National Institute for Research in Computing and Automation, in cooperation with CERN.

The stated goals of the W3C are to provide the Web with the following:

- A repository of information, including specifications about the Web for developers and users.
- A reference code implementation to promote standards.
- Various prototype and sample applications to indicate how new technology can be used.

W3C is a membership organization. While there is no official membership list, several companies have indicated their intentions to join, including AT&T, Digital Equipment Corporation, Enterprise Integration Technologies, FTP Software, Hummingbird Communication, IBM, IXI, MCI, NCSA, Netscape Communications, Novell, Open Market, O'Reilly & Associates, Spyglass and Sun Microsystems.

Expect to hear more from the W3C especially as privacy and security issues come more to the forefront of discussions about the WWW.

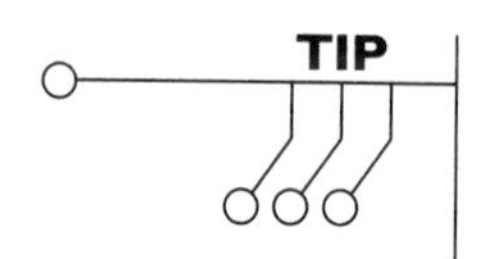

Check out the W3C pages for the latest standards developments and see why the Ws are green at http://www.w3.org/.

Internet Engineering Task Force (IETF)

The Internet Engineering Task Force oversees the general development and the evolution of standards for the Internet. The IETF meets three times a year to set directions for the Internet. The various teams and research groups of the IETF produce the official Internet standards documents called Requests for Comments or RFCs, as well as producing informative documents about the Internet and its history, culture and ways and means. The latter documents are called FYI RFCs or For Your Information RFCs.

According to the FYI RFC 1718 by G. Malkin, the IETF is the principal body engaged in the development of new Internet standard specifications. Its mission includes the following:

- Identifying, and proposing solutions to, pressing operational and technical problems in the Internet.
- Specifying the development or usage of protocols and the near-term architecture to solve such technical problems for the Internet.
- Making recommendations to the Internet Engineering Steering Group (IESG) regarding the standardization of protocols and protocol usage in the Internet.
- Facilitating technology transfer from the Internet Research Task Force (IRTF) to the wider Internet community.
- Providing a forum for the exchange of information among vendors, users, researchers, agency contractors and network managers within the Internet community.

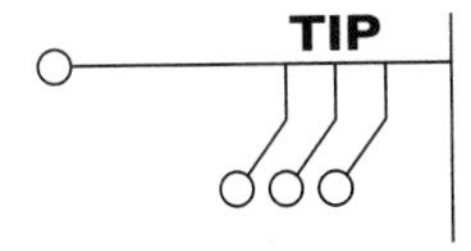

You can learn more about the IETF and, in particular, the "Tao of the IETF" at http://www.ietf.cnri.reston.va.us/home.html.

Keeping Current

As you may have noticed, the WWW was created and expanded through worldwide cooperation and as a result of discussions that began in the USENET newsgroup alt.hypertext and then spread to mailing lists and finally newsgroups specifically about the Web. The existing Web was built on top of the earlier web of newsgroup postings and of e-mail that was generated by mailing lists. Remember that the first WWW project was a project lasting only three months and that Netscape was released in late November 1994 and accounted for over 70 percent of the browsers by January 1995. The Web is growing very quickly. By the time this book is printed, the Web will have developed further and probably in

ways that we cannot predict (although we will make a few guesses at the end of the book). If you plan to be an active WWW provider, designer or publisher, it is imperative that you try to keep up with the latest Web happenings and that you be familiar with the appropriate newsgroups.

You can do this by beginning as the developers of the WWW began—by reading and participating in a number of newsgroups.

World Wide Web–Related Newsgroups

The most important newsgroups

comp.infosystems.www.misc—The discussion in this newsgroup includes just about anything concerning the WWW.

comp.infosystems.www.providers—This group discusses issues related to providing information on the WWW. Much of the discussion concerns servers and server side issues.

comp.infosystems.www.announce—This newsgroup is where new pages, collections, products and the like are announced. You can announce your latest developments for your service in this group as well.

comp.infosystems.www.users—Keeping an eye close on user issues, this group discusses how to use the WWW. It is also concerned with clients and external viewers.

Special interest newsgroups

bit.listserv.www-vm—This is a gateway of a Bitnet listserv that is concerned with the thankless task of managing a WWW server under VM, an IBM mainframe operating system.

bionet.software.www—This group discusses the WWW as it is used in the biological sciences.

Related important newsgroups

alt.hypertext—The discussion in this newsgroup covers hypertext, in general, and, specifically, every known hypertext implementation. You can obtain lots of information about the WWW and HTML in this group.

comp.internet.net-happenings—Gleason Slackman moderates this list of what's happening in the Internet-related world. This is the news gateway to his Net-happenings mailing list.

Need-a-life newsgroups

alt.culture.www—This group follows the tradition of alt.culture groups, which cater to every conceivable nationality, region, etc. It discusses how to live within the evolving culture of hypertext on the WWW and the consequences of doing so.

alt.life.internet—If you thought the folks on alt.culture.www were lamers, try this one out.

alt.destroy.the.internet—Read this group just when you think it can't get worse. Recent postings include "Corporate print-media weasels target Internet," "Internet whiners target corporate print-media weasels," "Longest known palindrome" and "Is Satan an April Fool's Joke." The last discussion refers to a suite of cracker programs. As the title indicates, these folks are concerned with what might wreck life on the Internet as we know it.

alt.best.of.internet—This group is a reposting of clever and otherwise important postings on the USENET newsgroups.

You might also participate in the WWW–related mailing lists. Mailing lists deliver the discussion directly to your e-mail address, which some people consider more timely and more convenient than reading newsgroups. Others of us find ourselves drowning in mail as it is and prefer to read discussions in newsgroups. Currently, the mailing lists are more technical and a bit more focused than the newsgroups. If you are a developer with a keen interest in a certain area, the WWW mailing lists are for you.

About the WWW Mailing Lists at W3.org

www-announce@w3.org contains general WWW–related announcements, such as announcements of new software releases. This list is intended to be low in volume and high in membership, so don't announce your new home pages here.

www-html@w3.org contains technical discussions regarding the design, development and implementation of HTML. Issues relating to style sheets and the like are also covered. Participants stress that this list is for designers of the language, not for beginners.

www-proxy@w3.org contains discussions of special-purpose servers, those that cache, those that act as proxies for other servers and those under development.

www-talk@w3.org contains technical discussion by and for those developing WWW-related software. Do not post questions about HTML; those should go to www-html. New user questions should go to the appropriate newsgroups. Such as comp.infosystems.www.misc.

www-rdb@w3.org contains technical discussions of issues relating to the use of the WWW with relational databases and, in particular, the various gateways to such databases.

To subscribe to the WWW mailing list of your choice, send a mail message to listserv@w3.org. The message should contain a single line in the following format:

subscribe *list-name your-name*

For example, if Gregor Samsa wanted to become a subscriber to the www-talk list, he would send an e-mail message to listserv@w3.org that contained the following line:

subscribe www-talk Gregor Samsa

To participate in the list, he would send e-mail to www-talk@w3.org.

Any **administrative requests, such as those that concern subscribing, unsubscribing, retrieving files from the archives, etc., should be sent to the listserv@w3.org address.**

To learn more about the listserv options, send a single line message of "help" to listserv@w3.org.

About Other WWW–Related Mailing Lists
www-security@nsmx.rutgers.edu is the official mailing list of the IETF HTTP Security Working Group. It is intended to be a forum on all aspects of security on the Web. Remember, this is a working group mailing list made up of people currently working on security products and policies; do not send new user or even novice questions to this list. To subscribe send a single-line message to www-security-owner@ nsmx.rutgers.edu. The message should contain the following:

subscribe www-security *your-email-address*

VRML@wired.com or the Virtual Reality Modeling Language mailing list has been pretty quiet as of this writing, but it got off to a good start in late 1994 and may revive. The list is dedicated to discussing the implementation of virtual reality viewers in a platform-independent environment. To join send the following single-line message to majordomo@wired.com:

subscribe vrml *your-email-address*

http-wg is the mailing list of the HTTP working group. Send subscription requests to http-wg-request@cuckoo.hpl.hp.com in the form of the following single-line mail message:

subscribe http-wg *your-full-name*

For additional mailing lists and archive information see http://www.w3.org/hypertext/WWW/Mailing/Mail/Overview.html.

W3 Interactive Talk or WIT was developed in 1994 as a means for those interested in various WWW topics to communicate entirely on the Web. WIT's stated intent is to be an improvement over newsgroups, in which old news evaporates into the ether in a few days, and over mailing lists that lack a reliable method of following a discussion thread. A short cruise of WIT will help you decide if it is actually much of an improvement. For us the jury is still out; we find ourselves returning to newsgroups and to the mailing list archives instead.

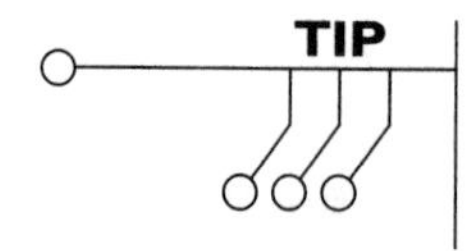

Take a look at W3 Interactive Talk at http://info.cern.ch/hypertext/WWW/WIT/User/Overview.html.

Moving On

Now you have some idea of what the Web is and how it came into being. We've provided a number of references to Web sites where you can learn more about the topics related to the Web and references to places you can go to keep current with Web happenings.

In the next chapter, you'll begin learning about the basic pieces of the Web, and you'll be on your way to participating in the Web. You'll be on your way toward becoming an information provider—not merely a passive consumer.

2 The Basic Pieces

Sparing the technical details of how HyperText Transfer Protocol (HTTP) works, it is useful from the outset to understand how data is transmitted on the World Wide Web. HTTP has been used since 1990 with the inception of the World Wide Web initiative (see Chapter 1, "What Is the Web?"). It is designed to provide a system that is fast enough to distribute multimedia information and flexible enough to use for very different purposes.

HyperText Transfer Protocol

HTTP is based on a client-server model of information distribution, or a "request/response paradigm," in the words of the Network Working Group's Internet Draft of HTTP specifications. This means that the information available on the World Wide Web is stored at central locations ("servers") and is accessed by user request via a program located on a user's personal computer (the "client").

Different ways of using the features HTTP makes available are explored in detail throughout this book. With the proper considerations, such as the power of your server, the capacity of your Internet connection and so on, HTTP allows you to present almost anything you could want to a global audience. This chapter examines the most basic elements of the Web server, with a brief introduction to Web page creation and details on how the Web browser processes the multimedia information that your server will provide.

How HTTP Works

HTTP operates by sending messages from the client to the server and from the server to the client. There are a number of different types of messages that a client can send to a server, but three types are most common: GET, HEAD and POST. These messages are "requests" from the client to send different types of information. The GET request is sent to retrieve a Web page, for example. The client sends a request in the format: GET *URL*, followed by a carriage return. This asks the server to return the document or file located at the specified URL. The response from the server consists of the body of the document, prefaced by information like the version of HTTP being used, the status of the request (e.g. OK, Not Found), and the MIME type of the document, as identified in the server's MIME types file (see Chapter 3, "Setting Up the Server").

The HEAD request prompts the server to send all of the same information as the GET request except for the body of the document or file. In an HTML document, this includes all of the information specified in the <TITLE>, <META>, <LINK> and <BASE HREF> tags (see "The Basics of HTML" later in this chapter). The HEAD request is used by programs called "robots," which request header information to verify that a URL is valid, to collect statistical information and to perform other functions that don't require the body of the Web page. Two examples, MOMspider and Anchor Checker, are detailed in Chapter 6, "Checking Your Work."

The POST request asks the server to accept information, whether in the form of a message posted to a newsgroup, a sub-

mission using a form (see Chapter 10, "Simple Forms"), or a submission to a database using a script interface between the Web page and that interface (see Chapter 11, "CGI: Advanced Forms for Programmers").

This client-server model has a number of characteristics. First, information can be transmitted only by request, and therefore, it is not possible to "force" a message on the user as is done in, say, advertisements on television. Users have to be convinced to access a particular server to get information, and if they are not interested in what is presented, they are not compelled to stay. Another important factor introduced by the client-server model is that virtually all information has to be provided from the server side of the equation. This means, perhaps obviously, that the server hardware should be sufficiently powerful to deliver all of the information that you make available, even to a large number of simultaneous users. For this reason certain factors, such as the size of images on a page, the length of a single page and the types of system calls made by a particular script, always need to be taken into consideration. The more effort required to load each page, the more heavily the server is taxed. The load on the server machine and the number of "hits" (requests from a client to a server) being taken by a server are factors that increase the amount of time it takes users to access your information.

An HTTP *daemon* (that is, the program that allows a machine to serve information to HTTP clients) fields requests from clients. Each time the daemon takes a request, it creates a new process to serve that particular request. Generally, creating a large number of new processes is not a problem because the processes respond to requests and finish extremely fast. However, since the majority of HTTP daemons create processes that can only respond to requests one at a time, the daemon can be overloaded in situations of heavy usage and not be able to create processes quickly enough to keep up with the requests. This situation is one of three major causes of *lag time* (the amount of time it takes a page to appear in the client browser). The one-at-a-time handling of requests is related to a second major cause of lag time, which is the *load,* or the amount of work that the CPU has to do at any one time. A machine taking a high number of hits must run simultaneous processes that compete for processor time. Both of these problems can be avoided or at least minimized by selectively promoting a site, by directing your promotions at particular populations among the Internet community (see "Choosing & Reaching Your Audience" in Chapter 12, "Fitting In: Joining the Virtual Community"). It is also important to select HTTP daemon software that is appropriate to your needs (as discussed in Chapter 3, "Setting Up the Server") and to keep up with the latest version of daemons because improvements are made on a regular basis that help reduce the impact of these problems.

The third major cause of lag time in accessing a server is the amount of bandwidth. Every connection to the Internet has a certain upper limit to the amount of information it can transmit at one time, and it is very easy for a server to exceed that limit in low-capacity connections. The type of connection (for example, SLIP, T1, 56 kbps) over which you will transmit your information should always be taken into consideration when you are deciding what to put up on the site. This is one of the ironic characteristics of a protocol as flexible as HTTP—it permits such a broad range of file types to be transmitted that it can tempt the provider into serving information that overreaches the hardware itself.

Having laid out the constraints of HTTP, it should be said that, by and large, most servers do not experience these problems in any serious way. HTTP is a very powerful protocol, capable of transmitting multimedia information to a client extremely fast.

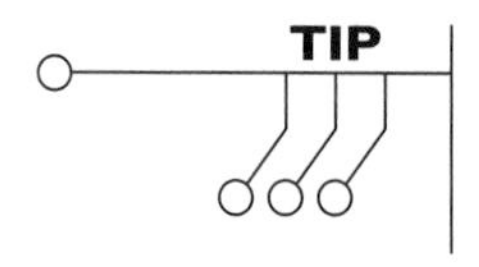

For full details and specifications of HTTP, look at "HTTP: A protocol for networked information," the draft of the Internet Engineering Task Force's paper on this subject, available on the WWW at http://info.cern.ch/hypertext/WWW/Protocols/HTTP/HTTP2.html.

Files on the Web

Throughout this book, reference will be made to certain types of multimedia files. These files are in common usage across the Internet, some by default, some for particular qualities that make them easier to transmit, and some through active promotion. Most require some sort of *helper application* so they can be launched automatically by a browser.

File Formats

The following tables list the types of text, image, sound, animation and compressed files commonly found on the Web.

Name	Extension(s)	MIME Type	Description
HyperText Markup Language (HTML)	.html, .htm	text/html	The basis for the World Wide Web
Text	.txt	text/plain	Plain ASCII text
Rich Text Format (RTF)	.rtf	application/rtf	An interchangeable text file type that preserves some formatting
PostScript	.ps, .ai, .eps	application/postscript	PostScript files

Text types commonly found on the Web.

Name	Extension(s)	MIME Type	Description
Graphics Interchange Format (GIF)	.gif	image/gif	The most common image format on the Web
Joint Photographic Experts Group (JPEG)	.jpeg, .jpg, .jpe	image/jpeg	A higher-resolution graphics format than GIF

Image types commonly found on the Web.

Name	Extension	MIME Type	Description
μ-law	.au	audio/basic	Sun mμ-law files, an 8-kHz audio format
Wave file	.wav	audio/x-wav	Microsoft's custom audio format
Audio Interchange File Format	.aiff, .aif, .aifc	audio/x-aiff	Audio formats commonly used by Macintoshes
Macintosh Sound File	.snd	audio/basic	Macintosh sound resource file
Moving Pictures Expert Group (MPEG)	layer-2	.mp2	audio/x-mpeg Digital-quality audio usable by all platforms

Sound types commonly found on the Web.

Name	Extension	MIME Type	Description
QuickTime	.qt, .mov	video/quicktime	Macintosh propri etary animation format with sound capability
Moving Pictures Expert Group (MPEG) layer-1	.mpg, .mpeg, .mpe	video/mpeg	High-quality video compression
Microsoft Video	.avi	video/x-msvideo	Microsoft's propri etary audio/ animation format

Animation types commonly found on the Web.

Name	Extension	MIME Type	Description
Gnu ZIP	.gz	Application/ x-gzip	Gnu ZIP compression
Compress	.Z	Application/ x-compress	Another type of compression, slightly more common than gzip
ZIP	.zip	Application/ x-zip-compress	Older form of compression, still widely used
Tape archive	.tar	Application/ x-tar	Format used to compile a number of files and directo ries into one file

Compression types commonly found on the Web.

MIME Typing

One of the most impressive aspects of the World Wide Web is how transparent the transmission of multimedia information can seem. A single link can bring up a text file, a document from across the world, a movie or a recording. The reason for this seeming transparency is that the server, when sending a file of any type, can tell the client how to process that file. For example, the server tells the client whether to run the file through an audio tool or an animation program or to simply load it as part of a new Web page. To tell the client how to process the file, the server sends the file with an attachment specifying its type. This attachment is referred to as the file's *MIME type*, which stands for Multipurpose Internet Mail Extensions.

This name comes from the original purpose of MIME typing, which was to allow for multimedia components to be sent with electronic mail messages by specifying their types in advance so that the mail program could display them as part of the message. MIME typing tells the browser what kind of file is being sent, so that the browser can then tell the client's computer how to display it. MIME types such as x-compressed, x-gzip, x-tar, and x-zip-compressed are understood to be compressed file types, and a browser saves files of these types to the client's drive.

Every HTTP server comes preconfigured to attach MIME types to certain files, but as you add new types of files, you'll want to specify their MIME types as well. In Chapter 3, "Setting Up the Server," the location and name of the MIME type file for each server is specified. A full listing of MIME types for different graphics formats is given in Chapter 7, "Images on the Web," and the MIME types for audio and animation files are listed in Chapter 8, "True Multimedia."

If you want to add a new MIME type, simply add the name and the extensions it uses to the end of this map file. Notice that some of the MIME types are preceded by an "x-". This prefix indicates that these types are not recognized by the agency responsible for setting file type standards on the Internet, the Internet Assigned Numbers Authority (IANA). This is the case with one of the more popular audio formats on the Web right now, MPEG layer-2, which usually uses the extension .mp2 and is mapped to the MIME type audio/x-mpeg. Most proprietary formats, like Microsoft's WAV, will also be unrecognized and as a result, need to be manually added to the server's map file.

While there is no way to specify from the server end what application the clients use to display multimedia files, you should be able to guide the clients to some application, preferably freeware, if they are unfamiliar with the type of file you are serving. Once you've set the MIME type of a file, the users have to set their browsers to automatically launch a helper application upon receiving a file of that MIME type. As with the servers, most clients have preconfigured a great deal of this, but if you are using a nonstandard multimedia format, it is a good idea to announce it on your Web pages and tell users that they need to configure their browsers accordingly. Every browser is configured differently, some with long text files called "mailcap" files, some with interactive menus. As long as you give the users the MIME type and perhaps recommend an application that can display the file, users should be able to configure their browsers appropriately.

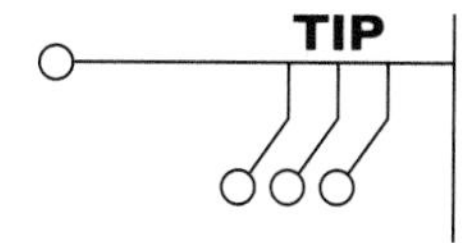

For further details on MIME types, check out "Introduction to MIME," at the URL http://www.cs.indiana.edu/docproject/mail/mime.html and the collection of documents available at CyberWeb, http://WWW.Stars.com/Vlib/Providers/MIME.html.

Compression

Transmitting files over the Web to be stored on the client's computer without displaying them is a very common practice, because browsers are capable of using FTP in the same way that they use HTTP. Since these files have no MIME type, the client's browser automatically saves them to disk. To cut down on transmission time, most files are stored in compressed formats, to be uncompressed when they are on the client's computer. Three of the most common compression programs are gzip, compress and zip. tar, a fourth program, is not a compression program per se, but can combine a large number of files into a single archive, called a tar file. This section provides a brief description of each program and instructions for compressing and uncompressing files. The instructions are abbreviated because these programs have a broad range of possible uses. To obtain complete information about gzip, compress and tar, use the following command:

```
$man filename
```

where *filename* is either gzip, compress or tar. When you use this command, you receive the manual pages for these files. To see the command-line options for zip, just type the following command:

```
$zip -h
```

This gives you access to a short help file.

tar

tar, or tape archive, is a program used to compile a set of files into a single file for storage on tapes, as the name might suggest. Usually this program is used for backups, but the fact that it can compress full directory trees as easily as single files makes it useful for file storage as well. tar is an extremely versatile command, so we'll cover only four functions—creating, adding to, listing and extracting tar files.

The simplest method to create a tar file is to first change to the top-level directory of the directory tree that you want to archive. If, for example, you want to archive everything in the directory /usr/src/xv3.0/, including the subdirectories docs and pics and all of their subdirectories, you would change directory to /usr/src/xv3.0/ and enter the following command:

```
tar cf xv.tar *
```

The c option means to create the tar file, and the f option means that the next characters you type will be the name of the tar file. In the example above, the name of the tar file is xv.tar. If you add any other options, such as the ones discussed below, make sure that f is always the last option specified so that tar correctly reads the name of the tar file. Finally, you enter an asterisk (*) as a wildcard character to indicate that you want to archive everything in the directory. When tar extracts this file, it puts all of the files from the directory /usr/src/xv3.0/ into whatever directory you were in when you ran the extract command. If you want the tar archive to store the directory name as well and create a new directory for the files being extracted, you should create the tar file one directory up from the files you are archiving. In other words, if you want to extract the files into a new directory called xv3.0 instead of their current directory, you need to specify what this new directory will be called. In this example, you would go to the directory /usr/src/ and enter the following command:

```
tar cf xv.tar xv3.0
```

Entering this command saves the files in the archive as, for example, xv3.0/README, xv3.0/INSTALL and so on, and when you extract the files, tar will create the directory xv3.0 for the new files and subdirectories.

tar works silently and doesn't tell you which files are being archived. If you want to see the status of the archive as it progresses, enter the option v between the options c and f. This option gives you a verbose listing of the files as they are added to xv.tar. If the directory tree that you want to archive contains symbolic links to other directories, tar doesn't follow those links unless you specifically tell it to. Use the h option to direct tar to follow symbolic links.

You can use gzip to compress a tar file, reducing the size even more. The easiest way to do this in a single command line is to send the tar information to standard output, rather than to a file, and to use a compression program to compress that information as it appears. gzip is discussed in greater detail later in this section, but in brief, to use gzip to compress a tar file, enter the following command line:

```
$tar cf - * | gzip > xv.tar.gz
```

In this example, the file name is specified with a hyphen (-), which tells the program to send the file output to stdout, or "standard output," and the pipe command sends stdout to the program gzip, which compresses the tar file into a gzip file. You must supply the file name for gzip to output, whereas it is not necessary when you compress an existing tar file (or any single file). gzip uses the name of the file that is being compressed to generate the name of the output file. For example, a file called xv.tar would be compressed and renamed xv.tar.gz. However, since gzip is reading the information to be compressed from stdin, or "standard input," the file name has to be given explicitly.

If you want to append a file to an existing archive, you can simply use the r option in place of the c option. Specify the name of the tar file that you want to add the file to and then the file or files to be added:

```
$tar rf xv.tar README.NEW
```

This command overwrites any file in the archive with that name. If you want to update the tar file, changing files that have been updated and adding new files, you can use the u option, as follows:

```
$tar uf xv.tar *
```

This command overwrites older files (using the date and time of creation to judge which file is newer) and appends new files to the tar file.

To check the contents of a tar file, use the t option as follows:

```
$tar tf xv.tar
```

This command gives you a listing of the files in the archive. Note whether the files are prefaced with a directory name, such as xv3.0/README, rather than appearing just as README. If a directory name is in front of the file, tar automatically creates this directory when it extracts the files.

To extract the files from an archive, change to the directory in which you want the new files to appear, and enter the following command:

```
$tar xf xv.tar
```

gzip

Like tar, gzip (Gnu ZIP) is an extremely versatile program. By and large, you will want to use it in two capacities: for compressing tar files or single files (such as binaries) and for uncompressing files with the extension .gz or .Z. gzip is an incredibly effective compression algorithm, reducing text files or source files containing code by as much as 70 percent. As noted previously, it is a useful follow-up compression for tar files. tar concatenates a large number of files into a single file, but the tar file can be further compressed as a single file. The format of the gzip command in its most basic uses is fairly simple. To compress a single file, such as our tar file xv.tar from the previous section, enter the following command line:

```
$gzip xv.tar
```

gzip replaces the file xv.tar with the file xv.tar.gz, preserving information like the date of creation. gzip should only be used to compress a single file—to compress multiple files, put the files into an archive using tar, and then use gzip to compress that archive. To preserve the original file being compressed, you can specify a non-destructive compress, which creates a gzip compressed file without overwriting the original. This option is specified with the -c option, as in the following example:

```
$gzip -c xv.tar > xv.tar.gz
```

Since you are not replacing the original file, you need to specify what file name to write the output to, just as you would if compressing multiple files simultaneously.

There are several options for uncompressing a gzip file. All of the following commands produce the same output:

```
$gzip -d xv.tar.gz
$gunzip xv.tar.gz
$zcat xv.tar.gz > xv.tar
```

The advantage to zcat is that it preserves the original compressed file, whereas the other commands replace the compressed file with the uncompressed version. In addition, unlike the others, zcat does not require a compressed file to have an extension specifying its format (such as, .gz, .Z, .tgz and so on). Any file that is indeed a compressed file is recognized and uncompressed by zcat. All of the commands recognize files compressed either with gzip or with standard compress, and some zip files. By and large, you will want to use gzip over both zip and compress, for a combination of efficiency and cross-platform compatibility.

compress

A file that has been compressed using the standard compress program can be recognized by the extension .Z. These files are widely used in FTP sites and can be uncompressed either with gzip or with the uncompress option of compress. The format for compressing a file using this program is fairly simple:

```
$compress xv.tar
```

This command line produces the output file xv.tar.Z, replacing the original xv.tar. When you specify the -c option, in exactly the same manner as with gzip, the original file is not replaced. To uncompress a file compressed in this fashion, use the following command line:

```
$uncompress xv.tar.Z
```

You can also specify a nondestructive uncompression, again with the -c option.

zip

zip is one of the older compression algorithms in use, but is constantly updated and improved. One benefit of using zip to compress files is that it can simulate PKZIP files, a format widely used on PCs. To create a standard zip compressed file, use the following command:

```
$zip xv.zip *
```

The asterisk (*) indicates the file name(s) to be added to the zip file, and xv.zip is the name of the zip file. If you want to add only specific files from a directory into a zip file, you can use the -i, or include option and then provide a list of file names to be added. zip defaults to adding files to a zip file, so it's not necessary to add any options in order to add to or to create a zip file. If you want to provide files readable by PCs, you should make the zip file PKZIP compatible, by adding the -k option, as follows:

```
$zip -k xv.zip *
```

To extract files from zip files, simply use the UNZIP command. The default action for this command is to extract files from the named zip file, so to do so you need only to enter the following:

$unzip *filename*.zip

To refine this command a bit, you can specify that you do not want to extract certain files by using the -x option at the end of the command line, as in the following:

$unzip *filename*.zip -x README

You can also specify a location for the files that are being extracted with the -d option,

$unzip *filename*.zip -d /usr/local/src

Finally, if you are extracting an update or software patch and want only the files that have been updated to be overwritten by the files in the zip file, you can use the freshen or -f option, which replaces a file with a newer version

```
$unzip -f newfiles.zip -d /usr/local/src
```

As noted previously, since the different types of compression programs have different functionalities, it is a good idea to be familiar with all of them. In general, the most efficient and transferable setup, if you are providing files on your server, is to create a tar file and compress it using gzip.

The purpose of the preceding sections is to give some background into the mechanism of the World Wide Web and the file types that compose it. All of the multimedia file types listed previously will be discussed in later chapters. The final basic piece of the

Web that you'll need to understand before diving in is the actual language in which Web documents are written, called HTML.

The Basics of HTML

The name "HyperText Markup Language" may be somewhat deceptive. HTML is not, properly speaking, a programming language. HTML is simply a set of codes that are placed around and within text to allow it to be displayed a certain way by browsers and to be given certain attributes, such as a link to another file. For the server, it is irrelevant what type of computer or browser will be accessing the information that is coded in HTML. All browsers can interpret HTML codes and use the codes to determine how the structure of the document is laid out—in other words, what the title is, what the headers are, where paragraph breaks are located and so on. There is, then, no need to try to design pages for certain types of hardware or software.

The process of marking up a document for presentation on the Web is a remarkably simple process. Including graphics, audio files or forms and linking to other multimedia resources or external files is somewhat more complicated but is by no means impossible to learn. The following is a brief explanation of some of the most common HTML coding, much of which will be elaborated upon in other chapters of the book. For example, forms, one of the most useful parts of a Web server, are discussed in Chapter 10, "Simple Forms," and in Chapter 11, "CGI: Advanced Forms for Programmers." This section is written simply to give you a feel for HTML and is not intended to be comprehensive.

Locating the Documents

The first order of business is to create the file itself. It can be named anything you want but make sure that the file extension is .html. This extension indicates to the browser that the file is a hypertext document. If the file is created on a PC and thus restricted to three-letter extensions, the extension should be .htm, which is also recognized by browsers. After you have created the file, you should put it in the area of your file system that is reserved for HTML pages. Your file's location and your machine's name or IP address provide that file's *URL,* or Uniform Resource Locator. The URL is the document's "address" on the World Wide Web. The following are hypothetical examples of standard URLs:

```
http://www.shoop.com/users/dobbs.html
http://www.nra.org/ak47.gif
ftp://sunsite.unc.edu/
gopher://gopher.foo.bar.org
```

All URLs have the following standard format:

protocol://machine address:port/path/filename

The port specification is optional, and if none is entered, the browser defaults to the standard port for whatever service is specified as the protocol. For example, if you are using HTTP, the default port is 80.

Other protocols in addition to the ones listed are news, mailto and telnet. Telnet has essentially the same format, but you can specify a login name before the machine name by using a command such as the following:

```
telnet://lynx@sunsite.unc.edu
```

For news and mailto, you simply enter the newsgroup to be read or the address to which you want to send mail:

```
news:comp.infosystems.www.announce
mailto:help@vmedia.com
```

In both cases, the client has defined the mail server and news server that it uses to execute these commands.

For your site, all URLs will probably begin with HTTP, because that protocol can access HTML documents and multimedia files. If you want access to a site's home page, the URL is all you need to enter. To access some other page at the site, just add the file path and the file name. The path for documents you create will be relative to whatever top-level directory you specify in your HTTP server software (see Chapter 3, "Setting Up the Server"). If you've told your server that the top-level directory is /html, a file located in /html/users/homepages/ would have the path /users

/homepages/. If the user does not know a document's file name, she or he can enter the file path and will be presented with an index page of available files in that directory.

Creating the Documents

Any HTML document should have certain features that mark it as HTML and that delineate its component parts. If, for some reason, you wanted to create a completely empty Web page, it would look something like this:

```
<HTML>

<HEAD>
</HEAD>

<BODY>
</BODY>

</HTML>
```

Note that each tag has a second tag that is identical to it, except for the addition of a forward slash. The first tag is the opening tag, and the second, with the forward slash, closes out the first one. Anything you put in between these two tags is affected by the characteristics that are specified by the opening tag. Anything before and after the tag is unaffected. One very common error in writing pages is to forget the closing tag, thereby giving everything the wrong characteristics.

The example page shown previously would display as a blank screen on a browser, with no title (or rather, with the document's URL as the title). The first tag, <HTML>, indicates that the document is to be read as an HTML format file. The reason this tag is necessary is because in the near future, different versions of HTML, and possibly documents in other languages, will be read through Web browsers. The <HTML> tag will tell the browser that the document is to be interpreted as HTML. The set of tags below (<HEAD> and </HEAD>) mark the area that serves as the header for the page. Anything in the header is located in between these two tags. The next set of tags, <BODY> and </BODY>, delineate—you guessed it—the body of the document. The information to be displayed on the browser should be placed in between this set of tags. The final tag marks the end of the document and should always be the last line of the file.

There are three tags that should be included in the header of the document, that is, between <HEAD> and </HEAD>, which will give important information about the document itself. The information defined in these tags, <META>, <LINK> and <BASE HREF> are not actually displayed on the browser, but are useful for users looking at the source of your document, and are used by programs that automatically gather information about Web pages. The <META> tag gives general information about the document, such as its expiration date (that is, when it should be considered obsolete), its owner, and how it was created. For example, the following tags define the owner of the document as "Bob," the program used to create it as "tkHTML 2.3," and indicate that the document should expire at midnight on July 5, 1998.

```
<META HTTP-EQUIV="OWNER" CONTENT="Bob">
<META NAME="GENERATOR" CONTENT="tkHTML 2.3">
<META HTTP-EQUIV="EXPIRES">Tue, 05 Jul 1998 00:00:00 GMT</META>
```

Note that the "generator" setting is specified using the NAME option, whereas the expiration date and owner are specified using the HTTP-EQUIV option. This is because the owner and expiration date are both variables recognized by the HTTP daemon when it sends or receives HEAD information, as described above in "Hypertext Transfer Protocol." The HTTP-EQUIV option indicates that this is a variable that the daemon software should recognize. The generator information is not understood or transmitted by the daemon, but is useful information, so it is specified using the NAME option, which means that this is a variable not necessarily recognized by daemon software.

The <LINK> tag is used to describe a document's relationship to other documents on the site. It identifies the relationship using the REL option, and identifies the document using the HREF option. So, for example, the following tag indicates that the document was "made" by a user that can be contacted at the URL mailto:webmaster@shoop.com.

```
<LINK REL="made" HREF="mailto:webmaster@shoop.com">
```

A complete listing of the different REL options that the LINK tag can contain is given in Chapter 6, "Checking Your Work."

The <BASE HREF> tag is used to include the URL of the document in the source of the document itself, so that a user viewing the source out of the context of the Web site can still locate it on the Internet. The syntax is simple—the following tag specifies the URL of the document as "http://www.shoop.com/index.html."

```
<BASE HREF="http://www.shoop.com/index.html">
```

A detailed discussion of these three tags, their uses and ways to incorporate them into a Web page to improve its accuracy and functionality, is contained in Chapter 6, "Checking Your Work."

Every Web page has a title, which generally displays at the top of the browser window. This is created using the <TITLE> tag and is generally located in the header of the document. This title is not usually displayed on the page itself but on the top of the browser window. If you want this title to be the heading of the page as well, you should include it at the top of the body of the page. To make it more prominent, you can identify it as a "header," specifying the size of the font that you want displayed. The sizes range from 1 (largest) to 6 (smallest), and the tags are <H1> through <H6>. As always, when you open with a tag <H1>, be sure to close with the closing tag </H1>.

To create a page with a title recognized by the browser and a large-font title across the top of the page, the code would look like this:

```
<HTML>

<HEAD>
<TITLE>ShoopSoft on the WWW</TITLE>
</HEAD>

<BODY>
<H1>The ShoopSoft Page</H1>
</BODY>

</HTML>
```

Putting plain text on a page requires no special formatting.

However, since browsers do not recognize spaces between lines or carriage returns in the code itself, you need to indicate where you want line breaks in the document. For a simple break, use the <BR> tag. To indicate that a section of text is to be interpreted as a paragraph, enclose the text inside the opening and closing paragraph tags, <P> and </P>. The <BR> or <P> tags are unnecessary inside a section of header text—a line is automatically inserted after a header closing tag.

You can format the plain text on an page in a number of ways. Enclosing text within the tags <B> and </B> makes it bold type, and enclosing text within <I> and </I> italicizes it. These tags, currently very common in HTML page design, may be gradually phased out in favor of more specific tags. For example, it is better to use the tags <EM>, for "emphasized" text, and <STRONG>, for text that is more strongly emphasized, than to use the more general <B>. Similarly, the tags <CITE>, for cited text, and <VAR>, which indicates a variable, are more useful than <I>, since they identify the text more exactly.

The layout of text on a Web page can be modified using the list functions. The three most commonly used types of lists are the *unordered list,* designated with the <UL> tag, the *ordered list,* designated with the <OL> tag, and the *definition list,* which is designated with the <DL> tag. The major difference between these tags is that all items in the unordered list are bulleted, the items in the ordered list are numbered, and the items in the definition list are unbulleted.

An unordered list is created by opening the list with <UL>, marking each item in the list with the tag <LI> and closing the list with </UL>. An ordered list is opened with the <OL> tag, and each item is also marked with the <LI> tag. The definition list is opened with <DL>, and each item in the list is marked with <DT>. That item can then be elaborated upon with text that follows the tag <DD>, and after the last item, the list is closed with the tag </DL>. The list items themselves, <LI>, <DT> and <DD> do not require a closing tag—they will be automatically closed when another item is started, or when the list itself is closed. Any of the lists can be *nested,* that is, you can place a list inside a list, simply by opening another list with <UL>, <OL> or <DL> before closing the first list.

The following is a sample page using the codes mentioned so

far. Figure 2-1 following this code provides a picture of how this page would look on a browser.

```
<HTML>

<HEAD>
<TITLE>ShoopSoft on the WWW</TITLE>
</HEAD>

<BODY>
<H1>The ShoopSoft Page</H1>
Welcome to the <B>ShoopSoft</B> page. This is our <I>very own home
page</I> on the World Wide Web.<P>
Here you can get information on the following services:

<UL>
<LI>Networking software
<LI>Custom hardware configurations
        <UL>
        <LI>Macintosh
        <LI>PC
        <LI>Workstations
        </UL>
<LI>HTML training seminars
</UL>

ShoopSoft's many virtues include:
<DL>
<DT>Reliability
        <DD>We guarantee quick response and 24/7
        accessibility.
<DT>Quality
        <DD>Our team has over 5 years of Internet
        experience.
<DT>Affordability
        <DD>Everything we do is free. Really.
</DL>

</BODY>

</HTML>
```

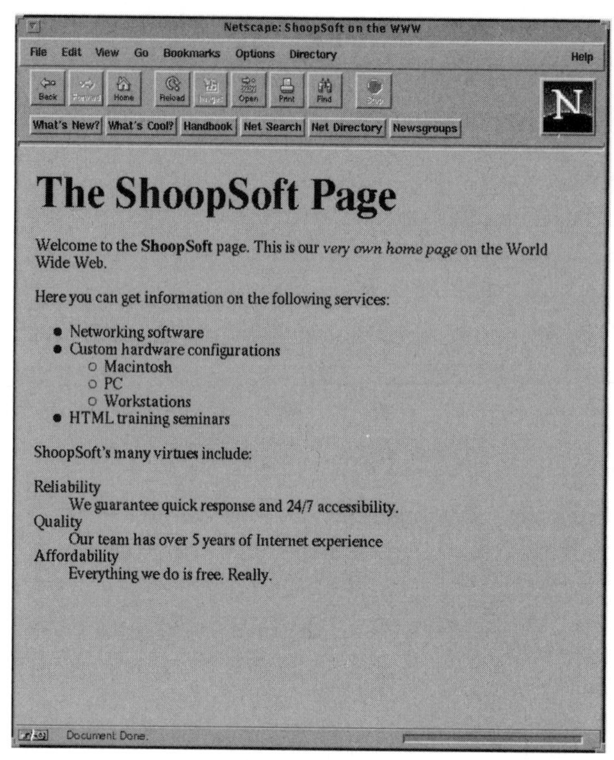

Figure 2-1: *A Sample Web Page.*

One of the added advantages of using an unbulleted list like <DL> is that, instead of the standard bullets, you can insert custom list bullets in your lists. The format for this uses a tag that we discuss later in this chapter, the <IMG> tag. In brief, this particular format allows you to load an image in front of each term. It also specifies an alternate character to display if the client's browser cannot load that image. The format for a two-item list using the <IMG> tag would be the following:

```
<DL>
<DT><IMG ALT="**" SRC="dot.gif"> Item I
<DT><IMG ALT="**" SRC="dot.gif"> Item II
</DL>
```

Note that DOT.GIF in the example can be any file name or location you choose. Simply create an icon for your list, and enter that file name in place of DOT.GIF. Using this tag and custom-designed list bullets, you can give your pages a personalized feel with relatively little effort on your part.

Three other tags are commonly used for page formatting. <BLOCKQUOTE> and </BLOCKQUOTE> indents a section of text to indicate that it is an extract—that it has been taken from some other source. Another commonly used tag is for preformatted text. It allows you to format text in your editor any way you choose and to display that formatted text. One of the limitations of HTML, for example, is that it cannot display more than one space between strings, so browsers cannot show text separated with a tab or display ASCII art. After formatting text the way you want it to appear on a browser, surround it with the tag set <PRE> and </PRE>, and it will display exactly as you have laid it out. Unfortunately, being "preformatted" means that formats like boldface and italics are not displayed and that the text will appear in the Courier font, which from a design standpoint, is not a particularly appealing option. Finally, to divide your page with horizontal lines, use the <HR> tag. It creates a line that extends across the page, which is an attractive way of delineating sections and does not slow the time required for a page to load.

Hyperlinks

After you have added the text to your page and formatted it appropriately, you can integrate the page into your site and other sites using links to other pages and to different resources like multimedia files. The hyperlink is an extremely versatile tool in HTML. It can link to any type of resource you choose, so long as your server can specify a MIME type and the client has software that can display data of that type (see the section "Files on the Web: File Formats & MIME Typing," earlier in this chapter). The most common links are to other HTML files, but links to different types of resources have the same format. If you wanted users to click on the words "our employees' resumes" to access a new Web page, you would insert a link similar to the following:

```
We're firing everyone. If you want to hire someone who works here, then
look at
<A HREF="resumes.html">our employees' resumes.
</A><P>
```

The <A HREF="..."> tag is closed with a </A> tag. The same is true of any tag that has more than one word in it. You can just use the first word or character string with a slash to close it. The tag in the example above references a document at the same site. To link to a document at another site, simply insert the full URL of that site:

```
Learn more about the
<A HREF="http://www.w3.org/">World Wide Web</A>.<BR>
```

You can use exactly the same format for linking to any other type of file:

```
Check out <A HREF="dobbs.gif">my photograph</A>,
<A HREF="/users/sounds/welcome.au">hear me say hi</A>, or look at an
MPEG movie of <A HREF="http://www.fbi.gov/data/rp003x.mpeg">me at
a political rally</A>.<P>
```

It's a good idea when presenting something other than an image or a standard audio file (Macintosh sound resource, PC WAV file or Sun AU) to state what kind of resource it is, so that users can determine if they have the capability to replay it on the machine being used. Finally, HTML can be used to provide links to files, like binaries or source code, that are not to be displayed. Links are made exactly the same way as with multimedia files, but when users try to download the file, they are asked where to save that file and are responsible for uncompressing the file themselves (since you will store all files for transfer in some sort of compressed format, as discussed in the section "Compression" earlier in this chapter). A link such as the following references a file that has been compressed with tar and gzip:

```
Try our <A HREF="/users/data/bin/recipe093.tar.gz">new recipe data-
base</A> for FREE!<P>
```

You can use hyperlinks to go to a specific location in an HTML document. You create an "anchor" in that document and then specify the file name and the anchor in the link. To create the anchors in the document to be accessed, insert the tag

<A NAME="*anchorname*">, where *anchorname* is replaced by whatever you want to call that anchor. Then, when building a link to the anchor on that page, reference it with the URL, the # symbol and the anchorname, as follows:

```
<A HREF="/users/data/matthews/book.html#ch2">
```

If you want to go to an anchor within the same document, you can make a reference to #*anchorname* without any file information.

```
<H2>Table of Contents</H2>
<A HREF="#ch1">Chapter 1</A><BR>
<A HREF="#ch2">Chapter 2</A><BR>
```

Images

The use of images within a Web page is a major element in creating a truly customized and impressive site. The use of images will be taken up extensively in Chapter 7, "Images on the Web," and this section will simply explain how to write the HTML code that puts the graphics on the page. The graphics format that all Web browsers can display on the page itself is called a GIF (Graphics Interchange Format), and the default extension for GIF files is .gif.

The tag for including images is rather obviously named <IMG>. A number of variables configure the <IMG> tag. The most basic format for including an image is <IMG SRC="*picture*.gif"> where *picture*.gif is replaced by the file name. As with the <A HREF> tag, you can specify the file name and draw an image from another server, simply by inserting the path or the full URL as the source file name. There is no closing tag for <IMG>.

Not all browsers, including the widely used text browser Lynx, can display graphics. It is a good idea to specify an alternate character or set of characters to load. Text-based browsers, by default, look for an alternate character, which is specified with ALT. For example, in our example custom bulleted list, the list items were coded as follows:

```
<DT><IMG ALT="**" SRC="dot.gif"> Item I
<DT><IMG ALT="**" SRC="dot.gif"> Item II
```

If a browser could not display the image DOT.GIF, it would preface each list item with the character string —> instead. Specifying an alternate for images is considered to be good form because a significant number of users use Lynx and other nongraphical browsers to access the Web.

Another way of customizing the layout of your page is to specify where you want the text beside a picture to be located. The ALIGN option aligns text beside the image with the top, middle or bottom of that image. Simply put ALIGN=top, ALIGN=middle or ALIGN=bottom inside the <IMG> tag. So, for example, to align the menu items listed in the previous example with the center of the list bullets, you could change the code for each to read as follows:

```
<IMG ALT="**" ALIGN=middle SRC="dot.gif">
```

HTML also currently recognizes an image that you've indicated is an *imagemap*, which is an image that has hyperlinks that are linked to certain coordinates in the graphic. By clicking on the graphic in a certain place, the user is taken to the link that is connected to that area of the image. To specify that an image should be recognized as an imagemap, add ISMAP at the end of the <IMG> tag. The graphic itself also needs to be linked to an imagemap file, and this process and the rest of the process of creating imagemaps is explained in the section "Clickable Imagemaps," in Chapter 7, "Images on the Web."

Graphics that are not imagemaps can be linked to a single file in the same way that text is. One very common way of presenting graphics on the Web is to have a small version of a graphic linked to the full size image. This is done in exactly the same manner as linking text, but in the place of the text, you insert the <IMG> tag. Two examples follow:

```
<A HREF="/users/data/pics/clinton.gif"><IMG ALT="Clinton!"
SRC="clinton-icon.gif"></A>
<A HREF="http://www.netscape.com/"><IMG ALT="*" ALIGN=bottom
SRC="mozilla.gif">Netscape Home Page
</A>
```

The second example links both the image and the text to the URL.

A number of editors write much of the code in HTML for you, using a menu-driven editor interface, one of which is included with this book. Many people find standard text editors perfectly adequate for writing HTML documents, others prefer to use special programs. If you find an HTML editor that you are comfortable with, by all means, use it. However, you should always have some sort of reference to the HTML code itself and be familiar with it, because no editor allows the full range of creative possibilities that HTML allows.

Netscape Extras

Netscape Communications, Inc., in 1994 introduced a new Web browser that can display a number of tags that are not yet supported by other browsers currently in use. The new tags have been proposed as additions to the HTML standard and may be globally supported at a later date, but for now, they are unique to Netscape users. There are several very nice features in the Netscape enhanced tags, and if you don't mind the current limitations on who can see their effects, they are worth checking out. A full listing of these tags is available at the URL http://www.netscape.com/home/services_docs/html-extensions.html. Some of the more interesting tags are described in the remainder of this section.

- **<HR>—Horizontal Rule.** The HR element, described earlier in "The Basics of HTML," can be configured in several different ways. For example, entering <HR SIZE=number> lets you define the thickness of the line, and you can modify the length of the line using <HR WIDTH=number | percent>, specifying the length of the line in pixels or the percentage of the page width it extends across. Using the tag <HR ALIGN=left | right | center>, you can specify the alignment of the line if you've made it shorter than the width of the page.
- **<IMG>—Image.** Most of the new Netscape extensions have to do with the <IMG> tag. We won't go into full detail in this chapter because all of the Netscape options are covered in Chapter 7, "Images on the Web."

- **<UL> and <OL>—Lists.** The unordered list, or <UL>, generally has a standard order in which bullets are displayed, depending upon the browser. A new option, TYPE, has been added so that, when creating the list, you can specify in advance the shape of that list's bullets as TYPE=disc, TYPE=circle or TYPE=square. For the ordered list, or <OL>, the TYPE option specifies the type of character to be used for ordering the list. Entering TYPE=A designates the use of capital letters (A, B, C . . .); TYPE=a, lowercase letters; TYPE=I, Roman numerals; TYPE=i; small Roman numerals; and not specifying this option defaults to using numbers. The <OL> option also has the new option START=, with which you can specify the starting value of the TYPE you have chosen. For example, setting START=4 would begin the list with D, d, IV or iv or 4, depending on the TYPE specified.
- **<NOBR>—No Break.** Since Web browsers, including Netscape, automatically wrap lines of text that are too long for the screen, lines occasionally lose the desired formatting. Text between <NOBR> and </NOBR> does not wrap around but continues off the side of the browser screen.
- **<WBR>—Word Break.** Using the <NOBR> tag, you can specify where you do want a line to wrap by using the <WBR> tag inside the no-break section. This is not the same as a line break tag; the word break tag tells the browser where a break could be placed, if needed.
- **<FONT SIZE=value>—Text Font Size.** This tag allows the font size of a character or string to be increased or decreased. You can either specify a size in a range of 1 to 7 or use a plus (+) or minus sign (–) to indicate a relative change, which is based on the standard font size 3. To change the standard size, you can use the <BASEFONT=value> tag. If you set <BASEFONT=4>, for example, a + would increase the size to 5, and text without the font size change would appear as 4.

- **<BLINK>—Blinking Text.** This tag is fairly self-evident. Anything enclosed between <BLINK> and </BLINK> blinks. Since it is kind of silly looking, this tag should be used in moderation.
- **<CENTER>—Centered display.** This tag allows any text or images to be centered on the page. Make sure to use the closing tag on this one so you won't center your entire page.

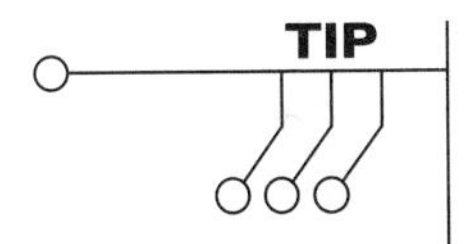

For an excellent introduction to writing HTML, check out NCSA's "A Beginner's Guide to HTML," at http://www.ncsa.uiuc.edu/demoweb/html-primer.html.

tkHTML: An HTML Editor

Included with this book is an HTML editor called tkHTML. tkHTML is a very comprehensive editing program, with a menu structure that includes almost every HTML tag. Using these menus, you can automatically insert tags into a document, or you can easily create a new document. tkHTML is written in a language called tcl/tk, which has a unique structure that allows users to make configurations and changes in the code itself and these configurations and changes immediately show up upon launching the program. The majority of configurations that you will want to make are in the file CONFIG.TCL, which you should browse before beginning. It is very clearly documented and easy to modify. Check to make certain that all of the options in this file are set correctly for your needs.

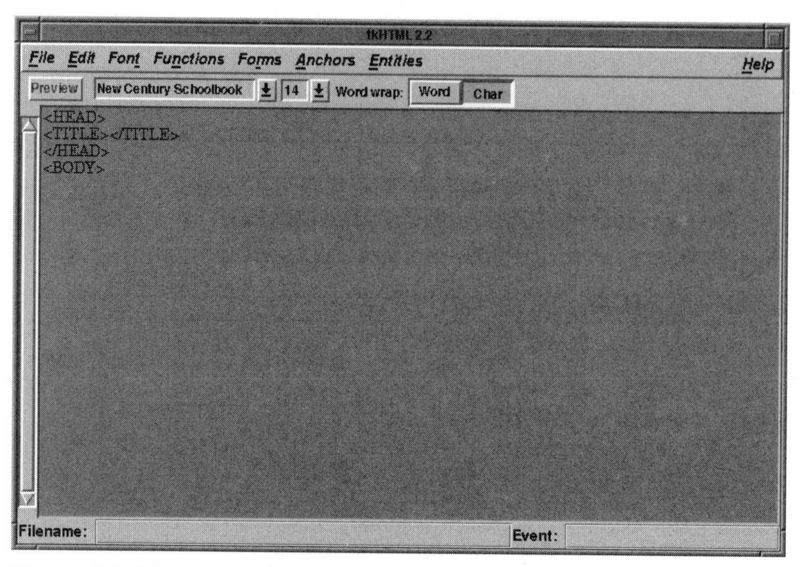

Figure 2-2: *The main menu in tkHTML.*

The menu-driven interface of tkHTML, shown in Figure 2-2, allows anyone who is generally familiar with graphical user interface (GUI) programs, like Macintosh or Windows applications, to learn the format fairly quickly. tkHTML contains virtually all of the HTML tags that are currently available in a simple pull-down menu structure. Basically, you are able to point and click to accomplish anything you want to do. This section briefly explains the capabilities of the various functions of tkHTML, with reference to some HTML tags not covered in the previous introduction to HTML.

The row of options below the menus themselves allows you to configure the editor window to your taste, setting the font style and size and so on. These changes do not affect the HTML document itself.

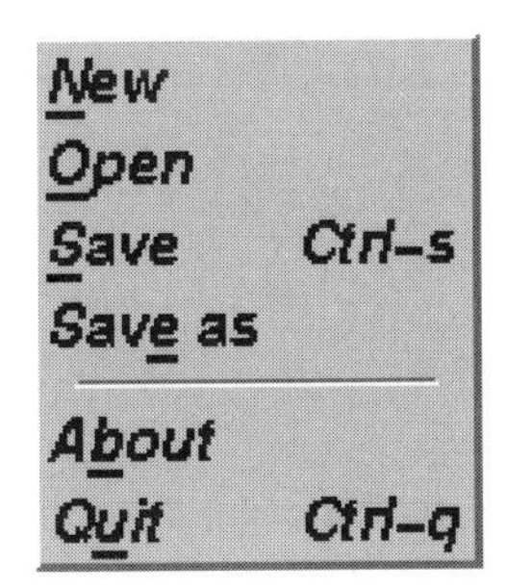

Figure 2-3: *The File menu in tkHTML.*

Cut Ctrl-X
Copy Ctrl-C
Paste Ctrl-V
Find ... Ctrl-S
Find again Ctrl-F
Replace Ctrl-R

Figure 2-4: *The Edit menu in tkHTML.*

The File and Edit menus (shown in Figure 2-3 and Figure 2-4, respectively) are fairly standard for GUI programs. The Find option in the Edit menu is sensitive to capitalization, so make sure to enter exactly the string you are looking for. The Font menu, shown in Figure 2-2, introduces several tags not mentioned in this chapter. A number of Netscape tags are available, but if you do not plan to use Netscape or are not designing your site to be Netscape enhanced, these tags may not be necessary. If this is the case and you don't want the Netscape tags to appear in your menus, you can change the last line in CONFIG.TCL to read as follows:

```
set netscape 0
```

Bold <B>	Alt-b
Italic <I>	Alt-i
Underline <U>	Alt-u
Center <CENTER>	Alt-C
Font <FONT>	▷
Typewriter <TT>	
Citation <CITE>	
Code <CODE>	Alt-c
Emphasis <EM>	Alt-e
Strong <STRONG>	Alt-s
Sample <SAMP>	
Keyboard <KBD>	
Variable <VAR>	
Definition <DFN>	
Address <ADDRESS>	Alt-a
Blink <BLINK>	Alt-B

Figure 2-5: *The Fonts menu in tkHTML.*

The <FONT>, <CENTER> and <BLINK> tags are the Netscape enhancements in the Font menu. The tags in the Font menu (shown in Figure 2-5), in order of appearance, are

- **<TT>—Typewriter.** This is similar to the <PRE> tag discussed earlier in this chapter, in that it returns a Courier, or typewriter-style font. However, unlike <PRE>, it requires tags for paragraph or line breaks and can use formatting like bold and italics. This tag is useful if you want some sort of font change in your document other than the font size.
- **<CITE>—Citation.** This is an italicized section of text, to indicate that it is being quoted from some other source.
- **<CODE>—Computer code.** This font is similar to the typewriter font, used to indicate computer code. It can use formatting and requires paragraph breaks.

- **<EM> and <STRONG>—Emphasis tags.** Both of these tags create a bold font, with <STRONG> producing a slightly larger font. On some browsers, <EM> appears as an italicized font.
- **<KBD>—Keyboard.** This font also produces a Courier-type font, requiring paragraph breaks and allowing for fomatting.
- **<VAR>—Variable.** <VAR> produces an italicized font.
- **<DFN>—Definition.** <DFN> indicates a word that is to be defined, and browsers should display that word in italics.
- **<ADDRESS>—Address.** Used for e-mail addresses, this tag displays the address in italics.

For now, many of the tags appear to be similar or even exactly the same on a browser, like italics <I> and address <ADDRESS>, but this situation may change in upcoming browser releases. It's always a good idea to use specific tags to delineate and define the items in an HTML document.

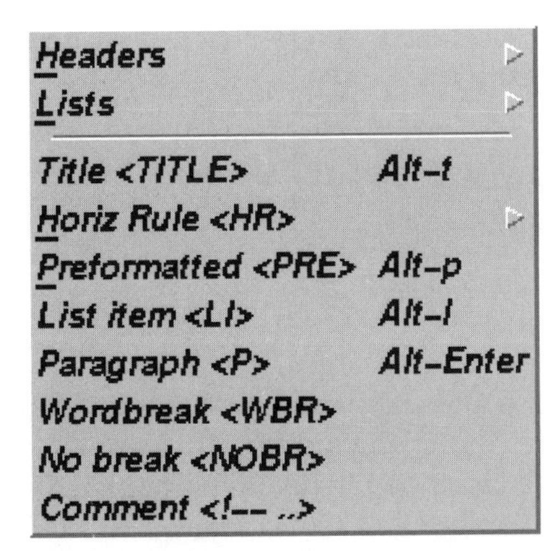

Figure 2-6: *The Functions menu in tkHTML.*

The Functions menu, as shown in Figure 2-6, allows for a wide range of configurations of an HTML document. The Headers submenu produces the header sizes 1 through 6, with both opening and closing tags. The Lists submenu allows you to produce either of the list types discussed earlier and insert list item tags, either <LI> or <DT> and <DL>. You insert the <TITLE>, <LI> (list item) and <P> (paragraph break) tags from the Functions menu as well. The comment tag can be used to insert in the code comments that will not be displayed on browsers , which is useful for marking changes from an original page or leaving notes for improvements that need to be made. The <HR> tag inserts the standard horizontal rule, and it also uses the Netscape enhanced options for the <HR> tag if the Netscape tags option is selected in CONFIG.TCL. Similarly, the word break <WBR> and no break <NOBR> tags, also Netscape enhancements, appear only if you have chosen to use them.

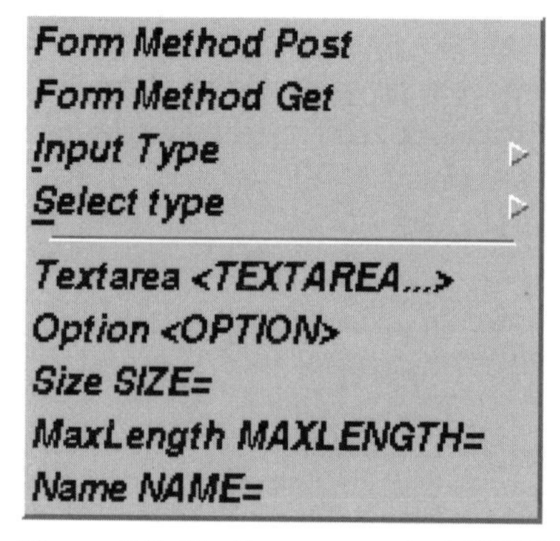

Figure 2-7: *The Forms menu in tkHTML.*

The Forms menu and submenus, as shown in Figure 2-7, allow you to create fill-in forms on your HTML documents. Creating and using forms is described in detail in Chapter 10, "Simple Forms," and in Chapter 11, "CGI: Advanced Forms for Programmers." Basically, you need to insert certain variables into the tags. tkHTML places your cursor exactly where your input is needed, and after reading Chapters 10 and 11, you should be able to create any type of form necessary for your site with the tkHTML menus.

Hyperlink	Alt-H
Inline image	Alt-I

Figure 2-8: *The Anchors menu in tkHTML.*

The Anchors menu, as shown in Figure 2-8, inserts the basic tags for hyperlinking documents and inserting inline images, but you need to fill out all of the file information. As with the forms, your cursor is placed where you need to add information. In the case of the file hyperlink, you are given the following text:

```
<A HREF="">CHANGE_ME</A>
```

You need to add the reference to the file itself, between the quotation marks, and the text for the link in place of the string CHANGE_ME. Also, you have to manually enter any additional options in the <IMG> tag, such as the ALT option. The same is true for hyperlinks to an imagemap; you need to manually insert the ISMAP option.

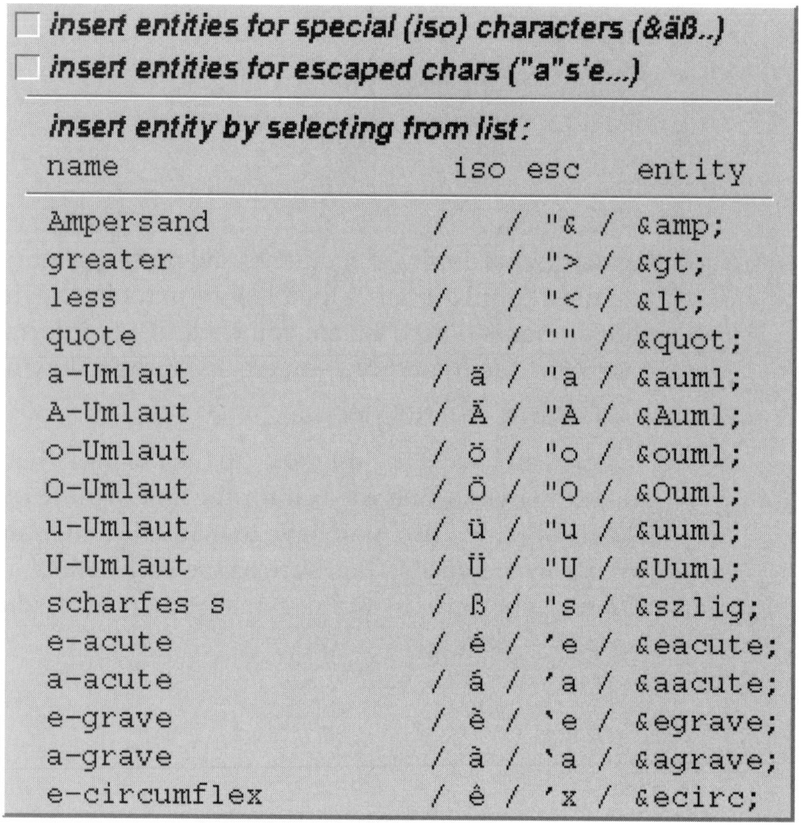

```
[ ] insert entities for special (iso) characters (&äß..)
[ ] insert entities for escaped chars ("a"s'e...)

insert entity by selecting from list:
name                  iso esc    entity

Ampersand           /   / "& / &amp;
greater             /   / "> / &gt;
less                /   / "< / &lt;
quote               /   / "" / &quot;
a-Umlaut            / ä / "a / &auml;
A-Umlaut            / Ä / "A / &Auml;
o-Umlaut            / ö / "o / &ouml;
O-Umlaut            / Ö / "O / &Ouml;
u-Umlaut            / ü / "u / &uuml;
U-Umlaut            / Ü / "U / &Uuml;
scharfes s          / ß / "s / &szlig;
e-acute             / é / 'e / &eacute;
a-acute             / á / 'a / &aacute;
e-grave             / è / `e / &egrave;
a-grave             / à / `a / &agrave;
e-circumflex        / ê / 'x / &ecirc;
```

Figure 2-9: *The Entities menu in tkHTML.*

Finally, one HTML function that we have not mentioned is the ability to insert *entities,* or special characters, that browsers can display. Essentially, by entering a certain string of characters, you can instruct a browser to display characters that are not on the keyboard itself or characters that cannot be displayed because the browser tries to interpret them as code. The first type, the nonexistent characters, includes vowels with accents, umlauts or circumflexes. The second type, characters that the browser tries to interpret as code, includes the ampersand (&) and the greater than (<) and less than (>) symbols. To insert these, you have to manually enter a string that the browser can interpret correctly. In tkHTML, you simply select the entity from the pull-down menu, shown in Figure 2-9.

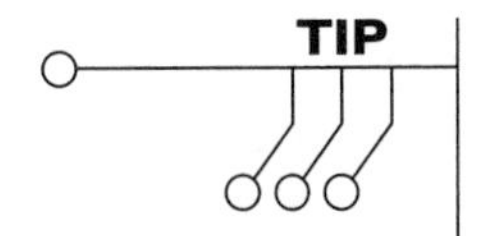

To create a new entity, look at the "Entities" on tkHTML's built-in Help function. You can add new entities to the editor by modifying the file ENTITIES.TCL, as the Help file explains. For a complete list of entities that WWW browsers can display, look at CERN's comprehensive listing at the URL http://info.cern.ch/hypertext/WWW/MarkUp/ISOlat1.html.

Once you have formatted your new HTML document, or as you are working on it and checking your progress, you can use the Preview button on the upper left-hand corner to show you the layout of your page. This button creates a new window, in which tkHTML displays the HTML document. The format appears, with some variation by browser type, exactly as it would on the World Wide Web browsers of users visiting your site. While you can't edit in the Preview window itself, when you make changes to the document in the tkHTML editor, the Preview window is updated each time you push the Preview button.

It should be noted that a number of features that are available in tkHTML do not actually appear in the Preview window, most notably, the Netscape extra tags. The best way to see how a document will look, in this and all cases, is to save it as a file and use several different browsers to view it locally. By seeing how different browsers display a document, you will have a better idea of what your world-wide audience will be seeing regardless of what browser software is being used.

Moving On

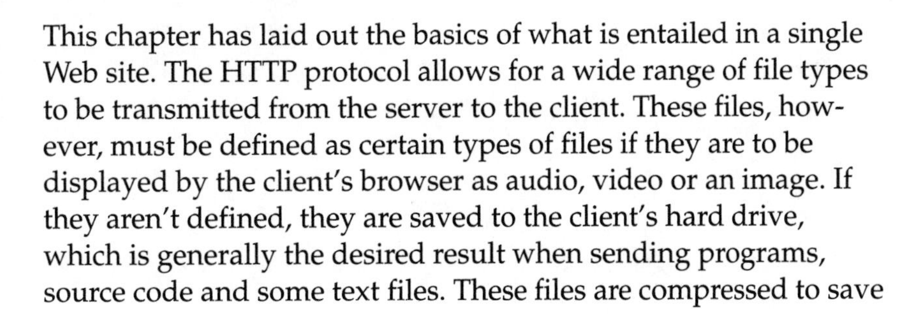

This chapter has laid out the basics of what is entailed in a single Web site. The HTTP protocol allows for a wide range of file types to be transmitted from the server to the client. These files, however, must be defined as certain types of files if they are to be displayed by the client's browser as audio, video or an image. If they aren't defined, they are saved to the client's hard drive, which is generally the desired result when sending programs, source code and some text files. These files are compressed to save transmission time, using one or more of the major compression programs like tar, zip or gzip. Finally, all of this information is laid out in the Web page, which is created using a series of codes called HTML. This code allows you to create formatted text, include images and create links to any files that you want the user to access.

Now that we've covered the basics of what a Web site comprises—the protocol, the files and the language itself—you should begin preparing to create your own site and pages. As noted previously, you need HTTP server software, or a daemon, to serve your documents to clients. The next chapter will describe several types of daemons and give instructions on how to set up and maintain each one. The rest of the book will be devoted to helping you develop the material on your server and make it accessible from your pages in as many ways as possible.

3

Setting Up the Server

If you're an active surfer of the Web, you're familiar with the client side of the client-server equation, but if you want to become an information provider, you'll need to know a bit about servers. Theoretically, the World Wide Web is a concept, a seamless way of integrating different Internet protocols and services. In practice though, the Web mainly involves the HyperText Transfer Protocol, or HTTP.

HTTP is a simple, stateless protocol; it was designed to be easy to implement, requiring little overhead. Because of this simplicity, many different people, companies and organizations have written HTTP server software; each with its own set of features and weaknesses. Although this diversity provides many choices to the interested Webmaster, it can also be confusing. This chapter reviews the available server software for UNIX, comparing the advantages and disadvantages of each.

Despite all of these alternatives, a straw poll conducted at the second WWW Conference showed that 90 percent of present Webmasters used the NCSA server. Its popularity comes from the ease with which it can be configured, its simple code and its light use of system resources. This chapter will completely describe how to install and configure the NCSA HTTP server.

If you don't quite feel ready to run your own Web server, you might try leasing space on someone else's machine. Many new companies will sell you space on their servers. This chapter also offers advice on choosing a Web provider, along with pointers to companies that offer this service and suggestions on making the transition from rented space to your very own server.

Comparing Servers

The HTTP protocol is intentionally easy to implement; a stripped-down server written in the perl programming language can have fewer than 50 lines of code. Because it's relatively easy to write one, many servers are out there. The vast majority of servers are research projects or toys, mostly written for the education or enjoyment of the author. Only a handful of UNIX HTTP servers are full featured and actively maintained, and the bulk of this section is devoted to describing and comparing them.

All of the reviewed servers share a common set of features. These represent the minimal level of functionality necessary to create and maintain a professional Web presence. All of the servers in this section support:

- Compliance with version 1.0 of the HTTP standard.
- Backwards compatibility with version 0.9 of the HTTP standard.
- Clickable imagemaps, which associate URLs with an area of a graphic image.
- Some method of extending the server's functionality with external gateways.

What is CGI?
All the servers discussed in this section, except for Plexus, implement the Common Gateway Interface (CGI), which is a programming standard that allows you to write and run external programs that interact with the HTTP server and Web browsers. CGI scripts can dynamically generate Web pages and handle interactive forms; the standard is indispensable for Web developers who wish to make their sites more than just flat pictures and text.

Despite CGI's usefulness, poorly written CGI programs can be a security risk to your site. For this reason, most servers (including NCSA servers, which we discuss in detail) impose restrictions on their use. The decision of who has permission to use CGI on the server is left with the server administrator, who can dole it out as he or she wishes.

Although the details of CGI are fully explained in Chapter 11, "CGI: Advanced Forms for Programmers," we often refer to CGI and CGI scripts in this chapter, so it's important that you have at least some idea of their implications.

The CERN Server

The Web and the HTTP protocol was invented at CERN, the European Laboratory for Particle Physics. The HTTP server written there is the original and the model for all the other servers. The CERN server shows its age in its stability, its long list of features and its complexity.

Although the CERN server can be complex to configure and administer, no other server offers its flexibility. Because it's built on the CERN WWW library code (which is used as the base for every Web browser), the CERN server can also act as an HTTP client, which is useful for users operating in a firewall environment, where only a single machine (the firewall) on the internal network can access the Internet at large. Users on firewall-protected machines can designate a CERN server on the firewall as their proxy. Rather than requesting URLs directly, clients send all URLs to the proxy server, which sends on the request to the intended server and then sends back the results to the original client.

This proxy architecture also allows an organization to maintain a caching WWW server. If users in an organization designate a CERN server as their proxy, their browsers send all requests to this dedicated server, which caches the returned object locally. When a user of the caching server requests a resource that was requested previously by another user, the server returns the saved copy. This avoids repeatedly retrieving the same Web resources from the external network, which speeds retrievals and saves wear and tear on other Web servers and the organization's own Internet connection.

In addition to its unique system of proxy caching, the CERN server offers an unparalleled number of configurable parameters. It allows you to:

- Finely limit the server's caching and proxy activity.
- Attach your own programs to handle unimplemented methods in the HTTP protocol.
- Control access to specific URLs by host, user authentication and access method.

In addition to these somewhat intimidating features, the CERN HTTP daemon (HTTPD) has the full package of features that most Web providers expect. You may ask the obvious question—if the CERN server has so many useful features, why does this chapter go into more detail about the NCSA server?

The answer is that the features of the CERN server incur costs in both the load that multiple copies of the daemon imposes on your server and in the amount of time it can take to figure out the dozens of options the CERN server offers. If you need a WWW cache or proxy, you have no alternative; you should use CERN. If you're a beginning Webmaster and you want to get your site up and running as quickly as possible, consider CERN something to investigate when you have some extra time.

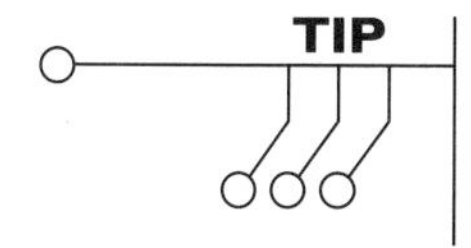

The CERN server source code and binaries are on the Companion CD-ROM for you to investigate yourself. You can also get copies of the software and its documentation at http://www.w3.org/hypertext/WWW/Daemon/Status.html.

Plexus

The Plexus server is written in perl, a dynamic, interpreted language. Along with the standard set of features, Plexus has its own abilities and its own way of doing things.

Since it's written in perl, you can write and seamlessly integrate extensions to the server in perl. Although it's easy to add new functionality to the server this way, the interface Plexus uses isn't compatible with the CGI standard; gateways written for other servers, such as the popular NCSA and CERN servers, won't run under Plexus. Instead, Plexus offers a much richer programming interface, which allows the experienced perl coder to access much of the server's own functionality from his or her script.

Perl is a wonderful language, and we proclaim its wonders at some length in Chapter 11, "CGI: Advanced Forms for Programmers," but there is a high overhead in using it for server applications. If you use Plexus, you can expect a slow response time and a heavy load on your hardware.

On the other hand, Plexus easily accomplishes feats that other HTTP servers find difficult. For example, it's easy to set up the searching of your archive with Plexus; it allows users to look for files in a particular directory or series of directories in your Web pages.

Plexus is an interesting package. It trades the efficiency and standards of the more popular servers for easy customization with a rich programming interface. If your Web development emphasizes dynamic response and you're not afraid of perl's overhead, you should give Plexus a try. The package and its associated documentation can be found at http://www.bsdi.com/server/doc/plexus.html.

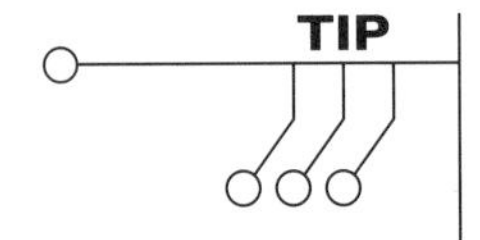

If you like the idea of HTTP servers in dynamic languages, you should check out John Mallery's Common LISP Hypermedia Server. This server, written in Common Lisp, is an attempt to combine the Web with Artificial Intelligence technologies. The server provides extensive support for the dynamic generation of HTML and other documents, as well as the full range of standard HTTP v1.0 features. A paper that describes the server and the Common Lisp source code can be obtained at http://www.ai.mit.edu/projects/iiip/doc/cl-http/server-abstract.html.

The WN Server

The author of the WN server, John Franks, says that his server is "for those who think the Web should be more than a user friendly interface to ftp." This statement represents WN's very different approach to serving.

Other popular HTTP servers take a fairly simple approach to server maintenance. They use the UNIX file system. The server has a data directory and serves files beneath that directory, according to requests from the client; access to these files is controlled by the regular UNIX file permissions (the server can't send files that it doesn't have permission to read) and special access control files.

WN borrows a few ideas from the Gopher server, combines them with a solid HTTP package, and ends up with a completely different way of doing things. Instead of relying on the UNIX file system, WN uses a flat text database file in each directory to control access to the files in that directory. If a file doesn't have an entry in the appropriate database, the server's default action is to deny access to it. Thus, making a file available through WN requires an explicit action by the server maintainer, which gives the Webmaster more control over who is accessing the server's resources.

In short, the server treats HTML pages as textual objects—documents that can be excerpted from, assembled and searched. This unique approach to server management has many advantages, especially for small sites. Larger sites may get bogged down in maintaining these databases, although WN comes with several useful tools for avoiding this.

If WN's unique approach sounds interesting to you, you can find a copy of the source and the well-written user manual at http://hopf.math.nwu.edu/.

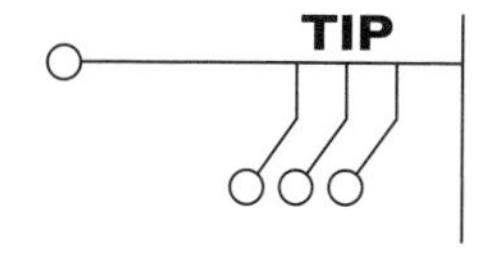

If you're trying to make the transition from Gopher to the Web, the GN server may be your best bet. GN is a dual protocol server; it recognizes both Gopher and HTTP requests and responds differently to each. For example, the GN server can present the HTML version of a document to a WWW client and a plain ASCII version to a Gopher client.

Using GN does have disadvantages. If you choose to run GN on the Gopher port, users may have a hard time finding your home page. Also, the HTTP URLs used by GN look suspiciously like Gopher URLs, which can be somewhat confusing to users.

Despite these disadvantages, GN is an excellent first step to take in setting up a server, if you already have a significant investment of time and effort in Gopher. You can find out more about GN at http://hopf.math.nwu.edu:70/.

Servers in Development

The field of server development seems to be accelerating. Several new HTTP servers in various stages of testing merit a mention in this section. Although none of these servers are currently (Spring 1995) "ready for prime time," some are quite close and may be ready by the time you read this book.

Apache

A group of WWW developers and Webmasters have announced the Apache project. Apache is a reaction to what many see as the lack of active maintenance of the NCSA server (although this situation has improved with the recent release of NCSA v1.4). Since, in the past, new versions of NCSA have been few and far between, many people have added features and fixed bugs in the NCSA server for themselves.

The Apache project is an effort to integrate these patches and coordinate further development of the NCSA server. The Apache group hopes to end up with a server that meets the needs of the Web's busiest sites and solves the problems that experienced Webmasters have found with all the other servers.

You can find more information about Apache at the Apache home page (Figure 3-1): http://www.apache.org/apache/.

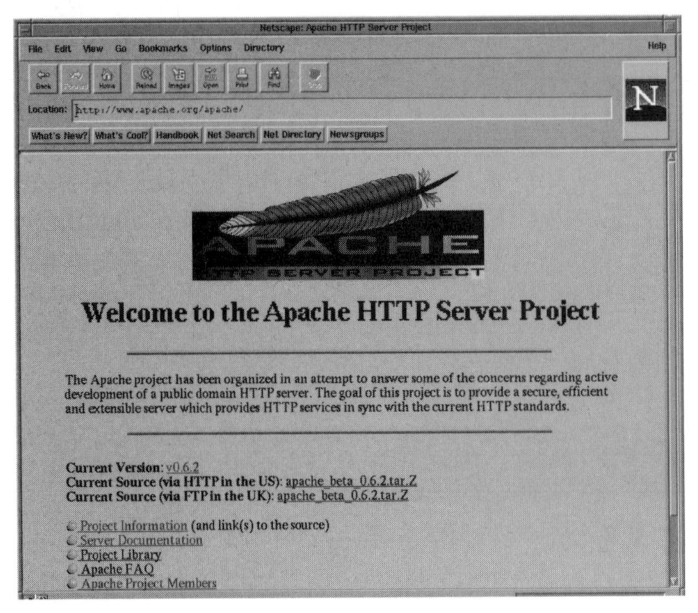

Figure 3-1: *The Apache server home page.*

MDMA

MDMA (Multi-threaded Daemon for Multimedia Access) is a new HTTP server for Solaris. It has been designed for use on busy servers such as SunSITE at the University of North Carolina, which handles over 300,000 requests a day.

The MDMA server's claim to speed is based on an examination of the bottlenecks in other servers and utilization of the technologies found in modern UNIX operating systems, such as multithreading (which avoids the overhead involved in "forking" a new copy of the server to handle each connection) and quick access to files through memory mapping. In addition to this,

MDMA's author, Simon Spero proposes and implements a new standard for dynamically extending the functionality of the server with BGI, the Binary Gateway Interface.

The currently available edition of MDMA is labeled "pre-alpha" and experimental. It hasn't been publicly updated for some time because MDMA has become the test bed for a potential replacement for the HTTP protocol known as HTTP-NG. You can find more information about HTTP-NG in Chapter 13, "Future Directions"; information and code for MDMA is at http://sunsite.unc.edu/mdma-release/mdma.html.

phttpd

Although MDMA hasn't been updated for quite some time, Peter Eriksson's phttpd captures much of its potential. Like MDMA, phttpd is limited to computers running the Sun Solaris version of UNIX, as it makes heavy use of Solaris multi-threading features. Unlike MDMA, the code is currently available and constantly improved, and several Web sites are using it.

The main disadvantage of phttpd (besides the fact that only Sun users can run it) is the complete lack of formal documentation. Although phttpd is extremely fast and fairly complete, it's currently used only by people who can figure it out from the source code. If that sounds like fun to you, you can get a copy of the source at ftp://ftp.lysator.liu.se/pub/phttpd/.

The NCSA Server

As previously noted, the NCSA HTTPD is the most popular server on the Web. In our opinion, it's the easiest free server to configure and install. Not only is it extremely easy to set up initially, but the NCSA server is also very flexible. The interested administrator can finely tune a number of parameters to optimize the server's performance and function. Most importantly, it provides all the functionality that you need to construct a first-class Web server. The NCSA server includes the following features:

- Easily configurable imagemaps.
- The original implementation of the CGI standard.
- Fine-grained control over client access and authentication.
- User-controlled directories for distributed administration of Web pages.

Just as important, the server is sufficiently stable to handle the heavy load that a popular site receives.

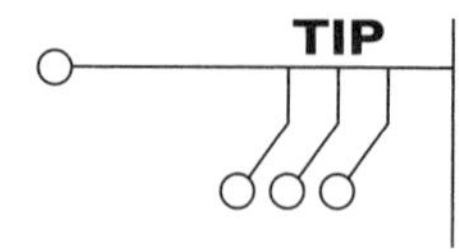

The original author of the NCSA HTTPD, Rob McCool, has left NCSA and joined Netscape Communications. In addition to its popular browser, Netscape sells a fast WWW server with commercial support. Recently, both Sun and SGI have announced plans to market the Netscape server with their hardware. For more information about the Netscape server, see http://home.netscape.com/comprod/netscape_products.html.

The current version of the NCSA server with binaries for most popular UNIX platforms is included on the Companion CD-ROM. If you install those binaries (following the instructions on the CD-ROM), you can skip ahead to the section "Configuring the Server." The next section will show you how to compile your own server (which is a useful experience).

Compiling the NCSA Server

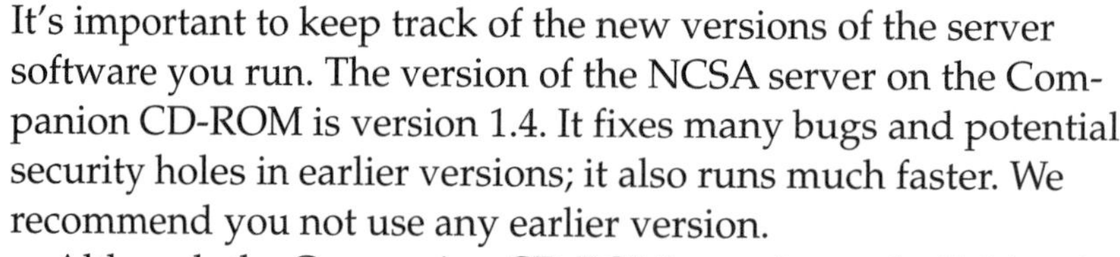

It's important to keep track of the new versions of the server software you run. The version of the NCSA server on the Companion CD-ROM is version 1.4. It fixes many bugs and potential security holes in earlier versions; it also runs much faster. We recommend you not use any earlier version.

Although the Companion CD-ROM contains prebuilt binaries for the current version, you'll need to compile newer versions yourself. Don't panic—the clever people at NCSA make this very simple. We'll briefly take you through the process with version 1.4—future versions will almost certainly be just as easy to compile. Follow these steps to compile the NCSA server:

1. Get the source code by pointing your Web browser at http://hoohoo.ncsa.uiuc.edu/docs/setup/Compilation.html or by anonymous FTP from ftp://ftp.ncsa.uiuc.edu/Web/httpd/UNIX/ncsa httpd/.
2. Move the source to /usr/local/etc/.
3. If you retrieved the source by anonymous FTP or with a browser that does not uncompress files on the fly, uncompress and un-tar the package as follows:

```
# zcat http_source.tar.Z | tar xvf -
```

4. XMosaic will uncompress files for you on the fly. If the file is already uncompressed, un-tar it as follows:

```
# tar xvf http_source.tar
```

5. This creates a directory named httpd_1.4. You can rename this directory to httpd:

```
# ln -s httpd_1.4 httpd
```

6. Or you can create a symbolic link to httpd:

```
# mv httpd_1.4 httpd
```

7. Go to the httpd directory.
8. Make a copy of the original Makefile located there for safekeeping.

```
# cp Makefile Makefile.dist
```

9. Edit the Makefile with your favorite editor. You need to check and set two key variables.
10. The first variable you need to change is CC. Uncomment the line (by removing the # in front of it) that refers to your ANSI C compiler and comment out the other CC line (by placing a # in front of it).

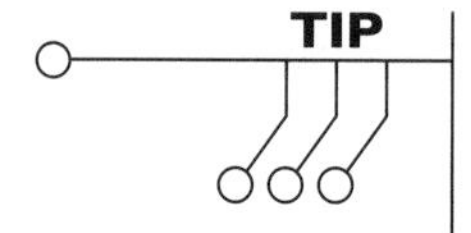

Unfortunately, there is an insidious trend in the computer industry to "unbundle" (that is, not include) a compiler with a system. For example, compilers no longer come with AIX and Solaris. The Free Software Foundation has written a portable, optimizing C compiler called gcc, which is available for free under the terms of the GNU Public License. gcc is available for a great number of operating systems, including Solaris and AIX. Take a look at ftp://prep.ai.mit.edu/pub/gnu for details.

11. The second variable that needs to be set is the CFLAGS value. Most people should set it to the following:

```
CFLAGS= -O2
```

12. You can also set several other options:

- -DMINIMAL_DNS This option prevents the server from doing a Domain Name Service reverse lookup for client connections. If you enable this option, the server logs only clients' numeric IP addresses, speeding up the server's response.
- -DMAXIMUM_DNS With this option, the server requires an authoritative response from client hosts. This option can slow the server significantly.
- -DPEM_AUTH This option enables the NCSA server's support for public key authentication for the PEM and PGP encryption programs, and is rarely used.
- -DXBITHACK This option tells the server that if the execute permissions bit is set on an HTML page, that page is a pre-parsed response.
- -DNO_PASS This option prevents the server from using the server pool described in the section "Configuring the Server" later in the chapter.

13. Save the Makefile, exit your editor and return to the main server directory.

14. Edit the Makefiles in the cgi-src and support directories. All you have to do is choose the proper compiler and CFLAGS.
15. You're ready now to compile the server. Type the following:

```
# make arch
```

16. Replace *arch* with one of the system architectures that the NCSA server supports: ibm (for AIX), sunos (for SunOS v4.x), solaris (for Solaris v2.x), hp-gcc (for HP-UX, using the gcc compiler), hp-cc (for HP-UX, using the ANSI HP compiler), sgi (for IRIX), decmips (for DEC MIPS machines, running Ultrix), decaxp (for DEC Alphas, running OSF/1), netbsd, linux or svr4 (for other System V Release 4 operating systems).
17. Copy the built httpd binary into /usr/local/etc/httpd.

```
# cp /usr/local/etc/httpd/src/httpd /usr/local/etc/httpd/httpd
```

You're finished! If you've followed the steps in this procedure, you've successfully compiled the server, as well as all of its CGI and support programs. Congratulations—now you must configure the server.

Configuring the Server

Three configuration files are associated with NCSA v1.4; you can find them in /usr/local/etc/httpd/conf. These configuration files control every aspect of the server's operation. When you've edited these files to your satisfaction, you can run the server. No further configuration is required.

First you go to the server's configuration directory, /usr/local/etc/httpd/conf. Inside that directory, you'll find distribution copies of the three configuration files. Since these copies are for your reference, you shouldn't edit them directly; make copies of them before you begin configuring the server:

```
$ for i in *-dist
> do
> mycopy = 'basename $i -dist'
> cp $i $mycopy
> done
```

At this point, you should have three files with the extension .conf. Table 3-1 gives the name and explains the purpose of each of these files. You should still have the original -dist files as well; keep these to refer back to in case you make a mistake customizing your configuration.

File Name	Purpose
httpd.conf	The server configuration file provides the most basic, technical description of how the daemon should run.
srm.conf	The server resource map file tells HTTPD how it should serve files.
access.conf	The server access configuration file controls who can access your server.

Table 3-1: *NCSA httpd configuration files.*

This section is intended to get you up and running as quickly as possible. We review the most useful options that the NCSA server offers, with an emphasis on those that are listed in the configuration files. The NCSA server supports a great many options that are rarely used and that this section doesn't cover. For complete documentation of every aspect of the server's configuration, see the official documentation for the NCSA HTTPD at http://hoohoo.ncsa.uiuc.edu/docs/.

Server Configuration File

The httpd.conf file is the server configuration file. Open it with your favorite editor and examine and change the following entries as appropriate. Use the following descriptions as a guide. They're not exhaustive descriptions, but they address the changes you'll have to make to get your server up and running.

ServerType

The default for this directive is ServerType standalone. Standalone servers are started from the system startup scripts at boot time. This setting is recommended to improve performance.

The NCSA HTTPD (like most traditional UNIX servers) requires a running copy of itself for each connection. UNIX is optimized for this behavior, and little overhead is required for a program to create a copy of itself. After the standalone server starts, it begins listening for connections; every time it detects one, it "forks" a copy of itself to service the request. When the copy has finished its work, it quits. This basic model changes somewhat if you use the StartServers and MaxServers directives, as explained later in this section.

The alternative to standalone is to use inetd; inetd is the Internet superserver for UNIX. Most network services are relatively rarely used, compared to the dozens of connections per second that busy HTTP servers endure. Even popular services like telnet usually get no more than a connection every few minutes. If you ran a separate standalone server for every possible Internet service, valuable system resources, such as CPU time and memory, would be needlessly wasted on idle services.

UNIX's solution to this problem is inetd. The file /etc/inetd.conf contains a list of network services for which inetd is responsible. It uses the file /etc/services to find which network port is associated with which service and listens for connections on those ports. When it receives one, it starts a copy of the appropriate server to handle it.

Although this is excellent for relatively rarely accessed services, the HTTP protocol doesn't really follow this model. Since a separate connection, and therefore, a separate copy of the server, is needed for every HTML page, every inline image and everything else that a client downloads, there will almost always be several new connections every minute, if not every second.

In addition, the NCSA HTTPD must reread and reparse the configuration files each time a copy is started from inetd. This overhead is unacceptable if you expect your site to be even marginally busy. Almost every site should use standalone for this directive.

Port

This directive specifies the network port on which your server is running if you're using standalone mode (if you use inetd, you must specify the port in /etc/services).

The default for this directive is Port 80, which is the default that Web browsers expect to connect to and the standard port for HTTP, and it is the recommended setting if this is the primary server for your site. You have to have system administrator (root) privileges on your machine if you want to run it there or on any other port lower than 1024.

If you don't have administrative privileges on your machine, you can still run a Web server on a port above 1024. You just need to announce and include the port in your URL (see Chapter 2, "The Basic Pieces"); common alternative ports are 8000 and 8080. The rest of the book assumes you have root access on your server and that you're running your server on the default port.

StartServers

This directive is a new addition to the NCSA server, as of version 1.4. It fundamentally changes the operation of the server when it is running standalone and this value is set higher than 1. Instead of a single master server starting, the server initially duplicates itself this number of times at startup, creating a *server pool*.

The original server acts as a master scheduler for all of the servers in the pool, accepting connections and passing them on to an idle duplicate. Theoretically, this strategy speeds the processing of requests by reducing overhead. In practice, some Webmasters say that the effects are negligible unless your server is very busy (greater than 100,000 requests a day).

For now, you can leave this value at the default and experiment with it later to find an optimal setting for your site. Since Linux v1.2 doesn't support the method NCSA uses to implement this feature, changing it will have no effect.

MaxServers

If you receive more simultaneous requests than the number of servers in your StartServers server pool, the server pool grows to handle them. These additional server processes don't die when they finish handling the requests that they were given; they stick

around. In this way, NCSA v1.4 adapts to your site's load.This value is the maximum number of servers the pool will grow to before resorting to the traditional strategy of spawning a server for each request.

User & Group

This entry determines the effective user and group permissions with which the server runs when you're using standalone. (If you're using inetd, most UNIX systems require you to specify a group in /etc/inetd.conf.) You can specify either a user and group name or the numeric equivalents, which are given in /etc/passwd and /etc/group, respectively.

The default user is nobody, which is an excellent choice in terms of security. It guarantees that the Web server will have access only to files and directories that are world readable. Alternatively, you may want to create a special Web or httpd user on your system and run the server under that ID. Whatever ID you use, make sure that it doesn't have a usable shell. Under no circumstances should you run your server with root privileges.

For group, you should use some innocuous group that exists on your machine; a common one is news. Alternatively, you can create a group specifically for the server.

Note that these directives are a common source of problems for beginning Webmasters. The server won't run if the user and group you name don't actually exist on your system. The default for the Group directive, for example, is the numeric group ID -1, which isn't a valid group on many systems.

ServerAdmin

This is the official e-mail address for the Web maintainer of your site. Generally, it's best to make this address in the form WebMaster@*yoursite*, in which *yoursite* is the well-known name of your server, which maintains a consistent address even if the person who maintains the site changes.

You need to add this address to the mail server's database of aliases in the file /etc/aliases. Edit this file as root and add the following entry:

```
webmaster: name
```

Replace *name* with the login name of the person who you wish to administer your Web server. Then execute the following command:

```
# newaliases
```

This command rebuilds the aliases database.

ServerRoot

This directive specifies the base directory where the NCSA HTTP software is installed. The default is /usr/local/etc/httpd.

ErrorLog, TransferLog, AgentLog

These three directives specify the location of the appropriate log files. The server assumes that values that don't begin with a slash are relative to ServerRoot.

These logs are fairly straightforward. The ErrorLog is where the server delivers diagnostic messages, including error messages from CGI scripts. The server logs every client request in the TransferLog. The AgentLog accumulates a list of all the clients that access your server.

RefererLog, RefererIgnore

These directives relate to the ability of NCSA v1.4 to keep track of which links clients are using to access your pages for clients that support it. The following is an example entry:

```
http://www.vpizza.com/greek/pesto.html -> /pine-nuts/order.html
```

This shows that the client followed a link from www.vpizza.com to the URL /pine-nuts/order.html on your server. Although not all clients provide this information, it can be useful for tracing bad links to your server because all requests, not only valid URLs, are logged. You should note though, that since Netscape v1.0 didn't always correctly transmit this information, you can expect some amount of incorrect data to be logged.

By default, the server stores all Referer data, including links from your own server. You can uncomment and define the ReferIgnore directive to be the same as ServerName, in order to prevent the server from logging Referer information from your own site. Since retrieving a page logs a Referer entry for every inline image loaded, this is an excellent idea.

PidFile

If you're running standalone, this directive specifies the name of the file where the original server process logs its process ID number. You can use this information to kill or restart your server (see "Miscellaneous Server Tasks," later in this chapter for more information).

ServerName

This entry should be the official hostname of your server as it appears in URLs (that is, http://www.*YourServerName*/). It must be a valid entry in the name server of your institution or service provider.

Finishing Up

Check over access.conf and make sure you've defined all the directives that need to be defined. When you're sure, quit, save the file and move on to the next configuration file: srm.conf.

Server Resource Map

The Server Resource Map, /usr/local/etc/httpd/conf/srm.conf, controls how the NCSA serves files. It translates between the abstract world of the URL, which clients deal with, and the actual files and directories on your server.

Open this file in your favorite editor and replace the system defaults with values appropriate to your site. As in httpd.conf, each directive and its value must be on a line by itself. Blank lines and lines that begin with a pound sign (#) are ignored by the server.

DocumentRoot

This directive specifies the directory from which your documents are served. The default directory is /usr/local/etc/httpd/htdocs. Files outside of this directory can still be served—you can use a symbolic link (see the section "Symbolic Links" later in this chapter) or the Alias directive (see the information on the Alias directive later in this section) to include them.

UserDir

This directive specifies the directory name in the user's home directory that is served if you choose to enable user-supported directories. The default directory name is public_html. If you don't wish to enable user-supported directories, you should specify

```
UserDir DISABLED
```

For more information about user-supported directories and how the server maps them, see the section "Setting Up Your Web Space" later in this chapter.

DirectoryIndex

This directive specifies which document is returned in a directory by the server when no document is specified in the URL. For example, no document is specified in the URL http://www.shoop.com/, so the document that the server returns is specified by the DirectoryIndex directive. Since the default document name is index.html, the server returns the document index.html from the server's DocumentRoot directory.

You should have a file named index.html in the DocumentRoot directory for both the site and the major document sections (and for the users' home pages, for example). This configuration presents an easier interface to the users of your site because they don't have to remember a specific document name.

It also gives you an important level of privacy. By default, when a client requests the URL for a directory, the NCSA server presents a listing of all the files in that directory. By creating a index file in a directory, you prevent users from getting a list of all the files in that directory.

You don't have to name the lead-in page for every Web project; you can create a symbolic link that points to the home document. For example, if your top-level document is named home.html, the following command creates a symbolic link named index.html, which points to MyHome.html.

```
$ ln -s MyHome.html index.html
```

AccessFileName

If the server administrator enables the AccessFileName directive (see the section "Access & Authentication"), the NCSA server allows a lot of control over the server's behavior when serving documents from individual directories. Owners of these directories can override many of the settings in the server resource map (srm.conf) by adding directives to a file named .htaccess in that directory. The AccessFileName directive changes the name of that file. Throughout the rest of the chapter, we assume you use the default for the AccessFileName.

FancyIndexing

As noted previously, the NCSA server responds to a client's request for a directory by

- Looking for the DirectoryIndex file and sending it, if it exists.
- Presenting a list of all files in that directory, if the DirectoryIndex file doesn't exist.

If FancyIndexing is on, the list uses icons and descriptions. If you specify off for FancyIndexing, the server presents a simpler listing.

AddIconByType

If you've enabled FancyIndexing, this directive tells the server which icon to use with which files, according to MIME type. The server uses the following format:

```
AddIconByType (ALT, URL) MIME
```

- *ALT* is a short bit of text that users with nongraphical clients should see instead of the icon.
- *URL* is the URL on your server where the icon is located.
- *MIME* is a MIME type or a wildcard-based set of MIME types.

The /icons URL is defined by an Alias later in the file.

You can probably skip this section, unless you have different file types on your server and want to create icons for them.

AddIcon, DefaultIcon

AddIcon tells the server which icons to use for presenting files and directories, while DefaultIcon is the URL of an icon to use with files that have no explicitly defined icon.

AddType

This directive is useful for adding new types of documents to be served, using MIME mappings (see the section regarding file formats and MIME typing in Chapter 2, "The Basic Pieces"). A good example of a new type of document you might want to add is the Adobe Acrobat format, which uses the .pdf file extension. You might need a way to tell the server the type of document an Acrobat file is (by the extension) and to send that type to the Web client so it knows to launch the Acrobat viewer. The AddType directive provides a way to do this. For example, you'd use the following command to tell your server to send the .pdf extension to the Web client:

```
AddType application/pdf pdf
```

The NCSA HTTPD also understands two special MIME types, which you can enable with AddType, that ease the maintenance of your server. These two types are commented out in the distribution srm.conf as follows:

```
#AddType text/x-server-parsed-html .shtml
#AddType application/x-httpd-cgi .cgi
```

The first AddType provides efficient server-side includes; if you uncomment this statement, you can use the .shtml extension to signal to the server that the document has an include.

Server-side includes allow you to instruct the server to embed another document or the output of a command into your Web page. Although you can enable them for your entire Web area, doing so forces the server to scan every HTML document for an include statement before sending it to the client, which wastes a lot of system resources. For information about using server-side includes, read http://hoohoo.ncsa.uiuc.edu/docs/tutorials/includes.html.

The second commented type, application/x-httpd-cgi, provides another file extension, .cgi. When this statement is enabled, this

extension tells the server that the file is an executable CGI script. This allows you to invoke scripts anywhere on the server, not just in those directories indicated by the ScriptAlias directive.

You can enable both of these types by removing the initial pound sign.

Redirect

Redirect is a useful feature when you're faced with the inevitable situation of documents moving to a different directory on your server or to a different server altogether. For example, if ShoopSoft spins off its Linux division to its own subsidiary, ShoopSoft might decide to put all of the related material on the new server there. If the former URL was http://www.shoop.com/Linux and the URL at the new division is http://www.shooplinux.com/, we could use the Redirect directive as follows:

```
Redirect /Linux http://www.shooplinux.com/
```

This enables all of the inquiries for Linux documents at the old URL to go to the server at the new division.

Alias

The Alias directive allows you to serve documents from a different directory than in or under the directory specified by DocumentRoot. By default, the server comes with one Alias defined—/icons, which is used by the AddIcon and AddIconByType directives.

See the section "Setting Up Your Web Space" later in this section for some useful applications for this directive.

ScriptAlias

The ScriptAlias directive controls which directories are allowed to execute CGI scripts. The following is the default ScriptAlias directive:

```
ScriptAlias /cgi-bin/ /usr/local/etc/httpd/cgi-bin/
```

This default allows the distribution CGI scripts, such as imagemap (see the section "Clickable Imagemaps" in Chapter 7, "Images on the Web"), to be executed. The first argument is the virtual path, or relative URL, that users can use to execute CGI scripts. The second argument is the actual path on your server that the URL accesses.

For example, /cgi-bin/ is the name of the relative URL and /usr/local/etc/httpd/cgi-bin is the directory where the scripts actually reside, so the following URL would refer to the CGI script /usr/local/etc/httpd/cgi-bin/imagemap:

```
http://www.shoop.com/cgi-bin/imagemap
```

You can add as many ScriptAlias directives as you like. Create one for every (trusted) user who wants to write and run his or her own CGI scripts. For example, if the user jem wants a CGI directory in /home/users/jem/html/cgi named /jembin, the following line would create it:

```
ScriptAlias /jembin /home/users/jem/html/cgi
```

If you trust all the users on your server to create and run CGI scripts with no examination or intervention by you, you can enable the CGI MIME type. See the description of the AddType directive earlier in this section.

ErrorDocument

This directive allows you to map HTTP error codes to URLs on this server. You can use this ability to replace and customize the servers' error messages. Until you want to do this, you can leave these server error messages commented out.

That's the last of the directives for the Server Resource Map. After you've defined the values you need to get started, quit and save srm.conf.

Server Access File

The NCSA HTTPD provides a wide range of features that can make maintaining your site more convenient; some of these features have implications for your site's security. The server access file (located in /usr/local/etc/httpd/conf/access.conf) allows you to enable and disable these features on a per-directory basis.

In addition, this file is also used for restricting access to your pages to certain hosts and users; these features will be discussed at length in the section "Access & Authentication." For now, let's configure it just enough to get your server working.

Open access.conf in your editor. Note that the file uses an HTML-like syntax, with the <Directory /usr/local/etc/httpd/cgi-bin> tag that declares the beginning of the section that describes the options for the server's default cgi-bin directory. This section ends with the </Directory> tag.

The access.conf file that is distributed with the server provides two access descriptions: one for the cgi-bin directory and a second for the document directory. This second directive should read as follows:

```
<Directory /usr/local/etc/httpd/htdocs>
```

If you changed your document root in srm.conf, you should change it in access.conf as well. Save the access.conf file and exit. You're now ready to map out your Web space.

Setting Up Your Web Space

You can choose to serve files in your Web space in a number of ways. As mentioned previously, the DocumentRoot in the srm.conf file controls the base directory where documents are served. The way the server maps the URLs to the file system of your machine is illustrated in the following example URL:

```
http://www.shoop.com/home.html
```

The server uses the path specified by DocumentRoot and appends the file home.html to the path. If DocumentRoot is set at the default, the server serves the file from the path/usr/local/etc/http/htdocs/home.html. You don't have to put all the files and directories that you want to serve under the ServerRoot directory. You have other options for organizing your site.

User-Controlled Directories

You can enable user-controlled HTML directories with the UserDir directive in the srm.conf file. This option allows a common directory entry in each of your user's home directories to be served. The default directory for this is public_html.

The directories are accessed with a URL path that begins with a tilde, followed by the user's login name. When the server receives such a URL, it retrieves the user's home directory from the

/etc/passwd file. We can see how the server maps this location from a URL by the following example URL:

```
http://www.shoop.com/~chris/index.html
```

If the home directory of user chris is /home/users/chris and the UserDir directory is the default directory public_html, the server would send /home/users/chris/public_html/index.html for this request.

Setting an Alias

You can map specific URLs to directories on your system with the Alias directive in the srm.conf file. This allows you to serve files that are not under the directory specified by the document root directive. For example, if you wanted to serve documents in the directory /public/ftp/multimedia, you could use the following line to allow documents in the directory /public/ftp/multimedia to be accessed on the ShoopSoft server via the URL http://www.shoopsoft.com/multimedia:

```
Alias /multimedia /public/ftp/multimedia
```

Currently, the NCSA HTTPD allows you to define a maximum of 50 aliases in this way. If you'd like to define more than this, you need to redefine the macro MAX_ALIASES in /usr/local/etc/httpd/src/httpd.h and recompile the server (see the section "Compiling the NCSA Server").

Symbolic Links

Symbolic links are one of the most valuable file system features of UNIX. They allow you to create a pointer within the file system that points to some other file or directory, making symbolic links an indispensable tool for managing Web space.

For example, you might decide to leave the default for the document root directive as /usr/local/etc/httpd/htdocs. You could then have your document root be actually located in the directory /public/html by typing the following command:

```
# ln -s /public/html /usr/local/etc/httpd/htdocs
```

A convenient convention for administrative purposes is to make a top-level directory link to the document root directory. If you were using the default /usr/local/etc/httpd/htdocs for the document root, you could make the top-level directory link with the following command:

```
# ln -s /usr/local/etc/httpd/htdocs /html
```

This command allows you to access directories under the ServerRoot easily and saves a lot of typing. The examples in the rest of the book assume you have such a link.

Other Considerations

The way you choose to set up your Web space has a lot to do with the nature of your organization and the purpose and users of your server. Many universities provide home pages for their students, for example. These accounts are, by definition, transient so the UserDir method (where the documents served are in the directory public_html within the users' home directories) works well. When a student matriculates and his or her account expires, removing the account's home directory also conveniently takes care of the Web document directory. Any quotas you have already established for student directories will also apply to their Web documents, making a separate quota for Web documents unnecessary.

If your site is a professional organization or company, you generally have a fairly stable set of documents to be served. In this case, it's better to have the majority of your documents in directories under the document root directory. You can still have different individuals contributing to the site by making symbolic links from their home directories to the directories under the document root that they'll be working on. If an individual then leaves the company, his or her account can easily be removed without the concern of deleting a Web document directory critical to the organization. In addition, a new symbolic link can be easily defined for the new maintainer of that section or directory without the need to move any of the associated documents. This setup lends itself to easier administration in that the majority of the Web documents are in a central location, which can often be maintained and backed up more easily.

The examples we used in this section are general examples and are not intended to suggest that only one method is appropriate for you, and the use of one method doesn't preclude the use of the other.

Starting the Server

Now that you've configured the server, it's time to start and test it. There are different techniques for starting the server, depending on whether you chose to run it standalone or from inetd.

Standalone

To run a standalone server, you simply have to add a line to the scripts that are executed at bootup. Under Linux, this script file is /etc/rc.d/rc.local; under another operating system, the file may be called /etc/rc.local, or you may need to create a separate script in the /etc/rc2.d directory. If you're not sure, consult your system administrator's manual.

After you've located the proper file, make yourself the superuser and open the script in your favorite text editor. Add the following lines to the end of the script:

```
if [ -x /usr/local/etc/httpd/httpd ]
then
echo "Starting HTTP server"
cd /usr/local/etc/httpd httpd > /dev/console 2>&1
else
echo "Can't start HTTP server!"
fi
```

When you're finished, save the file and exit your editor. These lines check to see if the WAIS server exists; if it does, the lines you added start it. Although you've added these lines to your system's startup scripts, they won't be run until the next time you reboot the computer. To start the server now, you should type the following as superuser:

```
# cd /usr/local/etc/httpd
# httpd
```

Assuming you get no error messages on your screen or in /usr/local/etc/httpd/logs/error_log, your server should be running successfully.

From inetd

To run the server from inetd, you must modify two files. The first of these, /etc/services, is used to define well-known ports and the protocols that use them. If you use NIS (also called YP) to share system databases on your local network, you need to update them with the yppush command for changes to this file to take effect. Become the superuser and open /etc/services with your editor, adding the following line to the end of the file:

```
http        80/tcp
```

The second file you need to modify is /etc/inetd.conf. This is the inetd configuration file; it tells inetd which ports to listen to and what action to take when it detects a connection. Still acting as superuser, open the /etc/inetd.conf file and add the following (all in one line) to the end:

```
http stream tcp nowait nobody /usr/local/etc/httpd/httpd/httpd
```

This entry should work on most UNIX systems. A notable exception is Ultrix, which uses the following format:

```
http stream tcp nowait /usr/local/etc/httpd/httpd/httpd
```

The fourth field, which is omitted under Ultrix, tells inetd which user to run the server under. Ultrix doesn't allow you to specify a user; servers started from inetd under Ultrix always run as root. Since this is a potential security problem, you should use User directive in conf/httpd.conf to set the user to nobody or some other appropriate user.

After you've added the appropriate lines to /etc/services and /etc/inetd.conf, you need to alert inetd that its configuration files have changed. To do this, find the process number (PID) of inetd and send it the HUP (hang-up) signal, as follows (on a System V system, such as Solaris and Irix, use the -aef options to ps, instead):

```
# ps -aux | grep inetd   root  11253  0.0   3.4   156  256    p 5 S  23:01    0:00
grep inetd               root     43  0.0   1.0    72   80   con S  Feb 1    0:00
/usr/sbin/inetd
# kill -HUP 43
```

When inetd receives the HUP signal, it rereads /etc/inetd.conf and begins listening for HTTP connections.

Testing the Server

When your server is running, you should give it a quick test. If you already have some pages ready, you could try to retrieve one in your favorite browser. If you haven't prepared any content or don't have a browser handy, you can test your server directly by entering the following:

```
$ telnet localhost 80
Trying 127.0.0.1 ...
Connected to localhost.
Escape character is '^]'.
```

This opens a connection to the server's HTTP port. When you've successfully connected, you can check to make sure everything is working by typing the following and pressing Return twice:

```
HEAD / HTTP/1.0
```

You should see a response similar to the following:

```
HTTP/1.0 200 OK
Date: Friday, 12-Dec-94 05:44:30 GMT
Server: NCSA/1.4
MIME-version: 1.0
Content-type: text/html
Last-modified: Sunday, 12-Dec-94 01:21:23 GMT
Content-length: 2342

Connection closed by foreign host.
```

Congratulations, you now have a working Web server. Now you can start developing the brilliant content that will make your site legendary!

Access & Authentication

By default, the NCSA server is very permissive from a security standpoint. In general, any file or directory that has the following characteristics is within the server's map and will be served if requested by a client:

- Beneath the ServerRoot directory.
- Linked into the ServerRoot directory.
- Referenced with the Alias directive.
- Within a user's public_html directory.

Despite this lax default security, the NCSA server provides fine-grain control over what a client can access and what a user on the system can provide.

NCSA provides this control in two ways. The first is the global server access configuration file, /usr/local/etc/httpd/conf/access.conf. Within this file, you set access policies for the server as a whole. You can restrict access to certain directories on your server, based on the IP numbers or hostnames of connecting clients. You can also protect directories with passwords, allowing only certain users or groups access to your server.

In contrast to these centralized restrictions on use and access, the second method is decentralized. Each individual user who maintains a Web directory on your site may control client access to that directory by means of an .htaccess file. In addition, users can override options from both srm.conf and access.conf if the global access file allows it.

Although NCSA requires this file to run, we barely touched on the access.conf when we were describing how to configure the server. To use authentication and access control, we need to understand more about the format of the directives in this file. Unlike the directives in the httpd.conf and the srm.conf file, the access.conf file directives use an HTML-like syntax, with separate elements marking the beginning and the ending of a section. These directives, which function to mark different areas of access control, are called "sectioning directives," and when we discuss them, we'll always show them between angle brackets (< and >).

The <Directory> directive delineates a directory to which you wish to apply access controls. You must specify the directory with an absolute path; wildcards are legal within the directive. The following is the basic syntax:

```
<Directory directory_name>
access control directives
</Directory>
```

These access *control directives* affect the sort of access that the server allows to that directory and all the files and directories beneath it.

Most of these same directives are valid in the user's .htaccess files as well, and the server overrides the global settings if that behavior is permitted by the AllowOverride directive.

AllowOverride

This directive, which is valid only within the access.conf file, controls the relationship between the global access file and the user's .htaccess files. Follow the directive with a space-separated list of access control features that .htaccess files beneath that directory can override. The following are the possible values:

- None The server ignores .htaccess files in this directory. If you don't need .htaccess files for a directory, you should explicitly set this option because it will improve the server's performance.
- All As the default, .htaccess files can override all global configuration access file settings for which they have an equivalent command.
- Options Allows use of the Options directive (see the section "Options" later in the chapter).
- FileInfo Allows .htaccess to use the AddType directive (see the previous section, "Server Resource Map," for a full description) and the AddEncoding directive, which is explained here: http://hoohoo.ncsa.uiuc.edu/docs/setup/srm/AddEncoding.html.
- AuthConfig Allows use of the AuthName, AuthType, AuthUserFile and AuthGroupFile directives, which are required to password-protect a directory.

- <Limit> Allows use of the <Limit> section directive. See the "<Limit>" section later in the chapter for a full description.

Options

The Options directive controls which server features are available within the directory specified by a <Directory> section or within a .htaccess file. The following are valid arguments to the Options directive:

- None No features are enabled in the specified directory.
- All All features are enabled in the specified directory (the default).
- FollowSymLinks The server follows symbolic links in the specified directory.
- SymLinksIfOwnerMatch The server follows symbolic links only if the target directory is owned by the same user as the link.
- ExecCGI Execution of CGI scripts is allowed in the specified directory.
- Includes Server-side include files are enabled in the specified directory. Enabling server-side includes requires the server to parse every HTML file before sending it to the client. Needless to say, this places a tremendous burden on the server, so we recommend disabling this option. If you need server-side includes, enable them per-file with an AddType directive, as described in the section "Server Resource Map" earlier in the chapter.
- Indexes The server allows users to request indexes in the specified directory. Disabling this option disables only the server-generated file listing, not the return of index.html.
- IncludesNoExec This directive enables server-side includes in the specified directory but disables the exec feature.

Resource Map Directives

There are several directives, derived from the server resource map configuration file (srm.conf), which you can specify on a per-directory basis. All of these directives function exactly as explained in the "Server Resource Map" section, overriding the server's global configuration for that single directory:

- AddType
- DefaultType
- AddDescription
- AddIcon
- IndexIgnore
- DefaultIcon

User & Group Passwords

The NCSA server allows you to enforce password protection for directories, either inside the global access configuration file or a user's .htaccess file. You must specify values for three different directives to password-protect a directory: AuthName, AuthType and AuthUserFile. A fourth directive, AuthGroupFile, is optional.

The AuthName directive should be a short string that tells the user the password for which they are being asked.

The second password directive, AuthType, is even simpler. AuthType identifies the authentication method the server is using. Currently, only the Basic type is defined. Since future versions of the NCSA HTTPD will implement other methods of authentication, this directive is required.

The AuthUserFile directive specifies the full pathname of the NCSA HTTPD user password file for that directory. To create a password file, use the htpasswd program, which can be found in /usr/local/etc/httpd/support. For example, to create a new password file for the user mdw, you enter the following command:

```
$ htpasswd -c /html/secured/.htpasswd mdw
Adding password for mdw.
New password:
Re-type new password:
```

The -c option tells htpasswd to create a new password file. If you omit this option, htpasswd attempts to edit an existing password file.

The fourth directive you can use to password-protect a directory is the AuthGroupFile. The file specified by this directive should contain a list of group names and entries from the AuthUserFile who are members of that group as illustrated in the following example:

```
smers: mdw ewt jem merry mgd
```

This entry creates a NCSA password group, smers, with five members.

<Limit>

Like <Directory>, <Limit> is a sectioning directive. It's used to put restrictions on HTTP access to the files within a directory. It can be used within a <Directory> section in access.conf or inside a user's .htaccess (assuming an AllowOverride directive doesn't prevent it).

This directive takes one or more HTTP methods as arguments—the methods to which its directives apply. There are four possible directives that can appear within the <Limit> section: deny, allow, order and require.

The deny and allow directives provide control over which hosts and domains access the affected directory. They have the same syntax; each should be followed by the word "from", followed by a list of hosts to which the server should either deny or allow access to the directory. The members of this list can be

- A domain name, such as shoop.com or cia.gov.
- A host-name, such as grumpy.shoop.com or bhurma.cia.gov.
- An IP host address, such as 115.23.42.5
- An IP domain, such as 115.23.42
- The word all, signifying all hosts.

The order directive determines the order in which the NCSA server evaluates any deny and allow directives. The following are the three valid values:

- deny,allow   The server evaluates the deny directive first, then the allow directive.
- allow,deny   The server evaluates the allow directive first, then the deny directive.
- mutual-failure   The server denies access to all hosts that aren't on the allow list.

The fourth directive is require. You can use this directive to enforce password protection over a directory. This directive should be followed by a list of "entities." These entities can be the name of a user or group defined with the AuthUserFile or AuthGroupFile directives. You can also use the keyword "valid-user", which tells the server that any user in the AuthUserFile should be allowed access if he or she provides a valid password.

The following is an example .htaccess file, which allows access only to authorized users from the nsa.gov domain:

```
AuthUserFile /home/users/onorth/www/secure/.htpasswd
AuthName SecurityTest
AuthType Basic
<Limit GET>
order deny,allow
deny from all
allow from nsa.gov
require valid-user
</Limit>
```

The server evaluates this <Limit> directive as follows:

1. It denies all access.
2. It allows access from the domain nsa.gov.
3. It requires users from the valid domain to give a username and password found in /home/users/onorth/www/secure/.htpasswd, as shown in Figure 3-2.

If a request passes all these tests it can retrieve files from that directory.

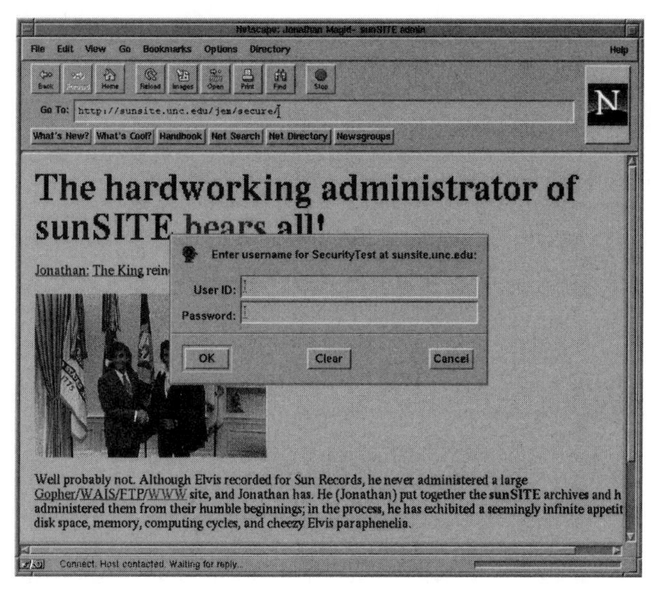

Figure 3-2: *An authetication challenge for login and password.*

Miscellaneous Server Tasks

Running an HTTP server is not all fun and glory. You must perform lots of everyday tasks in order to keep it running smoothly.

Killing & Restarting the Server

If the server runs from inetd and you need to turn off HTTP access to your site, you have to prevent inetd from starting additional copies of the server. Edit /etc/inetd.conf as root and comment out the server's entry, as follows:

```
#http stream tcp nowait nobody /usr/local/etc/httpd/httpd/httpd
```

Then save the file and exit your editor. To make this change take effect, you must send inetd a hang-up signal as detailed previously in the section "Starting the Server."

If you're running your server standalone and need to stop the server, enter the following as root:

```
# cd /usr/local/etc/httpd
# kill 'cat logs/httpd.pid'
```

If you're running the server standalone, you'll need to restart (or hang-up) the server when you want to rotate your log files (see the next section, "Logging & Log Analysis") or make any changes in the server's configuration. To do this you'll need the following simple variation of the previous command:

```
# kill -1 'cat logs/httpd.pid'
```

This command sends a HUP (hang-up) signal to the HTTP server. Upon receiving this signal, the original server does the following:

- It kills all the members of the server pool.
- It kills any other copies of the server.
- It rereads and parses its configuration files.
- It closes and re-opens its log files.
- It re-initializes the server pool, with the number of processes indicated by the StartServers directive in /usr/local/etc/httpd/conf/httpd.conf.

As you can see, this is a fairly complete list. Essentially, sending the hang-up signal to the server completely resets everything to initial conditions. If all goes well, a message similar to the following is sent to the ErrorLog file:

```
[Tue Apr 11 23:00:05 1995] httpd: successful restart
```

Logging & Log Analysis

The log files are kept by default in the logs directory located under the directory specified by the ServerRoot directive in the httpd.conf file (typically /usr/local/etc/httpd). The access_log file logs the transactions of connections to your server, and is the file used by the various logging programs to prepare reports of server usage. You'll want to set a policy of rotating your log files, usually at the start of each week or month. Use the following procedure to rotate them:

```
# cd /usr/local/etc/httpd
# mv logs/access_log logs/access_log.name_of_month.year
# kill -1 'cat logs/httpd.pid'
```

Most people want statistics on the usage of their site. The following list summarizes some of the log file analyzers available:

- Wusage by Thomas Boutell at http://siva.cshl.org/wusage.html.
- Fwgstat by Jonathan Magid at http://sunsite.unc.edu/jem/fwgstat.html.
- GetStats by Kevin Hughes at http://www.eit.com/software/getstats/getstats.html.
- wwwstat by Roy Fielding at http://www.ics.uci.edu/WebSoft/wwwstat/.
- gwstat, a program that graphs the output from wwwstat, by Qiegang Long at http://dis.cs.umass.edu/stats/gwstat.html.

Leasing Space

If, after reading all of this chapter, setting up your own server just seems like an overwhelming process, other options are available. Hundreds of businesses nationwide specialize in providing WWW server space for corporate and personal pages. Leasing Web space from an Internet presence provider can greatly simplify the process of setting up the server. Leasing space on a server can also provide a temporary home for your Web pages and online information while you are setting up your own server.

A number of factors should be taken into account when choosing an Internet presence provider. Primary among these, obviously, is price. There are no hard and fast standards for Web space pricing, and prices range from $10 a month to $35,000 a quarter, depending on the provider, the types of services available, the amount of creative work required and countless other factors. You will be able to create the majority of your site—graphics, searchable databases, text documents and more—using the information provided in this book. This means that your charge should be significantly less than someone who has to contract that work.

Providers who provide space alone with no development services generally charge by the megabyte of information to be stored. Including graphics, Web pages average about 50 kilobytes each, meaning that you can store a reasonable number of pages and graphics in a single megabyte. However, providers who charge an exceptionally low rate per megabyte of information probably provide little more than disk space and a link to their home pages. This is not a problem if you plan to do your own development, but if you want to work on more complex uses for your Web site, you will need more than just storage space.

The second main factor in choosing a Web space provider is the degree of control you will have over your pages and programs. CGI scripts, explained in detail in Chapter 11, "CGI: Advanced Forms for Programmers," can greatly extend the functionality of your Web pages, allowing dynamic content and interactivity that HTML alone cannot provide. However, the server has to be configured to allow CGI scripts in the users' directories, as detailed in the previous section, "Server Resource Map." Before leasing server space, make sure that a provider will allow you to create your own CGI scripts and that the provider will configure its software to accept the scripts.

The newest version of the imagemap program, described in "Clickable Imagemaps," in Chapter 7, "Images on the Web," allows users to place imagemaps in their own directories, rather than in server directories. When investigating service providers, make sure to ask if the provider is using the old or new version of imagemap—that is, whether it allows you to define your own imagemap information.

Another level of control that you will want to consider is the naming of your site. Some service providers can offer only a subdirectory, while others can create a unique machine name for your site's URL. In other words, some sites could create a URL such as http://www.shoop.com/ for a Web site. However, others could simply create a subdirectory, making your URL something similar to http://www.netshops.com/shoop/.

The final factor that you will want to consider in selecting a service provider is the value for your money. In other words, aside from services (such as CGI support, imagemaps, etc.) and server space, what are you paying for? Certain providers will get more traffic because of their reputations and because of other sites that they are hosting; although this can be an advantage in that it will bring people to your site, it's important to verify that they haven't oversold the bandwidth of their Internet connection. Others could have a focus on a particular subject or geographical area, which could complement your site well. Basically, this final criterion is a judgment call: what can their content and location offer you and your site?

Leasing server space is certainly not necessary: if you have an Internet connection and the software described in this book, there is no reason why you couldn't have your own Web server. However, for a temporary server or for those without a direct Internet connection, you might want to investigate leasing Internet presence provider space. The most up-to-date lists of Internet presence providers are available at the URLs http://www.yahoo.com/Business/Corporations/Internet_Presence_Providers/ and http://union.ncsa.uiuc.edu/HyperNews/get/www/leasing.html.

Moving On

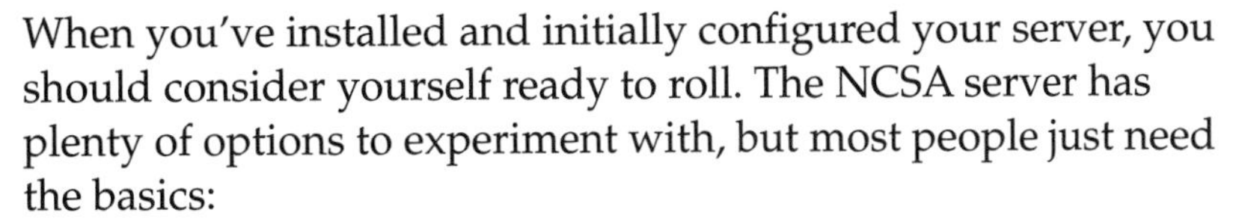

When you've installed and initially configured your server, you should consider yourself ready to roll. The NCSA server has plenty of options to experiment with, but most people just need the basics:

- A properly configured httpd.conf, with the server running under a safe user ID.
- A /cgi-bin directory, with the scripts that come with the server, including imagemaps.
- An srm.conf file and an access.conf file, which provide the basic functionality needed to set up your server so that it's convenient to administer.

Few people ever need to wander into the world of authentication and access. After all, most servers are started in order to *serve* files to an interested audience.

Still, security is a vital subject once you're connected to the Internet, especially if you're a highly visible site. In the next chapter, "System Security" you'll learn the basics of UNIX and Internet security, and how to protect yourself from an unfriendly world.

4 System Security

Security is one of the hottest topics in computing for several reasons. One of the most important is the sensationalist coverage the mass media have given to cases involving computer security, such as the 1988 Internet Worm virus and the exploits of Kevin Mitnick, who was arrested in 1995 for breaking into a number of prominent Internet hosts. This coverage has tended to increase everyone's concern about computer security: regular users are worried that they might be victimized by computer criminals, while security experts consider these incidents major embarrassments.

It is, of course, good to be concerned about security, but it's important to understand that a compromise is required. Increased security almost always comes at the expense of a reduction in the system's usefulness for legitimate users, and this is especially true for Internet servers. Each of the network services offers strangers some level of access to your computer; therefore, it's really impossible to be completely secure and still be a network server. Well-known hosts are especially tempting targets for crackers.

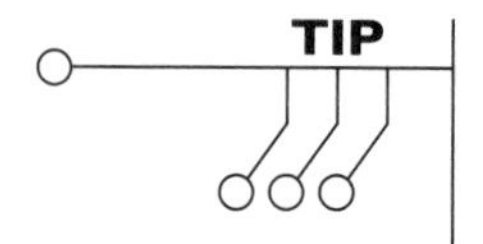

In the popular media, computer criminals are known as "hackers," which is a corruption of the word's original meaning—a hacker is anyone who enjoys working with computers and technology and stretching his or her technical capabilities. On the Internet, the original meaning still prevails. In this chapter, I'll refer to people who break into computers as "crackers" or "intruders."

System administrators must seek a balance between complete security (no network or modem connection and locking the machine in a vault) and being able to offer useful services. A good strategy toward this end is to isolate your risks. If multiple machines are on your local network, keep private or important data on a machine separate from your server platform; machines storing important data should not allow trusted logins from the server (see the section "Trusted Hosts" later in this chapter). You may also wish to separate your server from the rest of the network with a firewall (see the section "Advanced Internet Security Options" later in this chapter).

The essence of good security is vigilance. No configuration is perfectly secure, but if you take basic precautions and are constantly on the lookout for problems, you can make your system relatively secure and avoid being an easy target. You must have a thorough understanding of the security features of your system and of its weaknesses.

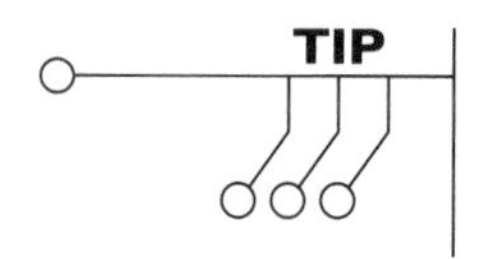

Computer security is a constant battle. You must stay up-to-date on the latest threats, bugs and tools. Reading USENET newsgroups is an excellent way to stay current. The following three newsgroups are essential reading for the responsible system administrator:

- comp.security.unix—discusses UNIX security.
- comp.security.misc—covers discussions of general computer and network security.
- comp.security.announce—discusses security bulletins from the Computer Emergency Response Team (CERT) (see the section "People to Contact" later in this chapter).

General UNIX Security

Good security begins at home. Before you worry about the vulnerabilities of being connected to the Internet, you need to have a firm grasp of traditional security mechanisms under UNIX. Although UNIX has the reputation of being an insecure system, this isn't really true. UNIX has many excellent security features; the problem is more often that administrators don't use them correctly. In the past, security features often went unused because UNIX first became popular in academic institutions, places where security is not the chief concern.

In this section, we'll review the mechanisms that UNIX uses to provide security. If you follow the secure practices outlined here, you'll be well on the way to keeping your system safe and secure.

Accounts

UNIX is a multi-user, multitasking operating system. Many different users can be logged in to the system at the same time, and UNIX shares the machine's resources among them. When a user logs on to the system, he or she must enter a username that identifies his or her account to the system. This username identifies the user to the login program, which is the first layer of security for accounts.

User IDs

The login program looks up this username in the file /etc/passwd. This file contains a table identifying all the users on the system. The following is an entry from a password file:

```
jem:YDonCj22dMOVDQ:100:150:Jonathan Magid:/home/jem:/bin/bash
```

Each user's entry is made up of seven fields, separated by colons. Table 4-1 contains an explanation of each of the fields in the password file.

Field	Description
jem	The account's username. Usernames can be only up to eight characters long.
YDonCj22dMOVDQ	The account's password in encrypted form.
100	The user ID (UID) is the number by which the operating system keeps track of the user.
150	The group ID (GID) is the number that identifies the user's primary group.
Jonathan Magid	The GECOS field. This field contains extra information about the user; in this case, it contains the user's full name. Some versions of UNIX also allow users to store their office and phone numbers in this field.
/home/jem	The account's home directory. The user is automatically placed in this directory when he or she logs in.
/bin/bash	The account's login shell. This program is run to interpret the user's commands.

Table 4-1: */etc/passwd entry fields.*

The login program retrieves the UID that corresponds with the username. This number is used by the operating system to keep track of the user; for this reason, UIDs should be unique. Two users with the same UID are treated identically by the system; they can read and write each other's files and kill each other's processes. In general, it's not recommended that two users have the same ID; make sure that every user has his or her own UID.

The UID 0 is reserved by the system. This UID identifies root, or the superuser. Although other users are capable of affecting only their own files and processes, the superuser can access any file and kill any process on the system. In addition, root is able to perform the following special functions:

- Mount and unmount file systems.
- Create special device files.
- Become any other user on the system.
- Access any device.
- Read and write any memory location.

- Configure the network interfaces.
- Execute any program.
- Write to the disk after it's full. (Most modern UNIX file systems reserve 10 percent of the partition's actual capacity for this purpose).
- Set the system time and date.

There is nothing special about the name "root"; in fact, some system administrators prefer the name "avatar." Any account with a UID of 0 will have superuser privileges.

Group IDs

The other number associated with a user is the GID. The GID indicates which group the user is in. UNIX uses the concept of groups to associate users who are working on the same project so they can share files easily without sharing usernames and passwords (which is not recommended). By changing the group permissions on a file, users can allow members of their group to access their files (see the section "File Permissions & Ownership" later in this chapter).

Group names and their associated GIDs are kept in a file named /etc/group. The following is an entry from an /etc/group file:

```
users::150:mdw,merry,mgd
```

Like /etc/passwd, this file contains several colon-separated entries. Table 4-2 provides descriptions for each of them.

Field	Description
users	The name of the group.
(null)	The encrypted password for the group. If the password field is empty (which is the default), no password is required.
150	The numeric GID.
mdw,merry,mgd	A comma-separated list of users who belong to the group. These users are in addition to users who are listed as members of the group in /etc/passwd.

Table 4-2: */etc/group entries.*

Under some UNIX systems (mostly System V-based systems), a user may be a member of only one group at a time. To change the GID under which he or she is operating, the user must execute the newgrp command:

```
$ newgrp compiler
```

This command changes the user's current group to the compiler group. Under normal circumstances, a user can change only to a group to which he or she already belongs. This rule is altered if the group has an associated password; in that case, the user may change to that group if he or she types the proper password when prompted.

Under modern UNIX systems, including System V release 4, a user may be a member of several groups simultaneously. When users log in, they are given access to all the groups they belong to in both their /etc/passwd file and in their /etc/groups file.

Passwords

Many, if not most, attacks on UNIX systems are directed at the password file. In most versions of UNIX, the encrypted password is stored in the file /etc/passwd. Since this file also stores all basic user information, such as the user's full name, home directory and login shell, it must be world-readable, allowing anyone with a login on the system to read its contents.

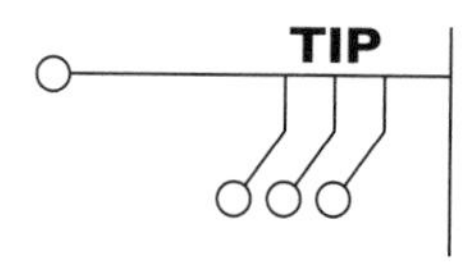

Some systems use the "shadow password" system. These systems store all the encrypted passwords in a file that can be read by root only and all the programs that have a need to check the password data operate with root authority. Although shadow passwords increase the system's security, they don't lessen the importance of choosing a good password.

Unfortunately, the world-readable /etc/passwd file is a major security problem. Although the passwords are stored in a more or less unbreakable form, access to even the encrypted password can give a would-be cracker way too much information. Most people choose very poor passwords. Once an attacker has access to the password file, he or she tries to guess the encrypted passwords.

A cracker guesses passwords by consulting a dictionary of common passwords (passwords created by not following the guidelines provided later in this section), encrypting them with the UNIX password algorithm and then comparing them with the encrypted passwords recorded in /etc/passwd. When a match occurs, a password has been correctly guessed, and the cracker has access to the system. Many programs have been written to automate this process, making it quick work to guess a poorly chosen password.

The UNIX password encryption algorithm is inherently secure—it has never been cracked. It's only the poor password choices of users that make it a weak link. You should require all users on your server to follow these simple guidelines in order to ensure that even if a cracker gains access to your password file, it does him or her little good:

- Don't use your login name in any form (by itself, doubled, reversed, etc.).
- Don't use any part of your full name in any form.
- Don't use a nickname or any other well-known made-up word.
- Don't use anyone else's name, including the names of spouses, children, friends and co-workers.
- Don't use the name of a computer.
- Don't use any easily gleaned bit of personal information, such as birthdays, Social Security numbers or license numbers.
- Don't use any word that appears in a dictionary, English or foreign.
- Don't use a word from the dictionary, preceded or followed by a single number.
- Don't use any word or name derived from science fiction or fantasy. All cracking dictionaries include "hobbit," "Tolkien," "Heinlein" and other similar words—avoid them like the plague.
- Don't use the same number or letter repeated several times.

- Don't use a password with fewer than seven characters.
- Do use a mixture of uppercase and lowercase letters.
- Do use numbers and non-alphanumeric symbols.
- Do choose a password that's easy to remember, so you won't be tempted to write it down.

If you follow these guidelines, your password file should be secure. If none of the passwords have these weaknesses, an attacker is forced to try every possible combination of characters in order to guess a password. Even with a fast machine, this might take a hundred years, and the cracker would surely move on to another target.

You can provide additional security by encouraging users to change their passwords on a regular basis. Many UNIX systems provide a mechanism for expiring passwords, which forces users to change them. You can check the passwd man page on your system for more information.

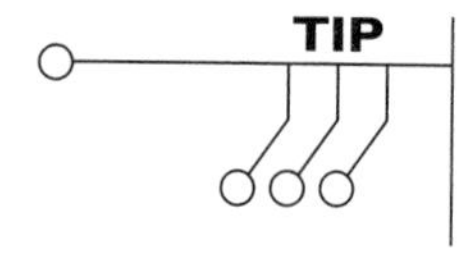

An excellent way to check the security of your users' password files is with the program crack. crack tries to break the security of your passwords with a series of attacks based on dictionaries and the information in /etc/passwd. You can get a copy of the source code for crack at ftp://ftp.cert.org/pub/tools/crack.

Protecting the Superuser Account

As noted previously, the superuser has complete access to every file and process on the system. Although this access makes system administration more convenient than on operating systems that divide system privileges among many different users, it means that any intruder who gains root access to your system may do anything he or she wishes. For this reason, it's important to use strong measures to protect the root account.

On most systems, there are two ways to gain superuser privileges: you can log in as root (or on some other account with an UID of 0) or you can change to root from your usual account with the su command. The su command (which stands for "set user" is used as follows:

```
$ su
Password:
#
```

As you can see, the system challenges you for the root password; if you give the correct password (which it doesn't echo), it gives you a root prompt. You should always log in to your system with your personal username and use su to get superuser access as needed, for the following reasons:

- The su command logs all attempts to change to root (or any other user) to /usr/adm/messages or /usr/adm/sulog (see the section "syslog & sulog" later in this chapter).
- Most modern versions of UNIX allow you to control which users are allowed to su to root. If the group "wheel" has members, only they may su to root.
- You can configure UNIX to disallow root logins from network connections (such as telnet or rlogin). If you do this, potential intruders must first gain access to a user's account before getting a chance to break root.

The file /etc/securetty contains a list of terminals from which you can log in as root. If the file is empty, or nonexistent, root may log in from any connection. It's an excellent idea to restrict root logins from terminals that aren't hard-wired to the computer. For example, a /etc/securetty file can look like the following:

```
console
tty1
tty2
tty3
tty4
tty5
tty6
```

This file allows root logins from the console and the six hard-wired terminals; all of which the administrator can personally keep an eye on. Telnet and rlogin users (which use the pty pseudo-terminal devices) may not log in as root.

When operating as the superuser, you have great power over the system. With great power comes great responsibility. You should always take precautions when operating as root to avoid security problems. A common gambit for crackers who have gained access to a user account (as well as for legitimate users with unfriendly intentions) is to try to trick root into running a Trojan horse program that creates a SUID shell (see the section "SUID & SGID" later in this chapter) giving the crackers effective root access. To prevent your system from falling victim to a Trojan horse, you should

- Keep your search path minimal, when operating as the superuser. It should contain only system directories, as in the following path:

  ```
  # echo $PATH
  /sbin:/usr/sbin:/bin:/usr/bin:/etc:/usr/etc
  ```

  These directories may vary from system to system, but the point remains the same: by restricting your search path, you reduce the chance that an intruder will trick you into running a security-breaching program.

- Never put the current directory (a single dot or empty entry) into your search path. If you do, a cracker may put a bogus copy of the ls program, for example, in a user's directory; if you have a dot in your search path, you may run the intruder's Trojan horse program as root.

- Always give the full pathname of all commands you run as root. For example, type /bin/ls instead of ls. Although it's an inconvenience, it goes a long way toward protecting your system from crackers.

Sometimes intruders find ways to replace system binaries. You should use the tripwire program (which can be found at ftp://ftp.cert.org/pub/tools/tripwire) on a regular basis to ensure that none of your system's files have been replaced with Trojan horses. tripwire generates a cryptographic checksum (using the MD5 algorithm) for your system files. By periodically comparing the files' current checksums with the original values, you can ensure that no unauthorized changes have been made.

File Permissions & Ownership

The UNIX file system can be thought of as an upside-down tree. At the top of the file system is the root directory. Inside the root directory resides a number of directories and files. These branches from the root can also contain directories and files, and so on.

File Information

Each of the files and directories are identified in a structure on the disk called an inode, which contains all the information about the files and directories except their names. You can list all the information about a file with the ls command:

```
$ ls -l chapter4.notes
-rw-r--r--  1 jem     10661 Mar 14 01:14 chapter4.notes
```

The ls command asks for a long listing of the file chapter4.notes. Table 4-3 explains each of the fields in the directory listing. You can add group information to the listing with the -g option; on UNIX systems running System V, the -g option replaces the user information with the group, while on BSD-derived systems, the group information is to the right of the user.

Field Contents	Description
-rw-r--r--	The file's type and permissions. See the section "File Permissions" later in this chapter for more information on permissions.
1	The number of links or names the file has.
jem	The username of the owner of the file.
10661	The size of the file, in bytes.
Mar 14 01:14	The time that the file was last modified.
chapter4.notes	The name of the file.

Table 4-3: *Information provided by ls -l.*

The ls command is the most important tool for investigating the status of the files on your system. It allows you to access all the information that UNIX keeps about your files—which is especially important if you suspect that your system security has been compromised. Table 4-4 contains a list of the file information kept by most UNIX file systems and the options for the ls command in order to get that information.

Inode Entry	Description	Option to ls
mode	The file permissions (see the next section "File Permissions").	-l
UID	The UID number for the owner of the file.	-ln
GID	The GID number for the group that the file belongs to.	-lgn
size	The size of the file in bytes.	-l
atime	The last time the file was accessed.	-lu
ctime	The last time the inode information of the file was changed.	-lc
mtime	The last time the file was modified.	-l
links	The number of names the file has.	-l

Table 4-4: *Inode information about files and how to retrieve it.*

If you're looking for recent skullduggery on your system, the ctime of a file is the most reliable indicator that a file has been recently changed in some way. Both the access and modification times can be easily changed with a simple program, but the kernel itself keeps track of ctime. This may not stop a wily intruder who has gained root access. He could temporarily reset the system time or make the change directly to the raw disk structures. Still, the ctime is the most reliable indicator there is (without using a checksum program like tripwire—see the previous section "Protecting the Superuser Account").

If you suspect a breakin has occurred, you should first check for files that have recently had their ctimes changed. On a large system, checking all the ctimes generates a lot of disk activity and creates a long listing for you to sort through. Still, it can be a fairly easy way to get a picture of recent changes to your system. You can generate such a listing by typing the following:

```
# find / \( -ctime 0 -o -ctime 1 \) -print
```

This command line creates a list of files whose ctimes have changed in the last two days (meaning the present day and the previous day). If your system supports the -xdev option, you may also want to use it to isolate the search to a single file system and then run it on the other partitions one at a time.

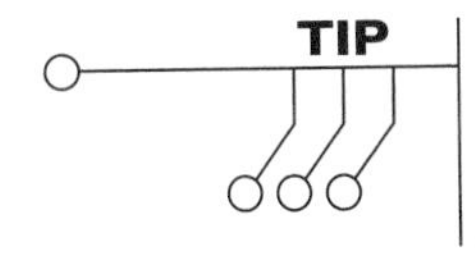

The best defense against data loss due to system crackers or an accident is a good backup policy. Not only will a reliable set of backups allow you to restore files that have been maliciously deleted or accidentally lost, but the log files archived on the backups may be your only evidence of the cracker's activities. A good backup policy should make a full (level 0) dump of the system at least once, and ideally twice, a month. You should do an incremental dump of files that have changed several times a week; once a day is ideal. For reliable backups, you should remember the following:

- *The only completely reliable backup is one that is done when the system is in single-user mode and the file systems are inactive. It's impossible to make a completely accurate backup of an active file system, no matter what the marketing information for your UNIX system says.*
- *Always keep multiple sets of working backup tapes, which you rotate through, round-robin fashion. If you always use the same set of tapes for backups, you may find that your most recent set is corrupted, and you have no recourse. Tape is cheap, especially compared to irreplaceable data.*

File Permissions

The first field in a long directory listing is a symbolic representation of the file's type and permissions. The format is 10 one-character fields. The following are examples:

```
drw-r-xr-x
-rw-------
-rwsr-xr-x
lrwxrwxrwx
```

The first one-character field indicates the file type. Table 4-5 contains a list of the possible file types and their symbols.

Symbol	Meaning
-	A plain file.
d	A directory.
l	A symbolic link.
b	A block device.
c	A character device.
p	A named pipe or FIFO.

Table 4-5: *Symbolic names for file types.*

The next nine fields can be broken down into three groups of three symbols. Each group specifies the permissions for a different type of access. The first group of three signifies the permissions for the user who owns the file; the second group of three is the permissions for the group that owns the file. The third group of symbols is the permissions for all the other users on the system (or the "world").

UNIX provides three levels of access that can be individually turned on and off for each group: Read, Write and Execute. Table 4-6 describes each of these types of access.

Symbol	Meaning	Description
r	Read	If a user is allowed Read access to a file, he or she can open the file and read its contents. For directories, Read access allows the user to list its contents.
w	Write	If a user is allowed Write access to a file, he or she can open the file to overwrite it or append to it. For directories, Write access allows the user to create and delete files in that directory.
x	Execute	If a user is allowed Execute access to a file, he or she can run that file as a program. Of course, this is meaningful only if the file is a binary program or shell script. For directories, Execute access allows the user to enter a directory with the cd command.

Table 4-6: *Types of file access.*

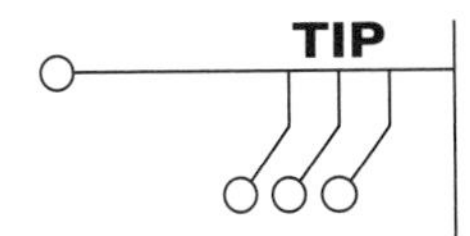

Some UNIX systems also use the "sticky bit" to control Write access in directories. If the sticky bit is turned on for a world-writable directory, anyone may create a file in it, but only the owner (or root) may delete the file. This feature is usually used with the system's temporary directories:

```
drwxrwxrwt   6 root   root      1024 Mar 14 16:15 /tmp
```

The "t" in the group execute spot shows that the directory is sticky. You can activate this bit with the chmod command, either symbolically or in octal:

```
# chmod o+t /tmp
or
# chmod 1777 /tmp
```

If you own a file, or are logged in as the superuser, you can change the permissions on a file with the chmod command. To do so, you merely specify the type of access you would like to change:

```
$ ls -l chapter4.notes
-rw-r--r--     1 jem    10661    Mar 14 01:14    chapter4.notes
$ chmod g+wx chapter4.notes
$ ls -l chapter4.notes
-rw-rwxr--     1 jem    10661    Mar 14 01:14    chapter4.notes
```

In this example, we use chmod to add Write and Execute permissions to the owning group. The first argument chmod takes is a string representing what permissions changes you want to make. This string is composed of the following:

- A character signifying the type of access you wish to modify (see Table 4-7).
- A character representing the type of change you wish to make (see Table 4-8).
- A string composed of the permissions modifications you wish to apply (see Table 4-9).

After the permissions string, you must give chmod a list of the files (or directories) to which to apply the changes. Under some versions of UNIX, chmod also accepts an -R option to allow you to make the changes recursively to all the files beneath a certain directory:

```
$ chmod -R o-wx my-dir
```

This command removes all Write and Execute permissions for the owner of the *my-dir* directory and everything beneath it.

Symbol	Meaning
u	The owning user.
g	The owning group.
o	All other users.
a	All users: owning user, group and others.

Table 4-7: *chmod codes for types of access.*

Symbol	Meaning
+	Add the following permissions.
-	Subtract the following permissions.
=	Explicitly set the following permissions.

Table 4-8: *chmod codes for types of changes.*

The chmod command also accepts another syntax for specifying permissions; most experienced system administrators find this syntax, even though it's somewhat confusing, more convenient to use. UNIX represents each of the possible permissions as an octal (base eight) code, and this code can be used to change permissions with the chmod command. Table 4-9 lists each of the octal permission codes.

Octal Number	Meaning
1000	Sticky bit.
2000	GID bit (see the next section, "SUID & SGID Files").
4000	UID bit (see the next section, "SUID & SGID Files").
0400	Read access for owner.
0200	Write access for owner.
0100	Execute access for owner.
0040	Read access for group.
0020	Write access for group.
0010	Execute access for group.
0004	Read access for others.
0002	Write access for others.
0001	Read access for others.

Table 4-9: *Octal permission codes.*

These codes can be logically ORd to give the full permissions of the files, as in the following example:

```
$ chmod 750 chapter4.notes
```

This command turns on rwx access for the owner (0400+0200+0100), and rx access for the group (0040+0010) and removes all access for all others. (The initial 0 can be left off.)

On most systems, files are created world readable by default. You can change this default with the umask command, which is built in to the various shells. The umask command specifies an octal permissions value to be removed from the default permissions (0777). So you can deny the group and the world Read, Write and Execute access to newly created files like this:

```
$ umask 077
```

Since most inexperienced UNIX users are surprised to find that most of the files they create are world readable, many system managers like to add such a line to the shell start-up files: /etc/profile, for Bourne-compatible shells, and /etc/csh.cshrc or /etc/.cshrc, for those based on the C shell. This increases the default security on the system and is recommended for installations in which users do little cooperative work.

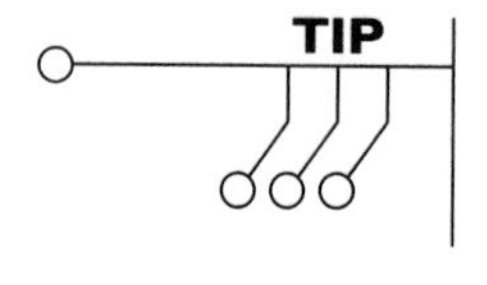

The default ownerships and permissions on systems shipped by many vendors are set incorrectly. These distribution bugs can open your system to attacks from remote intruders and unfriendly users. You should check with your vendor to make sure all permissions and ownerships on system software are set correctly. You can find a list of UNIX vendor security contacts at http://iss.net/~iss/vendor.html.

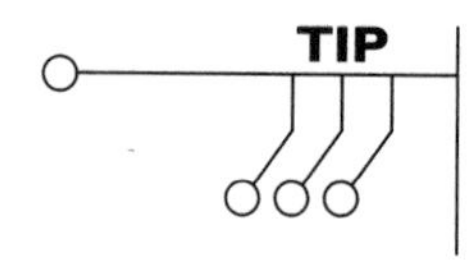

You should also use COPS on a regular basis. COPS is a system security auditor, which detects and reports common insecure configurations. You can get a copy of COPS at ftp://ftp.cert.org/pub/tools/cops.

SUID & SGID Files

The two special forms of execute access are SUID and SGID. SUID, or set UID, files execute with the permissions of the owner of the file rather than the user who is running the command. Similarly, SGID, or set GID, files are run with the permissions of the owning group. This feature allows the administrator of the system to grant special privileges to programs that need to access protected system resources.

An example of this feature in action is the ps command. Under most UNIX systems (Linux being a notable exception), ps must access the system memory—an area that is usually forbidden to regular users (see the next section, "Device Files"). For this reason, ps is usually SUID to root or SGID to a special group called kmem.

```
-r-sr-xr-x   1 root   sys   17800 Jul 16  1994 /usr/bin/ps
```

The s in the execute spot of the owner's permissions string shows that the program is SUID. On your system, you may find that ps is SGID, in which case, you would see an s in the group's permission's string, instead of the owner's string.

You can alter the SUID and SGID permission bits with the chmod command, as in the following examples:

```
$ chmod o+s execname
$ chmod g+s execname
```

The first command would make execname SUID, while the second would make it SGID. If you prefer chmod's octal notation, the SUID and SGID bits are numbered 4000 and 2000, respectively.

Although the ability to make executables set UID and set GID is a useful feature, it's also dangerous for system security. An intruder who makes a copy of a shell SUID to root can gain root authority any time simply by running the shell. This strategy is common among system crackers.

For this reason, it's important to keep track of all the SUID and SGID programs on your system. When you first install the system, you should make a list of all legitimate executables on your system with the set UID and set GID permissions; you can make such a list by entering the following command line:

```
# find / -type f \( -perm -4000 -o -perm -2000 \) -print
```

From time to time (especially if you think your system may have been compromised), you should rerun this command and compare the results to the output you received previously. You should regard any new programs that show up on the list with suspicion; if you can't account for them, they may be evidence of cracker activity.

Under no circumstances should you allow SUID or SGID shell scripts because there is no way to make such scripts secure. Allowing a SUID or SGID shell script on your system is an invitation for any marginally knowledgeable user to gain root access. There are many well-documented ways for a regular user to use a SUID script to gain root access. In fact, some systems, such as Linux, don't even honor the SUID and SGID bits on shell scripts.

Device Files

One revolutionary feature of UNIX is the convention of representing physical devices as files. These files can be (more or less) read and written normally, according to their ownership and permissions. This means that if you allow a user access to the file that represents the full system memory, he or she can read and write any area of the RAM, which is obviously not recommended.

It's important to keep track of all the devices on your system. By UNIX convention, all devices reside in the /dev directory. You should check the device files by doing a long listing of this directory to check their permissions and ownerships. In general, all devices should be owned by root with Read and Write access to the owner and group. The only exceptions (on most UNIX systems) are the special devices /dev/null, /dev/zero, /dev/console and /dev/tty; these will all probably be world writable.

Another exception to the rule that all devices should be owned by root are the tty and pty devices. When someone is logged in to a terminal or pseudo-terminal device, he or she owns it. These devices are also world writable by default, which allows users to communicate with each other with the write and talk commands. A user can remove world-write access to his or her screen by entering the following:

```
$ mesg n
```

Although all UNIX devices are found in the /dev directory, this is not a requirement. You can create a device file anywhere in the system with the mknod command, which, in fact, is a common tactic for successful intruders. By creating a hidden device file that gives them wholesale access to the system's memory or raw disk,

intruders can regain root access at any time. You should occasionally check for these rogue devices by entering the following command line:

```
# find / \( -type b -o -type c \) -print | grep -v ^/dev/
```

This command generates a list of all device files that aren't located in the /dev directory. If you find any, your system may have been compromised.

Security Logs & System Status

A busy UNIX system can be difficult to keep track of. Since most programs take advantage of a UNIX system's low overhead for creating new processes, it's not unusual to find hundreds of processes running on a busy server. Although it can be a chore, it's im-portant to keep on top of what's happening on the server you manage. Luckily, UNIX provides commands that allow you to get an overview of the activity on your system. It also provides for the copious logging of events of which the administrator should be aware. Of course, it's up to *you* to run the commands and read the logs.

The ps Command

The most important UNIX command for keeping track of system activity is ps, which stands for "process status." The ps command can give you a listing of all the programs running on the system, along with such vital information as their process IDs, the amount of CPU time and memory they've taken and which user ran which command. There are many options to ps, which determine the level of detail it goes into. Unfortunately, these command-line options differ from system to system. Most can be grouped into either System V (Solaris, AIX, IRIX) or BSD (Linux, SunOS, Ultrix) syntaxes.

A system administrator uses the ps command mostly to obtain a full listing of all the processes running on the system. If you're on a System V-based system, you enter the following:

```
$ ps -ef
UID       PID  PPID   C   STIME     TTY    TIME   COMD
root        0     0  80   01:40:26  ?      0:01   sched
root        1     0  80   01:40:29  ?      0:09   /etc/init -
root        2     0  80   01:40:29  ?      0:01   pageout
root        3     0  80   01:40:29  ?      15:14  fsflush
root      415     1  19   01:44:12  ?      0:00   /usr/lib/saf/sac -t 300
root      113     1  17   01:43:07  ?      0:00   /usr/sbin/kerbd
root      237   230  80   01:43:51  ?      4:06   lpNet
root      103     1  80   01:43:06  ?      0:10   /usr/sbin/rpcbind
root      105     1   2   01:43:06  ?      0:00   /usr/sbin/keyserv
root      215     1  80   01:43:50  ?      0:02   /usr/sbin/cron
root      111     1  80   01:43:06  ?      0:07   /usr/lib/netsvc/yp/ypbind
root      120     1  80   01:43:13  ?      0:44   /usr/sbin/in.named
root      124     1  80   01:43:13  ?      1:22   /usr/sbin/inetd -s
root      127     1  30   01:43:13  ?      0:00   /usr/lib/nfs/statd
root      129     1  70   01:43:14  ?      0:01   /usr/lib/nfs/lockd
nobody  10914  2749       06:50:04  ?      0:00   /opt/httpd_1.3/sbin/httpd
root     6016   124  80   04:10:53  ?      0:01   in.ftpd
jem     14737 14210  61   07:05:10  pts/8  0:01   ps -ef
```

This command generates a long listing, which you will probably want to redirect to a file or pipe to a pager, such as the more command.

We've included only the top few entries for the sake of brevity. As you can see, the output of the command includes eight fields, and the meaning of each is summarized in Table 4-10. You can add extra fields by including the -l option on the command line. Most of this extra information is fairly arcane; if you're interested, consult your man pages.

Field	Description
UID	The name of the user who is running the command.
PID	The unique process identification number.
PPID	The PID of the parent of the process, that is, the process that started the command.
C	The scheduling priority of the process.
STIME	At what hour and minute the process was started. If this time is more than 24 hours earlier, the month and day the process was started is printed.
TTY	The terminal from which the program is being run. If the program is a background daemon, and thus has no controlling TTY, a question mark is printed.
TIME	The total amount of CPU time the process has used since it started—in hours and minutes.
COMD	The name of the command and its arguments. If the process has been swapped out to disk, the arguments aren't printed.

Table 4-10: *The fields in the System V ps -ef.*

You can also get a full listing of process activity on BSD-based operating systems with the following command:

```
$ ps -aux
                %     %
USER    PID   CPU   MEM  RSS  SIZE  TTY  STAT START   TIME  COMMAND
jem   12553   0.0   0.5  117  332   ppd   S  07:46   0:00  telnet email
jem   12562   0.0   0.5  177  348   pp9   R  08:03   0:00  ps aux
jem   12563   0.0   0.3  105  244   pp9   S  08:03   0:00  less
root      1   0.0   0.3   48  236   con   S  Mar 7   1:20  init auto
root      6   0.0   0.2   28  160   con   S  Mar 7   0:00  bdflush (daemon)
root      7   0.0   0.2   28  164   con   S  Mar 7   0:02  update (bdflush)
root     41   0.0   0.4   61  272   con   S  Mar 7   0:36  /usr/sbin/syslogd
root     43   0.0   0.3   40  236   con   S  Mar 7   0:00  /usr/sbin/klogd
root     46   0.0   0.3   64  244   con   S  Mar 7   0:01  /usr/sbin/rpc.portmap
root     48   0.0   0.4   72  292   con   S  Mar 7   0:02  /usr/sbin/inetd
root     50   0.0   0.3   68  240   con   S  Mar 7   0:00  /usr/sbin/lpd
root     52   0.0   0.3   76  256   con   S  Mar 7   0:03  /usr/sbin/crond
root     54   0.0   0.3   60  220   con   S  Mar 7   0:00  /usr/sbin/rpc.ugidd -
root     65   0.0   0.4  100  288   con   S  Mar 7   0:00  /usr/sbin/rpc.mountd
```

As in the previous example, we've included only the first few lines of output. Table 4-11 summarizes the meaning of the various fields. You can add the -l option to the BSD ps, also, to obtain more information. Consult the man page for details.

Field	Description
USER	The name of the user who ran the command.
PID	The unique process identification number.
%CPU	The percentage of CPU time the process is taking. If the machine is a multiprocessor, the sum of these numbers may be equal to 100 percent multiplied by the number of processors.
%MEM	The percentage of real memory (RAM) used by this process.
SIZE	The combined size of the program's data and stack (in kilobytes).
RSS	The amount of real memory (RAM) used by this process (in kilobytes).
TTY	The terminal this process was run from. If it's a daemon and runs in the background, this value is equal to con, the system console.
STAT	The running status of the process. Common statuses are R for running, S for sleeping, I for idle and Z for zombie. Consult the man page for more details.
START	The time (in hours and minutes) that the command began running. If it's been running for more than 24 hours, the month and date are given.
TIME	The amount of CPU time (in hours and minutes) used by the process so far.
COMMAND	The name of the command, including the first few arguments. If the command is swapped out, the name of the command alone, in parenthesis, is given.

Table 4-11: *The fields in the BSD ps -aux.*

You can use the information given by both of these commands to track down suspicious processes. You should be especially sensitive to unknown programs that take a large amount of CPU time and memory. Intruders often use the CPU of one successful break in to crack the password file of another site.

Login Records

The three data files /etc/utmp, /var/adm/wtmp and /var/adm/lastlog contain information about users logging in and out of the system.

The system keeps track of users who are currently logged on in the /etc/utmp file. This file contains the following:

- The user's login name.
- The user's login time.
- The host from which the user is logged in.

This file is not a reliable indicator of who is really on the system because there are several ways to avoid being included in it. If you need a reliable indicator, you're better off using the ps command.

The /var/adm/wtmp file is similar in format to the /etc/utmp file, and it serves a similar purpose. Every login to and logout from the system is recorded in this file. The contents of the file can be parsed with the last command, which gives the following output:

```
$ last
ewt   ttyq3  mario12.ppp.ncsu   Thu Mar 16 14:10  - 15:14  (01:03)
ewt     ftp  mario12.ppp.ncsu   Thu Mar 16 14:07  - 14:10  (00:02)
ewt   ttyq3  cc00du.unity.ncs   Thu Mar 16 14:04  - 14:05  (00:01)
mgd     ftp  gatekeeper.glaxo   Thu Mar 16 13:22  - 13:22  (00:00)
ewt   ttyq2  netcom19.netcom.   Thu Mar 16 10:27  - 10:49  (00:22)
neb   ttyq2  marimba.cellbio.   Thu Mar 16 07:38  - 07:42  (00:04)
neb   ttyp9  marimba.cellbio.   Wed Mar 15 20:16  - 20:37  (00:21)
ewt   ttyp9  netcom6.netcom.c   Wed Mar 15 19:59  - 20:15  (00:15)
neb   ttypa  marimba.cellbio.   Wed Mar 15 18:45  - 20:00  (01:15)
giles ttyp9  c00313-11pa.eos.   Wed Mar 15 18:12  - 19:24  (01:12)
```

The meaning of these fields is fairly obvious, and the meaning of each of the fields in the first line of the output is summarized in Table 4-12. It's worth noting that on some UNIX systems, FTP logins also create a wtmp entry; for these, the FTP server enters the string "ftp" in the terminal field.

Field	Description
ewt	The username.
ttypq	The terminal (or pseudo-terminal) from which the user was logged on.
mario12.ppp.ncsu	The first 16 letters of the host from which the user established the network connection.
Thu Mar 16 14:10	The date and time that the user logged in.
15:14	The time that the user logged out.
(01:03)	Total time (hours and minutes) that the user was connected.

Table 4-12: *The fields in the output of the last command.*

Every time a user logs in to your system, he or she leaves a record in /var/adm/lastlog. These records are used by the finger daemon, which prints the last login time if you finger a user. They are also used by the login program, which prints the last time that the user logged in, which is illustrated in the following example:

```
Last login: Thu Mar 16 09:20:35 from bittyblue.oit.un
```

This information can be a valuable security tool. If you train your users to take note of their last login times, they can provide an early warning when someone else has used their account. Some System V-based UNIX systems also keep track of the last failed login attempt in the /var/adm/lastlog file, which is also an important security aid; a failed login can be a warning that a bad guy is trying to crack accounts.

syslog & sulog

The syslog daemon is used by BSD and SysVr4 systems to log errors from various daemons and services. Its output is controlled by the file /etc/syslog.conf and is in the following format:

type-of-message tab where-to-put-it

You can use this configuration file to route messages from all the services that use syslog for logging (the kernel, sendmail, system daemons, the printing daemon, the user authorization programs and many others) to output files where you think the messages will do the most good. By default, the most important messages are logged to both the system console and the file /usr/adm/messages. This file is usually your sole source of log information.

You should make a point of scanning this log file every day. All sorts of important security messages are logged to this file. For example, every time the su command is invoked, an indication of whether the user succeeded is logged to syslog, as illustrated in the following example output:

```
$ grep su: /usr/adm/messages
Mar 16 12:34:34 president su: 'su root' succeeded for macox on /dev/ttyp3
Mar 16 15:50:57 president su: 'su root' failed for jem on /dev/ttyp7
```

As you can see, this sort of message can give you essential information about the status of your system.

Not all versions of UNIX employ syslog. Many System V systems (before Release 4) log messages to separate files or only to system console. On these systems (and SysVr4) messages from the su command are logged to /usr/adm/sulog, as follows:

```
SU 03/16 09:07 - pts/47     sweet-root
SU 03/16 09:07 + pts/47     sweet-root
SU 03/16 11:21 + pts/138    harris-root
```

The meaning of these logs is fairly obvious. The time, date, terminal, the user attempting the su command and the user into which he or she was trying to change are logged. A plus sign in the fourth field indicates a success, and a minus indicates a failure.

The extendable logging features of syslog are extremely useful when trying to keep track of your system. Read the man pages on syslog and syslog.conf; you can then set your system to log in the manner most convenient for you.

Internet Security

Although security on any multi-user system is always an important concern, the advent of international data networks, like the Internet, has made it vital. As the manager of a host on the Internet, you have a responsibility to the rest of the Net to guard the security of your own box. This task is, of course, made more difficult by the added opportunities for cracking that your Internet connection provides to computer criminals. For this reason, careful attention to network security is of the utmost importance to the safety of your system and data.

Checking Services

A busy Internet server may offer dozens of different network services. The responsible administrator must have a solid grasp of the network daemons his or her server is running, the services the daemons offer and the security risks associated with running them. This section provides a service-by-service review of the most common network daemons and their vulnerabilities. If you find a problem with a network service you need to offer, you should contact the security representative for your vendor. A patch that fixes the problem is probably available. You can find a list of vendor contacts at http://iss.net/~iss/vendor.html.

Trusted Hosts

One of the most convenient features offered by the standard UNIX suite of networking programs is the concept of trusted hosts. When host A is trusted by host B, users on host A may use many network services on host B without authenticating themselves. This feature obviously has implications for system security; when all the machines on a local network trust each other, a single security breach may be replicated across the entire network.

The two main mechanisms for trust provided by UNIX systems are the /etc/hosts.equiv file and the individual .rhosts file. The /etc/hosts.equiv file contains a list of hosts and users who may access the system without supplying a password. The following is a sample copy:

```
groucho.shoop.com
chico.shoop.com
warners.animaniacs.com yacco
- evil.mynemesis.org
```

This /etc/hosts.equiv file allows unauthenticated logins from groucho.shoop.org and chico.shoop.org. The third line allows logins from the user yacco from the host warners.animaniacs.com. As shown in the fourth line, you can also explicitly remove permission from a host by prefixing a minus sign to its entry. When /etc/hosts.equiv contains a plus sign on a line by itself, all network hosts are allowed unauthenticated access, which is clearly a *very* bad idea. Unfortunately, in many versions of SunOS, this configuration is the default. It's important to make sure that your machine is not configured this way.

A similar format is used for the .rhosts file. This file goes into a user's home directory and controls who may log in to that user's account without a password. For a .rhosts file to be valid, it must be owned by the user who owns the account in which it resides.

When a user attempts a connection with rlogin, rsh or rcp, his or her username and hostname is validated against the contents of /etc/hosts.equiv and the .rhosts file of the account that the user is trying to access. An exception is made for the root user. The network daemons skip the /etc/hosts.equiv; unauthenticated root logins must be authorized in /.rhosts.

As is apparent, the trusted host feature can be very dangerous. It's of little use to encourage your users to choose good passwords, if the users are allowed to bypass them. On the other hand, controlled use of trust can make handling network service much more convenient. Also, use of trusted hosts can have a security advantage: most network programs pass the user's passwords unencrypted over the network. If a bad guy has direct access to your local network, these passwords can be captured with a "sniffer" program. With wise use of trusted hosts, you can keep unencrypted passwords from being passed over the network at all.

Still, if you're going to allow the use of this feature, we recommend that you follow these guidelines:

- Make sure that the /etc/hosts.equiv file or any .rhosts file doesn't contain a plus sign entry. Make sure you don't use comments beginning with a pound sign (#) in /etc/hosts.equiv or a .rhosts file. The file format doesn't allow comments, so an attacker could change their hostname to the commented string and gain access.
- Always give the fully qualified hostname for any trusted host.
- Never allow users to trust hosts that aren't a part of your organization. A trusted user from another site makes that site's security problems your security problems.
- If you have control of your site's router, configure it to drop packets from the outside network, which have IP addresses coming from inside your network. This configuration provides a defense against IP spoofing, an attack in which the intruder configures his or her local machine to have the IP address of a trusted host.
- Prohibit users from using .rhosts entries to give other people access to their accounts.

If you follow these guidelines, you can make the trusted hosts feature fairly safe. Read the next section, "inetd Services," for more information on securing the services that make use of the /etc/hosts.equiv or .rhosts files.

inetd Services

Originally, every network service had its own daemon, which ran on the system all the time waiting for connections. As the number of network services proliferated, a better solution was required. Even though a service might be inactive, the listening daemon used valuable system resources. The solution to this problem was inetd, the superserver.

The inetd reads in a table of network services from /etc/inetd.conf. This file contains a list of services, the network ports on which they operate and the programs that are responsible for servicing them. inetd listens on all the ports listed in the file and starts up the appropriate daemon when it detects a connection. The following is an example of an inetd.conf file:

```
#
# <service_name> <sock_type> <proto> <flags> <user> <server_path> <args>
#
#these services are primarily for testing the network
echo      stream  tcp  nowait  root    internal
echo      dgram   udp  wait    root    internal
discard   stream  tcp  nowait  root    internal
discard   dgram   udp  wait    root    internal
daytime   stream  tcp  nowait  root    internal
daytime   dgram   udp  wait    root    internal
chargen   stream  tcp  nowait  root    internal
chargen   dgram   udp  wait    root    internal
#
#these are production services
ftp       stream  tcp  nowait  root    /usr/sbin/in.ftpd      /usr/sbin/in.ftpd
telnet    stream  tcp  nowait  root    /usr/sbin/in.telnetd   /usr/sbin/in.telnetd
shell     stream  tcp  nowait  root    /usr/sbin/in.rshd      /usr/sbin/in.rshd
login     stream  tcp  nowait  root    /usr/sbin/in.rlogind   /usr/sbin/in.rlogind
#exec     stream  tcp  nowait  root    /usr/sbin/in.rexecd    /usr/sbin/in.rexecd
talk      dgram   udp  wait    root    /usr/sbin/in.talkd     /usr/sbin/in.talkd
#tftp     dgram   udp  wait    root    /usr/sbin/in.tftpd     /usr/sbin/in.tftpd
#bootps   dgram   udp  wait    root    /usr/sbin/in.bootpd    /usr/sbin/in.bootpd
finger    stream  tcp  nowait  daemon  /usr/sbin/in.fingerd   /usr/sbin/in.fingerd
```

An inetd.conf entry contains seven fields. The first four fields tell inetd how to set up the connection. The first field is the name of the service; this entry is an index into the /etc/services database that contains a list of services and their appropriate network ports. The second and third fields are related; services requiring a reliable connection use "stream" and "tcp", while datagram-based services use "dgram" and "udp". The fourth field has two possible values, "wait" and "nowait". Daemons using "wait" handle all incoming traffic after they are started. inetd must start a new copy of a "nowait" daemon for each new connection.

The fifth field is the name of the user under which the server should run. The sixth field tells inetd the name of the program to start when it receives a connection on the appropriate port. Some /etc/inetd.conf services are "internal"; these services are fairly simple and are usually used for testing networks. inetd handles these services itself, without starting a separate daemon. The seventh field is a space-separated list of arguments to start the daemon with; this list includes argument zero, which is the name of the program itself.

Now that you understand the meaning of the inetd entries, look at Table 4-13 for descriptions of the production services that it runs and the security implications of each. You should remember that there's always a trade-off between providing a network service and securing your system. When you're evaluating a network service, you should compare the security risks to your users' legitimate needs for that type of access.

Service	ftp
Description	File Transfer Protocol. Allows the interactive transfer of files to and from the host.
Security Concerns	Since FTP access requires a username and a password, FTP is fairly secure. If you allow anonymous FTP, make sure that your FTP daemon is newer than December 1988; older versions had security weaknesses. For more information on securing anonymous FTP, see Appendix F, "Legacy Technologies: FTP & Gopher."
Service	telnet
Description	Allows users to make a virtual terminal connection to your host, as if they were on a hard-wired terminal.
Security Concerns	Telnet presents two main security risks. One is the fact that telnet transmits the user's password unencrypted over the network; if someone has physical access to your local network, he or she can use a "sniffer" program to collect user passwords. The second risk comes from the actual function of telnet—it allows remote logins. A cracker can use this service to attempt to log in with a captured username and password.

Service	shell
Description	Used by the rsh and rcp commands, which allow users to run programs on remote hosts.
Security Concerns	This service uses the trusted hosts mechanism. See the previous section, "Trusted Hosts," for information about the security risks.
Service	login
Description	Used by the rlogin command, which allows remote logins from other UNIX machines.
Security Concerns	This service uses the trusted hosts mechanism. See the previous section, "Trusted Hosts," for information about the security risks.
Service	exec
Description	Not used by any built-in command but used for easy access to remote execution by custom programs.
Security Concerns	This service doesn't use the trusted hosts mechanism; instead, it transmits passwords unencrypted over the network. In addition, no system program uses the exec service, and its error messages can help a cracker find a valid username. For all these reasons we always disable this service on our system (by commenting it out of inetd.conf).
Service	talk
Description	Allows users to chat across the network.
Security Concerns	It presents no known security problems.
Service	tftp
Description	Allows the transfer of files from your system without a username or password. tftp is mostly used for booting diskless machines.
Security Concerns	Some versions of tftpd allow access to any file on the system. If you don't use this service for remote booting, definitely comment it out.

Table 4-13: *Production services run by inetd and their security implications.*

sendmail

Electronic mail is one of the most important services to Internet users. In fact, one might argue that without e-mail, Internet access is meaningless. No other Internet service provides the ease of e-mail for one-on-one communication.

Unfortunately, the reputation of this important service has been marred by the security holes in the most popular mail daemon, sendmail. This situation has been exacerbated by the tendency of major UNIX vendors to ship older versions of the sendmail program, in which these bugs aren't fixed. Currently, most UNIX vendors have become more responsive to network security problems and ship relatively bug-free copies of sendmail. Still, if you have an older system, it's important to make sure that none of the problems that have plagued sendmail in the past return to haunt you. The following is a checklist of ways to ensure that your system is safe from the well-known vulnerabilities of sendmail:

- Delete the uudecode or decode aliases from the file /usr/lib/aliases (/etc/aliases on some systems). Then run the newaliases command as root. These aliases have been shown to be insecure.
- If you have mail aliases sending mail to any other programs, make sure that no one can shell out of those programs or convince them to run arbitrary commands.
- Older versions of sendmail allowed you to send mail to random programs, which allowed crackers to trick sendmail into sending them a copy of your /etc/passwd file. You can test to see if you have this problem by entering the following command line:

```
mail "|/bin/mail < /etc/passwd root@yourhost.your.domain"
```

- If executing this command gains you a copy of /etc/passwd, upgrade sendmail.
- Make sure you have disabled the wizard's password feature. You can check for this feature with the wiz command, which the following example illustrates:

```
$ telnet localhost 25
Trying 155.127.0.0.1
Connected to yourhost.your.dom.
Escape character is '^]'.
220-yourhost.your.dom Sendmail 8.6.9/8.6.10 ready at Wed,
15 Mar 1995 23:52:21 -0500
wiz
500 Command unrecognized
quit
```

- If your system responds with "Command unrecognized", your version of sendmail doesn't support a wizard password. If the response is "You wascal wabbit! Wandering wizards won't win!", your sendmail supports it, but it isn't enabled. If the response is "Please pass, oh mighty wizard", the password is enabled, and your system is vulnerable; be sure to change the /usr/lib/sendmail.cf line, beginning with "OW" to "OW*".
- Make sure that your version of sendmail doesn't support the debug command. You can check for this command as follows:

```
$ telnet localhost 25
Trying 155.127.0.0.1
Connected to yourhost.your.dom.
Escape character is '^]'.
220-yourhost.your.dom Sendmail 8.6.9/8.6.10 ready at Wed,
15 Mar 1995 23:52:21 -0500
debug
500 Command unrecognized
quit
```

- If your sendmail replies "Debug enabled" instead of "Command unrecognized", you have an insecure version, and you must upgrade.
- Older versions of the /bin/mail delivery agent were insecure, allowing ordinary users to gain root privileges. If your version of this program is dated before February 20, 1991, you should upgrade it.

- A new security hole was recently found in recent versions of sendmail, which do IDENT lookups. Even if you are not subject to any of the previously listed sendmail bugs, if you haven't already applied the necessary patch or haven't upgraded, you are probably vulnerable to this one.

If any of the various sendmail security bugs apply to you, you should patch or upgrade your sendmail immediately. A list of sendmail patches for the major UNIX vendors is maintained at the URL http://iss.net/~iss/patch.html#sendmail.

We personally recommend replacing your vendor's sendmail system with the version available on the Net from the University of California at Berkeley. In general, the Berkeley version is updated and maintained much more actively than vendor sendmail. When a new security problem is discovered, a fix is usually available for Berkeley sendmail immediately. You can find the current Berkeley sendmail, version 8.6.12, at ftp://ftp.cs.berkeley.edu/ucb/sendmail.

Using netstat

Connections to network services are, by their nature, ephemeral. For this reason, it can be hard to get a lock on suspicious network activity. By the time you've noticed a network intruder, he or she may have already cut the connection. You should periodically check the state of your server's network activities with the netstat program.

The netstat program gives you a list of all active network connections to your host. The netstat output looks similar to the following:

```
# netstat
Active Internet connections
Proto  Recv-Q Send-Q      Local Address          Foreign Address        (state)
tcp        0      0   PRESIDENT.3143              CERT.ORG.ftp      TIME_WAIT
tcp        0      0   PRESIDENT.z3950            CALZONE.47709      ESTABLISHED
tcp        0      6   PRESIDENT.3141    SHADDAM.USB.VE.smtp      ESTABLISHED
tcp        0      0   PRESIDENT.login          BITTYBLUE.1018      ESTABLISHED
tcp        0      0   PRESIDENT.z3950            CALZONE.61543      ESTABLISHED
tcp        0      0   PRESIDENT.z3950            CALZONE.61043      ESTABLISHED
tcp     5840   4948   PRESIDENT.3044     193.221.170.196.smtp      ESTABLISHED
tcp        0      0   PRESIDENT.2868                       *.*      LISTEN
tcp        0      0   PRESIDENT.2865             CALYPSO-2.ftp      CLOSE_WAIT
tcp        0      0   PRESIDENT.login          BITTYBLUE.1017      ESTABLISHED
```

If you're running the X Windows system on your computer, you'll also see many entries in the output for UNIX domain sockets. We've deleted these entries from the output in the interest of saving space and because they don't really tell you anything about network utilization.

You can obtain a lot of information from this list. Look at the first line of the output. The local address is listed as the host PRESIDENT from port 3143, and the remote, or foreign, address is CERT.ORG using the reserved FTP port; the connection is in the TIME_WAIT state. Since netstat substitutes the service name from /etc/services for the port number when it's present in the database, you know that the connection netstat is reporting in this line is an FTP connection from PRESIDENT to CERT.ORG. As the state of the connection is TIME_WAIT, you can tell the FTP user has already closed the FTP session.

You can extract similar information from the second line of the output. This line reports that an ESTABLISHED connection is between the z3950 port (used for WAIS, which is described in Chapter 9, "Searching & Indexing") on PRESIDENT and some random port on CALZONE. This implies that the connection was initiated on the foreign host, which connected to the host's WAIS server.

You can use the -a option for netstat to obtain full information on all network activity on your host. You'll get output similar to the following:

```
# netstat -a
Active Internet connections (including servers)
Proto  Recv-Q  Send-Q  Local Address  Foreign Address  (state)
udp    0       0       *.daytime      *.*
udp    0       0       *.echo         *.*
udp    0       0       *.time         *.*
udp    0       0       *.talk         *.*
udp    0       0       *.syslog       *.*
udp    0       0       *.ntp          *.*
udp    0       0       *.sunrpc       *.*
tcp    0       0       *.z3950        *.*              LISTEN
tcp    0       0       *.imap         *.*              LISTEN
tcp    0       0       *.daytime      *.*              LISTEN
tcp    0       0       *.echo         *.*              LISTEN
tcp    0       0       *.time         *.*              LISTEN
tcp    0       0       *.finger       *.*              LISTEN
tcp    0       0       *.login        *.*              LISTEN
tcp    0       0       *.shell        *.*              LISTEN
tcp    0       0       *.printer      *.*              LISTEN
tcp    0       0       *.telnet       *.*              LISTEN
tcp    0       0       *.ftp          *.*              LISTEN
tcp    0       0       *.smtp         *.*              LISTEN
tcp    0       0       *.sunrpc       *.*              LISTEN
```

We've deleted the previously noted output for UNIX domain sockets from this example. The entries in the example all signify network services waiting for connections, either standalone or from inetd. The asterisks under the "Local Address" and "Foreign Address" columns show that the servers are waiting for connections from any host on any of the machine's network interfaces.

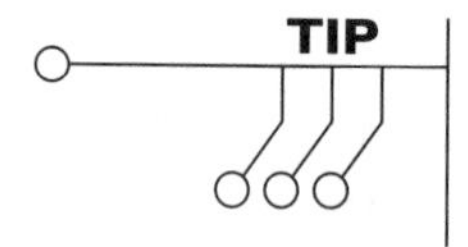

netstat lacks two network monitoring capabilities that we find useful when looking into network security:

- *netstat can't tell you which process is responsible for a network connection.*
- *netstat can't tell you the contents of a network transaction.*

You can use a freeware program called lsof to tell you which process is responsible for a network connection. It's available at ftp://ftp.cert.org/pub/tools/lsof. You can use a program called snoop to tell you the contents of a network transaction. If snoop isn't available for your system, a freeware program called tcpdump, available at ftp://ftp.ee.lbl.gov/tcpdump.tar.Z, can do the same things that snoop does, and even more.

NIS & NFS

NIS and NFS are standards introduced by Sun that govern the convenient sharing of information across networks. Although both standards have become popular, they have the potential to be real security problems. An in-depth explanation of how to use these services is beyond the scope of this section, but it's important to note the bugs and security pitfalls involved in using these services.

NIS

NIS stands for Network Information Services. (It was originally called YP, but that name infringed on a trademark of British Telecom.) It allows databases of information, such as password files, to be shared inside an organization. Thus, you can manage these databases centrally, without having to modify files on hundreds of different computers.

NIS works on a client-server basis. A collection of clients serving the same databases over NIS is called a domain. This use of the word *domain* is completely distinct from the use of *domain* as part of a machine's hostname. Be careful; it's easy to get the two usages confused.

An NIS domain is served by one or more NIS servers. The domain must have at least one *master* server, which contains the master copies of the databases being shared and can include several *slave* servers as well. Slave servers receive a copy of the NIS databases (called maps) when they change. These slave servers act as backup servers for times when the master server is down; clients direct their requests to a slave when they are unable to reach the master.

NIS presents several potential security problems. Some problems occur because of the design and implementation of the software. Others are merely easy-to-make mistakes, which can leave your host open to attack. The following is a list of the most important problems to guard against when using NIS:

- Clients indicate that they wish to use NIS for /etc/passwd lookups by putting the following line at the end of their /etc/passwd files:

```
+::0:0:::
```

- This line indicates to the client software that the contents of the server's password file should be inserted at this point in the file. Make sure that the plus sign exists. If it doesn't, this line becomes a password entry for an account that has an empty username, an empty password and root privileges. This situation can threaten the security of your system. Most implementations of NIS allow you to use the following syntax instead:

```
+:
```

  You should use this syntax because if the plus is deleted, the /etc/passwd entry is not valid.

- Similarly, this special line has no meaning to NIS if it's in the server's password file. In the server's password file, it creates an account with the username of a plus sign, no password and root privileges. Again, it presents a threat to your system security.
- Make sure your NIS maps are not world writable on the server. NIS maps usually reside in /usr/etc/yp. If they are world writable, change the Makefile in that directory to use chmod to fix the permissions.
- When choosing an NIS domain name, follow the guidelines for picking a password (see the previous section, "Passwords"). Most versions of the NIS server software allow anyone to access your NIS maps (including your password file!), if he or she knows the NIS domain name of the server. Most vendors can give you patches to fix this problem. Also, the free versions of the portmapper and rpcbind described in the section "TCP Wrappers," later in this chapter, don't suffer from this problem and have other enhanced security features as well.

If you follow these security guidelines, you'll find NIS to be an excellent service that saves you a lot of trouble. If you ignore them, your password file will be easily obtained by crackers.

NFS

NFS stands for Network File System, which is a protocol developed for transparently mounting and accessing file systems across the network as if they were local. This feature is very powerful, and with great power comes great security risks.

An NFS server is said to export its file systems to a client who mounts them. You can control which file systems the server exports to which hosts by modifying the file /etc/exports (SYSVr4 derived UNIX's list NFS exports in /etc/dfs/dfstab, which has a slightly different syntax). A typical /etc/exports file might look like the following:

```
/usr/local -access=www.shoop.com:doc.shoop.com,root=sneezy.shoop.com
/usr/man -ro,access=www.shoop.com:doc.shoop.com:sneezy.shoop.com
```

These lines export two directories (and all the files and directories beneath them) to several machines. The first line grants access to /usr/local to three machines: www.shoop.com, doc.shoop.com and sneezy.shoop.com. Only the latter is allowed access to the mounted directory as root; without the -root option, NFS converts all requests with root permissions to the nobody user. The second line grants read-only access to those same hosts. After you've written /etc/exports as you like, you must activate your changes on most systems with the program exportfs, as follows:

```
# exportfs -a
```

This command should force the NFS server to note your changes to the exports databases. The many other options that you can specify in /etc/exports are explained in the man page for /etc/exports.

If you run an NFS server, you should take the following into consideration:

- Most NFS servers honor options on a per-file system basis, not a per-directory basis. If you export two directories on the same file system, they use the same options.

- You should never export a file system that isn't needed.
- Don't export file systems that have system binaries on them. If you do, any breach in NFS security will have wider implications. If you must, export them read-only.
- Interestingly, the NFS server gives special treatment only to the root user. It relies on the client implementation to keep users from accessing each other's files in inappropriate ways. If a user is capable of writing his own NFS client, he or she can access the files of any nonroot user.

  If you have directories and files that are on an exported file system that you wish to protect from this risk, they should be owned by root.
- Regularly run the showmount command to find out who has your disks mounted.
- If your system supports it, run the fsirand command on your unmounted file systems. This program randomizes the inode numbers on a file system. NFS uses the inode numbers as the key to its (limited) security, but the default inode numbers for root and other directories are well known. By randomizing them, you reduce the chance that someone will be able to spoof the NFS authentication scheme.
- Older versions of BSD and Ultrix silently limited the length of the access line to be 255 characters. When a list was longer, anyone could mount the file system. If you have this bug, you should upgrade your system.
- You'll have increased security against unauthorized mount attempts if you run the enhanced version of the portmapper or rpcbind that is discussed in the next section, "TCP Wrappers."

This is a long list, but NFS is an inherently dangerous service. You should think carefully about how you want to use it and make sure the convenience is worth the increased risks.

Advanced Internet Security Options

Previously, we have concentrated on the native mechanisms of UNIX for increasing and ensuring network security. Several add-on packages are available, and they can dramatically increase the safety of your system. Although an in-depth discussion is beyond the scope of this brief introduction to UNIX security, a few points are worth mentioning. We also provide references for obtaining further information.

TCP Wrappers

TCP Wrappers is a security package written by Wietse Venema of the Eindhoven University of Technology in the Netherlands. The main part of the package is tcpd, which acts as a simple wrapper around each of the network daemons that are run by inetd. You can write rules in a simple configuration language, which accept or deny connections to any of these services based on various criteria. Also, you can associate actions with rules that deny connections. For example, you could finger a host that attempts an illegal rlogin request.

In addition, tcpd logs all attempted network connections to the wrapped services, which gives you an extra level of auditing that you can use to keep track of attempts against your machine's security. TCP Wrappers is an excellent package, and we recommend it to all system managers who are serious about network security. Slackware Linux systems come pre-installed with TCP Wrappers; all you need to do is to properly configure the hosts_access and hosts_options files. You can consult the man pages for both of them. The source code for TCP Wrappers can be found at ftp://ftp.win.tue.nl/pub/security.

The TCP Wrappers package comes with a support library named libwrap.a. This library is used by several other programs to provide wrapper-like defenses for other services. Of particular interest are the secure portmapper and rpcbind, which provide safe NIS and NFS serving. Also important is loginlog, which allows logging of all remote logins to your host. All of these programs can be found at ftp://ftp.win.tue.nl/pub/security.

Firewalls

A firewall is a special sort of gateway host that stands between the big, bad Internet and your local network. The firewall host is configured to stop most sorts of network traffic going into your LAN, while allowing some amount of traffic to go the other way.

If you want to keep important and confidential data on an Internet-connected host, a firewall is mandatory. A good firewall should be the first line of defense against professional crackers and data thieves. Unfortunately, building and maintaining an effective firewall is a complex subject, well beyond the scope of the introduction to security provided in this book. You can find more information about firewalls in the books referenced in the Bibliography. Also, Trusted Information Services not only sells a commercial firewall product but also has collected a page of pointers to general information about firewalls. In addition, it also offers a freeware Firewall Toolkit. All of this information can be found at http://ftp.tis.com/Home/NetworkSecurity.html.

Kerberos

Kerberos was invented at Project Athena at MIT by the same people who gave the world X Windows. Kerberos uses a complex system of encrypted "tickets" to solve the trusted host problem. An authentication server issues users a cryptographic ticket upon login, which does the following:

- It proves the identity of users to network services, allowing users to utilize all of the network services they have access to without resorting to a trusted hosts system or needing to reauthenticate themselves every time.
- It proves to users that the network services that are advertised are what they claim they are.
- It allows a distributed computing environment, in which a user may log in to any connected workstation and expect full access to their files, electronic mail, etc.

Unfortunately, Kerberos has disadvantages, too:

- It was developed in the United States, where cryptography is considered a weapon and can't be exported without a special license. This effectively limits use of Kerberos to the United States.

- Each individual network service must be recompiled to use the Kerberos protocols, which makes installing it fairly difficult, or impossible when working with a system for which the source code is not available.
- It works only if you allow only a single user per workstation.

The Kerberos software and documentation is available by anonymous FTP at ftp://athena-dist.mit.edu/.

When You've Been Cracked

It's a terrible feeling to know you've been cracked. Despite the fact that the vast majority of crackers do little or no actual harm to the system, you feel a sense of violation and betrayal. The annoyance and exasperation that comes from trying to track down an intruder are felt even stronger, in our experience. You can minimize this by keeping a firm grasp of the situation. This is not the time to fly off the handle and call in the marines (unless you're a military site, perhaps). Instead, you should do the following:

- Determine whether a breakin has indeed occurred.
- Minimize the damage.
- Close the hole through which the cracker entered.

Finding a Break In

Depending on how subtle the intruder is and how vigilant you are, it may be obvious that your system has been compromised, or you may learn about it only by accident. This section lists some warning signs that indicate your system may have been cracked.

New Accounts

You should occasionally browse your password file, looking for unfamiliar accounts. You should also be on the lookout for inactive accounts that have suddenly sprung to life, as well as for nonroot accounts with a 0 UID. The following command automates this check for you:

```
$ awk -F: '$3 == 0 && $1 != "root" {print}' /etc/passwd
```

If you use NIS, you should use the following command:

```
$ (cat /etc/passwd; ypcat passwd) | awk -F: '$3 == 0 && $1 != "root" {print}'
```

Unfamiliar Files

You should be suspicious if you find unfamiliar, unexplained files in your machine's system directories, such as /, /usr and /etc. Especially suspicious are unfamiliar hidden subdirectories, which often have spaces and other unprintable characters embedded in their names. Inside these directories, you may find cracking programs and other evidence of nefarious activities. You can look for hidden directories with the following command:

```
$ ls -lab
```

This command gives you a long format listing, which includes files and directories that begin with a dot. The -b option tells ls to rewrite unprintable characters as backslashed escape-characters (on systems that support it). The following is an example of a file that has a backspace character embedded in its name:

```
$ ls -lab
total 24
drwxr-xr-x    3 jem     staff    48    Mar 16 09:35    .
drwxrwxrwx    6 root    wheel   204    Mar 16 09:35    ..
drwxr-xr-x    2 jem     staff    32    Mar 16 09:35    ..\010
```

The combination of the usually ignored double dots and the control character causes most administrators to overlook this bogus directory. Most modern UNIX systems allow you to address such a directory by typing Ctrl-V and then the control character you wish to type. In this case, you would type the following:

```
$ cd ..^V^H
```

This input would allow you to enter the hidden directory. If you don't want to mess with doing this, you should keep in mind that the fsck program under most modern UNIX systems can flag this sort of hidden directory as an error and ask if you wish to remove it.

Poor Performance

As noted in the previous section, "The ps Command," unusually slow system performance may be a sign that a cracker is using your CPU time for his or her own purposes. You should use ps along with commands like top and vmstat to investigate suspicious activity on the system. You should be especially sensitive to unknown programs that take a large amount of CPU time and memory. Intruders often use the CPU of one successful break in to crack the password file of another site.

System Crashes

Like all operating systems, UNIX occasionally crashes. When it does, it usually prints a "Panic" message to the console, explaining the reason in fairly obscure, and usually undocumented, terms. If your system crashes, you should check to make sure a hardware error isn't indicated. If you need help understanding the panic, you may want to try asking about it on the appropriate comp.sys newsgroup.

If you find no legitimate reason for your system crashes, they may be caused by an intruder who is covering his or her tracks.

Denial of Service

Some attacks are aimed at just shutting a site down, by flooding its network interface, filling its disks or running self-replicating programs. If you think any of these strategies are aimed at you, you can investigate them with netstat, df and du, and ps, respectively.

Trojan Horses

If you're running tripwire (see the previous section "File Information"), you'll be alerted if any of your system programs have been replaced. If this happens, it's quite likely that you've been cracked and the intruder has replaced one or more of your system binaries with a tampered copy. Even if you're not running tripwire and if the cracker hasn't been too clever, you can look for Trojan horses by examining the ctimes of the files and comparing them against other system binaries.

Missing Log Files

Although the clever cracker merely eliminates his or her tracks in the log files, some take a wholesale approach and delete the logs altogether. If you find that your log files are missing, make sure that it isn't the result of an accident or the result of an automatic log rotation program. If you can eliminate these and other possible reasons, missing log files may be the sign of a successful break in.

Unexplained Logins

You should keep an eye on your users and become accustomed to their usage habits. If you see a user logging in at a strange time of day or from a strange site, his or her account may have been cracked.

Similarly, if your logs show repeated failed login attempts, failed logins to accounts such as sys, uucp, bin and sync, or inappropriate use of the su command from an account, these may be signs that the account is either broken or is being attacked.

Complaints From Other Sites

System crackers commonly jump from broken site to broken site. They do so to establish a reputation as well as to avoid being traced. If your system is being used as a platform for attacking another machine, you will probably get a call from the system administrator. Being notified by the system administrator of another site that his or her site is being attacked by a machine on your system is an indication (although not a perfectly reliable one—everyone makes mistakes) that your site has been cracked.

Things to Do

If the evidence seems to point to the conclusion that your server has been broken into, stay calm. You must carefully consider your options and the proper actions to take. This section discusses possible actions and their positive and negative implications.

Make Periodic System Checks

You can use the cron daemon, which allows you to repeatedly run a program at a certain time, to gather lists of who is logged on to the computer, what network connections exist and what processes

are running at certain times, with the who, netstat and ps commands, respectively. To find out how to use the cron system, consult the man pages on crontab or read the section "Incremental Indexing" in Chapter 9, "Searching & Indexing."

Make Hard Copies

As you track the wily cracker, remember that any information that you keep online is vulnerable. "Print it out" should be your motto. Keep a log book (on paper!) of the actions you've taken and the results you've found, along with the times and dates. This information could be important if you end up prosecuting the case, or if the case ends up being of interest to law enforcement officials.

Isolate the Problem

You want to keep the intruder from hopping from machine to machine in your network. You might want to separate the cracked system from the rest of the network with a firewall. At the very least, you should remove the cracked site from the lists of trusted hosts on other systems.

Talk It Out

If you manage to catch the intruder on your system at the same time that you're on, you might want to try to communicate with him or her with the talk or write command. You can take the following two approaches:

- The "We're All Reasonable Human Beings" approach. You might simply say that you don't appreciate this waste of your time and elaborate on that statement. Many crackers are just breaking into systems for the kicks and mean no real harm.
- The "Fear of God" approach. Offer veiled (or not so veiled) threats of charging the cracker with federal felonies or threaten to notify the long arm of the law.

Both of these approaches could backfire. On the other hand, just knowing that someone is aware of his or her presence may be enough to scare off your cracker. In any case, if you choose to "talk it out," be sure to document everything the intruder says; it may be valuable evidence later.

Kill the Cracker

If you catch an intruder on the system, you should change the appropriate password and kill the appropriate process. For example, assuming you find a known cracker logged in as "blake" on a BSD system, you could change his or her password and kill his or her process, as in the following example:

```
# ps aux | grep blake
blake     1692 0.0 0.6 479 408 pp2 S   Mar 8  0:00 -bash
# passwd blake
Enter new password for blake:
Re-enter new password:
# kill -9 1692
```

Or if you find the cracker logged in to your System V host, you could change his or her password and kill his or her process, as follows:

```
# ps -fublake
UID        PID    PPID    C    STIME      TTY    TIME  COMD
blake     3790    3783   80   09:20:34   pts/7    0:01  -bash
# passwd blake
Enter new password for blake:
Re-enter new password:
# kill -9 3790
```

These measures have the dual effect of patching the hole (hopefully) and kicking the intruder off the system at the same time.

Kill the Computer

If you're sufficiently worried about what a cracker is currently doing to your system, you can cut him or her off in one of the following ways:

- Unplug the network. If you remove the communications line over which the intruder is attacking, you should remove most immediate threats to the safety of your system.
- Unplug the computer. In general, precipitous power failure is very harmful to UNIX file systems. This measure should be a last resort for dealing with a very damaging cracker.

Patch the Hole

If you can identify the way the intruder entered the system, you should eliminate it immediately. If the intruder gained access through a broken account, you should disable the account or change its password. If a system bug allowed access, you should talk to your software vendor about a fix. You can contact CERT for help (see the section "People to Contact" later in this chapter).

Check for Damage

After you've assured the immediate safety of the system, you need to look for damage to data and for security weaknesses planted by the intruder:

- Check for new accounts or accounts that have a 0 UID.
- If you use tripwire, look for Trojan horses and replace them from your distribution media.
- Look for new SUID or SGID programs (see the previous section "SUID & SGID Files").
- Look for files with recent ctime, atime and mtime time stamps to find out what files the cracker replaced, examined or modified. Remember that the latter two time stamps can be easily spoofed (see the previous section "File Information").
- Look for changes in .rhosts and /etc/hosts.equiv.
- Look for hidden files and directories.
- Examine the /etc/exports table to make sure you aren't exporting NFS file systems to untrusted hosts.
- Use the showmount command to make sure that no unapproved hosts have mounted your file systems.

Restore From Backups

You have been keeping perfect backups, haven't you? If you keep daily incremental backups, you can always resort to them to repair damage to the system.

People to Contact

Who you talk to in case of a break in depends mostly on the policy of your organization. Some institutions prefer to keep all security problems completely internal. Others allow public discussion of the break ins.

Contacting Those at Risk

Regardless of organization policy, system administrators have a responsibility to inform others who are affected by the security problems. If you find that your server is being used as a platform for attacking other people's hosts, you should inform the parties responsible for those hosts. The question is how to contact them. You shouldn't use e-mail because it may be scanned or read by the intruder.

You may be able to find the administrator's telephone number by fingering the root account, as shown in the following example:

```
$ finger root@victim.sad.com
[victim]
Login     Name              TTY     Idle  When       Where
root      0000-Admin(0000)  pts/10  59    Thu 11:17  face.sad.com
```

If fingering the root account does not give you the telephone number, you can try using sendmail, as follows, to find the true identity of root:

```
$ telnet victim.sad.com 25
Trying...
Connected to victim.sad.com
Escape character is '^]'.
220-victim.sad.com Sendmail 8.6.9/8.6.9 ready at Thu,
16 Mar 1995 12:55:0
220 ESMTP spoken here
expn root
250 <dudley@victim.sad.com>
quit
```

You can then try fingering that account. If this fails, you can try using the whois command:

```
$ whois -h rs.internic.net sad.com
Sad Incorporated
Domain Name: sad.com

Administrative Contact:
        Doright, Dudley (DD999) dudley@victim.sad.com
        444-555-2323
```

If this method also fails, you should e-mail root on the host as a last resort. Don't mention any security concerns; merely invite the administrator to telephone you collect.

CERT

After the Internet Worm virus disaster in 1988, CERT was formed to act as a clearinghouse for information and efforts related to Internet security. If you're having security problems, CERT is the place to call. Not only does calling CERT allow it to keep track of security incidents on the network, but in most cases, CERT has seen your problem before and has suggestions for fixes.

You can contact CERT 24 hours a day, either by electronic mail (cert@cert.org) or by telephone (+1 412-268-7090). CERT also maintains an anonymous FTP site that's chock full of good Internet security tools. In fact, this chapter is full of references to them. The anonymous FTP site for CERT is at ftp://ftp.cert.org/.

Moving On

This chapter is just a brief introduction into the complex area of system security. Keeping a busy site secure from a determined, knowledgeable attacker is extremely difficult. Fortunately, most attackers are neither knowledgeable, nor particularly experienced. The most important key to everyday security is vigilance. Don't become complacent; you should constantly examine your system's logs and be on the look-out for suspicious files and processes. An actively maintained site tends to be a secure site.

Once you've set up your server and have the knowledge and tools to keep it secure, it's time to start populating your site with compelling content. Many organizations have already developed a large store of documents to put online. It's usually unnecessary to convert such documents by hand; the next chapter will show you how to automatically convert documents from popular word-processing and desktop publishing environments into HTML and effective Web pages.

SECTION II

Adding Content

5

Importing Documents to the Web

The majority of the information currently available on the World Wide Web is in textual format. Corporations put up descriptions of products and services, software developers offer documentation for software and hardware usage, linking the documentation with a table of contents and diagrams, individuals describe themselves and their interests on personal home pages and so on. Obviously, the majority of this information existed before the creation of a Web page or site. These documents had to be "imported" or translated into HTML. A wide range of programs and macros translate text, either unformatted ASCII or formatted in a word processor, into HTML format. This chapter will cover some of the major word processing and design programs and various text formatting styles that can be produced by almost any word processor.

Text to HTML

ASCII, or the standard character set, is the name for the file format of text files that have been saved as Text Only or created in a program like vi or pico, which does not attach formatting information. If you are converting unformatted ASCII text to a Web document, you will almost inevitably need to mark up much of the document manually or import the document into an HTML editor such as tkHTML (see Chapter 2, "The Basic Pieces"). However, a perl script, called txt2html.pl, is capable of doing some of the markup for you. txt2html.pl goes through the text and identifies certain text elements that should be marked up with specific HTML tags. Since the script contains options that are, to a limited degree, configurable, you can tell the program in the command line what to look for. Running the script from the command line requires you to redirect your text file to stdin for txt2html.pl and to redirect that output to the new HTML document, as in the following example:

```
txt2html.pl < textfile.txt> webpage.html
```

This command creates a marked-up version of *textfile*.txt with the name *webpage*.html. txt2html.pl contains a number of formatting tricks, which may be more useful in composing documents than in translating them but do provide some flexibility. For example, to create a head with an <H2> tag, in the text file you can enter the head with a row of equal signs beneath it, as follows:

```
This is header 2 text.
=================
```

txt2html.pl replaces those two lines with the following line:

```
<H2>This is header 2 text.</H2>
```

You can invoke the <H3> tag by entering a row of dashes directly underneath the head. This should not be confused with entering a row of dashes with no text or characters directly above it, which generates a horizontal rule tag (<HR>).

txt2html.pl is also capable of translating lists that include simple tabs and symbols (such as a dash, an asterisk, a letter or a number) into ordered or unordered lists, depending on the bullet type. txt2html.pl translates into HTML a section of a text file that looks like the following:

```
ShoopSoft's many virtues include:
        * Reliability
                - We guarantee quick response and 24/7
                  accessibility.
        * Quality
                1. Our team has over 5 years of Internet
                   experience.
                2. We have a money-back guarantee of
                satisfaction.
        * Affordability
                - Everything we do is free.  Really.
```

The output for this text would be:

```
<HTML>
<HEAD>
</HEAD>
<BODY>
<p>
ShoopSoft's many virtues include:<BR>
<UL>
<LI> Reliability
<UL>
<LI> We guarantee quick response and 24/7 accessibility.
</UL>
<LI> Quality
<OL>
<LI> Our team has over 5 years of Internet experience.
<LI> We have a money-back guarantee of satisfaction.
</OL>
<LI> Affordability
<UL>
<LI> Everything we do is free.  Really.

 </UL>
</UL>

</BODY>
</HTML>
```

Figure 5-1: *A list translated with txt2html.pl.*

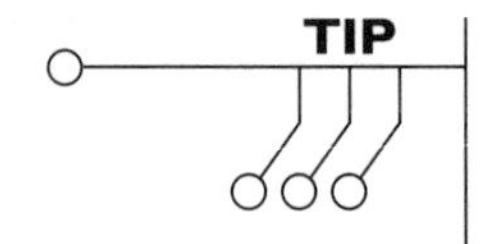

To obtain information about txt2html.pl and to check for new updates, see the developer's WWW page at the URL http://fs1.cs.wustl.edu:80/~seth/txt2html/.

Notice that txt2html.pl is capable of distinguishing between an ordered list (marked with numbers) and an unordered list (marked with asterisks, as in the subordinate items under item 1). You should separate the nested lists with tabs, but it is not necessary to change the type of text bullet that you use for txt2html.pl to recognize the nested list as a new list, so long as it is indented from the list level above it.

To configure txt2html.pl, you can either change the defaults in the program itself or select options from the command line. In all of the command-line options, you can either use an abbreviation for the option, such as -s, or the full name of the option, such as -shortline. In the following descriptions of command-line options in txt2html.pl, you can replace *n* with the numerical value of the variable you are setting.

The -s option allows you to set the maximum length for a short line that you want to preserve as a short line. In other words, if a line contains fewer than a certain number of characters, txt2html.pl inserts a line break at the end of the line to preserve its formatting.

```
[-s n ] | [—shortline n]
```

To mark a certain amount of text as preformatted (<PRE>), you can simply enter a certain number of spaces before that text. Using the -p option, you can define the number of spaces txt2html.pl should locate before switching to preformatting mode.

```
[-p n] | [—prewhite n]
```

Similarly, if your file contains text that "looks" preformatted (such as a chart with columns separated by spaces or tabs, a table with columns, etc.), txt2html.pl marks it as preformatted after finding a specified number of lines of this preformatted-looking text. The -pb option lets you designate the number of lines that txt2html.pl should encounter before inserting the <PRE> tag. For example, if you set the value of -pb to two, then the following line, standing alone, would not be marked as preformatted:

Bill Jones	118 Phillips Trace Road	Kalamazoo	MI	

because it only consists of one line of preformatted-looking text. However, a listing like the one below would be marked as preformatted.

Bill Jones	118 Phillips Trace Road	Kalamazoo	MI	
J.R. Dobbs	P.O. Box 1	Quantico		VA

Finding the required number of preformatted lines—in this case, two—causes txt2html.pl to insert the opening tag for preformatted text, <PRE>. The next option, -pe, defines the number of lines that do not look preformatted that have to be found for txt2html.pl to insert the closing tag for preformatted text, </PRE>.

[-pb *n*] | [—prebegin *n*]

After you have defined how to begin a section of preformatted text with the -pb option, you can also define how to end the section. Using the -pe option, you can set the number of lines that do not look like they should be preformatted, and after finding that number of lines, txt2html.pl inserts the </PRE> closing tag at the end of the preformatted-looking section. As an example, if the -pe option were given a value of two, then the following section of text would all be marked as preformatted.

```
Bill Jones         118 Phillips Trace Road  Kalamazoo     MI
J.R. Dobbs         P.O. Box 1               Quantico      VA
The above clients should receive mailings. The following clients should
not:
Raymond Williams      Route 3, Box 10 Birmingham     AL
Desmond Dekker       101 Q. Elizabeth Kingston       Jamaica
```

However, if the value of the -pe option were reduced to one, then the above paragraph would only mark the addresses as preformatted, and leave the single line of text separating the addresses as regular text. It is useful to set -pe to a higher value if you want to include some lines of text that don't look like preformatted text inside a section of preformatted text.

[-pe *n*] | [—preend *n*]

The -e/+e option, when entered at the command line, removes the standard headers that frame a complete HTML document, such as <HTML>, <HEAD> and <BODY>. Removing these headers makes it easier to insert the text into an already existing HTML document. Since the default is for every document to contain these tags, if you are planning on using txt2html.pl to insert text into other HTML documents, you will want to change the value of the default in the script itself (line 186).

```
[-e/+e] | [—extract / —noextract]
```

To create a horizontal rule (<HR>) in a document, you can enter a line of dashes. Use the -r option to set the number of dashes that txt2html.pl should find before replacing them with the <HR> tag.

[-r *n*] | [—hrule *n*]

txt2html.pl formats a line composed of all capital letters any way that you specify with the -ct option, discussed below. To tell txt2html.pl what kind of line you want to have recognized as all capitals, you can set the -c option to indicate the number of capital letters at the beginning of a line necessary for the line to be treated as all caps. In other words, if you set the -c option to have a value of 5, then the following line would not be treated as "all caps" and so would not be marked up with the tag that you set with the -ct option:

```
HEY! Check out this site: http://www.shoop.com
```

This line would not be recognized because there are only three capital letters, and by setting -c to 5, you have told txt2html.pl that there have to be five capital letters. However, if you set the value of -c to 2, then the line above would be recognized as a line of "all caps." This might be confusing, since you know that it is not actually all capital letters, but what you are doing is telling how many capital letters in a row it will need to find before treating the line as something special. This "special treatment" means that, after encountering the specified number of capital letters, txt2html.pl marks that entire line with the tags you set with the -ct option.

After telling txt2html.pl what is to be treated as a line of all capitals, you can set the HTML tag with which that line is to be marked up. Set the -ct option to the HTML tag surrounded by quotes, and txt2html.pl marks up all capitals-only lines accord-

ingly. This option is one that you might want to set in the program itself. Change the entry on line 144 of the script to set the default for this option. The default for capitals is for them to be marked as <STRONG>. To continue with the example above, let's assume that we have set the option -c to 2. This means, as explained above, that any line with more than two capital letters in a row will be marked up with whatever tag has been set in the -ct option. Assuming we have not changed the default value of the -ct option from "<STRONG>" then the following line:

```
HEY! Check out this site: http://www.shoop.com
```

would be translated into

```
<STRONG>HEY! Check out this site: http://www.shoop.com</STRONG>
```

So the two options, -c and -ct, have to be used in concert. The first, -c, tells txt2html.pl when to activate the second, -ct. If you have lines of text with a number of capital letters that you do not want specially marked up, then you should set the -c option to a fairly high number.

[-c *n*] | [—caps *n*]

[-ct "*tag*"] | [—capstag "*tag*"]

You can use the append option to include a file at the end of any documents translated. If you include a file with HTML codes in it, they are interpreted as HTML codes and not as text. If your e-mail address in your signature file is surrounded by brackets, for example, the brackets are interpreted as indicators of an HTML tag. For characters such as the ampersand, quotation marks or brackets, try to use the HTML entities, the codes that tell a browser to display these special characters (see the discussion of entities in the section "tkHTML: A Web Browser & Editor" in Chapter 2, "The Basic Pieces"). However, any HTML markup, such as a hyperlink to a home page or a mailto tag, included in the file you want to append to your translated documents would be correctly interpreted by the browser. For example, if you wanted to include a link to your home page at the bottom of a translated document, you could enter the HTML tags and text "as-is":

```
This document is part of <A HREF="http://www.shoop.com/bob/
index.html">Bob's Pages</A>.
```

This line would be interpreted as containing a hyperlink. If you didn't want an HTML browser to think characters like "<" or ">" were meant as HTML—in other words, to interpret them as text characters—then you would need to use the HTML entities for those characters, for example:

This page has been created by >>SHOOPSOFT<< Enterprises.

The string ">" tells the browser to insert a greater-than symbol, and the string "<" tells the browser to insert a less-than symbol. Therefore, on an HTML browser, this line would appear as:

This page has been created by >>SHOOPSOFT<< Enterprises.

[-a *file*] | [—append *file*]

The +a option turns off the append option if it is turned on in the script itself. By default, the append option is turned off, but if you change the default in the script, you can use the +a option to turn it back off.

[+a] | [—noappend]

The -t option allows you to specify the title of your document. By default, the document is left untitled. Make sure to enclose the document title in quotation marks.

[-t "*title*"] | [—title "*title*"]

The -tw option sets the number of spaces that are equivalent to a tab. This option is most useful when creating nested lists, since txt2html.pl uses the tabs to determine where to place lists in an HTML document. The default is set to 8 spaces, which might be too many for some word processors. Again, you might want to consider setting this variable in the program itself (line 177).

[-tw *n*] | [—tabwidth *n*]

The -iw, or indent width, option determines the number of spaces to indent a nested list in the HTML document. Since a browser automatically determines where to place nested lists, this option is necessary only for the formatting of the source itself, to make it more readable as HTML code. The default is set to two spaces.

[-iw *n*] | [—indent *n*]

The final two options determine how to treat underlined text in which the underline extends beyond the words themselves. The default is set to one character, which seems to work fine.

[-ul *n*] | [—underlinelong *n*]

[-us *n*] | [—underlineshort *n*]

Using txt2html.pl can help you translate your documents into the most basic HTML format, but as mentioned at the outset, for attractive customized documents, you are better off formatting by hand or using an advanced editor. One other possibility is saving your documents in Rich Text Format, which is a file format that preserves all of the formatting codes of a document. A document saved in Rich Text Format, or RTF, can be converted with an extremely powerful and versatile program called rtftohtml and, with some configuring, will end up being as attractive as the output from any editing you do manually. By and large, though, txt2html.pl, rtftohtml and other converters are best used to convert a sizable body of documents, rather than an individual document or small group of documents, simply because of the amount of time involved in properly configuring any conversion program.

RTF to HTML

RTF, or "Rich Text Format," is a file format that lies somewhere in between pure ASCII and a word processor format. RTF saves the formatting of a document in codes that can be interpreted by other word processing programs and allows a wide range of word processed documents to be translated into other formats. Rich Text Format documents contain both the text of a document and all of the formatting codes that are used in that document, and these codes can be interpreted by many word processors and other applications. For example, the following is the first sentence of this section, saved in Rich Text Format:

```
\par \pard\plain \s15\sa240\tx360 \f4 RTF, or \ldblquote Rich Text
Format,\rdblquote  is a file format that lies somewhere in between pure
ASCII and a word processor format.
```

You can see a number of the RTF codes embedded in the sentence, such as those telling the word processor to insert double quotes (\ldblquote, \rdblquote) around the string "Rich Text Format". The rtftohtml program has been included on the Companion CD-ROM. rtftohtml converts these codes into HTML tags. The program is usable as is, with a number of prespecified codes that cover the majority of styles used in standard word processors. However, if you are using specially configured styles, you can update the html-trans file that contains translation rules to include your styles. By configuring rtftohtml to work with your in-house word processor, you can quickly translate your documents into custom-formatted HTML documents.

A number of formatting styles in rtftohtml are predefined. rtftohtml converts any text that you write using the font Courier into typewriter-style text (<TT>) on the HTML page. Tables, not yet supported in HTML, are converted into preformatted text (<PRE>).

rtftohtml can be incredibly intuitive in its conversions. For example, if you have a table of contents at the beginning of your document, rtftohtml makes it a separate file and creates hyperlinks between that document and the chapters and sections to which it refers. rtftohtml will make all of the entries already in your table of contents into hyperlinks, pointing to the appropriate locations in your document. In addition, any paragraph headings that use the header tags <H1> through <H6> will be inserted into your table of contents as new entries, and this text will also be linked to the appropriate location. Similarly, rtftohtml moves any footnotes in your document to a separate file and hyperlinks the footnote markers in the main document to the appropriate footnote text in the separate file. As when using any conversion features, you need to make sure that you are using the correct styles so that rtftohtml will recognize them. For the most part, rtftohtml will correctly interpret any styles that come with your word processor. Make sure that you use a different style for each new format that you want to see in an HTML document. If you create any new styles, or if your documents use custom styles, then you will need to add these styles to the configuration file for rtftohtml. You can check what styles rtftohtml already under-

stands, and add new ones, using the configuration file for translation rules, which will be discussed in "Defining New Styles" later in this chapter. If rtftohtml encounters a format it does not recognize, it generates an error message and leaves the text untranslated (including it as regular text).

Graphics

When rtftohtml finds a graphic embedded in the RTF document, it does two things. First, it creates a hyperlink to that graphic in the HTML document at the location where it found the graphic in the word processor file. Since this link is an <A HREF> link, rtftohtml does not embed the graphic itself in the HTML document. As noted in the section "Command-Line Options," it is possible to use the -i option to change this feature, so that all graphics are referenced with an <IMG SRC> tag, which does imbed the graphic. Aside from simply creating the link, rtftohtml actually exports any included graphics and saves them as separate files. The filename is the name of the RTF document, the number of the graphic and an extension that indicates the format that the graphic is in. For example, converting a file called CATALOG.RTF that contained three embedded Microsoft Windows bitmapped images creates the graphics files CATALOG1.BMP, CATALOG2.BMP and CATALOG3.BMP. The extension depends on the format that rtftohtml exports to. The three formats that rtftohtml is capable of creating are Windows bitmaps (.bmp), Windows meta-files (.wmf) and Macintosh PICTs (.pict). The link created in the first step, either <A HREF> or <IMG SRC>, is made to a GIF file (CATALOG1.GIF, in the example). This means that you have to use a separate program to convert the bitmap, meta-file or PICT to a GIF.

You can convert the extracted PICT and BMP files with the Netpbm toolkit, included on the Companion CD-ROM. To use the toolkit conveniently, you need to include its binary directory in your search path:

```
$ PATH=$PATH:/usr/local/netpbm/bin; export PATH
$ MANPATH=$MANPATH:/usr/local/netpbm/man; export MANPATH
```

These pathnames tell your shell where to look for the Netpbm binaries and documentation. After you set your path, you're ready to convert the extracted images to GIFs, suitable for your Web pages:

```
$ for i in *.pict
>do
>foo='basename $i .pict'
>picttoppm $i | ppmtogif > $foo.gif
>done
```

This script converts a directory of files ending with the .pict extension to GIFs with the same file name. Similarly, you can use the Netpbm toolkit to convert Windows BMP images:

```
$ for i in *.bmp
>do
>foo='basename $i .bmp'
>bmptoppm $i | ppmtogif > $foo.gif
>done
```

Netpbm itself cannot handle Windows meta-files (.wmf). You have to convert these files to bitmaps (.bmp) using the Windows application wmf2bmp, included on the Companion CD-ROM. This application is fairly self-explanatory and comes with a detailed instructions file (WMF2BMP.WRI). Basically, you need to copy the driver VBRUN200.DLL to the directory \WINDOWS\SYSTEM if it is not already there and launch wmf2bmp. In the lower right-hand corner window, select the file that you want to convert. The scrollbar beneath the image window controls the width of the image, which proportionally increases or decreases the height. Click on the Convert button to create a bitmap formatted graphic with the extension .bmp. Then follow the directions given earlier in this section for converting this file to a GIF.

Since rtftohtml automatically uses the GIF file extension for inline images, the files created by the scripts described in this chapter will automatically work in the HTML documents.

Command-Line Options

Assuming that you have no updates to the translation rules file, you can run rtftohtml using the following command-line options:

rtftohtml [-i] [-V] [-o *filename*] [-P *extension*] [-T] [-G][*file*]

-i	Indicates that embedded graphics should be linked to the main document using an <IMG> tag. The default is to use the <A HREF>-style link.
-V	Prints the current version to stderr.
-o *filename*	Indicates that the output file name should be *filename*. If any other file is created (such as for graphics) the base name of the other file will be *filename* without the .rtf extension if it is present in the original file name.
-P *extension*	Use *extension* as the extension for any links to graphics files. The default is .gif.
-T	Indicates that no table of contents file is to be generated.
-G	Indicates that no graphics files should be written. The hypertext links to the graphics files are still generated. This is a performance-enhancing feature for when you are retranslating a document and haven't changed the graphics.
file	The *file* to be processed. If no *file* is given, standard input is used. If standard input is used, the body of the document is written to standard output (unless overridden by the -o option). If a file name appears, the output is written to *filename* with .html as the extension. (If .rtf appears as an extension on the original input file, it is stripped before the .html is appended.)

Defining New Styles

While the translation file that comes with rtftohtml has a number of styles already configured, you will probably want to add more to allow for cleaner translations of your pages. You need to modify two sections of the configuration file, called html-trans, when you add a new style. You modify either the paragraph style table or the text style table and either the paragraph match table or the text match table. Essentially, these tables define what sort of input to match with the appropriate HTML tag and how the HTML tag should be inserted into the HTML document. The tables are labeled .PTag, .TTag, .TMatch and .PMatch in order of their appearance in the html-trans file.

.PTag

The paragraph tag, or .PTag, table will probably require very little modification. This table controls how various paragraph formatting tags are exported into the new HTML document. Suppose you wanted to add the Netscape extension <CENTER> as a new paragraph tag. You would add the following line to the .PTag table:

```
"center","<center>/n","</center>/n","/t","/t","<p>/n",1,1,0,1,0
```

The html-trans file contains an abbreviation for each of these items. The following is a brief definition of what each item indicates to rtftohtml:

- The first item gives the name of the style itself. This is defined in the paragraph match, or .PMatch, table.
- The second and third items are the opening and closing tags for the HTML markup. Note that both are followed by the string "/n". This string causes a new line to be inserted after the tags are written to the new HTML file. Note that if you are using a tag that does not require a close tag, such as the horizontal rule <HR>, you can enter a null string by just putting two quotation marks in place of the third option.
- The fourth and fifth items are the replacement strings for tab characters. The fourth is the replacement tag for the first tab in every paragraph, the fifth for tabs anywhere else. In this case, they are both replaced with the "/t" command string, which places a string of spaces into the new HTML document.

- The sixth item gives the paragraph marker to be used inside any text with this format. It should be set either to <BR>, for a line break, or <P>, for a paragraph break. The "/n" string, again, causes a new line to be inserted after the tag is written to the HTML source file, for easier reading.
- The next four items are binary switches that turn them on or off. If the value is 0, the option is turned off; if it is 1, the option is on. The seventh option, if turned off with a value of 0, will not allow any text formatting markup (such as <STRONG>, <EM>, <TT>, etc.) inside this tag. For example, if bold text is placed inside text defined as a header (using the <H1> through <H6> tags), it will confuse browsers. The eighth option allows nesting, such as when you want a list and a subordinate list within that list. The ninth option, if turned on with a value of 1, will cause rtftohtml to delete all of the text up to the first tab in a paragraph. This is useful if your text document has an ASCII character like * as a list bullet, since you will not actually want that character as a part of the list item. It would be deleted and replaced with a tag like <LI> if this value were turned on. The tenth option automatically inserts a new line in the HTML source document when a line exceeds 80 characters. This new line is only visible in the source document itself, and will not be displayed as a new line when the document is viewed by a browser. This option is simply to make it easier to read the HTML source code itself, since it has no effect on the way the document will appear on the Web. The only exception is in the case of the preformatted text tag <PRE> which tells the browser to display the layout of the text exactly as it appears in the source code. If you are using the <PRE> tag in this line of your .PTag table, then make sure that this value is set to 0.
- Finally, the last option determines the level at which an item should be listed in the table of contents. The default is that a paragraph marked <H1> gets top-level listing, <H2> is a subhead of that and so on, down to <H6>. Simply set this final option to 1 if you want the style in question to be given a table of contents entry.

.TTag

The text tag, or .TTag, table, is straightforward. It is composed of the name of the tag, the opening tag and the closing tag. If, for example, you wanted to add the Netscape tag <BLINK> as a new style, you would add the following line to the .TTag table:

```
"blink","<BLINK>","</BLINK>"
```

.TMatch

In contrast to the .TTag table, the text matching, or .TMatch, table, is probably the most difficult to grasp, but also one of the most versatile. It is composed of five options. The first two are the font and font size, which you can use to select the style based only on those characteristics. This is how rtftohtml knows to translate all Courier fonts into <TT>, or typewriter, style in the HTML document. You can enter a null string ("") for the font and/or a 0 for the font size to configure rtftohtml to ignore either or both in matching the text to a particular style. The line that rtftohtml uses to translate Courier fonts into typewriter-style text is:

```
"Courier",0,00000000000000,00000000000000,"tt"
```

The third and fourth items, the long string of 0's, are the match and the mask options. The match option determines exactly what type of formatting to look for (i.e., bold, italic, hidden, etc.) by using a string of binary switches. If the switches are set to hidden, double underline, it returns a match. The mask option also uses binary switches. In the mask option, the switches determine which switches to recognize. For example, using the mask option, you could tell rtftohtml to look at the settings for bold, underline and hidden. In the match option, you could determine what those should be set to for a match to be returned. This makes it possible to tell rtftohtml "if a string is bold and underlined, but not hidden, match it to strong." A more concrete example will be provided later.

You set the switches in a long list of switches, with each switch corresponding to a particular formatting type.

You should think of the match and mask options as charts, with each column of the chart representing a different formatting type.

PostScript to HTML

The existing methods of converting PostScript files to HTML documents are somewhat limited. Since a PostScript file is simply a file that contains the data that is sent to a printer, it is not capable of containing information like styles and formatting, other than font type and size. It is far more efficient to obtain the file that generated the PostScript document, such as a text document or graphics file, and convert it using a tool like rtftohtml or the Netpbm Toolkit for graphics. Two programs are available that convert PostScript files in different ways, but it is not within the scope of this book to go into either one in detail, and they are not included on the Companion CD-ROM. If you need to convert PostScript files, your best bet is to visit the home pages for these programs, and determine if the application meets your needs.

One program is called Webify. It converts a PostScript file to an inline graphic. If the file contains more than one page, each page is made into a separate graphic. Webify also produces smaller graphics, which you can put on a Web page as links to the full-size graphics. To find out more about Webify, visit the URL http://cag-www.lcs.mit.edu/~ward/webify/webifydoc/.

If it is the text of the PostScript file that you want to preserve, rather than the graphics, you might want to look at a utility called ps2html. ps2html strips the text from a PostScript file and produces a text file that is then converted to HTML. Unfortunately, you must specify each different font type for ps2html, making it unwieldy unless you are working on a large body of documents with identical text formatting. To learn how to use ps2html and to see some samples of how it works, look at the URL ftp://bradley.bradley.edu/pub/guru/ps2html/ps2html-v2.html.

Word Processor Converters

While it is possible to save your documents as Rich Text Format in almost any word processing package and to use the program rtftohtml to convert them to HTML, as explained previously, a number of add-ons for commercial packages are available on the World Wide Web or via anonymous FTP for people who prefer a more direct route from their word processors to HTML. This book will cover add-ons for three of the more popular desktop publishing programs: Microsoft Word for Windows, WordPerfect and QuarkXPress. Since these are commercial programs, a number of the add-ons are proprietary and cannot be included on the Companion CD-ROM.

Word for Windows & Internet Assistant

Never one to miss out on a new development, Microsoft has released its own add-on for Microsoft Word for Windows version 6.0a and later versions. This tool, called Internet Assistant, incorporates the graphical interface of Word for Windows with WYSIWYG (what you see is what you get) capability for viewing the documents using the built-in browser. This application is freely available for downloading from ftp.microsoft.com or off their Internet Assistant home page (the URL is provided later in this section). Internet Assistant represents part of what seems to be a broad move on Microsoft's part toward the Internet and networked applications as the Microsoft Network comes online. However, the documents that it creates are not limited to the Microsoft Network but are perfectly usable as HTML documents.

Since Internet Assistant is self-explanatory to Word for Windows users and since the main focus of this book is on UNIX applications, Internet Assistant is not discussed in much detail here. Anyone who is familiar with Word for Windows should be able to use Internet Assistant. After installing Internet Assistant, converting Word for Windows documents is incredibly simple. Just load the document into Word for Windows, select Save As... from the File menu and select HTML from the file type listing.

This accurately converts the majority of the Word styles into HTML tags. To modify any tags that might not be correctly interpreted, or to add new HTML tags, use the Style menu to select the appropriate type. Each type of HTML tag, except for such text tags as bold, italics and underline, has its own style. Text tags can be selected in the same way that text is formatted from the menu bar.

To install Internet Assistant, you need to double-check that you have the correct version of Word (anything after 6.0a) and then download the software from the URL ftp://ftp.microsoft.com/deskapps/word/winword-public/ia/. The file is WORDIA.EXE. After you download the file, it installs itself when you run it from the Program Manager in Windows.

If you have a version of Word that is earlier than 6.0a or 6.0c, your best bet is to save the file or files to be converted into Rich Text Format and to use rtftohtml. Since all of the style tags are preserved in RTF, your documents will be formatted correctly after you have configured the translation file to match your documents.

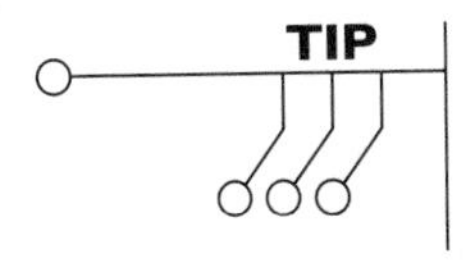

To retrieve Internet Assistant via anonymous FTP, FTP to ftp.microsoft.com, and go to the directory /deskapps/word/winword-public/ia/, or use the URL ftp://ftp.microsoft.com/deskapps/word/winword-public/ia/.

Microsoft does not yet provide support for Internet Assistant, but it does maintain a Web site where you can report bugs and find out about any software updates at the URL http://www.microsoft.com/pages/deskapps/word/ia/default.htm.

WordPerfect

Given the prominence of WordPerfect in the business world, it is not surprising that an application has been developed that converts documents directly from WordPerfect to HTML. It is also possible, as with Word for Windows, to save WordPerfect output to Rich Text Format, and then to convert that output with rtftohtml. This route may provide you with some extra flexibility in terms of defining your particular word processor styles and customizing the HTML output tag that they are matched to. However, for a quick and efficient conversion, wp2x does a remarkably good job. The authors of the program note that the conversion may require some manual updating, but by and large, wp2x marks up most of the WordPerfect text into quite acceptable HTML.

wp2x requires two files: an input file in WordPerfect format and a configuration file defining the HTML markup. You can create the input file in either WordPerfect version 5.1 or 6.0. When creating a new input file that you intend to mark up, you should observe a number of formatting details. First, if you enable the display of hard returns, you can get a better idea of what the output document will look like. According to the authors of the program, this can be done using the following WordPerfect command sequence:

```
Shift-F1 , 2 (Display), 6 (Edit-Screen Options), 4 (Hard Return), Control-V
```

Enabling the display of hard returns allows you to see the difference between hard returns, which are translated into the HTML tag <P>, and soft returns, which translate to <BR>.

Bold and italicized text is also translated directly into <B> and <I> in the new document. wp2x, unlike rtftohtml, does not interpret changes in fonts when creating the markup. It does, however, use the scaled fonts to create different sizes of header tags. ExtraLarge font is matched to <H1>, VeryLarge to <H2>, Large to <H3>, Small to <H4> and Fine to <H5>.

The authors of wp2x also recommend a standard format for citing references, because later versions of the program are able to interpret them more cleanly. The standard format for references is a bold reference, an italicized title and plain text for the author and publication information, as in the following example:

```
<b>[Moron80]</b> <i>Preparing a document with WordPerfect</i>,
Moron, J. et al., Cat's Quarterly, V. 3 winter, pp. 14–57.
```

This standardized format is optional, however, because the current version of the software does not depend on it, and references are not widely used in HTML documents.

The second necessary component for converting WordPerfect documents with wp2x is the configuration file HTML.CFG. This

file probably requires little editing unless you have a specific document formatting setup or style that you want to appear on an HTML page. One line that you will want to edit is the signature at the end that wp2x automatically inserts. This signature is in line 24 of the HTML.CFG file and can be anything you want, including a hyperlink or image source call. You can also modify the lines above and below the signature, which provide links back to a home page or a table of contents.

Since you have to know the name of the output that WordPerfect writes to its output files, setting the configurations themselves can be more complex. However, if you know the name of the output, you can simply use a straight equivalence setting, as in the following:

```
ExtraLarge="<H1>"
extralarge="</H1>"
VeryLarge="<H2>"
verylarge="</H2>"
```

The opening tag is capitalized and the closing tag is in lowercase, or in the case of a particular function being used or not used, the capitalized option represents an enabled function, and the lowercase option represents a disabled one.

After you have composed and/or uploaded your WordPerfect files, you can run a single command to convert the WordPerfect files into .HTML format. The command line reads the configuration file, applies it to the WordPerfect document and redirects that output to the new HTML document, as follows:

```
wp2x html.cfg textfile.txt > webfile.html
```

In the process of converting the files, wp2x returns the error messages it receives, but often the best method of error-checking is for you to look at the completed product and see what formats wp2x did not recognize. The error messages display on the screen by default. To turn them off, simply use the -s option after the command wp2x. If you receive error messages that are significant, or some part of a document is not being correctly formatted, you can either modify those formats in the HTML.CFG file or add them to it in the same format as the other configuration settings.

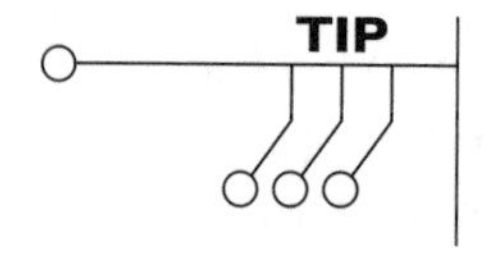

For more information about wp2x, especially information on how to use it as a converter to file types other than HTML, look at the home page at the URL ftp://journal.biology.carleton.ca/pub/software/wp2x.html.

qt2www.pl

qt2www.pl is a perl script that allows you to convert the text of a QuarkXPress document directly into HTML. It operates in a manner similar to rtftohtml in that it has one file with tables that match styles to HTML markup tags, and the styles themselves are set up in QuarkXPress. You run qt2www.pl from the command line with the following variables:

qt2www.pl *mapfile textfilename HTMLfilename*

For example, you can convert the QuarkXPress file SAMPLE.TXT with the following command:

```
qt2www.pl map sample.txt sample.html
```

The map file is probably the only part of this program that you need to configure, but first, you need to create different styles in QuarkXPress for each of the text types that you will be using. Any time you want to see a different style of HTML markup, you must change your QuarkXPress style. Then create an entry in the map file that matches the QuarkXPress style to an HTML tag, a paragraph or line break and, optionally, a type style. This entry can be delimited with commas or with tabs, as in the following:

```
Body        Normal    P
Citation    CITE      BR
Title       H1        P
Subheading  H2        P
References,Normal,BR,I
```

Both types of entries, delimited either with tabs or commas will work within the same file. The value "Normal" simply tells qt2www.pl to leave the text unmarked.

To create the text file, use QuarkXPress to export the file to Quark Tags, because all of the formatting tags from QuarkXPress must be maintained for qt2www.pl to correctly translate the file.

qt2www.pl is set to look for perl in the directory /usr/local/bin/. If you have perl somewhere else, you need to change the first line of the file qt2www.pl to point to the correct location.

One other change that you might want to make is to suppress status messages that the script generates. You can do this by setting the option $status_output to no in line 62 of the script. However, since the output from the program is minimal, this change is not necessary.

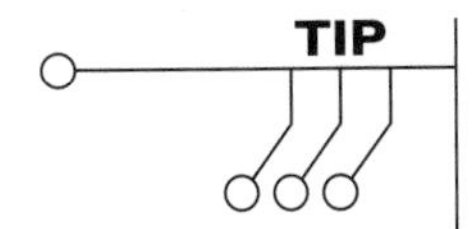

For more information on qt2www.pl, look at the home page for the program at the URL http://the-tech.mit.edu/~jeremy/qt2www.html.

Other Word Processors

There are a number of word processing programs that cannot be discussed in this book. The following is a list of URLs that have information on converting to HTML from word processors that we did not discuss.

FrameMaker
Frame2HTML (freeware): ftp://ftp.nta.no
WebMaker (commercial): http://www.cern.ch/WebMaker/

LaTeX
LATEX2HTML (freeware): http://cbl.leeds.ac.uk/nikos/tex2html/doc/latex2html/latex2html.html

PageMaker
Dave (freeware for Macintosh): http://www.bucknell.edu:80/bucknellian/dave/

troff
troff2html (freeware): http://dcpu1.cs.york.ac.uk:6666/jim/troff2html.html

Texinfo
texi2html (freeware): http://wwwcn.cern.ch/dci/texi2html

Electronic mail
MHonArc (freeware): http://www.oac.uci.edu/indiv/ehood/mhonarc.doc.html

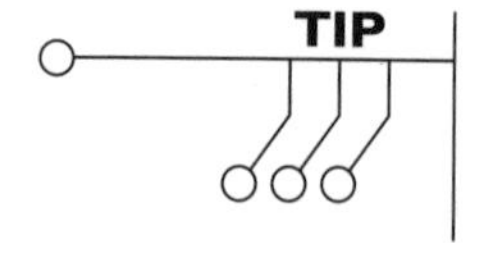

For updated lists of available converters, check the list of converters at the URL http://www.w3.org/hypertext/WWW/Tools/Word_proc_filters.html, and SunSITE UK's translator archive at the URL ftp://sunsite.doc.ic.ac.uk/computing/information-systems/WWW/tools/translators/.

Moving On

A number of possibilities exist for converting your documents from their current format into HTML. Almost every application is capable of producing ASCII text format and RTF output, and both of these file types have quite efficient translators that are easy to customize to your document type. Finally, a number of add-ons and converters are application-specific and can be used to quickly bring documents into HTML as well. Even with the wide range of possibilities that these applications present, manual markup should always remain an option, especially if you have only a document or two to convert. Every program requires time to configure, and if you need it for only a few conversions, you might actually save time (and get valuable experience in authoring HTML) by simply running through the text of the document and entering tags manually.

When you have used the authoring information contained in Chapter 2, "The Basic Pieces," and the document conversion tools explained in this chapter, you should be ready to move beyond text into the wide world of multimedia. In Chapter 6, "Checking Your Work," we explain how to check your pages and links for HTML style and accuracy and how to check the sites and files that

you are linked to. In Chapter 7, "Images on the Web," we explore the possibilities of including multimedia files in your Web documents and on your site. These chapters will explain everything from putting a graphic on your home page to including full animations in your site, and how to go about all of it most efficiently and impressively. Combining carefully created text with high-quality graphics and audio is what distinguishes an excellent WWW site, and this chapter and the upcoming ones show you just how to accomplish it.

6

Checking Your Work

As you will no doubt discover upon launching your World Wide Web server, the primary source of feedback about broken links and ineffective sites will come directly from your site's users. In some basic sense, all Web pages are perennially "under construction," or perhaps, in beta test. In the near future, however, there will be a fundamental problem with having Web pages perennially under construction. As the Internet and the Web become more important in commercial transactions, personal interactions and information distribution, the unfinished quality of a Web site—a broken link here, an HTML error there—will no longer be an expectation on the part of the user. Soon, if not already, a Web site will be an organization's primary point of interaction with users on the Internet, and the quality of that site will determine the kind of impressions that visitors to the site will make about that organization. An error on Web pages will be no less noticeable than a typo in a magazine advertisement—and no less damaging.

Aside from the standard errors that are inevitably made when creating a new Web site, working in HTML presents special complications. As with the Web itself, HTML is a constantly evolving and changing structure. Every effort is made, when HTML is changed in some way, to ensure that older versions of correct HTML continue to be understood by Web browsers and HTML editors. Unfortunately, what is "correct" and "incorrect" has become blurred somewhat in general usage, since browsers like Netscape support a number of "incorrect" types. This means that tags that are perfectly valid HTML will be phased out as the language becomes more strict and more specific (and simultaneously more efficient and refined). To keep abreast of these changes and to ensure a site's integrity in the face of them, it is vital that you check your site thoroughly for accurate and stylistically valid HTML. This chapter will outline a number of ways to check your work and will present some automated alternatives to manual checking. This type of validation work can help you avoid discovering, one visit too late, that your site has embarrassed you on what may become one of the most public, and global, forms of mass media.

HTML Style

As mentioned briefly in Chapter 2, "The Basic Pieces," HTML is not a programming language per se. It is a markup language, based on Standard Generalized Markup Language (SGML) standard. This has an important implication for developing Web documents: the configuration of the display of a markup language is largely up to the author. In a programming language that defines the GUI, such as the code that created Netscape or NCSA Mosaic, the code clearly defines the layout and presentation. However, a markup language defines only how a string of information, such as a section of text, is different than other strings of information. It provides, as the language implies, markup codes. That information is then passed on to an interpreter, such as a Web browser, that specifies its format.

Platform Independence & HTML

From a stylistic point of view, there are two major reasons why it is important that HTML defines the structure of a document rather than its design. One is that, as browsers develop, more specific ways to display certain tags are created and used, which is why it is a good idea to use tags that are as specific as possible. In other words, use the <CITE> and <ADDRESS> tags for citations and addresses instead of the <I> tag, for italicized text, which currently on most browsers produces seemingly identical output to the <CITE> and <ADDRESS> tags. The paragraph tag <P> also produces seemingly identical output; it appears to simply create a paragraph break but is actually a marker that contains the structure of a full paragraph. As HTML evolves, it is likely that both the <P> opening tag and the </P> closing tag will be necessary for the paragraph to be recognized.

The other design consideration raised by HTML's creation of structural markup, rather than design specification, is the difference between browsers. If you design your pages with a single browser in mind—for example, by overemphasizing the use of Netscape's new HTML extensions—your pages run the risk of becoming obsolete when new browsers come online and new HTML specifications are adopted.

One effective way of avoiding the potential problems of designing for a single-browser is to check all of your pages on a range of different browsers, making sure that the design is acceptable on all of them. More important, you should look at how different machines, Macs, PCs and workstations running UNIX, display pages, since moving from platform to platform often results in very different types of displays even when you use the same browser. This test alone may not be enough, however, since users can configure their browsers differently with regard to image loading, colors and fonts. Your best bet to ensure that the widest variety of browsers will display your pages attractively and, by extension, to ensure that users will find your pages useful, is to treat HTML as a language for marking structure, and not as a language for specifying the design of your pages.

Using HTML to mark structure means avoiding a number of pitfalls. Primary among these is the temptation to use markup tags for "effect"—in other words, using the eccentricities of certain browsers to create a specific type of display or layout. One example of this is using header text to emphasize certain sentences, instead of using header text as titles for sections and subsections of a document. This practice will seldom create the same effect on different browsers and platforms, and the emphasized text will incorrectly appear as part of the tables of contents in those programs that automatically generate tables of contents from header text. Essentially, you should create HTML documents as if each user will be reading the source code and determining what to do with it on his or her own—not as a graphics or page design system but as a set of instructions that specifies how text is to be read and defines its relationship to the rest of the document.

Designing With Style

To design pages that conform to HTML style standards and, more important, that are broadly usable and appealing, you should keep a number of considerations in mind. While several of these considerations are explained in the "Site Unity & Traffic Control: Design & Content Considerations" section of Chapter 12, "Fitting In," a number of them deserve repeating in this chapter. By responsibly designing your pages according to a set of acceptable standards, you will ensure long life and limited maintenance for your Web site, and you will have more time to improve the site because you are spending less time fixing it.

One of your first considerations should be, as noted earlier, the types of HTML markup that you use. With apologies to Thoreau, we urge you to "Specify, specify." You will appreciate the benefits that using specific markup tags for different parts of a document will bring as the Web evolves. In this regard, you should make sure that several tags, mentioned briefly in Chapter 2, "The Basic Pieces," are on every document. These tags are the <META> tag, the <LINK> tag and the <BASE> tag, which give the user, browser and maintainers of a site a great deal of important information about your Web pages.

The <META>, <LINK> and <BASE> tags contain information about your document that is similar to the comments that are placed in a well-written computer program or script. These tags contain information about the authors of the document, about its relationship to other documents and about the document itself. All of the tags should be located in the header of the document (between the <HEAD> and </HEAD> tags).

You can use the <META> tag to name certain variables in a document, such as the author and the program that was used to generate the document. The latter is important to specify if you are using an HTML editor. This information, as is the case with the information specified by the other tags, is not displayed on the screen itself but is available to users who view the source of your documents, and it can be read by information-gathering programs that read Web files over the Internet. The following is an example of <META> tags being used to define document characteristics:

```
<META NAME="GENERATOR" CONTENT="tkHTML 2.3">
<META NAME="AUTHOR" CONTENT="webmaster@shoop.com">
<META HTTP-EQUIV="OWNER" CONTENT="Bob">
```

Some HTML authoring software, such as Microsoft's Internet Assistant, automatically generates these <META> links.

There are two types of <META> definitions, HTTP-EQUIV and NAME. The <META> attribute HTTP-EQUIV setting links the information in the CONTENTS setting to an HTTP response header, as described in Chapter 2, "The Basic Pieces." However, if you do not know the exact name of the HTTP response header that you want to identify, you are better off using the NAME setting because it simply creates a variable name.

Another useful <META> definition is the identification of an expiration date for documents. To set this date, you can use the <META> tag as follows:

```
<META HTTP-EQUIV="EXPIRES">Tue, 04 Dec 1993 23:59:00 GMT
</META>
```

In this example, the <META> tag flags certain error checkers, such as MOMspider (discussed later in this chapter), after the expiration date has passed. A browser receives this information from the server before the page is loaded, so that if a document has expired and a browser is configured not to load expired documents, the server would return an error message.

The <LINK> tag indicates the relationship of the HTML document to other documents and objects (for example, images and mailto links) on the site. You should use a different <LINK> tag for each object that you want to link to. For example, the following set of <LINK> tags would define information about a document.

```
<LINK HREF="mailto:webmaster@shoop.com" REL="made">
<LINK HREF="http://www.shoop.com/pricing/section2.html" REL="next">
<LINK HREF="http://www.shoop.com/pricing/index.html"
REL="previous">
```

In the first tag, the author is defined as webmaster@shoop.com, and the contact URL is a mailto link to this address. Alternatively, this URL could have provided a link to the author's home page. Browsers can use this link information to show where comments can be sent to the author or to display more information about the author. The second <LINK> tag defines the next document to be accessed if the documents are being read in order, and the third defines the previous document in the hierarchy. A number of other relationship definitions are possible, all of which take the following format:

```
<LINK HREF=URL REL="relationship">
```

Other relationships that you can define with the <LINK> tag are "parent," which indicates that the specified URL is one level up in the HTML document hierarchy, and "bookmark," which defines the specified URL as a bookmark, or "frequently used page," at that site.

The <BASE> tag allows you to put the URL of the file into the text of the document itself, so that if a file is saved or exported out of the context of the Web site, its original location is preserved. The format of a <BASE> tag takes the following form:

```
<BASE HREF="http://www.domain.com/path/filename.html">
```

As noted at the beginning of this section, these three header tags do not currently produce any output on browsers, but they provide valuable information to robots, users viewing the source and document maintainers. Since future releases of browsers will

incorporate these tags into dynamically generated toolbars and links, specifying them in advance of their implementation by browsers gives your site a leg up in the development of the Web.

Information that should be included on every page, preferably at the bottom, is the name of the author of a page or Webmaster of the site with a mailto link or a link to that person's home page; a link to the home page of the site; a "last revised" date (in standard format, such as 9 December 1994, since readers worldwide will have access to the document); and if applicable, a statement of copyright. The copyright statement should simply state that the copyright is held by a particular person or institution, and the statement could contain a link to a copyright or legal disclaimer page. A sample footer, with a horizontal rule above it to delineate it from the body of the page, would look something like the following:

```
<HR>
<A HREF="mailto:webmaster@shoop.com">F. Nietzsche
</A>, ShoopSoft Webmaster, <ADDRESS>webmaster@shoop.com
</ADDRESS>. Last Revised: 9 Dec 94.<BR>
All contents copyright 1994, ShoopSoft Enterprises<BR>
<A HREF="http://www.shoop.com/">Return to the ShoopSoft Home
Page</A><P>
</BODY>
</HTML>
```

Note that the final tags mark the end of the document—first the end of the body, then the end of the document itself. No other text or markup should be entered after these two tags.

Another HTML style consideration that you should keep in mind is that images are always optional on browsers. Users on low-speed connections generally choose to turn image loading off, and if they are forced to use the images on a page for navigation, they will be frustrated by the increase in the time each page takes to load. This means that button bars, imagemaps and other graphics-dependent navigational tools, even something as simple as a gray button marked "Previous" that returns the user to the previous page, are not always visible to a user. For users not viewing graphics, or unable to view graphics (as in the case of text-based browsers), you should include two types of text options. The first is to always specify an ALT setting in your image tag, such as the following:

```
<IMG ALT="Previous Page" SRC="pics/previous.gif">
```

This setting enables text-only browsers to automatically load the alternate text instead of leaving a meaningless string like [IMAGE] in its place.

Since browsers in the future will probably load ALT settings when image loading is turned off, using this option will become more important as browsers evolve. However, since a browser capable of displaying graphics will not load the ALT text, you should duplicate any links made to a graphic or icon in text. For example, if a page contains a row of buttons for navigation, you might want to put a row of text links to those same pages beneath the row of buttons, giving the user the option of using either buttons or text links. In addition, make sure that you list all of the links in an imagemap in close proximity to the imagemap, because without the coordinate information, the HTTP daemon generates a server error when a user clicks on the imagemap when image loading is turned off.

Finally, remember that hyperlinked text is always emphasized in some manner on a browser, and that to most users, these links are intuitive. The combination of emphasis and obvious usage makes a link such as the following somewhat unnecessary and silly looking:

```
you'll find info on monkeys <A HREF="monkeys.html">here</A>
```

Using "here" or "click here" as the text for a link is bad form because it distracts the user from the information in the document and makes the document appear as a sort of interface and not as a source of information. Hyperlinked text should be as transparent as possible and not call attention to itself with link text, as in the previous example. A better design, one that integrates the linked text and the information, would take the following form

```
we also have <A HREF="monkeys.html">info on monkeys</A>
```

Use these style considerations to create professional-looking documents. In doing so, you will increase their viability and longevity and save yourself and others considerable work and discomfort with the appearance of your pages.

Absolute & Relative URLs

An ongoing debate in the Web authoring community is over whether to use absolute URLs or relative URLs when creating hyperlinks between documents on the same server. To date, no unequivocal resolution has been reached in favor of either type. In brief, an absolute URL takes the following form:

```
<A HREF="/users/shoop/docs/pricing.html">
```

A relative URL would take the following form:

```
<A HREF="docs/pricing.html">
```

In some ways, the debate is rather trivial because using absolute or relative URLs does not affect performance. However, each type of link does afford some design advantages.

An advantage of using relative URLs is the portability of a body of documents linked together relatively. If, for some reason, you need to move an entire HTML hierarchy, either to another machine or simply to another directory, a relatively linked body of documents requires minimal updating because the links are expressed in terms of their relationship to that document. Using relative URLs also allows a user to download an entire HTML hierarchy to another machine, either to be viewed locally or to provide a mirror of the same information at a different site, with minimal changes. This design technique is especially useful for large documents that are divided into separate pages, because a user can obtain the entire body of documents and browse the documents as local files without having to connect to your site—saving time for the user and CPU and bandwidth for the server.

Absolute URLs, however, provide a consistent structure to the HTML hierarchy. More importantly, they allow for a more consistent method of accessing documents that might be higher on a directory tree or in a different directory tree altogether. For example, if you wanted to provide a link from a document in /html/users/bob/sermons/ to the document in /html/users/shoop/pricing/services.html, a relative link would have to express this path as the following:

```
<A HREF="../../shoop/pricing/services.html">outrageously low prices</A>
```

An absolute link would be in the following more intuitive format:

```
<A HREF="/users/shoop/pricing/services.html">outrageously low prices
</A>
```

An absolute URL also allows users looking at the source to easily identify the location of particular documents that are linked to a Web page.

In either case, it's a good idea to employ a standard method of hyperlinks, at least between clearly defined sections of your Web documents. For example, you might want to use absolute links for your menu system, to provide easier definition of horizontal and vertical movements across documents, but relative links within particular sections, such as catalogs or paginated text information.

Following the nuances of HTML style is not always an intuitive or easy process, and it may at times seem easier to use more design-intensive approaches or shortcuts to coding. However, we cannot emphasize enough that by following HTML style as closely as you can, you will be saving yourself and the people who maintain your site a great deal of time and effort as HTML standards evolve. More than that, now that automated information-gathering programs wander the Web in search of content for indexing, a malformed HTML document is overlooked in popular indexes. Since these robots and wanderers can read only correct HTML, in a general way, the accuracy with which you create your documents will determine your accessibility. Keeping style in mind throughout the Web-authoring process will allow your site to remain high quality, both aesthetically and technically, as the Web grows and changes.

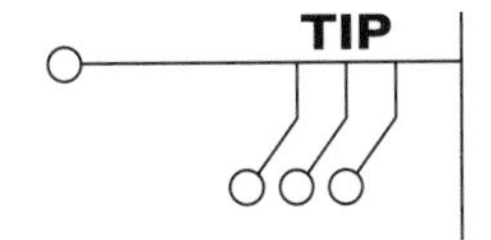

For a collection of style guides and authoring information, look at the compilation of links at the URL http://coombs.anu.edu.au/SpecialProj/QLTY/QltyHome.html. One of the best style manuals in this collection, from the Yale Medical School, is located at the URL http://info.med.yale.edu/caim/StyleManual_Top.HTML and should be consulted often throughout the authoring and design process.

Validation Programs

It is a lot to ask of any one HTML author that she or he check each document and tag for the appropriate style specifications. There are, though, many reasons for doing so, as noted in the beginning of this chapter. Since not everyone is familiar with the nuances of HTML, especially insofar as HTML v3.0 is concerned, it is a good idea to find some help. In this particular case, help comes in the form of automated document checkers, or validation programs, that parse your documents according to style and accuracy standards. These programs are capable of giving your HTML documents a thorough going-over, checking style and alerting you to a stylistic faux pas or a link that just doesn't work. These programs are comprehensive and sometimes more rigorous than is necessary for the majority of existing browser software. However, you should bring your documents in line with the recommendations of these programs, since the HTML standard will become more tightly enforced as browsers and editors themselves conform more closely to HTML.

In this section, we give you the details of four of these programs. Two programs check for content and style, one checks for links, and the fourth acts as a Web-wandering robot, starting with a home page and following all of the links in your pages recursively until it has checked all of the documents that you have linked on your Web server. Using these programs will cut down greatly on the time that you need to spend manually checking your pages, and they will catch errors that might not even be apparent at first glance.

Content & Style Checkers

This section describes two programs that parse the content and style of your Web pages. Checking content does not mean that a program runs through the grammar of the text of your document and warns you about dangling participles. The content of the Web page that these programs check is the content of the tags themselves and the text that is included between tags (such as the ever-threatening <A HREF="*filename*.html">Click here</A>). These programs also check the way that the document is arranged. Weblint and HTMLCHEK will probably catch many of the same errors, and they can be used exclusively or interchangeably. Each program has distinctive features that make running them in combination a very thorough error-checking practice, and we highly recommend doing so.

Weblint

Weblint is described by its author as "a program which picks fluff off of HTML pages." This description is perhaps too humble because Weblint monitors both style and validity when parsing an HTML document. Weblint currently checks for a wide range of potential errors and, by default, returns warnings when it comes across any errors. To run Weblint without excluding any of these errors, simply enter the following command line:

```
$weblint filename1.html filename2.html
```

On the command line, you can list as many HTML documents as you want to check. You can also use a wildcard (*.html) to have Weblint check all of the HTML files in a particular directory, or you can search directories recursively with the -R option. If you run it without any options, Weblint does not check whether your tags are uppercase or lowercase, and it won't check for a <LINK> tag, which is discussed earlier in "HTML Style," at the end of the document. Weblint does check the structure of your document, the syntax of tags, the validity of those tags and the stylistic layout of your documents.

When checking syntax, Weblint checks that all of your tags have a closing tag, that inappropriate elements do not overlap, that elements are correctly formatted (it checks for too few or too many quotation marks, for example) and that you are not nesting elements that are not supposed to be nested. These checks are the most valuable because the errors that they find inevitably result in browsers displaying error messages.

When checking a tag's validity, Weblint ensures that the tag is not obsolete or unknown and checks to see if a tag is used in the appropriate context (such as an SRC element inside an <A HREF> tag). Weblint checks other details that would not necessarily appear as errors when browsers view the document.

Finally, Weblint makes a number of style checks on a document, which includes checking for an ALT specification in an image tag, looking for a title in the header of the document, checking that headers appear in order (<H3> after <H2> and so on) and warning you if you use "here" (as in "Click here") for the text of a hyperlink. Catching these stylistic problems really just helps you create good pages, because these errors won't necessarily create problems for a user, except perhaps in an aesthetic sense. The best way to find out exactly what Weblint does, though, is to run it on a set of test documents and examine the complaints it makes about them. If you decide that the problems it identifies should not be changed, you can eliminate those criteria in the configuration file or on the command line. You can configure Weblint either on the command line or in a configuration file. By default, Weblint looks for a configuration file with the name .weblintrc in your home directory. However, you can define a new location by setting the environment variable WEBLINTRC to the correct location and file name, as in the following setting:

```
$WEBLINTRC=/users/bob/lint-config.conf
$export WEBLINTRC
```

The possible settings you can put in your .weblintrc file are detailed in this chapter. These settings can enable specific warnings, disable specific warnings (such as warnings about obsolete tags) and enable language extensions. Currently Weblint supports only Netscape extensions, but plans are in the works to check HTML v3.0 as well.

The format of the configuration file is fairly straightforward. Simply enter the commands and the settings, each on a separate line, that you want Weblint to follow. For example, if you want to enable Weblint's search for the <LINK> tag, disable the warnings for obsolete tags and enable Netscape language extensions, you would create the following configuration file:

```
enable mailto-link
disable obsolete
extension netscape
```

We have listed the identifiers for enabling or disabling warnings, because some of the identifiers are not intuitive—for example, "mailto-link" is not necessarily an intuitive name for the <LINK> tag. You can enter these identifiers either on the command line or in the configuration file to specify the types of warnings that are and are not generated.

Weblint can accept five command-line settings that configure the type of checking it does. The -d option in the command line is the same as the disable command in the configuration file. When you enter -d and an identifier, separated by a space, Weblint does not generate a warning message for that particular element. The -e option in the command line is the same as the enable command in the configuration file and generates warnings for any identifier that you list. By default, all of the warnings are enabled except for the case of tags (uppercase or lowercase) and for the <LINK> tag. The -x option is the same as the extension command in the configuration file. Currently you can enter only the element netscape to direct Weblint to check Netscape tags.

The -R option directs Weblint to check directories recursively when you provide a directory name rather than a file name, as in the following command line:

```
$weblint -R /html
```

When you enter this command, Weblint checks all of the files in the directory /html, then checks for any subdirectories and checks those files and then goes to the subdirectories of those subdirectories and so on. If you are going to check all of your files in this manner, it is a good idea to redirect the output of Weblint to a file that you can read more slowly, rather than having the errors

displayed across your screen too fast for you to read. To redirect the errors, you simply enter a command line similar to the following:

```
$weblint -R /html > all-errors.txt
```

Finally, to generate shorter error messages, you can use the -s option to direct Weblint to omit the file name of the document being checked when it identifies an error. Using the -s option in this way is obviously a good idea only when you are checking a single document.

To enable or disable certain types of warnings, you need to use their identifiers. Place the identifiers after the -e or -d options in the command line or after the enable or disable commands in the configuration file. The identifiers and the warnings associated with them are listed in the man page as follows:

tag <...> is not in upper case.
Identifier: upper-case
Default: disabled

tag <...> is not in lower case.
Identifier: lower-case
Default: disabled

foo attribute is required for <...>
Identifier: required-attribute
Default: enabled

expected an attribute for <...>
Identifier: expected-attribute
Default: enabled

unknown element <...>
Identifier: unknown-element
Default: enabled

Unknown attribute "..." for element <...>.
Identifier: unknown-attribute
Default: enabled

Should not have whitespace between "<" and "...>"
Identifier: leading-whitespace
Default: enabled

bad form to use 'here' as an anchor!
Identifier: here-anchor
Default: enabled

no <TITLE> in HEAD element.
Identifier: require-head
Default: enabled

tag <...> should only appear once. I saw one on line XX!
Identifier: once-only
Default: enabled

<BODY> but no <HEAD>.
Identifier: body-no-head
Default: enabled

outer tags should be <HTML> .. </HTML>.
Identifier: html-outer
Default: enabled

<...> can only appear in the HEAD element.
Identifier: head-element
Default: enabled

<...> cannot appear in the HEAD element.
Identifier: non-head-element
Default: enabled

<LI> can only appear in DIR, MENU, OL or UL elements.
Identifier: list-item
Default: enabled

<...> is obsolete.
Identifier: obsolete
Default: enabled

unmatched </...> (no matching <...> seen).
Identifier: mis-match
Default: enabled

IMG does not have ALT text defined.
Identifier: img-alt
Default: enabled

<...> cannot be nested.
Identifier: nested-element
Default: enabled

<...> can only be used in definition list (<DL>..</DL>).
Identifier: defn-list-elements
Default: enabled

<...> can only appear in a FORM element.
Identifier: form-item
Default: enabled

<OPTION> can only appear within a SELECT element.
Identifier: select-option
Default: enabled

Did not see <LINK REV=MADE HREF="mailto:..."> in HEAD.
Identifier: mailto-link
Default: disabled

</...> on line XX seems to overlap <...>, opened on line YY.
Identifier: element-overlap
Default: enabled

No closing </...> seen for <...> on line XX.
Identifier: unclosed-element
Default: enabled

Markup embedded in a comment can confuse some browsers.
Identifier: markup-in-comment
Default: enabled

odd number of quotes in element <...>.
Identifier: odd-quotes
Default: enabled

heading <H?> follows <H?> on line N.
Identifier: heading-order
Default: enabled

target for anchor "..." not found.
Identifier: bad-link
Default: enabled

unexpected < in <...> — potentially unclosed element.
Identifier: unexpected-open
Default: enabled

Use these identifiers in the command line or configuration file to define the warnings you want enabled or disabled. For example, you can enter the following line in your .weblintrc file:

```
disable unexpected-open
```

Or you can specify the option -d unexpected-open in the command line for Weblint to suppress the error message "unexpected < in <*tagname*> — potentially unclosed element".

After configuring Weblint according to these options, you will be almost ready to run it. Test it on a few of your documents to determine which errors are useful to identify, set the disable options accordingly and you will be ready to use Weblint.

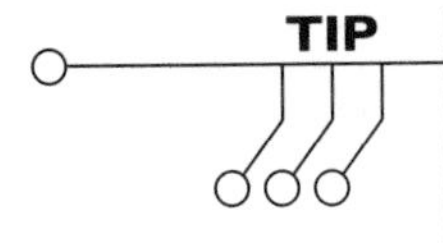

For information and updates about Weblint, check out the Weblint home page at the URL http://www.khoros.unm.edu/staff/neilb/weblint.html.

HTMLCHEK

As discussed earlier, both the style and the syntax of HTML are important factors in determining a document's validity on the Web. Obviously, it is more important to ensure that the syntax of the coding is correct because incorrect coding causes a number of browsers to generate errors. However, as the Web moves further toward a unified standard, those practices of coding that are currently classified as style, such as the use of certain tags within other tags or the use of tags that define the structure of a document but don't affect its appearance (such as <HTML> and <BODY>) will become syntactical requirements for browsers and editors. Included on the Companion CD-ROM is a perl script called htmlchek.pl (and an awk equivalent) that checks both style and syntax in a single run-through of a document. While both the awk and the perl files produce the same output, we will discuss only the perl version of the program. All configurations and file names are the same in both versions of HTMLCHEK.

htmlcheck.pl is an especially useful program because it allows you to specify HTML v3.0 checking (see Chapter 13, "Future Directions") and allows you to include Netscape tags for checking. In addition, you can configure it in a wide variety of ways using command-line options or a configuration file.

To run HTMLCHEK as is, without any special configurations, you enter a simple command line similar to the following:

```
$perl htmlchek.pl webfiles.html > errors.txt
```

If you are using awk, enter a command line similar to this one:

```
$awk -f htmlchek.awk webfiles.html > errors.txt
```

You can specify multiple file names or use wildcards on the command line to check multiple files.

Before going into detail about the possible configurations that you can specify for htmlcheck.pl, we will explain the output so that you will know what you are turning off or turning on while configuring the program.

The output file is divided into two parts. The first section gives you an outline of the warning and error messages that are generated by the program, according to the sort of errors that you have instructed the program to look for. There is a difference between warning messages (which contain the string "Warning!") and error messages (which contain the string "ERROR!"). Warnings are usually generated by style errors, which do not necessarily prevent the document from displaying correctly on a browser but may cause problems later. Errors indicate an error in the HTML markup itself and cause an inaccurate display when your document is viewed.

The second section of the output file lists all of the tag types that you have used in a particular document and all of the options that you specified for these tags.

You can specify a third type of output to list the files and references that are made in all of the HTML documents. This optional function of htmlchek.pl, called "cross-reference checking," is discussed later.

Configuring Your Output

Three options configure the output of HTMLCHEK when it comes across an error or generates a warning. You enable these options with a setting of 1 and disable them with a setting of 0, or you can simply omit them from the command line or configuration file.

- **inline=1** By default, HTMLCHEK generates error messages with references to the file names and line numbers where the errors are located. To include the actual text of that line in the error messages, set the option inline=1.
- **nowswarn=1** Since extra white space can generate errors on some browsers, HTMLCHEK generates a warning when it encounters extra white space. However, since some documents legitimately contain white space, you might want to turn these warnings off just to save yourself some time. Setting nowswarn=1 disables the white space warnings.
- **sugar=1** This option adds a prefix of "*filename*: *linenumber*:" to each error message, making it easier to quickly read the messages and making the output compatible with some editors that can interpret it, such as emacs.

Tag Definition Options

Four options allow you to define a new tag to be accepted by HTMLCHEK. Using one of these options tells HTMLCHEK how to treat the new tag: whether the tag requires a closing tag, whether a closing tag is optional, if no closing tag should be used or when a closing tag is not only required but also when no other identical tags can be enclosed in that element (for example, no <A HREF>...</A> set can include another <A HREF> tag). All of these options are tag lists, defined by listing the tags and separating them with commas.

- **nonpair=** Defining a tag as nonpair tells HTMLCHEK that no closing tag should be used. Tags already defined as nonpair are <BR> and <HR>.
- **loosepair=** The option loosepair defines the closing tag as optional. For example, the <LI> tag in lists can optionally have an </LI> at the end of the item in HTML v2.0, but it is not required.
- **strictpair=** A strictly paired tag (strictpair) must have a closing tag to be accurate. A common example is the accidental omission of </STRONG> at the end of an <STRONG> tag, which formats all the text after that tag in boldface. The majority of HTML tags are strictly paired.
- **nonrecurpair=** This type of tag is both strictly paired and cannot contain any identical tags, as in the example of <A HREF> cited previously.

The following is an example of a tag definition option:

```
strictpair=b,i,em,strong,p
```

Since the first four extensions are already defined as strictly paired, this configuration line would be redundant. Defining the paragraph tag as strictly paired would change it from the default loosepair. In all tag lists, the case is not important—tags can be either uppercase or lowercase.

Other Tag Options

HTMLCHEK also allows you to modify tags that have already been defined. These modifications allow you to configure HTMLCHEK to your particular style of authoring. In some cases, the recommendations that HTMLCHEK makes by default should be considered advance notices of changes in HTML. You can specify three types of settings for these tag options. You can specify a tag listing, just like the tag definition options given earlier. You can specify a listing of tags with allowed options in the following format:

```
tag,option:tag,option...
```

For example, enter the following to allow the <P> tag to contain the options align and nowrap:

```
tagopts=p,align:p,nowrap
```

Finally, you can specify a numerical option, which establishes levels of strictness, used in the dlstrict option. The following command-line options take tag listings as arguments:

- **lowlevelpair=** This option, followed by a list of tags, defines strictly paired tags as low-level markup, or in other words, markup that is allowed to contain certain types of other tags. For example, a low-level markup tag that is already understood by HTMLCHEK is the use of boldface text inside a hyperlink, as in

```
<A HREF="http://www.shoop.com/">Check out the <EM>ShoopSoft
Home Page</EM></A>
```

Tags that are not low-level markup include lists, headers and paragraph markers, and these tags should not be defined as low-level markup because including them inside of low-level markup tags will confuse browsers and may generate errors.

- **lowlevelnonpair=** This option produces the same effect as lowlevelpair for tags that are not strictly paired, such as <BR>, the line break tag.
- **nonblock=** The nonblock option also allows a strictly paired tag to contain low-level markup. However, if an option is defined as nonblock, it cannot contain any other elements that are also included as nonblock. For example,

the address tag (<ADDRESS>) cannot contain a header tag because both are defined as nonblock.

- **deprecated=** By specifying a tag in this option, you mark it obsolete or "deprecated" (obsolete but still supported). You might want to include tags like <B> and <I>, the bold and italics tags, in this category, because these tags may become deprecated in future versions of HTML, so that you can replace them with more specific tags like <STRONG> or <VAR>.

Three settings define allowed or required options in the following format for certain tags:

```
tag,option:tag,option...
```

- **tagopts=** This setting allows tags to have additional options, as in the optional settings for the paragraph tag for alignment and line wrapping. The following line would allow both of these options and their configurations (for example, ALIGN=center) to be accepted by HTMLCHEK:

```
tagopts=p,align:p,nowrap
```

- **novalopts=** To allow a tag option without any setting, such as the image option ISMAP for imagemapping, it should be listed in the same format as a tagopts setting, as in the following example:

```
novalopts=img,ismap
```

- **reqopts=** Pairing a tag with an option in the reqopts listing causes HTMLCHEK to generate a warning whenever that option is not included. One use of this specification that is useful for future planning involves the WIDTH and HEIGHT specifications for inline images, which is currently supported only by Netscape but will be part of the HTML v3.0 specification. The following setting tells HTMLCHEK to warn you of any place where the dimensions of an inline image are not defined using the WIDTH and HEIGHT settings:

```
reqopts=img,width:img,height
```

The final tag option supported by HTMLCHEK uses a numbering system to determine the strictness of the program in generating a warning. The dlstrict setting determines how strictly HTMLCHEK checks the definition list, defined by the <DL> tag. A setting of dlstrict=1, which is the default for HTMLCHEK, allows the tags <DD> and <DT>, the tags for the text of a definition and for a term that is being defined, to be placed anywhere inside a definition list. A setting of dlstrict=2 requires that the two tags coexist, but the definition term can indirectly precede the definition itself. The strictest setting is dlstrict=3, which requires that every tag that marks the text of a definition, <DD>, be immediately preceded by the definition term itself, indicated with the tag <DT>. Definition lists are explained in detail in Chapter 2, "The Basic Pieces."

Parsing Options

Two settings control the way that an HTML document is parsed, both with regard to the use of the less than (<) and more than (>) characters. The metachar option is similar to the dlstrict setting in that you use a 1 to 3 setting to specify the strictness, except in the case of the metachar option, 1 is the most strict and 3 is the least strict.

Setting the option metachar=3 will allow either the less than character (<) or the greater than character (>) inside a comment (such as <!—<HR>—>) to pass without warning. However, including these characters inside a comment can sometimes confuse browsers. The stricter setting metachar=2 does not allow these characters inside comments. However, it allows a comment to extend over more than a single line, which can generate an error on the strictest of browsers. The strictest setting, then, metachar=1, does not allow comments to extend past a single line.

The other parsing option is more of a style setting. If you set nogtwarn=1, HTMLCHEK warns you of any loose less than or greater than characters in the text of your document. You should simply replace these characters with the correct ISO Latin-1 entity ">" for the greater than character (<) and "<" for the less than character (>).

Language Extensions

By default, HTMLCHEK checks your documents according to the HTML v2.0 standards currently in place. However, you can have it check according to the Netscape extensions or the HTML v3.0 standard (see Chapter 13, "Future Directions"). In your command line or configuration file, you can specify one of the following options:

```
netscape=1
html3=1 (or arena=1 or htmlplus=1)
```

Each of the three options html3=1, arena=1 or htmlplus=1 uses the latest revision of the HTML v3.0 standard. The option html3=1 is a reference to HTML v3.0, arena=1 is a reference to the only currently existing browser that can understand HTML v3.0, and htmlplus=1 refers to an older upgrade of HTML, which has been included in the HTML v3.0 upgrade.

Cross-Reference Checking

Cross-reference checking, that is, the capability of checking the references that you have linked into your document, should be the last step of the document-checking process using HTMLCHEK. While HTMLCHEK is not capable of actually going to sites that are linked to your pages and checking if the links are valid, it does collect all of the links to off-site resources in a single file for you. It also lists unreferenced locations in your documents, such as the inclusion of an <A NAME="Section_1"> anchor without any link to that anchor. Optionally, you can use HTMLCHEK to generate a "dependency map," that is, a full listing of the files that reference resources, so that you can check those resources as well.

Seven command-line options control cross-reference checking: four control the output, and three determine the input by defining how to resolve the URL of links. Two of the four options are necessary for cross-reference checking to be stored in output files, one for each document:

- **xref=1** This option turns on cross-reference checking in the first place, and, unless you enable the next option, refsfile, error messages are sent to the screen as the program runs.

- **refsfile="*prefixname*"** This option creates reference files with three suffixes. The first, *prefixname*.href, lists the references using the HREF option (that is, <BASE>, <A HREF>, etc.); the second, *prefixname*.src, lists all of the inline images (<IMG SRC>, and the third, *prefixname*.name, lists all of the destination locations that are specified in the HTML documents.

The optional dependency map is generated using the map=1 option, which generates a file called *prefixname*.map. You must also include xref=1 in the command line or configuration file for the option to work.

HTMLCHEK automatically overwrites any old reference files. To prevent this, you can use the command-line option append=1 to append entries to the files that contain reference information. Three options determine the URL prefix of documents to be checked.

- **dirprefix="*pathname*"** By specifying this option, you give HTMLCHEK the information it needs to complete relative URLs in your documents. Enter the beginning of any relative URLs that you are using, such as dirprefix= "http://www.shoop.com/" or dirprefix="/users/bob/". You can enter the protocol type or simply specify the full path.
- **usebase=1** This option directs HTMLCHEK to obtain the URL from the <BASE> tag rather than from the name of the file and a directory prefix. This option requires that <BASE> be the first tag in the header of your document.
- **subtract="*pathname*"** Specify this option if you are running HTMLCHEKon files outside the current directory. For example, if you are running HTMLCHEK from /html/stats/htmlchek/ to check files in /html/users/bob/, you would enter a command line similar to the following:

```
$perl htmlchek.pl xref=1 refsfile="bob-check" subtract="/html/users/bob/"
dirprefix="http://www.shoop.com/users/bob/" /html/users/bob/*.html >
outfile.check
```

This command line would strip off the directory name /html/users/bob/, and whenever HTMLCHEK encountered a relative URL, it would preface it with the following:

```
http://www.shoop.com/users/bob/
```

HTML would not return "file not found" errors by trying to search for relative URLs in the working directory.

One of the limitations of cross-reference checking is that it can work only within a single directory tree. If, for example, you wanted to check the references that exist in the trees /html/users/bob/ and /html/pricing/, you could not do so from one command line. The easiest way around this limitation is to use multiple command lines, the same refsfile= "*prefixname* " and the append=1 option, which creates large reference files with information about all trees, as in the following example of two command lines run in sequence:

```
$perl htmlchek.pl xref=1 refsfile="output" subtract="/html/users/bob/"
dirprefix="http://www.shoop.com/users/bob/"
/html/users/bob/*.html > outfile-bob.check
$perl htmlchek.pl xref=1 refsfile="output" append=1 subtract="/html/
pricing/" dirprefix="http://www.shoop.com/pricing/" /html/pricing/*.html >
outfile-pricing.check
```

These command lines would create three files: output.href, output.src and output.name. These files would contain the information from both directory trees and two separate output files, outfile-bob.check and outfile-pricing.check. To produce a single output file and a single set of cross-reference checking output files, change the redirect command in the second command line to append to the output file as follows:

```
$perl htmlchek.pl xref=1 refsfile="output" subtract="/html/users/bob/"
dirprefix="http://www.shoop.com/users/bob/"
/html/users/bob/*.html > outfile-all.check
$perl htmlchek.pl xref=1 refsfile="output" append=1 subtract="/html/
pricing/" dirprefix="http://www.shoop.com/pricing/" /html/pricing/*.html
>> outfile-all.check
```

Using Configuration Files

After getting a sense of how extensive a single command line must be for you to thoroughly check your HTML documents, you may want to use configuration files for checking sets of documents. Since a configuration file specifies only the language definition options, you can't configure certain options there. Specifically, you have to define the append, dirprefix, refsfile, sugar and usebase options all on the command line and not in the configuration file. The configuration file should have the extension .cfg. In the configuration file, you list the command-line options much as you do in a command line, with a separate option on each line.

Aside from the options that cannot be defined in the configuration file, there are a few additional differences between what you can specify in it and what you can specify on the command line. Primary among these is the ability to create cumulative definitions—that is, to define a particular option more than once and have all options apply. In the command line, the last option that you define overrides any definitions of the same option given earlier in that line. However, in the configuration file, a series of definitions, such as those listed below, allows documents marked up with either HTML v3.0 or Netscape extensions to pass without returning an error:

```
html3=1
netscape=1
```

To use a configuration file, enter the option configfile="*filename*" (or cf="*filename*") in the command line. If you choose to override an option in your configuration file, you can do so in the command line, after the configfile option. For example, to turn off HTML v3.0 checking after it has been turned on in the configuration file, you could enter a command line similar to the following to override the option "html3=1".

```
$perl htmlcheck.pl configfile="pricing.cfg" html3=off /html/pricing/
index.html > outfile.check
```

We suggest you combine the checking capabilities of Weblint, which are more rigorous stylistically, and those of HTMLCHEK, which is more rigorous in terms of syntax and HTML validity.

These two programs checking in concert will ensure that there are few, if any, potential problems in your Web pages.

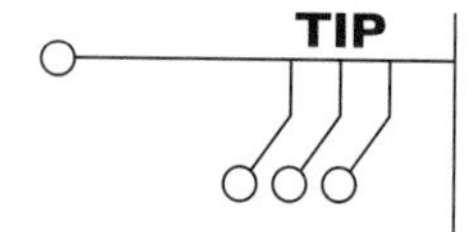

For extensive documentation of HTMLCHEK, see the Users Guide *at the URL http://uts.cc.utexas.edu/~churchh/htmlchekprog.html.*

Checking Your Links With Anchor Checker

While HTMLCHEK and Weblint check your HTML documents in a number of ways, which include checking the integrity of links to local files, Anchor Checker is a program that is capable of following external links and checking their integrity, which neither HTMLCHEK or Weblint can do. We have included Anchor Checker (or checker from the command line) on the Companion CD-ROM. This program follows each link, relative or absolute and internal or external, resolves the hostname and checks to confirm that the document in question actually exists.

Anchor Checker is easy to use and requires only a few command-line configurations. The standard command line is in the following format:

```
checker [options] filename filename ...
```

The configuration options that you specify on the command line can be stored in a configuration file, which can save you the work of re-entering the options each time that you run the program itself. Two options that you can pass to Anchor Checker affect the way that it checks particular documents.

- **-base-address** By specifying a URL after the -base-address option, you pass the first part of all absolute URLs to Anchor Checker (see the section, "Absolute & Relative URLs," in this chapter). For example, if a document references the file /users/bob/pipe.gif, Anchor Checker knows to prefix that location with the URL that you give it in the command line.

- **-current-address** This option determines the host and directory information that Anchor Checker puts at the beginning of a relative URL. For example, if your Web page contains a reference to a file such as <A HREF="pics/pipe.gif"> and you specify a -current-address value of http://church.bob.org/users/bob, Anchor Checker looks for the existence of http://church.bob.org/users/bob/pics/pipe.gif.

These two options allow you to check a document from a remote machine (a remote machine would not usually be able to locate files without knowing the hostname) and to check documents that use a relative referencing system for hyperlinks. However, if you are running Anchor Checker on the machine where all your Web documents are located and are not using relative pathnames, using these options is unnecessary. One limitation of Anchor Checker is that it has to be run on the same machine as the document that is being checked. This limitation does not mean that all of the files referenced in the document have to be on that machine, so long as you have specified the -base-address option correctly, but that the HTML document itself needs to be on the same machine that Anchor Checker is on.

Anchor Checker uses two options to configure its output.

- **-only-errors** If you run Anchor Checker without this option, it notifies you about both successful links and links that have failed. As you might guess, when you have enabled the -only-errors option, Anchor Checker returns only the error messages and suppresses the success messages.
- **-trace** If you have found a link that is not working, you might want to run Anchor Checker with the -trace option specified. This option provides a detailed breakdown of how the machine name is being resolved, where the files are located and what error is causing the file or directory to be inaccessible. This option generates a lot of text, however, so it is a good idea to dump the output to a text file and browse that text file. You can direct the output to a text file errors.txt with the following command line:

```
$checker -trace index.html > errors.txt
```

If you will be running Anchor Checker with a single configuration on a regular basis, you should create a configuration file. By default, Anchor Checker looks in your home directory for a file called .checkercfg. If you want to give this file a different name or put it in a different location, you can use the -config-file option to specify the configuration file and location. The configuration file should contain one configuration option per line, formatted exactly as the command-line options would be, as in the following example:

```
-only-errors
-base-address http://church.bob.org
-current-address http://church.bob.org/users/bob
```

Note that both on the command line and in the configuration file, the options and the settings are separated by a single space. To run the configuration specified in the previous example of a configuration file, you could enter the following command line to produce exactly the same result:

```
checker -only-errors -base-address http://church.bob.org
-current-address http://church.bob.org/users/bob index.html
```

Using Anchor Checker, you can verify your documents for accuracy by checking the hyperlinks. After you use a combination of style and link checkers and give your documents a manual once-over with style considerations in mind, your documents should be quite sound and as ready as any hypertext document can be for the rigors of Web usage.

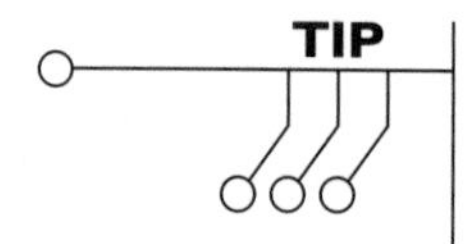

The Anchor Checker home page is located at the URL http://www.ugrad.cs.ubc.ca/spider/q7f192/branch/checker.html.

Wandering Through Your Site With MOMspider

After you finish a document, Anchor Checker is an excellent program for proofing all of the links that you have included. However, it does present some problems, and a program called MOMspider, which is included on the Companion CD-ROM, is

designed to overcome some of the problems that repeated use of a program like Anchor Checker might present. Anchor Checker functions by sending a HEAD request (see "Hypertext Transfer Protocol," in Chapter 2, "The Basic Pieces") to all of the URLs that are listed in an HTML document and verifying that they respond correctly. The problem with using this system for maintenance is that doing so results in a waste of Internet resources, such as bandwidth and CPU time. As an alternative, MOMspider executes this test once and keeps a log of those links that returned a successful response. Also, MOMspider has an advantage over Anchor Checker in that it recursively follows the links in all of your HTML documents, beginning at the top document in an index and ending at the "dead end" documents (non-HTML files or HTML files without any links) at the bottom of the document hierarchy. MOMspider checks the site the way that a user would experience it and does not check documents that are not linked to your HTML tree even if those documents are located in the same directory as other HTML documents.

Before running MOMspider, you will need to set the location of all of the files that MOMspider will be using as an environment variable for your shell. These files include all of the perl scripts and configuration files that are included in the MOMspider distribution. The location for the MOMspider files themselves should be named in the MOMlib environment variable. For example, the following sequence of commands would identify the directory /users/bob/bin as the location of MOMspider's files:

```
$MOMlib=/users/bob/bin
$export MOMlib
```

The other location that will need to be specified using an environment variable is the directory containing the special perl libraries used to run MOMspider. This library is called libwww-perl-0.40 in the current release. If you are using the Linux operating system that is included on the Companion CD-ROM, you don't need to set this environment variable, since the library will be in a place where perl already looks. However, if you are running MOMspider on your own operating system and have put the directory containing these libraries in another directory, you will need to identify this location in the environment variable

WWWlib. For example, if the library directory is in the directory /users/bob/lib/perl, you should use the following sequence of commands:

```
$WWWlib=/users/bob/lib/perl
$export WWWlib
```

You can configure MOMspider with incredible specificity. You should begin by setting your default configurations in the file momconfig.pl. Most likely, the only line that you need to change is the line that defines the "local network" domain (line 72). Replace the following with your domain suffix:

```
"\.uci\.edu";
```

Use the backslash to make the periods readable by the program, as in the following:

```
"\.shoop\.com";
```

The rest of the options in this file set the locations of various files, applications and directories on your system. Double-check them to make sure that they are accurate, but since they are fairly standard settings for UNIX systems, you should not have to change many. One group of settings that you might want to adjust, especially if you want only a certain type of document browsed, is the Allowed settings (line 129), which can restrict the files that are browsed by MOMspider. The options are quite straightforward: you turn them on with a 1 and off with a 0.

Another group of settings that you should adjust according to your server's speed and the nature of your Internet connection are the controls that determine time settings. The variable $Timeout (line 177) indicates the number of seconds to wait for before timing out on a connection, $Pausetime (line 183) defines the number of seconds that make up a long pause, which should be increased for a slow server, and $Betweentime (line 186) sets the amount of time to wait between two requests to the same site.

After configuring momconfig.pl to your site, you can build an instruction file for MOMspider to follow when checking the site. By default, MOMspider looks for this file, .momspider-instruct, in your home directory. The format of the file is fairly intuitive. An instruction file would look similar to the following:

```
AvoidFile  /users/bob/MOMspider/.momspider-avoid
SitesFile  /users/bob/MOMspider/.momspider-sites
<Tree
Name                  Sample_Test
TopURL                http://www.shoop.com/users/bob/index.html
IndexURL              file://localhost/users/bob/MOMspider/short-
index.html
IndexFile             /users/bob/MOMspider/short-index.html
IndexTitle            A Short Example MOMspider Index
EmailAddress          webmaster@shoop.com
EmailBroken
EmailRedirected
EmailChanged 7
EmailExpired 1
ExpireWindow 1
Exclude               file://localhost/users/bob/sermons/conspire.html
>
```

The AvoidFile and the SitesFile entries will be discussed in greater detail later in this section. The first entry in the bracketed section, Tree, defines the type of checking that you want MOMspider to do. Checking a document tree means that MOMspider recursively checks all of the files linked into the URL specified in TopURL, down to the bottom of the directory tree. The other possible options are Site and Owner. Specifying Site directs MOMspider to begin at the top level of a site and check all of the links on that site. When you specify Site, MOMspider checks every external link in the documents at that site, stopping with the first off-site document that it reaches. When you specify Owner, MOMspider searches all of the files that have an owner name specified in the <META> tag, such as <META HTTP-EQUIV="OWNER" CONTENT="Bob">. To specify the owner name to be used in choosing which documents to check, use the next configuration setting, Name. The Name option in the configuration file should be set to any name you want to give the search. The only special case for this is when you are searching by owner, in which case, you provide the owner name in the Name option.

The TopURL setting defines the HTML document to begin the search with. In the case of a Site search, TopURL defines the machine name, which marks the limitation of the search. The TopURL setting can be either relative (to the working directory) or absolute, in the form of a complete URL.

The IndexFile setting defines the location of the HTML document that is generated as output, and the IndexTitle setting defines the name of that document.

The EmailAddress setting gives an e-mail address to which all errors are mailed. This setting should be followed by lines indicating what types of errors merit e-mail notification. Including the EmailBroken tells MOMspider where to send e-mail reporting broken links, and including EmailRedirected directs it to do the same for redirected links. Neither of these settings need to be followed by any other information—including them enables that function and not including them disables it.

EmailChanged followed by a number of days determines when MOMspider generates an e-mail message warning when a link has changed within that number of days. EmailExpired, followed by a number of days, tells MOMspider to send an e-mail message if a link is set to expire within that number of days. This allows users and Web site administrators to remove information that has become obsolete, or to update that information. For example, if a page contained an announcement that became irrelevant after a certain date, the owner of that page or the site administrator would be notified when the expiration date was coming up so that the page could be removed or changed. The expiration date, as noted above, is set using the <META> tag.

Finally, the Exclude setting indicates the URL or URLs that should be treated as dead-end documents, even if they contain other links. To specify a number of different URLs, you can enter multiple Exclude settings, and to exclude an entire range of documents, you can enter a prefix to be excluded. MOMspider treats anything with that prefix as a dead-end for the browser.

Note that the configuration file ends with a greater than character (>) on a line by itself. If you want MOMspider to run a sequence of searches, you can enter a second set of configurations after this greater than character, such as:

```
AvoidFile          /users/bob/MOMspider/.momspider-avoid
SitesFile          /users/bob/MOMspider/.momspider-sites
<Tree
Name               Users_Test
TopURL             http://www.shoop.com/users/index.html
IndexURL           file://localhost/stats/MOMspider/short-index.html
IndexFile          /html/stats/MOMspider/files-index.html
IndexTitle         File Stats for User Pages
EmailAddress       webmaster@shoop.com
EmailBroken
EmailRedirected
EmailExpired 1
ExpireWindow 1
Exclude            file://localhost/users/bob/sermons/conspire.html
>
<Owner
Name               Bob
TopURL             http://www.shoop.com/
IndexURL           file://localhost/users/bob/MOMspider/user-
index.html
IndexFile          /users/bob/MOMspider/files-index.html
IndexTitle         File Stats for User "Bob"
EmailAddress       bob@shoop.com
EmailBroken
EmailRedirected
EmailExpired 1
ExpireWindow 1
Exclude            file://localhost/users/bob/sermons/conspire.html
>
```

The two files that are identified at the beginning of the instructions file, the AvoidFile and the SitesFile, contain information that MOMspider uses to determine which sites not to check, either because the checking is unnecessary or because it's prohibited by that site. There are two copies of each file—one for individual traversals, and one system file that MOMspider uses every time that it is run. The traversal-specific files can be named each time a new instruction file is created and, in the previous example, are called .momspider-avoid and .momspider-sites. The systemwide files are named in the momconfig.pl program, and the default names are system-avoid and system-sites. As mentioned earlier, these files should be located in the directory named in the MOMlib variable.

The AvoidFile defines two types of sites: the dead-end sites, also called Leaf sites, and sites to be avoided altogether. The following is the format for the AvoidFile:

```
EntryType      URL      [ExpireDate]
```

ExpireDate can be either a date in the same format as the Expires setting in the <META> tag or a wildcard, indicating that the expiration date is irrelevant. The *EntryType* is either Avoid, which directs MOMspider to avoid the site altogether, or Leaf, which defines any page with that prefix as a dead end. Finally, you put any expiration date in brackets at the end of the line, as in:

```
Avoid http://www.wais.com/      [*]
```

The .momspider-sites file is an automatically generated file that is created whenever MOMspider encounters a file specifically designed to send instructions to robots. This file is essentially a list of sites that cannot be traversed by Web-walking robots like MOMspider. Since the .momspider-sites file is automatically generated, you do not need to edit it. Both the .momspider-avoid and .momspider-sites files are intended to be user specific, and you should also create a systemwide equivalent that you set in momconfig.pl, which should be located in the directory named in the MOMlib variable. You should name these systemwide equivalents system-sites and system-avoid. Examples of both files are included in the software distribution on the Companion CD-ROM.

Finally, after having configured an instruction file to determine how to check your documents and having set up your momconfig.pl script, you are ready to enter the command itself. You can enter a final set of options at the command line that enable you to validate your documents. You will probably use three settings the most often. The first is the error log, which you can name using the -e option, as in

```
$momspider -e errors.txt
```

The second is the output history file, specified using the -o option. Finally, you need to name the instruction file that you want MOMspider to use. You can specify this file in the file momconfig.pl, but if you want to conduct a search other than what you have defined in your default configuration, you can use the -i option to specify a new instruction file. Keep in mind that since all of the options on the command line override configuration options, it is acceptable to specify one file on the InstructFile line of momconfig.pl and to use the -i option to specify another. A command line redirecting errors and output to different files, and naming the instruction file, would look similar to the following:

```
$momspider -e errors.txt -o history.txt -i site_instruct
```

The rest of the command-line options are generally duplications of information that is in momconfig.pl and can override anything in that file. The -d option is the same as the MaxDepth variable in momconfig.pl. It provides the maximum number of levels that MOMspider can traverse. The -a option is the same as the AvoidFile variable in either momconfig.pl or in the instruction file. It defines the file that contains the list of URLs that MOMspider should avoid checking. The -s option specifies the location of the sites file for the user; it is equivalent to the SitesFile variable in the instruction file. The -A and -S options give the location of the systemwide equivalents of the AvoidFile and the SitesFile, respectively. As noted earlier, however, you can specify this information more easily elsewhere, either in the momconfig.pl file (for all usage) or in the instruction file (for specific traversals).

After having configured MOMspider thoroughly, giving it information about the system and file locations in momconfig.pl, providing specific instructions for searching in the instruction file and giving command-line options, you can run MOMspider. When this process is complete, you will have an HTML document with stats about all of the files checked, and e-mail will be sent to the appropriate page maintainers if any pages are not functional. If different people will be maintaining Web spaces on your server, MOMspider is an excellent tool for checking all of these hierarchies and automatically notifying the appropriate people.

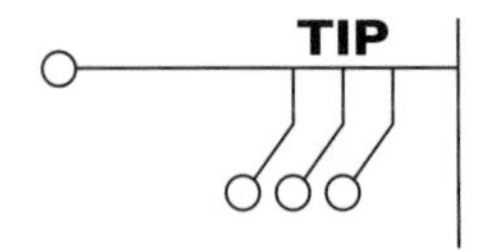

For more information about MOMspider, look at the provided documentation on the Companion CD-ROM, and go to the developer's MOMspider pages at the URL http://www.ics.uci.edu/WebSoft/MOMspider/.

Moving On

HTML authoring can be a more difficult process than might be apparent from the simplicity of the codes themselves. Since the Web and the HTML standard are constantly evolving, page design and authoring must follow a rigorous standard so that pages do not become obsolete. Primary in these design considerations should be the types of tags that you use. You should take special care to use each tag in the correct context and sequence and as specifically as possible in delimiting the structure of an HTML document. A number of tags that are not necessarily apparent to the browser, or that seem extraneous, such as the inclusion of tags that contain authoring information on each page, are features that will make your site appear more standardized and easier to maintain. A number of programs can help automate the process of validating both the HTML and the links between documents and files on the Web. Using these programs in conjunction with manual checkups will ensure that your site has the integrity that is necessary to create a useful and long-lived site.

After having taken care of the basics of server setup and Web page authoring and after checking your work, you should consider creating an aesthetically interesting and innovative site. Using other features of HTML, such as the forms and cgi scripts, you can create a high level of interactivity on your site. Also, the ease with which Web browsers handle multimedia—images, sounds, animation and so on—mean that you should give them a prominent place in your site design. The following chapters are devoted to helping you develop a high level of innovation for your site using these impressive features of the World Wide Web.

7 Images on the Web

Many factors caused the great explosion of growth in the World Wide Web in 1993, but probably the single most significant was the release of Mosaic for X version 0.10 from the National Center for Supercomputing Applications (NCSA).

Not only did the programmers at NCSA create an easier-to-use and more intuitive interface for Mosaic, but they also took the liberty of enabling it to display pictures, right in the midst of text. This feature made Mosaic attractive to the many thousands of people on the Internet who had never heard of the World Wide Web and, more importantly, made the Internet interesting to millions who had never heard of it before.

Inline images have made the WWW useful for advertisers who want to include pictures of their products and graphics of their trademarked logos, as well as for scientists who want to share figures and diagrams with their colleagues. Inline images have also sparked the imagination of artists, who use WWW servers as centers of collaboration, and they have inspired teachers to develop entire courses of study and virtual museums on the Web. All of these would have been difficult or impossible without the ability to easily embed images into Web pages.

Comparing Links & Inlines

You can integrate images into your Web pages in two ways: by linking them to your pages with hyperlinks (*linked images*) or by placing them directly on the page (*inline images*). Linked images use the hypermedia and MIME-typing capabilities of the WWW client (see Chapter 2, "The Basic Pieces") to let the user click on a hyperlink and download an image. You can include such a hyperlink with the HTML anchor code, like this:

```
Here's a <A HREF="/pics/linked-image.gif">picture.</A>
```

The word *picture* is a hyperlink, and the user can activate it to download the image. After the client downloads the image, the client usually executes a "helper application" to display it. The Netscape family of clients handles this process differently, by displaying images from invoked links inside the browser window.

Graphical browsers display inline images right on the page. This useful ability allows the author of the page to add illustrations, logos and diagrams in the context of the surrounding text. Adding an inline image is very simple; the <IMG> tag signals the browser that a graphic should be inserted, like this:

```
<IMG SRC="vmedia.gif" ALT="Ventana Online Logo"> This inline represents the Ventana Online Visitor's Center.
```

Figure 7-1: *An inline image.*

When it encounters the <IMG> tag, the client retrieves the URL that follows the SRC element. Note that the <IMG> tag is standalone; there is no equivalent closing tag. If you omit the host and protocol parts of the URL, the client assumes this image is on the same server as the document, and when it encounters a URL whose pathname lacks the initial forward slash (/), the client assumes the URL is relative to the document's directory.

If the user is running a client that cannot display inline images (such as Lynx, a client commonly used by UNIX and VMS terminal users as well as by MS-DOS users who aren't running Microsoft Windows), the client displays the text assigned to the ALT tag. If there is no ALT tag for an <IMG> tag, Lynx users see

"[IMAGE]" instead. Always provide an ALT specification with any inline image; you can either use it to describe what the picture illustrates or leave it blank (ALT="") so people using text-only clients won't see the distracting "[IMAGE]".

Inline images are often used in combination with hyperlinked images. For example, a page could include a small, icon-sized copy of an inline image and a larger, photograph-quality copy of the same image could be hyperlinked to it for people who want a better look. To do this, simply include an ordinary hyperlink anchor around the <IMG> tag, as in the following markup:

```
<A HREF="/pics/urizen.jpg"><IMG SRC="/pics/urizen.gif" ALT="image
from Urizen"></A> In this etching from <cite>Urizen</cite>, you can see
the inter-relation of Blake's poetry and art.
```

This creates a hypertext anchor for the inline image itself, which the user can click to get the larger version. As noted previously, if the client cannot display inlines, the hyperlink is anchored to the text specified with the ALT setting. If there is no ALT specification, the link is anchored to "[IMAGE]".

Placing Inlines on the Page

HTML gives the author of a page a certain amount of flexibility in specifying how inline images are displayed. Unfortunately, this flexibility falls far short of the capabilities professional designers are accustomed to, but with a little practice, you will be able to understand and utilize these basic capabilities to create efective pages.

Common HTML

The most commonly implemented version of HTML is version 2.0, which is the first version to support inline images. As a default in HTML v2.0, the client aligns the bottom of the image with the bottom of the text. You can change this default by adding the ALIGN setting. If you add ALIGN=top to the <IMG> tag, the top of the image is aligned with the top of the tallest item in the line, including other pictures, and *not* with the top of the text as you might expect. Similarly, ALIGN=middle aligns the middle of the image with the bottom of the text, not with the middle of the text. ALIGN=bottom gives you the default placement.

Netscape Extensions

The release of Netscape has included some HTML extensions that increase the options for the alignment of images. These extensions aren't part of the HTML v2.0 specification and are available only in Netscape; all other clients ignore them (implementing the default placement of ALIGN=bottom).

It's difficult to predict when or even whether other clients will implement these HTML extensions. Although they are becoming commonly used, they aren't part of any formal standard developed by the HTML Working Group. Despite the fact that the emerging HTML v3.0 standard (see Chapter 13, "Future Directions") allows even better image placement, an established Internet tradition favors the adoption of the first practical and implemented solution to a problem as an "official" standard.

All of the HTML extensions that the authors of Netscape provided either add functionality to HTML as a page layout language or fix poorly designed features in the original HTML. Since the primary authors of Netscape are also the original implementers of inline images in NCSA Mosaic, their additions to HTML in this area carry considerable weight.

The first of these additions is the use of ALIGN=texttop to correct the strange behavior of ALIGN=top. When you use ALIGN=texttop, Netscape aligns the top of the image with the top of the text, rather than with the top of the tallest element on the line. Likewise, ALIGN=absmiddle aligns the middle of the image with the middle of the text, rather than with the bottom of the text. To allow you to align the bottom of the image with the bottom of the lowest element in the line (including other images), Netscape also adds ALIGN=absbottom. The last of these variations on top, middle and bottom alignment is ALIGN=baseline, which does the same as ALIGN=bottom.

Two additional Netscape extensions to ALIGN are the left and right settings. When you specify ALIGN=left, your image is displayed in the next available space in the left-hand margin and text is wrapped around it, if necessary. ALIGN=right has the same effect, but Netscape places the picture in the right-hand margin. This effect is commonly known as "floating" the image. Table 7-1 lists all the Netscape ALIGN extensions.

ALIGN tag	Function
ALIGN=texttop	Aligns the top of the image with the top of the text.
ALIGN=absmiddle	Aligns the middle of the image with the middle of the text.
ALIGN=absbottom	Aligns the bottom of the image with the lowest element on the line.
ALIGN=baseline	This extension does the same as ALIGN=bottom.
ALIGN=left	Drops the image into the left-hand margin and wraps the text around it.
ALIGN=right	Drops the image into the right-hand margin and wraps the text around it.

Table 7-1: *Netscape ALIGN extensions.*

The <BR> tag, which tells the client to insert a carriage return and break the line, has been extended for use with floating images. As you can see in Figure 7-2 and from the HTML markup that follows, the <BR CLEAR=left> tag indicates to the client to break the line and move far enough down the page to avoid wrapping subsequent lines of text around images in the left margin. It's used as follows:

```
<IMG SRC="/pics/girl.gif" ALIGN=left ALT="Picture of pretty
girl">This is a picture of a good friend of mine, who often poses for
layouts in technical books. The hat was a gift from me!<BR
CLEAR=left><P>
I'm just kidding of course, this is an example picture from the xv soft-
ware package, which we will talk about later in the chapter. <P>
```

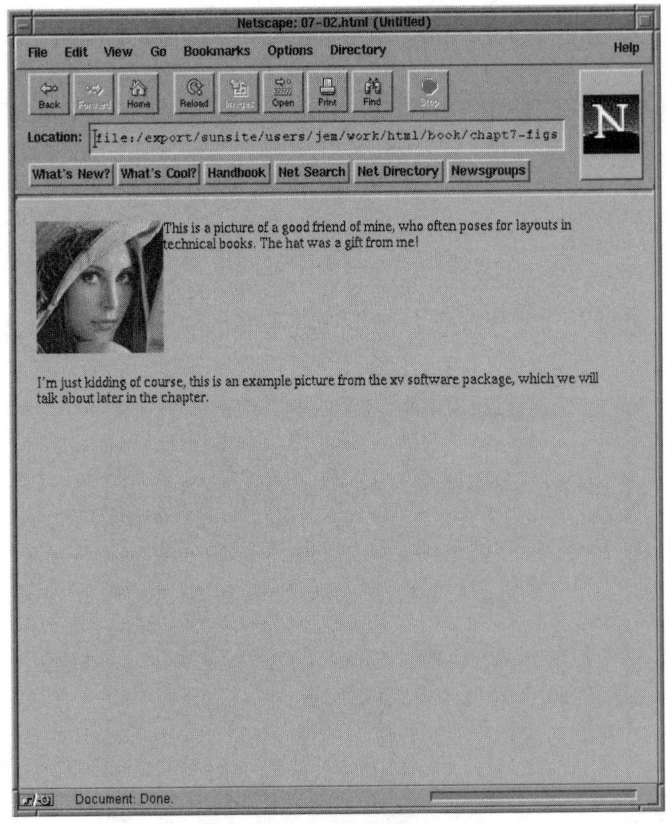

Figure 7-2: *Use of left alignment with the <BR CLEAR> tag.*

In the same way, the CLEAR=right tag spaces the subsequent text to avoid obscuring any images that are right aligned. You can avoid images on both sides by using the CLEAR=all setting.

The LEFT and RIGHT ALIGN extensions to the <IMG> tag, along with the addition of the CLEAR element to <BR> have been included in HTML v3.0, so other browsers will support them in time.

Netscape also adds two more settings, HSPACE and VSPACE, for the <IMG> tag. These settings are especially useful with floating images. Although Netscape honors these settings for use with all inline images, they are most often used with ALIGN=left and ALIGN=right. They allow you to specify the horizontal and vertical spacing, in pixels, between the floating image and the text that wraps around it.

You can see this effect in Figure 7-3, which is a page from an imaginary computer company's catalog. The alignment and spacing of the text and image in Figure 7-3 was created with the following ALIGN=left setting:

```
And here you see our top-of-the-line model, the SteamShoop 5000.
<IMG SRC="/pics/steamshoop.gif" ALT="" HSPACE=5 VSPACE=5
ALIGN=left>
This computer currently is in the Guinness Book of World
Records as the fastest steam-powered computer.
```

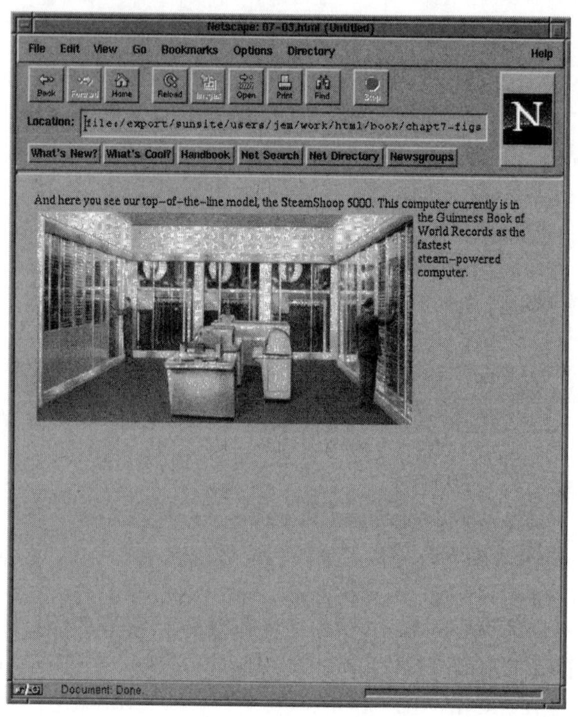

Figure 7-3: *Left-aligned image with horizontal and vertical space.*

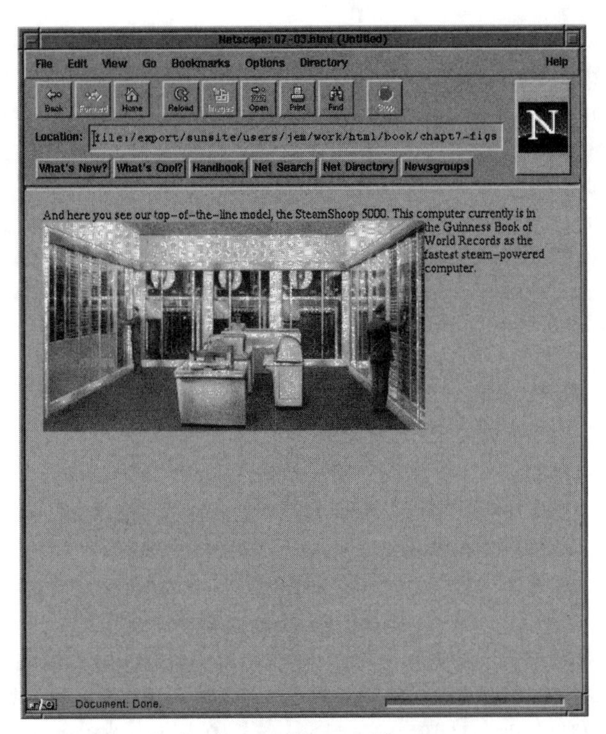

Figure 7-4: *Left-aligned image with no space.*

When you compare Figures 7-3 and 7-4, you can see that adding white space dramatically improves the clarity and readability of the page in Figure 7-3.

Two additional settings, WIDTH and HEIGHT, to the <IMG> tag that Netscape implements can help improve the performance of a client with a slow connection to the Internet. These settings allow you to specify, in pixels, the size of the image and they let browsers like Netscape, which display pages as they arrive at the browser, render the text next to an image without having to wait to download the image. Without these settings, the rendering is delayed because the client must retrieve the image in order to calculate its size on the page. These settings also allow you to rescale images on the fly; you can simply specify different HEIGHT and WIDTH settings for an image's actual size, and Netscape scales the image to those dimensions.

Although Netscape is currently the only client to implement them, these extensions are part of the HTML v3.0 standard, and other browsers will support them in time. To use these settings, you need to know the dimensions of your image. If you don't know the dimensions, you can use the Netpbm Toolkit to find these values. (See the sections "Manipulating Colormaps" and "Scaling Images" later in this chapter to learn how to use Netpbm.) When you know the dimensions of your image, you can add them to the <IMG> tag as follows:

```
<IMG SRC="/pics/girl.gif" ALT="" HEIGHT=125 WIDTH=125>
```

Another Netscape extension, BORDER, lets you create a black border around an inline image. The value you provide is the thickness of the frame (in pixels):

```
<IMG SRC="/pics/girl.gif" ALT="" BORDER=4>
```

Although few people use BORDER to put frames around regular inlines, this setting is often given a value of 0 to remove the border around a hyperlinked inline that serves as a button (see "Commonly Used Inlines") and around a transparent inline imagemap (see "Transparent GIFs" and "Clickable Imagemaps" later in this chapter).

Netscape also allows you to specify a lower resolution version of your inline image with the LOWSRC setting for the <IMG> tag. You can use this setting as follows:

```
<IMG LOWSRC="lowres.jpg" SRC="hires.gif" >
```

When Netscape reads the page on which this tag appears, it displays lowres.jpg on its first pass through the document as it renders the text. It makes a second pass through the document, retrieving hires.gif and displaying it in the place of lowres.jpg. If the two images take up different amounts of space on the page and you don't explicitly specify a size with the HEIGHT and WIDTH elements, the second image is scaled to the size of the first one.

Net.mavens (including ourselves) often deprecate the use of these extensions. One of the Web's strengths is its openness and the cross-compatibility of documents across different platforms and browsers. There is a risk that nonstandard HTML implementations will splinter the Web between incompatible pages and viewers. Despite this, more people are using these extensions in their pages, because the extensions address the needs of page designers. Although using them increases the risk that some people viewing your pages won't see what you originally intended them to see, the fact remains that perhaps as many as 70 percent of Web users, as of January 1995, are using a Netscape client. Many Web authors feel that the increased effectiveness of their pages for that majority outweighs the possibility of alienating a minority of their audience.

On the other hand, this high percentage of Netscape users will probably not last forever. Although Netscape is currently the most popular client, the Web is a young, and quickly changing technology. If Internet users abandon Netscape for some hot new browser, you may have to rewrite pages that heavily rely on Netscape extensions. By adhering to the standards, you ensure the long-term viability of your pages.

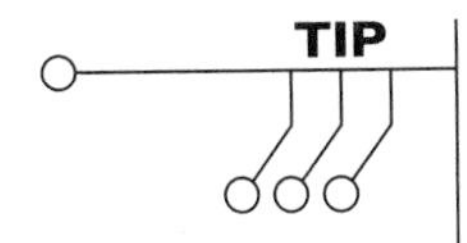

You can find more information about using the Netscape HTML extensions at http://www.netscape.com/home/services_docs/impact_docs/creating-high-impact-docs.html.GIFs & JPEGs

Although the miracles of MIME typing allow you to send any file format across the Web, only two graphics formats, GIF and JPEG, are commonly found on the Web. One sees the occasional XBM or even an XPM and, on the rarest of occasions, an IFF, but most authors use these two formats.

GIF

These acronyms can be fairly confusing at first, but you can sort them out pretty quickly. GIF is an acronym for Graphics Interchange Format. GIF was developed by the CompuServe Information Service in 1987. There are two variations on the format: GIF87a, which was the original specification, and GIF89a, which added some interesting features. These variations aren't important on the Web (but see the section "Transparent GIFs" later in this chapter for an exception). All Web browsers that support inline GIFs understand both varieties of GIF.

As a graphics format, GIF has many advantages. First, it's not difficult to write a program that decodes and displays GIFs, so this format enjoys a wide level of support; almost every image processing and drawing program can read and write graphics in GIF format. Also, the graphics information in the GIF is compressed with the LZW algorithm, so images in GIF format take a fourth or a fifth of the space taken by images in equivalent, uncompressed formats. This saves space on your server and saves time in transferring them over the network. An added bonus is that the compression used for GIFs is relatively fast to decode; once they're downloaded, GIFs can be displayed quite quickly on most computers.

The greatest disadvantage to using GIFs is that you are limited to only 256 colors in a single image. On the other hand, icon and cartoon-like images often use only a few colors, and GIF especially excels at compressing these sorts of images. For complex images though, such as scanned photographs, this limitation can lead to unattractive dithering. Dithering uses contrasting colors for adjacent pixels in order to create the illusion of additional colors. This process almost always degrades the quality of the image.

JPEG

The other commonly used graphic standard is JPEG. JPEG isn't really an image format; it's a compression standard. Usually though, JPEG refers to the JFIF format, which uses JPEG encoding. JPEG stands for Joint Photographic Experts Group, which is the name of the organization that developed the standard for the storage and transmission of photograph-style images with subtle gradations of color.

JPEG compression is "lossy"; this means that some of the information in the image is lost in the compression. This loss takes advantage of the natural limitations of the human eye, which perceives gradual changes in color with less accuracy than changes in brightness.

JPEG is the format of choice for storing complex real-world images. It supports "true-color," which is 24 bits of color information per pixel; this gives you a maximum of 16,777,216 colors, compared to the 256 offered by GIF. Not only does JPEG allow images much richer in color than GIF, but its compression algorithm really excels at compressing images that have subtle gradations of color. It's common for JPEG compression to shrink this sort of image to a tenth or a twentieth of its original size.

This clever algorithm has its downside: many clients are relatively slow when decoding JPEGs because the process is rather complex. For people downloading images over a slow connection to the Internet, the smaller size may make up for the greater time needed to display it. Another consideration to keep in mind when using JPEGs is that most computer displays are currently only 8 bit; therefore, they can display only 256 colors at a time. Programs displaying 24-bit images on 8-bit screens must dither them, which requires additional time. This situation is quickly changing; many new computers have true-color monitors, and as hardware standards change, JPEG will become more popular.

The most important consideration to remember when deciding whether to use JPEG for your image is that JPEG stores simple images poorly. If your image includes only a few colors (fewer than 16) or large areas of the same color, JPEG's lossy compression will distort it. Also, applying JPEG's lossy compression to this sort of image often results in a final product that is larger than the GIF version.

Further Thoughts on GIF vs. JPEG

Other considerations as to whether you should use GIF or JPEG images have nothing to do with the intrinsic merits of the formats. They concern the state of browser technology and legal issues. Until recently, graphical browsers allowed only GIFs as inlines. If you wanted to use JPEGs in your documents, you had to include them as hyperlinks. This situation has started to change. The current versions of the most popular graphical browsers (Netscape and Mosaic) support inline JPEG, and most other clients have plans to support them soon.

Until everyone has upgraded to browsers that support inline JPEGs, an excellent compromise is to link your high-quality JPEG images to icon-sized GIF inlines (see the next section, "Getting the

Best From Inline Images," to learn how to do this). Linking JPEG images to GIF inlines allows those interested in seeing greater detail to click the link and download the JPEG. Not only does this allow anyone with a graphical client to get the full benefit of your page, but the small GIFs usually load faster than JPEGs.

A recent controversy has risen about the legal future of the GIF format, which uses a patented compression technology. In the future, developers that use the GIF format in their programs may have to license the technology from the Unisys Corporation, which owns the patent. When Unisys announced this possibility in January 1995, a great outcry was heard from client developers, and many have started to look for a new format that could replace GIF.

Several new formats have been prototyped; all of them share the lossless compression and other features of GIF, and many sport added features, such as 24-bit color. One of these, the Portable Network Graphics (PNG) format, seems to be enjoying fairly wide support and has recently been embraced by CompuServe as its next-generation GIF24 format. You can learn more about the specification on the author's home page at http://sunsite.unc.edu/boutell/. Whether or not this specification becomes a new standard for the Net, some benefit has come from the disagreement because the controversy seems to have accelerated the development of browsers that support JPEG inlines.

Getting the Best From Inline Images

Adding an inline image or two to your page is quite easy, and every page designer likes using them. Unfortunately, many of the pages you see on the Web look awful. By taking care in selecting and manipulating your images, you can dramatically improve the appearance and clarity of your pages.

Manipulating Colormaps

Although 24-bit, true-color displays are becoming more popular, most clients will be running on 8-bit color displays, which means that only 256 colors can be on the user's screen at one time. Once the sum of all the colors used on the display exceeds this limit, the machine does its best to substitute an existing color for new requests. This attempt usually fails pretty miserably, and the result is often extremely distorted images.

Many browsers that display colored inlines try to alleviate this problem by limiting each image to a maximum number of colors. For example, NCSA XMosaic allows only 50 colors per image. This policy usually allows the client to display four or five inline images with minimal distortion, depending on the number of colors that are already being used by other applications. This solution is still less than satisfactory because many browsers dither rather poorly. In any case, you may want to include more than five inlines on a page at one time.

Luckily, all of the inline images on a single page can share a colormap. The easiest way to accomplish this is with the Netpbm Toolkit.

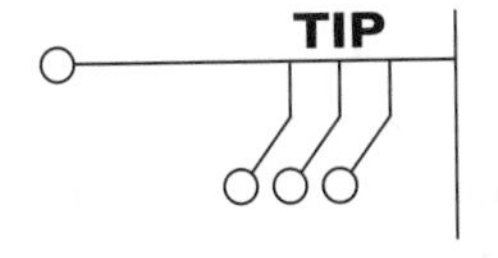

The current version of the netpbm tools can be found at ftp://ftp.x.org/contrib/utilities. The current version of the Independent JPEG Group's JPEG utilities can be found at ftp://ftp.uu.net/graphics/jpeg.

File Conversion With the Netpbm Toolkit

The Netpbm Toolkit contains dozens of programs, and each one does a single image-processing task. By using the Netpbm programs with UNIX pipes, you can easily manipulate an image in many different ways with a single command line.

To use this collection of programs, you must convert your image to one of the internal image formats that Netpbm supports. The toolkit includes many programs for this purpose. Other tools are available in the toolkit for converting images from the internal image formats to almost any graphic formats you choose. Of course, the toolkit includes more than conversion programs; it also has a large number of tools that can improve the appearance of your inlines.

To use the toolkit conveniently, you need to include its binary directory in your search path, as follows:

```
<cd>$ PATH=$PATH:/usr/local/netpbm/bin; export PATH
$ MANPATH=$MANPATH:/usr/local/netpbm/man; export MANPATH
```

This command line tells your shell where to look for the Netpbm binaries and documentation. After you set your path, the first step in manipulating images with the Netpbm Toolkit is to convert your files. The toolkit performs all of its image processing on files in one of its three internal formats, listed in Table 7-3.

Format	Full Name	Type of Image
PBM	Portable BitMap	black-and-white bitmap image
PGM	Portable GrayMap	grayscale image
PPM	Portable PixMap	full-color image

Table 7-3: *The internal graphic formats supported by Netpbm.*

The GIF conversion tool is part of a family of tools in the Netpbm Toolkit called the PNM (Portable aNyMap) tools. PNM tools can read and write all three Netpbm formats. Since GIFs can be color, black and white, or grayscale, the GIF conversion tool automatically picks the correct format and writes it. Since all the inlines that we're converting are color GIFs, we first translate them to PPM files, as follows:

```
$ giftopnm shoop.gif > shoop.ppm
```

This command converts a color GIF named shoop.gif to a color PPM named shoop.ppm. If you have an entire directory of GIFs that you wish to convert, you can use the built-in programming language of the UNIX shell to convert them all at one time:

```
$ for i in *.gif
> do
> file='basename $i .gif'
> giftopnm $i > $file.ppm
> done
```

You can easily convert JPEG images to PPM files as well. Although the Netpbm Toolkit doesn't have its own tools for handling JPEGs, there are JPEG tools that understand PPM. One consideration to keep in mind about JPEGs is that every time you convert to and from JPEG format, additional information is lost. Thus, you should minimize conversions by storing only the final product as JPEG. To convert a directory of JPEGs to PPM, you can use the following script:

```
$ for i in *.jpg
> do
> file='basename $i .jpg'
> djpeg -ppm $i > $file.ppm
> done
```

You can also convert images that aren't in GIF or JPEG format. Since the Netpbm Toolkit includes 52 different programs for converting images to its native formats, the format your images are in is probably included in the toolkit. See Table 7-4 for a list of popular image types and the proper Netpbm tool to use to convert them.

File Type	Conversion Tool
TIFF	tifftopnm
PCX	pcxtoppm
BMP	bmptoppm
PICT	picttoppm
SGI	sgitopnm
XPM	xpmtoppm
Targa	tgatoppm
MacPaint	macptopbm*
FITS	fitstopnm
Postscript	pstopnm**
Raw RGB	rawtoppm***

* Only converts the original, monochrome MacPaint format.
** To use pstopnm, you must have GhostScript, the PostScript interpreter, installed. It is installed with Stackware Linx and is available from ftp://prep.ai.mit.edu/pub/gnu.
*** PPM files read from raw RGB data may be upside down or transposed from left to right. If this is the case, the files can be corrected with pnmflip, which is also part of the Netpbm Toolkit.

Table 7-4: *Image formats and Netpbm tools that convert them.*

Table 7-4 includes most of the images that you're likely to encounter. If you do find some strange image format not included in this list, you can try converting it with anytopnm, another tool in the toolkit. anytopnm tries to detect the image type based on its structure and file extension. Since it's making a not-so-educated guess, don't expect great results from anytopnm. If anytopnm fails to detect your file type, you can check to see if a program for the format of your files exists by entering the following command:

```
$ apropos filetype
```

Replace *filetype* with the format that you think your image is in. Failing all else, you can post to the USENET newsgroup comp.graphics and ask if anyone knows how to convert your image to PPM.

Generating a Colormap

After you have converted all the images on a page to PPM, you need to find a common set of colors for them. This set should be large enough to avoid distortion but small enough that the Web client can display it on an 8-bit monitor. You can generate a new colormap for a directory of converted inlines with the pnmcat command.

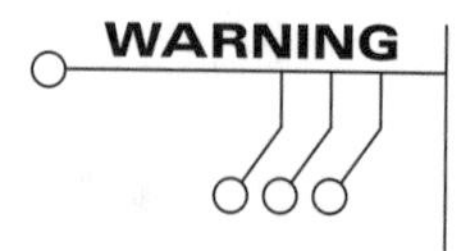

The map file that this step generates will be 10 to 20% percent larger than the sum of the sizes of all the images.

```
$ pnmcat -lr *.ppm | ppmquant 150 > mapfile
```

The pnmcat command combines any number of images into a single image. If you were to redirect the output of pnmcat to a file and view that file, you'd see all of your inlines combined, left to right, into a single image. Instead, the pnmcat command pipes that super image into ppmquant.

ppmquant tries to pick colors intelligently (using Heckbert's "median cut" algorithm) from the colors that you give it. It picks colors that accurately represent the original image. ppmquant then writes the same image as it read in, except the image has been modified to use its chosen colormap.

In the previous command line, we've told ppmquant to use only 150 colors, because that allows users with color monitors that support 256 colors to display without color distortion several other programs in addition to the Web client. Using only 150 colors also reduces the chance that any one image uses more than 50 colors, since 50 colors is the maximum number of colors per inline image that XMosaic allows.

Remapping the Images

At this point you need to modify your original images to use this new colormap. A script like the one that follows dithers an entire directory of PPM images, using the map file you created with the pnmcat command, while converting them to GIFs:

```
$ for i in *.ppm
> do
> file='basename $i .ppm'
> ppmquant -map mapfile $i | ppmtogif > $file-inline.gif
> done
```

At this point, you have three copies of your images: the original image file, the intermediate PPM file (which, unlike a GIF, isn't compressed) and the final color-corrected inline GIFs, not to mention having a map file that's a bit larger than the sum of all the PPM files. The lesson here is that image processing can require a lot of disk space! Luckily, you can now delete the PPM files and the colormap.

```
$ rm *.ppm
$ rm mapfile
```

Sometimes the colors that ppmquant chooses distort the final product. If you find the final product of this process unsatisfactory, you may wish to try generating a map file with more colors. Using more than 200 colors is probably a bad idea because it leaves few colors for the user's display.

In addition, you might want to try enabling the "Floyd-Steinberg error diffusion" step in ppmquant. This algorithm often produces dramatically better results when mapping a large number of colors to very few. Unfortunately, it's a computationally intensive process and can take a long time. You can enable this step by adding the -fs option to ppmquant, both when choosing a colormap and when using that map to convert the PPMs to GIFs.

Choosing a common colormap for the inline images on a page has a multitude of advantages. Not only does it improve the appearance of your page, but GIFs with fewer colors are smaller and are downloaded faster. Also, as long as the images are within the limits of a client's ability to display color, the client doesn't have to dither them itself, speeding the rendering of the page.

Interlaced GIFs

Another advantage of using GIFs for your inline images is interlacing. Interlaced GIFs hold the same contents as regular GIFs, but the rows of pixels aren't encoded from top to bottom. Instead, the lines of the image are interlaced, like a television display, so that the complete image appears in stages. The encoding software breaks the image down into four groups, starting from different points.

It's easiest to understand interlacing by studying an example; imagine an image with 20 rows, numbered from 0 to 19. The interlaced image begins with every eighth line of pixels and always starts with row 0; in the test image, this first group includes rows 0, 8 and 16.

The second group begins at row 4 and includes every eighth row from there. This group is rows 4 and 12. After the second group of rows, the third starts with row 2 and includes every fourth row from there: 2, 6, 10, 14 and 18. The final group begins with row 1 and contains every odd row; a complete listing of the four groups is in Table 7-5.

Group	Rows
1	0, 8, 16
2	4, 12
3	2, 6, 10, 14, 18
4	1, 3, 5, 7, 9, 11, 13, 15, 17, 19

Table 7-5: *Interleaved encoding for a 20-row GIF.*

This permuted encoding allows users to see the image decode as it arrives, getting more detail as the process continues. This especially favors viewers with slow connections because it allows them to decide when they've seen enough of an image and to terminate the connection before the client downloads the entire image.

Currently, not all clients decode and display interlaced GIFs as they arrive. Older browsers still wait until they've received all rows of the interlaced GIF and then display the image in its entirety. Still, as more clients fully support interlacing, it will be a real boon to users with slow connections. Not far in the future, users will be able to specify how much resolution they want in their interlaced images.

The actual process of activating interlacing in your inline images is very simple. The commands that follow convert a directory of inline GIFs to PPM format and then immediately pipe the output to ppmtogif to convert them back, with interlacing turned on:

```
$ for i in *.gif
> do
> file='basename $i .gif'
> giftopnm $i | ppmtogif -interlace > $file-i.gif
> done
```

This process is faster than first converting the files to an intermediate PPM file, and it takes less disk space. Still, you may wish to add a conversion step if you're going to further manipulate the images (see the section "Putting It Together" later in this chapter).

Scaling Images

As noted earlier, it's a common practice on the Web to have pages with icon-sized inline images (usually GIFs), each linked to a full-sized, high-quality image (usually a JPEG). The Netpbm tools make it simple to scale an image larger or smaller, while preserving the ratio between its X and Y dimensions (the aspect ratio).

Scaling by Factor

Suppose you have a directory of JPEG images that you wish to scale down to icon-sized inlines. You could use the following commands:

```
$ for i in *.jpg
> do
> file='basename $i .jpg'
> djpeg -ppm $i | pnmscale .25 >$file-inline.ppm
> done
```

First, these commands convert the JPEGs to PPM format using djpeg, with the -ppm option this decompresses the JPEG into a 24-bit PPM image. The converted output is piped to pnmscale, which reads a PBM, PGM or PPM file and scales it by a factor that you specify. In this example, since the factor is .25, the image is reduced to one quarter of its original size. The factor that you should choose depends on the size of the original image and how small you want your icon to be. After scaling, pnmscale writes the reduced image in the same format as the original. The result of the script is a directory of full-sized JPEGs and quarter-sized PPM files. Since PPM files are 24-bit, these files must be color-quantized before converting them to 3-bit GIFs. These considerations are explained in detail in "Putting It Together" later in this chapter.

Scaling JPEGs

You can use almost the same series of commands to generate icon-sized inline JPEGs. All you need to do is pipe the output to the JPEG compression tool, cjpeg, as follows:

```
$ for i in *.jpg
> do
> file='basename $i .jpg'
> djpeg -ppm $i | pnmscale .25 | cjpeg -Q 75 > $file-inline.jpg
> done
```

It's important to remember that each time you convert an image from JPEG to PPM and then back again, additional image quality is lost. You can control the "lossiness" of cjpeg's compression and, therefore, control the quality of the image with the -Q option. The number following the option should be between 50 and 95. Higher numbers lose less detail but result in poorer compression and larger images, while lower numbers improve compression at the expense of image quality. In the previous example, we use the default 75, which produces good results most of the time. If the loss of quality is visible, try increasing the value by 5 or 10 points at a time. If you want smaller files, decrease this value. Values below 50 are fairly useless if you want legible images; values between 95 and 100 make no real improvements in quality but dramatically increase the size of the final product.

Other Ways to Scale

You can use pnmscale in several other ways to reduce the size of an image. Rather than indicating a factor by which to scale both dimensions, you can specify the final size (in pixels) of either the X or Y dimension, and pnmscale adjusts the other dimension to preserve the aspect ratio. You can find the current dimensions of a PBM, PGM or PPM image by using the pnmfile program. For example, suppose you have a PPM file, image.ppm.

```
$ pnmfile generic-image.ppm
generic-image.ppm:   PPM raw, 640 by 480 maxval 255
```

The resolution of the image is 640 x 480, and you want to scale it so that the image is 200 pixels wide. The following command line would give you a 200 x 150 image:

```
$ pnmscale -xsize 200 generic-image.ppm > image-200x150.ppm
```

Similarly, to scale an image to a particular height, you can use the -ysize option, and pnmscale automatically adjusts the width.

You can use pnmscale to scale an image to fit within a certain number of pixels without disturbing the aspect ratio. Simply use the -pixels option followed by the number of picture elements that you want to include in the final image.

You can also scale images to a particular resolution by using the -xysize option:

```
$ pnmscale -xysize 200 150 generic-image.ppm > image-200x500.ppm
```

This command line scales the image to as close to 200 x 150 as possible, while retaining the aspect ratio.

Using pnmscale, you may also change the image without preserving the ratio of the sides. You can do this by scaling the width or height of the image by some factor; the other dimension will not be scaled at all. Thus, you can use the following command on a 640 x 480 image:

```
$ pnmscale -xscale .25 generic-image.ppm > image-ugly.ppm
```

The result will be an extremely distorted 160 x 480 image. Although there's no obvious use for this ability, you may need it to produce special effects.

Similarly, you can scale an image to any particular resolution you wish, regardless of aspect ratio. To do this, use the -xsize and -ysize options together, as follows:

```
$ pnmscale -xsize 740 -ysize 230 generic-image.ppm > image-weird.ppm
```

This command would write an 740 x 230 image, no matter what the original dimensions were.

Enlarging Images

Implicit in all of the examples in the previous section is the fact that you can use pnmscale to enlarge an image, as well as to reduce it. Both scaling factors larger than one and pixel counts greater than the original give you a larger copy of your image. Unfortunately, the problem with enlarging images is that the amount of information in the original image isn't actually increased. The pixels get bigger, and the image looks grainy and artificial. This distortion becomes extremely noticeable when the image is three times greater than its original size. You can mitigate this effect by combining pnmsmooth with pnmscale, as in the following command line:

```
$ pnmscale 3 image.ppm | pnmsmooth > big-image.ppm
```

This example enlarges image.ppm 300 percent and then smoothes the result before writing the final product as big-image.ppm. pnmsmooth takes the color value of each pixel and replaces it with the average of each of its nine neighbors. This "smoothing" reduces the distinctiveness of the border between pixels, at the expense of reducing the overall sharpness.

Transparent GIFs

As you start spiffying up your pages, you'll want to add special effects to them. A common desire is a fancy logo, flush to the page, but most image formats allow only rectangular borders. Fortunately the GIF format provides a way around this annoying limitation—the transparency index.

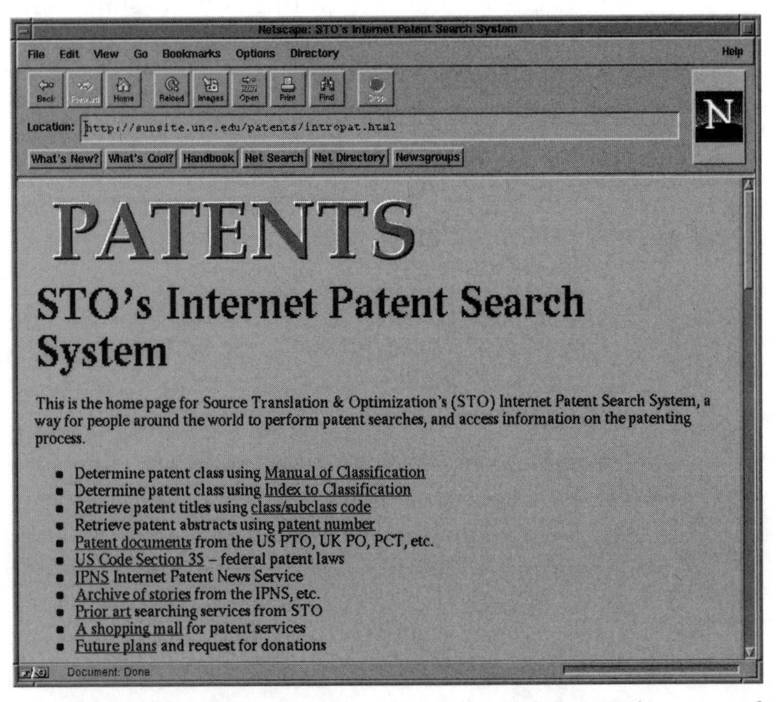

Figure 7-5: *A logo using transparency on the STO Patents home page, http://sunsite.unc.edu/intropat.html.*

The transparent color index is a field in the GIF header that indicates to the browser that one color in the image's colormap should be changed to a "color to be named later." The browser encounters this field when rendering the GIF and changes all occurrences of the transparent color to whatever color the background color of the page is. This feature is only available in the GIF89 version of the GIF standard; tools that allow you to use it will silently translate GIF87a images to the newer standard.

Turning on Transparency

The easiest way to take advantage of the transparency index is to make sure your image has a single background color that appears nowhere else in the image. This is important because any part of the image with the transparent color will disappear when the image is displayed by the browser. An easy way to ensure that your image has a single background color that appears nowhere else in the image is to use a paint program, like the free program xpaint, to change the background color to something unlikely to appear in the rest of the image. We find that bright pink or lime green is usually a good choice.

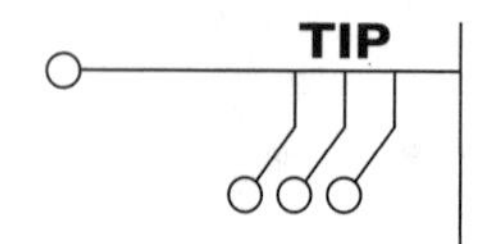

If you're using Slackware Linux, you should already have xpaint installed. If you're using another OS, or you want the newest version, go to ftp://ftp.x.org/contrib/utilities.

Another strategy is to cater to the few clients that don't understand the transparent GIF extension. To do so, make the transparent background of your image neutral gray (RGB values 190, 190, 190). Since this color is the default background on most browsers, it blends smoothly with the background of clients that don't support transparency.

After you've made sure that all the parts of the image that you want transparent are the same color and that color appears nowhere else in the image, you're ready to begin. The first step is to find out exactly what color, in terms of its RGB components, you're trying to turn transparent. The easiest way to do this is in X Windows with xv. xv is a powerful (and free!) WYSIWYG image-processing program that has a great number of useful features, almost none of which we are going to use. Load your GIF in xv as follows:

```
$ xv image.gif
```

After a moment, your image should appear in a window. Click the left mouse button in the window that contains the image while dragging the pointer about; a series of numbers, similar to the following, appear at the top of the window:

```
22, 104 = 111, 32, 68 (332 71 43 HSV)
```

If the image is so small you can't see at least the first five numbers, press the greater than key (>) while your pointer is inside the image. This doubles the size of the window and scales the image to fit inside it.

The first two numbers in the string are the X and Y coordinates of the pixel that the pointer is touching. The next three numbers are the RGB values for the pixel, and the final three are the hue, saturation and color values for the pixel. The only numbers we're concerned with are the RGB values; these are the red, green and blue components that make up the color of that pixel.

Left-click in the part of the image you want to make transparent and note the RGB values. By dragging the pointer around with the left mouse button pressed, you can check and make sure that the area is all the same color. All the pixels in the area should have the same values.

As mentioned previously, xv is a powerful program and an excellent piece of free software. We heartily recommend you explore its image-processing abilities. We don't discuss them here because they are mostly outside the domain of this book. You can click the right mouse button inside the image to access the xv control panel and explore the features on your own. xv also has an excellent manual in PostScript, which you can find in /usr/local/lib/xv. If you don't have access to a PostScript viewer (GhostView, for example) or a PostScript printer, the man page for xv contains the same manual minus appendixes and figures. To access the xv man page, type the following:

```
$ man xv
```

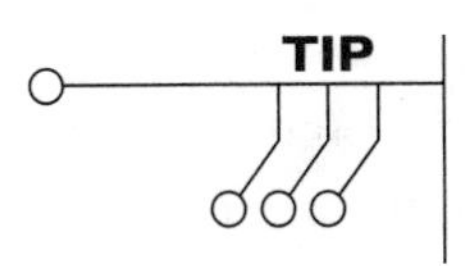

Newer versions of xv are available, but they are affordable shareware, not freeware. If you want to check them out, you can get the newest version at ftp://ftp.cis.upenn.edu/pub/xv.

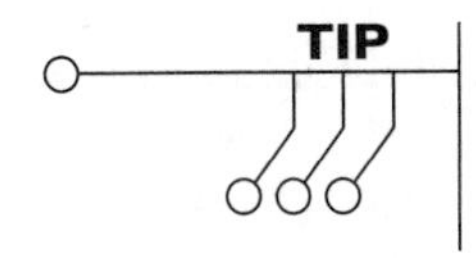

GhostView is an X-Window PostScript viewer that uses the free GhostScript interpreter. You can find the portable source for it at ftp://prep.ai.mit.edu/pub/gnu.

In any case, after you have determined the RGB value of the color you want to make transparent, you are ready to use transgif.pl to add the transparent color index to your GIFs. Since this program is written in perl, you need to have perl installed on your system to run it. Using it is quite simple, as the following command line illustrates:

```
$ transgif.pl -rgb R G B image.gif > trans-image.gif
```

R, G and B are the three values you noted in xv; transgif marks the color this represents as transparent and writes a new GIF on its output.

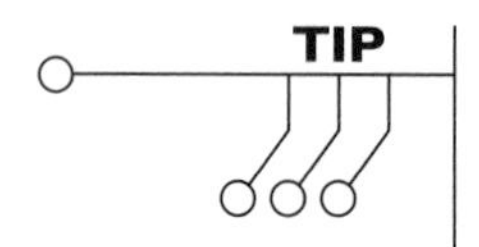

The transgif.pl script was written by Jeffrey Friedl (jfriedl@omron.co.jp). You can find the newest version of it at http://www.mit.edu:3001/people/nocturne/etc/trans.transgif.html.

Other Uses for Transparency

Some page designers use one-pixel-thick, transparent GIFs as blank space between adjacent inline images. We think this is a bad idea. Not only will the page's appearance differ depending on the browser used, but it will also change depending on the dimension to which the user has resized his or her viewing window. If you do want to experiment with using transparent GIFs for blank space, it's easy to create them with the Netpbm tools. The following command creates a one-pixel-high, black, transparent GIF:

```
$ ppmmake 0,0,0 width 1 | ppmtogif -transparent 0,0,0 > padding.gif
```

Substitute the length of the GIF you wish to create for *width*. Although, ppmtogif can also be used to add transparency to a GIF, since it accepts only the RGB components in hexadecimal or a strange decimal notation, we wanted to spare you the anguish of dealing with it here. You can read the ppmmake man page for information on the RGB notations that Netpbm finds acceptable.

In any case, we strongly discourage you from using transparent GIFs to provide blank space. The results are unpredictable, and it's all around bad HTML style. If you must add space, you should use the Netscape HTML extensions, HSPACE and VSPACE, to the <IMG> tag, which give you better effects in browsers that support them (see the section "Netscape Extensions" earlier in this chapter).

Transparent GIFs open all sorts of possibilities in your page design; you can use them for a variety of effects, including fancy headings, diagrams and screen captures of tables and charts, created in other programs. The appropriate use of transparent GIFs can give your page a professional appearance, while careless abuse of the feature might make people wonder about your eyesight.

Putting It Together

One of the nicest features of the UNIX command line is that it allows you to build complex scripts from simple tools. By linking commands together with pipes and the built-in command language of the shell, you can accomplish a great deal at one time. The orthogonal nature of the Netpbm tools lets you easily take advantage of these features, but you should consider several points before trying to integrate all of the above steps into a single command.

Before you begin manipulating your images, you need to decide whether you want a transparent background in any of the inlines on the page that you're currently creating. If you do, you should have already used your favorite paint program to make sure that all of the bits you want transparent are the same color. To make it easier on yourself (and avoid garishness on clients that don't support transparency), use the same background color for all of the transparent images on the same page.

After you finish touching up your pictures, you first have to convert the images to the proper Netpbm format, usually PPM. What might not be obvious is where to go from there. Since the length of time most graphic manipulations take is proportional to the number of pixels in the image, an excellent candidate for the second step is reducing the size of the image with pnmscale. Even if you are going to increase the image's size, you should scale the image before manipulating the color maps, because the scaling and smoothing operations will change the color values of individual pixels. For this reason, you should postpone all of the other operations that we've discussed in this chapter until after you've settled on a size for the inline.

After you've scaled the image to an appropriate size, the next step should be color quantization. Since this is a two-step process—first choosing a colormap, then actually changing the individual images to use that map—you need to write down the scaled PPMs before starting. We'll consider this a temporary stopping point and list the commands for what you've done so far:

```
$ for i in *.jpg
> do
> foo='basename $i .jpg'
> djpeg -ppm $i | pnmscale .25 > $foo.ppm
> done
```

Now that you have a directory of reduced PPM files, you can continue with the color quantization. Remember that the map file that you create will be 10 to 20 percent larger than the sum of all the images put together, so make sure that you have enough disk space before starting. Simply create the map file by entering the following command line:

```
$ pnmcat -lr *.ppm | ppmquant 150 > mapfile
```

After you create the map file, you can quantize each image in turn. Although each of the new quantized images will be as large as the input files, you can delete the originals as you go:

```
$ for i in *.ppm
> do
> ppmquant -map mapfile $i > $i-q
> mv $i-q $i
> done

$ rm mapfile
```

After scaling and quantization, the colormaps of your images shouldn't change any further. Now it's safe to use xv on these new PPM files to look for the RGB value of the color you want to make transparent. Since the previously taken steps may have changed the RGB value for the background, don't use any color information you might have gotten from your paint program. You should wait until you've finished the rest of the image processing before finding the RGB values.

After you've determined the RGB value that you want to make transparent (let's say it's 230, 23, 23—an attractive lime green), you're ready to convert the images to GIF and add interlacing if you want to:

```
$ for i in *.ppm
> do
> foo='basename $i .ppm'
> transgif -rgb 230 23 23 $i | ppmtogif -interlace > $foo.gif
> rm $i
> done
```

This script assumes you want to add transparency to every image, and you probably don't. As long as your chosen transparent color doesn't appear in any of the other images, you'll be okay running transgif on all of them. If the chosen transparent color is being used in other images, you'll have to add transparency and convert the images separately.

When you're through, you should have a directory containing the original images (in this example, JPEGs) and the inlines that you want to use, properly scaled, quantized, transparent and interlaced. Although you probably won't want to apply every manipulation to every inline you create, you can link the steps you do desire as long as you follow these guidelines:

- Scale your images first.
- Color quantize before adding transparency.
- Avoid temporary files when possible by piping the output of one command to the input of another.
- To save space, delete unnecessary temporary files.

Commonly Used Inlines

If you've done a fair amount of surfing on the Web, you've probably noticed that certain styles of inlines, as well as a few specific icons and images, pop up again and again. Although many people create these from scratch, several collections of images, icons and clip art are archived on the Web. As we take a quick tour of these servers, we'll introduce you to the common uses of some of these simple, but useful, images.

Pretty Little Dots

Probably the most commonly used type of inline on the Web is what we call PLDs—Pretty Little Dots. These small, 3D shaded spheres are often used in combination with the <BR> tag in place of HTML's bulleted lists, like this:

```
<h2>My Grocery List</h2>
<IMG SRC="pld.gif" ALT="*">Milk.<BR>
<IMG SRC="pld.gif" ALT="*">Honey.<BR>
<IMG SRC="pld.gif" ALT="*">Tofu.<BR>
<IMG SRC="pld.gif" ALT="*">Milkbones.<BR>
```

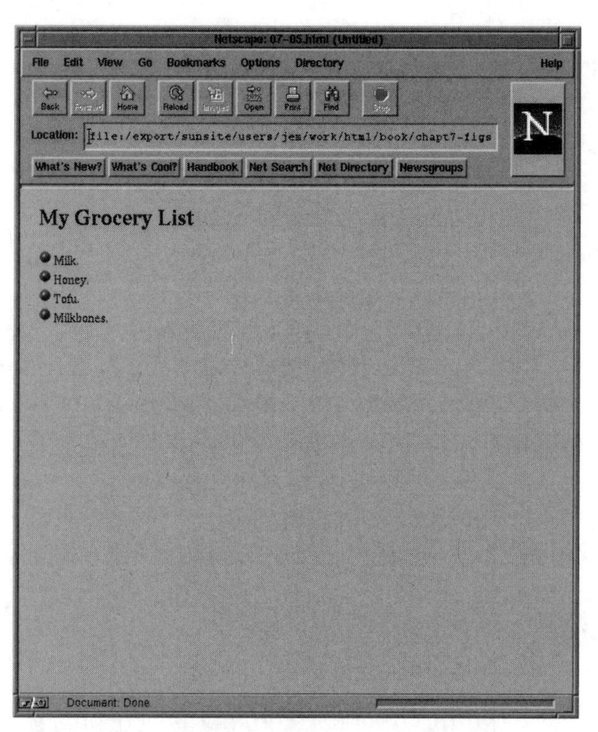

Figure 7-6: *A pseudo-list using dots and <BR> tags.*

As you can see in Figure 7-6, the previous markup gives you a fairly satisfactory looking result, but it has a serious problem—it's not a real unordered list. Although some clients may render it identically to an unordered list, others use special indenting to set lists off from the rest of the text. More importantly, this usage violates HTML's purpose as a structural markup language. If you don't use HTML's ability to indicate content and concentrate on appearance instead, the client loses its ability to treat your text intelligently.

Unfortunately, HTML v2.0 doesn't allow you to retain strict structural markup of your lists while using graphics for bullets. (HTML v3.0 does—see Chapter 13, "Future Directions.") There is a compromise, though, that retains some structure and improves the appearance of your page on many clients. You can use HTML's defining lists (see Chapter 2, "The Basic Pieces") without definitions, to achieve the appearance of a bulleted list. The following is an example of how to do it:

```
<DL>
<DT><IMG SRC="pld.gif" ALT="*">Quail
<DT><IMG SRC="pld.gif" ALT="*">Pheasant
<DT><IMG SRC="pld.gif" ALT="*">Grouse
</DL>
```

This markup creates a three-item list with these attractive dots as bullets. Although the list is not really the proper type (<UL> would be the correct tag), at least this markup more closely represents the actual structure of the text.

URL	http://www.jsc.nasa.gov/~mccoy/Icons/balls/
Description	Lots of dots are in Daniel's Icon Archive.
URL	http://www.idb.hist.no/~geirme/gizmos/gizmo.html
Description	Mosaic Gizmos has color dots, lines, buttons, pointers and illustrations.
URL	http://melmac.corp.harris.com/images.html
Description	This site prefers color squares to color dots.

Table 7-6: *Sources for pretty little dots.*

Color Bars

Another very common convention on the Web is the use of brightly colored horizontal bars, which take the place of the HTML <HR> tag that draws a horizontal rule across the page. Unfortunately, this usage also goes against the structural guidelines of HTML in the same way that using little dots for bullets does. Even worse, no semi-structural workaround is available for this usage; if you want to use color bars to divide your pages, you'll have to break the rules. Here's how to do it:

```
<IMG SRC="bar.gif"
ALT="-------------------------------------------------------------------------------------------">
```

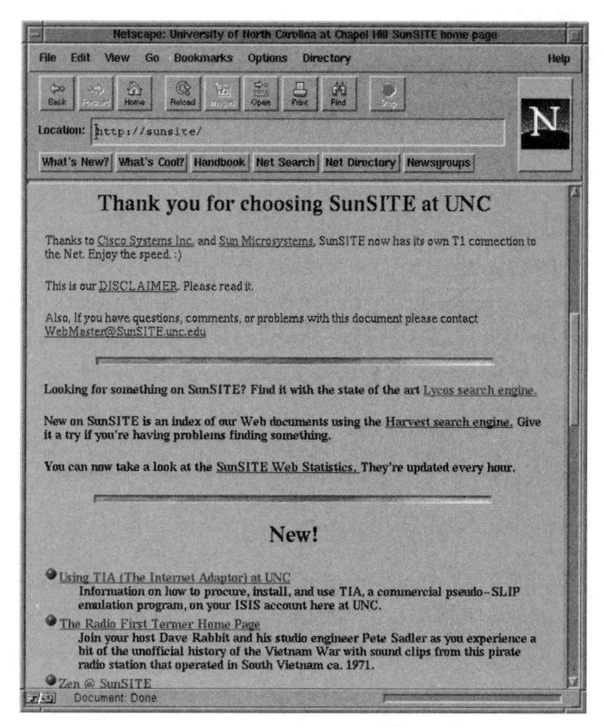

Figure 7-7: *Color bars on the sunsite.unc.edu home page.*

This ALT specification at least gives users of nongraphical browsers some sort of divider, although it's not identical to the horizontal rule that Lynx uses. Again, we'll have to wait for HTML v3.0 to be widely implemented for the structural solution to this problem (see Chapter 13, "Future Directions").

URL	http://www.jsc.nasa.gov/~mccoy/Icons/lines/
Description	Many bars are available in Daniel's Image Archive.
URL	http://www.cs.vu.nl/~dsbouma/grab/rulers.html
Description	Mosaic Rulesz [*sic*] specializes in color bars.
URL	http://melmac.corp.harris.com/images.html
Description	You can find a few pretty bars at this site.

Table 7-7: *Sources for color bars.*

Navigation Buttons & Icons

The Apple Macintosh and other GUIs have made the icon-laden desktop a familiar metaphor to most users. This paradigm has also become prevalent on the Web; thousands of icons are out there, used in many different ways.

One of the most common uses for these icons is as buttons for navigational aids. Often, HTML pages are linked in series, like pages in a book. Thus, it's useful to add little buttons to the top and bottom of each page, so the user can simply click them to move to the previous or next page.

There are many different styles of navigation icons, but we especially like the look of 3D shaded buttons, with no borders (see the section "Netscape Extensions," earlier in this chapter), as shown in Figure 7-8. This is, of course, just our personal preference, and many variations are available, including pointing fingers and colored arrows. When using this type of navigation aid, don't forget to include ALT settings, such as the following, for users on nongraphical browsers:

```
<A href="page3.html"><IMG SRC="/pics/prev.gif" ALT="[Previous]"
BORDER=0></A> <A href="toc.html"><IMG SRC="/pics/home.gif"
ALT="[Back Home]" BORDER=0></A><A href="page5.html"><IMG SRC="/
pics/next.gif" ALT="[Next]" BORDER=0></A>
```

Figure 7-8: *A navigation button bar.*

If you position such a button bar at the top and the bottom of each page in your text, you give the user a quick and attractive way to navigate your pages. HTML v3.0 (see Chapter 13, "Future Directions") provides the <LINK> tag as a standard way to present these navigation buttons so that they'll always be visible on the page.

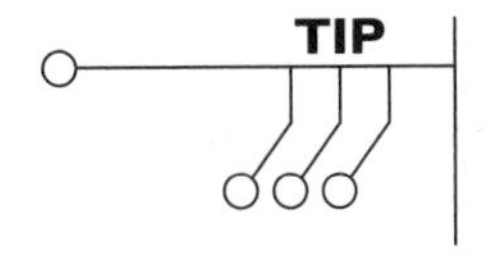

You can also use icons to announce new features (as shown in Figure 7-9), work in progress (see Figure 7-10), hyperlinks to sounds and movies (as shown in Figures 7-11 and 7-12, respectively) and whatever else you desire.

Figure 7-9: *Exclamation mark icon.*

Figure 7-10: *"Under construction" icon.*

Figure 7-11: *"Audio hyperlink" icon.*

Figure 7-12: *"Film reel" icon.*

In Table 7-8, you'll find a list of icon archives. Not all of the icons found at the sources listed in Table 7-8 will be in GIF format; quite a few, in fact, are XPM and XBM images, which are easy to convert to GIF with the Netpbm Toolkit (see the section "File Conversion With the Netpbm Toolkit" earlier in this chapter).

URL	http://www.jsc.nasa.gov/~mccoy/Icons/
Description	Daniel's Icon Archive.
URL	http://www.yahoo.com/Computers/ World_Wide_Web/
Description	Programming/Icons/ the Yahoo Icon Page.
URL	http://www.di.unipi.it/iconbrowser/icons.html
Description	University of Pisa Searchable Icons.

Table 7-8: *Sources for buttons and other icons.*

The icons at the sites listed in Table 7-8 are excellent ways to spruce up your page, especially if you're not particularly gifted artistically. Before using them, be sure to carefully read their copyright statements. Even if free use is granted, it's always good manners to give credit to the people whose work has helped you.

In addition, remember that many users have slow network links. They'll be annoyed if it takes a ridiculous amount of time to load your page because you've added too many spiffy icons. A picture is worth a thousand words, but that's only 5000 bytes; many icons are much larger.

Clickable Imagemaps

HTML provides a special type of inline image—the imagemap. You indicate that an inline is an imagemap with the ISMAP attribute. When a user activates the imagemap's hyperlink, the client sends the server the coordinates of the point on which the user clicked. These coordinates are processed by a special program that returns a URL to the client based on how you've mapped the image.

The use of imagemaps on Web pages gives the user the impression of real interactivity. The use of a creative imagemap, over and above simply embedding buttons in a background, can be a very impressive addition to the page. However, do not rely exclusively on imagemaps to provide links to various parts of your site because not all clients load images or are even able to. After you have constructed an imagemap, include links below the image to all of the pages that the imagemap is referencing or provide a link to a text page with those links on it. Doing so prevents your page from being nonfunctional when a text-based browser accesses it.

An imagemap contains three components. One is the image itself, which must be in GIF format. This image can be anything you want. Outside of sensible design standards, there are no restrictions on how the image must look or on how large it must be.

Another component is the link that is put in whatever document contains the imagemap. The newest version of the imagemap program allows you to place the imagemap file (described later in this section) in any location. This means that you simply make a hyperlink to the imagemap program itself and provide the map file information in that reference. For example, if a map file called people.map is located in /html/users/homepages/, and the imagemap program is located in the server's cgi-bin directory (see Chapter 3, "Setting Up the Server"), the link would be the following:

```
<A HREF="/cgi-bin/imagemap/users/homepages/people.map">
<IMG ALT=""SRC="faces.gif" ISMAP></A>
```

This markup links the file faces.gif to the imagemap file people.map. The version of the imagemap program that allows this is installed with the server package and is included on the Companion CD-ROM. However, if for some reason you are using an older version of the imagemap program, you need to identify the map file in a different way.

For the older version, shipped with version 1.3 and earlier, a file called imagemap.conf is located in /usr/local/etc/httpd/conf. If it's not, you'll need to create one. This file contains the names of aliases that point to the location of the map file. Again, assuming that the map file is located in /html/users/homepages/ and is called people.map, you would make the following entry into the imagemap.conf file:

```
people : /html/users/homepages/people.map
```

The word *people* acts as an alias to the correct location of the map file. Then, in the reference that you make in the Web page itself, you should enter the following link:

```
<A HREF="/cgi-bin/imagemap/people">
<IMG ALT="*" SRC="faces.gif" ISMAP></A>
```

This link passes the command people to the imagemap program that then turns to the imagemap.conf file, which sends it to the map file itself. The current imagemap program is backwards compatible with the old method; if you don't provide a valid map file, the program looks in imagemap.conf.

Using either type of imagemap reference, you can put the file that contains the imagemap coordinates anywhere. This file, the map file, is the third component of the imagemap. It is standard to give a map file the extension .map. The map file should have the following format:

```
default         http://www.domain.com/
# Send users to the House of Debuggin'
rect    http://house.debuggin.com/info/index.html          101,234 152,300
circle  gopher://gopher.doc.ic.ac.uk:7001/          53,42 53,96
poly    index.html          25,10 39,1 52,29 45,40 28,40
```

The first line of the map file, beginning with "default", should give the location that the user goes to if he or she clicks outside of any of the shapes that you identify in the imagemap. Subsequent lines are broken down into the shape of the range of coordinates to be linked, the location to which they are linked and the coordinates that the program uses to construct the boundaries of the range. The imagemap program ignores comments, which begin with the pound sign.

The example gives the three types of shapes that the imagemap program can recognize: the rectangle, the circle and the polygon. The coordinates for each shape should be identified differently. For rectangles, you should enter the coordinates of two diagonally opposite corners (left top corner and right bottom corner, in this case). For circles, give the coordinates of the center and any point on the circumference. For polygons, enter the coordinates of all of the corners. It is possible to overlap the coordinates for two images. Whichever set of coordinates comes first in the map file is the link that is followed. For example, if you want to create concentric circles that will have different links assigned to them, you could make a map file similar to the following:

```
default http://www.floofco.com/map-links-text.html
circle  http://www.floofco.com/products/ 100,100 100,135
circle  http://www.floofco.com/services/ 100,100 100,150
circle  http://www.floofco.com/info/     100,100 100,175
circle  http://www.floofco.com/index.html        100,100 100,199
```

If the user clicked inside the centermost circle, with a radius of 35, he or she would be sent to the file index.html in the directory products; the second circle would take him or her to the services directory and so on. Clicking outside the circles would take the user to the file map-links-text.html, which could contain the text links to the various files or directories. It should be noted that the full URL, *http://www.domain.com*, is optional. If the file or files are on the same server as the imagemap, you can simply enter the path and file name, and the imagemap program assumes that it is opening a local file.

Assuming that, like most of us, you're not very good at counting pixels in an image to get the coordinates, you'll need to use a program that provides them. At the risk of sounding primitive, the most reliable way to obtain these coordinates is to use xv with a pen and piece of paper. If you need to review using xv, reread the introduction to it given earlier in this chapter in the section "Turning on Transparency."

After you have loaded an image into xv, you can use the mouse to get the coordinates by following these steps:

1. Simply hold down the left mouse button and move the mouse to the first point for which you want the coordinates. In the corner of the image window, you'll see a line of numbers similar to the following appear:

   ```
   22, 104 = 111, 32, 68 (332 71 43 HSV)
   ```

The first two numbers are the coordinates for that point. The numbers in this line change as you move the mouse.

2. Write down those coordinates because they disappear when you let go of the mouse.
3. Repeat this process for the rest of the points you need to identify.

After you've identified the coordinates for the corners or center and circumference of all of your included shapes, you can use a standard text editor to make your map file.

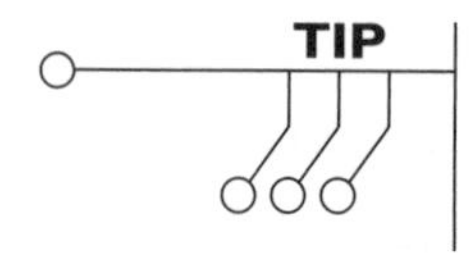

There are a number of programs that automatically generate the map file for you. In most of these programs, you simply click on the corners of the shape or draw the box or circle that you want to serve as your linked area. A collection of these programs can be found at the URL http://www.stars.com/Vlib/Providers/Imagemaps.html.

Moving On

This chapter has moved us into the wonderful realm of image processing for HTML. Although we've covered a lot of material, not all of it is immediately important. After you have learned the basic principles of image formats, of the HTML <IMG> tag and of simple image processing, you can pick up new skills and ideas as your pages become more complex.

Images have been an important part of traditional publishing for centuries. The next chapter introduces a capability that's really an electronic publishing innovation: the embedding of audio and animation directly onto the page. After you've grasped the essentials of electronic sound and movies, combined with your understanding of images, you'll have truly arrived in the world of networked multimedia.

8

True Multimedia: Adding Audio & Animation

The proliferation of graphical and intuitive user interfaces based on hypertext technologies has spawned an increasing interest in the use of computer networks for audio and video file distribution. While the basic technologies that permit such distribution have been around for quite a few years now, the Web has encouraged numerous individuals and companies that once shied away from multimedia technologies to examine the ways in which the addition of sound and animation might enhance the content of their Web pages. In turn, this increased interest has intensified the efforts of many software developers and media producers to customize their products for distributed-media environments.

The ability to embed audio and animation files into hypertext documents has astounding implications. Numerous high-quality media archives are already on the Net, and as the speed, storage capabilities and available bandwidth of computer networks increase, we're sure to witness the continued migration of traditional media to the digital realm.

In order to understand the (r)evolution that media and communication are currently undergoing, it is imperative that you gain a basic working knowledge of the technologies involved. This chapter introduces the various audio and video file types currently in use on the Internet, the underlying concepts that have led to the proliferation of multimedia technologies online and the software tools necessary for you to use these files. Finally, we discuss the ways in which you can incorporate audio and video files into your own pages so that you can get started right away.

Digital Audio on the Internet

The introduction of digital audio recording and playback techniques has revolutionized the ways in which music is made, stored and transmitted. Since digital information can be copied and manipulated without degradation, digital audio recording technologies have placed the holy grail of audio engineers in the hands of the many, and with a few simple tools, the grail can be yours, too.

Before discussing the various audio file formats in use on the Net, it's important that you gain an understanding of the basic underlying concepts of digital audio. We only scratch the surface in this section, but the information we provide should be enough to get you started and to help you decide which file formats are right for you.

Obviously, the first step in getting audio onto the Net is transferring it into your computer. In order to digitize an analog audio source, such as the output from a tape deck or microphone, the signal must be processed through an analog-to-digital (A/D) converter. Many workstations come equipped with sound cards that have A/D converters on them. If your computer has a sound input jack, it already has an A/D converter. If your computer provides only a sound output jack (usually a female 1/8" jack on the rear panel of the machine) or an internal speaker, you may only have digital-to-analog conversion capabilities.

Even if you're recording audio from a digital source, such as a digital audio tape (DAT) or compact disk (CD), some kind of A/D conversion is usually involved because most computers do not come equipped with digital audio inputs yet. In this case, the digital signal is converted to an analog signal within the hardware of the DAT or CD and sent through the analog output (usually a 1/8" jack). The analog signal travels along the line plugged into your computer and is redigitized by the workstation's sound board. The same is true of most CD-ROM players with regular audio-CD playback capabilities. Even though some CD-ROM players have digital outputs, most often the sound cards to which they connect do not.

The basic tenets of how audio is digitized are quite simple. An A/D converter utilizes a "sample and hold" circuit that records the voltage levels of the input signal at a fixed interval. This interval, or rate, at which the signal is sampled is determined by the A/D converter's "sampling rate." The sampling rate determines the highest frequency that can be recorded or played back, which can be found by dividing the sampling rate in half. This is based on the Nyquist theorem, which basically states that a sampling rate must be twice that of the highest frequency to be sampled. For instance, if an audio source is sampled at 44.1kHz, the highest frequency that can be accurately recorded is 22.05kHz.

Many hard disk audio recording and playback packages allow sampling rates to be user-defined. It's a common mistake for people to play back audio files at a sampling rate different than the ones at which they were sampled. This mistake results in the alteration of the file's pitch and duration. For instance, if you play back an audio file at 44.1kHz that was originally sampled at 22.05kHz, the output pitch will be much higher than the original, and the output length will be half of what it's supposed to be. This is similar to playing a 33 rpm album at 45 rpm (the Alvin and the Chipmunks effect). Likewise, if you play back a file at 22kHz that was recorded at 44.1kHz, the pitch will be much lower than the original, and the length will be twice what it's supposed to be.

Table 8-1 lists the most frequently used sampling rates.

Sampling Rate in Hertz (Hz)	Descriptions
8k	8kHz is a telephony standard that is emerging as a standard for 8-bit µ-law (.au) mono files (you'll find more information on the µ-law forms in the section "Audio File Formats" later in this chapter).
11k	11kHz is used to refer to either 11.025kHz (one quarter of the CD sampling rate) or 11.1272727 (half the Mac sampling rate).
22k	22kHz refers to either 22.05k (one half of the CD sampling rate) or 22254.545454545454k (the Mac sampling rate—the horizontal scan on the original 128k Mac). This is emerging as a standard for 8-bit unsigned mono and stereo file formats.
32k	The sampling rate of long-play (LP) digital audio tape decks, also of Japanese HDTV (high-resolution television) systems.
44.056k	Used by professional audio hardware to fit an integral number of samples into a video frame.
44.1k	The standard audio CD sampling rate. This is emerging as a standard for 16-bit linear signed mono and stereo file formats.
48k	The primary DAT sampling rate.

Table 8-1: *Popular audio sampling rates.*

Another concept you frequently encounter is that of "bitrate" or "resolution," which indicates the number of bits allocated for each "sample" or output value from the A/D converter. Most audio files on the Net have been recorded at a resolution of 8 or 16 bits. To find the number of discreet values at which audio source was sampled, apply the indicated bit integer as the exponent of 2. For instance, 8-bit audio files are sampled at 2^8 (256) discrete levels, and a 16-bit audio files are sampled at 2^{16} (65,536) discreet levels.

The resolution bitrate determines the overall dynamic range of the output from an audio source. The dynamic range is a measure of the span between the quietest and loudest sounds an audio device is capable of recording or reproducing. Each bit of resolution contributes approximately 6 *decibels* (a decibel, or dB, is a measure of the ear's response to sound pressure levels) of dynamic range to the recording. Eight-bit audio files are therefore able to reproduce a dynamic range of 48dB, roughly that of an analog cassette deck, while 16-bit audio files are capable of yielding the 96dB of dynamic range found in CDs.

The sampled audio file formats currently in use on the Net usually have either one or two channels. Naturally, single-channel files are often labeled mono, and dual-channel files are labeled stereo. This is important to consider when making your audio files available. Stereo files are twice as large as equivalent mono files, and often it is not necessary to distribute the stereo version of a recording.

File Format Considerations

Before placing your audio files on the Net, you should consider all of the parameters previously discussed. Since higher sampling rates and resolutions require more storage and throughput, you need to decide if you can sacrifice disk space and bandwidth for high-quality audio files. While one minute of an 8-bit mono file sampled at 8kHz is approximately 150k in size, a 16-bit stereo file of the same duration sampled at 44.1kHz can take up 10mb. Sometimes the low-fidelity version of an audio clip may well serve the purposes for which the clip is intended. Also keep in mind that many Web browsers do not yet have their computer audio outputs plugged into stereo amplifiers, and lower resolution mono files are ideal for playback via internal computer speakers.

It's a *very* good idea to keep multimedia files as small as possible if you intend to distribute them over the Net. For this reason, many net.music archives are primarily using MPEG layer-2 (.mp2) and μ-law (.au) audio files. MPEG layer-2 files are generally one-tenth the size of an equivalent AIFF or WAV file, and since MPEG audio compression schemes are based on psycho-acoustic models of how we perceive sound, there is minimal loss in sound quality during the compression process (see the section "MPEG" later in this chapter).

Using Audio Equipment

The audio hardware setup on UNIX machines varies quite a bit, so it's best for you to become familiar with your specific setup before you install the applications we discuss later in this chapter. Computers equipped with their own audio hardware often come with audio recording, editing and playback software tools. Sun Microsystems OpenWindows comes packaged with AudioTool on machines that have audio-input capabilities. Likewise, many Silicon Graphics workstations are equipped with the excellent graphical recorder/editor SoundEditor (see Figure 8-1) as well as the sound converter utility Soundfiler. Also, NeXT workstations come with the standard sndplay application for playing numerous types of audio files. If your workstation came with its own audio card, check the manufacturer's documentation to see if audio tools that are already compiled are available.

The ways in which you actually get the sound into your computer are dependent on the audio hardware/software setup installed on your machine. To edit audio files, most people use graphical audio editors. These programs graphically display the waveform of the audio file in various ways, allowing users to use a mouse to manipulate the audio data by cutting, pasting and adding effects.

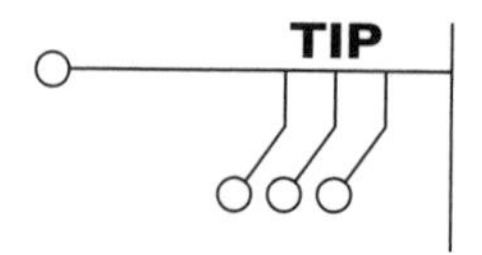

If you're installing Linux on your PC and have questions about compatible sound cards, see the Linux Sound HOWTO at http://sunsite.unc.edu/mdw/HOWTO/Sound-HOWTO.html.

This source provides detailed explanations for configuring Linux for sound support, picking the best sound card, how to play audio files and dealing with common problems.

Figure 8-1 is a typical audio editor interface, in this case Silicon Graphics SoundEditor. The audio waveform is displayed along with controls for modifying and playing it back. It shows the waveform fully zoomed out, displaying the entire 30-second waveform, as is indicated in the box next to Selection. Figure 8-2 shows what the waveform looks like when it is enlarged to display a smaller chunk of the file, in this case 0.125 seconds of the sample. The ability to zoom in allows levels of editing precision previously unavailable with analog tape-based editing systems.

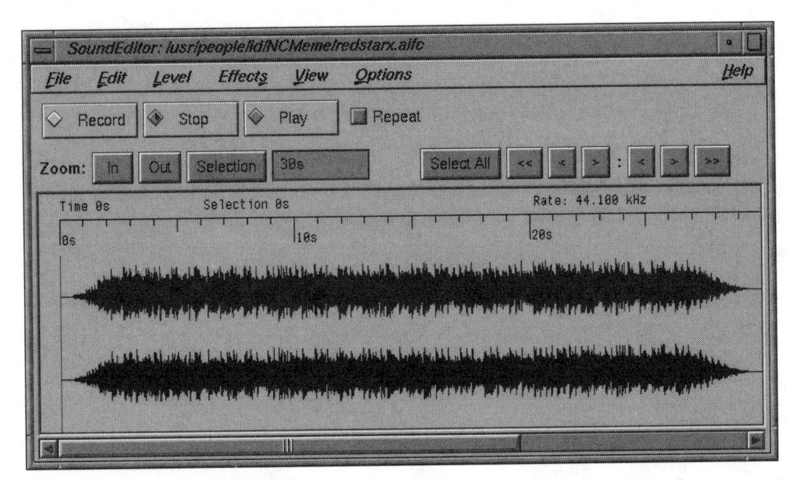

Figure 8-1: *Silicon Graphics SoundEditor showing a graphical representation of a 30-second audio sample.*

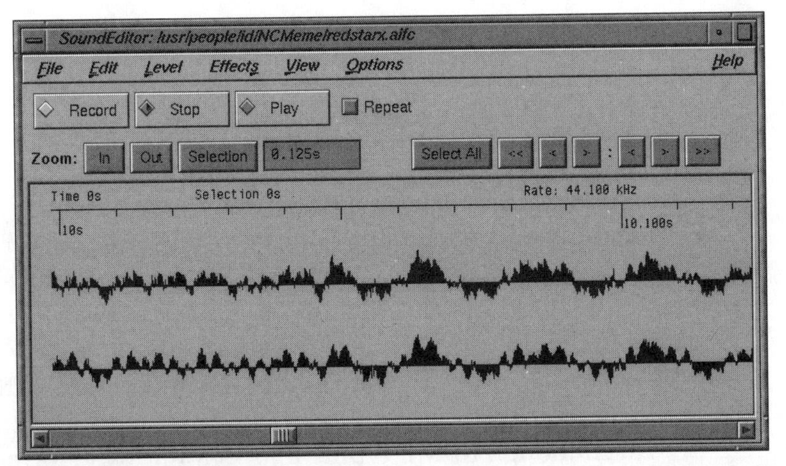

Figure 8-2: *SoundEditor displaying the same audio clip, zoomed in to display 0.125 seconds of the sample.*

It's important to keep in mind when recording and working with audio files that *digital distortion is very nasty.* Analog recording devices can be fudged a little bit past their maximum recording levels without too much damage to the audio signal. Actually, many people *like* a slightly distorted analog signal, especially guitar players. However, digital distortion is quite different. Once you have crossed the distortion threshold with digital recording gear, you have gone too far. Most audio recorders provide input meters that graphically display the audio levels coming into your sound card.

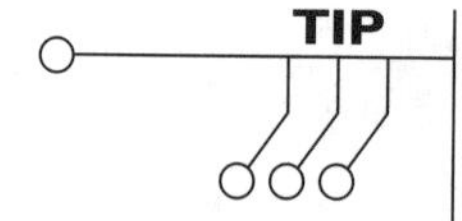

Looking for examples of music sites? The following are great indexes of lots of music-related links:

- *http://www.yahoo.com/yahoo/Entertainment/Music—music resources at Yahoo, the mother of all World Wide Web directories.*
- *http://syy.oulu.fi/music.html—World Wide Web Virtual library of music.*
- *http://www.music.indiana.edu/misc/music_resources.html—music resource on the Internet.*
- *http://www.timeinc.com/vibe/mmm/—the Mammoth Music Meta-List.*

Audio File Formats

Numerous digital audio file formats, many of which you will probably never encounter, have been introduced over the years. As computer platforms have come and gone, so have their proprietary file formats. This section provides you with a brief introduction to the file types that are commonly used on the WWW today, as well as the ways in which you can convert files to these various formats.

Even though MIME typing allows for any file format to be transmitted between a client and server, only a handful of prominent multimedia file types are commonly used on the Web. Since every new file type requires an appropriate helper application on the client end, simplicity and practicality have necessitated a decrease in commonly used file types. The formats discussed in this section are the ones that you are likely to run across on the Net. Each format is followed by its appropriate MIME type.

μ-law

audio/basic au snd

The μ-law (pronounce mu-law) file format, is the most frequently used audio file type on the Internet. Even though it's not the highest quality audio file format available, its relatively small file size and the availability of players for just about every operating system have made it a favorite for Net users. At a sampling rate of 8kHz, its sound quality is roughly equivalent to that of standard telephone receivers. Some systems, such as NeXT, use a sampling rate of 8.013kHz for the μ-law format. Since both Sun and NeXT machines commonly use this format, it is often referred to as the NeXT/Sun format.

Many people have found that the level of audio quality provided by μ-law files is sufficient for their particular applications, especially since most WWW users are still listening to audio they retrieve from the Internet through a monophonic computer speaker. For this reason, many sound archives now provide audio samples in both μ-law and higher quality formats like MPEG.

Most UNIX machines equipped with an audio device can play μ-law files with the following command:

```
$cat filename.au>/dev/audio
```

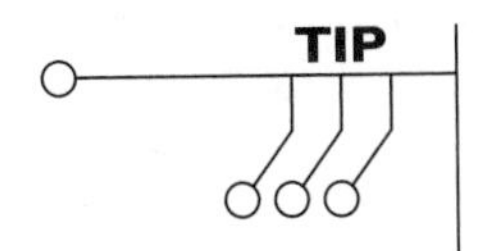

For a great archive of μ-law audio files, check out the WWW TV Theme Songs home page at http://ai.eecs.umich.edu/people/kennyp/sounds.html.

For hundreds of μ-law samples, see http://sunsite.unc.edu/pub/multimedia/sun-sounds/.

AIFF & AIFC

audio/x-aiff aif aiff aifc

The Audio Interchange File Format (AIFF) allows for the storage of monaural and multichannel sampled sounds at a variety of sampling rates. Since it is an interchange format, it is easily converted to other file formats. For these reasons, it is often used in high-end audio recording applications when storage space is not a concern. Originally developed by Apple, this format is used predominantly by Silicon Graphics and Macintosh applications.

AIFF files can be quite large. One minute of 16-bit stereo audio sampled at 44.1kHz usually takes up about 10 megabytes. Since AIFF does not allow for compressed audio data, Apple introduced the AIFF-C, or AIFC, format, which allows for the storage of compressed and uncompressed audio data. AIFC supports compression ratios as high as 6:1 but at the cost of the file's signal quality. Most of the applications that support AIFF playback also support AIFC.

Since AIFF supports multiple sample rates, some sites offer AIFF files roughly equivalent to standard μ-law files. These files are usually labeled as 1-channel, 8-bit, 8kHz AIFF files. Notice that when downsampled, AIFF files usually give a sample rate of 8kHz, not the 8.013kHz sampling rate of some μ-law files.

RIFF WAVE

audio/x-wav wav

A proprietary format sponsored by Microsoft and IBM, the Resource Interchange File Format Waveform Audio Format (.wav) was introduced in MS Windows v3.1 and is most commonly used on Windows-based PCs. WAVE files support multiple encoding methods, most often ADPCM (Adaptive Differential Pulse Code Modulation) and all WAVE files follow the Rich Information File Format (RIFF) specification. Don't worry if these encoding techniques sound alien to you—you won't need to know these things for day-to-day use of the format.

This format is *very* similar to the AIFF format in that it supports monaural and multichannel samples and a variety of sample rates. Like AIFF, WAVE files require approximately 10mb/min for 16-bit samples with a sampling rate of 44.1kHz, but 8-bit, 8kHz, single channel versions are often offered by sites.

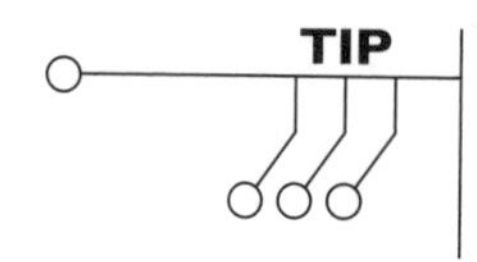

A large archive of WAVE sounds can be found at http://sunsite.unc.edu/pub/multimedia/pc-sounds.

MPEG

audio/mpeg mp2

The International Standard Organization's Moving Picture Expert Group is responsible for one of the most popular compression standards in use on the Internet today. Designed for both audio and video file compression, the MPEG codecs have become a favorite of Net users working with audio/video files over the past couple of years due to the scheme's ability to compress large files without sacrificing much quality.

MPEG-I audio compression specifies three layers, and each layer specifies its own format. The more complex layers take longer to encode but produce higher compression ratios while keeping much of an audio file's original fidelity. Layer I takes the least amount of time to compress, but layer III yields higher compression ratios for comparable quality files.

Numerous sites that offer high-quality music distribute it in the form of MPEG-compressed audio samples. The use of this compression technique is quite desirable because players have now been developed for just about every platform and operating system, and since MPEG audio compression is based on psycho-acoustic models, it is an ideal format for distributing high-quality sound files online. Most sites with MPEG audio files offer layer II encoded files, which can compress files anywhere from 1/3 to 1/24 their original file size (with higher compression ratios, resulting in more data loss). The quality of an MPEG-I layer II-compressed audio file remains very similar to the original uncompressed file at ratios from 5:1 to 12:1. These files are usually identified with the .mp2 extension, which does *not* mean they are compressed with the MPEG II standard. MPEG-II is still predominantly used for video compression, since the MPEG-II audio compression standard is still being worked out. This is often confusing to many new Net users.

In addition to the numerous WWW sites that are using MPEG-1 to encode audio files, Phillips uses it for their new digital video CDs, and it has also been adopted by some digital radio standards bodies for use with digital radio broadcasts.

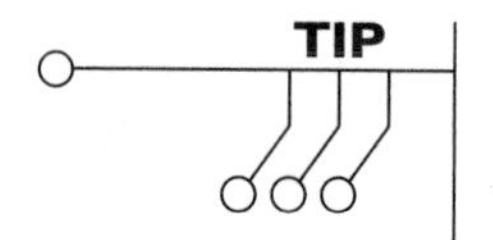

For more information on the MPEG compression standard, see the following Web sites:

- *http://www.crs4.it/~luigi/MPEG/—the MPEG FAQ.*
- *http://www.crs4.it/~luigi/MPEG/mpeg1-a.html—information about MPEG-1 audio encoding.*
- *http://www.crs4.it/~luigi/MPEG/mpeg2.html#What is MPEG-2 AUDIO—information about MPEG-2 audio encoding.*
- *ftp://ftp.crs4.it/mpeg/—an extensive MPEG software archive.*

Creative Voice

audio/x-voc voc

Creative Voice (.voc) is the proprietary sound file format that is recorded with Creative Lab's Sound Blaster and Sound Blaster Pro audio cards. This format supports only 8-bit mono audio files up to sampling rates of 44.1kHz, and stereo files up to 22kHz.

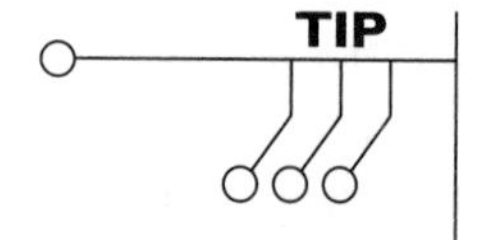

Creative Labs has a home page at http://creaf.com.

There is a Sound Blaster 16 programming information guide at http://www.xraylith.wisc.edu:80/~ebrodsky/sb16doc/sb16doc.html

IFF/8SVX

audio/x-iff iff

IFF/8SVX is the standard Amiga sound file format. Like AIFF, it is an interchange file format, meaning that it was designed for easy conversion to other formats. However, the IFF/8SVX format supports only 8-bit samples. The header section of an IFF/8SVX file differentiates it from other IFF format types (see IFF/ILBM in the section "Animation File Formats" later in this chapter). This format is rarely used for audio file distribution on the Net.

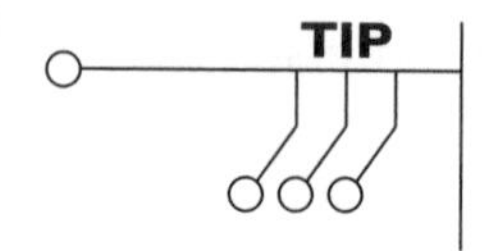

For the IFF standard, see gopher://ftp.std.com:70/0R0-182411-/obi/book/Standards/Electronic.Arts.

SND

The extension .snd is a bit ambiguous. Sun/NeXT sound files are sometimes identified with the .snd extension when they are actually μ-law files. Macintosh system sounds also have the .snd extension, as do some PC sounds. They vary in sample rate from 5.5kHz to 22kHz, with 11kHz being the most popular.

Macintosh .snd files are assigned the SFIL (sound file) in the 'type' field of the Mac resource fork. These files can consist of AIFF/AIFC samples and/or of synthesized sounds that can take advantage of the System 7 sound hardware and software.

Raw PCM data

Raw Pulse Code Modulated data is sometimes identified with the .pcm extension, but it sometimes has no extension at all. Since no header information is provided in the file, you must often specify the waveform's sample rate, resolution and number of channels.

MIDI & MOD

Not all audio file formats on the Net perform the sole function of storing digitized audio. In the following section, we discuss two unique file formats that you might consider using if you're interested in electronic music composition.

MIDI

audio/x-midi mid midi

Unlike the above formats, the Musical Instrument Digital Interface is not a specification for sampled digital audio. Instead, it is a serial communications protocol designed to allow the transmission of control data between electronic music instruments. It has been likened to a PostScript language for music. Since MIDI contains only instructions for controlling how and when devices, most frequently electronic synthesizers or samplers, produce sounds, the files are *much* smaller than digitized audio files. The MIDI Manufacturer Association (MMA), a group of electronic music instrument manufacturers, has been responsible for the evolution of the MIDI protocol since its inception in 1983.

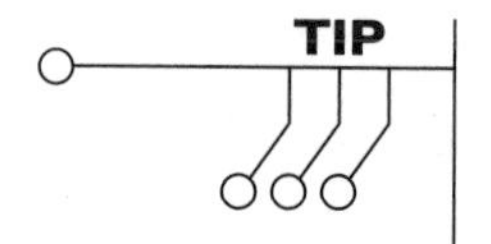

For information on MIDI, see the MIDI home page at http://www.eeb.ele.tue.nl/midi/index.html.

Links to electronic music software on the Net can be found at the Arachnaut's Internet E-Music Software List at http://www.webcom.com/~hurleyj/music/emusic-sw.html.

Modules

audio/x-mod mod

Modules, usually identified by the .mod extension, are somewhat like a cross between MIDI files and digitized audio files. Instead of consisting solely of sampled audio or control information, this format contains a bank of digitized sounds as well as control information for controlling the ways in which the sounds are sequenced upon playback. The samples are raw, 8-bit audio data. The format also has simple digital signal processing (DSP) capabilities for adding effects.

Modules originated on the Amiga, but their relatively small file size and impressive breadth of usage has made them a favorite of many composers on the Net. Thanks to the readily available playback tools and gigantic collections of these files on the Net, module composition has in itself become an art form.

Even though we've listed a MIME type with this entry, modules are usually compressed, so it may not be necessary for you to add the entry to your mime.types file.

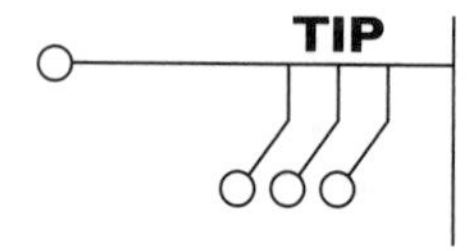

For detailed information on the MOD file format, see the MOD FAQ at http://www.cis.ohio-state.edu/hypertext/faq/usenet/mod-faq/top.html.

Consult the following newsgroups to find out more about the various aspects of audio on the Internet:

- *alt.binaries.multimedia—encoded audio and video files.*
- *alt.binaries.sounds.midi—encoded MIDI files.*
- *alt.binaries.sounds.mods—encoded MOD files.*
- *alt.emusic—general discussions about electronic music.*
- *comp.music—discussions about computer music.*
- *rec.music.makers.synth—discussions about music synthesizers.*

- *http://sunsite.unc.edu/emusic-l/—the home page for the EMUSIC-L list, including the MIDI specification, a section about building MIDI triggers, tons of reviews of electronic music equipment and tips on buying your first keyboard.*
- *http://mitpress.mit.edu:/Computer-Music-Journal/CMJ.html—the Computer Music Journal archives at MIT, an* excellent *resource for technical articles about electronic music as well as a long list of links to other emusic sites.*
- *http://ftp.ircam.fr/index-e.html—the Institut de Recherche et Coordination Acoustique/Musique (IRCAM) WWW server.*
- *http://akebono.stanford.edu/yahoo/Computers/Music/MIDI/—MIDI links at Yahoo.*

Audio Software

The Companion CD-ROM contains many audio software packages. Each of these packages performs different functions, and the best way to become familiar with them, as with any software package, is to tinker with them for hours on end. Keep in mind that many of these are beta releases (or even earlier), so be sure to exercise the fine art of patience when working with them. Many UNIX workstations come with their own audio editing and playback software, such as Sun's Audio Tool and Silicon Graphics' SoundEditor, so check with your computer's manufacturer, or post a question to a relevant newsgroup.

After the application names we've listed the appropriate entries for your personal mailcap file, should you choose to use these applications for playback file, if applicable. We've also included the URLs for the sites from which you can find updates for the programs.

maplay

```
audio/x-mpeg   maplay %s
```

ftp://ftp.crs4.it/mpeg/programs/
maplay, an MPEG audio player, decodes layer I and layer II MPEG audio streams and plays them in real time. Written by Tobias Balding, it supports single channel, stereo, joint stereo and dual-

channel MPEG streams. It can also output the decompressed file to a 16-bit signed PCM file for further conversion.

Sox/Sound Tools

http://cuiwww.unige.ch/OSG/AudioFormats/a07.html

According to its creator, Lance Norskog, Sox (SOund eXchange) is intended to be the "Swiss Army knife of sound processing tools." It is actually one of the most useful tools for working with audio on UNIX-based computers because it allows you to use shell commands to convert between numerous audio file formats. Sox supports conversion between .snd (NeXT), .voc (Creative Lab's Sound Blaster), .iff (Amiga 8SVX), .au (Sun ADPCM), .aiff (Apple/SGI), .wav (Microsoft Windows), CD-R (used in mastering compact disks), .hcom (Macintosh), .sf (IRCAM sound files), .smp (Turtle Beach Samplevision files), and numerous others.

Sox also allows you to apply many effects to a sound file, such as changing the sampling rate, adding echo and delay, filtering frequencies, reversing samples and averaging sound channels.

The Sox command-line structure is as follows:

```
sox [options] from-file-args to-file-args [ effect [effect-args]]
```

Many of the command-line options require you to know the charateristics of the sound file you are converting, such as its sampling rate and whether it has one or two channels. If you're not sure of these, you can get Sox to try to auto-determine the file parameters with the *-auto* option. For instance, if need to convert a WAVE file called *chicken.wav* to a µ-law file, you would type the following:

```
$ sox -t auto chicken.wav -b -c 1 -U -r 8000 chicken.au
```

This tells Sox to determine the audio characteristics of *chicken.wav* and convert it to *chicken.au*. The command-line options tell Sox to output a single channel (*-c 1*) µ-law file (*-U*) with a sampling rate of 8000Hz (*-r 8000*), with the sample data in bytes (*-b*). There are numerous other options available, all of which are outlined in the Sox man page that comes with the program.

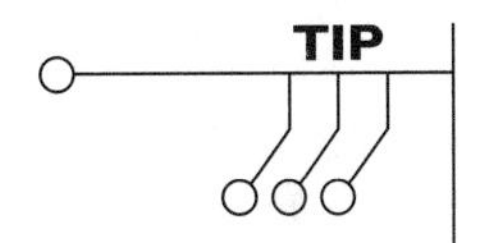

For a brief overview of Sox, see http://cuiwww.unige.ch/OSG/AudioFormats/a07.html.

MpegAudio

ftp://ftp.crs4.it/mpeg/programs/

MpegAudio is an MPEG-1 layer II audio compressor. It compresses 16-bit mono or stereo audio files sampled at 32, 44.1 or 48kHz. It usually compresses a file to one-tenth its original size with very little signal loss, but compression takes quite a while on slower machines. MpegAudio accepts input in raw PCM format (16-bit signed integer) or in WAVE format.

MPEG layer III encoder/decoder

ftp://fhginfo.fhg.de/pub/layer3/

Even though just about everyone on the Net is working with MPEG layer II audio compression, a shareware MPEG layer III encoder/decoder is available. The encoder accepts raw PCM and WAVE formats, and the decoder can output WAVE, IFF and µ-law formats. Binaries are available for Suns, Hewlett-Packards and Silicon Graphics platforms and for PCs running Linux or NeXTSTEP.

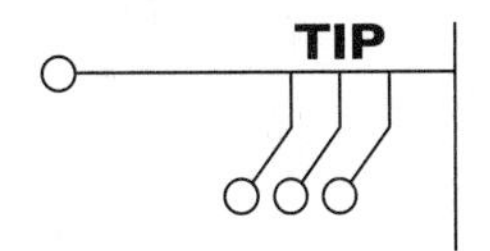

For more information about MPEG Audio layer III, see ftp://fhginfo.fhg.de/pub/layer3/MPEG_Audio_L3_FAQ.html.

MiXViews (mxv)

```
audio/*;  mxv %s
```

ftp://foxtrot.ccmrc.ucsb.edu/pub/MixViews/

MiXViews is one of the first shareware graphical audio editors available for UNIX. It allows you to play, record, edit, process and analyze numerous types of audio files, including µ-law, AIFF, AIFC and WAVE. With MiXViews's powerful editing capabilities, you can mix, crossfade, splice, reverse, transpose and filter

samples, as well as add special effects like reverb and phase vocoder resynthesis. It can also convert between numerous audio formats. The program is loaded with features, so the best way to become familiar with them is to open an audio file and start playing around. Files are opened with the command
$ mxv *filename.wav.*

You will be presented with a graphical representation of the audio file like the one in Figure 8-3. To hear the file, select Play from the Sound menu.

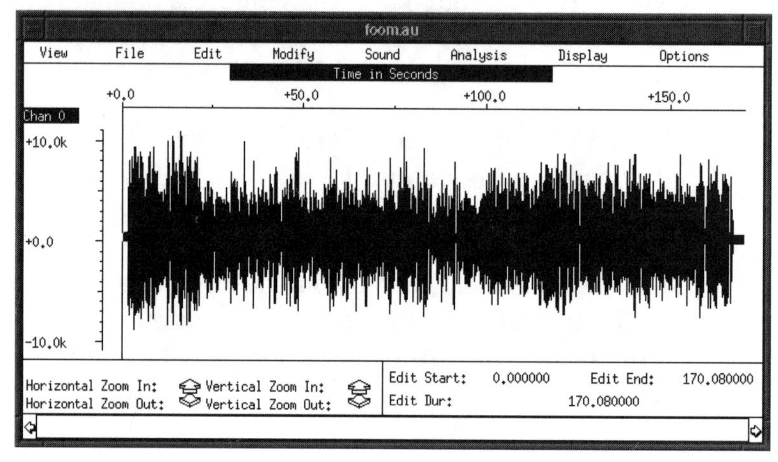

Figure 8-3: *The MiXViews audio editing interface.*

tracker

audio/x-mod; mod %s

ftp://sunsite.unc.edu/Linux/apps/sound
Even though no MOD editors are currently available for UNIX machines, tracker is an excellent MOD player. It plays music modules from the Amiga-based Soundtracker, a family of music composition programs. tracker emulates the Amiga sound hardware, enabling numerous platforms to play the modules if the machine on which tracker is running has sufficient horsepower.

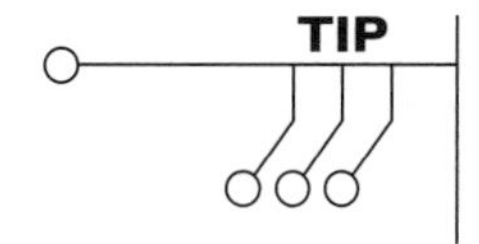

For more MOD files than you'll know what to do with, see ftp://ftp.funet.fi/pub/amiga/audio/modules or its mirror at ftp://sunsite.unc.edu/pub/multimedia/mods.

MP for Linux

```
audio/x-midi;   mp %s
audio/x-mid;    mp %s
```

ftp://sunsite.unc.edu/pub/Linux/apps/sound

MP (MIDI play) allows Linux users to play back MIDI files on a sound card equipped with a frequency modulator (FM) synthesizer. It can also send the MIDI commands to the card's external MIDI port. Since the program comes with many of its own percussion voices, it can use your sound card's synthesized drum voices or its own.

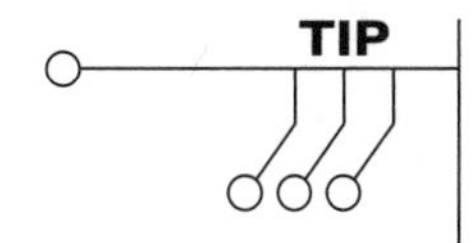

If you've got a Roland MPU-401 MIDI adapter card and are looking for a Linux MIDI sequencer so that you can make your own MIDI files, check out ftp://sunsite.unc.edu/pub/Linux/apps/sound/jazz-1.0.tar.gz.

XPlaycd & XMixer for Linux

ftp://sunsite.unc.edu/Linux/apps/sound

XPlaycd and Xmixer by Olav Woelfelschneider provide X Windows interfaces for control over CD-ROM audio playback and the amplitude level from an audio card's sound inputs. XPlaycd (the interface is shown in Figure 8-4) provides the typical controls for a CD player, such as play, stop, record (just kidding), skip track, eject, elapsed time and loop. XMixer (the interface is shown in Figure 8-5) provides several sliders for adjusting the overall volume, synthesis modules, line-in, microphone-in, headphone volume and other values, depending on the sound hardware your system supports.

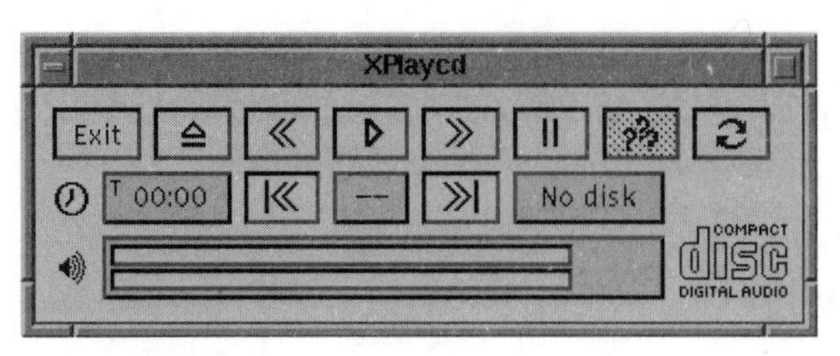

Figure 8-4: *XPlaycd interface.*

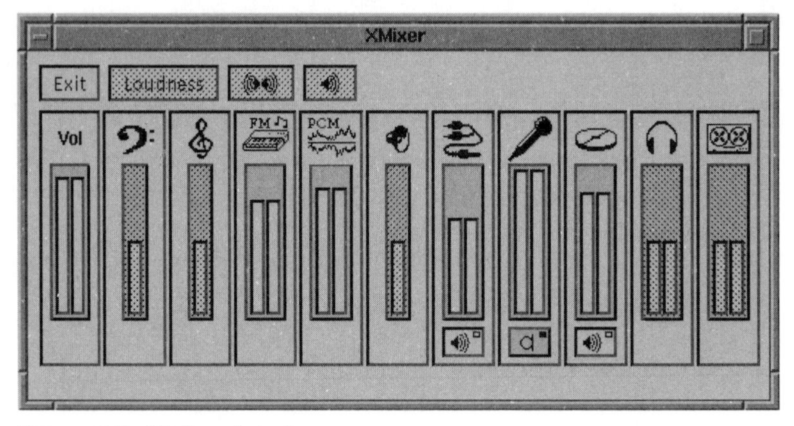

Figure 8-5: *XMixer interface.*

XPlaycd and XMixer run only under Linux, but numerous applications are available that perform the same functions for just about every flavor of UNIX.

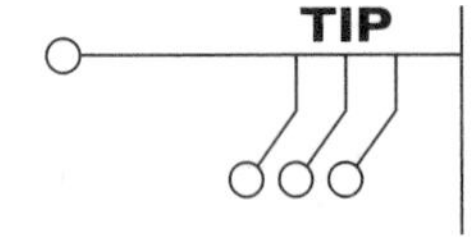

For X Windows applications galore, see ftp://ftp.x.org.

OggSQUISH

http://deskfish.cs.titech.ac.jp/squish/alpha.html

If you're interested in other forms of audio compression, check out Christopher Montgomery's OggSQUISH. It's optimized for 16-bit, CD-quality audio files. Although OggSQUISH is only in its alpha release stage, the author claims that it "is faster than MPEG and generally surpasses it in quality," and that at 13:1 compression, it is comparable to MPEG-1 layer III quality.

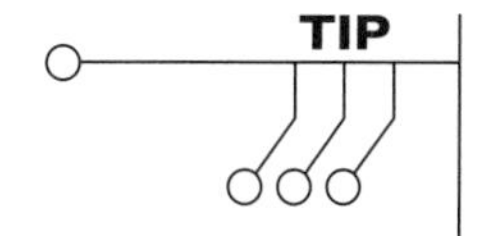

See the OggSQUISH home page at http://deskfish.cs.titech.ac.jp/squish/squish_index.html.

Digital Video on the Internet

Most video signals (including videotapes and cable and off-air transmissions) in North America *are broadcast quality* as defined by the National Television Standards Committee. The NTSC standard dictates that the signal be displayed at 30 frames per second in an interlaced fashion, with the odd and even horizontal lines alternating during each pass. This process divides each frame into two fields, thus producing 60 fields per second. The vertical resolution of the video image is determined by the number of scanlines (defined as 525 by the NTSC standard).

Needless to say, digitizing and reproducing broadcast-quality video signals requires processing speed, hard disk storage space and RAM at capacities typically unavailable on computer workstations. Even though some high-end digitizing systems are capable of meeting these requirements, the sheer volume of data would overwhelm most machines. One second of NTSC-equivalent digitized video consists of 30 full-screen (640 x 480 pixels), 24-bit images, which take up approximately 26mb of disk space. That's over 1.5 gigabytes a minute *without* audio!

These prohibitive requirements have generated the acceptance of lower-quality video clips on the Net. These files differ from analog and high-end digital video sources in that they are not displayed as interlaced fields but instead as a series of images. For this reason, digitized video files on the Net are often referred to as *animations*, because the method with which they are displayed resembles that of cartoons more than traditional video. Since animation playback software provides the illusion of movement by rapidly (or not-so-rapidly) displaying a series of individual images, the terms *video, animation* and *movie* are often used interchangeably.

Making Movies Under X

Like its audio counterpart, video hardware on UNIX machines varies greatly. Most (if not all) video recording software is commercially distributed because it has to be tailored for specific video input cards. Many Silicon Graphics machines come with the MovieMaker and MoviePlayer applications, and Sun distributes video recording and editing software with some of its video input boards. To find out if a video recorder/editor is available for your machine, it's best to contact the manufacturer or post questions to a relevant USENET newsgroup.

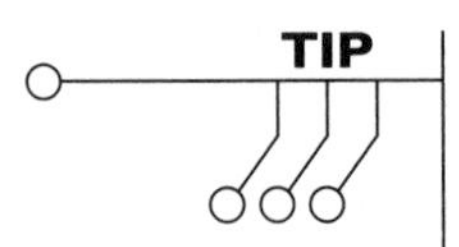

The following applications, all available from ftp://sunsite.unc.edu/pub/Linux/apps/video, provide support for some video-capture boards under Linux:

- *PMS-grabber.tgz—support for Pro MovieStudio, a commercially available video digitizing board for PCs.*
- *ScrMachII_1.0.tar.gz—driver and utilities for FAST Screen Machine II video capture card.*
- *ScreenMachineII_1.1.tgz—driver for FAST Screen Machine II live video overlay.*
- *fgrabber-1.0.tgz—driver for the WinVision B&W (black-and-white) video capture card.*
- *vid_src.tgz—Video Blaster video capture card usage under Linux and DOS.*

You don't necessarily have to have a video digitizing board in order to make a movie. Since animations are nothing more than a sequence of images, it is possible to string together a series of

images and convert them to a movie. Of course, doing this is much more time consuming than capturing video from an input board, but it's fun to experiment with if you don't have access to any video digitizing equipment. If you're interested in doing this, check out http://www.eit.com/techinfo/mpeg/mpeg.html.

Animation File Formats

This section reviews most of the animation file formats in use on the Internet today. These don't represent every available animation or video file format out there, but they're the ones that you're most likely to encounter in day-to-day use. Actually, many of the formats covered are fading into obscurity and are discussed as points of reference so that you can get a better idea about the differences among the various formats. We've listed the appropriate MIME type following each file format.

QuickTime

video/quicktime mov moov qt

QuickTime is Apple's proprietary dynamic data format originally implemented on the Macintosh. This format has become an increasingly popular animation file format on the Net since Apple has released QuickTime enablers for both the Microsoft Windows environment and Silicon Graphics machines. These movies can be played on Silicon Graphics machines with MoviePlayer under IRIX v5.1 and later versions or just about any other UNIX-based system with Xanim (see the next section "Video Software" for information about Xanim).

The most important thing to remember about QuickTime movies is that they are often created under the Macintosh operating system, which divides files into two separate "forks": *data forks* and *resource forks*. The resource fork contains small chunks of program code that describe various attributes of the file necessary for the Macintosh interface, while the data fork contains the actual numerical and textual data of the file. Since HTTP does not provide support for transferring multi-forked files, it is necessary for

QuickTime movies made on a Macintosh to be converted before they can be distributed over the WWW to be played on multiple platforms. This conversion process combines the resource and data forks into a single-forked file, commonly referred to as a "flattened" file. The resultant file can be stored on non-Mac file systems without the loss of important data.

The latest version of QuickTime supports both digitized audio samples and MIDI (see the previous section "Audio File Formats"), so it is possible to include soundtracks that take up very small amounts of space. Most video files on the Net that include a soundtrack are in the QuickTime format.

Xanim (see "Video Software" later in this chapter) plays both the video and audio segments of flattened QuickTime movies under X.

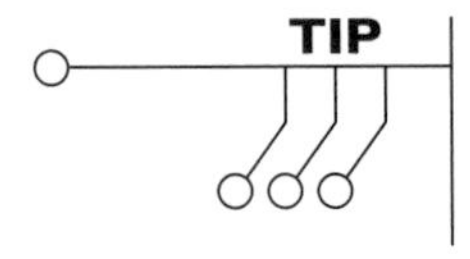

If you have access to a Mac, this conversion can be accomplished with the Movie Converter utility that comes with the Macintosh QuickTime Starter Kit or the publicly available Flattmoov from http://www.astro.nwu.edu/lentz/mac/qt/.

Apple has a Web site devoted to QuickTime at http://quicktime.apple.com.

MPEG

video/mpeg   mpeg mpg mpe

MPEG compression, discussed in the previous section "Audio File Formats," can be used for both audio and video files. With the appropriate combination of hardware and software, real-time compression and decompression is possible on numerous platforms. The use of MPEG compression reduces the bandwidth necessary for high-quality audio/video file transfer without excessively sacrificing the original signal quality, making it an ideal way to efficiently distribute multimedia files online.

Most MPEG movies on the Internet do not have soundtracks, but some of them support MPEG-1 layer II audio. MPEG movies that contain audio data are sometimes called Xing movies, referring to the Xing Technology Corporation. Xing has introduced many inexpensive MPEG audio/video recording and playback tools for Windows-based PCs and is currently working on similar applications for Linux-based and Solaris-based machines.

mpeg2play (see "Video Software" later in this chapter) plays MPEG movies under X Windows.

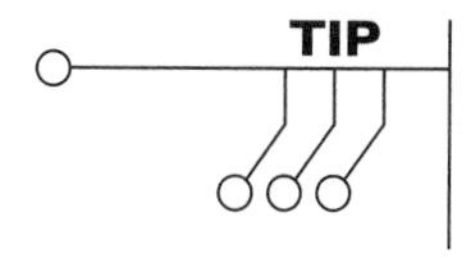

There are a few different ways to convert QuickTime movies to MPEG files.

- *http://www.eit.com/techinfo/mpeg/mpeg.html—MPEG technical information from Enterprise Integration Technologies.*
- *ftp://mm-ftp.CS.Berkeley.edu/pub/multimedia/mpeg/—mpeg_encode from the UC Berkeley Plateau Multimedia Project.*
- *ftp://ftp.crs4.it/mpeg/programs/—mpeg_encode mirror and mpeg archive.*
- *http://www.arc.umn.edu/GVL/Software/mpeg.html*—How to Make MPEG Movies *from the University of Minnesota's graphics and visualization lab.*
- *http://www.mcs.anl.gov/home/plassman/movie/howto.html—Making an MPEG Movie for your XMosaic Application.*

AVI

video/x-msvideo avi

AVI is Microsoft's proprietary video format, also known as video for Windows. Its performance features are similar to those of QuickTime's, and numerous freely available AVI to QuickTime and QuickTime to AVI converters are available. Like QuickTime files, AVI files are capable of having an audio track.

Xanim (see "Video Software" later in this chapter) plays both the video and audio segments of AVI movies under X.

FLI & FLC

video/x-fli fli,flc

FLI and FLC are Autodesk's "Flick" formats. FLI, the original format of Autodesk's Animator, is limited to a maximum resolution of 320 x 200 pixels, a 64-color palette and 4000 frames per file.

FLC, the second generation of Autodesk's animation formats introduced with Animator Pro, supports larger images (up to 65,536 pixels in width and height) but is limited to a 256-color palette for each frame. Neither of these formats support audio.

Xanim (see "Video Software" later in this chapter) plays AVI animations under X.

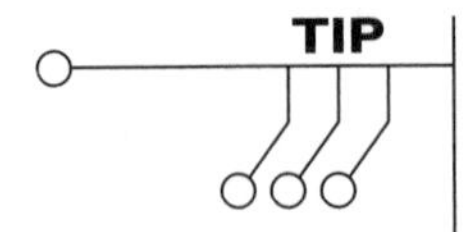

More detailed information about animation file formats is available from ftp://avalon.vislab.navy.mil/pub/format_specs/.

IFF/ILBM

video/x-iff iff

The IFF/ILBM (Interchange Format File) format was defined by Electronic Arts as a multimedia file standard to facilitate the transfer of images, text, audio and other data. It was designed specifically to work efficiently with Amiga hardware. The IFF/ILBM (Interlaced Bitmat) format is both a graphics format and an animation format.

Xanim (see "Video Software" later in this chapter) plays IFF animations under X.

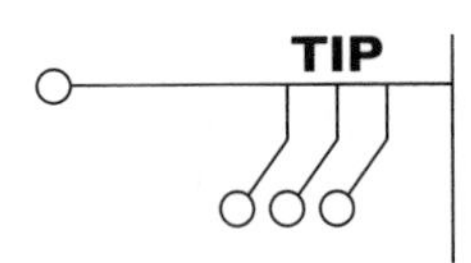

For the IFF standard, see gopher://ftp.std.com:70/0R0-182411-/obi/book/Standards/Electronic.Arts.IFF.

Video Software

In order to view large animation files with any of these playback utilities, it is *imperative* that you have plenty of RAM. For instance, you can expect problems if you've got a Linux box with 8mb of RAM, running X Windows, and you're trying to play back large animation files (over 2mb). Lots of folks running X have reported that without sufficient RAM, the sound on flattened QuickTime movies cuts in and out with each hard drive access.

Some of the applications discussed in this section are available only for certain platforms, so it's best to familiarize yourself with the different options available and then decide which tools are best for you. After the name of each program, we provide the entry that you need to put to your mailcap file, as well as the URL for the site from which you can get updates.

Xanim

```
#This maps all non-MPEG video types to Xanim
video/*;   xanim %s
```

http://www.portal.com/~podlipec/home.html

The X11-based animation viewer Xanim is a wonderful little program that lets you view just about any animation file format on the Net. It displays numerous animation and graphics formats, including FLI, FLC, IFF, AVI and QuickTime (see Figure 8-6).

The latest release of Xanim also supports AVI (raw and ADPCM) and QuickTime audio. Under Linux, it compiles on both 8- and 16-bit audio cards. Also, WAVE files can be played with any animation file type if the audio file is specified after the animation file, as in the following command line:

```
$ xanim animation.avi audioclip.wav
```

When calling Xanim, you can add numerous options to the command line, which add functionality to the application. For example, you can enable on-the-fly resizing of animations by adding the following call for Xanim in your mailcap file:

```
xanim +Sr
```

The Xanim man pages outline all of the available commands.

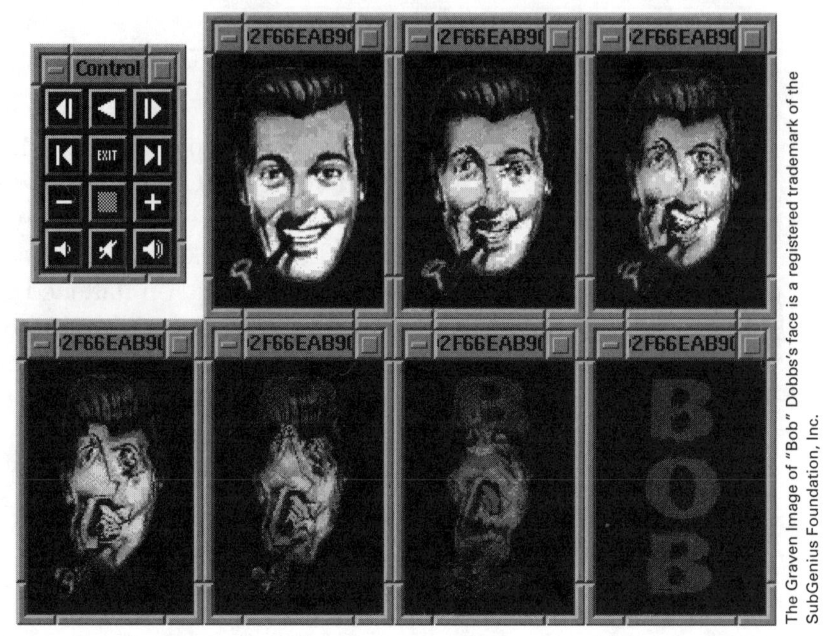

Figure 8-6: *The Xanim controls and a series of screen captures from a flattened QuickTime animation.*

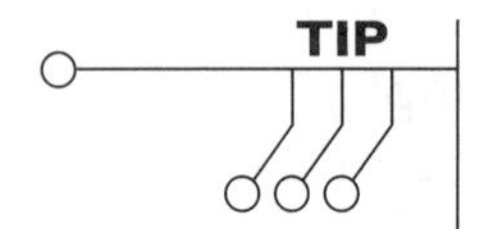

The Xanim home page is at http://www.portal.com/~podlipec/home.html.

Additional Xanim information can be found at http://www.univ-rennes1.fr/ASTRO/fra/xanim.html.

mpeg2play

```
video/x-mpeg; mpeg2play %s
```

ftp://ftp.netcom.com//pub/cf/cfogg/mpeg2

This movie player for 8-bit color X Windows plays both MPEG-1 and MPEG-2 video streams. It not only plays back MPEG video files, but also allows you to rewind and loop them. It even allows you to view the movies one frame at a time with a Step control (see Figure 8-7). The application can be started from the command line with the following command:

```
$ mpeg2play filename.mpg
```

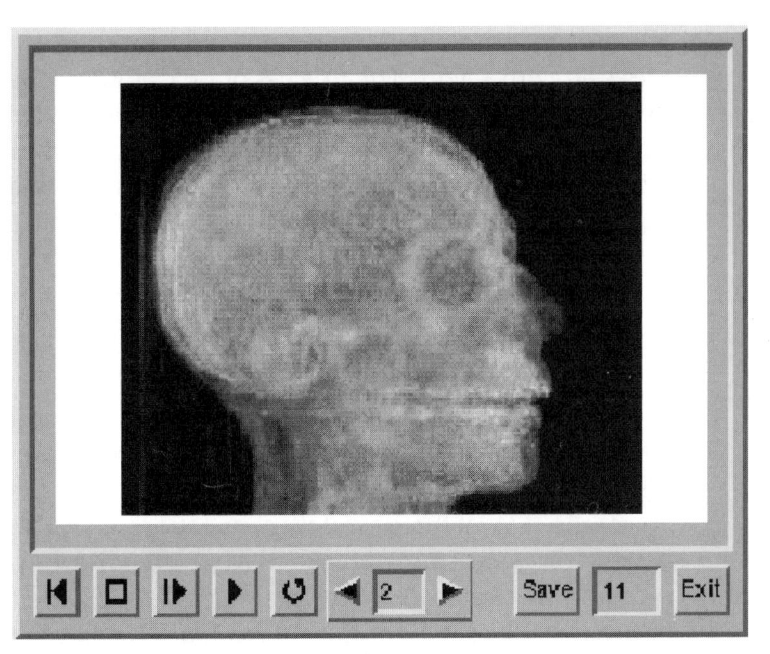

Figure 8-7: *The mpeg2play interface.*

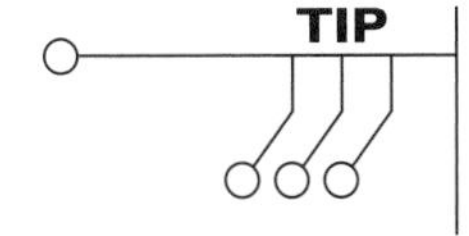

The mpeg2play home page, complete with binaries for multiple UNIX platforms and example MPEG audio and video files, is at http://macke.gris.informatik.uni-tuebingen.de:4712/projects/mpeg2play.html.

mpeg_play, an application similar to mpeg2play, has a home page at http://www.geom.umn.edu/docs/mpeg_play/mpeg_play.html.

Serving Multimedia Files

Before the World Wide Web, audio and animation files were usually distributed on the Internet by either posting them to USENET newsgroups or making them available at FTP sites. Both of these methods are still widely used today, but the Web is quickly becoming the preferred method for distributing multimedia files.

Don't be intimidated by the idea of incorporating multimedia files into your pages. The process of linking these files into your documents is *exactly* like the one described for linked images in Chapter 7, "Images on the Web." You simply need to call the file with the <A HREF> tag, as illustrated in the following examples:

```
<A HREF="/audio/bob.mov">"Bob"'s Loop of Endless Slack.</A>
(QuickTime movie - 3300 Kb)

Say, why don't you check out the 3.3Meg QuickTime movie <A HREF="/
audio/bob.mov">"Bob"'s Loop of Endless Slack</a>?
```

Notice that the file type and size of bob.mov is indicated somewhere near the link, either next to it or in the sentence before it. It's important to supply this information because some users access the WWW through slow connections and/or they may not have the software necessary to playback the file. Including the file type and size helps them decide whether they have the time and/or capabilities of initiating the download. Also be sure to indicate the file format, sampling rate and resolution of any audio files you have available for download. It's not written in stone anywhere that you have to do this, but this courteous gesture will save you the headache of dealing with irate users and tons of hate e-mail.

Other than the ones just mentioned, there aren't many "guidelines" for distributing audio/video files over the Net. If you plan to make multimedia files available on your server, the guiding force of your plan should be *common sense*. Obviously, larger files take up more disk space and increase the demand on the throughput of your system. If you observe that your server is incredibly loaded down and that your connection to the Net is perpetually maxed out, make sure that your entire system is not being choked by the transfer of large files that you could reduce in size or remove.

You can decrease the sizes of the files you offer by using the compression techniques discussed earlier in this chapter and/or reducing the resolutions of the files. For example, if you've got numerous 16-bit AIFF audio files that you need to make available, consider converting them to the 8-bit μ-law format with Sox/Sound Tools, or better yet, compress them with MpegAudio so that they lose very little of their original quality. Likewise, you can limit the size of the animations on your server by reducing the pixel resolution (frame size) of the files. You can also reduce the number of bits allocated for each frame's color display, such as reducing a 24-bit movie to 8-bit, or you use the animation compression techniques discussed previously to decrease their file sizes.

Again, exercise common sense. This can't be stressed enough. Even though the Internet was designed to withstand a nuclear assault, it's having a hard time standing up to the barrage of multimedia files flowing through its wires. This problem will be partly remedied by the introduction of increasingly faster computers and the dissemination of high-bandwidth lines, but for now we need to take all the precautions we can to make sure that file sizes are kept to a minimum.

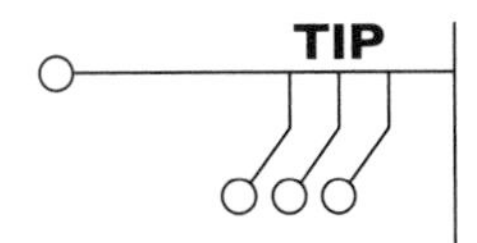

The following are multimedia indexes and related newsgroups:

- *http://viswiz.gmd.de/MultimediaInfo/—an* excellent *index of sources categorized by subject.*
- *http://cuiwww.unige.ch/OSG/AudioFormats/a11.html—information about posting sounds to USENET.*
- *alt.binaries.multimedia—encoded binaries of animation and audio files.*
- *alt.binaries.pictures.utilities—encoded binaries of various graphic applications.*
- *alt.comp.compression—general discussions about computers and compression.*
- *comp.graphics—discussions about computer graphics.*
- *comp.graphics.animation—discussions about computer animation.*
- *comp.compression—discussions about compression.*
- *comp.multimedia—general discussions about multimedia.*
- *rec.video.desktop—discussions about desktop video applications, hardware and related issues.*

Moving On

This chapter has reviewed the most popular file formats currently in use on the Web for audio/video file transfer, as well as the ways in which you can include audio and video in your Web documents. Multimedia on the Net is still in its infancy, and we hope this overview has provided you with enough information, tools and jumping-off points to explore audio/video technologies and the ways in which they can be integrated into your Web documents.

As the available bandwidth on the Internet increases, so will your ability to utilize new communication technologies to transmit high-quality multimedia files. Actually, in this chapter, we haven't discussed many of the exciting developments in the field of distributed media currently in use on the Net. Don't worry. Chapter 13, "Future Directions," discusses advancements in real-time audio/video conferencing, improved protocols that support distributed computer-generated graphical environments and the general directions in which the Net is headed.

Most of the information in this chapter is available on the Net, and it's important that you learn how to efficiently search for the materials you need. The next chapter focuses on various search engines that are available to assist you in your information hunting and gathering, as well as on the ways in which you can organize and index the resources available on your own server.

SECTION III

Adding Interactivity

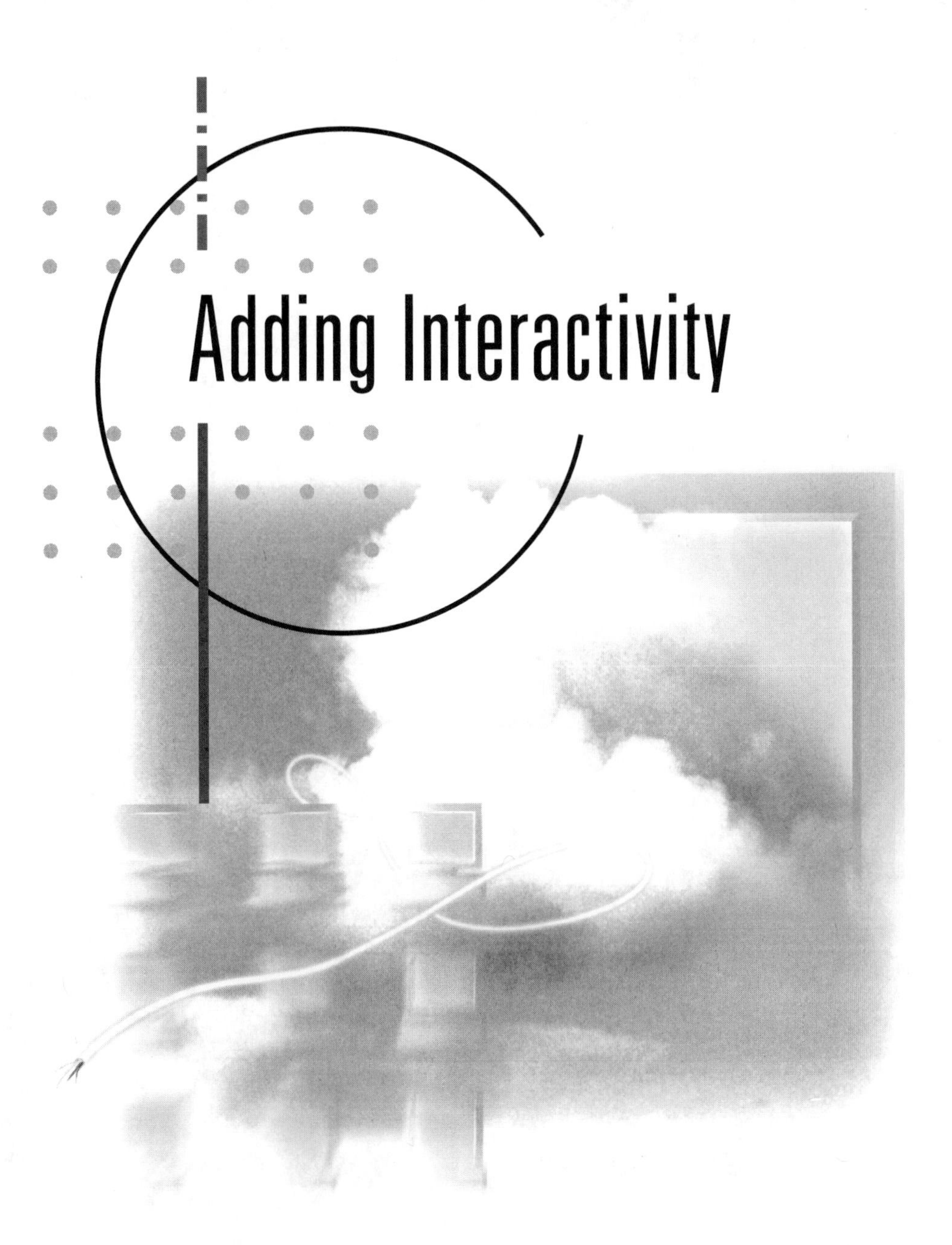

9

Searching & Indexing

Most of the world's best computer scientists have worked on the problem of searching; it's one of the most important topics in computing. When applied to the Internet, this field of study is often referred to as Networked Information Discovery and Retrieval (NIDR). Computer scientists in the area of NIDR are working to apply the ideas and algorithms of computer-based searching to tools that will allow users to easily and intuitively find information on the Net.

Like many of the best ideas in computer science, the approach to most of these tools is an extension of a familiar concept. When you're looking for a particular bit of information in this book, you probably check the index. This index has been prepared by a professional; while the indexer's expertise isn't specific to the Web, he or she understands how to organize the topics of a book so that they are easily searched. In creating the index, he or she combines her understanding of the way people read computer books with the author's knowledge of the material. The result is a table of ideas and concepts that are important to the author and the reader.

Similarly, most of the Internet's searching tools are broken into separate modules: an indexer and a search engine. The indexer reads the documents and builds several files containing tables of all the words within the collection. The search engine is like a reader leafing through a book. It understands the tables created by the indexer and uses them to quickly locate documents that match the user's query. Of course, the software indexer can't duplicate the experience and knowledge of a human being. Instead, it substitutes thoroughness for understanding, by giving every word or phrase an entry in the index. This full-text indexing allows users to search the database in English, without having to learn a complex query language.

The explosive growth of the Internet has made these searching and indexing technologies even more important. The Net gives you access to a great amount of information, but it can be difficult to find the exact bit that you need. This was true when most data on the Net was in text files, and the problem has grown with the explosion of hypertext on the Web, because each link represents another possible path to the information you seek. Full-text indexing allows you to create searchable databases of any large collection of documents, including all the Web pages on your server. Doing so makes accessing the content of your site more convenient.

The easiest way to create searchable indexes on your server is to use freeWAIS. freeWAIS is one of the most powerful and widely used full-text indexing packages on the Net. WAIS stands for Wide Area Information Servers and refers to a protocol standard for search and retrieval over a network. The WAIS protocol is based on Z39.50, the 1988 version of the ANSI standard for communicating with electronic library catalogs.

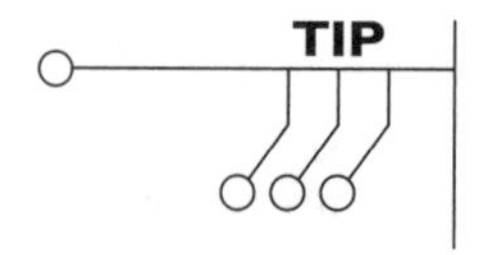

CNIDR is working on a next-generation replacement for freeWAIS called Isite. This package will feature faster searching, an extendable API and compliance with the current Z39.50 standard. For more information look at the URL http://vinca.cnidr.org/software/Isite/Isite.html.

WAIS was first designed and implemented by Thinking Machines, Inc., for the enormous text databases needed by customers like Dow Jones. Thinking Machines generously donated an implementation of the protocol and its full-text search and index system to the public domain. Eventually, the programmers who designed WAIS left Thinking Machines to found WAIS, Inc., a company devoted to further developing the WAIS technology. Support for the public domain version of WAIS passed to the Clearinghouse for Networked Information Discovery and Retrieval (CNIDR), who changed the package's name to freeWAIS.

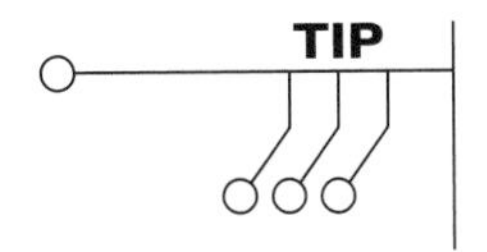

The newest version of the freeWAIS package can be found at ftp://ftp.cnidr.org/pub/NIDR.tools/freewais.

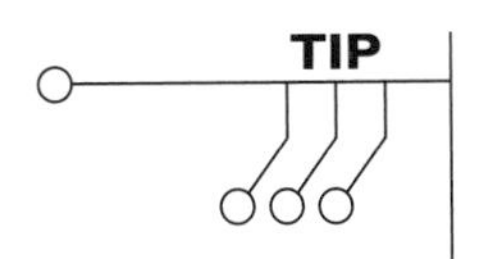

You can keep up with new developments in WAIS by subscribing to the WAIS newsgroup, comp.infosystems.wais. You may also want to read the WAIS developers mailing list, wais-talk@wais.com. To subscribe, send a message with "subscribe wais-talk" in the message text to wais-talk-request@wais.com.

Overview of WAIS

Although the WAIS protocol can be used to ask questions of any sort of database, this chapter discusses only the full-text indexes that freeWAIS creates. In these databases, the basic retrievable unit is called a *document*. A document consists of a file, or a piece of a file, and is associated with a DocID, a type and a headline.

The DocID is like a URL; it uniquely locates a document within the database. The headline functions as the document's title, and the freeWAIS search engine gives a higher priority to search terms found in the headline than in the rest of the document. The document type has the same function as the MIME type in HTTP; you can configure WAIS clients to execute helper applications (called viewers) to display nontext documents, based on their type.

WAIS, like HTTP, follows a client-server model. The user of a WAIS client selects one or more "sources" to search; each source contains all the information the client needs to find the database on the network. After the user has selected the proper sources, he or she enters the terms for which he or she wants to search. WAIS queries can be stated in plain English; often they take the form of a question or request: "What is the population of Mozambique" or "Tell me about Scientology in Utah." Many WAIS servers (including freeWAIS version 0.4) also understand simple Boolean queries like

```
(dingo and cat) or ginko not aardvark
```

This query would result in a set of documents with either the word "ginko" or with both "dingo" and "cat." None of the returned documents would contain the word "aardvark."

The freeWAIS server also supports literal and partial-word queries. Literal queries are placed inside quotation marks; the server returns only documents that contain the entire phrase. Because of the way the WAIS index is implemented, these queries are usually much slower than normal searches. Partial-word queries allow the user to search for only the first part of a word as in the following:

```
anim*
```

This query would match documents, for example, with words that begin with the string "anim", "animal", "animus" or "anime".

The WAIS client does no parsing of the query; it has no way of knowing what query syntaxes the WAIS server recognizes. It merely constructs a WAIS request out of this information and queries each of the servers in the sources the user has selected. Each server searches the databases for which it's responsible and notes documents that contain the query words. It ranks these documents based on the quantity and placement of the hits and returns a list of their headlines and DocIDs to the client.

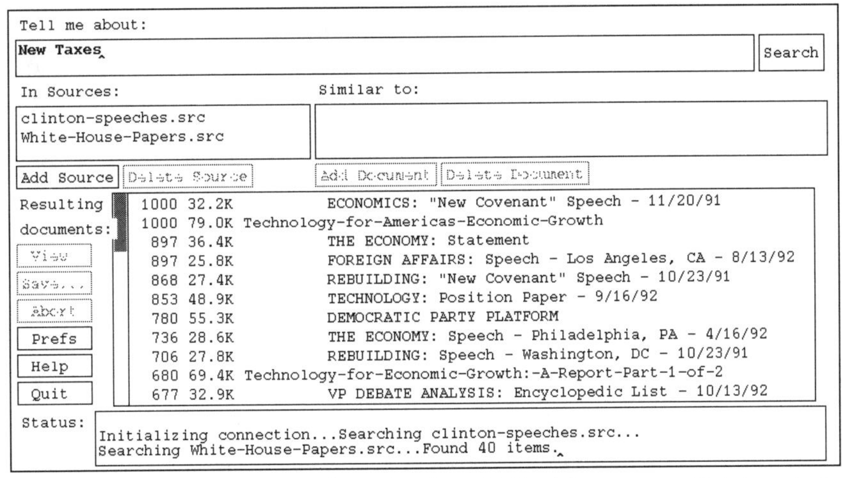

Figure 9-1: *The WAIS client (here the client is Xwais) presents a list of ranked results.*

The client is responsible for merging the lists it receives from the various servers. It presents the final results to the user, listing the documents' headlines and computed rankings, as shown in Figure 9-1. The user then selects interesting-looking documents from the list, and the client retrieves the appropriate DocIDs from the server. While this is all the functionality that some WAIS clients provide, advanced clients allow the user to refine his or her search using relevance feedback.

The relevance feedback feature allows the user to mark documents, or pieces of documents, as relevant to his or her search, and to resubmit the query. The client transmits this added information to the server, asking it for documents that are similar to those that the user noted. The freeWAIS search engine adds the words in the relevant text to its search criteria and runs the search again; since freeWAIS is searching an index, this approach is fairly fast. Once the new search is complete, the server collects the results and sends them to the client. From there, the user can mark further documents as relevant, repeating the process until he or she is satisfied with the information collected.

As you can see, the interaction between client and server in WAIS can be complex. Their dialog allows researchers to quickly narrow and refine their searches as they work through large amounts of indexed material. Although WAIS offers these abilities to the advanced user, its speed and easily phrased queries make it a good choice for simple searches as well.

A wide variety of WAIS clients are available. Their interfaces vary widely, from simple command-line clients to advanced clients for every windowing system. The freeWAIS distribution includes the following five clients:

Client	Description
waissearch	A simple command-line client
waisq	Another command-line client, suitable for use by other programs, like fwais (see Chapter 10, "Simple Forms")
xwais	A client for the X windowing system
swais	A full-screen, text-only, client
wais.el	A client for use with the Emacs editor

Table 9-1: *Clients included in the freeWAIS distribution.*

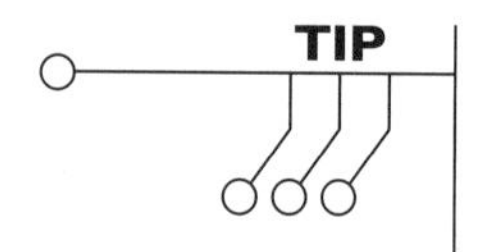

More WAIS clients (for every platform) can be found at ftp://sunsite.unc.edu/pub/wais/clients.

The WAIS Indexer

The WAIS indexer creates the special full-text databases used by freeWAIS. These indexes are roughly the same sizes as the original files, and the process of building them requires twice as much space. For this reason, it's important to make sure you have enough room on your disk before building a new database.

Creating an Index

To begin, make sure the WAIS binary and documentation directories are in the appropriate search paths:

```
$ PATH=$PATH:/usr/local/freeWAIS-0.4v/bin; export PATH
$ MANPATH=$MANPATH:/usr/local/freeWAIS-0.4v/man; export
MANPATH
```

Once you've set your paths, you're ready to index some files. Since I receive a lot of e-mail, I find it useful to index my mailbox occasionally. This lets me track down lost messages and overlooked questions without wading through my backlog of 500 messages. All you need to do to create a local index of your mail, named mymail, is to enter the following:

```
$ waisindex -d mymail -t mail_or_rmail /usr/spool/mail/jem
```

You can substitute your own mailbox for /usr/spool/mail/jem. waisindex has a large number of built-in filters that break files down into their component documents and locate the appropriate headlines. The index in the example was created with the mail_or_rmail filter in waisindex, which can parse out the individual message from a mail file; it also creates a headline composed of the sender's address and the message subject. (For a discussion of waisindex's many other filters, see "waisindex Filters" later in this chapter.) When waisindex has finished parsing and indexing the documents, it creates seven files. The names and functions of these files are listed in Table 9-2. Of the files described there, only the catalog and the source file are human-readable; the rest contain binary data.

File	Description
mymail.dct	The dictionary file holds a list of all the words in the indexed documents and pointers to their entries in the index file.
mymail.inv	The inverted index lists all the words in the documents, along with their locations in the original file and their relative importance.
mymail.doc	The document file includes all necessary information for extracting WAIS documents (each mail message is a different document) from the mailbox.
mymail.fn	The filename table lists all files that make up the index and their WAIS types.
mymail.hl	The headline table lists all WAIS headlines and where to find them in the file. For mail, a headline is composed of the sender and the subject.
mymail.src	The source file includes all the information that a WAIS client needs to find and search this database. Since this is a local database, only local clients can search it.
mymail.cat	The catalog contains a human-readable list of all the WAIS documents in the index, including their headlines, DocIDs and types.

Table 9-2: *Files created by waisindex.*

You can search the index you've just created with waissearch, a simple, command-line WAIS client:

```
$ waissearch -d mymail book release party in May
```

This command searches your database for the words "book release party May" and returns a list of messages that contain some or all of those words. The word "in" is not relevant to the search because WAIS ignores short and extremely common words. Read "Stop Words" later in this chapter to learn how to configure and fine-tune this feature.

Exporting a Database

The mymail database, which we have just created with waisindex and searched with waissearch, is local. Only users with accounts on your server can search it, and since your mail file isn't world-readable, only you can access this database. To create a database that anyone can search, you need to use the -export option with waisindex:

```
$ waisindex -export -d mymail -t mail_or_rmail /usr/spool/mail/jem
```

If you're running a WAIS server and you put the resulting database files in the index directory on the server (see "The WAIS Server" later in this chapter), anyone on the Internet can search them. CNIDR keeps a central directory of all the publicly available WAIS databases on the Internet. If you think your database has general appeal, you can add its source record to CNIDR's "server of servers" with the -register option:

```
$ EDITOR=vi; export EDITOR
$ waisindex -export -register -d mymail -t mail_or_rmail /usr/spool/mail/
jem
```

When waisindex is finished, it opens the source file in the text editor you've defined in the EDITOR environment variable. The WAIS source file contains a series of fields separated by colons (see Figure 9-2). Although the standard lists a great number of possible fields, the indexer actually uses only a few. A list of these is in Table 9-3.

Field	Description
version	The version number of the protocol; the current version is 3.0.
ip-address	The IP address of your server.
ip-name	The hostname of your server; exported sources must have either an ip-name or an ip-address.
tcp-port	The WAIS server's port; the default is 210.
database-name	The name of the database.
cost	The cost for searching this database. Since the freeWAIS server doesn't implement for cost searching, this field is usually ignored.
cost-unit	The unit for which the cost is charged. Possible values include free, dollars-per-session, dollars-per-minute, dollars-per-query and dollars-per-retrieval.
maintainer	The contact information (e-mail address, etc.) of the database's maintainer.
description	A description of the database's contents. The indexer automatically fills this in with a list of the files it indexed; you should replace this with a proper description.
keywords	A list of important words relating to the database. The indexer automatically chooses the top 15 words found in the documents.

Table 9-3: *Entries in the automatically generated source file.*

```
(:source
   :version  3
   :ip-address "198.86.40.81"
   :ip-name "sunSITE.unc.edu"
   :tcp-port 210
   :database-name "Dr-Fun"
   :cost 0.00
   :cost-unit :free
   :maintainer "wais@calypso-2.oit.unc.edu"
   :keyword-list (
                  bizarre
                  humor
                  funny
                  cartoon
                  jpg
                  )
   :description "Server created with WAIS release 8 b5 on Jan 31 18:02:14 1994 b
y root@sunsite.unc.edu
   This database indexes the captions of all the Dr. Fun cartoons published
   on sunsite. You can search the database by caption, and retrieve the
   associated cartoon.
"
)
```

Figure 9-2: *A WAIS source description.*

Editing the source file is your opportunity to make sure all the information is accurate before the source is registered. You should also write a good description of your database and add any keywords you consider important. Internet users often search CNIDR's directory of servers for databases that are pertinent to a specific problem; adding keywords and a complete description makes your source easier to find.

When you've finished modifying this source record, save the file and exit your editor. Since waisindex creates a new source file only if one doesn't already exist, you don't need to worry that it will overwrite your edited source. When you're finished, waisindex mails the modified source to wais-directory-of-servers@cnidr.org. If you forget the -register option, or wish to update your record, you can mail the source there yourself. Remember that exporting and registering a database makes it available to the entire Internet community; you don't want to do this with private information, like your mailbox!

Other waisindex Options

You can use a number of command-line options to modify the behavior of waisindex. A list of the most useful options is in Table 9-3. Most of these options are self-explanatory, but a few require additional explanation.

As Table 9-4 states, the -T option allows you to set the WAIS type when indexing files for which waisindex has no built-in filter This option can be used along with the -nocontents option, for example, to create an index of JPEGs:

```
$ waisindex -nocontents -T JPEG *.jpg
```

This command would build an index of all the file names ending in ".jpg". WAIS would not index the (all binary) contents of the JPEGs, and the files' type would be set to JPEG in the index.

Another interesting option is -nopairs. Usually, waisindex indexes adjacent capitalized words as a pair, as well as individually. This allows greater accuracy in searches for proper names. Turning this feature off reduces this accuracy but can make a dramatic difference in index size.

By default, WAIS sends the catalog (see "Creating an Index," earlier in this chapter) to clients with unsuccessful queries. Since this file contains three lines of text for each document in the index, it can be very large. You can save space on your server, and download time for the user by using the -nocat option to inhibit creation of the catalog. If you do this, you should manually edit the catalog file, adding useful instructions for searching the database.

Option	Description
-a	Adds new material to the index. Without this switch, waisindex overwrites an old index of the same name. The new index is appended to the old, but old entries aren't deleted. Thus, it's a good idea to completely re-index the entire set of files every so often to save space.
-t	Selects a filter type (see the next section, "waisindex Filters").
-r	Indexes directories recursively. With this switch, waisindex traverses all subdirectories of the directory you specify, looking for files to index.
-mem	Roughly controls the amount of memory waisindex uses (in megabytes). The default is 10mb. Other valid values are 2, 3, 4, 5, 10, 20 and greater than 20. The more RAM you allow waisindex to use for its internal tables, the faster it runs.
-e	Takes the name of a file to log onto as an argument. If you specify the –e option without providing the name of a file, the output is discarded.
-l	Sets logging level. Level 1 logs only errors and important warnings, level 5 adds messages for each file indexed and 10 (the default) logs everything (which is important if you wish to collect statistics on WAIS traffic). You can suppress logging by specifying level 0.
-v	Prints the version number for waisindex.
-stdin	Causes waisindex to take its list of files from the standard input. This option lets you pipe a list of files to be indexed from another command.
-nopairs	Turns off word pairs.
-nocat	Disables creation of the catalog.
-contents	Forces indexing of contents, which is useful for filters (like gif and pict) that usually index only the filenames.

-nocontents	Disables indexing of file contents. Only the file name is indexed.
-hlweight	Changes the additional weight given to search terms found in the headline. The default value is 10.
-T	Sets the WAIS type for the documents in the index.
-export	Causes waisindex to write a WAIS source file which can be used to access your database remotely.
-register	Registers your database with CNIDR's public Directory of Servers.

Table 9-3: *Commonly used options inwaisindex.*

waisindex Filters

Although the only text we've indexed so far has been mail folders, the WAIS indexer understands many more formats. As you saw above, the -t option is used to tell waisindex which of its internal filters to apply to the text. These filters have the following functions:

- Extract a headline from the text.
- Separate documents for formats that have more than one document per file.
- Assign a type to the indexed documents.

Although there are over 50 filters built in to the freeWAIS indexer, many of these were designed for very specific projects; they aren't important to most users. The filters that are generally useful can be broken down into four groups. The first three groups all parse documents with the TEXT type: filters for free-form text, filters for special applications and filters for the various Internet message formats. The fourth group of filters are grouped together because the documents they parse use a non-TEXT type.

Free-Form Text

Most common indexing tasks use a free-form text filter. These filters do what WAIS does best; they index text files with no real internal structure and break files into separate documents on some simple criteria. Table 9-4 contains a list of the filters that fall into this category; most are self-explanatory. You should be aware that very large databases that use the one_line type are likely to hit an internal limit in WAIS because WAIS is incapable of indexing more than 16mb of headlines.

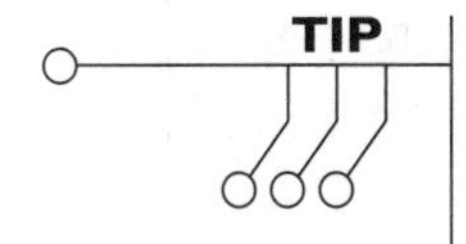

waisindex can also index files that have been compressed with the compress or gzip command. It uses the zcat command to uncompress the files before indexing them. The WAIS server also uncompresses compressed files before sending them to the client, as long as zcat is in its search path.

Even if none of the filters in Table 9-5 fits your needs exactly, one of them can often be easily adapted. For example, you may have a collection of files, with sections delimited by a series of equal signs. With a little bit of UNIX shell programming, you can change the data to fit the filter:

```
$ for i in *
> do
> sed 's/^=+/----------------------------------------/' $i > $i.tmp
> mv $i.tmp $i
> done
```

These commands run through all the files in a directory, substituting your equal signs with a row of dashes. You could then use the dash filter to waisindex the documents.

Filter	Description
text	(Default) Each file is a document; headline is the file's full name (including path).
filename	Each file is a document; the headline is the filename only.
first_line	Each file is a document; the headline is the first line of the file.
one_line	Each line is a document; the headline is also that line.
dash	Documents are separated by lines of at least 20 hyphens; the headline is the first line after the dashes.
redbook	Documents are separated by a line beginning with a pound sign (#); this line is also the headline.
formfeed	Documents are separated by Ctrl-L; the headline is the first line after the separator.
para	Documents are separated by a single blank line; the headline is the first line of the paragraph.

Table 9-5: *Free-form text filters in waisindex.*

Structured Data

The second group of filters allows you to index several structured data formats that are popular on the Internet. These filters are summarized in Table 9-6. In general, these filters are useful only for the specific data format for which they're intended.

The two exceptions are the phonix and soundex filters. These special indexers are similar to the one_line free-form text filter, but there's an important difference: they store words in a special code, based on their component sounds. They were added to freeWAIS for use in online phone books; users can look for names that they know how to pronounce, even if they don't know how to spell them.

The two filters differ in how they convert words to sounds. Neither algorithm is perfect; if you want to use this ability, index the data with both filters, allowing users to select the one that gives them the best results. On the client side, users must put "soundex" or "phonix" (as appropriate) before every word in the query. Although doing so is inconvenient, it's the price of using WAIS for an application for which it wasn't designed.

Filter	Description
BibTeX	Each reference in BibTeX format is a document; the headline is the reference's title. This filter also indexes latex files, in which the headline is document's title.
Refer	Each reference in Refer format is a document; the headline is composed of reference's title, author and date.
Medline	Each reference in Medline format is a document; the headline is composed of the reference's title, author and date.
emacsinfo	Documents are in GNU TeXInfo format; the headline is the name of the Info node.
oneline_phonix	Each line is a document; the headline is that same line. Entries are stored in the index phonetically.
oneline_soundex	Each line is a document; the headline is that same line. Entries are stored in the index phonetically.

Table 9-6: *Special application filters in waisindex.*

Internet Message Formats

Indexing mailboxes was the first application for which we used WAIS in this chapter. We explained how to index your mail for a good reason! Overflowing electronic mailboxes and USENET news queues are a leading cause of info-glut on the Internet. By indexing your archives of mail and news, you can quickly access the information they contain without spending the time to read each message one by one.

Many people have found this use of WAIS to be invaluable. In fact, Brewster Kahle, the original designer of WAIS, saves every bit of mail he's ever sent or received and indexes all of it. WAIS has a wide assortment of filters for parsing the various message types popular on the Internet; this third group of filters is summarized in Table 9-7.

Filter	Description
mail_or_rmail	Each mailbox message is a document; the headline is composed of the sender and subject.
mime	Entirely the same as mail_or_rmail. The document's type is specified as MIME, allowing multimedia mail agents to handle it specially.
mail_digest	Each message in Internet standard mailing list digest format (messages separated by 30 dashes) is a document; the headline is the same as the headline in mail_or_rmail.
listserv_digest	Each message in a digest produced by Listserv (message separated by 40 equal signs) is a document; the headline is composed of sender and subject preceded by "Re:".
rn	Documents are messages saved by the rn or trn newsreaders; the headline is the same as the headline in mail_or_rmail.

Table 9-7: *Message filters in waisindex.*

Non-TEXT Filters

The fourth and final set of filters that WAIS provides are grouped together because they assign some type other than TEXT to the documents they index. WAIS types are used for the same purpose as MIME types in HTTP: to allow the client to launch a helper application to view data that it can't handle itself. Although all the filters discussed in this section use a non-TEXT type, they don't have much more in common; the summaries in Table 9-8 require further explanation.

With the html filter, WAIS indexes HTML files. WAIS treats them like ordinary text files, except that the indexer extracts any text between the <TITLE> tags for use as a headline. In addition, the indexer gives these documents the HTML type. With this information, standalone WAIS clients can start a Web browser with which to view them, and WAIS gateways, like fwais, can treat them properly.

WAIS also reserves a special filter, called server, for indexing WAIS source files, which you can use by invoking the server filter. Meta-servers, like CNIDR's directory of servers, use this type to index the source files that are registered with them. This allows users who do searches on the directory to add the sources it returns to their library of WAIS sources.

The ps and dvi filters are both brute-force applications of WAIS to complex formats. WAIS makes no attempt to extract the actual text in a PostScript document; it indexes the PostScript commands as well as the actual words. It gives a similar treatment to TeX's DVI format, relying on its (imperfect) ability to extract text from the surrounding binary data.

The gif, tiff and pict filters are even cruder. They index only the filename, leaving the data untouched. Of course, this limited indexing is understandable; indexing images is really outside of WAIS' domain. To get vaguely acceptable results, use long, descriptive filenames like sad-clown-with-flower.gif for images you wish to index; WAIS understands dashes as word separators.

Filter	Description
html	Each HTML file is a document; the headline is the HTML <TITLE>. The document type is HTML.
server	Each WAIS source file is a document; the headline is the filename of the source. The document type is WSRC.
ps	Each PostScript file is a document; the headline is the filename. The document type is PS.
dvi	Each TeX DVI file is a document; the headline is the filename. The document type is DVI.
gif	Each GIF is a file; the contents aren't indexed, only the filename is, which is also the headline. The document type is GIF.
pict	Each PICT is a file; the contents aren't indexed, only the filename is, which is also the headline. Document type is PICT.
tiff	Each TIFF is a file; the contents aren't indexed, only the filename is, which is also the headline. Document type is TIFF.

Table 9-8: *Non-TEXT typed filters in waisindex.*

Multi-Type Indexing

Although WAIS does a poor job of indexing files that aren't mostly text, you can use WAIS' multi-type feature to correct this problem. Multi-type indexing allows you to index together two files with the same name and different extensions. When a user searches the database, the server searches the indexed text of one file, but when the user retrieves a document, the server sends the other.

For example, you can use this feature to provide a database of GIFs and accompanying text files. For each GIF, there should be a descriptive text file with the same name but ending in .TEXT, rather than .GIF. Although the capitalized extensions are awkward, multi-typing requires that the file's extension be the same as its WAIS type.

You invoke the multi-type feature with the -M option, followed by the two WAIS types you're indexing. Suppose you have four GIFs to index: car.GIF, truck.GIF, bike.GIF and skateboard.GIF; The following command indexes them along with their text descriptions:

```
$ waisindex -d transport -M GIF,TEXT -t text car.TEXT truck.TEXT
> bike.TEXT skateboard.TEXT
```

This command line creates the multi-type transport database, with the primary type TEXT and the secondary type GIF. WAIS indexes the files of the primary type that you tell it to index but returns the secondary type files when the hits are returned.

One disadvantage to this approach is that GIFs without a TEXT description won't get added to the database. You can remedy this disadvantage by creating an empty TEXT file for GIFs without real descriptions:

```
$ for i in *.GIF
> do
> foo='basename $i .GIF'
> touch $foo.TEXT
> done
```

These commands create zero-length TEXT files for every GIF in the directory. If a GIF already has an accompanying description, the touch command merely updates its timestamp.

The WAIS indexer is a powerful program that can parse and extract text in many different ways. By no means though, does it do everything. Read "Extending the Indexer" later in this chapter to learn how to add new filters to WAIS.

Incremental Indexing

Often WAIS is used to index a collection of documents that grows on a regular basis. For example, every day I make a copy of all the new articles in the newsgroups I'm interested in and add them to a WAIS index. freeWAIS comes with delta-wais.sh, a shell script that automates the indexing of new material. You can use delta-wais as follows:

```
$ delta-wais.sh mydb /usr/spool/news -mem 2 -t netnews
```

This command starts at the top of /usr/spool/news and looks for files that have been added since the last time delta-wais was run. Any new files are indexed and added to a database named mydb. You can add any additional arguments to waisindex at the end of the command line. I've used the -mem option to limit the amount of memory that waisindex uses, and I specified the proper filter with the -t option.

You can run delta-wais from cron to fully automate the process. The cron daemon is used under UNIX to run a command at some regular interval. This is what a cron entry looks like:

```
0 3 * * * delta-wais.sh mydb /usr/data -mem 2 -t netnews
```

This cron entry runs the listed command at 3:00 a.m. every morning.

Cron runs commands based on the following first five fields in the cron entry:

- Minutes—this field should be a number from 0–59.
- Hours—this field should be a number from 0–23.
- Day of the month—this field should be a number from 1–31.
- Month—this field should be a number from 1–12.
- Day of the week—this field should be a number from 0–6. The week begins on Sunday.

If any field is an asterisk, the command is run at every appropriate value of that field. For example, the above cron entry would be run at 3:00 a.m. of every day.

The method for adding a new entry to the cron tables varies among operating systems. In general, you must use the crontab command; you can investigate the local options by reading the crontab manual page. Under Linux, you add a new entry like this:

1. Change to the user that you wish the command to run under. I use root to run my indexing jobs.
2. Get a list of all the current cron jobs in the table by entering the following:

```
# crontab -l > mycrontab
```

3. Open mycrontab in your favorite editor and add the new entry.
4. Save the modified file.
5. Replace the old cron entries with the new one, as follows:

```
# crontab -r mycrontab
```

When you've completed these steps, the cron daemon reads the table and starts executing the commands at the proper time. Output from the commands is e-mailed to the user. Since waisindex's output can be fairly verbose, you may wish to redirect this output to a file with the -e switch.

Stop Words

Not all words are created equal to the WAIS indexer. The indexer eliminates any word that occurs more than 20,000 times in a collection of documents, because words that are common probably occur in every indexed document. In addition, the indexer maintains a list of almost 400 words that it ignores. This list is mostly composed of prepositions (such as "at" and "from"), articles (such as "the" and "a"), contractions (such as "can't" and "I'd") and other words that have no real semantic content. Ignoring these words serves several purposes:

- It keeps the indexes from being bloated with words for which no one wants to search.
- It allows the search engine to reserve "and," "or" and "not" for Boolean queries (see the section "Overview of WAIS" earlier in this chapter).
- It allows users to phrase their questions in English without the extra words distorting the results of the search.

Although this feature is useful (searching under WAIS wouldn't work half as well without it), specialized documents often require different behavior. For this reason, the indexer allows you to specify an alternate list of stop words with the -stop option. This list should be in alphabetical order, with one word per line, as follows:

```
aardvark
beetle
cat
dingo
emu
finch
ginko
halibut
```

When you've created your list, you can alphabetize it with the sort command:

```
$ sort stop-list > stop-list-in-order
```

When using your own stop list, it's important to remember that your list supersedes WAIS' internal list, so the indexer will index words that it usually ignores.

Synonym Lists

One of the problems with full-text indexing is that it can be difficult for the user to find the right words with which to search. This is especially true when nonspecialists search indexes of technical documents; the user knows what he or she wants but can't get past the jargon. WAIS addresses this problem with a synonym list that acts like a built-in thesaurus for your index.

To create a synonym list, edit the file my_index.syn, so that my_index is the name of the database with which the list is associated. Each line of the file consists of equivalent terms. A search for any word in the synonym list matches any other word on the same line; all terms should be lowercase, because that's how WAIS stores words. The list should look like the following (lines beginning with a pound sign are ignored):

```
#synonym list for PC-hardware database
memory ram rom cache sram dram simm sipp
cpu processor intel 8088 8080 286 386 486 pentium 68k
```

In a database indexed with this list, a search for "what is memory" would match a document that discusses SIMMs or SRAM. The way this works is simple: the indexer merely substitutes an occurrence of any word in the list with the first word of the list. Since the indexer is responsible for processing the synonym tables, you must re-index all the documents in the database when you modify the list.

If you build your indexes with a well thought out synonym list, you add your own understanding of the material to the index, making it act much more like the index of a book. Using a well-written synonym list dramatically improves the user's chance of finding information.

Extending the Indexer

Although the WAIS indexer includes a wide range of filters, you may have an indexing task for which it's unsuited. If this is the case, you have several options:

- You can try massaging the data to fit one of the built-in filters. See "waisindex Filters" earlier in this chapter for a simple example of this strategy.
- You can use WAIS' multi-type abilities to associate free-form text descriptions with your data. The section "waisindex Filters" contains an example of this.
- You might want to try freeWAIS-sf. This offshoot of freeWAIS includes an extension language that you can use to define new filters. freeWAIS-sf is available at ftp://sunsite.unc.edu/pub/packages/infosystems/wais/servers/sf-alpha. You can extend the freeWAIS indexer if you program in the C programming language.

This section provides a brief explanation of extending the indexer in C. Although you have to have some C programming ability to write a new filter for freeWAIS, you don't have to be a C wizard; the code is very simple and well-defined.

Of course, to add code to freeWAIS, you must have its source tree installed. If you haven't already installed the source to freeWAIS, follow the installation instructions provided on the Companion CD-ROM. These instructions explain how to unpack the source code and Makefiles into /usr/local/src/freeWAIS-0.4v/src. You should become the super user (if you aren't already) and move to that directory:

```
# cd /usr/local/src/freeWAIS-0.4v/src
# ls
Makefile client/ indexer/ ir/  server/
```

As you can see, there are four directories in /usr/local/src/freeWAIS/src. Each contains the source code for a different part of the freeWAIS distribution:

- **client** This directory contains the source for the various WAIS clients that come with freeWAIS, including waissearch and waisq.
- **indexer** This directory contains the source for the WAIS indexer; it parses only the command line and sets up your options before calling the routines defined in ir.
- **ir** This directory contains the source for all the indexing and searching routines used by freeWAIS.
- **server** This directory contains the source for the WAIS server; it contains the code for handling network connections and interfaces to the search routines defined in ir.

Since you're defining to indexing functions, you need to add them to the work-horse code in the ir directory. After you've defined the functions and linked them to the WAIS libraries, you need to add a little code to the WAIS indexer to add a command-line option to call your new filter.

There are four simple functions that WAIS uses to define a filter. You should create a new C source file in the ir directory to store your implementations of them. Since my example code parses an HTML file in which sections are divided by a named anchor, I call my file aname.c. The following four functions need to be defined to add this new filter to the indexer:

- **boolean aname_separator_function(char *line)** This function is called on every line of the datafile and returns True if the line marks the end of a document. Otherwise, it returns False. My function returns True when it finds the string "<a name=" or "<A NAME=".

- **void aname_header_function(char *line)** This function is called on every line of the datafile. It should look for text to add to the headline and accumulate it in a global variable. My function uses the first header in the section as the headline.
- **void aname_finish_header_function(char *header)** This function is called when the separator_function returns True. It's responsible for copying the accumulated headline into the header variable and resetting any global variables your functions use for the next document.
- **time_t equal_date_function(char *line)** This function is called on every line of the datafile. It looks for a date for the document. When it finds one, it returns the date in standard UNIX format (seconds since midnight, Jan. 1, 1970). I'm not actually going to define this function, allowing WAIS to set the date according to the file's timestamp.

Here are some sample routines. Example 9-1 is the C module that contains the code for them, while the header file that contains function prototypes for them is Example 9-2. After you read the code in iraname.c, you may want to compare those functions with the filter functions that come with freeWAIS. You can find those in freeWAIS-0.4v/src/ircfiles.c.

Example 9-1: freeWAIS-0.4v/src/ir/aname.c—Routines to add named anchor parsing to waisindex.

```
/*
 * jem@sunsite.unc.edu 2-23-95
 *
 * aname.c: ircfiles module to split an HTML file on named anchors
 * headline is the first  header in the section.
 *
 */
#include <string.h>
#include "cutil.h"
#include "aname.h"
```

```
boolean aname_separator_function(char *line) {
        if (strstr(line, "<a name=") != NULL || strstr(line, "<A NAME=") !=
NULL) {
                return true;
        }
        else return false;
}

char aname_header[MAX_HEADER_LEN+1];
boolean haveheader=false;

void aname_header_function(char *line) {
char *h1ptr;
const int h1size = sizeof("") - 1;

        if (!haveheader && ((h1ptr = strstr(line, "")) != NULL ||
         (h1ptr = strstr(line, "")) != NULL)) {

                h1ptr += h1size;
                fs_strncpy(aname_header, h1ptr, MAX_HEADER_LEN);

                if ((h1ptr = strstr(aname_header, "</h1>")) ||
                 (h1ptr = strstr(aname_header, "</H1>"))) {
                        *h1ptr = '\0';
                }
                haveheader = true;
        }
}

void aname_finish_header_function(char *header) {
        if (strlen(aname_header) == 0) {
                strcpy(header, "No Title");
        }
        else {
                fs_strncpy(header, aname_header, MAX_HEADER_LEN);
        }
        aname_header[0] = '\0';
        haveheader = false;
}
```

Example 9-2: freeWAIS-0.4/include/aname.h—Header file for aname.c.

```
/*
 * jem@sunsite.unc.edu 2/23/95
 *
 */

#ifndef _H_aname
#define _H_aname

#define MAX_HEADER_LEN 100

boolean aname_separator_function( char *line );
void aname_header_function( char *line );
void aname_finish_header_function( char *header );

#endif
```

As you can see, this code is fairly simple. You should note :

- cutil.h is included in order to define the Boolean type.
- cutil.h also contains the prototype for fs_strncpy().
- fs_strncpy() is a WAIS defined routine. It's the same as strncpy, except that it guarantees that the target string is null-terminated.

The include file, aname.h, should go in /usr/local/freeWAIS-0.4v/include. When you have all the pieces, you add these routines to the WAIS indexer like this:

1. Compile the new module: # cc -c aname.c.
2. Add the new module to the wais.a library as follows:

```
# ar r ../../bin/wais.a aname.o
# ranlib ../../bin/wais.a
```

3. Add aname.h to the list of files included in src/ir/indexer/waisindex.c: #include "aname.h"
4. Add code to src/ir/indexer/waisindex.c in the appropriate place (see Figure 9-3) to print a usage message for the new option:

```
fprintf(stderr, "   | aname  /*split html files on <a name=>,title is the first */
\n");
```

5. Add code to src/ir/indexer/waisindex.c in the appropriate place (see Figure 9-4) to parse the new option:

```
else if (0 == strcmp("aname", next_argument)){
 dataops.type="HTML";
 typename = next_argument;
 dataops.separator_function = aname_separator_function;
 dataops.header_function = aname_header_function;
 dataops.finish_header_function = aname_finish_header_function;
 }
```

6. Move to the top of the freeWAIS tree and remake the indexer

```
# cd /usr/local/src/freeWAIS-0.4v
# make waisindex
```

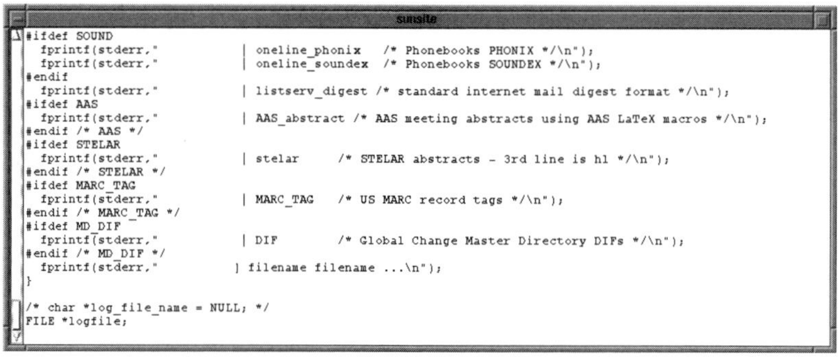

```
sunsite
#ifdef SOUND
  fprintf(stderr,"              | oneline_phonix   /* Phonebooks PHONIX */\n");
  fprintf(stderr,"              | oneline_soundex  /* Phonebooks SOUNDEX */\n");
#endif
  fprintf(stderr,"              | listserv_digest /* standard internet mail digest format */\n");
#ifdef AAS
  fprintf(stderr,"              | AAS_abstract /* AAS meeting abstracts using AAS LaTeX macros */\n");
#endif /* AAS */
#ifdef STELAR
  fprintf(stderr,"              | stelar     /* STELAR abstracts - 3rd line is hl */\n");
#endif /* STELAR */
#ifdef MARC_TAG
  fprintf(stderr,"              | MARC_TAG   /* US MARC record tags */\n");
#endif /* MARC_TAG */
#ifdef MD_DIF
  fprintf(stderr,"              | DIF        /* Global Change Master Directory DIFs */\n");
#endif /* MD_DIF */
  fprintf(stderr,"             ] filename filename ...\n");
}

/* char *log_file_name = NULL; */
FILE *logfile;
```

Figure 9-3: *Usage messages in src/indexer/waisindex.c.*

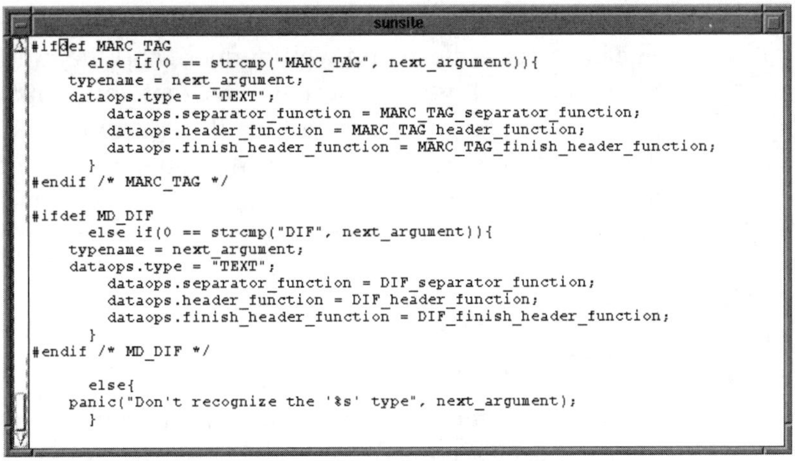

```
#ifdef MARC_TAG
      else if(0 == strcmp("MARC_TAG", next_argument)){
    typename = next_argument;
    dataops.type = "TEXT";
        dataops.separator_function = MARC_TAG_separator_function;
        dataops.header_function = MARC_TAG_header_function;
        dataops.finish_header_function = MARC_TAG_finish_header_function;
      }
#endif /* MARC_TAG */

#ifdef MD_DIF
      else if(0 == strcmp("DIF", next_argument)){
    typename = next_argument;
    dataops.type = "TEXT";
        dataops.separator_function = DIF_separator_function;
        dataops.header_function = DIF_header_function;
        dataops.finish_header_function = DIF_finish_header_function;
      }
#endif /* MD_DIF */

      else{
    panic("Don't recognize the '%s' type", next_argument);
      }
```

Figure 9-4: *Option parsing in src/indexer/waisindex.c.*

When you're finished, waisindex is ready to index the new "aname" type. I wrote this filter to index stories in an online newspaper, like the one in Example 9-3. You can test the new filter on that file, if you like.

Example 9-3: testdata/newspaper.html—A sample file for "aname" indexing.

```
<A NAME=sports>UNC Wins National Championship Again!</H1>
<P>
The University of North Carolina won the NCAA Collegiate Basketball
tournament once again.
<P>
<A NAME=national>Large Monster Eats New York</H1>
<P>
        Once again, a large radioactive beast has gobbled most of
Manhattan's important landmarks.
<P>
```

As you can see, adding a new filter to waisindex is not difficult. The interface is clean and well-defined, and the functions are easy to implement. If you add a new filter that you think others would find useful, you should contribute it to the main distribution. Send your patches to freewais@cnidr.org. You may also want to post them to the WAIS newsgroup, comp.infosystems.wais, and the WAIS developer's mailing list, wais-talk@wais.com.

The WAIS Server

The WAIS server is responsible for responding to incoming WAIS requests. A new copy of the server is started for each connection; if the request is a search, the server looks in its index directory (/usr/local/freeWAIS-0.4v/indices), opens the appropriate index and searches for the user's query. If the client asks for a DocID, the server checks the index to find the file name that goes with that DocID and sends that document to the client.

Standalone Servers

You can run the WAIS server in two ways: standalone or from inetd. If you configure it to run standalone, the WAIS server is started at system boot-up and begins listening for connections to the WAIS port. When there is a new connection, the main WAIS server forks, creating a copy of itself to deal with the client's requests. This copy exits when it has finished serving the client.

To run a standalone WAIS server, you merely have to add a line to the scripts that are executed at boot-up. Under Linux, this file is /etc/rc.d/rc.local; under another operating system, the file may be called /etc/rc.local, or you may need to create a separate script in the /etc/rc2.d directory. If you're not sure, consult your system administrator's manual.

When you've located the proper file, designate yourself as superuser and open the script in your favorite text editor. Add the following lines to the end of the script:

```
if [ -x /usr/local/freeWAIS-0.4v/bin/waisserver ]
then
echo "Starting WAIS server"
cd /usr/local/freeWAIS-0.4v
bin/waisserver -p 210 -e adm/server.log -u nobody -d indices -l 10 &
else
echo "Can't start WAIS server!"
fi
```

When you're finished, save the file and exit your editor. These lines that you entered in the script check to see if the WAIS server exists; if it does, they start it, with several command-line options that configure its behavior (see Table 9-8). Although you've added these lines to your system's start-up scripts, they won't be run until the next time you reboot the computer. To start the server, as superuser you should type the following:

```
# cd /usr/local/freeWAIS-0.4v
# bin/waisserver -p 210 -e adm/server.log -u nobody -d indices -l 10 &
```

Check the server's log to make sure it started correctly:

```
# cat /usr/local/freeWAIS-0.4v/adm/server.log
11142: 0: Feb 15 20:19:36 1995: -2: Warning: No SRC's found in directory
foo. IN
FO db not created
11142: 1: Feb 15 20:19:36 1995: 100: Running server freeWAIS Release
0.4v
```

If the log contains no errors, and you see the "Running server" line, the server is running and listening for requests.

Option	Description
-p	Specifies the port to listen to. The "well-known" port for WAIS is 210.
-e	Indicates a file to log connections and errors to.
-u	Specifies a username to run under. By using the "nobody" user, you ensure that the server can only access world-readable files.
-d	Directs the server where to look for its indices and database files.
-v	Tells the server to print version information on start-up.
-l	Sets logging level. Level 1 logs only errors and important warnings, and level 5 adds client initialization information, and 10 (the default) logs everything (which is important if you wish to collect statistics on WAIS traffic). You can suppress logging by specifying level 0.

Table 9-10: *waisserver options.*

Using Inetd

You can also configure the WAIS server to run from inetd. Inetd is the "super server"; it listens for connections on many different ports and runs the appropriate server when a client makes a connection to one of them. If you add WAIS to inetd's list of services, it starts a WAIS server when one is needed. Although using inetd adds a bit of additional overhead for each connection, it saves system resources on servers with few WAIS queries, because the WAIS server is running only when it's needed.

To run the server from inetd, you must modify two files. The first of these, /etc/services, is used to define well-known ports and the protocols that use them. If you use NIS (also called YP) to share system databases on your local network, you need to update them with the yppush command for changes to this file to take effect. Become the superuser and open /etc/services with your editor, adding this line to the end of the file:

```
z3950   210/tcp     # Z39_50 protocol for WAIS
```

The second file you need to modify is /etc/inetd.conf. This is the inetd configuration file; it tells inetd which ports to listen to and what action to take when it detects a connection. Still as superuser, open this file and add this (all one line) to the end:

```
z3950 stream tcp nowait nobody /usr/local/freeWAIS-0.4v/bin/waisserver
waisserver.d -e /usr/local/freeWAIS-0.4v/adm/server.log -d
/usr/local/freeWAIS-0.4v/indices -l 10
```

This entry should work on most UNIX systems. A notable exception is Ultrix, which uses this format:

```
z3950 stream tcp nowait /usr/local/freeWAIS-0.4v/bin/waisserver
waisserver.d -e /usr/local/freeWAIS-0.4v/adm/server.log -d
/usr/local/freeWAIS-0.4v/indices -l 10 -u nobody
```

The fourth field, which is omitted under Ultrix, tells inetd which user to run the server under. Ultrix doesn't allow you to specify a user; servers started from inetd under Ultrix always run as root. Since this is a potential security problem, I've added the -u option to have the WAIS server change its own user ID to the "nobody" ID, which has no system privileges. You can find the meaning of the other options in Table 9-10.

After you add the appropriate lines to /etc/services and /etc/inetd.conf, you need to alert inetd that its configuration files have changed. To do this, find the process number (PID) of inetd, and send it the HUP, or hang-up, signal; this will make inetd re-read its configuration files (on a System V system, like Solaris and Irix, use the -aef options to ps, instead):

```
# ps -aux | grep inetd
root  11253  0.0  3.4  156  256  p 5 S 23:01  0:00  grep inetd
root  43     0.0  1.0  72   80   con S Feb 1  0:00  /usr/sbin/inetd

# kill -HUP 43
```

When inetd receives the signal, it rereads /etc/inetd.conf and begins listening for WAIS connections.

Server Security

By default, the WAIS server allows anyone to access exported databases. You can change this with the SERV_SEC and DATA_SEC control files, which go in the server's indices directory. If either of them exist, WAIS validates every connection against the information in the file. The server rejects connections from any host that isn't given specific permission to do the search.

The SERV_SEC control file contains a list of hosts and domains that are allowed to connect to the server:

```
grumpy.shoop.com 115.23.42.5
foobar.org 127.96.17
```

This SERV_SEC would allow connections only from grumpy.shoop.com and machines with the foobar.org domain. Listing the IP address of the machines and domains is optional; only the hostname is required.

The DATA_SEC file allows you to control access on a per-database basis. It includes a list of databases that you wish to make available for searching; if a database isn't in the list, no remote client can access it.

The first field is the name of the database that you're making accessible. The second field is the name of the host or domain that you want to allow to search that database; the third, and optional, field is the IP address for that domain or host. Here's an example:

```
mydb  grumpy.shoop.com 115.23.42.5
mydb  fast.vpizza.com 197.13.7.53
telephone-numbers floofco.com
support * *
```

This sample DATA_SEC file gives access to three databases: mydb, telephone-numbers and support. Access to mydb is granted to two hosts, grumpy.shoop.com and fast.vpizza.com, while only hosts in the floofco.com domain may search the telephone-numbers index. The asterisks after "support" are wildcards; that database is publicly available, and any host on the Net can search it.

Of course, these files don't overrule the usual permissions of the system. If you're running your WAIS server as "nobody" or some other unprivileged user, it can't serve any files that aren't world readable.

Indexing Your Web Server

One of the problems with the Web is that it can be difficult to navigate. Although hypertext is easy to browse and can take you to unexpected places, it can be frustrating if you're looking for something specific. One way to solve this problem is to use freeWAIS to create an index of all the HTML pages on your Web server.

You can create such an index like this:

```
# cd /usr/local/freeWAIS-0.4v/indices
# find /usr/local/etc/httpd/htdocs -type f -name \*.html -print | waisindex -
stdin -d siteindex -t URL /usr/local/etc/httpd/htdoc \
http://www.shoop.com && touch/usr/local/etc/httpd/INDEXTIME
```

The find command starts at the top of my Web area, /usr/local/etc/httpd/htdocs, and looks for files that have the .html extension. I use the real pathname instead of /html, because under most operating systems, the find command doesn't cross symbolic links. Linux is an exception; it uses the GNU find which crosses them if you use the -follow option.

The output of find is piped to waisindex. Since I've specified the -stdin option, waisindex reads the list of files that find generates and indexes them, creating a database called siteindex. It does this with the URL filter, a special type that we've not yet discussed.

When you index files with the URL filter, waisindex creates a headline that's equivalent to the file's URL on your server. To use this feature, you must give waisindex two additional arguments after specifying the filter:

- the text to remove from each file's pathname
- the text to add in its place

In the previous example, I've told waisindex to clip "/usr/local/etc/httpd/htdocs" from the beginning of each path, and to replace it with "http://www.shoop.com". So a file like /usr/local/etc/httpd/htdocs/homepage.html will have "http://www.shoop.com/homepage.html" as its headline.

You may be wondering why I don't use the HTML filter that was described in "waisindex Filters" earlier in this chapter. The HTML filter uses the document's <TITLE> for the WAIS headline. Although this would work fine for searching, users would have no way of finding the document later. Documents indexed with the URL filter have the correct URL attached to them, so users can collect references to successful search results.

Now you've indexed your Web area for the first time. If your indexing was successful, the touch command creates a file with a timestamp recording when the indexer finished. This file, INDEXTIME, will be used later.

The next step is to set up a cron entry that adds any new or changed pages to your index. To do this, you'll need the following command, which is slightly different:

```
cd /usr/local/freeWAIS-0.4v/indices; find /usr/local/etc/httpd/htdocs \
 -newer /usr/local/etc/httpd/INDEXTIME -type f -name \*.html -print |
waisindex -stdin -a -d siteindex -t URL /usr/local/etc/httpd/htdocs \
 http://www.shoop.com && touch /usr/local/etc/httpd/INDEXTIME
```

The find command looks for HTML files that are newer than the timestamp file that we created last. Also, in this example, waisindex uses the -a option to add new entries to the existing database. You should use the cron daemon to run this command on a daily basis. Adding entries to the cron tables was explained previously in "Incremental Indexing."

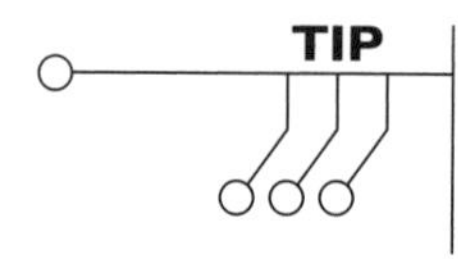

Several packages have been developed specifically for the task of indexing WWW sites. Two of the best are Harvest and Lycos. You can find more information about them at http://harvest.cs.colorado.edu/ and http://fuzine.mt.cs.cmu.edu/mlm/lycos-home.html, respectively. See Chapter 12, "Fitting In," for more information.

Moving On

By now, you should be able to use freeWAIS to create full-text indexes of any collection of documents. You should be able to

- select an appropriate filter,
- export and register your databases,
- use delta-wais to update your indexes regularly,
- set up and install the WAIS server, and
- use WAIS to index your WWW area.

When you've mastered those skills, you may want to look into the more advanced topics discussed earlier in this chapter:

- synonym lists,
- stop words, and
- extending the indexer.

Of course, having an index of your pages does you little good if users can't search them. In the next chapter, you'll learn how to create and use interactive forms in HTML. Forms allow the user to interact with your HTML pages and send information back to your server. When you've mastered the material in Chapter 10, you'll know how to set up fwais, a forms-based gateway, which allows users to search your WAIS databases from their WWW browsers.

10

Simple Forms

Most of the traditional publishing media communicate in only one direction. People read newspapers and watch television; they don't interact with them because these media are designed to carry information or entertainment from the provider to consumers. The distributed design of the Internet has the potential to break that mold and allow people to develop new patterns of communication. The recent emergence of embedded forms in HTML has realized some of this potential.

Forms allow the page designer to mix the traditional elements of the printed page with the user interface of a modern windowing system. They let you place pull-down menus and pushbuttons in the midst of formatted text and pictures. These user interface devices, or widgets, give those viewing your pages the opportunity to communicate upstream, allowing users to respond to what they are seeing, rather than being passive viewers.

Web pages are often merely static catalogs of information and pretty pictures, but the proper use of forms can make your pages dynamic. For an excellent example of dynamic Web pages, check out the Internet Underground Music Archive (IUMA) at http://www.iuma.com. Figure 10-1 is a form from IUMA that allows the user to look at the archive's music databases in several different ways: by artist, location and genre. In other words, a form like the one in Figure 10-1 lets users get the information they want, organized the way that they want it.

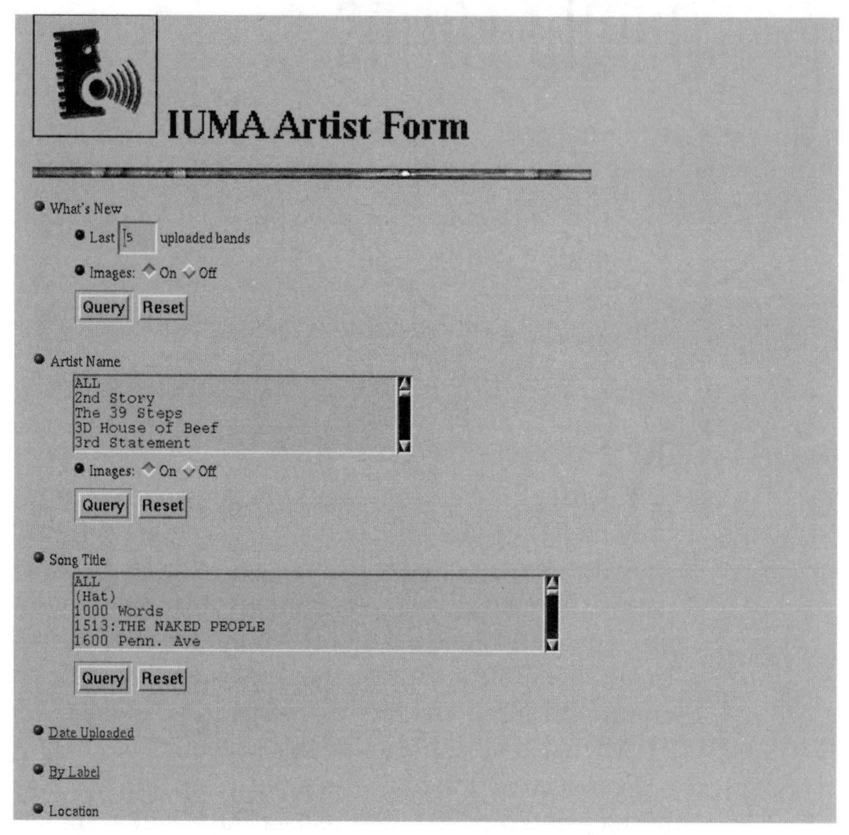

Figure 10-1: *An excellent example of the use of forms from IUMA.*

Forms can also provide feedback on the job you are doing. Although you can attach your e-mail address to every page and ask for comments, users are more likely to give you useful information about your efforts if you give them an immediate, in-context opportunity to express their views.

Another important benefit is psychological; forms can remove some of the feeling of faceless anonymity on the Net. This oppor-

tunity for feedback and interactivity reminds the user of the people on the "other side" who are responsible for the content that the user is enjoying. This somewhat intangible benefit is important, especially if you want your Internet presence to provide the basis of a dialogue or continuing relationship with a client, customer or fellow-traveler.

Although they are extremely useful, forms have a few basic limitations. The major limitation is a result of the stateless design of the HTTP protocol. Web clients make a new connection to the server each time they download a page or upload the contents of a form, and the HTTP server keeps no record of the clients' previous transactions. Although some programming tricks can get around some of the stateless limitations of HTTP (see Chapter 11, "CGI: Advanced Forms for Programmers"), the interactivity of forms cannot be used for tasks that require real-time control, such as arcade-style games. Additionally, since clients currently have to wait until they receive all of the expected data before displaying any of it, they can't use an HTTP connection for displaying video in real time, for example.

You should also keep in mind that the interactive tags that are the basis of forms are like the rest of HTML; they define functionality, rather than actual appearance. As you can see in Figures 10-2, 10-3 and 10-4, the exact implementation of these tags varies from client to client, depending on what makes sense for the platform. Although you can be assured that the user will be able to enter the appropriate data in each device, you should be careful not to depend on a particular implementation.

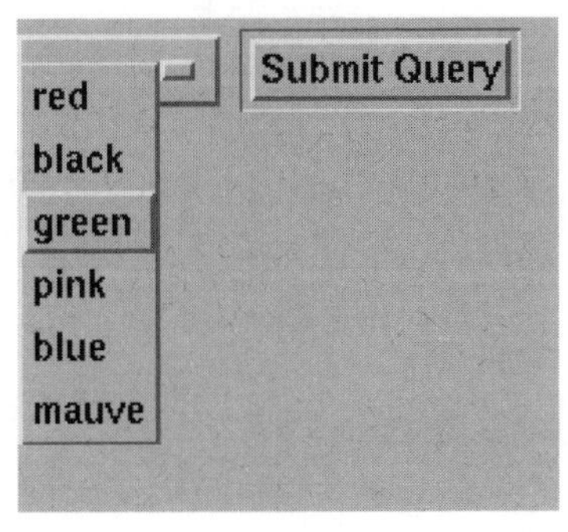

Figure 10-2: *A pull-down menu in Netscape for X.*

Figure 10-3: *A pull-down menu in MacMosaic.*

Figure 10-4: *A pull-down menu in Lynx.*

The Basic Structure of a Form

Unfortunately, HTML forms have gained a reputation for complexity, and many people believe that it takes great expertise to write and understand them. In reality though, you need to learn only a few simple elements to master the art of putting them together effectively. Every form has the same basic structure, which follows:

```
<FORM ACTION="/cgi-bin/post-query" METHOD=POST>
Hi! Welcome to palace of Glinda the Good.<P>
Where are you trying to go? <INPUT NAME=home> <BR>
<P>
<STRONG>Thank you</STRONG> for taking the time to complete this
form. </FORM>
```

Hi! Welcome to palace of Glinda the Good.

Where are you trying to go? kansas

Thank you for taking the time to complete this form.

Figure 10-5: *A simple text-entry form with a response.*

As you can see in the example, it all begins with the <FORM> tag. This tag tells the client that an interactive area has begun and will continue until the client reaches the </FORM> end tag. Since the <FORM> tag has no effect on what the page looks like to the user, it's a good idea to use <HR> tags before and after the form to visually separate it from the rest of the page.

Every <FORM> tag must have an ACTION element that specifies the program that the server should send the form's data to (the process is described in Chapter 11, "CGI: Advanced Forms for Programmers"). The program used in the previous example, post-query, is a utility for testing forms; it prints all the data that it receives from the client.

For security reasons, post-query and other programs that process submitted data are usually kept in a special directory that has the URL /cgi-bin. To learn how to set up this directory, as well as other options for keeping forms secure, see Chapter 3, "Setting Up the Server."

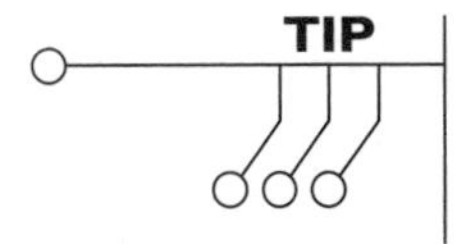

The CGI in cgi-bin stands for Common Gateway Interface, a programming standard for accessing data from HTML forms. Although programs that use this standard are commonly called CGI scripts, you should remember that CGI is not a scripting language, but an interface that any programming language can use. We'll talk about CGI in detail in Chapter 11, "CGI: Advanced Forms for Programmers."

The other element, METHOD, in the header of the example form tells the client how to send the entered data to the server. This element is optional; if you leave it out, browsers assume the default value GET. GET tells the client to embed the data from the form inside the URL; in fact, you can create hyperlinks that run CGI programs that use METHOD=GET directly. The section "fwais: A Forms Interface to WAIS," later in this chapter, contains an example of this.

When a form uses the POST method, the server sends the submitted data as if it were typed by the user. The distinctions between these two methods and the particulars of choosing the proper one, is an advanced topic; it's covered in Chapter 11, "CGI: Advanced Forms for Programmers." For now, it's enough to know that we'll be using the POST method in all of the examples in this chapter.

You can put any text or markup between the beginning and ending elements of a form, except for another <FORM> tag; you can't nest forms. In addition to regular markup, several special HTML tags are legal only inside a form; adding them elsewhere may even crash some (very poorly written) clients. Browsers render these special tags as areas for user interaction and input.

In the previous example, the form contains a question to answer, followed by two tags, <INPUT> and <BR>. As you can see in Figure 10-5, the client's rendering includes the text, followed by an embedded text-entry box into which the user has already typed his or her response. To finish the form, the user presses Return, which tells the browser that the form has been completed. The browser assigns the entered text to the tag's NAME element, which is "home," and sends this data to the server.

Every interactive tag should have a unique NAME that distinguishes it from the rest of the fields in the form. If you give two interactive elements the same NAME, the client sends both values, but the CGI program won't be able to distinguish which one came from which element. This is a result of the way that forms work in HTML; all the intelligence for understanding the entered data resides in the program that processes it. Neither the browser nor the Web server have any way of knowing if all the elements have been filled out properly, or even if they've been filled out at all—the CGI standard leaves this task to the CGI script to figure out.

Although this example is simple, it demonstrates all of the basic elements of a form; it asks for information from the user and provides a widget in which to enter it. Of course, you can choose from many more interface elements; adding any of them is as easy as inserting the appropriate HTML tag.

Submit & Reset

We discuss these two settings first because they serve an important purpose in almost every form. The first of these settings allows the user to signal that he or she has finished the form:

```
<INPUT TYPE=submit>
```

All forms require a submit setting; without it, the user has no way to send his or her responses to the server. For historical reasons, most browsers make an exception for forms that contain only a single text input (as shown in Figure 10-5). This behavior is not required by the HTML v2.0 standard, and future browsers may not support it. For those that do, pressing Return in the entry field completes the form if no Submit button is available.

Although the second of these settings, reset, is not required, it's usually a good idea to add it because it allows the user to change every element back to its default value (we'll learn how to set defaults for each interface element later in this chapter). Adding the reset setting is simple:

```
<INPUT TYPE=reset VALUE="Reset to Defaults">
```

The label on both reset and submit varies from browser to browser; for example, Lynx uses the simple "submit", while Mosaic and Netscape both use the more technical-sounding "submit query". You can easily change the text on both submit and reset with the VALUE element.

The <INPUT> Tag

The most versatile of the tags that allows user input is, appropriately, the <INPUT> tag. Not only does it provide text-entry fields like the one you saw in the simple form at the beginning of the chapter, but it is also the source of toggle buttons, password fields and hidden state information. You differentiate among all these options by adding the TYPE element to the <INPUT> tag.

Text-Entry

Text-entry widgets are the workhorses of the forms world. They are used for any fairly short, free-form response. In the following example, they are used for the fields of an address in a subscription form:

```
<FORM METHOD="POST" ACTION="/cgi-bin/post-query">
<EM>Enter your address below:</EM>
<P>
First Name: <INPUT TYPE=text NAME="first" SIZE=15>
Last Name: <INPUT TYPE=text NAME="last" SIZE=15><BR>
Street Address: <INPUT TYPE=text NAME="address" SIZE=40><BR>
City: <INPUT TYPE=text NAME="city" SIZE=15>
State or Province: <INPUT TYPE=TEXT NAME="state" SIZE=2
MAXLENGTH=2>
Country: <INPUT TYPE=text NAME="country" VALUE="USA">
Area Code: <INPUT TYPE=text NAME="zip" SIZE=5><BR>
<P>
<STRONG>OR</STRONG>
<P>
<EM>Enter your secret subscriber's code:</EM>
<INPUT TYPE=password><BR>
<P>
<INPUT TYPE=submit>
</FORM>
```

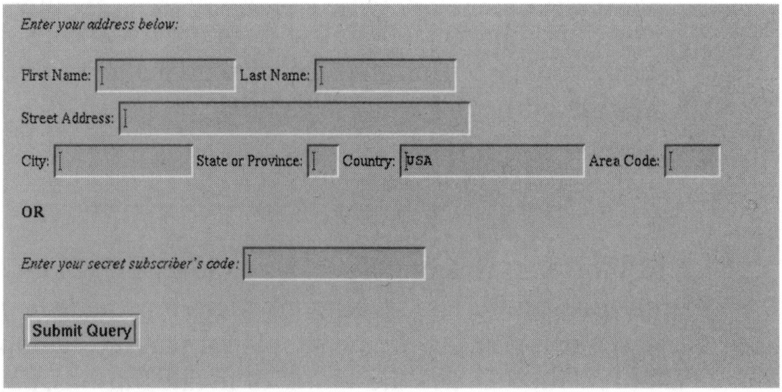

Figure 10-6: *An address form.*

This form allows the user to enter an address in a series of text-entry fields or to enter a special code, which must be kept secret for security reasons. For the address fields, we use a regular text-entry <INPUT> tag. Even though text-entry is the default, we explicitly specify text-entry with TYPE=text, which is a good idea because it clarifies the intentions of the author of the page and makes it obvious when he or she has forgotten the TYPE element in other INPUT tags.

For the subscriber's code, we use a special type of text-entry field, the password-entry field. This type of input type is identical to the regular text-entry type, except that characters typed into this box aren't echoed; instead, the client displays asterisks.

As you can see in the example, a number of elements modify the behavior of a text-entry widget. The first of these is SIZE, which changes the length of the field from the default of 20. If the user types more than this number of characters, the field scrolls left to provide more space; the SIZE value isn't a maximum limit on input.

The MAXLENGTH element, on the other hand, is such a limit. The user can't type more than two characters into the state field, for example. Although it stops the user from adding further input, MAXLENGTH doesn't automatically limit the length of the entry box; you must explicitly set that with SIZE.

The last of the optional elements that are valid with text-entry widgets is VALUE, which allows you to provide a default response for a field. You can see an example of this element in the country field in the example. When the client renders this form, shown in Figure 10-6, it places the text "USA" inside the area; if the user wants a different response, he or she must delete this default text first. The VALUE element is useful for providing examples of the type of input you desire, as well as for saving the user the trouble of typing the typical response.

Pushbuttons

The <INPUT> tag isn't only for text-entry; it can also be used to create toggle buttons. These buttons allow the user to select one or more options from a series of choices. There are two varieties of pushbuttons: the checkbox and the radio button. The first of these creates a simple button that can be toggled on and off by the user.

You can create a checkbox in your form using markup similar to the following:

```
Choose as many of the following toppings as you desire:
<P>
<INPUT TYPE=checkbox NAME="sausage" CHECKED>
Italian Sausage? (our favorite!)<BR>
<INPUT TYPE=checkbox NAME="mush">Mushrooms?<BR>
<INPUT TYPE=checkbox NAME="olive">Olives?<BR>
<INPUT TYPE=checkbox NAME="garlic">Garlic?<BR>
<INPUT TYPE=checkbox NAME="fish">Anchovies?<BR>
```

Choose as many of the following toppings as you desire:

Italian Sausage? (our favorite!)
Mushrooms?
Olives?
Garlic?
Anchovies?

Figure 10-7: *A checkbox pizza menu.*

As you can see in Figure 10-7, this HTML markup creates four options, each preceded by a button that the user can select to add that topping to his (virtual) pizza. Each button has its separate NAME element and can be independently chosen, and you can preselect a button with the CHECKED element. By default, browsers assign selected checkboxes a value of on; you can elect to give the buttons a different value with the VALUE element, as in the following example:

```
What commercial browser(s) do you use? (choose any that apply)
<P>
<INPUT TYPE=checkbox NAME="client1" VALUE="spyglass" >
Spyglass Mosaic.<BR>
 <INPUT TYPE=checkbox NAME="client2" VALUE="netscape"> Netscape
Mozilla.<BR>
 <INPUT TYPE=checkbox NAME="client3" VALUE="sesame"> Ublique's
Sesame.<BR>
```

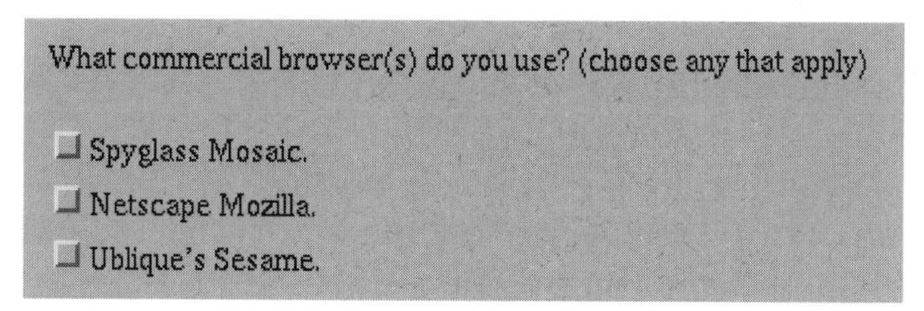
What commercial browser(s) do you use? (choose any that apply)
Spyglass Mosaic.
Netscape Mozilla.
Ublique's Sesame.

Figure 10-8: *A form with a preselected checkbox.*

Each checkbox in this example has its own specified value; when the user submits the form, the browser sends the NAME and the assigned VALUE for each button that the user invokes instead of the string "on." Browsers send no data at all about nonactivated checkboxes.

Unlike checkboxes, radio buttons aren't independent entities. Multiple radio buttons are usually grouped together, all sharing the same name. Only one radio button of a group can be selected at any one time because they behave like the presets on an old-fashioned car radio. When the user pushes a button, the last selection pops up. Radio buttons are used to select one from several exclusive options:

```
What is your sex?
<P>
<INPUT TYPE=radio VALUE="male" NAME="sex">Male<BR>
<INPUT TYPE=radio VALUE="female" NAME="sex">Female<BR>
```

This example creates two exclusive choices, each with its own radio button. Although this sort of either-or option excludes those who may be feeling confused about which option to select, it is often the easiest way to give the user concrete choices. If you want to suggest a choice, you can specify a preselected option for a single radio button with the CHECKED element.

As with all the interactive tags, you must give each button a NAME, but radio buttons are somewhat special; since the tags have the same NAME, radio buttons within the same form are linked together, no matter how far apart they appear on the page. And since radio buttons share NAME elements and the VALUE element is what distinguishes one button from the rest of its group, you always have to specify a VALUE element.

Hidden Fields

Besides text-entry and pushbuttons, the <INPUT> tag has one other important role, the hidden field. Although a hidden field is rarely important for simple forms, it allows the advanced forms author to get around one of the major obstacles to writing interactive applications for the Web: its statelessness.

Since the Web server keeps no information about a client's previous connections, any information that the application needs to remember between transactions must be kept by the client. You can keep such information either by embedding the data itself, or a key to it, in the hidden fields of a form where it is invisible to the user unless he or she views the page's HTML source. These fields aren't really interactive. (The user can't even see them, let alone interact with them!) Rather, they are more like variable assignments in a programming language; they let you equate a NAME with a VALUE:

```
<INPUT TYPE=hidden NAME="gamestate" VALUE="o--x-----">
```

This example might be from some imaginary WWW tic-tac-toe game. It declares a variable named "gamestate" and assigns it a value that represents the status for each of the nine squares. In this hypothetical application, the user would initially pull down a form that contained three rows of three single character text-entry fields (although using the <SELECT> tags might be a better choice, see the next section, "The <SELECT> Tag"). The user would enter an X in the center square, and press the Submit button.

The forms-processing program on the server's end would find the user's move and make its own, perhaps in the upper left hand corner. It would then write out a new form, like the one in Figure 10-9, with the hidden field that is shown in the previous example. By keeping track of the game's progress inside of the hidden field, the program can remember whose turn it is. It can also ensure that a user doesn't change his or her moves later in the game or try to make two moves in a single turn.

Figure 10-9: *A Tic-Tac-Toe form.*

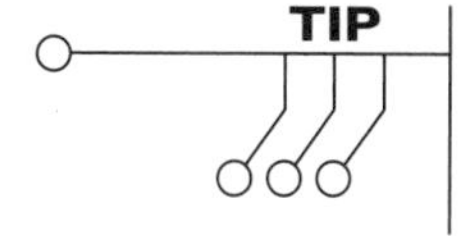

Hidden fields have an additional use in forms that serve applications: they can hold information that might change between sessions but that you don't want the user to have to supply. For example, if a user has to enter a password to read a set of pages, he or she should have to enter it only on the entry page. On each subsequent page, the password can be embedded in a hidden field, and the user can press the Submit button to request the next page of the series. For another example of this use of hidden fields, see the section "fwais: A Forms Interface to WAIS" later in this chapter.

The <SELECT> Tag

Another special interactive tag is the <SELECT> tag, which allows the user to choose one or more options from a menu. Although you can use radio buttons and checkboxes to provide similar functionality, the <SELECT> tag is often a better choice if you want to present lots of options. Too many pushbuttons can make your interface appear cluttered and can confuse the user. Like the <INPUT> tag, every <SELECT> tag requires a NAME to hold the selected option or options. The following is a brief, and absurd, example:

```
Which of the following performers do you like? <P>
<SELECT NAME="favbands" MULTIPLE SIZE=2> <OPTION> Culture Club
<OPTION> Beastie Boys
<OPTION> Negativland
<OPTION SELECTED> Tito Jackson
</SELECT>
```

Figure 10-10: *A SELECT widget as a scrollable list with two options visible.*

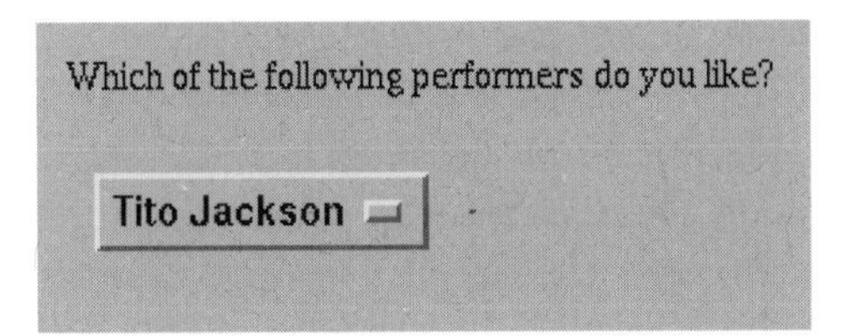

Figure 10-11: *A SELECT widget as a pull-down menu.*

As you can see, the <SELECT> tag requires both a beginning and an ending tag. Between these, you list each possible choice with the <OPTION> tag, indicating default choices with the <OPTION SELECTED> tag. All other HTML tags are illegal inside of an area enclosed by <SELECT> tags; most browsers ignore them, but some are so impolite as to crash when encountering an illegal tag.

In addition to NAME, there are also two optional elements that control the behavior and appearance of the <SELECT> tag. SIZE determines the number of menu options visible to the user at a time. In many clients, the default value of 1 (a single option visible) causes the SELECT widget to be rendered as a pull-down menu as in Figure 10-11, while values greater than 1 make it a scrollable list as in Figure 10-10. Although you can use SIZE to control the amount of vertical space that the widget occupies, browsers like Lynx, which render the <SELECT> tag in an odd way, won't honor it.

The other optional element, MULTIPLE, allows the user to choose more than a single option from the menu. Usually, this element forces the browser to give the user access to more than one option at a time, and most graphical clients display such a menu as a browsable list. If the user selects more than one option, the client sends multiple copies of the same variable NAME, each with a different VALUE.

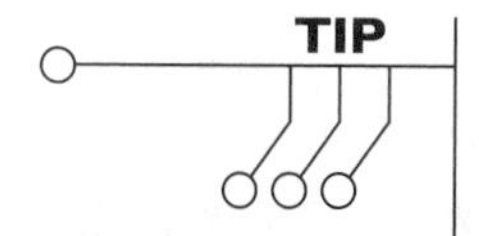

You can specify more than one default choice with the <OPTION SELECTED> tag with the MULTIPLE element. Without the MULTIPLE element, the client usually uses the first SELECTED option as the default.

The <TEXTAREA> Tag

The last of these special form tags is <TEXTAREA>, which gives you a multiple line version of the text-entry field. This area is suitable for any sort of free-form writing, and it's often used to give users a chance to send comments or e-mail to the author of the page. Although there is no official limit on the amount of text you can enter into this widget, individual clients will have their own limits, so we don't advise pasting in Shakespeare's complete works.

Like the <SELECT> tag, the <TEXTAREA> tag requires both a beginning and an ending tag; any text that you place between them becomes the default response, as shown in Figure 10-12. If the user wants to fill the area with his or her own musings, he or she must delete the default text. In many clients, deleting the default text is a pain, and since there is rarely a need for default text, most page designers leave this space empty.

The <TEXTAREA> tag has three mandatory elements that control its use and size. Like the rest of the interactive tags, every <TEXTAREA> tag requires a NAME that tells the client where to store the results. The other two elements, ROWS and COLS, give the dimensions of the writing area in characters. The following is a brief example of the use of the <TEXTAREA> tag:

```
<TEXTAREA NAME="poem" ROWS=12 COLS=80> I've never seen a
purple cow.
I never hope to see one.
But I can tell you anyhow,
I'd rather see one, than be one.
—Gelett Burgess 1866–1951
</TEXTAREA>
```

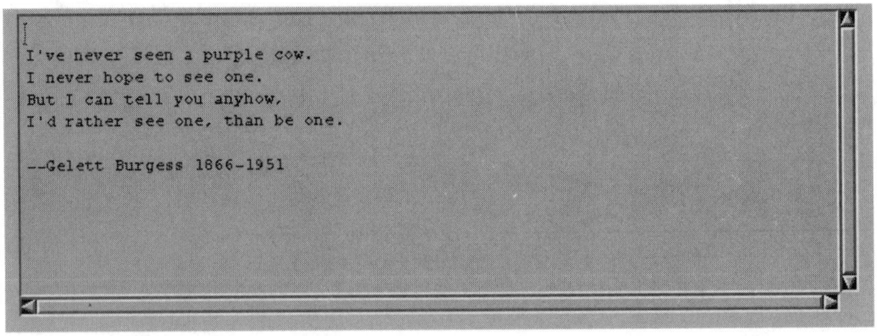

Figure 10-12: *A TEXTAREA widget with sample text.*

As you can see, the <TEXTAREA> tag pays attention to line breaks, both in the default text and in text entered by the user. Another important point is that ROWS and COLS specify the amount of space that the area occupies on the page, not the maximum amount the user can write. For example, if the user wrote a poem with 23 lines of 90 characters, the client would scroll the TEXTAREA widget both horizontally and vertically to make space for the additional characters.

Putting It Together With gform

Although designing an interface with HTML forms is fairly simple, writing a program to process the entered data can be quite complex. In the past this problem has limited the use of forms to programmers, and unfortunately, most Web authors aren't programmers. Luckily, Harry Raaymakers of Swinburne University has solved this problem with gform, a generic form-handler for the nonprogrammer.

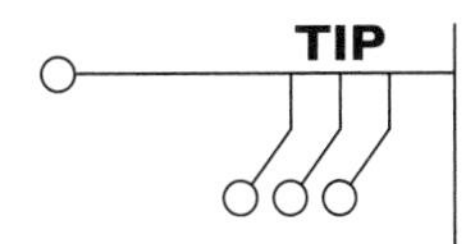

You can always find the newest version of gform at ftp://swin.edu.au/pub/cwis.

Using gform

The most common destination for form data is a log file or someone's mailbox. gform lets you design the form that *you* want and then lets you easily specify how the submitted data should be formatted and recorded. You write your form, using any of the interactive tags discussed in this chapter.

```
<FORM ACTION="/cgi-bin/gform?/pathname" METHOD=POST>
```

Replace */pathname* with the directory and filename of your page, and write the form as you please. After you've finished writing your form and have added the ending tag </FORM>, you can start adding commands to gform in this format:

```
<!gform >
```

Since the gform conmmand is in the form of an SGML directive, browsers ignore it. When the client uploads the forms data, the Web server runs gform and hands it the path of your page as an argument. gform then opens that page and reads it, assuming that anything within the <!gform > tag is a command. gform understands two types of commands: deliverable text and keywords.

Deliverable Text

Deliverable text is a string surrounded by quotation marks. This string contains text and NAMEs from the interactive tags that you used in your form. To tell gform that some part of the deliverable text is a variable, you precede it with a dollar sign, like this:

```
<FORM ACTION="/cgi-bin/gform?/pathname" METHOD=POST>
<INPUT TYPE=text NAME="job">
</FORM>
<!gform "The user's job is $job">
```

gform reads this command and makes the proper substitutions. If the user entered "fireman" in the text-entry field, gform would deliver this text: "The user's job is fireman".

gform also recognizes special escape sequences. These begin with the escape character, a backslash, and represent items that you can't otherwise include in quoted text, such as newline, tab and the literal dollar sign (which must be escaped to keep gform from interpreting it as the beginning of a variable). Table 10-1 contains a list of the escape characters that gform recognizes and indicates whether gform considers them white space.

Escape sequence	Meaning	White Space
\n	Newline	yes
\t	Tab	yes
\f	Form-feed	yes
\r	Carriage Return	yes
\$	Escape a dollar sign	no
\\	Escape a backslash	no

Table 10-1: *Escape characters recognized by gform.*

gform defines a variable as all the text between an unescaped dollar sign and the next white space or end quote. Suppose that the gform command in the previous example was this:

```
<!gform "The user's job is $job!\n">
```

gform would interpret "job" as the name of the variable and try to find an interactive tag with the NAME, "job!". It would fail, returning an error. You can get around this limitation by putting parentheses around the variable, as in the following example:

```
<!gform "The user's job is $(job)!\n">
```

This syntax would give you the results that you want. In the delivered results, gform substitutes these variables with the NAME and VALUE data that it receives from the client and writes to the output:

```
The user's job is fireman!
```

Although you don't have to use every NAME in the form, references to NAMEs that don't actually exist result in errors, and gform stops processing the submitted form.

Keywords

After you specify the text that you want gform to deliver, you have to tell gform where to put that text after it has swapped the variables with their appropriate values. To do this, you use the DELIVER keyword, which can either send the results by e-mail or append them to a file. The following command sends the results by e-mail (the quotation marks are required!):

```
<!gform DELIVER=mail SUBJECT="ATTENTION- "shoop@foo.org">
```

This command mails the text to the address shoop@foo.org with the subject line "ATTENTION". The SUBJECT keyword is optional; if you leave it out, gform sends the mail with the subject "Form */pathname* submission", where */pathname* is the location of the form. The command for appending these results to a file is also very simple:

```
<!gform DELIVER=file "/pathname">
```

This example would add the form's results to the end of a file called */pathname*; you can replace this path with the full path to a log file on your own system. It's important to make sure that the file that you tell gform to write to already exists and is world-writable; otherwise, gform won't have the necessary permissions to append to it. At the shell prompt, type:

```
$ touch /pathname
$ chmod o+w /pathname
```

This command should create a zero-length file and make it writable by gform, as well as by anyone else who has an account on your system. Unfortunately, this security risk is currently a fact of life when using forms.

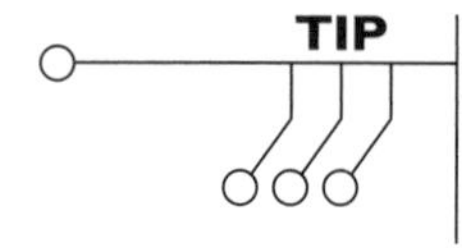

If you tell gform to deliver the results to a file, it's a good idea to add a line of dashes as the last line of deliverable text to help you separate one response from another.

The final keyword that gform understands is REPLY, which is used as follows:

```
<!gform reply="pathname.html">
```

This optional keyword specifies an HTML file, relative to the top of your HTML data area, that gform should send back to the client upon successfully processing the submitted form. If you leave this out, gform sends a simple "Thank You" as its default response.

Putting It Together

This section serves as a quick review of the various interactive elements in HTML and of how you can use them with gform. It includes two full-length examples, both of which were automatically installed when you installed gform from the Companion CD-ROM.

You can find the first example in /html/examples/gform-bridge.html. This form, shown in Figure 10-13, asks the user a couple of important questions and writes the submitted answers to a log file in the /tmp directory. In real life, writing the answers to a file in the /tmp directory might not be a good idea because everything in the /tmp directory is usually deleted when the system is rebooted.

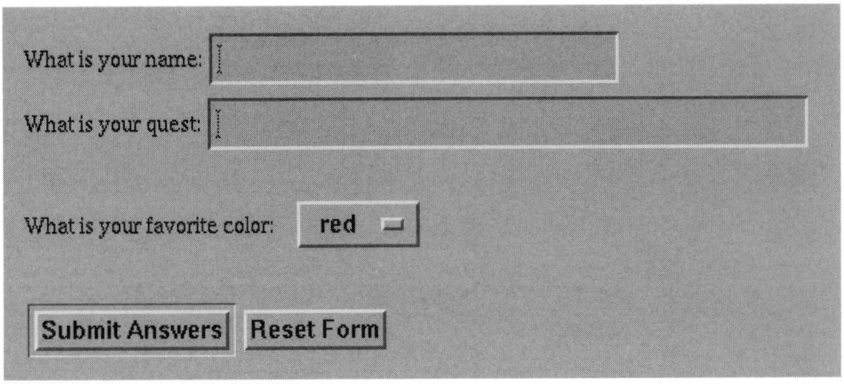

Figure 10-13: *Simple form using gform.*

Example 10-1: Example form from /html/examples/gform-bridge.html.

```
<HTML>
<FORM METHOD=POST ACTION="/cgi-bin/gform?/html/examples/gform-
bridge.html">
What is your name: <INPUT NAME="yourname" SIZE=30><BR>
What is your quest: <INPUT NAME="quest" SIZE=45><BR>
<P>
What is your favorite color:
<SELECT NAME="color">
<OPTION> red
<OPTION> blue
<OPTION> green
<OPTION> pink
<OPTION> puce
</SELECT>
<P>
<INPUT TYPE=submit value="Submit Answers"> <INPUT TYPE=reset
value="Reset Form"> <P>
</FORM>
<!gform "The knight's name is $(yourname), and his quest is (quest).\n">
<!gform "More importantly, he really likes $(color)!\n">
<!gform "--------------------------------------------------------------------------------"
<!gform DELIVER=file "/tmp/bridge-log.txt">
</HTML>
```

This form includes two text-entry fields and a select box. Assuming the user types "Galahad" and "to seek the grail" in the two input fields and chooses "blue" from the pull-down menu, gform would write the following in /tmp/bridge-log.txt:

```
The knight's name is Galahad, and his quest is to seek the grail. More
importantly, he really likes blue!
------------------------------------------------
```

The second example is a mailer that lets the user send a message to the author of the page, a common task on the Web. The page can be found in /html/examples/gform-mailer.html.

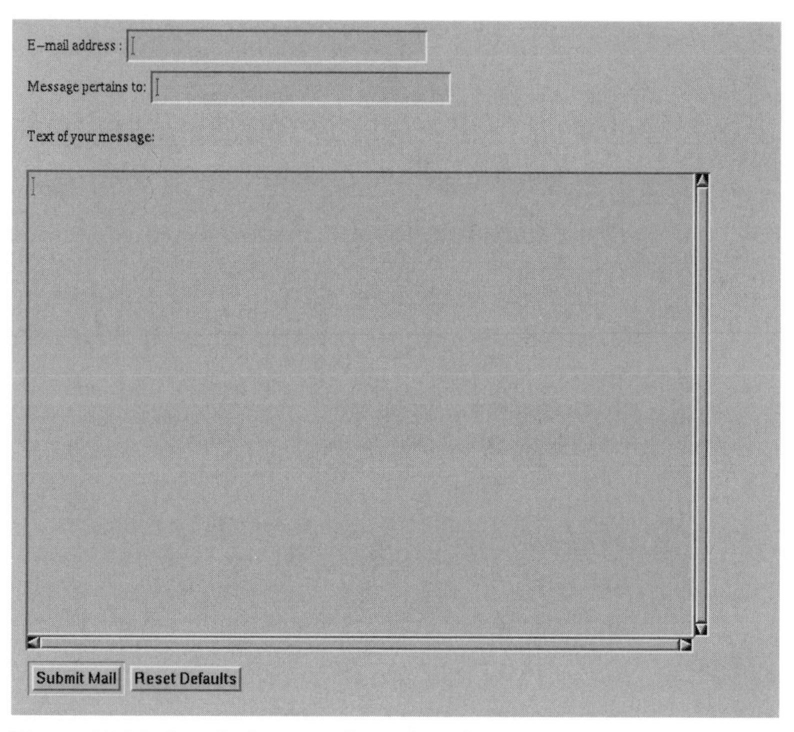

Figure 10-14: *Sample forms mailer using gform.*

Example 10-2: A sample forms mailer using gform.

```
<HTML>
<FORM METHOD=POST
ACTION="/cgi-bin/gform?/html/examples/gform-mailer.html">
E-mail address : <INPUT SIZE=35 NAME="e-mail"><BR>
Message pertains to: <INPUT SIZE=35 NAME="subject"><BR>
<P>
Text of your message:
<P>
<TEXTAREA NAME="body" ROWS=45 COLS=80>
</TEXTAREA>
<INPUT TYPE=submit VALUE="Submit Mail">
<INPUT TYPE=reset VALUE="Reset Defaults"> <P>
</FORM>
<!gform "Message From: $e-mail\n">
<!gform "Regarding: $subject\n\n">
<!gform "Body of Text:\n\n $body">
<!gform DELIVER=mail "webmaster@shoop.com">
</HTML>
```

The e-mail you receive from this form might look like the following:

```
From: nobody@shoop.com
To: webmaster@shoop.com
Subject: Form /html/sample-mailer.html submission
Message From: jem@sunsite.unc.edu
Regarding: quick comment
Body of text:
I really enjoyed reading your material, but I thought you would want
to know that you put three a's in "aardvark" on the second page.
```

Since gform won't allow you to put a variable within a DELIVER or REPLY keyword, you can't let the user specify his or her own subject for e-mail. Instead, we give the message two subjects: an official one and a secondary one.

As you can see, it's quite easy to build a form and use gform to process it. Not only is using gform easier than writing a different program to handle every form, but this approach has the additional advantage of associating the form's action with its interface. gform's embedded commands tell you at a glance what the form is doing.

Using Forms for Gateways

Although most Web browsers already support a wide range of protocols, new information services pop up everyday. It's too difficult to add every new service to every browser, and doing so would make browsers slow and unwieldy. Instead, you can use forms to provide gateways between the World Wide Web and other network services.

The forms gateway to Archie is an excellent example. Archie lets you search for a file in a database of all the filenames in several hundred FTP servers. Traditionally, access to Archie was through dedicated clients that used the Prospero protocol or through a clumsy (and slow) telnet interface. Fortunately Martin Koster (m.koster@nexor.co.uk) of NEXOR developed a WWW gateway to Archie (shown in Figure 10-15), providing a standardized form interface to this important service.

ArchiePlexForm

This is a Forms based version of ArchiePlex, an Archie gateway for the WWW. See also information on ArchiePlex.

Please remember that Archie searches can take a long time... Tip: store this document on your host for faster access! **You need a Forms Browser to use this** (if you haven't use alternatives).

What would you like to search for?

There are several types of search: Case Insensitive Substring Match

The results can be sorted By Host or By Date

The impact on other users can be: Very Nice

Several Archie Servers can be used: ANS archie server

You can restrict the results to a domain (e.g. "gov"):

You can restrict the number of results (default 95):

Press this button to submit the query: Submit .

To reset the form, press this button: Reset

Figure 10-15: *The Archie gateway at http://www.lerc.nasa.gov/Doc/archieplexform.html. You can find a full list of ArchiePlex gateways at http://web.nexor.co.uk/archie.html.*

This sort of gateway makes it simple to access Internet services that aren't native to the Web: all you have to do is choose the URL from your browser's hotlist and submit the form. On the other hand, forms gateways have some disadvantages. The server that runs the gateway can become heavily loaded, slowing access to the service. A common workaround, which the Archie gateway uses, is to offer the same form on many machines around the world. Another disadvantage is that some network services don't lend themselves to the forms interface; gateway users may not be able to access some of the advanced features of these services. Finally, gateways are limited by the stateless HTTP protocol, which can't exchange and display real-time data.

WAIS is a good example of a service that is difficult to effectively bridge to the World Wide Web. Although it's relatively easy to write a form and CGI script that perform a simple query on a single database, it's very difficult to access all the powers of WAIS through the Web. Some features, such as relevance feedback on a piece of a document, are completely impossible through a forms gateway.

It's the session-oriented nature of WAIS that makes it difficult to access all the features of WAIS. The WAIS server expects a query from a client, followed by a series of requests for documents, or pieces of documents, all without ever disconnecting from the server. Despite this, the URL standard defines a WAIS type, and many early browsers had built-in support for WAIS queries.

So you might wonder why the WAIS gateway is necessary. The problem is the great length and complexity of the WAIS client code; including it often doubled the size of browsers, which was fine as long as most clients were running on workstation class machines. On Macs and PCs, however, memory is often a precious commodity.

Because of the memory problem, many browsers started using a WAIS proxy to handle WAIS URLs. A proxy is a sort of gateway, which the client asks to do the search and return the results. Unfortunately, all the clients would be configured to use the same server as their proxy, and this server became swamped by the load. Although users had the option of configuring their clients to use different servers for their proxies, few did so, and there were few choices for those who did.

Today, not all clients even support these WAIS proxies, and it's a bad idea to use WAIS URLs at all. By using a gateway like fwais, you can avoid all the problems of WAIS URLs, and give users greater power and flexibility in their queries as well.

What fwais Is

Although a number of WWW gateways have been written for WAIS, the best, in our opinion, is fwais. It has several features that put it at the top of the list:

- You can use it to present a list of several searchable databases.

- It allows the user to select more than one database to search at a time.
- It can search both local and remote databases.
- fwais presents the score alongside each document that is found.
- When a retrieved document is text, fwais adds HTML tags to emphasize keywords before returning the document. Unfortunately, stop words in the query are also emphasized, even though they didn't actually contribute to the search. Emphasizing stop words is a limitation of WAIS, not fwais.
- By using hidden fields to provide information to fwais, you can limit the user's options and make fwais useful for very specific tasks, such as searching a single database or searching on a preselected phrase. This method isn't a secure way to exclude the user from sensitive material, though; it's simply an easy way to set up a preconfigured search.

After you've installed fwais on your system, you need to edit the script itself to configure it. Follow these steps to edit the fwais script:

1. If you're the administrator of your server and you installed fwais in the main /cgi-bin directory, you need to log in as root before starting.

   (Note: If you are a user on someone else's server and installed fwais in your own personal CGI directory, use this path instead of /usr/local/etc/httpd/cgi-bin in the next step.)

2. Open /usr/local/etc/httpd/cgi-bin/fwais.pl in your favorite text editor. We'll use vi in this example:

```
$ vi /usr/local/etc/httpd/cgi-bin/fwais.pl
```

3. Scroll down until you find the following lines:

```
# common configuration variables
# this is where you put waisq
$waisq = "/usr/local/freeWAIS-0.4/bin/waisq";
# this is the default WAIS source directory. It is overridden with
# the "Directory" argument
$waisd = "/usr/lib/wais-sources/";
# this fully qualifies a host name from a WAIS source file (if needed)
$defaultdomain = "vmedia.com";
```

4. Make sure that $waisq correctly points to the waisq program, which fwais uses to perform the searches. If you installed freeWAIS from the Companion CD-ROM, this should already be correctly configured.
5. Edit the $waisd section to point to the directory that stores the WAIS source files that you want fwais.pl to access.
6. Delete vmedia.com from the $defaultdomain section, and replace it with the Internet domain of your server. If, for example, your server's hostname is www.shoop.com, change it to shoop.com.

   By changing this line, you allow fwais to search local WAIS databases that you don't export (for an explanation of the differences between local and exported indexes see Chapter 9, "Searching & Indexing").
7. Make sure that all of the new values are surrounded by quotation marks and that each line ends with a semicolon. In perl, the programming language that fwais is written in, every line must end with a semicolon.
8. Quit and save the file.

That's all the configuring you'll need to do in order to use the fwais gateway.

What fwais Does

fwais is a complex script, and its behavior depends on the information that you give it. Since a WAIS query usually consists of three steps, fwais is usually run three times in the process of completing a query. Its action and interface changes in each of these steps:

1. The first time the user runs fwais, it provides a form for setting up the search. The user uses this form to select which databases to query, how many hits to return and which keywords to search with (see Figure 10-16).
2. After the information in Step 1 is provided, fwais performs the search and returns a list of hyperlinks to the results (see Figure 10-17).
3. Each WAIS document title is a link that runs fwais again.

   When the user activates a link, fwais retrieves the document that link represents. If the document is text, fwais adds HTML tags to emphasize keywords (see Figure 10-18).

To allow users to set up their own searches, all you need to do is provide a hyperlink to fwais, like the following:

```
<A HREF="/cgi-bin/fwais.pl">WAIS searching</A>
```

When the user activates that link, the server runs fwais.pl. fwais writes an HTML page, like the one in Figure 10-16, containing a forms interface to all the databases it finds in the directory /usr/lib/wais-sources. As you can see, this form contains two SELECT boxes, one that lists all searchable databases and another to choose the maximum number of hits the search should return. It also provides a text-entry field in which to enter the search terms, as well as Submit and Reset buttons.

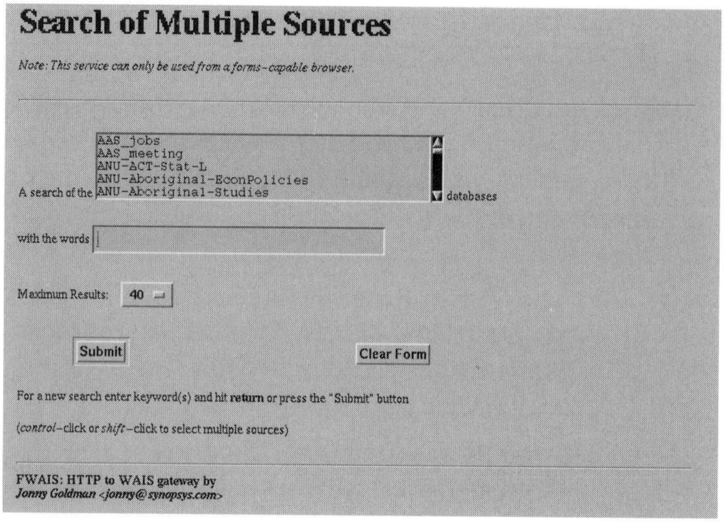

Search of Multiple Sources

Note: This service can only be used from a forms-capable browser.

A search of the
AAS_jobs
AAS_meeting
ANU-ACT-Stat-L
ANU-Aboriginal-EconPolicies
ANU-Aboriginal-Studies
databases

with the words

Maximum Results: 40

Submit   Clear Form

For a new search enter keyword(s) and hit **return** or press the "Submit" button

(*control*-click or *shift*-click to select multiple sources)

FWAIS: HTTP to WAIS gateway by
Jonny Goldman <jonny@synopsys.com>

Figure 10-16: *Default form from fwais.*

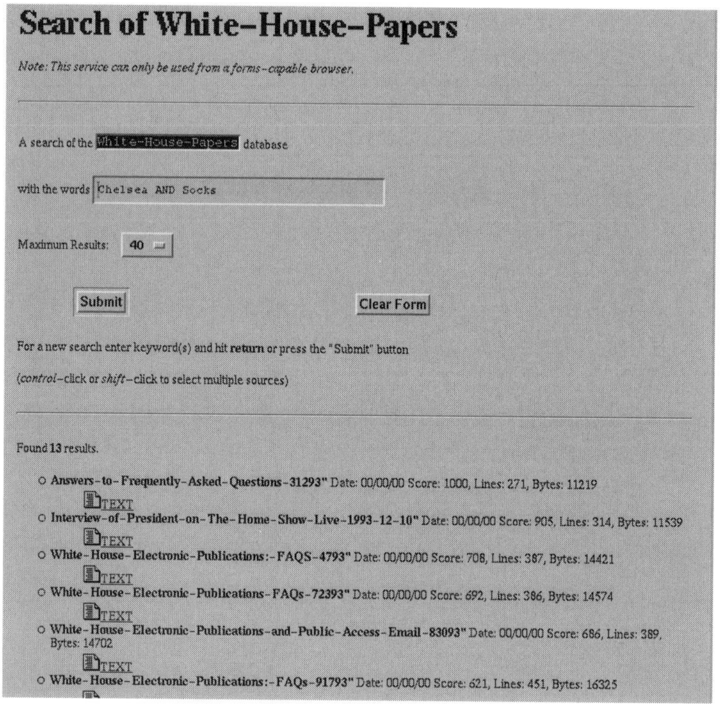

Search of White-House-Papers

Note: This service can only be used from a forms-capable browser.

A search of the White-House-Papers database

with the words Chelsea AND Socks

Maximum Results: 40

Submit   Clear Form

For a new search enter keyword(s) and hit **return** or press the "Submit" button

(*control*-click or *shift*-click to select multiple sources)

Found **13** results.

- **Answers-to-Frequently-Asked-Questions-31293"** Date: 00/00/00 Score: 1000, Lines: 271, Bytes: 11219
  TEXT
- **Interview-of-President-on-The-Home-Show-Live-1993-12-10"** Date: 00/00/00 Score: 905, Lines: 314, Bytes: 11539
  TEXT
- **White-House-Electronic-Publications:-FAQS-4793"** Date: 00/00/00 Score: 708, Lines: 387, Bytes: 14421
  TEXT
- **White-House-Electronic-Publications-FAQs-72393"** Date: 00/00/00 Score: 692, Lines: 386, Bytes: 14574
  TEXT
- **White-House-Electronic-Publications-and-Public-Access-Email-83093"** Date: 00/00/00 Score: 686, Lines: 389, Bytes: 14702
  TEXT
- **White-House-Electronic-Publications:-FAQs-91793"** Date: 00/00/00 Score: 621, Lines: 451, Bytes: 16325

Figure 10-17: *Hyperlinked and ranked results.*

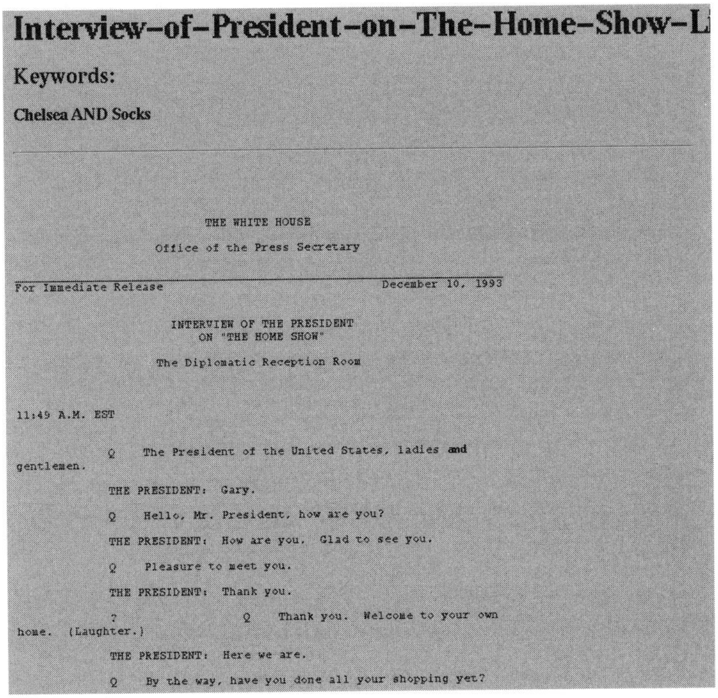

Interview-of-President-on-The-Home-Show-L

Keywords:

Chelsea AND Socks

```
                    THE WHITE HOUSE

                Office of the Press Secretary

For Immediate Release                          December 10, 1993

                INTERVIEW OF THE PRESIDENT
                    ON "THE HOME SHOW"

                The Diplomatic Reception Room

11:49 A.M. EST

           Q    The President of the United States, ladies and
gentlemen.

           THE PRESIDENT:  Gary.

           Q    Hello, Mr. President, how are you?

           THE PRESIDENT:  How are you.  Glad to see you.

           Q    Pleasure to meet you.

           THE PRESIDENT:  Thank you.

           ?               Q     Thank you.  Welcome to your own
home.  (Laughter.)

           THE PRESIDENT:  Here we are.

           Q    By the way, have you done all your shopping yet?
```

Figure 10-18: *A retrieved document.*

fwais writes this form when the only information it has is the defaults that you coded into the perl script. You can change the form that fwais writes by providing values for the CGI variables it's looking for. The following are the CGI variables that fwais understands (they are case sensitive):

- Directory: The directory on the server that contains the sources that you want fwais to use. If this directory is not specified, fwais uses the default directory that you defined when you installed it.
- Source: The WAIS sources to search; you can define multiple sources. If you provide this information, fwais won't list all the sources in Directory.
- keywords: The words to search the database(s) for. When these are given, along with the source(s) to search, the query is performed.

- numres: The maximum number of hits to return. If not specified, this variable defaults to 40.

For example, suppose you want to allow the user to search in three technical support databases. Since fwais uses the GET method (see the section "The Basic Structure of a Form," earlier in this chapter), we can encode this information into the URL:

```
You can <A HREF="/cgi-bin/fwais.pl?Directory=/usr/lib/support-sources&
Source=end-user-support.src&Source=technical-support.src&
Source=programming-information.src">Search</A>our technical support
databases.
```

You separate the name of the program, fwais.pl, from the list of its variables with a question mark. After the question mark, list each variable, an equal sign and then its value. Separate pairs of variables and values with an ampersand. The example hyperlink runs fwais and returns a form offering the user a choice of three databases from the directory /usr/lib/support-sources: end-user-support.src, technical-support.src and programming-information.src.

Search of Multiple Sources

Note: This service can only be used from a forms-capable browser.

A search of the end-user-support / programming-information / technical-support databases

with the words

Maximum Results: 40

Submit Clear Form

For a new search enter keyword(s) and hit return or press the "Submit" button

(control-click or shift-click to select multiple sources)

FWAIS: HTTP to WAIS gateway by
Jonny Goldman <jonny@synopsys.com>

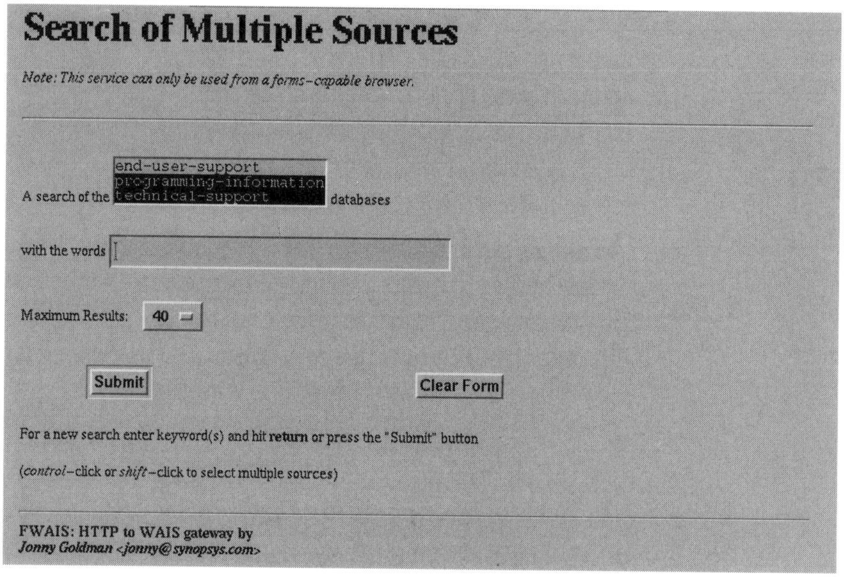

Figure 10-19: *Fwais interface to technical support databases.*

Similarly, you can use fwais to offer a "canned" search, where the user runs fwais with preselected keywords. A canned search is an easy way to provide a standard search on a database that changes often. All you have to do is encode the keywords in the URL, along with the Source information:

```
<A HREF="/cgi-bin/fwais.pl?Directory=/usr/lib/sports-sources&
Source=college-basketball.src?keywords=UNC%20tarheel%20wins">
Recent victories by the University of North Carolina Tarheels</A>
```

Activating this link searches the database college-basketball.src with the keywords "UNC tarheel wins". Notice that the spaces in the keywords have been replaced with the string "%20". This is because the space is one of the characters that can't appear in a URL. The CGI standard specifies that clients should replace these special characters with a percent sign, followed by the ASCII code for that character, in hexadecimal. This may seem rather complicated, but unless you are writing your own CGI scripts (see Chapter 11, "CGI: Advanced Forms for Programmers), all you need to remember is that spaces in URLs must be replaced with "%20".

As you can see in these examples, fwais, like all other CGI scripts, doesn't care how the variables it uses are defined. They can come from its own self-generated form, or you can encode them directly into the URL. A third way to gather this information is in your own form that invokes fwais as its ACTION.

By embedding a form that calls fwais into your own HTML page, you can gain better control over the interface and integrate the functionality of the search with your own text and images. For example, you may want to add a WAIS search to your page but don't want to add all the visual clutter of the full fwais form. You can save some vertical space by eliminating the numres SELECT box and by using checkboxes for choosing the Source. Examine Example 10-3 (which was automatically installed in /html/examples/fwais-custom.html, if you installed fwais.pl from the Companion CD-ROM) to learn how to eliminate the numres SELECT box and to use checkboxes for choosing the Source.

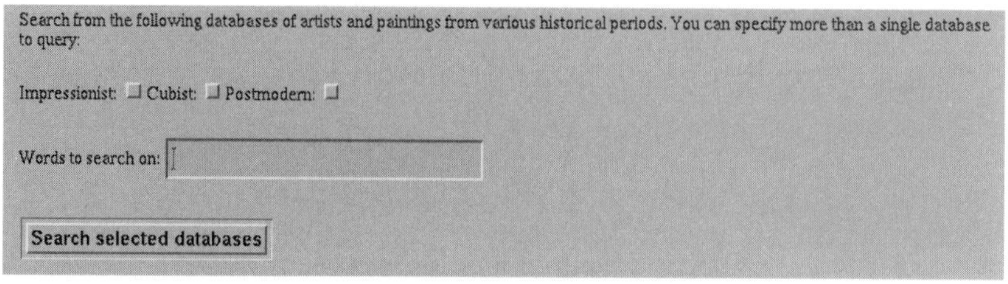

Search from the following databases of artists and paintings from various historical periods. You can specify more than a single database to query:

Impressionist: ☐ Cubist: ☐ Postmodern: ☐

Words to search on:

Search selected databases

Figure 10-20: *Alternate WAIS interface using fwais.pl.*

Example 10-3: Example form from /html/examples/fwais-custom.html.

```
<HTML>
<FORM METHOD=GET ACTION="/cgi-bin/fwais.pl">
<P>
Search from the following databases of artists and paintings from
various historical periods. You can specify more than a single database
to query:
<P>
Impressionist:
<INPUT TYPE=checkbox NAME=Source VALUE=impress.src>
Cubist:
<INPUT TYPE=checkbox NAME=Source VALUE=cubist.src>
Postmodern:
<INPUT TYPE=checkbox NAME=Source VALUE=postmod.src>
<P>
Words to search on: <INPUT TYPE=text NAME=keywords SIZE=30><BR>
<INPUT TYPE=hidden NAME=numres VALUE=10>
<INPUT TYPE=hidden NAME=Directory VALUE="/usr/lib/art-sources">
<P>
<INPUT TYPE=submit VALUE="Search selected databases">
</FORM>
</HTML>
```

This form is a good example of a custom interface to the fwais gateway. It lets the user select sources to search with a row of three checkboxes, while the numres and Directory information is specified in hidden fields. As this example illustrates, you can use fwais in any form you want, as long as you provide the proper NAMEs.

Moving On

Now that you've read this chapter, you are a true Webmaster. With your knowledge of HTML forms, you can write pages that are both attractive and interactive. By now you should

- Know the structure of a form: how it begins and how it ends.
- Understand the various interactive elements in HTML.
- Begin to understand how to interface these elements with applications like fwais and gform.

If you're not a programmer, the information in this chapter may be all you need to know about forms, but if you have a little programming experience (or aspirations), you should read the next chapter. Chapter 11, "CGI: Advanced Forms for Programmers," shows you how to write CGI programs that process forms results, provide gateways to other Internet services and generate pages dynamically. It is these skills that separate the everyday Webmaster from the true Web wizard.

11

CGI: Advanced Forms for Programmers

You can make your pages somewhat interactive by using form handlers like gform or by setting up prewritten gateways like fwais, but if you want to create complex effects, you'll have to write the program yourself. Fortunately, server developers have crafted a simple way to write programs that process forms and generate documents on the fly—CGI.

As we explained in Chapter 10, "Simple Forms," CGI stands for Common Gateway Interface; it defines a method for the HTTP server and an outside program to share information. When the server receives a request from a client to run a gateway program (often called a CGI script), it summarizes the pertinent information about the request in a standard set of environment variables. The script then examines these environment variables in order to find the information it needs to respond to the request. In addition, CGI standardizes methods for the CGI script to give the server information that it needs, such as the MIME type of the script's output.

CGI scripts are used for any task that requires a dynamic response from the server. The main purpose of CGI is to let you write programs that talk to Web browsers. Using CGI, you can write programs that

- Dynamically create new Web pages on the fly.
- Process HTML forms input.
- Bridge the gap between the Web and other Internet services.

Programming With CGI

The CGI standard is very simple. Any programming language that can access UNIX environment variables can use it. CGI programs are most commonly written in C, C++, perl, and Bourne and C shell scripts. Other languages also becoming popular for CGI programs are TCL, Python and Scheme.

All of these languages, except C and C++, are interpreted. Interpreted languages, like perl, have several advantages for writing CGI programs. Many CGI programming tasks require a lot of string handling, and most interpreted languages have powerful built-in functions for manipulating text. In addition, most interpreted languages let you write code for the interpreter on the fly, which is extremely useful for many gateways.

Of course, there are also disadvantages to writing CGI programs in interpreted languages. Although it's convenient to use the dynamic interpretation features of these languages, they can also be a security hazard if you aren't careful (more on this later in this section). In addition, programs written in scripting languages often run slower than those written in a compiled language like C.

In any case, since you can write CGI programs in almost any language for which you have a compiler or interpreter, you should use the language you're comfortable with. We like perl; it's fairly easy to learn and very powerful. For this reason, most of the examples in this chapter are written in perl. We've tried to avoid the more esoteric features of the language, so anyone with programming experience can understand the examples. If you don't know perl but would like to learn it, we recommend *Programming perl*, by Larry Wall and Randal L. Schwartz.

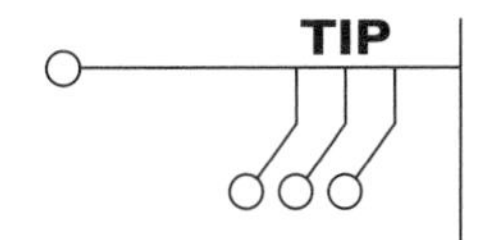

There are libraries available that make CGI programming easier for most popular programming languages. The following list contains recommended languages and where you can access them:

- *For programming in C, try Enterprise Integration Technology's CGI library at http://wsk.eit.com/wsk/dist/doc/libcgi/libcgi.html.*
- *As easy as CGI programming is in perl, there is a library to make it even easier. Try Steven Brenner's cgi-lib.pl at http://www.bio.cam.ac.uk/web/form.html.*
- *A CGI class library by Michael McLay is available for the interpreted, object-oriented language Python. You can find documentation about it at http://www.eeel.nist.gov/python/cgi.html.*

You'll probably want to test the CGI programs that you write. Most servers have restrictions on who can create CGI programs and from which directories they can be run. Allowing clients to run arbitrary programs on the server is quite dangerous from a security standpoint, and wise server administrators don't give this permission to everyone on their systems.

If you are running the NCSA HTTPD, the file /usr/local/etc/httpd/conf/srm.conf controls who has the right to run programs on that server. By default, most servers have a single valid directory for CGI scripts, which is represented by the URL /cgi-bin/. Usually only the server administrator can write to this directory, but he or she can give other users their own CGI directories in srm.conf with the ScriptAlias command. Alternatively, the system administrator can use the AddType directive to make a special MIME type for CGI programs, allowing them to reside anywhere on the server. For more information on both of these options, see Chapter 3, "Setting Up the Server."

In any case, if you want to try the examples in this chapter, you'll need access to some part of a server that allows CGI scripts. Speaking of examples, it's time for our first CGI program. Like any good first program, it prints "hello, world":

```
#!/usr/local/bin/perl
print "Content-type: text/html\n\n";
print "hello, world\n";
```

Although simple, this program illustrates two important rules to follow when writing CGI programs:

- You write any data or text for the client to the standard output.
- Any output *must* be preceded with a Content-type line, defining its MIME type, followed by a blank line.

Both of these rules are very important. They are the reason that generating new pages with CGI scripts is so easy. You simply write any data you want the client to receive to the standard output, preceded by its MIME type, and the server does the rest! Don't forget the Content-type and the blank line though; the server returns an error when it can't find them.

The <ISINDEX> Tag

One of the most common applications for CGI programs is to bridge the gap between the Web and other Internet services. The easiest way to do this is to provide a simple CGI wrapper around a UNIX command-line program, which can perform the actual work needed for the request. This fits well with the UNIX philosophy of combining simple tools to do complex tasks. There's often no need for a gateway program to re-invent the wheel and completely re-implement a service when you can build on the work of others.

HTML and the CGI standard have conspired to make this approach as simple as possible with the <ISINDEX> tag. When a browser notes the <ISINDEX> tag within an HTML document, it marks the document as a searchable index and allows the user to enter terms for which to search. When the user's reply is submitted, the client retrieves the same URL as the document that included the <ISINDEX> tag, adding the user's search terms as follows:

http://www.vpizza.com/cgi-bin/isindex.pl?*arg1+arg2+arg3*

The words that the user entered in the search box follow the question mark; the browser replaces spaces with the plus sign. Furthermore, non-alphanumeric characters are specially encoded;

although this encoding is relatively easy to undo in perl, it can be very annoying to have to decode in other languages, such as C or the Bourne shell. To make <ISINDEX> scripts easier to develop, the server converts the information received from a client's <ISINDEX> query into command-line arguments for the CGI script; each word of the input is a different argument. For example, this silly little Bourne shell script simply echoes the terms that the user enters:

```
#!/bin/sh
echo Content-type: text/plain
echo
echo $@
```

As you can see, this feature makes <ISINDEX> scripts fairly simple and to the point; to create more complex applications, most people use HTML forms. Because they're simple, <ISINDEX> scripts are often written quickly and somewhat carelessly. You should remember that all CGI scripts have the potential to be a security hazard and always follow these guidelines when writing your <ISINDEX> scripts:

- Check whether the script is being run with command-line arguments. If it is, it should print out searching instructions, including the <ISINDEX> tag.
- Check the validity of the arguments before executing the action (this is important if you're using an interpreted language like perl or a shell script, in which some characters have a special meaning to the interpreter).
- Perform the proper action, and return the results, properly preceded by a Content-type header.

Example 11-1 shows a CGI script that uses <ISINDEX> to provide a gateway to the finger service, which lets you obtain information about a user on any host that supports it. If you've installed the cgi-exam package from the Companion CD-ROM, you should find a copy of the source in /usr/local/etc/httpd/cgi-bin/finger.pl.

Example 11-1: finger.pl, a WWW finger gateway using the <ISINDEX> tag.

```
#!/usr/local/bin/perl
#
# finger.pl An <ISINDEX> gateway to the finger service
#

# the location of finger on your system
$finger='/usr/bin/finger';

if ( $#ARGV < 0 ) {
	&print_header("Finger2Web Gateway");
	&print_form;
	&print_footer;
	exit;
}
elsif ( $#ARGV > 0 ) {
	&print_header("Finger2Web Error");
	&print_form;
	print "The Finger Gateway takes only a single argument.";
	print "Please try again.\n";
	&print_footer;
	exit;
}
else {
	$user = $ARGV[0];
	if (! &safety_check($user)) {
		&print_header("Finger2Web Error");
		&print_form;
		print "You've submitted a request with an illegal character.";
		print "Please try again.\n";
		&print_footer;
		exit;
	}
	unless(open(FINGDATA,"$finger $user|")) {
		&print_header("Finger2Web Error");
		&print_form;
		print "Fatal Error executing the finger command.\n";
		&print_footer;
		exit;
	}
```

```
		&print_header("Finger2Web Results for $user");
		&print_form;
		print "<PRE>\n";
		while (<FINGDATA>) {
				print $_;
		}
		print "</PRE>\n";
		close(FINGDATA);
		&printfooter;
}

#####################
#####################
##
## SUB-ROUTINES
##

# make sure that argument is made up of only "safe" characters.
sub safety_check {
		local($tocheck) = @_;
		($tocheck =~ /^[a-zA-Z0-9_+\-%@\t ]+$/)
}

# print HTML header data. Takes 1 argument, which is printed as both the title
# and a level-1 header.
sub print_header {
		local($title) = @_;
		print "Content-type: text/html\n\n";
		print "<HTML>\n";
		print "<HEAD>\n";
		print "<TITLE>$title</TITLE>\n";
		print "</HEAD>\n";
		print "<BODY>\n";
		print "<H1>$title</H1>\n";
}

# finish off the HTML page.
sub print_footer {
		print "</BODY>\n";
		print "</HTML>\n";
}
```

```
# print ISINDEX and search instructions
sub print_form {
        print "<ISINDEX>\n";
        print "<P>This is a finger to Web gateway. Enter the name of a user\n";
        print "for whom you need information, in the form: “;
        print "<VAR>user@hostname</VAR>";
        print "<HR>\n";
}
```

When you examine the code in Example 11-1, you can see that the finger script performs all the essential actions of an <ISINDEX> CGI script. The main code of the program is a block of if statements, which check the number of arguments that the program has received. If none are found, it prints the <ISINDEX> tag and the search instructions as shown in Figure 11-1, while more than one argument causes the gateway to print an error message.

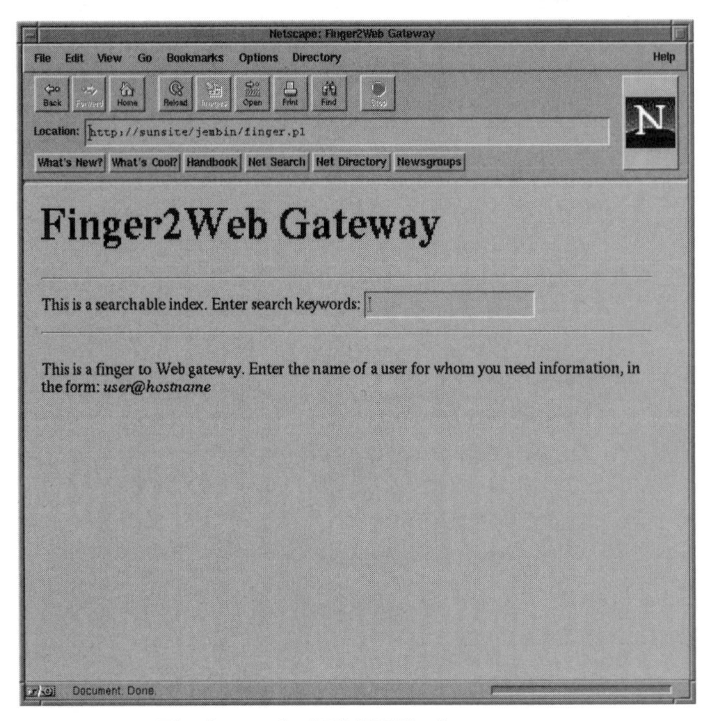

Figure 11-1: *The finger.pl <ISINDEX> input page.*

If the program receives only a single argument, the gateway makes sure that the argument is safe to interpret. In this case, "safe" means that it contains no characters that have a special significance to the perl interpreter, which is an important security safeguard. Without it, a malicious user might be able to fool the CGI script into violating system security. The NCSA HTTP server is kind enough to escape these meta-characters with a backslash when it decodes them into command-line arguments. Since other servers don't do this and you'll have to do it anyway for all other types of CGI scripts, you should get in the habit of always checking user-supplied input for dangerous characters.

After the script has checked the supplied input, it opens a pipe to the finger command and prints the output between the <PRE> tags. A more advanced program might try to parse the output and add more interesting HTML markup, but since different finger daemons have extremely varying output, this would be difficult to implement. After the script has finished with its output, it closes the pipe and sends the closing <BODY> and <HTML> tags.

This simple finger gateway shows what's required to write a simple <ISINDEX> script. Like all such scripts, this one checks its arguments in order to find how it's being called. These arguments can be supplied in two ways. You can link the URL of the gateway to the document and allow the user to use the search input box, as follows:

```
We offer a <A HREF="/cgi-bin/finger.pl">finger gateway</A>
```

You can also directly add them to the URL in a hyperlink:

```
Want to see if I'm online? <a
href="/cgi-bin/finger.pl?jem@sunsite.unc.edu">
Finger me</a>
```

Each time it returns a result or an error message, the gateway reprints the <ISINDEX> tag and the search instructions, separated from the rest of the text with a horizontal rule. This makes it easy for a user to check multiple addresses without needing to use the Back button on the browser to return to the search page.

Handling HTML Forms

In Chapter 10, "Simple Forms," you learned how to use the <FORM> tag to create interactive areas in your HTML pages. Although you can use prewritten CGI programs, like gform, to process the results, they are limited by their simplicity. You gain a lot of flexibility by "rolling your own" CGI scripts to process the forms that you create.

Form Structure & CGI

A browser may pass data from an HTML form to the server in two ways, GET and POST, which you specify with the METHOD attribute of the <FORM> tag, as follows:

```
<HTML>
<HEAD>
<TITLE>Sample Guestbook</TITLE>
</HEAD>
<BODY>
<H1>Sample Guestbook</H1>
<FORM METHOD=POST ACTION="/cgi-bin/guest.pl" >
Full name:
<INPUT TYPE=TEXT SIZE=30 NAME="fullname"><BR>
E-mail address:
<INPUT TYPE=TEXT SIZE=20 NAME="e-mail"><BR>
<P>
Comments:<BR>
<TEXTAREA COLS=60 ROWS=15 NAME="comments">
</TEXTAREA>
<BR>
<INPUT TYPE=SUBMIT VALUE="Sign Guestbook">
</FORM>
<HR>
You can see <A HREF="/guests/guestbook.txt">
what other people have written</A>
</BODY>
</HTML>
```

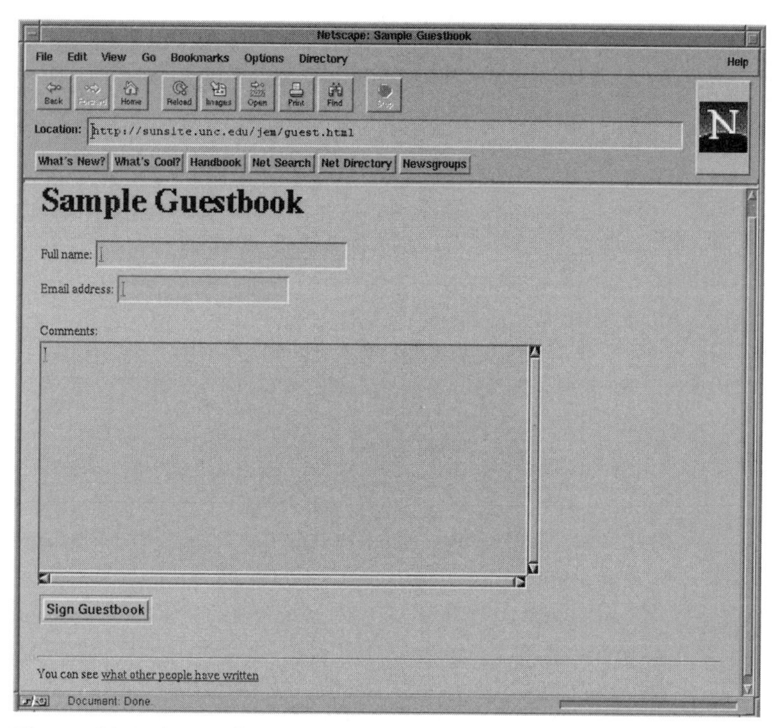

Figure 11-2: *A sample guestbook form.*

This sample guestbook form provides three different areas for user input; each of these areas contains a variable (given by the NAME attribute) to which the browser assigns whatever the user enters. If the user leaves a widget blank and the widget has no associated default, the browser doesn't bother to transmit that widget's NAME. CGI programs that process forms are responsible for making sure that the user has completed all the required parts of the form; there is no way to tell the client which bits must be filled out.

Browsers would invoke this guestbook with the POST method. When a browser submits form data with this method, it transmits the data in a way that's similar to that which the server uses to send HTML and other objects to clients.

You could change this form to use the GET method by modifying the METHOD element of the <FORM> tag. When form data is submitted with the GET method, the client attaches it to the end of the URL that is named by the ACTION tag; the encoded information (see the next section, "URL Encoding") is separated from the name of the CGI script by a question mark. As you can see, this is identical to the browser's method for sending data from an <ISINDEX> query; in fact, both of these types of scripts use the HTTP GET method (see Chapter 2, "The Basic Pieces").

Deciding which method to use with your form and program can seem somewhat arbitrary. Some Web developers consider any use of the GET method a bad idea. They say that attaching dynamic information to the end of the URL is a distortion of the URL's purpose because the writers of the standard had intended the URL to be a unique *locator* for network resources.

In addition, this feature is a liability when dealing with forms that hold information that the user might want private. Most browsers boldly display the current URL at the top of the window, and few people like having embarrassing information broadcast across the office.

Although all these objections may be valid, we believe that the GET method does have its place. By using this method, you allow users to store their responses to commonly used forms on the hotlist, or bookmark file. The GET method is particularly useful for queries in databases that change regularly, for example.

The POST method, on the other hand, is preferred when creating forms that users rarely complete or always send with different data. The POST method is more efficient and more reliable than the GET method because different operating systems have different limits on the maximum amount of data that can be passed that way. For example, forms that contain <TEXTAREA> boxes, which allow users to enter large amounts of text, should always use the POST method.

URL Encoding

Although browsers transmit the data to the server differently depending on the method the form specifies, they encode that data in the same way, regardless of whether they're using GET or POST. The client gathers the user's input from all the widgets and packages it with its corresponding NAME; variables are separated by ampersands. Data from the form in Figure 11-2 might be encoded as follows:

```
fullname=Fred+Mbogo&e-mail=mbogof@zappa.shoop.com&
comments=hi+ya%27ll
```

In this example, you see the three HTML variable names in the form. An equals sign separates each one from its proper value.

Since the GET method adds form data to the end of the URL, the form information must be specially coded so as not to conflict with the URL standard. In the URL standard, several characters (such as the ampersand) are reserved; they have a special meaning to clients and servers. Other characters are simply illegal. The following list describes the characters that can't be used.

- The following reserved characters have special meanings in a URL:

  = ; / ,#,? :

- Any nonprintable ASCII control character can't be used.
- The space character is also illegal.

Browsers replace the space character with a plus sign and replace reserved and control characters with a percent sign followed by their ASCII code in hexadecimal. Browsers also often encode characters that have special meanings, either in the URL or to most UNIX-based interpreted languages in this hexadecimal format. For this reason, the apostrophe in the previous example, "hi ya'll," is replaced by the ASCII hexadecimal code of %27.

Although most browsers properly encode these special characters, your program shouldn't count on it. Not only may a buggy browser fail to change them to their hexadecimal equivalents, malevolent crackers may directly send improperly encoded data to your script hoping to trick it into performing a security-breaking action. To ensure the robustness of your program and the integrity of your system, always make sure that any user-provided data that will be interpreted by a shell is free of any characters with special meaning to the shell.

The POST Method

When an HTML form uses the POST method, the server sends the data that it received from the client to the handling CGI script on its standard input. It also sets the REQUEST_METHOD environment variable to POST. Your script should check this variable to ensure that it's receiving POST data; it can then read this data almost as if it were being piped to the script from the command line:

```
cat form-data | cgi-script
```

A major difference between writing a normal UNIX utility that reads data from the standard input and a CGI script for use with the POST method is that the HTTP server sends no signal that it has finished transmitting data. Usually, when a utility has finished reading all the available data from the standard input, it receives a special end-of-file value; CGI programs never receive this notification.

Instead, the HTTP server sets the CONTENT_LENGTH environmental variable, which gives the amount of input the script should read in bytes. When your script has read that amount of data, it should stop; the results of further reads are not defined by the CGI specification and therefore may vary from server to server.

Like the data that the server sends to the client, this information that the client transmits with the POST method has a MIME type. Currently, only one possible MIME type is defined for client-transmitted data: application/x-www-form-urlencoded, which defines data from an HTML form. The server records the MIME type of the client-sent data in the CONTENT_TYPE environment variable. Although there is currently only a single type for data from an HTTP POST, this will change in the future (see the section "HTML v3.0 Forms," in Chapter 13, "Future Directions"), so you should check the value of this variable in order to make sure that your scripts will work in the future.

After you've finished checking that the REQUEST_METHOD and CONTENT_TYPE variables have the expected values and you've read the number of bytes indicated by CONTENT _LENGTH from the standard input, you're ready to process the actual data from the form. Processing the data requires that you undo the URL encoding that's been described previously and includes four steps:

1. Break up the pairs of HTML form variables and their values, which are separated by ampersands.
2. Separate each HTML form variable from its value; the variables and their values are linked by equal signs.
3. Convert all hex sequences (escaped by a percent sign) in each of the variables and the values to their ASCII equivalents.
4. Replace all plus signs in each of the variables and values with spaces.

After you've gone through these permutations in order and extracted the HTML variables and values in their original form, you can do whatever you like with them. The output of a CGI script always follows the same guidelines; you must precede data with a Content-type header, specifying the MIME type, and a blank line.

Example 11-2 is a simple CGI script that processes the POSTed data from the sample guestbook form in Figure 11-2. It appends the user-supplied name, e-mail address and comments to a text file. When it is finished, it prints a simple but friendly message expressing its thanks. If you've installed the cgi-exam package from the Companion CD-ROM, you should find a copy of the source in /usr/local/etc/httpd/cgi-bin/guest.pl.

Example 11-2: guest.pl, a CGI script to process the results of the simple guestbook form.

```
#!/usr/local/bin/perl
#
# guest.pl: A cgi script to handle user input from guestbook.html
#

# The server's document root
$root = '/html';

# path, relative to $root, to the guestbook file
$guestbook = '/guests/guestbook.txt';
```

```
# e-mail address of the server's administrator
$webmaster = 'webmaster@www.shoop.org';

# copy the values of these environment variables
$method = $ENV{"REQUEST_METHOD"};
$type = $ENV{"CONTENT_TYPE"};

# make sure the script was called with the POST
# method and the HTML form's MIME-type
if ($method ne "POST" || $type ne "application/x-www-form-urlencoded")
{
        &print_header("Guestbook Method Error");
        print "Guestbook data must come from a form and be invoked ";
        print "with\n"
        print "the POST method.\n";
        &print_footer;
        exit;
}

# read form data from standard input
%input_values = &break_input;

# convert from the strange URL syntax to normal ascii
# and translate non-UNIX (MAC, PC) line endings to UNIX convention
$fullname = &normalize_query($input_values{"fullname"});
$e-mail = &normalize_query($input_values{"e-mail"});
$comments =
&unixify_eols(&normalize_query($input_values{"comments"}));

# you must log at least your name or your e-mail address
if ($name eq '' && $e-mail eq '') {
        &print_header("Guestbook Input Error");
        print "You must give either your full name or an e-mail address\n";
        print "to sign the guestbook.\n";
        &print_footer;
        exit;
}
```

```
&log_entry("$root/$guestbook", $fullname, $e-mail, $comments);

&print_header("Thanks!");
print "Thanks for your comments...\n";
&print_footer;

####################
####################
##
## SUB-ROUTINES
##

# read CONTENT_LENGTH bytes from the standard input and decode
# the URL format input, breaking it into an associative array
# of HTML variable names and their values.
sub break_input {
        local ($i);
        read(STDIN, $input, $ENV{'CONTENT_LENGTH'});
        @form_names = split('&', $input);
        foreach $i (@form_names) {
                ($html_name, $html_value) = split('=', $i);
                $input_values{$html_name} = $html_value;
        }
        return %input_values;
}

# given a title, print the return header
sub print_header {
 local($title) = @_;
 print "Content-type: text/html\n\n";
        print "<HTML>\n";
        print "<HEAD>\n";
        print "<TITLE>$title</TITLE>\n";
        print "</HEAD>\n";
        print "<BODY>\n";
        print "<H1>$title</H1>\n";
}

# finish off the HTML page.
sub print_footer {
```

```
        print "</BODY>\n";
        print "</HTML>\n";
}

# URL syntax converts most non-alphanumeric characters into a
# percentage
# sign, followed by the character's value in hexadecimal. this function
# undoes this weirdness.
sub normalize_query {
        local($value) = @_;
        $value =~ tr/+/ /;
        $value =~ s/%([a-fA-F0-9][a-fA-F0-9])/pack("C",
hex($1))/eg;
        return $value;
}

# clients don't translate the end-of-line from TEXTAREA widgets to
# the server's convention. this function does it for this program.
sub unixify_eols {
        local($string) = @_;
        $string =~ tr/\n\r/\n/;
        $string =~ tr/\r/\n/;
        return $string;
}

# given a filename and user data, this function logs it.
sub log_entry {
        local($log, $fullname, $e-mail, $comments) = @_;
        unless (open(BOOK, ">>$log")) {
                &print_header("Guestbook Open Error");
                print "Failed to open $guestbook. Please inform
        $webmaster\n";
                &print_footer;
        }
        print BOOK "Entry by: $fullname\n";
        print BOOK "E-mail address: $e-mail\n\n";
        print BOOK "$comments\n\n";
        print BOOK "------------------------------------------------------\n";
        close BOOK;

}
```

Although we've made the program and its comments mostly self-explanatory, you should note the following:

- Look at the subroutines break_input and normalize_query. See how easy it is to do this sort of complex text processing in perl? That's why we like to write as many CGI scripts as possible in perl. Writing this sort of script can be painful in other languages.
- The subroutine unixify_eol translates the end-of-line characters inside the input from the <TEXTAREA> box to the UNIX convention (a single newline). Since browsers send text using the characters appropriate to their operating systems (MS-DOS uses a linefeed followed by a carriage return, and the Mac operating system uses only a carriage return, for example), you should always translate before you write the input to a file.
- The script checks to make sure that essential HTML variables (such as *fullname* or *e-mail*) are present. It's always the responsibility of the CGI script to verify that the user has correctly filled in the form.
- Unlike Example 11-1, <ISINDEX> finger gateway, this form-processing script doesn't bother to check for illegal characters in the input. Since the script never employs the user input in a way that could possibly interpret the input as a command, it's not necessary to check for illegal characters.

Except for the previous few points, this is a simple script for a simple form; it merely processes the data that the browser sends and acknowledges it. More complex scripts write the form itself, without relying on a pre-written page.

The GET Method

A CGI script that's written to be used with the GET method works essentially in the same way as a POST-based script except for the way that the server passes the data. Instead of sending browser-submitted data to the standard input of the script, the server encodes this data in the environment variable QUERY_STRING, using the steps described previously, in the section "URL Encoding." An additional difference is that the CGI variable REQUEST_METHOD is defined as GET rather than POST.

So whether you use the GET method or the POST method makes little difference in the amount of work that you need to do to write your script. That's one of the appealing features of the CGI standard— simplicity. The interface between the script and the server that runs it is unobtrusive; usually only a few lines of code (at least in perl!) are required in order to access the submitted data or to gather information about the server that is running the script (see the section "CGI Environment Variables," later in this chapter, for details).

Since it's so easy to provide support for both methods, many scripts support both by changing their behavior depending on the value of the REQUEST_METHOD variable. Although supporting both methods is an excellent way to increase the flexibility of your program (especially if you're going to make the program publicly available), you should keep in mind the guidelines provided in "Form Structure & CGI" that explain when each method is most appropriate.

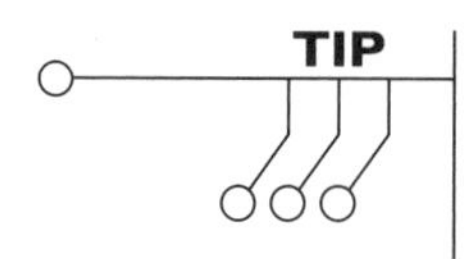

One of the most common questions CGI novices ask is, "How do I debug my script?" The answer is simple—fake it. You need to define (and export) all the CGI environment variables that your script is looking for; you must also provide data on the standard input for scripts that use the POST method. An easy way to do this is to write a simple shell script that defines the proper environment variables and echoes your script's input; you can run this script before using your debugger.

Since there are so few differences between CGI scripts that process the results from the GET method and those that use the POST method, the Example 11-3 script, audioconv.pl, which you'll find later in this section, concentrates on demonstrating some of the more interesting things you can do with CGI. Audioconv.pl is a simple interface to the sox sound conversion program described in Chapter 8, "True Multimedia: Adding Audio & Animation." This script was designed for a hypothetical audio archive on the Web; it allows the user to select a sound sample and the audio format he or she prefers, and audioconv.pl converts it on the fly.

Rather than relying on a static HTML page, containing a static form, audioconv.pl generates the HTML form itself when the QUERY_VALUE variable contains no data. This is similar to what the <ISINDEX> finger gateway did for its search index, but audioconv.pl goes a step further. The form that it generates is dynamic because the script writes the page based on the audio samples that it finds available in the archive, listing them with radio buttons, as shown in Figure 11-3.

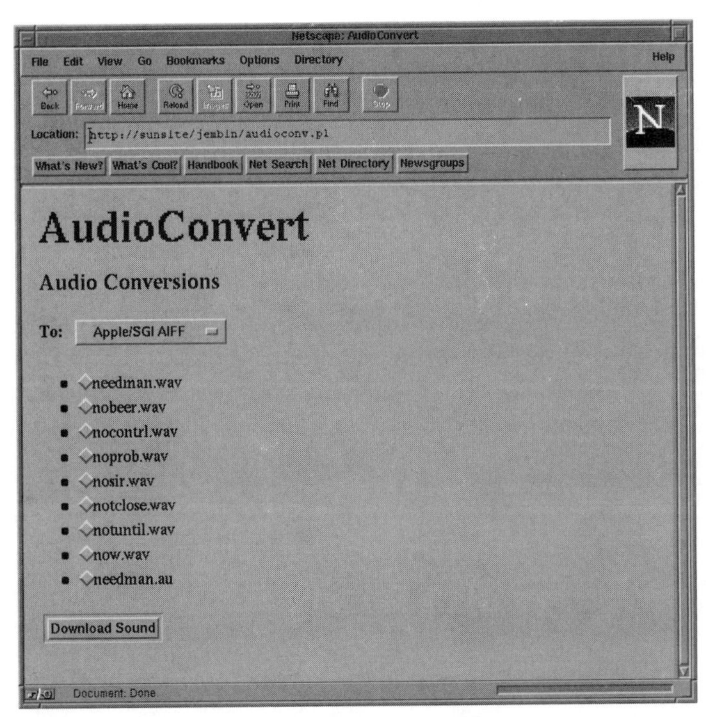

Figure 11-3: *The form generated by the audioconv.pl script.*

In addition, this script demonstrates the utility of MIME types. When it converts an audio sample, it doesn't just generate a page with a link to a file with the selected format; instead, audioconv.pl does the following:

1. Selects the proper MIME type for the converted sample.
2. Transmits that type, followed by the mandatory blank line.
3. Outputs the converted sample directly, without ever writing a temporary file.

Since the script is sending audio objects, rather than HTML files, the user's browser remains on the audioconv.pl form page. The user can conveniently select additional file and format combinations until he or she is sick of the page.

In this way, audioconv.pl acts as a gateway to the Sox conversion program, just as finger.pl, described in the earlier section "The <ISINDEX> Tag," is a gateway to a finger client. This is an excellent model to follow when looking for innovative services to implement. It makes it easy for you to build complex Web-based applications with little work, and it allows remote users to share your unique resources.

The main disadvantage to this sort of gateway is the load that it can inflict on your server. If your server is popular, you may find one morning that your computer is performing audio conversions for most of southern California. To avoid inflicting a heavy load on your server, you could either keep copies of every sample in every format or encourage your users to obtain their own copies of the sox package. Practicality aside, this example should get you started writing your own "real world" CGI applications. If you've installed the cgi-exam package from the Companion CD-ROM, you should find a copy of the source in /usr/local/etc/httpd/cgi-bin/audioconv.pl.

Decoding Forms With uncgi

Although breaking up a QUERY_VALUE and decoding the values within is fairly simple in perl, it can be a difficult task in other languages. One solution to this problem is the program uncgi, which does the job for you. To use it, set the ACTION of your form to /cgi-bin/uncgi/*your-cgi-script*, where *your-cgi-script* is the name of your forms processing script (it must be in the same directory as uncgi).

uncgi decodes the query string (if the request is a GET) or the standard input (if the request is a POST) and defines environment variables equivalent to the name of the HTML forms variables, preceded by the string "WWW_". For example, a shell script to process the results of the guestbook form in the previous section might look like this:

```
#!/bin/sh
# A simple Bourne shell script to process the results
# of the Sample Guestbook in "Form Structure and CGI," above

guestbook="/guests/guestbook.txt"
separator="--------------------------------------------------------"
echo "Entry by: $WWW_fullname" >> $guestbook
echo "E-mail address: $WWW_e-mail" >> $guestbook
echo >> $guestbook
echo $WWW_comments >> $guestbook
echo $separator >> $guestbook
```

As you can see, using uncgi is an easy way to quickly write CGI scripts for forms processing. If you want to try uncgi, you can install it from the Companion CD-ROM and read the documentation at http://www.hyperion.com/~koreth/uncgi.html.

Example 11-3: audioconv.pl, a CGI script that gives users access to sounds in several formats.

```
#!/usr/local/bin/perl
#
# audioconv.pl: A cgi script to translate audio formats
#

# this is the location of the sox binary
$sox = "/usr/local/bin/sox";

# directory on the server in which to look for sound files
$sound_dir = "/html/sounds";

# a regular expression of sound files in sounddir
#
$incl_patt='\.au$|\.aiff$|\.wav$|\.voc$';

# an associative array of the audio sample types that
# we can convert to, and their extensions
%format_ext=( "Apple/SGI AIFF", "aiff",
        "Sun u-law", "au",
        "MS-Windows WAV", "wav",
        "Sound Blaster VOC", "voc",
);

# an associative array of those same extensions and
# their appropriate MIME types
%format_type=( "aiff", "audio/x-aiff",
        "au", "audio/basic",
        "wav", "audio/x-wav",
        "voc", "audio/x-voc",
);

# copy these CGI environment variables
$method = $ENV{REQUEST_METHOD};
$query_string = $ENV{QUERY_STRING};

# check access method
if ($method ne 'GET') {
        &print_header("text/html", "AudioConvert Method Error");
```

```
        print("AudioConvert must be invoked with the GET method.\n";
        &print_footer;
        exit;
}


# if there is no query string, print form
if ($query_string eq '') {
        &print_header("text/html", "AudioConvert");
        &print_form("GET", "/cgi-bin/audioconv.pl");
        &print_footer;
        exit;
}

# otherwise, convert the desired sound
else {
        # unpack the user's input into an associative array
        %query_values = &break_query($query_string);

        # ensure that both the file and format HTML variables exist
        if ($query_values{"file"} eq '') {
                &print_header("text/html","AudioConvert Input Error");
                print "Name of file to convert not found.\n";
                &print_footer;
                exit;
        }
        if ($query_values{"format"} eq '') {
                &print_header("text/html","AudioConvert Input Error");
                print "Name of format to convert to not found.\n";
                &print_footer;
                exit;
        }

        # convert from the strange URL syntax to normal ascii
        $file = &normalize_query($query_values{"file"});
        $format = &normalize_query($query_values {"format"});

        # check to make sure that $file has no "dangerous" symbols
        # before we use it to open a file
        if (! &safety_check($file)) {
```

```
                &print_header("text/html","AudioConvert Input Error");
                print "Name of file contains illegal
                characters.\n";
                &print_footer;
                exit;
        }

        # find the proper file extension of the format we're converting *to*
        if (($ext = $format_ext{$format}) eq '') {
                &printheader("text/html", "AudioConvert Input Error");
                print $format, ": Unknown Sound Format.\n";
                &print_footer;
                exit;
        }

        # open a pipe to the sox audio conversion program, using
        # the -t auto option which auto-detects the format
        # of the original file- strangely this works better than
        # telling sox the actual type... even when we know it!
        open(SOUND, "$sox -t auto $sound_dir/$file -t $ext -|");

        # turn off buffering of output
        $| = 1;

        # send the output of sox to the standard output and close the pipe
        &print_header($format_type{$ext}, "");
        while (<SOUND>) {
                print $_;
        }
        close SOUND;
}

####################
####################
##
## SUB-ROUTINES
##

# given a MIME type and title (if text/html), print the return header
sub print_header {
```

```
local($type, $title) = @_;
print "Content-type: $type\n\n";
        if ($type eq "text/html") {
                        print "<HTML>\n";
                        print "<HEAD>\n";
                        print "<TITLE>$title</TITLE>\n";
                        print "</HEAD>\n";
                        print "<BODY>\n";
                        print "<H1>$title</H1>\n";
        }
}

# given the method and action, print the main body of the form
sub print_form {
        local ($method, $action) = @_;
        print "<H3>Audio Conversions</H3>\n";
        print "<FORM METHOD=$method ACTION=\"$action\">\n";
        print "<STRONG>To:</STRONG>\n";
        &format_select("format", (keys %format_ext));
        print "<P>\n";
        &list_files($sound_dir, $incl_patt);
        print "<INPUT TYPE=\"SUBMIT\" VALUE=\"Download Sound\">";
        print "</FORM>\n";
}

# finish off the HTML page.
sub print_footer {
 print "</BODY>\n";
 print "</HTML>\n";
}



# given a URL format query string, break it into an associative array
# of HTML variable names and their values
sub break_query {
        local($query_string) = @_;
        local ($i);
        @form_names = split('&', $query_string);
        foreach $i (@form_names) {
```

```
                ($html_name, $html_value) = split('=', $i);
                $query_values{$html_name} = $html_value;
        }
        return %query_values;
}

# URL syntax converts most non-alphanumeric characters into a
# percentage sign, followed by the character's value in hexadecimal.
# this function undoes this weirdness
sub normalize_query {
        local($value) = @_;
        $value =~ tr/+/ /;
        $value =~ s/%([a-fA-F0-9][a-fA-F0-9])/pack("C", hex($1))/eg;
        return $value;
}

# ensure that all the characters in a query string are
# safe to pass to the perl interpreter
sub safety_check {
        local($tocheck) = @_;
        ($tocheck =~ /^[a-zA-Z0-9_+\-%@\t\. ]+$/)
}



# given a directory and a pattern, print a sorted HTML list of those files
sub list_files {
        local ($dir_name, $incl_patt) = @_;
        print "<UL>";
        @sound_files = sort &get_dir($dir_name, $incl_patt);
        foreach $file (@sound_files) {
                print "<LI>", &format_input("radio", "file", $file), $file, "\n";
        }
        print "</UL>\n";
}


# print an INPUT widget of some type, variable name, and default value
sub format_input {
        local($type, $html_name, $html_value) = @_;
```

```
        return("<INPUT TYPE=$type NAME=\"$html_
        name\" VALUE=\"$html_value\">");
}

# given an HTML variable name and an array of options,
# print a <SELECT> widget
sub format_select {
        local ($html_name, @options) = @_;
        local ($i);
        print "<SELECT NAME=\"$html_name\">\n";
        foreach $i (@options) {
                print "<OPTION>", $i, "\n";
        }
        print "<\SELECT>\n";
}



# given a directory and a regular expression, return a list of files
# in that directory which match that pattern.
sub get_dir {
        local($dir, $incl_patt) = @_;
        opendir(DIR, $dir);
        if ($incl_patt ne '') {
                grep(/$incl_patt/, readdir(DIR));
        }
        else {
                readdir(DIR);
        }
}
```

The audioconv.pl script can operate in two possible modes, depending on the state of the QUERY_STRING CGI environment variable:

- If the variable is empty, audioconv.pl assumes that the user has connected to the AudioConvert page for the first time and prints the form shown in Figure 11-3.
- If the variable contains HTML forms values for the *file* and *format* HTML variables, audioconv.pl opens a pipe to the

Sox audio conversion program, sends the appropriate MIME type and transmits the sound data to the client.

Although this example is quite a bit longer than the one for the POST method, its interface with the server is just as simple. In fact, if you examine the subroutines that are responsible for processing the HTML form data in both programs, you'll notice they're almost identical. That's another appealing aspect of writing CGI scripts: since the tasks that must be done are repetitive, once you've written code to complete a task the first time, the code is almost infinitely reusable.

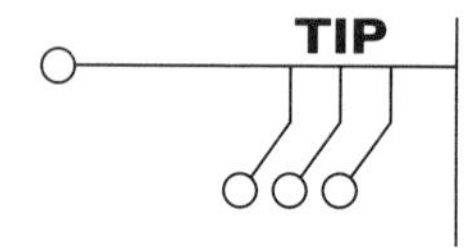

Sox is a great program if you're interested in digital audio. Not only will it convert audio files to many different formats, you can also use it to change the basic characteristics of the audio file, such as sampling rate and volume. Sox can also apply various filters to the sample to remove noise and add special effects. As an exercise in both using Sox and programming CGI, add an interface from audioconv.pl to one or more of Sox's other features. To get a full description of the sox syntax and features, check out the Sox man page.

Generating Pages Dynamically

CGI can be used for much more than writing forms and handlers. You can also use CGI programs to generate new HTML pages on the fly, which is an incredibly useful and powerful capability. With dynamic documents, you can alter the appearance, interface and features of your Web pages as you desire. You can also use them to extend the functionality of the Web, adding features that are difficult or impossible to get from traditional media.

In Example 11-3, the audioconv.pl script writes a page with a form because the QUERY_STRING variable was empty. This is a simple example of a dynamic document, since the contents of the page are dependent on the files present in the sounds directory on the server. The script generates a new list of files every time it

runs; it does so to save you the trouble of maintaining a separate list in a static page, which might become out of sync with the actual contents of the directory.

Although the HTML that audioconv.pl generates is for a form, you can write CGI scripts that take no input to solve similar problems. The main reasons to create a document dynamically instead of by hand are

- To present the current state of some changing resource.
- To save you the trouble of writing pages that would be difficult, annoying or impossible to write by hand.

The task might be as simple as appending the current date and time to a page, or it could be as complex as constructing a personal newspaper from the hundreds of megabytes in a day's Usenet news. Of course, the price that you pay for this flexibility is the overhead of running the CGI program every time someone retrieves the page.

In addition, dynamically created documents have a further disadvantage in that they can't be cached (the server automatically marks them as un-cacheable). This problem will become more important as more organizations direct all their Web requests through a locally caching server to reduce outside traffic.

Despite these disadvantages, using CGI programs in this way is the best (or only) solution to many of the problems you encounter in maintaining a large, complex Web site. One such problem is the major differences from user to user in client software, available bandwidth, and the data formats they prefer. Although the HTTP protocol contains some support for negotiating such things and HTTP-NG (see Chapter 13, "Future Directions") has even more, few WWW clients and servers take real advantage of it.

From WWW to SQL

More companies and organizations wish to gateway their traditional MIS departments and databases to the Web. For this reason, CGI interfaces to SQL-based relational databases have become increasingly important. Currently, some CGI scripts can provide at least read-only access to all of the major relational databases, but fully integrating a complex database and Web site is a difficult undertaking. The following are some links to get you started:

You can access the Web/DB Gateway Discussion mailing list at http://www.w3.org/hypertext/WWW/RDBGate/Overview.html.

Papers and talks on WWW-database gateways from the first International WWW Conference are available at http://www.tns.lcs.mit.edu/call/specialized.html#Database.

The Genera gateway lets you present data from Sybase databases by simply writing formatting instructions in an easy-to-use, high-level format. You can get a copy of the software and instructions for its use at http://gdbdoc.gdb.org/letovsky/genera/genera.html.

WDB is a framework for writing Web-database (WDB) gateways. Currently WDB gateways are available for Sybase, mSQL and Informix Relational Database Management Systems (RDBMS). Check them out at http://arch-http.hq.eso.org/bfrasmus/wdb/wdb.html.

The oraywww gateway allows search, insert, update and delete access to Oracle databases. You can find information about it at http://www.nofc.forestry.ca/oraywww/.

Oracle has collected some Net-written software (including oraywww) and some that they have written and called the "The Oracle World Wide Web Interface Kit." You can find more information about it at http://dozer.us.oracle.com:8080/.

You can find lists of links to similar resources at http://www.charm.net/~web/Vlib/Providers/Database.html and http://www.yahoo.com/Computers/World_Wide_Web/Databases_and_Searching/.

The example CGI script included near the end of this section, condit.pl, helps solve the problems associated with matching the client's preferences with the capabilities of the user's browser by allowing you to

- Embed one or more Boolean flags in a URL.
- Test for these flags in a simple conditional macro language.

You can use condit.pl to maintain a single set of HTML pages that have different sets of features. You could use this ability to implement a pre-home page (discussed in Chapter 12, "Fitting In: Joining the Virtual Community"), which presents links to two or more alternative main pages—one that uses graphics extensively, for example, and one that is text only. The markup for such a page might look similar to the following:

```
<HEAD>
<TITLE>The SHOOP Home Page</TITLE>
</HEAD>
<BODY>
<!-- INCLUDE-IF-NOT NOGRAPHICS
        <!-- INCLUDE-IF USEJPEG
        <A HREF="/cgi-bin/imagemap/homemap"><IMG
SRC="graphics/home-map.jpg ISMAP>
        </A>
        -->
        <!-- INCLUDE-IF-NOT USEJPEG
        <A HREF="/cgi-bin/imagemap/homemap"><IMG
SRC="graphics/home-map.gif ISMAP>
        </A>
        -->
-->
<!-- INCLUDE-IF-NOT NOTEXT
        <OL>
        <LI>We have lots of <A HREF="goodstuff/first.html">good stuff</a>.
        <LI>Most people find this <A HREF="boringstuff/first.html">
        boring</a>.
        <LI>This is all very <A HREF="importantstuff/first.html">
        important</a>.
        </OL>
-->
</BODY>
```

This markup creates a home page that supports multiple types of access, so users can choose the one that is most appropriate for the abilities of their clients and the speeds of their Internet connections. You could create a list of links to this document, offering the same page in many different ways, as illustrated in the following markup:

```
Choose which homepage:
<UL>
<LI>Graphical Interface Only (imagemap)
	<OL>
	<LI><A HREF="/cgi-bin/condit.pl/NOTEXT/ home.html">
	GIF graphics</A>
	<LI><A HREF="/cgi-bin/condit.pl/USEJPEG:::NOTEXT/home.html">
	JPEG graphics</A>
	</OL>
<LI>Graphical Interface with text
	<OL>
	<LI><A HREF="/cgi-bin/condit.pl//home.html">GIF graphics</A>
	<LI><A HREF="/cgi-bin/condit.pl/USEJPEG/home.html">
	JPEG graphics</A>
	</OL>
<LI><A HREF="/cgi-bin/condit.pl/NOGRAPHICS/home.html">
Text-only Interface</A>
</UL>
```

When a user activates one of the hyperlinks in this markup, the server runs condit.pl, stuffing all the URL information after /cgi-bin/condit.pl into the PATH_INFO environment variable. condit.pl interprets the PATH_INFO variable as a list of option flags, followed by a relative URL. This relative URL points to an HTML document to which the options should be applied.

The script opens that document and scans it for commands within the HTML comment tag, <!-- >. Each command tests for the presence of one or more flags and includes a section of text if the command and its flags evaluate as true. Commands to condit.pl must be on a line by themselves and followed by a comma-separated list of flags to test. You can find a full list of condit.pl commands and their functions in Table 11-1. The audioconv.pl script writes a page with a form because the QUERY_STRING variable was empty.

Command	Description
INCLUDE-IF	Include this section if all flags match.
INCLUDE-IF-ANY	Include this section if any flags match.
INCLUDE-IF-NOT	Include this section if no flags match.
INCLUDE-IF-NOT-ALL	Include this section if not all flags match.

Table 11-1: *Commands understood by condit.pl.*

Example 11-4: condit.pl, a CGI script that allows conditional inclusion of markup code.

```
#!/usr/local/bin/perl
#
# condit.pl: A cgi script to handle conditional includes
# Written for The Web Server Book by: Simon E Spero (ses@eit.com)
#

# root of document space
$root="/usr/local/etc/httpd/htdocs";


# regular expression identifying html files
$html = '\.html$|\.htm$|/$';

# the default page to load, if the URL
# represents a directory
$default = "index.html";

# Get the path info and split off the flags
$path_info = $ENV{"PATH_INFO"};
($slash,$flags_given,$rest) = split('/',$path_info,3);

# set $key{$flag} to true for each flag
for (split(/:::/,$flags_given)) { #
		$key{$_} = 1;
}

# Check to see if the request is for an html file
unless($rest =~ /$html/) {
		# If it isn't, let the system handle the request directly
```

```
        print "Location: /$rest\n\n";
}

# Otherwise, we need to try and open it. Let's find the filename
else {
        $filename = "$root/$rest\n";
        if($filename =~ /\/$/) {
            $filename .= $default;
        }

        # and try and open it
        unless(open(INPUT,"$filename")) {
            # couldn't open the file - let the system have a go.
            print "Location: /$rest\n\n";
            exit;
        }


        &print_header;

        #
        $print_it will be used to enable and disable printing. At first,
        # we'll want to print anything until we get told otherwise
        # we'll also be keeping a stack of old print_it's so we can nest
        # conditional includes.
        $print_it = 1;
        @print_it_stack = ();

        # now, for each line in the file
        while(<INPUT>) {

            #is this a command for us?
            if( /^\s*<!--\s*INCLUDE-IF/) {
                #yes it is - if we're printing at the moment, we
                #need to parse it - otherwise, we'll just push the
                #current state onto the stack to make sure we
                #keep track of nesting
                if($print_it) {
                    # ok, we do have to check it -let's parse the
                    # request into command and requirements
```

```
                ($command,$requirements) =
                    /^\s*<!--\s*(INCLUDE-IF[^\s]*)\s*(.*)$/;

                # We'll test the requirements as requested.
                # &satisfy_all is true if all requirements match
                # &satisfy_any is true if any requirements match

                if($command eq "INCLUDE-IF") {
                    $should_include=
                    &satisfy_all
                    ($requirements);
                }
                elsif ($command eq "INCLUDE-IF-ANY") {
                    $should_include =
                    &satisfy_any
                    ($requirements);
                }
                elsif ($command eq "INCLUDE-IF-NOT") {
                    $should_include =
                    !&satisfy_any
                    ($requirements);
                }
                elsif ($command eq "INCLUDE-IF-NOT-ALL") {
                    $should_include =
                    !&satisfy_all
                    ($requirements);
                }
            }
            # let's save the current value of print_it and set
            # print_it to its new value. If we're not printing
            # now, this won't start us printing; we're just
            # balancing brackets

            push(@print_it_stack,$print_it);
            $print_it = $print_it && $should_include;
        }
        elsif (/^\s*-->\s*$/) {
            #this wasn't a command - but it was the end of a
            #conditional. we'll restore print_it from the stack
            $print_it = pop(@print_it_stack);
```

```
                }
                else {
                        # It's a real line - if print_it is set, let's, er, print it
                        print $_ if $print_it;
                }
        }
}


####################
####################
##
## SUB-ROUTINES
##

# print the MIME type, and # add a comment saying how
# this document was created
sub print_header {
        print "Content-type: text/html\n\n";
        print "<!-- This file generated by condit.pl\n";
        print " original source was /$rest\n";
        print " keys used were ",join(", ", keys(%key))," --
>\n\n";
}

# given a comma-separated list of requirements, return
# true if all exists in %key
sub satisfy_all {
        local ($requirements) = @_;
        local ($all_match);
        $all_match = 1;
        for $i (split(/,\s*/,$requirements)) {
                unless($key{$i}) {
                        $all_match = 0;
                }
        }
        return $all_match;
}
```

```
# given a comma-separated list of requirements, return
# true if any exists in %key
sub satisfy_any {
        local ($requirements) = @_;
        for $i (split(/,\s*/,$requirements)) {
              if($key{$i}) {
                    return 1;
              }
        }
        return 0;
}
```

Although condit.pl is a good example of a CGI script that dynamically writes HTML, it also demonstrates two features of CGI that we haven't yet discussed:

- The PATH_INFO variable
- CGI redirection

If a slash follows the name of the script in the requested URL, the HTTP server puts everything between this slash and the beginning of the query string into the PATH_INFO environment variable. condit.pl uses this string to store both the list of options and the name of the file to which to apply them.

If the relative URL doesn't seem to point to an HTML document, the script asks the client to retrieve the URL directly. It sends the client to that document with an HTTP redirect, which you can create in CGI scripts by printing the string "Location:", followed by a URL and a blank line.

You should note that clients place the URL for the condit.pl before any relative links in the documents that it generates, which has both advantages and disadvantages. Although this automation allows you to easily use the condit.pl macros in the pages beneath the top directory of the hierarchy, it also means that condit.pl is run for every link the user follows. To avoid this, use a full URL (including the protocol and hostname) in the hyperlinks.

condit.pl gives you an idea of the power of CGI in generating and modifying documents on the fly. It also illustrates an approach to solving programming problems on the Web. By implementing a general solution, you gain a lot of flexibility; not only is condit.pl a good way to maintain a set of pages with different interfaces, but you could use it to take advantage of the new HTML v3.0 tags that only some browsers support (see Chapter 13, "Future Directions").

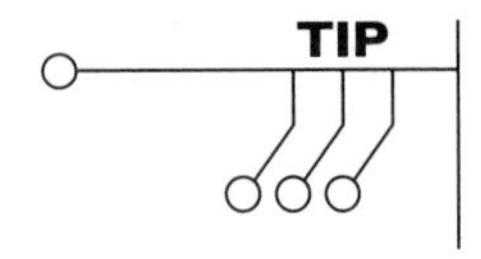
TIP

The natural complement to dynamic documents is dynamic graphics. Thomas Boutell's gd library allows you to easily create GIFs on the fly from your C program. You can then use these GIFs as inline images in your dynamic pages! The URL is http://siva.cshl.org/gd/gd.html.

CGI Reference

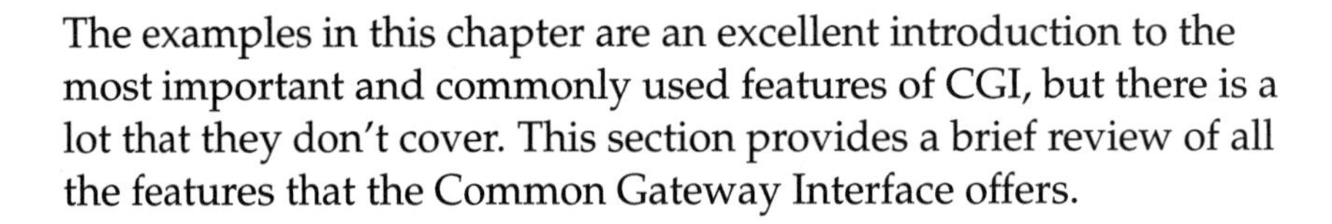

The examples in this chapter are an excellent introduction to the most important and commonly used features of CGI, but there is a lot that they don't cover. This section provides a brief review of all the features that the Common Gateway Interface offers.

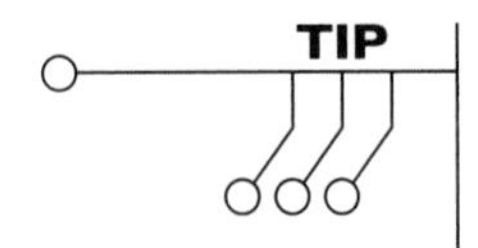
TIP

You can find a formal specification for the CGI v1.1 standard at http://hoohoo.ncsa.uiuc.edu/cgi/overview.html.

CGI Environment Variables

As you've learned throughout the chapter, the CGI standard mandates that servers pass information to scripts through environment variables. Although the example scripts in this chapter demonstrate how to use most of the important CGI variables, many more aren't discussed. You can investigate these variables with the test-cgi script if you're running the NCSA HTTPD. Try pointing your Web client to the URL http://www.shoop.com/cgi-bin/test-cgi/friendly/.

Substitute the hostname of your server for www.shoop.org. Your browser should display something similar to the following:

```
CGI/1.0 test script report:


argc is 0. argv is .


SERVER_SOFTWARE = NCSA/1.4
SERVER_NAME = www.shoop.org
GATEWAY_INTERFACE = CGI/1.1
SERVER_PROTOCOL = HTTP/1.0
SERVER_PORT = 80
REQUEST_METHOD = GET
HTTP_ACCEPT = */*, image/gif, image/x-xbitmap, image/jpeg
PATH_INFO = /friendly/test
PATH_TRANSLATED = /usr/local/etc/httpd/htdocs/friendly/test
SCRIPT_NAME = /cgi-bin/test-cgi
QUERY_STRING = hello+world
REMOTE_HOST = grumpy.shoop.org
REMOTE_ADDR = 115.23.42.5
REMOTE_USER =
AUTH_TYPE =
CONTENT_TYPE =
CONTENT_LENGTH =
```

CGI Variable	Description
SERVER_SOFTWARE	The name and version of the HTTP server that accepted the request, separated by a slash.
SERVER_NAME	The advertised hostname of the server.
GATEWAY_INTERFACE	The version of the CGI standard that the server implements.
SERVER_PROTOCOL	The name and version of the protocol that sent the request. Currently, only HTTP supports the CGI standard.
SERVER_PORT	The number of the port on which the request was received.
REMOTE_HOST	The hostname of the machine from which the request originated. If reverse lookups are disabled, this variable isn't defined.
REMOTE_ADDR	The IP address of the machine where the request originated.
REMOTE_USER	The authenticated username of the user, if the script is protected by client authentication.
AUTH_TYPE	The type of client authentication (if any) that protects the script.

Table 11-2: *Simple CGI environment variables.*

As you can see, test-cgi prints each of the environment variables that are a part of the CGI standard along with their value. Most of the variables are quite simple; they are summarized in Table 11-3. These simple variables give the gateway information about the server's configuration and the origin of the request.

CGI Variable	Description
REQUEST_METHOD	The HTTP method the client used to make the request (GET, POST or HEAD). CGI gateways receive data from the client differently depending on the method (see the sections "The GET Method" and "The POST Method" earlier in this chapter).
HTTP_ACCEPT	A comma-separated list of MIME types that are acceptable to the client. Asterisks are wildcards and signal that any type of data is acceptable. Most servers and clients make no use of this data; in the future, servers may do on-the-fly conversions to the client's preferred type.
PATH_INFO	The extra pathname information that follows the name of the CGI script. This is an easy way to send information to your gateway.
PATH_TRANSLATED	The pathname information from PATH_INFO preceded by server's root data connection. If PATH_INFO specifies the name of a file beneath the server's directory, a gateway can use this variable to get the full pathname to that file on the system.
QUERY_STRING	The data from the browser, if the client invokes the gateway with the GET method (see the sections "URL Encoding" and "The GET Method" earlier in this chapter).
CONTENT_TYPE	The MIME type of the transmitted information. Currently, only one value, application/x-www-form-urlencoded, is valid for data from a submitted HTML form.
CONTENT_LENGTH	The number of bytes of data sent from the browser if the client invokes the gateway with the POST method (see the sections "URL Encoding" and "The POST Method" earlier in this chapter).

Table 11-3: *Client data CGI variables.*

The CGI environment variables summarized in Table 11-2, are, in general, more important because they relate to the actual contents of the client's request. Most of these are explained and used in the examples throughout this chapter; the only two exceptions are PATH_TRANSLATED and HTTP_ACCEPT.

The PATH_TRANSLATED variable is closely related to the PATH_INFO variable. The latter consists of everything within the URL, from the end of the name of the script to the query string (which begins with a question mark). This string is often used to pass a relative URL on which to operate to the CGI script. The server sets the PATH_TRANSLATED variable to be the same as the PATH_INFO variable, modified to represent a valid path on the system.

For example, if the URL were http://www.shoop.com/cgi-bin/test-cgi/user/jem/test.html, the server would set PATH_INFO to /user/jem/test.html and PATH_TRANSLATED to /usr/local/etc/http/htdocs/users/jem/test.html (assuming the default document root). The server makes all necessary translations—if your server supports tilde expansion for user document directories, the requested URLs are also converted to their proper paths. For this reason, it's a good idea to use the PATH_TRANSLATED variable when getting the name of a file from a CGI program.

The other important CGI variable we haven't really covered is HTTP_ACCEPT. This variable contains a comma-separated list of the MIME types that the browser is prepared to accept from the server. The list is ordered from most welcome to least welcome. Although this feature has great potential, no Web client or server really takes advantage of it; most clients just give a long list of data types, followed by */*, which signifies any and all MIME types, which obviously isn't very useful.

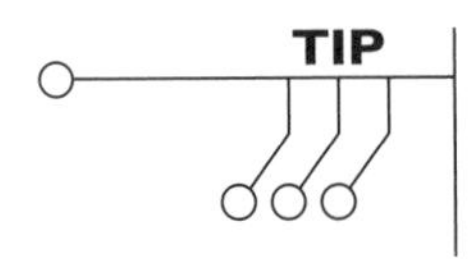

Although HTTP_ACCEPT is the only variable specifically mentioned in the CGI v1.1 standard, the server creates environment variables for every line of HTTP header information that the client sent with the request. Each variable is the name of the HTTP header field preceded by the string "HTTP_". You can find a full list of possible HTTP headers at http://www.w3.org/hypertext/WWW/Protocols/HTTP1.0/draft-ietf-http-spec.html.

CGI Headers

While the HTTP server communicates with the CGI program through environment variables, CGI programs write to the standard output to send information to the server. The CGI standard describes three header lines that a CGI script can use. Table 11-4 lists these headers.

Header	Description
Content-type	Specifies the MIME type of the following output. If the script generates any output at all, other than a CGI header, Content-type must be the very first line it sends.
Location	Specifies that the output is the location (a URL) of another document, rather than a document itself.
Status	The HTTP status code that the server should return with the response. You'll find a list of HTTP status codes at http://www.w3.org/hypertext/WWW/Protocols/HTTP/HTRESP.html.

Table 11-4: *Standard CGI headers for script to server communication.*

Each of these headers must be sent on a line by itself, followed by another blank line. The server then interprets this output and generates a proper HTTP response from it, thus saving the programmer the trouble of learning the full HTTP v1.0 standard. This also provides a layer of data abstraction, preventing future upgrades to the HTTP standard (such as HTTP-NG—see Chapter 13, "Future Directions") from breaking pre-existing CGI scripts.

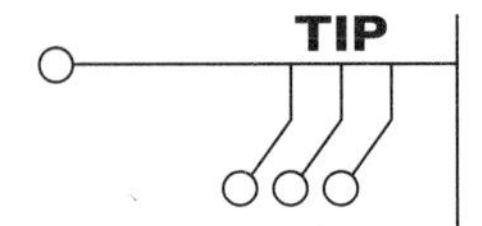

TIP

If you really need to generate your own HTTP headers in order to get complete control of the dialogue between the client and your CGI script, the CGI standard provides for this situation. If the name of your script begins with the string "nph-" (for no parse headers), the server sends the output of your script straight to the client with no further interpretation. You can find the complete HTTP standard (including all possible headers and status codes) at http://www.w3.org/hypertext/WWW/Protocols/HTTP/HTTP2.html.

Moving On

The CGI standard provides an easy way to extend the basic functionality of your Web server. The standard gives your programs a simple way to access information about the server's configuration and the client's request from any programming language; this allows you an incredible amount of flexibility in expanding your pages from a static catalog of documents into a dynamic, interactive presence on the Web.

Although the standard is simple in concept, it defines a lot of variables that can be difficult to keep track of. Fortunately, most scripts require only a few that are easy to remember. After reading this chapter, you should have a basic understanding of the following important CGI techniques:

- Writing scripts that output and handle the <ISINDEX> tag.
- Decoding URL-encoded data from the QUERY_VALUE variable, or the standard input, in order to process HTML forms data.
- Dynamically generating HTML and other output, using a properly defined MIME type.

When you can do these tasks in your CGI scripts, you'll be able to complete 90 percent of the tasks that you need to do with CGI, and you can count yourself among the most technically proficient Webmasters.

Technical proficiency isn't the only skill required to produce a successful Web site. As in all human endeavors, design and promotion are at least as important. In the next chapter, you'll learn how to use these skills to create an effective site. You'll also learn about the various channels and forums that are available for advertising and promoting your site.

SECTION IV

Final Considerations

12

Fitting In: Joining the Virtual Community

You can approach putting a new site on the World Wide Web in two ways. One is to have a relatively isolated site, with little publicity and few external links. For some sites, there is little reason to encourage users from all over the Web to connect. For example, if your site is providing technical support for specific products, it would probably be enough to include the URL for the site in your product documentation, along with instructions on how to connect and access information. However, the majority of sites will want to use their presence on the Web both for publicity and for information distribution. This chapter will focus primarily on this second approach, providing information on how to create a site that is easy to locate and use and that encourages users to come back often.

Location & First Impressions

The location of your site—that is, both the machine name and the file name—determines, in part, how easy it is for a user to find you without using any search tools or Web indexes (which are discussed later in this chapter). It has become standard for the machine that is hosting a Web site to be named "www". Ventana Communications Group's site, for example, is running on the machine www.vmedia.com. This does not mean that the host machine has to be renamed. To create an alias that sends a user to the correct machine, simply add a CNAME entry in your nameserver. Alias www.*domain*.com to the machine that you will be using to serve your information, and from that point on, using either the machine's real name or its new alias will enable a user to access your site. If you are working with a service provider who handles your name service, contact them and ask them to do this for you.

The file name itself can also help users get to your information more easily. All World Wide Web browsers are configured to look for a file called INDEX.HTML when entering a new directory. If this file is present, the user does not need to enter a file name at all. The directory or machine name alone will take her or him to this default page. Using these two features, a URL like http://foobar.shoop.com/index.html could be accessed by simply pointing a browser at http://www.shoop.com/.

This first page, index.html, provides a sort of conceptual center for your site. It is commonly referred to as the "home page" of the site. The home page provides users with their first impressions both of the site itself and of the company, department or individual that is being represented there. Assuming that you are not operating entirely on name recognition to draw users, you will want to make sure that the presentation of your home page encourages exploration of the content presented throughout the rest of the pages. There are, obviously, an infinite number of potential layouts for home pages. Several different types are seen consistently throughout the Web:

- the graphical interface
- the graphics/text hybrid
- the pre-home page

Each of these types is discussed in more detail below.

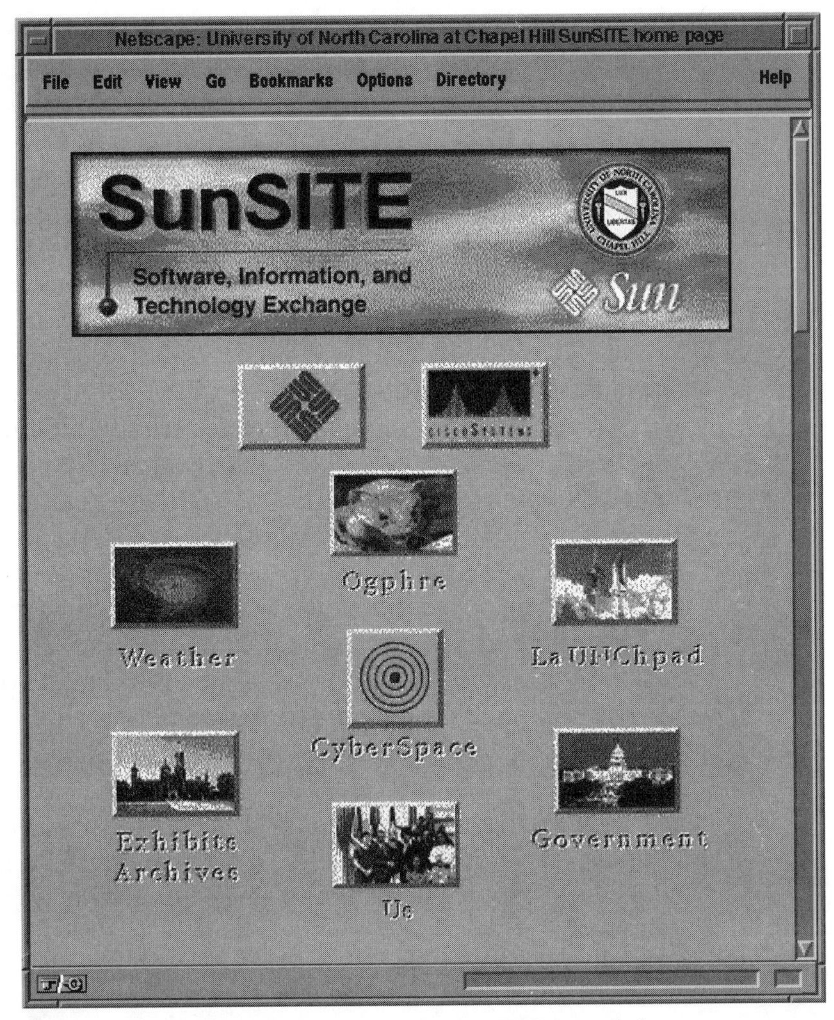

Figure 12-1: *A graphical interface—the SunSITE.unc.edu home page (http://sunsite.unc.edu/).*

Graphical Interface

The graphical interface, shown in Figure 12-1, attempts to present, in one image or set of images, all of the categories into which information is organized, using the graphics themselves as the links to different areas of the site (see "Clickable Imagemaps" in

Chapter 7, "Images on the Web"). This sort of layout should be used by designers who are expecting high-speed output on the server end and users with high-speed connections, who are looking specifically for impressive graphics layouts. One way to determine whether a large-scale graphical interface on your home page is practical is to analyze in advance the type of information that the site will be serving. If you are primarily focused on distributing text information or have limited multimedia content (a few audio clips or photographs of a small number of products, for example), having a complex front end limits the number of people who go beyond your first page. Users who could benefit from text files, such as catalogs or news briefs, or from small images alongside product descriptions, could very well be frustrated by a detailed home page. Since many users on the Web use the Web through SLIP connections or text-based browsers like Lynx, it is a good idea to remember that for every large graphic you include on a page, you are substantially increasing the time the page takes to load.

If, on the other hand, your focus is on multimedia products, graphic design or other, more technically oriented materials, you will, and will want to, draw users who are looking for impressive page design and layout. The graphical interface, in this context, can convince users at first glance of your ability. Even in cases where it is appropriate to use the graphical interface, however, you should provide a text menu at the bottom of the page as an alternative.

Figure 12-2: *A graphics/text combination—the NCSA home page (http://www.ncsa.uiuc.edu).*

Graphics/Text Hybrid

The graphics/text hybrid, as shown in Figure 12-2, is used by the majority of sites on the Web. This layout integrates hyperlinked text and graphics, primarily for visual effect. This layout can have two advantages over a straight graphical interface. One advantage is the amount of time required for the page to load because, by and large, the graphics are relatively smaller at a site with the graphics/text combination layout. However, a number of small graphics can take as long to load as a larger graphic because each has to load in turn. Since most browsers cache images after loading them, it is advisable to use a bulleted list with a single icon (as described in "The Basics of HTML" in Chapter 2, "The Basic Pieces") or to include a small number of pictures repeated throughout the page. This allows images to be loaded out of the client's memory instead of off the server itself.

The second advantage to the graphics/text combination format is that it can establish a sense of consistency beyond the home page. A banner on the top of the home page can be repeated on all of the pages in the site or can be modified slightly to indicate one's location relative to the home page. Also, icons can be reused to link to pages with similar content, furthering design continuity.

Finally, the inclusion of text obviously allows for greater elaboration about the site and the products than does the use of a completely graphical interface. In both layouts, however, it is a good idea to include an "About this site" link, which provides the user with detailed information separate from the home page about the site itself and the parties it represents.

Figure 12-3: *A pre-home page—the Internet Underground Music Archive (http://www.iuma.com/).*

Pre-home Page

A pre-home page is shown in Figure 12-3. Given that no site designer can fully anticipate the capacities or interests of his or her potential audience, a number of sites have put up pre-home pages. This page still uses index.html, but it does not immediately present the main menu. Instead, it gives the user the option to view a full-fledged graphics display or to view a scaled-down text/graphics combination or sometimes a straight text menu.

Including a pre-home page is generally the best way to go if your site seeks to cater to a wide range of users, from those using Lynx to those connecting on full T1s. Generally, the pre-home page is little more than a menu allowing the user to select which view of the home page to go to.

One mistake a number of sites have made in implementing a pre-home page is that only the home page or a few pages have the reduced number of graphics, and as the user moves through the site, she or he encounters pages full of graphics even though she or he selected the option of a limited graphics display. To create a truly flexible site, all the pages should be accessible in the format selected by the user. One easy way of doing this, which requires time and disk space, is to create separate directory hierarchies with identical pages, one with the image tags and one without. A more complex method in the short term, but certainly easier in the long run, is to use a cgi-bin script at the outset, which would tell the browser not to load images on any page in the site if a user selected a "text-only" option. This process is explained in Chapter 11, "Advanced Forms for Programmers."

Once your design and layout skills have drawn users to the first page, your next considerations have to be how to keep them at your site, and after they have left, how to encourage them to come back. In the next section, we will provide some suggestions on how to structure your site to keep the users' attention after they have entered the site and how to develop the content and presentation of your site to encourage repeated usage.

Site Unity & Traffic Control: Design & Content Considerations

One of the most compelling and exciting aspects of hypertext is its ability to create the appearance almost transparently of a unified body of information across machines and domains. For example, by clicking on a link while reading information in California about networking software, the user can pull up a technical document about the World Wide Web located on a machine in Switzerland, without any sense of a break in continuity. However, this sense of continuity can present a problem for some sites. If a software vendor desires that the user browse through its catalog, look at screen captures of the software interface and read reviews by users of the software, all to get a sense of the company's products and ability, the user's early departure from the site may represent lost potential in terms of exposure or interaction. One way to avoid this problem from the outset is to be conscious of any external links that you build within the body of the site. For example, if the first line of your home page reads as follows

```
<h2>Welcome to ShoopSoft Netware's Home on the <a href="http://
info.cern.ch/hypertext/WWW/TheProject.html">World Wide Web</a></h2>
```

you run the risk of losing the visitor to the wealth of information that CERN offers about the World Wide Web. The problem is not that these links are not valuable—in some basic sense, any site that does not inform users of the WWW project is leaving out the most important information available on the Web—but that these links should be relegated into a particular area, and anyone creating a Web site should understand that these links are a possible draw away from the site.

The best strategy to allow users to sample the information available about similar topics is to present a "links" page somewhere in the site. It is a good idea to provide a significant amount of hyperlinked text throughout your pages and to configure these links so they move the user around your site in a nonlinear way—allowing the user to choose how and when to receive the information you provide. However, you should limit the information available to what you choose to provide, at least, so long as you want to keep the user on-site.

It is fairly standard to include a link on the home page of a document. The link is labeled something like "Other resources" or "Links to the WWW" and provides an organized listing of topics that you feel anyone interested in your site would want to explore. It is a good idea to include links to resources that provide services similar, or identical, to your own because it allows the user to judge your site against others in the field. By extension, then, if competition is your goal, it is up to you to ensure that users will prefer your site to the others. However, if you are working toward building a general knowledge base, regardless of where the user obtains the information, adding links to similar sites allows the sites to complement each other and collectively cover issues that no single site could fully address. The links page, then, should be accessible as part of the site, but as a marginal part, so that the information you provide can be clearly delineated as your own.

Another way of creating a site that gives the sense of a unified body of information is to use a standard design and layout for your pages. A number of sites standardize their pages through the use of menu bars that allow users to navigate through the various screens, encountering a standard header for every page or a signature and contact line at the bottom of every page. It's always a good idea to include a mailing address, such as webmaster@www.domain.com, on every page, linked to a mail script or a mailto tag if possible. Standardizing your site this way makes certain the user is constantly aware of his or her location and knows when he or she is leaving the site via an external link.

Also, every page on a site should have a "Back to the home page" link with some sort of recognizable icon. This link allows the user to start again at the top and explore new areas of information, without having to use the browser's Back function to page all the way back to the top.

Finally, the most important element of the site, above and beyond all design and presentation concerns, is the content. Sites on the World Wide Web can take a number of forms, as discussed in the opening chapter. They can be little more than virtual billboards with pretty pictures and promotional information or online catalogs giving essentially the same information available from a mail-order catalog. However, it is unfortunate—and unprofitable—to use the technology of the Web to such limited ends.

Throughout this book, we provide a number of tips on how to interface your Web site with various features available on the Internet, such as multimedia resources or different types of database programs. When you're developing the ideas for your site, look closely at the resources available to you that you can offer the Internet community. A database of information, such as collections of news articles about certain topics, technical specifications for products or scientific work and so on, can draw a large number of users to your site, especially if the information is unavailable or difficult to get elsewhere.

This kind of service can establish your site's Web presence—ironically, perhaps—by drawing more potential customers by giving away your services for free. Companies that release information or entertainment that can be used by visitors to their sites generally see those same visitors return as consumers who recommend the site and, by extension, the company, to others. Also, as discussed in the next section, "Choosing & Reaching Your Audience," providing services is its own form of promotion, both online and off. Consider what you have to offer as a company, as a department or as an individual Web provider, and decide what would be the most valuable information to give away. Using the technologies described throughout this book, you should be able to convert almost any resource at your disposal into data accessible via the World Wide Web. By doing so, you establish yourself both as an entity present on the World Wide Web and as a participant in the benefits that it confers upon both users and providers.

Choosing & Reaching Your Audience

Strange as it may be to say toward the end of a book about creating a World Wide Web presence for yourself, there are no guarantees that the Web will be the "next big thing." The reason it is necessary to keep this point in mind is that, as a new participant in the Web, it is part of your responsibility to make sure this new technology remains an important medium. In this media-driven society, the primary means to working toward this goal is the generation of interest through publicity—both for individual sites and for the Web itself. By talking about the Internet and the Web and by demonstrating the vast potential that it presents to business, education and individual users, you serve the dual purpose of encouraging the use of a particular site and of the Web itself. While this section focuses primarily on publicity within the Internet itself, it should be remembered that publicity in the print or broadcasting media draws new users to the Internet and broadens the potential audience for your site.

One of the first decisions that has to be made about publicity, online and off, is how much publicity is necessary and who will comprise the target audience. Some sites require very little publicity, such as those serving a particular need for a select group of people. For example, a site that provides software patches and updates for a particular line of products should consider inserting its URL into the documentation distributed with the software, along with information about how to get onto the Web in the first place (that is, where to download a browser or how to use Lynx over dial-up connections).

To publicize the site over all available channels would create more traffic than might be desirable for some sites. If a server is running over a slow connection or expects a large number of FTP accesses, too much traffic will adversely affect the performance and access time of the machine hosting the information. Educational sites, such as university departments running their own servers, would probably want to publicize within the university itself and link to the university's home page, but these departments probably would not want to post to a large number of newsgroups. These are a few examples to encourage thought about an issue that is becoming increasingly important, especially online—namely, that too much publicity can be detrimental to the site and to the Internet community at large, as in the case of "spamming," discussed at the end of this section.

The use of print media to promote a Web site can be extremely helpful in some cases, and in others, its effect is negligible. Some basic steps requiring very little effort can raise general awareness about your site. A number of companies include a line at the bottom of their standard print advertisements saying something like "Be sure to visit us on the Internet at our World Wide Web site: http://www.*domain*.com." This publicity encourages people who are already familiar with the Web to go to the site and engenders curiosity in those who are not. Simply putting a line like "WWW: http://www.*domain*.com/" in conspicuous places like letterheads or business cards can achieve the same effect.

As a more proactive way of getting attention for a new site, many companies issue press releases announcing the opening of the site. A press release for a Web site should include several

items. First, include an explanation of what the World Wide Web is. This explanation can be as simple as "the multimedia front end for the Internet" or as complex as you feel is appropriate for your audience. Second, include an explanation of how to access the site for people on the Internet but unfamiliar with the World Wide Web. Again, this can be as simple as: "Using software like NCSA Mosaic or Netscape, people connected to the Internet can simply enter our new address (URL) and see all our site has to offer." Finally, some discussion of the implications of this new technology is appropriate, if as nothing more than a way to answer the reader's question, "Why should I care?"

If you are distributing products online, presenting special information to Internet users or even just allowing consumers to get product information without having to make a telephone call, discuss these advantages as a way to encourage people to investigate how they can get access to this resource. Keep in mind that, unlike online promotion, any promotion done via print media must assume that the majority of readers are unfamiliar with the technology being described. That is why there is no guarantee that using newspapers or magazines will significantly increase your site's usage. Print media should be viewed as a way of drawing new users online, and to get their attention, you must offer something that is worth their efforts. Publicity in print should, above all, emphasize the significance of this new medium to someone who is not yet online but should be.

An easy way to draw people online is to provide a unique service to users, either something new to the Internet or something otherwise not achievable through standard channels like telephone or mail-order. The most obvious benefit of the Web in this regard is multimedia capability. Photographs of your products, brief audio clips of staff or "satisfied customers" discussing whatever your site is focused upon, and other ways of creating a rich description of your goals and organization are all easy to achieve within the context of a Web site. This alone, though, will be purely promotional, and promotional sites are inherently limited. Even if users are so interested in your product or site content that they have come online as a result, their visits will last only long enough for them to look at what they might want and possibly to order the products. A site that is little more than glorified advertising does not encourage repeated usage and does not hold the attention of users who are not interested in a particular product or service.

Another way to create a site that will draw people online is to explore new technologies in the context of a Web site. For example, improvements in audio and video compression and distribution are occurring daily (see Chapter 8, "True Multimedia"), and if you can use the newest technology, your site will be of interest by default, as it is exploring the cutting edge of the Internet. This sort of approach can be promoted through print media, and your site will gain a reputation as "one to watch" for users who are excited by the potential of Internet technologies.

This is also true in industries that are not heavily represented on the Web. For example, a film company using high-quality video compression to distribute audio/visual clips would be seen in industry press as a site to watch to find out how this technology can affect or benefit others in the field. If the site also encouraged collaborative efforts—allowing users to edit and upload these clips, creating a sort of community-made film project— the press might use the site as an exemplary case study in articles about the potentials of Web technology. This example is provided simply to reinforce what should be on every Web designer's mind: the draw to a Web site will be in direct proportion to the site's levels of substance, interactivity and innovation. By emphasizing the new and exciting, you can effectively use print and broadcast media as "free" advertising and, in so doing, increase the population of the Internet itself.

Promoting a New WWW Site: The Case of the Mammoth Records Internet Information Center

When North Carolina-based Mammoth Records put up its Mammoth Records Internet Information Center on the WWW, it was still a fairly new idea for record companies. Karen Booth, Mammoth Records's Internet coordinator, focused announcements on nontechnical publications. "If anyone was going to talk about the site being innovative, it was going to be a business journal, if they were running an Internet issue or interactive multimedia issue," she explained, adding that recording industry trade publications also took that approach.

In a press release, Mammoth emphasized unique details of the site ("full-length singles, video, artist photos, CD art, up-to-the-minute tour schedules, and mail order information") and emphasized some technical details, such as its use of MPEG2 audio compression "which provides CD quality music samples." To draw attention to the potential of the Web as a medium, Mammoth stated that "the Internet is fully global," citing accesses from Russia, Japan, New Zealand and Australia within the first days of operation. And to help writers who were not familiar with the Web itself, Mammoth distributed several pages of a book about the Web.

The focus on nontechnical press had a two-fold effect. First, in the industry, Karen noted, "you get a reputation as a trailblazer." Second, it encouraged users who were not yet connected to the Internet to seek a connection so that they could get the information, such as touring schedules for bands.

Publicity on the Internet itself is vital to promoting your site. Print and broadcast media will draw new users to the Internet, the Web and to your site, but since a substantial population already inhabits the Web, drawing these existing users to your site can establish your presence very quickly. Most Web users check for new sites on a regular basis, both at announcement sites and on newsgroups. While there is no centralized registration process for Web sites, there are some newsgroups and pages that are recognized as informal centers for new developments.

Catalogs & Announcements on the WWW

Where do Web users look to learn what's new on the Net? This section provides a rundown of locations most users check.

What's New at NCSA Mosaic
http://www.ncsa.uiuc.edu/SDG/Docs/whats-new.html

What's New at NCSA Mosaic was the first of the "What's New" pages on the Internet and has remained one of the most active. Mosaic was the first of the World Wide Web browsers, and it included from the outset a link to a page where the NCSA staff would list new sites. The page is now updated almost daily, and all of the updates for the current month are kept on a single page. There are two ways to submit to What's New. The first, and probably the simplest for a single page or site, is to go to the URL http://www.ncsa.uiuc.edu/SDG/Docs/whats-new.html and fill out the form. When you submit the form it is automatically added to the list. If you don't have forms capability on your browser or are trying to avoid going from site to site to add to every different What's New page, you can send e-mail. The e-mail should be marked up in HTML with one or two links to your site. The maintainers of NCSA's What's New page ask that submissions be formatted in the following way:

Title (name of resource):

Primary URL (main link to resource):

Organization sponsoring resource:

Location of resource:

City:

State (two-letter code if in US):

Country:

Contact person:

  Name:

  E-mail:

Category (put an X next to the one that best describes your organization):

Commercial

Educational

Government

Independent

Description:

A single paragraph (30-word limit) that briefly describes your service. You can include HTML links in the description (no repeat of the main link) but please, no bolds, italics, all-caps.

Yahoo
http://www.yahoo.com/

Originally run from Stanford University, Yahoo has rapidly developed into one of the most comprehensive subject-based catalogs on the World Wide Web since its recent inception. Netscape has recently made Yahoo its default subject index and new page listing site, and it will probably be (if it is not already) one of the most frequently accessed sites on the WWW. Yahoo is a hierarchical menu organized by subject headings that allows users to submit their sites in the area or areas that they feel are appropriate. One can add a site from anywhere in Yahoo by selecting the Add button on the menu bar, but it is a good idea to go to the area you want to have your site included in first. Unless you are already familiar with Yahoo's menu structure, it is not always immediately apparent where to place your new site, and by wandering through the index to find the best location, you save the maintainers of Yahoo the work of placing your entry for you. Be sure to keep in mind that sites can be added in multiple categories, thereby increasing your exposure. The Add form is quite straightforward, and will even assume that you want to add your site to the menu area that you selected Add from and lists that as the default in your form. You receive a confirmation message soon after Yahoo adds your site.

EINet Galaxy
http://www.einet.net/
The maker of MacWeb and WinWeb, EINet Galaxy has a listing for new sites attached to its home page for the EINet browser software. While MacWeb and WinWeb have declined in popularity as Netscape has risen in prominence alongside Mosaic, a number of users still reference this site for its extremely valuable hierarchical subject menu. As with Yahoo, to submit to EINet Galaxy, wander through the subject tree until you have found an appropriate place for your site. Click on Add on the EINet menu bar, and fill out the form. If you cannot determine a place for your site, simply submit it from the home page, and the EINet staff will create a new heading. For help on adding information to EINet Galaxy, look at the page http://www.einet.net/annotate-help.html.

The GNN Whole Internet Catalog
http://www.gnn.com/gnn/wic/
A product of the Global Network Navigator, The GNN Whole Internet Catalog is the World Wide Web outgrowth of the O'Reilly book *The Whole Internet User's Guide & Catalog*. On the "About this site" page for the catalog, GNN describes the site as "a collection of links to 1000 or so of the best resources on the Internet, divided into easy-to-surf subject areas." The catalog is manually updated, and all submissions to the catalog are checked out by the GNN staff before being added. To submit your site, simply send e-mail with the URL and a description of the site to wic@ora.com.

The WWW Virtual Library
http://www.w3.org/hypertext/DataSources/bySubject/Overview.html
The WWW Virtual Library is an index of resources on the Web, organized by subject. Unlike the other catalogs, it is made up of separate departments that are maintained by volunteer users. It is intended more as an index of informational sites than an index of commercial sites. However, it does have a separate section for commercial services, and commercial servers that address one of the other informational topics can and should be added to the listings for that topic. To add your site to the library, you should contact the maintainer of the particular area into which your site

fits. For example, the majority of commercial servers would want a listing in the "Commercial Services" area. To submit to this section, send e-mail with a description of the site to www-request@mail.w3.org. For a complete listing of subject areas and the people maintaining them, look at http://www.w3.org/hypertext/DataSources/bySubject/Maintainers.html.

The Web of Wonder
http://www.digimark.net/wow/
The Web of Wonder, maintained by Weicomp Consulting, Inc., is a relatively new hierarchical catalog of WWW resources. For now, new sites should be submitted to Lance Weitzel (lweitzel@netcom.com) by e-mail, but the WOW is currently working on a submission form similar to the ones for Yahoo and EINet Galaxy.

Robots & Web-Walkers on the WWW

Here is a listing of some robots and Web-walkers on the WWW.

Lycos
http://lycos.cs.cmu.edu/
Developed by Michael Mauldin at Carnegie-Mellon University, Lycos is possibly the most efficient and extensive indexer available on the Internet. Like other automatically updating indices, it "wanders" the Web and registers the pages that it finds. Lycos locates a home page and follows the links from that page, down to the end of that site, registering the URL, title and a portion of the text from each page. It is incredibly efficient (and even more popular) and has the vast majority of sites on the Web within its database. It does, however, need to be told about new domains with Web servers, so that it can add those to its wandering patterns. To add your site to Lycos, go to the URL http://lycos.cs.cmu.edu/lycos-register.html, and fill out the form to submit your home page.

The World Wide Web Worm
http://www.cs.colorado.edu/home/mcbryan/WWWW.html
The World Wide Web Worm is a robot designed by the University of Colorado Computer Science Department and is similar to Lycos

in function. It follows links through Web documents and catalogs its findings in a searchable database. Also like Lycos, it requires that the URL of your top-level document be submitted, and from that point on, the process is automatic. To submit your home page, and by extension, all of the pages at your site, go to the URL http://www.cs.colorado.edu/homes/mcbryan/public_html/bb/13/42/summary.html and fill out the form on that page.

The WebCrawler Index
http://webcrawler.cs.washington.edu/WebCrawler/
Based at the University of Washington, the WebCrawler Index is another Web-walker designed to maintain a dynamic database of World Wide Web pages. To submit your site for indexing, fill out the WebCrawler URL submission form at http://webcrawler.cs.washington.edu/WebCrawler/SubmitURLS.html.

USENET

Here are some USENET newsgroups you might wish to explore on the Web.

news:comp.infosystems.www.announce
Originally there was a single newsgroup on USENET for discussions of the World Wide Web. That group has been split into four groups, which have separate purposes. The group currently used for announcements is comp.infosystems.www.announce. It is considered bad form to post announcements of a new site to the other three groups, even though it happens with some frequency. The comp.infosystems.www.announce newsgroup is moderated, meaning that an administrator clears all posts before they go up on the group itself. Announcements should be sent via e-mail to www-announce@medio.com. The announcements should be in plain text, not marked up in HTML. At the beginning of the message, you should include a single line, in the following format:

<URL:*protocol://site*[:*PORT*]/*path/to/file/or/directory/*>

For example: <URL:http://sunsite.unc.edu/mdw/linux.html> is a valid entry for the beginning of the message. The [:PORT] option should be used only if your http daemon is running on a port other than the default port (80). In the subject line, use one of

the following categories as your first word, in all capital letters, followed by the title of the resource:

ARCHIVE	ART	BOOK
BROWSER	COLLECTION	ECONOMY
EDUCATION	ENTERTAINMENT	ENVIRONMENT
FAQ	GAMES	HEALTH
HUMANITIES	INFO	LAW
MAGAZINE	MISC	MUSIC
NEWS	PERSONAL	POLITICS
REFERENCE	RELIGION	SCIENCE
SERVER	SHOPPING	SPORTS
SOFTWARE		

The newsgroup's charter makes the following recommendations: "The announcement should be short—less than 75 lines—and to the point. The author's signature should be four lines or shorter; the moderator will trim longer signatures. Announcers should not include surveys, polls, application forms, or the like in their posts; such addenda will be excised. Likewise, announcers should not quote price lists or extensive catalog-style descriptions. Instead, a post should provide pointers, in the format described above, to those resources."

news:comp.internet.net-happenings

Originally, the newsgroup net-happenings@is.internic.net was a mailing list started by Gleason Sackman as a way to keep people updated, via e-mail, on the latest developments from all over the Internet. However, user after user complained of the thirty to fifty messages a day that poured in about Gophers, FTP sites, legal updates and the Web, and so the newsgroup comp.internet.net-happenings was created as an alternative means of retrieval. There are also several FTP mirrors and a WWW site with a searchable index of postings to net-happenings. Net-happenings still remains one of the largest mailing lists on the Internet and is a major source of information for events and new additions to the World Wide Web.

There is not really a standard format for messages on comp.internet.net-happenings, but you can do a few things to help the moderator organize the messages. First, the subject line should begin with the protocol, in this case "www". The subject line itself should contain a one-line description of the event to be announced, such as "ShoopSoft WWW Site Online." In the body of the message, you can describe your site, services to be offered, interesting features, and include the URL and a contact person. The URL should be in the same format as in messages to the comp.infosystems.www.announce newsgroup, <URL:*protocol*://*site*[:*PORT*]/*path/to/file/or/directory/*>.

news:alt.internet.services

This newsgroup is generally used for announcements about new services being offered to the Internet community at large. New sites are occasionally posted here but far less frequently than on a group like comp.infosystems.www.announce. You should especially consider posting here if your site offers a unique service to the Web community and is not simply a promotional site. The subject line should begin with "ANNOUNCE:" and should include, at the beginning of the message, the URL of your site in standard format: <URL:http://www.*domain*.com/*location*/*filename*.html>.

More on Newsgroups

You'll want to publicize your site on a number of newsgroups in addition to these. Since USENET is patronized very selectively by most users, the more newsgroups you're visible on, the more attention your site gets.

However, this statement must be qualified: if your site is publicized on inappropriate groups to which it is irrelevant or even tangential, you will certainly receive attention but not the sort that you might be seeking. It is absolutely imperative that promotional posts, especially for commercial sites, not be made recklessly. This type of behavior, called "spamming" in Net lingo, is considered one of the worst infractions that users can commit against the Internet population for a number of reasons. One is that, contrary to what many users may think, USENET is not free to maintain or distribute. Every post takes up disk space and CPU time that has to be paid for by each news host. This is not a problem for information and news, but begins to be a problem for commercial advertisements. Every unnecessary post can be encouragement for news hosts to limit the amount of news that they provide, a limitation which would damage both the users using that particular host and USENET as a community and a resource.

That said, there is no reason why you shouldn't address appropriate newsgroups when a new site, relevant to the interests of the readers, is created. After posting to the standard announcement sites, think about what newsgroups you read on a regular basis, and decide whether those groups would find this information relevant. Also remember that electronic mailing lists are a valuable means of distribution for new site announcements.

While no advice can be given as to where to begin looking, or exactly which groups would or would not be receptive to an announcement, you can use several methods to determine how you should approach them. Primary to all of these methods, though, is your taking time to read through the group, participating in discussions unrelated to promotion and getting a feel for the community of the group. Ask yourself these questions: first, have other sites been announced on this particular group, and how have those postings been received? Second, is the population of this newsgroup inclined toward Web usage in this first place? If they are not, should they be, for your site or in general, and might your announcement help encourage them? Finally, how would the members benefit from using your site, outside of being just consumers? Are you providing information that would help them, given that they, as customers and interested investigators, will benefit you by their presence and participation?

This final question should always be considered, not only in your promotional strategies, but in the way that you design your site. As mentioned previously (in "Site Unity & Traffic Control: Design & Content Considerations"), the quality of the informational content and the general benefits of using your site will be directly proportional to its use by the Internet community. Before promoting your site, and perhaps even before creating it at all, think in terms of mutual benefit: the benefit you will get by establishing a Web presence and having a new body of potential customers or contacts, and in return, the benefit that you will give them by providing a new resource for information and ideas. From the outset, we have stressed that the World Wide Web can be much more than a series of billboards or online catalogs. As a new citizen of the Internet (a "Netizen"), it is your responsibility to ensure that it indeed is much more.

Moving On

This book outlines a number of ways to create an excellent Web site, from authoring and style techniques to full multimedia. After creating the site, you should decide how it is to be found and how it will appear upon first impression. Naming your machines and creating an appropriate and attractive home page will lead users to your site and please them upon arrival. The links in your document, laid out with foresight, will guide your users to the pages that you want them to see.

After everything is finished, or at least presentable, new sites should be "advertised" to the Net, using USENET newsgroups and World Wide Web indices. A number of sites announce their presence on the Internet in the areas listed throughout this chapter, and then place an "Under Construction" icon on their pages. In a way, this is redundant. Every site on the World Wide Web is, and should be, under construction all the time. Instead of putting an "Under Construction" notice on your pages, make it obvious that your site is under construction by providing the newest functions available. The final chapter of this book, "Future Directions," describes the ways that the World Wide Web is changing, and what is becoming possible. Using this information, you can make sure that your site is always under construction, and by extension, on the cutting edge.

13

Future Directions

The World Wide Web is evolving at a faster rate than probably any other medium in history. Between the time that this book is written and when it is on the shelves of bookstores, browsers will be capable of displaying new features of Web pages, merchants will be selling new products for the Web, Web sites will be selling products in new ways, and discussions will be occurring across the globe about how to change the face of the Web.

This chapter is largely based on speculations—speculations made by developers working on the cutting edge of Internet technology. The discussions in this chapter are intended to give you a peek into the future of the Web, including:

- Developments in HTTP, the protocol that clients and servers use to communicate. These developments include an upgraded version and enhancements to HTTP security that are changing commerce on the Web.
- Additions to, and renovations of, HTML.
- A new language, called the Virtual Reality Modeling Language (VRML), describing three-dimensional space on the Web.

- New technologies and Web sites that allow new levels of collaboration across the Internet.

All of our discussions will be based, to some degree, on ideas that are still being developed and should not be seen as definitive statements of what the Web will be like. Instead, the sections in this chapter contain informed speculations about the directions in which the Web is moving. You should consider these speculations as indications of what to watch for and where to watch it and how to prepare for and participate in the future directions of the Web.

HTML v3.0

It should be noted at the outset of any discussion of HTML v3.0 that most of the current plans for development could change. The document that describes HTML v3.0 is an "Internet Draft," a working document that contains proposals, and not definitive statements of language standards. However, a number of the proposals contained in the HTML v3.0 Internet Draft have already been implemented—for example, tables are supported by Netscape as of v1.1 and Mosaic as of v2.5.

The description of HTML v3.0 contained in this section, then, should be seen as a theoretical one—in other words, a look at the potential of HTML v3.0 as it has been proposed. Our purpose is to give you an idea of what changes might be taking place so that you can structure your documents accordingly. After HTML v3.0 is implemented as an WWW language standard, certain stylistic elements, such as the <!DOCTYPE> tag, discussed later in this section, will be important in distinguishing documents written with older versions of HTML so that browsers can correctly display those documents as well as newer ones.

HTML v3.0 will be fully backward compatible with older versions of *correct* HTML. However, incorrect HTML, or HTML that does not contain all of the necessary elements to be correctly interpreted, will be dealt with more strictly by HTML v3.0 browsers. Even the experimental browser Arena, developed to test HTML v3.0 markup, will flag old and new versions of HTML that

are incorrect with a "Bad HTML" warning at the top of the browser window.

As HTML v3.0 moves closer to its final form, you should consider experimenting with it. Incorporate some of the new tags and the improvements contained in the already existing tags, and check it with a browser like Arena, which is discussed later in this chapter. By getting practice early on and by guaranteeing that your documents will be compatible with the versions of HTML to come, you will ensure that your site is flexible and enduring.

Defining Your Documents

HTML v3.0, as with a new version of any language or software package, is designed to improve upon, but not to eliminate, older versions. To guarantee this compatibility, you need to appropriately define your documents as to whether they are marked up in HTML v3.0 or HTML v2.0. You can define a document by setting a document type in the header of the document, using a standard file extension for HTML v3.0 documents and by setting an appropriate MIME type on the server side to type files before they reach the browser itself.

MIME types are not only used for defining multimedia file types, but they also define the file type of any input that is received by a browser. Pages designed using the HTML v3.0 language standard use a different MIME type from older HTML documents because they must be interpreted differently by a browser. The current MIME type for an HTML document is simply text/html, which a browser interprets as "This document is an HTML v2.0 (or earlier) document and has certain formatting configurations that I understand." To distinguish HTML v3.0 documents, while retaining the MIME type text/html, an addition to this MIME type will be added. The MIME type for all HTML v3.0 documents is text/html; version=3.0. This MIME type tells the browser that the document is to be interpreted as HTML but is in a different version, requiring a different type of interpretation. Browsers that can interpret only HTML v2.0, or variants of it, such as older versions of Netscape and Mosaic, will not attempt to display a file of this MIME type but will save it to a file.

This new MIME type will be specified in the same way that all of a server's MIME types are specified, in the global MIME-types file for the daemon software (see Chapter 3, "Setting Up the Server"). To simplify the automatic MIME typing of HTML v3.0 documents, it has been proposed that files in this format be saved with the extension .html3, or .ht3 for PCs. Since the file that determines MIME types for a server does so by matching a MIME type to the file extension, this would be a quick way to get around the problems of potential incompatibility if servers that could display only HTML v2.0 attempted to display HTML v3.0. Another option is to use the information in HTTP requests to determine, before a document is loaded, whether a browser can support HTML v3.0 markup. This makes the information contained in the header of the document all the more important because it will ease the transition to HTML v3.0 for users still using older browsers.

You can use the HTML markup itself to indicate that a document is in HTML v3.0 format. Inside the header of a document, that is, between the <HEAD> and </HEAD> tags, you should include the appropriate document type tag. For HTML v3.0, the document type tag is

```
<!DOCTYPE HTML public "-//W3O//DTD W3 HTML v3.0//EN">
```

This type tag essentially tells the browser to use the W3O's (the World Wide Web Organization) HTML v3.0 standards document, or DTD (Document Type Definition), to understand the markup. We recommend you include a document type tag in documents marked up with HTML v2.0 to indicate to newer browsers that your document should be interpreted as HTML v2.0. The following is the document type tag for an HTML v2.0 document:

```
<!DOCTYPE HTML public "-//W3O//DTD W3 HTML 2.0//EN">
```

There are alternate proposals for the syntax of this phrase, such as the inclusion or omission of the "W3", the use of either W3O or IETF (The World Wide Web Organization or the Internet Engineering Task Force) as the name of the standard developer and so on. In all likelihood, a number of syntaxes for setting the document type will be permitted.

In addition to the document type, another type of document definition should be set in the header of a document. The document's relationship to other documents, that is, what it depends on and how it is positioned in the document hierarchy, needs to be provided, using the <LINK> tag, as is discussed in Chapter 6, "Checking Your Work." The <LINK> tag takes a wide range of arguments in HTML v3.0. The following <LINK> elements are proposed as additions to the HTML v2.0 <LINK> elements in the HTML v3.0 Internet Draft:

- REL=Home If a <LINK> tag contains this element, it references a home page or the top of a hierarchy.
- REL=Copyright A <LINK> tag containing this element references a copyright statement for the current document.
- REL=Up When the document forms part of a hierarchy, a <LINK> tag containing this element references the immediate parent of the current document.
- REL=Help A <LINK> tag with this element references a document offering help. The help document describes the wider context and offers further links to relevant documents. This element is aimed at reorienting users who have lost their way.
- REL=StyleSheet This element, described later in this section, references a style sheet that defines the way that certain text types are displayed by the browser.
- REL=Banner This element references a banner that appears at the top of all documents, even while you scroll up or down through the document.

Using these new <LINK> tag elements, you can define your documents both in terms of relationships to other Web pages and with stylistic elements, such as the style sheet and the banner. HTML v3.0 will allow for changes in the way that style and content are implemented. These changes make it necessary to understand how style and content are treated in HTML v3.0 and, by extension, how the component parts of a Web page will be treated by browsers in the future.

Designing Your Documents

The MIME type of HTML v3.0 reflects what will not change about HTML as it evolves—namely, that version 3.0 is based on older versions of HTML and is simply an upgrade. Version 3.0 is fully backward compatible with older versions of HTML. However, the new additions will make the Web a far more interesting and diverse space and will force designers and developers to change the way that documents are created and defined. Specifically, the new features of HTML reinforce an idea that this book has presented throughout: HTML is a structural language, not a graphic or design language. Even more so than HTML v2.0, HTML v3.0 will require attention be paid to the structure of the document and will encourage the development of a fully platform-independent method of distributing documents. This focus is reflected in a central difference between HTML v2.0 (and especially variants, such as the Netscape extensions) and HTML v3.0—the nearly total separation of style and content in documents marked up with HTML v3.0.

Style

To allow a combination of user and provider input in the presentation of a document, HTML v3.0 will implement two levels of presentation, one of which will be the user's own preferences that he or she selects in the browser. The first way to configure presentation sitewide is through a style sheet, which is a document that a number of different HTML documents can link to that will define a number of presentation characteristics of the document.

The introduction of style sheets, which allow the separation of presentation from content, is one of the more notable changes in HTML v3.0. The style sheets for a document are "cascaded." In other words, a top-level document is used to define a wide range of documents. Specific changes to that document—either additions to or overrides of the top-level style sheet—are made in the document itself. Finally, the user has control over the styles displayed by the browser. At the top level, one or more style sheets are designed and referenced using the <LINK> tag as a "global" style sheet. The <LINK> tag can take a new relationship definition

in HTML v3.0, which provides a link to the global style sheet. The following tag tells the HTML browser to use the formatting information in the file stylesheet.dsssl to format the document:

```
<LINK REL=StyleSheet HREF="stylesheet.dsssl">
```

Style sheets will likely be written using a language called DSSSL (Document Style Semantics and Specification Language), or more specifically, a subset of that language called DSSSL Lite. Using this language, you can map the content tags in the body of an HTML document to style tags such as those defining paragraph alignment, text color, font size and other formatting styles. DSSSL will not be the only language in which these codes can be defined, but it will probably be something of a standard as HTML v3.0 develops.

While it is outside of the scope of this book to go into DSSSL Lite style sheets and other types of style sheets, you can check out the growing body of HTML v3.0-based materials that address the development of style sheets. A collection of documents about style sheets is maintained at CERN, at the URL http://www.w3.org/hypertext/WWW/Style/.

Aside from the style sheet, HTML v3.0 will make it possible to include style information inside the document itself. The <STYLE> tag, located inside the header of the document, is capable of overriding any outside style tags that are used in the global style sheet. It can use either the DSSSL Lite language for defining styles, or it can use a browser-specific language. In the case of Arena, which is the only currently available HTML v3.0 document browser, the notation is referred to as "experimental" notation. The style tag can take an argument that tells it what language the style information will be composed in. For example, the following tags could be used to enclose a set of style formatting definitions that would be composed using the "experimental" language format:

```
<STYLE NOTATION="experimental">
</STYLE>
```

To use the DSSSL Lite style notation, replace the string "experimental" with the string "dsssl-lite".

The introduction of style sheets will allow for a broad range of possible formatting configurations. Style sheets will be able to define the following characteristics of a file:

- Font family, the base font used for documents, modified by tags like <EM>, <STRONG> and other text-formatting tags.
- Font color, which can be different for any text font or format.
- Font size, which can also vary according to each type of text format.
- Paragraph alignment.
- Document background color.
- List indention.
- List numbering style.

These may be added to, or subtracted from, as HTML v3.0 is implemented. However, it is likely that the range of style-formatting possibilities will only increase and that the NOTATION element for the style tag will allow for different languages with different abilities and limitations to define an HTML document's style. This will make the global style sheets a useful base point from which they can be modified as you develop the unique feel of your pages.

Structure

Designing the content of your document—that is, laying out the structure in the most efficient and useful way possible—is an important concern in HTML v3.0. By skillfully setting up the structure of your document, you will be able to do a great deal more with it in terms of style, presentation and management (that is, indexing, cross-referencing, etc.). This section will cover some of the ways that HTML v3.0 is used to define the structure of an HTML document. (We will discuss the tags themselves in the section "Refining Your Documents.")

Two attributes, ID and CLASS, can be used in almost any tag in the body of the document, and you can then refer to using these tags in the header or style sheet. The attributes define a certain area or string in a way that other tags can reference.

Defining something as ID="idname" defines it in a similar way to the <A NAME> tag; in other words, it gives it a unique identi-

fier within the document. However, the ID attribute is not only an anchor but can be used to define any sort of entity within an HTML document: a paragraph, a table, a header or even the document itself. This definition can be used as a point of reference by several different types of tags. In the following example of the ID attribute, it is used with the <RANGE> tag to identify two points in a section of text.

The header tag that uses the ID attribute is <RANGE>, which marks a range of a document between two identifiers. The format of the <RANGE> tag is

```
<RANGE CLASS=classtype FROM=id1 UNTIL=id2>
```

The CLASS variable, which replaces *classtype* in the example, defines how the range located between id1 and id2 would be identified. For example, you could match the CLASS setting to a style type in your style sheet, which would then define how that particular region of the document would be interpreted. To use a very basic example, the following is a sample document that would have one sentence defined as "text.important" and a second defined as "text.extra".

```
<HTML>
<HEAD>
<!DOCTYPE HTML public "-//W3O//DTD W3 HTML v3.0//EN">
<TITLE>ShoopSoft News Bulletin</TITLE>
<RANGE CLASS=paragraph.important FROM=spot1 UNTIL=spot2>
<RANGE CLASS=paragraph.extra FROM=spot3 UNTIL=spot4>
</HEAD>
<BODY>
<P>
<SPOT ID=spot1>This is absolutely vital information! ShoopSoft will be
closing its doors on July 5, 1998.<SPOT ID=spot2> Please read on.
</P>
<P>
<SPOT ID=spot3>
All of our software will be heavily discounted for two months in advance.
<SPOT ID=spot4> Make plans to take advantage of this offer now!
</P>
</BODY>
</HTML>
```

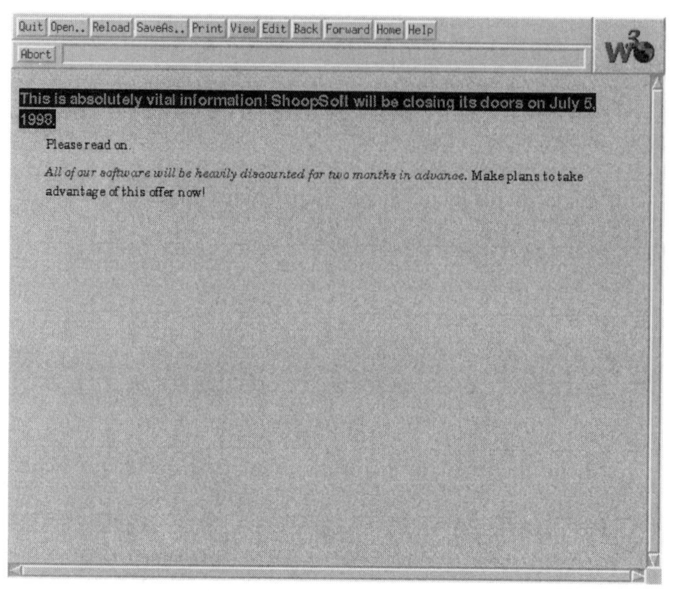

Figure 13-1: *A Web page, designed using a style sheet.*

Each section of the sample document begins with the opening <SPOT> tag containing an ID attribute, which simply marks a point in the text and then assigns an identifier to that point. The <RANGE> tag says that all of the area between spot1 and spot2 should be identified as "text.important" and the area between spot3 and spot4 should be identified as "text.extra." The classes are in this format because it is the standard format understood by style sheets and other functions that use the "class" of an entity: the most general category is given first (text) and the most specific category is given second (important), with the two categories separated by a period. After setting the class like this, it would be relatively simple to match those two text types to a particular style—for example, displaying the text designated as "text.important" in red and the "text.extra" in a smaller font size.

The CLASS setting can be used in virtually every tag in the body of a document as well. If you want to mark any element in the body of the document with a certain class, you can simply put the CLASS setting inside the tag for that element. For example, to

mark an entire paragraph as "text.important," you could add the following lines to a document:

```
<P CLASS=text.important>
This is important text.
</P>
```

Aside from marking certain sections with an identifier that associates formats with a class type, a number of new tags can be used to lay out and structure your Web pages. These new and improved tags will serve to refine your pages and allow a wide range of functions that HTML v2.0 did not allow.

Refining Your Documents: The New & Improved Tags

It would be inappropriate to go into much detail about the specific tags and features that HTML v3.0 will introduce, because they haven't been finalized yet. This section outlines a number of tags to give you a sense of how changes in the language might affect HTML authoring after HTML v3.0 is formally adopted as a standard. However, the tag set we discuss is neither comprehensive nor definitive. We explain the tags so you can use them in advance of their implementation, and by using them informally, you can anticipate how they will be used when they are adopted.

The tags and settings that we discuss in this section are not part of the HTML v2.0 specification. Some browsers, like Netscape v2.5, have already implemented them or have created tags that produce the same effect, but we don't recommend using tags that have been designed for a single browser. Even if the tags are supposed to be a part of the HTML v3.0 standard, the syntax of the tags might change, meaning that you will have to revise the tags to incorporate the new syntax.

You will be able to use more complex layouts in documents marked up with HTML v3.0. The new version will allow you to use page layouts similar to magazine or newspaper layouts. A number of new tags, some for marking structure and others for designating text and image formatting, can be used in conjunction to make this possible.

Three tags explicitly define the layout of a page: the old tags <P> and <BR> for defining paragraphs and lines and the new tag <DIV> that defines larger sections of a document. The paragraph tag, as discussed previously, can take a setting called CLASS, which allows you to give that paragraph a "name." The name can then be referenced by other tags in the document or by an external style sheet.

You can use the <DIV> tag in a similar manner. It can enclose a number of paragraphs and other elements, such as forms and tables, and define the enclosed section with a class. So, for example, a section of an HTML document like the following could be defined as a preface:

```
<DIV CLASS=Preface>
This document seeks to outline ShoopSoft's accomplishments in the
world of networking software and services. It is not intended to be a final
copy, but will give you a sense of our abilities and potential.</P>
Special thanks to J.R. Dobbs, Bill Jones, Akbar, and Jeff for their
invaluable contributions to this work.</P>
</DIV>
```

To make the preface designation meaningful, you have to tell the HTML browser what to do with a preface. It can be indented, displayed in boldface or displayed in a chartreuse color. As noted in the discussion of style sheets, this is defined either in a separate file or in the <STYLE> tag in the header of the document.

You should use the <DIV> and <P> tags to define the sections of your documents as specifically as possible and then give these sections special characteristics in your style sheets. Both <DIV> and <P> share a number of settings in common, such as CLASS and ID, and both can also take the two formatting settings ALIGN and CLEAR.

Both ALIGN and CLEAR determine how text is arranged on the page. The ALIGN option aligns the specified paragraph or division with the left margin or the right margin or the center of the page. The syntax of the setting is, simply enough, ALIGN=left, ALIGN=right or ALIGN=center. ALIGN can also be set to justify the text in the paragraph. These settings have already been implemented in Netscape v2.5, along with other possible settings that are not currently part of the HTML v3.0 Internet Draft. Since a

paragraph is aligned at left by default, explicitly setting ALIGN=left is unnecessary for paragraphs and divisions.

The paragraph and line break tags, <P> and <BR>, can take the CLEAR setting, which is used in conjunction with a new feature of inline images, the ability to wrap text around the image. You can use the CLEAR setting to wrap text around the left or right margin of an image and start the next text line or paragraph below the image rather than alongside it, as described in Chapter 7.

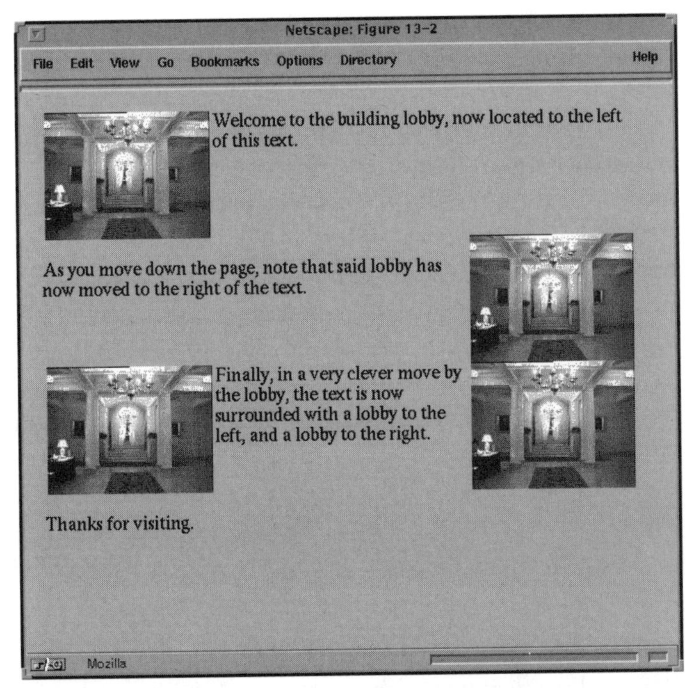

Figure 13-2: *Graphics and text using the ALIGN option.*

Aligning the images is as simple as aligning sections of text. The HTML v3.0 Internet Draft contains additional settings for the <IMG> tag, which designate this alignment. The <IMG> tag in HTML v2.0 uses the settings ALIGN=top, ALIGN=middle and ALIGN=bottom to determine the vertical location of text alongside the image. The additional settings for this tag, ALIGN=left and ALIGN=right, determine the horizontal location of the image on the page, aligning it with either the left or the right margin, respectively. Figure 13-2 shows graphics using the ALIGN-left and ALIGN-right settings. Other settings for the <IMG> tag and a new <FIG> tag are discussed in the section "Graphics" later in this chapter.

After defining your document's structure with <DIV> and <P> and the layout of the text with <P> and <BR>, you can define other formatting settings with the HTML v3.0 markup. These other settings include placing a stationary banner at the top of your pages, which will not scroll with the rest of the document; creating custom lists and new types of text design; and a range of new features, from graphics with wraparound text to forms that take input from a microphone.

The banner element is a simple tag to implement, but one that will make a significant difference in the way that your pages appear and the way that they are used. The banner is an HTML document, or a section of an HTML document, that appears at the top of the screen and remains there when you scroll down a page or to the left or right. The banner is an ideal place for a corporate logo, navigation aids and other information that anyone looking at a page might need. Since banners appear at the top of a document that is being viewed, they should be kept as small as possible. A banner can be set up in two ways: as an external document, linked in with the <LINK> tag, or as an internal section of the HTML document itself, bracketed by the beginning and ending <BANNER> tags. The syntax of the <LINK> tag for a banner is

```
<LINK REL=Banner HREF=filename.html>
```

You replace *filename* with the name of the banner. Markup enclosed by the opening and closing banner tags can be identical to any other markup in the document—just remember to keep it short.

Text Formatting

The implementation of HTML v3.0 will improve lists in several ways. One way is purely visual: you can replace the standard list bullet (•) with any one of a set of simple graphics called "dingbats." These graphics are selected from the new HTML v3.0 icon entities, which are simple graphics that HTML v3.0 browsers will include as local graphics. Essentially, icon entities are similar to the alphabet entities that are used to display characters like the less than symbol (<), which cannot be displayed from the source code alone. These icons are included in a document by using the tag <!ENTITY>, or in the case of the list dingbat, by using the DINGBAT markup. For example, the following list would appear on a browser with a computer monitor icon next to each list item, using the DINGBAT=display markup.

```
ShoopSoft supported platforms include:
<UL DINGBAT=display>
<LI>UNIX
<LI>Macintosh
<LI>PC
</UL>
```

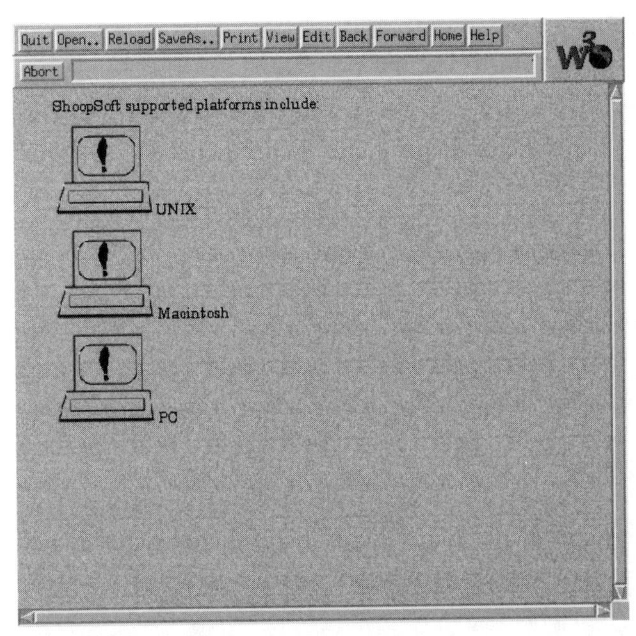

Figure 13-3: *A list using the "display" dingbat.*

You simply set the DINGBAT option to the name of the icon, which is usually a fairly obvious one-word description of the icon. HTML v3.0 icons are discussed in detail in the next section, "Graphics." If you don't want the standard list bullet or any of the

HTML icons, you can use the tag <UL PLAIN> to open an unbulleted list.

You can use the DINGBAT setting only in unordered lists, that is, lists opened with the tag <UL>. The ordered list, which is marked up with the <OL> tag and uses numbers or letters to indicate the order of list items, has also changed. Primary among these changes is the capability to start the list at whatever point you want (for example, starting a numbered list at item 5) and the capability to continue the numbering from a list earlier in the document. These two settings, SEQNUM and CONTINUE, are very easy to implement. The SEQNUM setting, which sets the starting value for an ordered list, uses the following syntax:

```
<OL SEQNUM=n>
```

The *n* is replaced with the number of the starting value. For example, a list with the following code would produce a list in the format shown in Figure 13-4:

The panel recommended adding the three new items to the four cardinal directions.

```
<OL SEQNUM=5>
     <LI>Left
     <LI>Right
     <LI>Under
</OL>
```

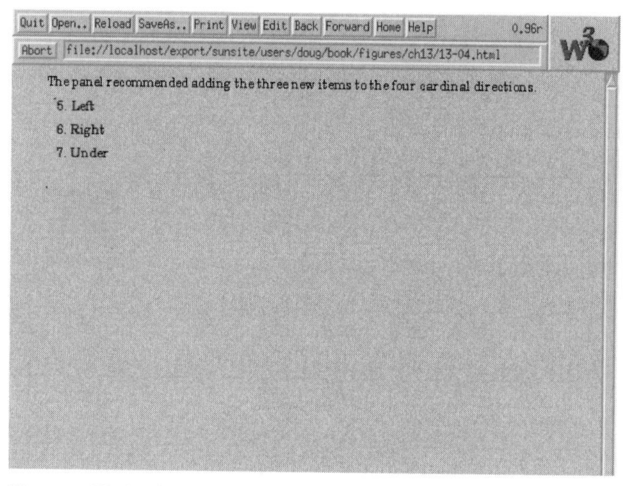

Figure 13-4: *A numbered list beginning with list item 5.*

The CONTINUE setting for ordered lists allows an ordered list to continue the numbering from the previous ordered list in a document. The syntax for this tag is simply <OL CONTINUE>.

Finally, both ordered and unordered lists can take a list header, a description or title of the list. The tag <LH> should be the first item after the list is opened. It will start a list header, and the tag </LH> will finish it.

In addition to special text formats like lists, a number of new formatting tags for text are introduced in HTML v3.0. These tags, however, are the ones most likely to change as the Internet Draft is revised. The remainder of this section discusses formatting features that are likely to be implemented.

Four new tags have been proposed to format specific types of textual information. The <AU> tag will be used to indicate the name of the author. The <ACRONYM> tag, as you might guess, is the formatting style for acronyms. The <ABBREV> tag will indicate an abbreviation. Finally, the <PERSON> tag will be used to surround the names in a document. The draft recommends that this last tag be used by search engines, to extract and display the names of people associated with particular documents.

Nine additional general text-formatting tags can be used for less specific purposes than the ones we've discussed previously. The <Q> tag can be used to place quotation marks around short quotations, as opposed to the <CITE> tag, which put citations in italicized and indented text. The <U> tag, for underlining text, is part of the HTML v2.0 specification but is not yet widely supported. Tags for superscripts and subscripts, <SUP> and <SUB>, respectively, have also been added. The <S> tag is a strikethrough tag that designates the text be displayed with a line through it. The <BIG> and <SMALL> font tags have been proposed as additions to the standard; they will display text in a font that is larger or smaller in proportion to the standard font size. Finally, the <INS> and <DEL> tags, for inserted and deleted text, will indicate that text has been added to or deleted from a particular document, while still including that text as part of the document.

One final text formatting tag that has been proposed is the <TAB> tag, which will allow you to set the horizontal alignment of a particular word or string. The <TAB> tag is used in two phases. First, the tab width is set using the ID setting within the tag. Then, another <TAB> tag below the first uses the TO setting that takes the name of the ID setting as a reference and indents the text to that position.

The following lines of HTML code set up two tab stops, one called "Tab1" and the second called "Tab2," and the second line refers back to those tab stops to align sections of text.

```
There are two typog<TAB ID=Tab1>arphical errors contained in this one
l<TAB ID=Tab2>nne.
<TAB TO=Tab1>Here <TAB TO=Tab2>and Here.
```

On an HTML v3.0 browser, this text would be displayed with the two phrases lined up underneath the tab stops identified by "Tab1" and "Tab2," as is shown in Figure 13-5.

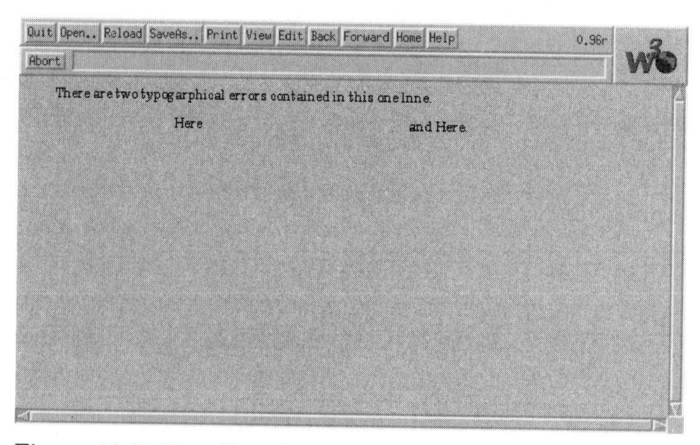

Figure 13-5: *Text aligned with the <TAB ID> and <TAB TO> tags.*

The <TAB> tag can also take an ALIGN setting, which will align a particular word or line at the left, right or center of a page with the settings ALIGN=left, ALIGN=right or ALIGN=center, respectively. Finally, paragraphs or lines can be indented by using the INDENT setting. For example, a setting of <TAB INDENT=6> would indent the text following that tag a distance of 6 units.

Graphics

The standard tag for imbedding a graphic in an HTML document, <IMG>, will be changed significantly with the implementation of HTML v3.0. One change, the ALIGN setting, is discussed in the previous section. Another change is that you will be able to specify the size of a graphic in the <IMG> tag itself. The WIDTH and HEIGHT settings will set the dimensions of a graphic, and when that graphic is displayed, it will be automatically resized regardless of the original size of the graphic itself. This automatic resizing means that you will not have to spend time resizing your graphics manually, and it will be much easier to establish a standard size for all of your images. The WIDTH and HEIGHT settings take numerical values, which will indicate the number of pixels for each dimension. You can also use a different unit, the en space, which is a typographical unit equal to half the point size. For example, the following <IMG> tag would produce a graphic 100 pixels wide by 100 pixels high:

```
<IMG WIDTH=100 HEIGHT=100 SRC="bob.gif">
```

Probably the most significant change to the tags that allow the inclusion of graphics has nothing to do with the image tag but, rather, is the introduction of the figure tag, <FIG>. <FIG> includes the graphic itself and other information, including captions and credits, within the beginning and ending <FIG> tags. An example of these features is provided in the following lines of code, which include a graphic, a caption and credits:

```
<FIG SRC="bob.gif">
<CAPTION>J.R. "Bob" Dobbs and a friend</CAPTION>
<CREDIT>Source unknown</CREDIT>
</FIG>
```

Note that the closing tag for <FIG> follows the <CAPTION> and <CREDIT> tags. These tags need to be used inside the <FIG> tag. You can also use ALIGN set to any setting other than center, which is the default, to insert lines of text next to a figure, with the text wrapped around the figure. For example, the following markup consisting of a graphic aligned to the left text margin, a caption, and some lines of explanation, would produce the output seen in Figure 13-6.

```
<FIG ALIGN =left SRC="bob.gif">
<CAPTION>J.R. "Bob" Dobbs and a friend</CAPTION>
<P>This is a rare photograph of J.R. "Bob" Dobbs and an otherwordly
visitor, discussing the shape of things to come.
</FIG>
```

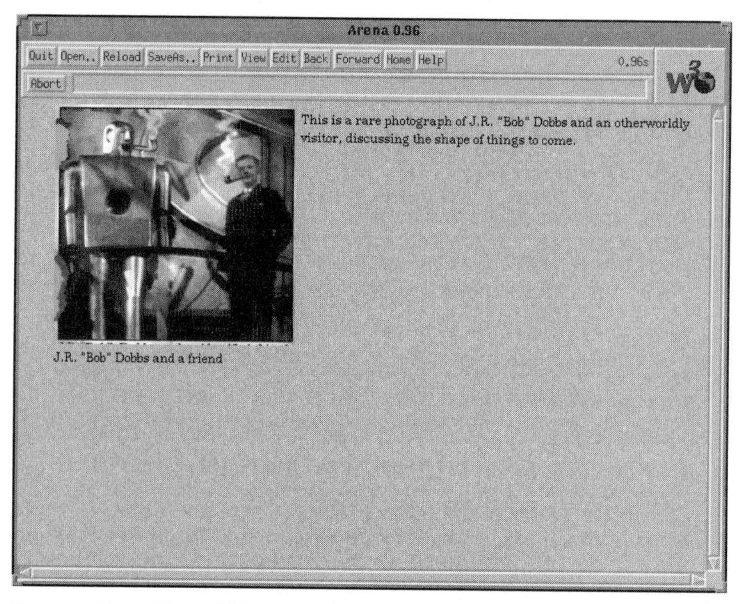

Figure 13-6: *The <FIG> tag with caption and wraparound text.*

The <FIG> tag can take all of the ALIGN settings that the <IMG> tag can, as well as a number of others. By default, figures are aligned to the center, which disables wraparound text. Aside from left, right and center, ALIGN can take the following settings:

- justify This option increases or decreases the size of the figure to fill all of the space between the left and right margins. Text wraparound is disabled when this setting is used.

- bleedleft While the ALIGN=left setting aligns the figure to the left text margin, the ALIGN=bleedleft setting aligns the figure to the left edge of the window itself, beyond the text margin.

- bleedright This setting affects the graphic similar to the bleedleft setting, except the figure is aligned to the right edge of the window.

One other appealing feature of how HTML v3.0 handles figures is the <OVERLAY> tag, which, like <CAPTION> and <CREDIT>, is used inside the figure tags. For example, the following section of

HTML markup will load the first image, mona_lisa.gif and, after loading that image, overlay a second image, mustache.gif:

```
<FIG SRC="mona_lisa.gif">
    <OVERLAY SRC="mustache.gif">
</FIG>
```

This feature is especially useful if you will be loading one figure a number of times and want to overlay different images on top of it.

In the following example, the markup would cause the browser to load mona_lisa.gif only once and then cache that image so it would be ready to be displayed immediately. The only images that would then need to be loaded in subsequent figures are the images to be overlaid.

```
<FIG SRC="mona_lisa.gif">
    <OVERLAY SRC="mustache.gif">
</FIG>
<FIG SRC="mona_lisa.gif">
    <OVERLAY SRC="goatee.gif">
</FIG>
<FIG SRC="mona_lisa.gif">
    <OVERLAY SRC="monocle.gif">
</FIG>
```

Unfortunately, unless you design overlay pictures specifically to be used with the figure, just entering the <OVERLAY> tag will not position the overlaid graphic correctly. To correctly place the overlaid image, use the X and Y settings inside the <OVERLAY> tag to specify the horizontal and vertical coordinates for the upper left-hand corner of the image. A setting such as the following would place the upper left-hand corner of the overlay image, mustache.gif, at the coordinates 100,150.

```
<FIG SRC="mona_lisa.gif">
    <OVERLAY X=100 Y=150 SRC="mustache.gif">
</FIG>
```

Finally, HTML v3.0 supports a feature that the authors of the Internet Draft call "graphical hotzones." The hotzone is a way to overcome the problem of using imagemaps on pages that might be viewed by text-only browsers. A clickable imagemap allows a user to select a particular link by clicking on some region of an image. However, since a text-only browser could not view that image, the imagemap is totally disabled. In HTML v3.0, this problem no longer exists because for every link specified in a graphic, a corresponding text link is displayed on nongraphical browsers. For example, on a nongraphical browser, each of the links within the following <FIG> tags would be displayed as a hyperlinked string of text, such as the string "The Alumni Center" linked to the file alumni.html.

```
<FIG SRC="campusmap.gif">
<H1>Welcome to State University!</H1>
<P>Come and visit our campus:</P>
<UL>
<LI><A HREF="visitors.html" SHAPE="rect 30,200,60,16">
SU Visitors Center</A>
<LI><A HREF="sports.html" SHAPE="rect 100,200,50,16">
SU Gymnasium</A>
<LI><A HREF="students.html" SHAPE="rect 160,200,30,16">
The Student Union</A>
<LI><A HREF="academics.html" SHAPE="rect 200,200,50,16">
The Academic Departments</A>
<LI><A HREF="alumni.html" SHAPE="rect 260,200,80,16">
The Alumni Center</A>
</UL>
</FIG>
```

However, on a graphical browser, the area of the graphic campusmap.gif delineated by the coordinates set with the SHAPE setting would be linked to the file in the HREF setting. In the case of "The Alumni Center," this area would be a rectangle with the corners 260,200 and 80,16. The SHAPE setting takes coordinates in the same way that the map file for an imagemap takes coordinates, but the two coordinate pairs are separated by a comma rather than a space. Figure 13-7 shows a graphical hotlink as it appears on a browser with graphics (13-7a) and on a text browser (13-7b).

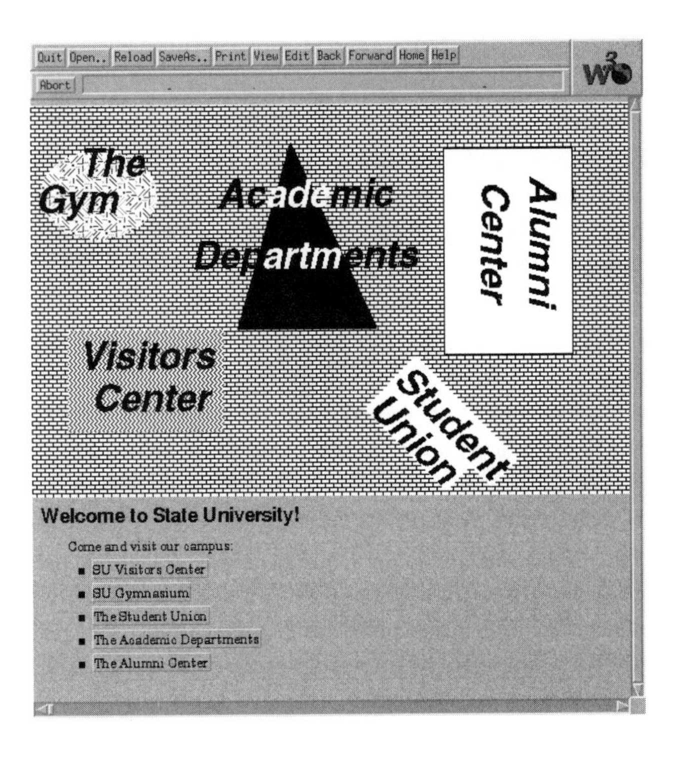

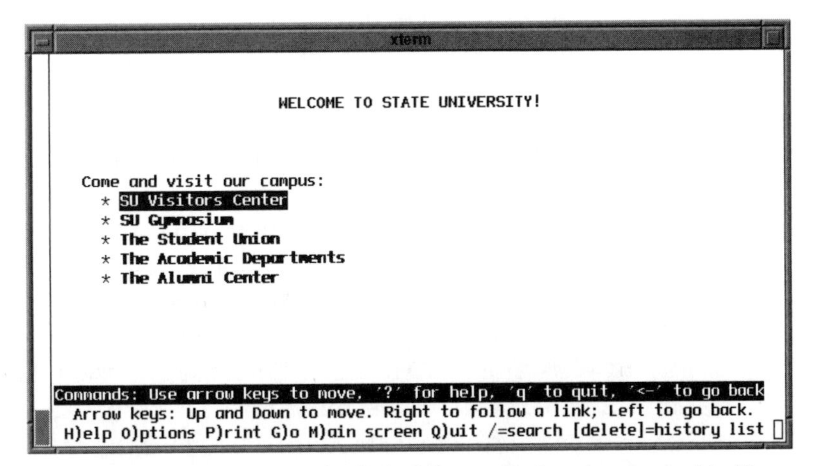

Figure 13-7 a (top) & b: *A hotlinked figure displayed on a graphical browser and nongraphical browser.*

The use of fancy images and detailed markup for these images has been complemented in HTML v3.0 by the introduction of a way to display images, or icons, quickly and simply. These icons are not graphics that are downloaded from a server but are actually part of the browser. An icon is identified by a name in the <!ENTITY> tag, which passes the name from the document to the browser. When the browser reads which icon entity to load, it uses one of a set of locally defined images in the display. For example, the DINGBAT setting used in the example near the beginning of the previous section "Text Formatting" also calls an icon entity, the "display" icon. When Arena, the browser that displays the list in Figure 13-3, reads that the "display" icon is needed, it loads a local image (in this case, a small computer monitor) and puts it in place of the DINGBAT option.

The case is the same for the <!ENTITY> tag. When an HTML v3.0-compliant browser sees the <!ENTITY> tag, it loads whatever icon is named in that tag and displays it in place of the <!ENTITY> tag. Using these tags will allow a limited number of small graphics to be loaded quickly, cutting down on the need for servers to supply every graphic on a page. The list of icon entities is still being developed, but an updated listing is available at the URL http://www.hpl.hp.co.uk/people/dsr/html3/icons.txt.

Tables

Even though tables are still being revised in the HTML v3.0 Internet Draft, both Mosaic and Netscape have implemented them in their current releases. This section will provide instructions on how to construct HTML v3.0-compliant tables, but these instructions are not necessary for the exact implementation being used by Mosaic v2.5 or Netscape v1.1. However, you should code for the future. Netscape and Mosaic will release browsers that are compliant with the HTML v3.0 standard once it is finalized, so creating tables according to that standard, which we describe in this section, is best.

Tables are extremely simple to set up and customize. The opening tag for the table is, not surprisingly, <TABLE>. If you want to include a border, you can use the BORDER setting inside the <TABLE> tag. The ALIGN setting in the <TABLE> tag can use all of the same settings that are available in the <FIG> tag: left, right, center, justify, bleedleft and bleedright. The CLEAR setting can also be used with the <TABLE> tag and can take the same settings that we described in the previous discussion of the <P> tag: left, right and all.

Aside from these more basic settings, you can use other settings as a part of the <TABLE> tag, which will configure it before the actual layout of the information in the rows and cells is specified. The COLSPEC setting allows you to configure the width of each column and the alignment of the information in that column to the left, right or center. It isn't required that you use the COLSPEC setting to configure the widths of columns in a table. In a table in which the COLSPEC setting is not given, the column width is automatically sized according to the contents of the cells. If you wanted to create a three-column table in which one column had text aligned to the left and was 30 units wide, another column had text in the center and was 15 units wide and the third column had text aligned to the right and was 45 units wide, you would enter the following opening tag:

```
<TABLE COLSPEC="L30 C15 R45">
```

For each new column, enter an L, R or C setting for the alignment and a number indicating the width of the columns. The width is measured in en spaces, a unit equal to half the point size.

After creating a border and setting the widths and alignments of the columns, you will want to enter the <CAPTION> tag next, which will give the table a title. You can then mark each row in the table with the table row tag, <TR>. The table row can contain one of two types of cell tags, either <TH> or <TD>. The <TH> tag will produce a cell with a table header, in other words, to create a row that contains headers for the other cells in that column. The <TD> tag will indicate that the text is to be table data, in other words, information about the items named in the header row. The following example uses the <BORDER>, <CAPTION>, <TR>, <TH> and <TD> tags to create a simple table, which is shown in Figure 13-8.

```
<TABLE BORDER>
    <CAPTION>Produce in stock</CAPTION>
    <TR><TH>Apples<TH>Oranges<TH>Bananas
    <TR><TD>13<TD>15<TD>5
</TABLE>
```

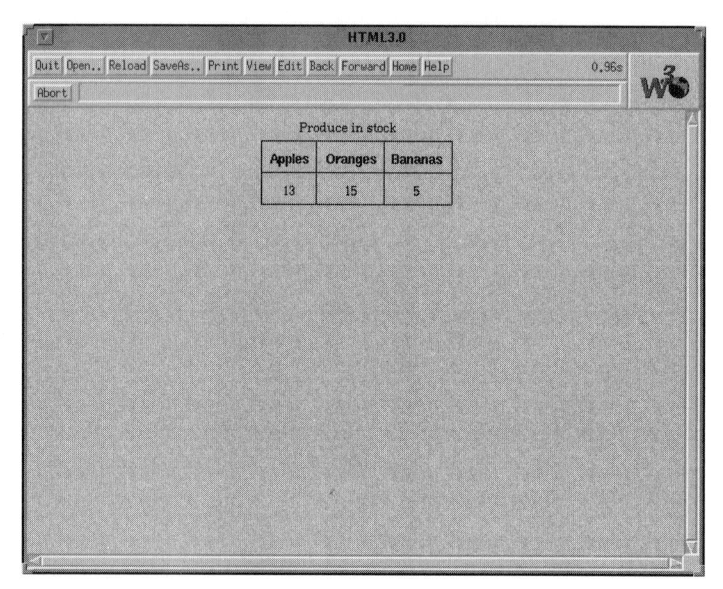

Figure 13-8: *A simple table.*

You can align the cells in a column with the COLSPEC setting, but we recommend you set the alignment separately for each cell with the ALIGN setting inside any of the <TD> or <TH> tags. If you want to set the alignment in an entire row, use the ALIGN option inside the <TR> tag.

One cell can extend over any number of rows or columns. The ROWSPAN and COLSPAN settings designate the number of rows or columns that a cell will occupy. For example, a table row with the following setting has two columns, one that is two column widths across and a second that is the normal size.

```
<TR><TD COLSPAN=2>400,000<TD>10
```

A table row with the following setting would have a table cell that is two rows tall, and another that is normal size.

```
<TR><TD ROWSPAN=2>Hi!<TD>there
```

Since tables are automatically sized according to the contents of the cells, it is not necessary to increase a cell's width for a large amount of information. The ROWSPAN and COLSPAN settings simply allow you to control a table's appearance.

You can include anything inside a cell, not just text. Images, lists, forms and any other objects that can be specified with HTML markup can be included by putting the appropriate markup tags after the <TH> or <TD> tag. For example, the following markup creates the table in Figure 13-9. The table includes two images, a list and headers that are hyperlinked to other Web pages.

```
<TABLE BORDER>
<TR><TH><A HREF="bob.html">Bob's Picture</A><TH><TH><A
HREF="http://www.shoop.com/services/">ShoopSoft Services</A>
<TR><TD><IMG ALT="Bob" SRC="bob.gif"><TD><IMG ALT="Shoop"
SRC="logo.gif">
<TD>ShoopSoft supports:
    <UL>
    <LI>Macintosh
    <LI>PC
    <LI>UNIX Workstations
    </UL>
</TABLE>
```

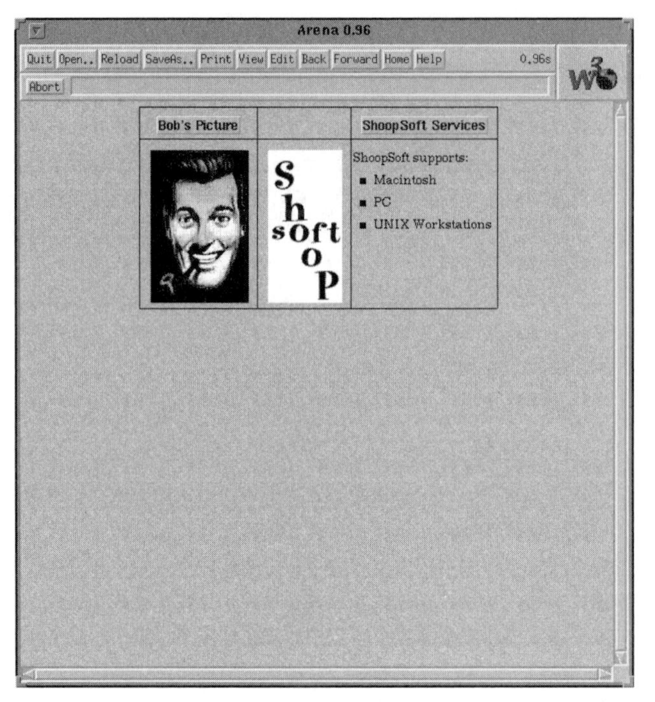

Figure 13-9: *A table with hyperlinks, images and a list.*

Note that the second use of the <TH> tag, between the headers "Bob's Picture" and "ShoopSoft Services," has no text or HTML markup after it. This markup produces the filled-in cell that appears in the top row of the table in Figure 13-9. You can use this feature with either the <TH> or the <TD> tag. Also, you can see in the example markup that all of the information for a cell does not have to appear on a single line, as in the case of the imbedded list, which contains several lines of entries.

Using these tags and options, you can produce lots of different types of tables. Inside the cells, you can include anything that a browser is capable of displaying. A number of tutorials on table design are on the Web. One of the best is the NCSA Mosaic Tables Tutorial, which includes some fancy examples of table design, at the URL http://www.ncsa.uiuc.edu/SDG/Software/Mosaic/Tables/tutorial.html.

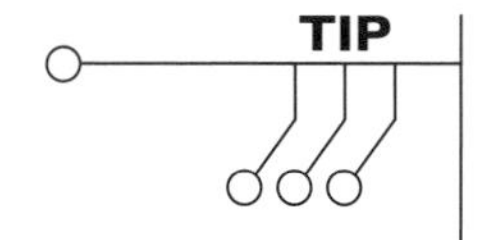

The two most popular Web browsers, NCSA Mosaic and Netscape, both currently support tables but implement them slightly differently. To see how tables are implemented in Netscape, look at the help page at the URL http://home.netscape.com/assist/net_sites/tables.html. To see how tables are implemented in Mosaic, see the "Tables Tutorial," at http://www.ncsa.uiuc.edu/SDG/Software/Mosaic/Tables/tutorial.html.

Forms

HTML v3.0 also features many improvements in forms. The major improvements are in the types of input allowed. The forms are still structured in the same way that we described in Chapter 10, "Simple Forms," and Chapter 11, "CGI: Advanced Forms for Programmers." However, a number of new tags and settings extend the functionality of forms.

The most significant extensions of forms are the new settings that the <INPUT> tag can take. As noted in Chapter 10, "Simple Forms," the <INPUT> tag can accept a number of TYPE elements: TYPE=text for text input, TYPE=radio for radial buttons, TYPE=checkbox for checkbox options, TYPE=hidden for hidden input and TYPE=submit and TYPE=reset to submit or clear the entries in a form, respectively. There are four new elements that have been added to these types.

TYPE=range will let you set a range of numbers, from which the user will be asked to select one. For example, the following <INPUT> tag asks the user to select a number between one and ten and passes that value to the variable name "luckynumber".

```
<P>Pick a number between one and ten: <INPUT NAME="luckynumber"
TYPE=range MIN=1 MAX=10></P>
```

TYPE=scribble is one of the more interesting additions. This input type will allow you to drag the mouse over an area to draw a picture and then submit that picture as the input for the form. The tag will set a background image and then record clicks and drags on that image. For example, to start with a background image called "mona_lisa.gif" and allow users to submit mustache styles, you could enter a tag such as the following:

```
<P>Draw your favorite facial hair on Mona! <INPUT NAME="dada"
TYPE=scribble VALUE="Text entry:" SRC="mona_lisa.gif"></P>
```

Obviously, the use of this tag will be restricted to browsers that can display graphics. On nongraphical browsers, the field will appear as a text entry field, and the VALUE setting will enter the default text for that field. The setting of VALUE will be ignored on browsers that can display graphics.

TYPE=file allows the user to submit a file from his or her local file system as form input. The file would be essentially uploaded and attached to the contents of the form submission. The file is matched to a MIME type according to its file extension. It is possible to screen the MIME types of file to be submitted. For example, the following <INPUT> tag would ask for file submissions and accept any type of audio file that is submitted:

```
<P>Add to our Verbal Guest Book—submit a recording of your voice
here!</P> <INPUT TYPE=file NAME="greetings" ACCEPT="audio/*">
```

TYPE=image performs the same function as the TYPE=submit setting, except that you specify an image, in place of the submit button, to be clicked on. When a user clicks on this image, the form will record the location where the user clicked and pass on that information with the contents of the form. This particular input type may be replaced in favor of a more efficient implementation of the same function.

One element in the implementation of HTML v3.0 forms, the SCRIPT setting, is still in the most preliminary stages but may in the end allow the highest degree of interactivity than any other option. The SCRIPT setting will contain a reference to a script that will be downloaded to the client's browser software and run locally. The HTML v3.0 Internet Draft suggests that uses for these scripts might include submitting a limited amount of user information in the form (like the user name and time of day), initializing and cleaning up fields in a form upon entry or exit, or monitoring mouse or keyboard input. Since the scripts will be written with a limited library set, functions that might pose a security threat, such as reading or writing files on a host machine or transmitting information over the network (rather than as a form submission), will be impossible to perform.

Math

Documents marked up with HTML v3.0 will be able to display mathematical characters and equations in great detail. HTML v3.0 includes an extensive set of math characters as entities, just like the icon entities described previously in the section "Graphics." While it is beyond the scope of this chapter to describe every mathematical tag that HTML v3.0 offers, a complete listing and explanation is available in the HTML v3.0 Internet Draft, at the URL http://www.hpl.hp.co.uk/people/dsr/html3/maths.html. In this section, we will briefly describe some of the math features in HTML v3.0.

The <MATH> tag allows you to enter a number of abbreviations for mathematical symbols and syntactical markers for formulas and, in combination with the math entities, creates a complete system for displaying functions. You begin a section of mathematical markup with the <MATH> tag. You then use combinations of the other tags to lay out your information in correct mathematical syntax. The HTML v3.0 Internet Draft currently lists the following tags for mathematical markup:

- <BOX> Used for hidden brackets, stretchy delimiters and placing one expression above another (as in numerators and denominators), the <BOX> tag can take a number of internal settings, which allow formatting of complex fractions, placing functions above or below one another and other layout specifications. The shortcut characters for the opening and closing <BOX> tags are { and }, respectively. An example demonstrating the use of the shortcut characters is provided at the end of this list.
- <SUB> and <SUP> The subscript and superscript tags are also used for limits. The shortcut character for the superscript tag is ^, and the shortcut character for the subscript is _.
- <ABOVE> and <BELOW> The <ABOVE> tag is used to draw an arrow, line or symbol above an expression, and the <BELOW> tag draws the same elements below the expression.
- <VEC>, <BAR>, <DOT>, <DDOT>, <HAT>, <TILDE> These tags are convenient for marking common accents as an alternative to using the <ABOVE> tag.

- <SQRT> and <ROOT> These tags are used for square roots and other roots of an expression.
- <ARRAY> You can use the <ARRAY> tag for matrices and other kinds of arrays.
- <TEXT> Used to include a short piece of text within a math element, the <TEXT> tag is often combined with the <SUB> or <SUP> tags.

The use of the shortcut characters for <SUP>, <SUB> and <BOX> makes simple equations reducible to a single line of HTML code. The following lines are separate functions and equations, which are shown in Figure 13-10.

```
<MATH>{1<OVER>1 + x}</MATH><P><HR>
<MATH>2^3^</MATH><P><HR>
<MATH>{x^2^<OVER>1 + {3<OVER>y - z}}</MATH><P><HR>
```

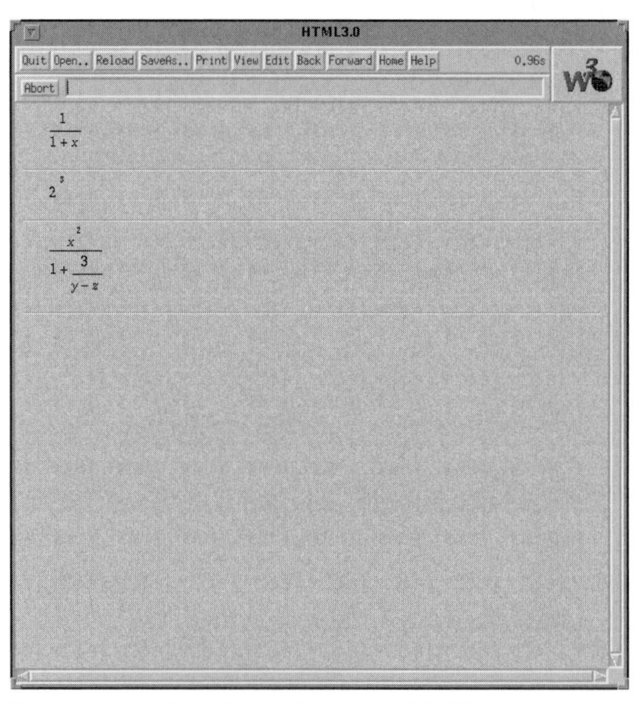

Figure 13-10: *Equations using the <MATH> tag and shortcut characters.*

Note that the character for superscript (like subscript, which is not shown in the example) has to be used twice, once as an opening tag and once as a closing tag. The first function is "one over one plus x," which must be enclosed in the <BOX> tags (or their shortcut equivalents) because it is rendered as a fraction. The second function is "two to the third power." The third equation is "x squared over one plus three over y minus z." In this function, the fraction "three over y minus z" must be put inside the <BOX> tags even though it is in the denominator of another fraction.

The level of complexity of the <MATH> tag increases with the complexity of the functions being expressed. Every level of expression is possible, from simple algebra and arithmetic, as shown in the example, to complex matrices and chemical notations. To explore the possibilities of mathematical symbols using the new functions in HTML v3.0, watch the specification for mathematical notation as it develops at the URL http://www.hpl.hp.co.uk/people/dsr/html3/maths.html.

Arena: A Sneak Preview

The HTML v3.0 standard will develop and be revised by users and providers, people who look at pages developed with the standard and people who create pages with it. One way to watch the development of the standard and to become a part of the process is to look at pages that use the language.

A browser called Arena, which is being developed by the World Wide Web Organization, is capable of viewing documents that have been marked up in the version 3.0 standard. Since Arena is changed when the HTML v3.0 Internet Draft is revised, its development will always correspond with the latest developments in HTML. Information about Arena is available at the URL http://www.w3.org/hypertext/WWW/Arena/.

HTTP-Next Generation

HTTP, as noted in Chapter 2, "The Basic Pieces," is an extremely fast and efficient protocol that, nonetheless, has some serious limitations. A limitation causing the most problems is the fact that HTTP can process only one request at a time, which causes long delays when a large number of users are accessing the same site. Other limitations of HTTP are in the area of security. Anonymous access of documents by clients poses a security threat because users are untraceable and no freely available servers support authentication and encryption, which are other security features. (A number of servers that support authentication and encryption are available commercially, as explained in the section "Security & Commerce" later in this chapter). Simon Spero, a software developer at Enterprise Integration Technologies (EIT) and author of MDMA, is developing a standard for a new version of HTTP, which would meet these needs. He states:

> Any new protocol needs to meet the needs of three different groups. Individual users want to be able to browse the Web without being forced to wait for pages to be delivered. Information providers need to be able to support large numbers of users, and to restrict access to authorized users, and to get money from their paying customers. Software developers need a system which is easy to implement, but which can be optimized and enhanced to differentiate between products. (From HTTP-NG Architectural Overview)

This new version of HTTP is called HTTP-Next Generation, or HTTP-NG. Although it is still under development, HTTP-NG is designed with a number of criteria in mind to meet the goals that Spero listed.

To allow for an improvement in speed, HTTP-NG supports "asynchronicity," which is the ability of a client or server to initiate a new request without waiting for previous requests to complete. Asynchronicity will eliminate the lag time created by servers having to start a number of processes one at a time. Essentially, the way that HTTP generates and completes requests is by opening a separate connection for each request: get this document, get that image, post this message, etc. Each time one of these requests is completed, a new request can be made, but not before. HTTP-NG opens only a single connection and divides that connection into a number of virtual connections that can handle separate requests. Within one real connection to a server, different virtual connections can be simultaneously making requests from the client to the server, passing meta-information (information contained in the <META> tag) from the server to the client and downloading text and multimedia files to the client.

Another feature of HTTP-NG that improves the speed of Web usage is the compression of the messages between the client and the server. HTTP uses text messages, or "methods," such as GET, HEAD or POST, to communicate between the client and the server, as described in Chapter 2, "The Basic Pieces." HTTP-NG sends messages that are compressed and encoded. While compressed and encoded messages are not easily interpreted by human readers, they are far more efficient for the client and server software to use.

HTTP-NG also contains a number of improvements upon HTTP that are little more than simplifications. For example, HTTP allows clients to send to the server a list of all possible types of objects (such as text files, images, sound files, etc.) that can be requested. However, because of the number of possible file types that this list contains, requests are prefaced with a large amount of type information—over 1k. Even though transactions between clients and the server could have been simplified by limiting the possible file types that could be sent, the complexity and length of the type information preface prevented most servers from ever implementing this feature.

HTTP-NG gets around this problem by allowing a client to send a short list of commonly used file types to the server, meaning that a client can specify the file types it can process in advance. This short list is encoded in a bitmap file, drastically reducing the file length. The vast majority of users will use only the most common file types (GIF, JPEG, MPEG, AU, etc.) and will not need to add special types. If a user does want to add new types, they can be encoded into the bitmap.

The types of information that can be transmitted over the Internet have expanded a great deal over the last year, and HTTP has, by and large, not been able to take advantage of these new media. For example, the only way to receive a live video feed using a Web client with HTTP is to launch a separate application from the client. That application, after being started, is independent of the Web client. HTTP-NG is able to refer a user to another service, such as a video or audio client, while still retaining control from the client software itself. In other words, the Web interface could not only tell an application when to start but also when to stop.

Finally, both HTTP-NG and Secure HTTP, another project of Enterprise Integration Technologies in cooperation with NCSA, attempt to address the issue of how to conduct safe transactions over a Web client. HTTP-NG uses a message wrapper with fields that tell a client how to encrypt or decrypt information so that the information cannot be intercepted and used by a third party. HTTP-NG also allows a server to launch external applications that allow commercial transactions to take place securely over the Internet, such as DigiCash, CyberCash and First Virtual (see the next section, "Security & Commerce"). HTTP-NG does not specify the type of security to be used but leaves that decision up to the provider. HTTP-NG simply allows the HTTP server to tell the client that the information is secure and how to access it. Secure HTTP, also discussed in the next section, is another approach to the issue of security and follows a model similar to HTTP-NG. As HTTP-NG and Secure HTTP are finalized, it is likely that they will be merged, with the best elements of each protocol being incorporated into a new and better version of HTTP.

Security & Commerce

Thus far, the focus of this book has been to show you how to provide information that can be freely accessed by anyone on the Internet. However, a number of businesses use the Web for commercial transactions as well, selling goods, such as software and information, that can be sent over the Internet and goods that are ordered over the Internet and physically shipped to the consumer.

There are, however, security issues involved with transactions over the Web. Using forms, as described in Chapter 10, "Simple Forms," and Chapter 11, "CGI: Complex Forms for Programmers," a user can select his or her order, enter a credit card number and a shipping address and send that information to a vendor. However, submitting that information using HTTP is relatively insecure. A third party could intercept the information and use it. In addition, there is no way to verify the card owner using forms as they are currently implemented—anyone could be ordering goods with someone else's credit card number.

Two new protocols are being developed to get around these problems: Secure HTTP and Secure Socket Layer (SSL), developed by Netscape. Since Netscape will probably phase out SSL in favor of Secure HTTP in the near future, this chapter focuses primarily on the features and current implementations of Secure HTTP. In addition to these protocols, which would be a part of the client and server software, alternative methods of transmitting secure information are being developed by other companies. These strategies for commercial transactions will make commerce on the Web far safer than sending your credit card number in the mail or giving it to an operator over the phone.

Security Protocols

Both Secure HTTP and SSL use encryption to protect secure information. Encryption is, simply put, the process of encoding information so that only parties who understand the code can read that information. The type of encryption in Secure HTTP and SSL uses keys. Each party has two keys, a public key and a private key. If you want to send information to someone, you obtain his or her public key. Some people make their public keys available when you finger their accounts and others have it listed in directories. You can use this public key to encrypt information. Once the information is encrypted with the recipient's public key, only his or her private key can decrypt it.

With the Secure HTTP and SSL protocols, a client obtains a public key (or a session key) from the server and uses it to encrypt a message, and the server uses its private key to decrypt that message, and vice versa. Secure HTTP and SSL are different in one basic way: Secure HTTP is an application protocol, meaning it can be used only for HTTP transactions, whereas SSL is a protocol that can be implemented with any application protocol: HTTP, FTP, Gopher, telnet and others.

Secure HTTP

Secure HTTP is a variation of HTTP, the standard protocol used on the World Wide Web. It is implemented in the same way that HTTP is implemented on current browsers and servers, but Secure HTTP provides the ability for both servers and clients to send encrypted information. Secure HTTP is capable of communicating with both secure and insecure servers and clients (the security functions are disabled when Secure HTTP communicates with the latter).

One of the more important features of Secure HTTP is that it does not require the client to use a public key. Secure HTTP supports three types of protection: encryption, which is discussed in detail in this section; authentication, which verifies that a message has not been changed since it was sent and that the name of the sender is accurate; and signature, which is the inclusion of a unique digital signature identifying the sender of the message.

The signature on a document is a certificate that verifies the identity of a particular individual or organization. The certificate is unique and is distributed by data security organizations, such as RSA Data Security, Inc. RSA Data Security is one of the pioneers of electronic cryptography and, as we describe in this section, has an arrangement with Netscape Communications to provide certificates for Netscape's Secure HTTP server software. The certificate is attached to a document, and this signature verifies the source of a document.

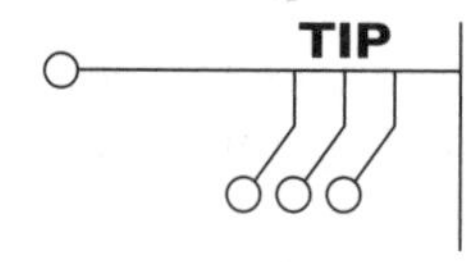

To find out more about digital signatures and certificates, look at RSA Data Security's home page at http://www.rsa.com/.

The process of authentication uses a message transmitted between a server and a client called a Message Authentication Code, or MAC. The MAC is not encrypted using the public and private keys as described previously, but instead is encrypted with what is called a "shared secret" that, for example, can be in the form of a password. The server creates a MAC by encrypting both the message itself and the timestamp of when that message was transmitted. The shared secret is used to encrypt the MAC so that only a provider who knows the shared secret can create that particular MAC. A user or client who wants to verify the integrity of a document can use that same shared secret (which has to be communicated to the user via some secure means) and check it against the MAC. Essentially, this process eliminates the need to have a third party verify that a message is authentic. A user says, "I don't believe you sent this," and the sender replies, "Check the MAC with this password: shoop!3." When the password and the MAC match up, the document is considered valid.

The most vital element of protecting a document, however, is encryption. Encrypting information allows it to be sent securely without any danger of its being intercepted by a third party. Information can be encrypted in one of two ways, either by assigning a key when a session is started and transmitting that key between the server and the client, or by using a prearranged key that is selected using information in a document header.

With the first method, the server either uses a client's public key or, if that client does not have a public key, generates a temporary key for that session. This session key is generated in the following way: a text string is generated by the client software, and the client sends the text string, encrypted with the server's public key, to the server, saying, "This is my session key." The server then encrypts secure information using that session key and sends it to the client, and the client uses the same session key to decrypt the message.

In the second method, the server sends a code naming a particular key and tells the client, "Select this key out of the keys you already understand, and use it to decrypt the following information." This method is useful for repeated transactions between a particular client and server.

Both methods should be transparent both for the user and for the server administrator. The software will choose the most appropriate method.

How It Works

Secure HTTP, like regular HTTP, communicates by sending text messages between clients and servers. In regular HTTP, these text messages include header information, the HTML documents themselves and information about files, such as their MIME types. In Secure HTTP, these text messages establish a secure session between a client and a server before the server sends the document itself.

A client starts a secure session by sending a request for a secure document, and the server replies that the document being sent is a secure document. This reply is followed by header information about the document being sent. Two header lines are mandatory: the first names the type of encryption being used, and the second contains MIME type information for the document. The Secure HTTP Internet Draft recommends the MIME type application/http for secure documents. Other optional header lines can contain information about prearranged keys, MACs and specific settings for different encryption types.

This information, and another set of transactions between the server and the client called the "negotiations," allow encrypted information to be successfully received and decrypted. The negotiation headers describe the capabilities of the client to the server, telling the server what encryption formats can and cannot be understood, for example. After all of this information is transferred, the content is sent, encrypted in whatever format is named in the first mandatory header line. The content is optionally followed by a digital signature to verify the source of a document.

Using these methods, Secure HTTP allows clients and servers to perform a range of functions not possible with regular HTTP, including verifying a document's validity and ensuring the secure transmission of information. This standard will probably be adopted by most servers and browsers in the near future. One other protocol, SSL, which we previously explained was developed by Netscape Communications for its client and server software, presents an alternative model to Secure HTTP. However, it is very likely that Netscape products will move toward support of Secure HTTP and phase out SSL, helping establish an Internetwide security standard.

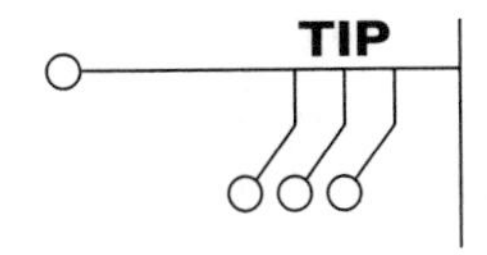

For a description of Secure HTTP, look at EIT's information pages at the URL http://www.eit.com/projects/s-http/index.html. To see how it is being implemented, check out the Secure NCSA HTTPD home page at http://www.commerce.net/software/Shttpd/.

A number of companies are beginning to market server software and services using Secure HTTP. These companies include Spry, Inc. (http://www.spry.com/secure/feat.html), Open Market, Inc. (http://www.openmarket.com/webserve.html#secureweb), and a consulting and development company, Terisa Systems (http://www.terisa.com/).

SSL

SSL was developed by Netscape Communications and integrated into the Netscape Web browser and the Commerce Server, which is Netscape's commercially available server software. To use SSL, a server first has to have a certificate, that is, a verification of the identity of the individual or organization that is accepting secure transactions. Certificates for Netscape Commerce Servers are handled by RSA Data Security in a joint arrangement with Netscape.

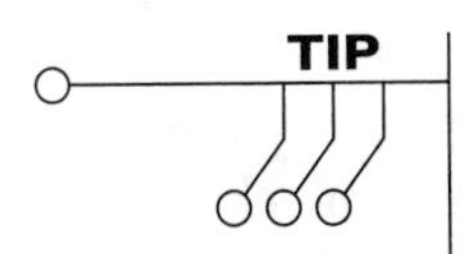

For information about acquiring an RSA certificate for use with the Netscape Commerce Server, see RSA's Web pages at the URL http://www.rsa.com/netscape/.

During the process of acquiring a certificate, the server software generates a public and private key code. The server's public key will be used to generate a session key in the same way that Secure HTTP does. The client generates a session key and uses the server's public key to encrypt and send that session key to the server. The user does not have to have his or her own public key, because SSL generates a temporary session key on the fly.

SSL and Secure HTTP have similar uses, even though the syntax of the messages sent between the server and client is different. SSL has the same security capabilities as Secure HTTP—authentication, encryption and signature. (Theoretically, these features can be used in any TCP/IP protocol, not just HTTP.) The only implementation of SSL that currently exists is in the Netscape Commerce Server, but Netscape has provided SSL reference tools for developers wanting to implement SSL elsewhere. These reference tools are available at the URL http://home.netscape.com/info/sslref.html.

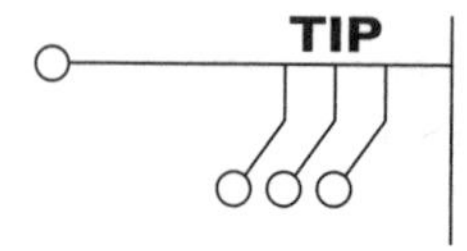

Full details about the SSL protocol are available from Netscape at the URL http://www.netscape.com/info/security-doc.html.

Other Approaches to Security on the Web

CyberCash

CyberCash (http://www.cybercash.com/) is a method that complements having a secure HTTP daemon running at a merchant's site and a secure browser submitting information to that site. CyberCash uses encryption to protect private messages and then sends those messages on top of another protocol, like Secure HTTP or SSL. A user establishes a "CyberCash persona," which sends information about the user to CyberCash after downloading the client application via anonymous FTP. The CyberCash client application is a standalone interface on a user's machine that is launched whenever a purchase needs to be made using CyberCash. When a purchase is requested, the user is sent an online invoice form with the total charge for that purchase. The user then enters her or his credit card number and credit card information and submits it to the CyberCash server. All of this information is encrypted using public and private key encryption technology. When the CyberCash server receives this request, the credit card is authorized by a bank or credit processing center, and the merchant's account is credited.

CyberCash can also be used between individuals, not just between a merchant and a consumer. CyberCash maintains accounts for every user who registers his or her client software. Any two CyberCash users can send money between CyberCash accounts. The electronic cash can be exchanged for real cash through a demand deposit in a bank, and the funds in CyberCash accounts are certified by participating banks (currently only Wells Fargo Bank).

Figure 13-11: *The CyberCash home page.*

DigiCash
http://www.digicash.com/

Figure 13-12: *The DigiCash home page.*

DigiCash uses another model for electronic financial transactions, "ecash," or electronic cash. The idea behind ecash is that ecash users have an account at an ecash bank, from which they can withdraw ecash, in the form of electronic coins. Each coin carries a bank signature to authenticate it. The ecash is certified by a bank, and the bank can exchange real money for whatever amount of ecash is spent. Like CyberCash, DigiCash uses its own client and server software, which can be used in conjunction with any Web browser.

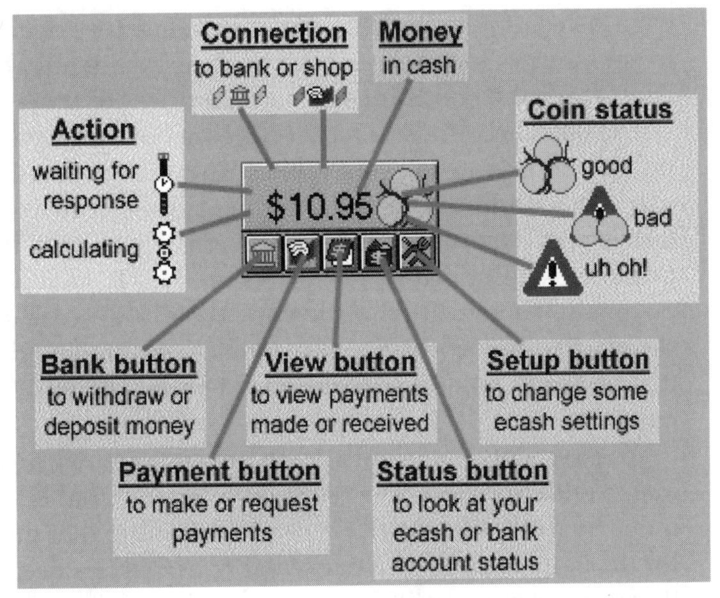

Figure 13-13: *The DigiCash client, with explanations.*

The client software can be used to withdraw a certain amount of cash from the bank account, in other words, taking ecash from a server and storing on the local disk of the user. Then, the client software can send the ecash from the local disk to a vendor to pay for a product or service. The user makes a connection to a vendor's "shop" using a regular Web client. When the user selects a link that requires payment, a CGI script launches the DigiCash shop software, which then makes a request to the user's DigiCash client for payment.

The DigiCash shop software is simply the text-based version of the DigiCash software, which can be used as either a server or a client, in other words, for a vendor or for a customer. The graphical interface, shown in Figure 13-13, is a client-only program. Currently, UNIX servers are the only servers that can use DigiCash shop software, but software is being developed for Macintosh and Windows HTTP daemons. For HTTP servers than cannot run the DigiCash software, DigiCash runs a remote shop server which will automatically handle transactions. The remote shop server uses a special directory set up on the Web server.

DigiCash's remote server accesses this directory over the Internet to get information about a store, such as the identity of the shop and owner, the goods for sale and the prices of those goods.

The bank account and local ecash are both protected using public and private key encryption. This means that no one but the user can withdraw money from their bank account or from their local ecash. Also, every payment in ecash is unique, using authentication (as described above in "Secure HTTP") to identify the payment. If a user attempts to copy their local ecash supply into a second file, and spend that ecash twice, the bank will recognize that the ecash coins have been used before, and will not clear the payment.

All payments made with ecash are anonymous, just like payments with real cash. The ecash is "blinded," that is, made anonymous by the bank, when it is issued, meaning that there is no way for the bank to connect a particular coin that has been issued to that same coin when it is spent. The value of the coin is verified by the bank without any reference back to the user. In essence, the bank says, "Yes, this is real money," without asking, "Who are you and where did you get this money?"

A user includes an e-mail address when setting up a DigiCash account, allowing the bank to communicate with the user. The contact address is for adminstrative purposes only, not for purposes of identification. For example, if a bank needed to tell a user to look at a set of transactions, or to tell them that their key needed to be changed, this e-mail address would be used to get in touch with the user.

DigiCash is working on other ways of using ecash, aside from transactions over the Internet. For example, a card with a computer chip on it, or "smartcard" can read an amount of ecash from a user's disk, and then that card can be used to make payments like a credit card. While the cards with computer chips were developed by DigiCash several years ago, DigiCash's cooperation with major credit card companies is leading to a wider acceptance of the ecash system. This type of innovation could fully integrate electronic financial transactions and real-world purchases, in effect, making every personal computer a automatic teller machine combined with a shopping mall.

First Virtual

The First Virtual (http://www.fv.com/) solution to secure financial transactions on the Web uses no encryption whatsoever. Users establish an account with First Virtual by sending it electronic mail with information about themselves. After this information is submitted, the user calls a toll-free number and enters his or her credit card number using a touch-tone phone. After these two steps, the user is sent an account number and complete details about using the new account. Whenever a purchase is made using First Virtual, the user transmits only the account number, and First Virtual automatically charges his or her credit card for that amount.

The process is not much more complicated for vendors. First, the vendor submits the initial application just like a regular user. Then, the vendor sends information about its checking account to First Virtual, and from that point on, any purchases made using First Virtual will be deposited directly to that e-mail account.

To prevent people from intercepting and using a First Virtual account number to make unauthorized purchases, every First Virtual purchase is confirmed by e-mail. A user makes a purchase, submitting only his or her account number. FirstVirtual uses that account number to retrieve the user's e-mail address and automatically send a letter requesting confirmation. Charges are made only after a reply is received from that user's e-mail address.

There is one major restriction on using First Virtual to authorize purchases, however: the only thing that can be paid for with a First Virtual account is information, in the broadest sense of the word. Nothing that First Virtual merchants sell is ever physically shipped to the consumer—it is sent over the Internet. This means that First Virtual can be used to buy anything from electronic artwork to software to literary works, so long as that information can be transmitted to an electronic mail account. Also, First Virtual can be used to make donations and pay fees. This specialization reduces the possibility of fraud, because any information purchased will be sent to the account holder's electronic mail address, and not to a third-party imposter, even if the account number was used without authorization.

First Virtual hosts all of its merchants in its "InfoHaus," at the URL http://www.infohaus.com/. However, First Virtual purchasing capability can also be built into Web pages on a merchant's server. Essentially, Web pages have to be configured to mail a MIME-typed message that is recognized by First Virtual's InfoHaus software, which initiates the automated electronic mail confirmation process. Full technical information about First Virtual, including documentation on the implementation of First Virtual purchasing on your own pages, is available at the URL http://www.fv.com/tech/.

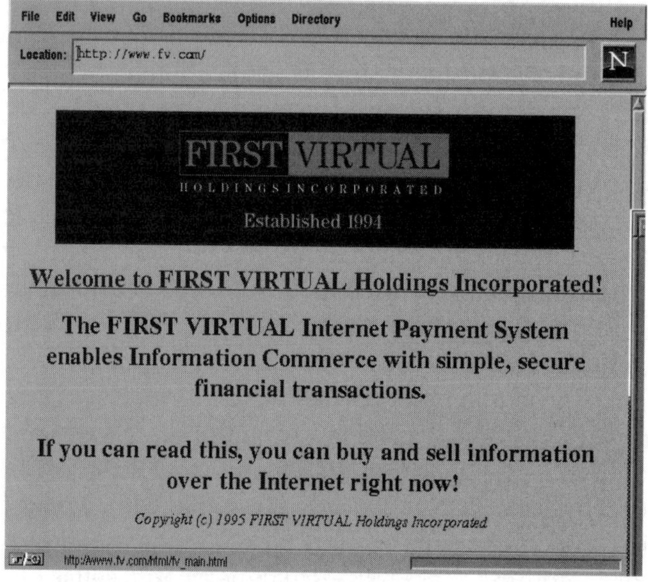

Figure 13-14: *The First Virtual home page.*

CommerceNet http://www.commerce.net/

CommerceNet was founded in 1993 with a federal grant designed to promote the commercial use of defense-related technology. It is, primarily, a consortium of corporations, organizations and individuals committed to developing commerce on the Internet.

CommerceNet has organized a number of task areas and working groups to develop different resources and technologies involved in Internet commerce. These areas include topics from Internet connectivity and engineering groups to marketing and payment services, and participants are drawn from CommerceNet member organizations. The consortium of organizations has also provided funding for the development of new technologies for commercial usage. One of the technologies developed with CommerceNet funding is Secure HTTP, which is discussed in the previous section "Security Protocols."

CommerceNet's WWW site has a broad collection of information about commerce gathered from across the Web, as well as a number of original documents. Some of this information, however, is restricted to subscribers. Subscribers can participate in CommerceNet under a number of different subscription plans that allow access to different types of information and subscription benefits. For full information about subscribing to CommerceNet, send e-mail to subscriber-info@commerce.net or look at the CommerceNet subscriber information page at the URL http://www.commerce.net/information/sb/overview.html.

TIP

For discussions about buying and selling on the Web, check out the archives of the www-buyinfo mailing list at the URL http://www.research.att.com/www-buyinfo/archive/, or subscribe to the list by sending the message "subscribe www-buyinfo" to the e-mail address www-buyinfo-request@allegra.att.com.

Virtual Reality Modeling Language

There has been quite a bit of speculation and, dare we say, hype about the emergence of "virtual reality" as a widely used communication medium. The image of complete immersion in a three-dimensional, computer-generated virtual world is indeed a strong one, and many media outlets and entrepreneurs have romanticized about and capitalized on this vision. The increasing popularity of the Internet has only furthered the romanticization of this ideal, as can be seen lately by (often outlandish) portrayals of VR technology in popular media.

The obvious problem with implementing virtual reality communication systems is the amount of computing power and bandwidth they would require. Thankfully, computers with enough processing power to display complex graphical environments are dropping in price and becoming more commonplace. However, the networks that connect these machines are becoming increasingly strained by the growing demand for bandwidth as multimedia applications become more popular. Even though these networks are limited by the amount of information they can transfer, the demand for distributed 3D environments and "sensualized" interfaces of virtual reality is stronger than ever.

Not satisfied with waiting for high-bandwidth fiber-optic networks, some software developers have proposed techniques for distributing 3D graphical worlds over the existing Internet infrastructure. In the spring of 1994, Tim Berners-Lee (see Chapter 1, "What is the Web?") and Dave Raggett organized special sessions at the First International Conference on the World Wide Web (see http://www.w3.org/) to encourage discussion about virtual reality interfaces to the Web. At the conference, Mark Pesce and Tony Parisi first proposed a networked 3D Web interface based on previous virtual reality and networking research. Since many of the conference participants were already working on 3D visualization tools, they agreed upon a need for a common protocol with which different visualization applications could communicate over the Internet. The participants realized that the maturation of the virtual reality industry would bring with it the need for some method of utilizing existing technologies and protocols for shared virtual environments.

An electronic mailing list was set up soon after the conference to facilitate discussion among the numerous researchers who expressed an interest in the proposed interface. After much debate, it was decided that the Virtual Reality Modeling Language (VRML) would be based on Silicon Graphic's Open Inventor ASCII file format. Open Inventor and its predecessor, IRIS Inventor, are 3D modeling toolkits that have been used for a number of commercial 3D graphics applications.

The current VRML implementation is designed to function as a platform-independent language for three-dimensional graphic scene design. It describes 3D objects much like the PostScript language describes images and text. Objects' descriptions, not their entire graphic representations, are communicated between machines. This technique greatly reduces the amount of bandwidth necessary for distributing virtual worlds. It also enables objects to be infinitely scalable, meaning that as you navigate within a 3D environment and move closer to objects, greater levels of detail emerge. Once an object's parameters (description and coordinates) have been defined, it can be viewed from every imaginable range and orientation.

To handle 3D objects, VRML defines a set of objects called nodes. Objects can theoretically contain any file format type, but nodes are designed specifically for 3D graphics. Each node is defined with certain characteristics, including

1. type: This could be a cube, sphere, cone, light source, texture map, transformation, etc.
2. fields: These are characteristics that differentiate the node from other nodes of the same type, such as the radius of a sphere, the intensity of a light source or the image used for a texture map.
3. name: Although not necessary, naming nodes can assist in the manipulation of the scene. Named nodes are commonly used within worlds that are hyperlinked to other worlds.
4. node hierarchy: This allows parent nodes to contain children nodes, the combination of which are referred to as group nodes.

For example, a blue sphere would be described by VRML as

```
Separator { # The blue sphere
 Material {
  diffuseColor 0 0 1 # Blue
 }
 Translation { translation 3 0 1 }
Sphere { radius 3.3 }
```

The "material" node specifies the surface material property of all subsequent shapes; in this case, it specifies with "diffuseColor" that the sphere be rendered the color blue. The "translation" node defines a translation by a 3D vector, which, in this case, is the three floating point values of 3, 0 and 1. Finally, the "sphere" node specifies the shape of the object and the radius of the sphere.

The example in itself is not a complete VRML world. All VRML files must begin with the following so that VRML viewers can properly identify the file type:

```
#VRML V1.0 ascii
```

The pound sign (#) preceding the text indicates that it is comment, not to be graphically interpreted by the VRML viewer.

To enhance the functionality of the language, it was decided early on that VRML should incorporate certain aspects of the Internet that have made it so popular. Since so many information resources are currently available within hypermedia documents on the Web, VRML developers have incorporated the ability to hyperlink objects within VRML worlds to information sources outside of the model. This will greatly enhance the usefulness of VRML as a tool not only for information display, but also for information retrieval.

The previous VRML code didn't contain hyperlinks. Hyperlinks are added with the WWWAnchor node as follows:

```
WWWAnchor { # Hyperlinked WWW page about Connie:
 name "http://www.connie.com/connie.html"

 Separator { # The blue sphere
  Material {
   diffuseColor 0 0 1 # Blue
  }
```

```
 Translation { translation 3 0 1 }
Sphere { radius 3.3 }
 }
}
```

WWWAnchor specifies that whenever one of its children, or nodes that are contained within itself, is chosen, a new scene is loaded into the VRML browser. The way objects are chosen is up to the browser, but it's usually accomplished by clicking on an object with a mouse. In the previous scene, the page http://www.connie.com/connie.html would be loaded whenever the blue sphere is selected.

If this explanation is intimidating to you, don't worry. Remember, VRML is not a program for designing 3D worlds. It is a protocol for describing them. Much like the WYSIWYG editors that have become available for HTML, graphical editing tools for working with VRML are sure to be introduced, as will translators for converting commonly used 3D file formats to VRML.

Since VRML is designed to be used in conjunction with existing Web protocols, the file extension for VRML files is .wrl (world), and the MIME type is world/x-vrml | vrml.

```
world/vrml  vrml
```

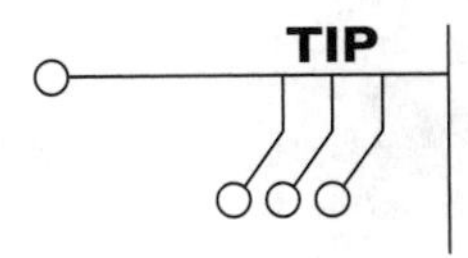

This has been only a brief introduction to VRML and should by no means be considered complete. For more complete details, see the VRML version 1.0 Specification at http://www.eit.com/vrml/vrmlspec.html.

To learn more about the theories behind the development of VRML, see the EIT VRML overview at http://www.eit.com/vrml/.

The main VRML forum is at http://vrml.wired.com.

The VRML mailing list Hypermail archive is at http://vrml.wired.com/arch/.

Curious about actual uses of VRML? Check out WAXweb at http://bug.village.virginia.edu/. It's a hypermedia version of David Blair's feature film "WAX or the Discovery of Television Among the Bees," which incorporates multimedia clips, MOOs and VRML worlds.

The decision of the VRML developers to base the modeling language on Open Inventor has prompted Silicon Graphics to strongly support the VRML standard. The company has officially announced the planned release of WebSpace, the first commercially available VRML viewer (see Figure 13-15). In its announcement, Silicon Graphics stressed the broad support VRML is receiving from numerous members of the business and research communities, including CERN, Brown University, NEC Technologies and Netscape Communications. By the time you read this book, beta versions of the WebSpace VRML viewer should be available for most platforms.

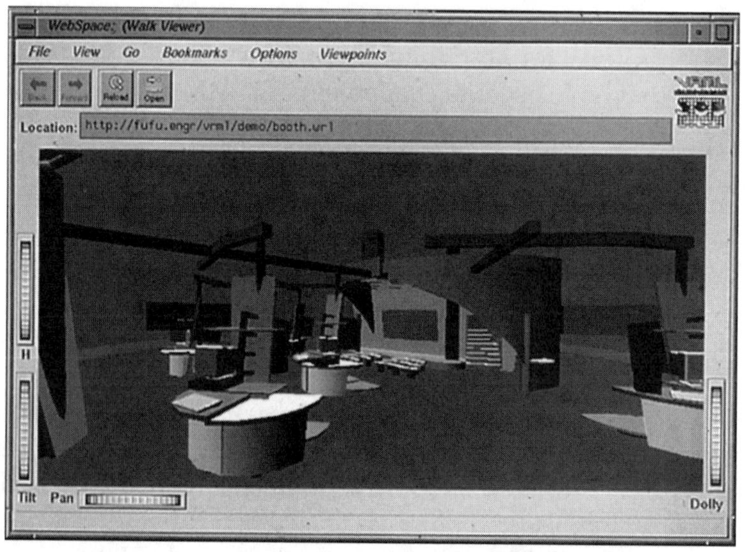

Figure 13-15: *The Silicon Graphics WebSpace VRML viewer.*

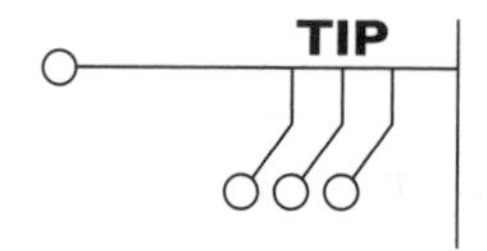

For more information on Silicon Graphics's WebSpace, see http://www.sgi.com/Products/WebFORCE/WebSpace/.

You can obtain more information on the Silicon Graphics Open Inventor toolkit at http://www.sgi.com/Technology/Inventor/.

The VRML specification is still very much in its infancy, and it is by no means the only possible path to the development of large-scale distributed virtual worlds. Numerous other developers have proposed methods of 3D object distribution, many of which were early contenders for the VRML standard.

The Web Object Oriented Graphics Language, or WebOOGL, developed over the past few years at the University of Minnesota Geometry Center, was one such contender. WebOOGL and VRML are very similar and perform many of the same functions. However, the Geometry Center released Geomview (shown in Figure 13-16), the WebOOGL viewer, long before VRML viewers were publicly available. For this reason, many people have gotten their first glimpses of distributed 3D graphical worlds courtesy of WebOOGL. Binaries of Geomview are available for numerous platforms, and the WebOOGL developers have announced filters to translate between WebOOGL and VRML files.

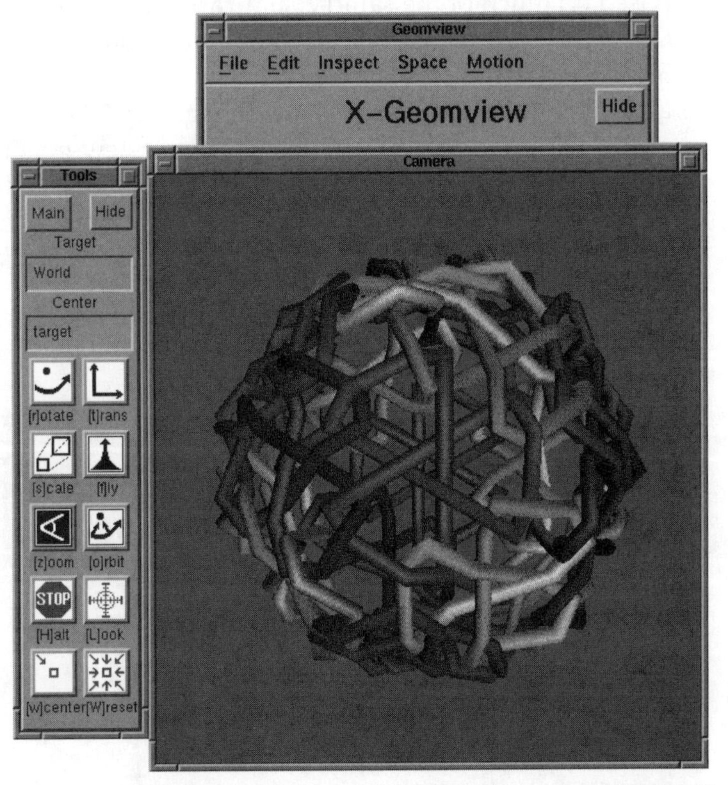

Figure 13-16: *The UMN Geometry Center's Geomview WebOOGL viewer.*

Like VRML, WebOOGL is designed to be compatible with existing Web technologies. WebOOGL worlds have the extension .oogl, and their MIME type is world/oogl.

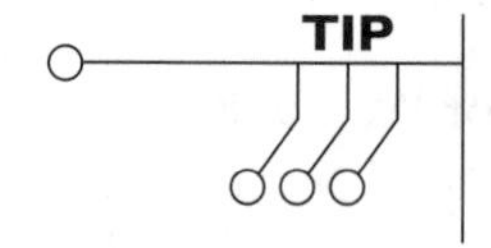

For more information on WebOOGL, see http://www.geom.umn.edu/software/weboogl/welcome.html.

W3Kit, an object-oriented toolkit for building interactive WWW applications can be obtained at http://www.geom.umn.edu/docs/W3Kit/W3Kit.html.

For a listing of the numerous proposed VRML file formats, see http://www.cica.indiana.edu/graphics/3D.objects.html.

If you're interested in adding easily manipulated 3D objects to your site without waiting on the wide acceptance and use of VRML, you should definitely check out the Geometry Center's Cyberview 3D Documents Generator (shown in Figure 13-17). Based on much of the same visualization research as WebOOGL, Cyberview is a Web server add-on that automatically generates 3D images based on variables that can be changed by the user. It also automatically generates new images of 3D objects when a user clicks on different sections of a Cyberview-generated imagemap (see Chapter 7, "Images on the Web"). Cyberview binaries are currently available only for Irix, Solaris and SunOS, but the author provides source code to qualified individuals.

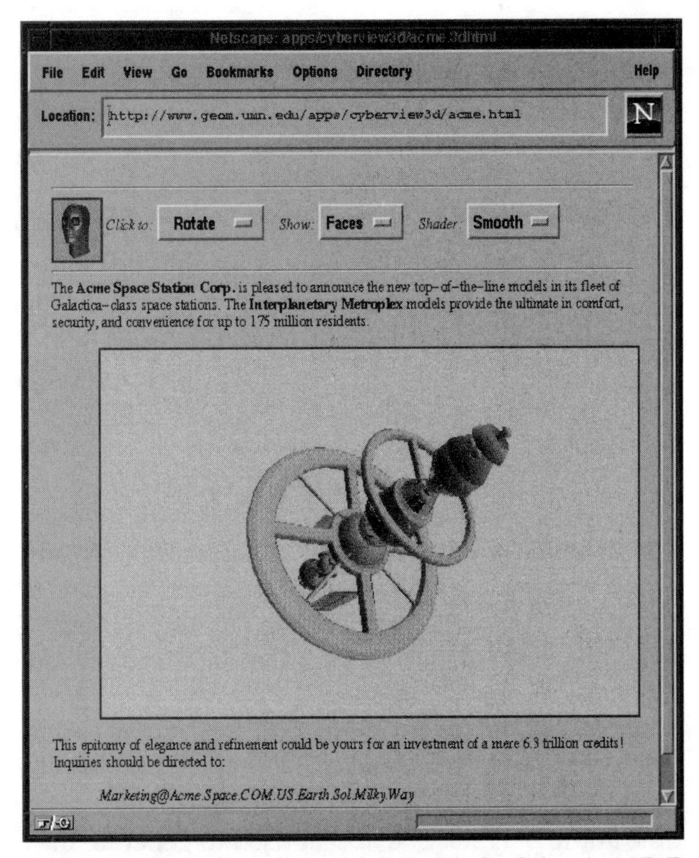

Figure 13-17: *A 3D model generated with the Cyberview 3D Documents Generator.*

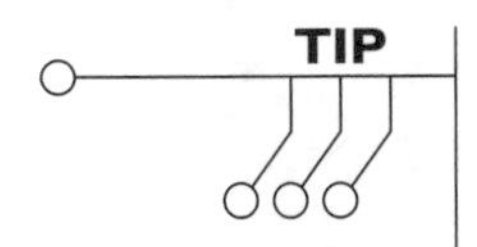

Cyberview 3D Document Generator information is at http://www.geom.umn.edu/apps/cyberview3d/about.html.

HotJava

Sun Microsystems has taken a different approach to distributing 3D objects with its HotJava Web browser. The approach enables Web developers to transfer independent applications called "applets" to work with Web browsers whenever HTTP requests are sent. Whereas most browsers must be configured with external applications to deal with unknown file formats, HotJava can internally display the file type after it has downloaded the appropriate applet. Since the downloading process occurs at the same time a request is sent for the unknown file type, the user does not have to worry about preconfiguring his or her browser to deal with it. For instance, if you develop a new compressed audio file format called MePEG, it is not necessary for you to distribute MePEG players across the Net and get people to add MePEG player entries to their browsers' mailcap files. Under the HotJava paradigm, you would simply need to write a MePEG applet that would be downloaded by users automatically when they request MePEG-compressed files.

The possible uses for imbedded applets are endless. Within a few weeks of HotJava's release, numerous applets have appeared on the Web, ranging from an interactive hangman game to real-time audio players. The applet used to generate the object shown in Figure 13-18 allows users to manipulate wire-frame objects in real-time on their screens. The objects are rotated by clicking the mouse and dragging the pointer around the screen.

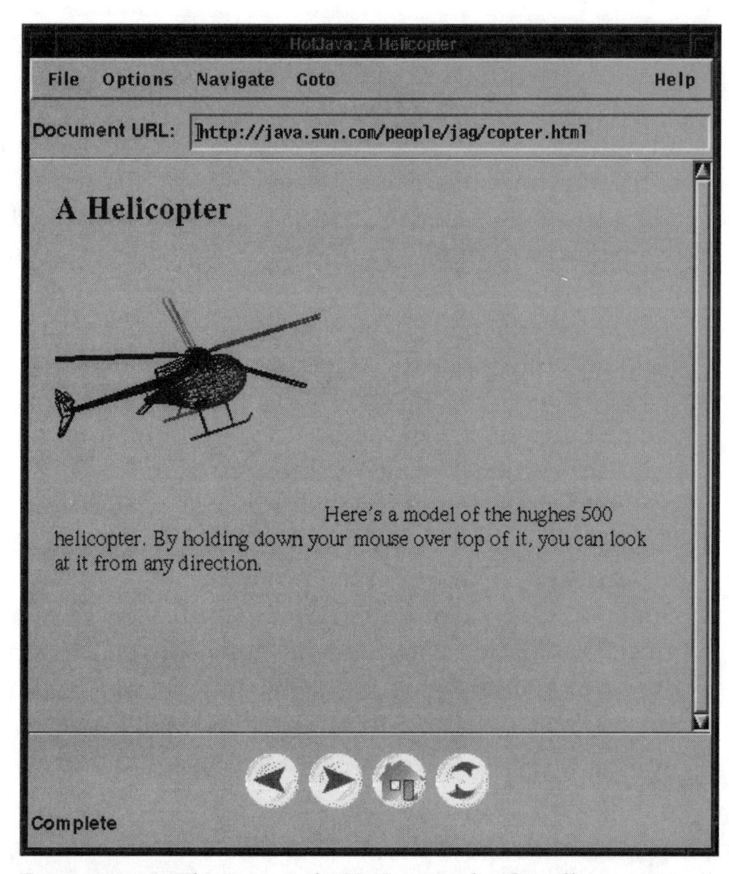

Figure 13-18: *The output of a HotJava applet that allows users to manipulate 3D wire-frame objects.*

The way that HotJava handles these small applications is simple. Applets are placed on the host computer within the HTML tree, usually in the path-to-html-root/classes directory. The applets are then called by individual pages when they are needed. In the example of the 3D helicopter viewer, the applet is called with the following markup:

```
<APP CLASS="ThreeD"
  SRC="doc:/classes/"
  model=hughes_500.obj
  scale=1.7
  width=200
  height=200>
```

This APP HTML tag specifies that the applet "ThreeD" be called every time the page is loaded. "SRC" specifies the location of the classes directory in which the compiled applet resides. Since all compiled Java applets end with the .class extension, the name of the application is ThreeD.class. "Model" tells the applet which 3D file is to be displayed. "Scale" defines how large the image is to be displayed, while "width" and "height" give the browser an indication of how much space the model will occupy on the completed Web page. This is necessary for HotJava to lay out the page properly while the applet is downloading.

Even though many of the applets are quite simple, they have astonishing effects. The ability to view animations and listen to real-time audio *within* a Web browser is quite exhilarating. If you're interested in writing your own Java applets, everything you need to know is on the Web. All applets are currently written in Java, Sun's object-oriented programming language, which is similar to C++. Java source code, identified by the .java extension, must be compiled with the freely available Java compiler. As of the writing of this book, the Java compiler and HotJava browser are available only for Sun workstations, but Sun has promised future releases that will run on most major platforms.

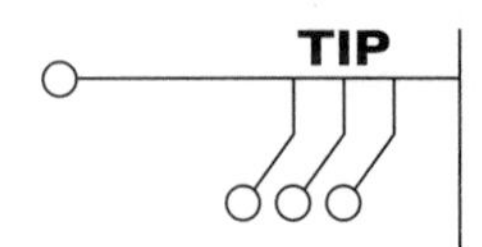

For more information on the HotJava browser and applets, see http://java.sun.com.

Teleconferencing Technologies & Advanced Multimedia

As discussed earlier in Chapter 8, "True Multimedia," audio and video file distribution has become increasingly common over the Net. Most multimedia file transfers require initiating a download, waiting for the full file to arrive and playing it back when the download is complete. However, software and hardware developments have made possible real-time audio/video transmissions over the Net. These transfers are not affected by download delays because packets that are sent out by a server are displayed by the client as they are received. The resultant communication flow is often referred to as a real-time data *stream*.

MBONE

As the Internet has matured, new and innovative ways of transmitting real-time multimedia information have been introduced. The majority of these new technologies have evolved out of efforts by the Internet Engineering Task Force to hold IETF conferences over the Internet. Since IETF members are spread out all over the world, they have developed a "virtual network" that uses the same physical wiring and hardware as the rest of the Internet to connect conference participants. This network has come to be known as the "Multicast Backbone," or MBONE, and it's truly a shining example of Internet ingenuity.

The MBONE relies on multicasting for transmitting information. Multicasting is a method of delivering real-time data streams to multiple network hosts simultaneously. Multicasts are to computer networks as CB transmissions are to radio, so think of the MBONE as kind of a digital CB network that allows numerous people to talk to and see one another simultaneously. Unlike CB radio users, however, multicast participants are not limited by the strength of their transmitters—they can be seen and heard wherever the MBONE reaches.

Even though the principles of multicasting existed long before the MBONE, engineers have had to optimize multicasting technologies to work with existing Internet technologies. Since all Internet traffic is delivered in the form of Internet Protocol (IP) packets, MBONE communications have been custom-tailored to work efficiently over IP-based networks. In order to distribute the network load so that no single part of the network has to handle a disproportionate amount of MBONE traffic, multicast hosts are organized into groups, which are in turn networked to other groups. Groups communicate with one another through designated multicast tunnels that are set up along the network. Tunneling provides dedicated paths that can assure delivery of the data streams, even if the hardware over which they travel does not specifically support IP multicasts.

Since MBONE groups distribute multicast traffic among themselves, duplicate information is reduced and much-needed bandwidth is preserved. Even low-resolution MBONE traffic requires quite a bit of bandwidth (a 128-kilobit video stream is usually only 1 to 4 frames of very low-resolution video), so it's imperative that network traffic be handled as efficiently as possible. Also, groups work together to decide on the best paths for multicast traffic to take. Since most multicast applications are time critical, meaning that there cannot be too much of a lag between the sender and receiver, it is important that the information be routed along the shortest paths possible.

The most commonly used types of applications for which the MBONE is used are audio and video conferencing. Both of these are susceptible to delays caused by high network loads, but delays in audio transmissions are much more noticeable because broken-up audio signals tend to be more annoying than low frame-rate video signals. However, the use of efficient audio encoding techniques has minimized this problem. Audio and video signals are sent as two separate data streams through two different applications. Audioconferencing is usually accomplished through the use of VAT (the Visual Audio Tool shown in Figure 13-19), while videoconferences usually utilize NV (the Network Video tool shown in Figure 13-20). Since the two signals rarely sync up during an MBONE session and both are severely limited by the amount of bandwidth available, the resultant signal is nowhere near the broadcast-quality of traditional video transmission channels.

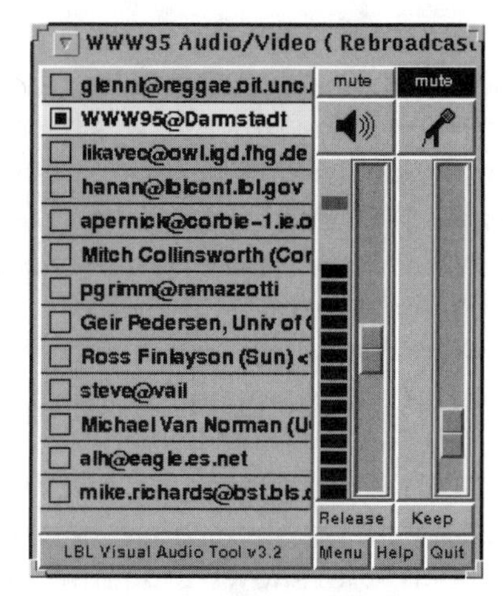

Figure 13-19: *The Visual Audio Tool (VAT) for audioconferencing over the MBONE.*

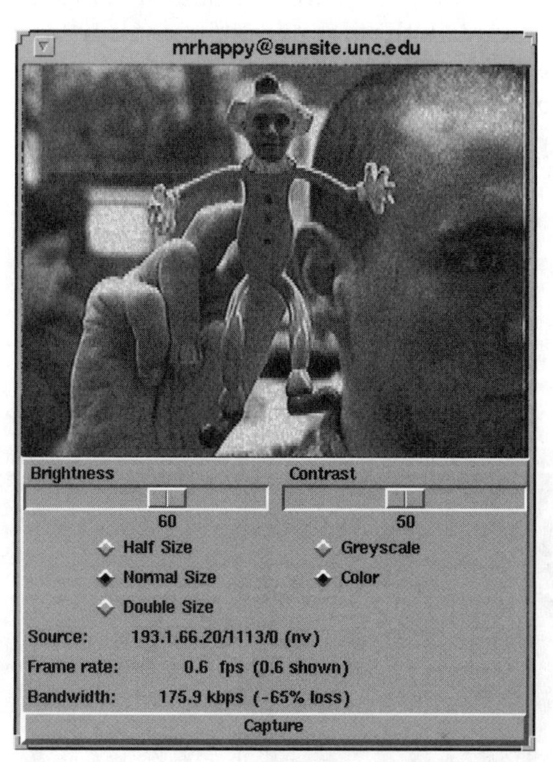

Figure 13-20: *The Network Video (NV) tool for videoconferencing over the MBONE.*

What the MBONE lacks in signal quality has been made up for by the innovative applications for which it has been used. Since the first transmissions in early 1992, the MBONE has been a constant source of numerous worldwide communication "firsts." Users have been willing to deal with choppy audio and video in order to watch live reports from NASA's Mission Control and the Space Shuttle, sit in on talks by famous personalities and, more recently, remotely attend rock concerts and live performances. And yes, some folks even occasionally participate in IETF conferences.

Numerous other less bandwidth-intensive applications are commonly used on the MBONE. Conference participants can communally work on graphical problems on a shared whiteboard by using the WB (Whiteboard tool shown in Figure 13-21). This is commonly used during engineering and brainstorming sessions over the network. Some developers are also working on ways to use the MBONE for efficient delivery of USENET news, and still others are developing ways to distribute 3D virtual environments over it. Even though these applications don't get as much media attention as the teleconferencing programs, the levels of interactivity they provide are truly what makes the MBONE more than just a computer-based television system.

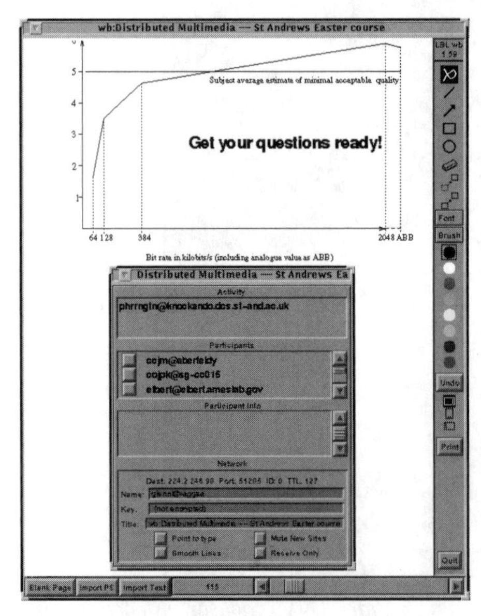

Figure 13-21: *The Whiteboard tool (WB), which provides a shared graphical working space over the MBONE.*

All of these events are usually monitored using the SD tool (see the Session Directory tool in Figure 13-22), which displays active multicast groups and launches multicast applications on its host computer. This way, MBONE participants can keep track of who is transmitting information and who is participating in any particular session.

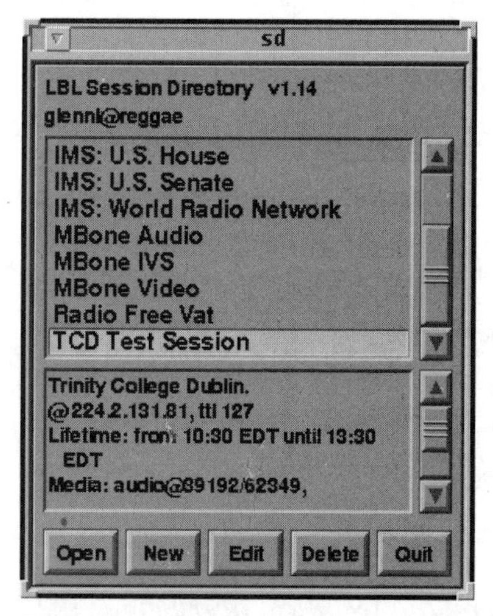

Figure 13-22: *The Session Directory (SD), which keeps track of events and groups on the MBONE.*

Numerous factors are contributing to the further growth of the MBONE. Multicast capabilities are now being incorporated into many UNIX operating systems, including Linux, Solaris, IRIX and many others. Much of the networking hardware on which the Internet is built is being optimized for use in a multicast environment, reducing the need for dedicated tunnels that can sometimes cause inefficient use of network bandwidth.

If you're interested in joining the MBONE, a number of resources are available on the Internet that provide step-by-step instructions on how to do it. You should start by reading "Dan's Quick and Dirty Guide to Getting Connected to the MBONE" at EIT, which gives you all the links and information you'll need to get started. The guide outlines the numerous steps you must take before you can participate in MBONE-based multicast conferences, as well as the ways in which MBONE events are scheduled, coordinated and announced. Configuring your server to receive MBONE multicasts is no small task, but with a little effort (and a sufficiently high-bandwidth multicast feed), it can be a rewarding experience. And, like many other Internet tools, most of the software packages you'll need to get started are free.

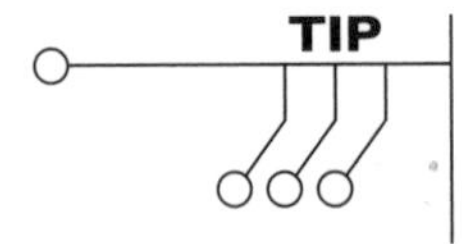

Yahoo's MBONE index is at http://www.yahoo.com/Computers/Multimedia/MBONE/.

Dan's Quick and Dirty Guide to Getting Connected to the MBONE can be obtained at http://www.eit.com:80/techinfo/mbone/how-to-join.html.

You can find the MBONE Information Web, including links to MBONE archives, mailing lists, products and more, at http://www.eit.com/techinfo/mbone/mbone.html.

Read "MBONE Provides Audio and Video Across the Internet," a hypertext version of a paper that first appeared in IEEE Computer Magazine at ftp://taurus.cs.nps.navy.mil/pub/mbmg/mbone.html.

You can learn about videoconferencing over IP for Linux (including ports of NV for use with ScreenMachine II) at http://www.hrz.uni-giessen.de/~l018/nig.html.

An easy-to-understand technical overview of the MBONE can be found at http://www.unige.ch/seinf/mbone.html.

MBONE multicasting technology has spawned numerous other real-time conferencing projects. Software developers at Cornell University, in conjunction with a broad consortium of researchers, have developed CU-SeeMe, the first free desktop videoconferencing tool for Macs and PCs. CU-SeeMe provides a way for Net users without access to the sophisticated servers necessary to utilize the MBONE to experiment with real-time videoconferencing applications. The Macintosh version also supports audioconferencing, and an audio-capable Windows version is promised for the near future. In addition, the newest version of CU-SeeMe supports the exchange of text and slides to further enhance communication.

CU-SeeMe is unique because it doesn't use the multicast tunnels set up by MBONE subnets. Users can connect directly to each other by establishing one-on-one communication channels, or multiple users can hold a conference through the use of a "reflector," which is a UNIX workstation running the CU-SeeMe reflector software. Reflectors can be configured by system administrators to allow limited and/or invitation-only conferences. If so desired, chains of reflectors can be linked together to form a multicast network completely autonomous of the MBONE.

Unlike MBONE hosts, which are constantly communicating with every other host on a multicast channel, reflectors send out data streams only when requests are made. This model, commonly called unicasting, is based on one-to-one or one-to-many conferences and therefore doesn't require as much bandwidth as MBONE multicasting. This is ideal for Internet users who don't have access to high-bandwidth connections but wish to experiment with real-time IP multimedia applications.

CU-SeeMe is somewhat compatible with existing UNIX-based MBONE tools. Reflectors can send CU-SeeMe video streams to NV, and depending on the audio encoding technique used, VAT can sometimes receive CU-SeeMe audio streams.

Linux users can finally take advantage of some of these multicasting technologies, thanks to the recent addition of multicast support to the Linux kernel. The CU-SeeMe reflector has been compiled for Linux, as well as for a Linux version of NV that works with the ScreenMachine II frame grabber. If you are at all interested in multicast technologies, you should definitely read up on these applications and become familiar with what they could offer you.

MBONE and CU-SeeMe technologies have hinted at the incredible potential of computer network-based media distribution. As bandwidth constraints become less of an issue, the Internet will be increasingly used for real-time multimedia applications. Radio stations are already being simulcast 24 hours a day over the Net, and hundreds of people have discovered the joy of becoming their own worldwide video transmission station. As networking technologies evolve, so too will the numerous purposes for which they are used. Gaining an understanding of how real-time, network-based transmissions operate will help you stay ahead of the game as new transmission techniques and applications are introduced.

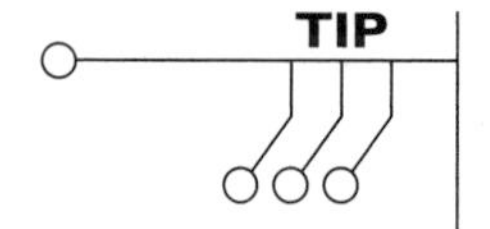

To learn more about the CU-SeeMe project, see http://cu-seeme.cornell.edu.

The CU-SeeMe reflector FAQ is at http://www.indstate.edu/msattler/sci-tech/comp/CU-SeeMe/faq-reflectors.html.

For a complete list of freeware, shareware and commercial desktop videoconferencing applications, see http://www2.ncsu.edu/eos/service/ece/project/succeed_info/dtvc_survey/products.html and http://www.hrz.uni-giessen.de/~l018/nig.html.

Real-time radio over the Internet is available at http://sunsite.unc.edu/wxyc.

Conclusion

The future of the World Wide Web is promising. The protocol that clients and servers use to communicate is undergoing major changes; changes that will improve the speed, efficiency and security of the Web. HTML, the language in which Web pages are designed, will expand dramatically and change from being a simple layout language to a language capable of complex interactions and flexible design. Other developments on the Web, from teleconferencing to commercial transactions, will change the face of the Web, allowing for a broad range of uses that no other technology has made possible.

Using the information in this book, you can create a site that is among the best on the Web. By using advanced features like multimedia, databases and complex forms, you can make your Web pages rival those of the largest companies with an Internet presence. By incorporating developing technologies, and by looking ahead to the newest advances on the Internet, you can also make sure that your site never becomes obsolete. So put your best out there for the world to see, and you will enjoy the rewards of building a strong presence on the World's fastest growing medium—the World Wide Web.

SECTION V

Appendices

About the Online Companion

Serve up some Web fun with the *Web Server Book Online Companion*. It's an informative tool as well as an annotated software library. It aids in your understanding of setting up a Web server while at the same time providing you with the resources and utilities you need to accomplish these tasks. *The Web Server Book Online Companion* hyperlinks Chapter 8 of the hard-copy book to the World Wide Web sites and utilities that it references. So you can just click on the reference name and jump directly to the resource you are interested in.

Perhaps one of the most valuable features of *The Web Server Book Online Companion* is its Software Archive. Here, you'll find and be able to download the lastest versions of all the freely available software mentioned in *The Web Server Book*. This software ranges from a link to the complete Slackware distribution of Linux, which is everything you need to set up a UNIX workstation on a PC 386 or better, to Web server software from NCSA and CERN. Also with Ventana Online's helpful description of the software you'll know exactly what your getting and why. So you won't download the software just to find you have no use for it.

The Web Server Book Online Companion also links you to the Ventana Library where you will find useful press and jacket information on a variety of Ventana Press offerings. Plus, you have access to a wide selction of exciting new releases and coming attractions. In addition, Ventana's Online Library allows you to order the books you want.

The Web Server Book Online Companion represents Ventana Online's ongoing commitment to offering the most dynamic and exciting products possible. And soon Ventana Online will be adding more services, including more multimedia supplements, searchable indexes and sections of the book reproduced and hyperlinked to the Internet resources they reference.

To access the Online Companion, connect via the World Wide Web to http://www.vmedia.com/wsb.html

About the Companion CD-ROM

The CD-ROM included with your copy of *The Web Server Book* contains all the software you need to create your very own platform for interactive electronic publishing on the Internet. Not only does the CD-ROM include all the Web-related software discussed in-depth in the book, it also includes the popular Slackware distribution of Linux, a multitasking, UNIX-compatible operating system for 386 or better PC-compatible computers.

With Linux and a fast PC, you have a powerful 32-bit platform for your World Wide Web server and page development. To install Linux, first check Appendix C, "The Linux Hardware Compatibility HOWTO" for the long list of hardware that Linux v.1.2.3 supports. Once you're certain that you have the right hardware, you're ready to turn your PC into a Linux workstation.

Load the CD-ROM and change to the appropriate drive while running MS-DOS. Read Appendix D, "Installing Linux," for step-by-step instructions on selecting the appropriate Slackware *boot* and *root* disk images and writing them to floppy disks with the included RAWRITE program. You can then use those disks and the Companion CD-ROM to install Linux on your PC. Once you've done so, you can then use the rest of the software on the CD-ROM to build your World Wide Web site.

Of course, you don't have to use Linux for your server platform. The CD-ROM includes the source code for all the programs discussed. In addition, for most of the programs, the CD-ROM includes precompiled distributions for AIX, Irix, OSF/1, Solaris, SunOS, Linux and Ultrix. For a few of the programs discussed, precompiled distributions are not provided on the CD-ROM, but are available from the Web Server Book Online Companion.

To install the included Web-related software, you must mount the CD-ROM as an ISO-9660 format filesystem. The exact steps to do so vary from OS to OS, so consult your manual if you're not sure. Under Linux, you can mount the disk, as root, with this command:

```
# mount -r -t iso9660 device /mnt
```

where *device* depends on the type of supported CD-ROM drive you have:

CD-ROM Drive	Device
SCSI	/dev/scd0 or /dev/scd1
Sony CDU31A	/dev/sonycd
Sony 531/535	/dev/cdu535
Mitsumi	/dev/mcd
SoundBlaster Pro, Panasonic	/dev/sbpcd
Aztech, Orchid, Okano, Wearnes	/dev/aztcd
IDE CD-ROM on first interface	/dev/hda or /dev/hdb, IDE
CD-ROM on second interface	/dev/hd1a or /dev/hd1b

Once you've mounted the CD-ROM, you can access the software it contains. In addition to several directories containing the Slackware distribution, you'll find the booksoft directory, which contains all the other software discussed in this book. The booksoft directory contains the netscape subdirectory (which includes several versions of Netscape Navigator), the perl subdirectory (which includes an interpreter required to run several of the programs on the CD-ROM), and a separate subdirectory for each chapter that discusses a software program.

Inside each chapter directory, there is a collection of directories: one for every package discussed in that chapter. These package directories contain the binaries and source for that piece of software, as well as a README file that briefly describes the package and tells you how to install it. For the latest information on the software packages and other topics related to this book, refer to *The Web Server Book Online Companion.*

The following list describes the software contained in each of the chapter subdirectories included on the CD-ROM. You can find these subdirectories under the booksoft directory.

Directory	Program	Description
chapt2		
tkhtml	tkHTML	An HTML editor that allows for easy editing and Web page creation. (The CD-ROM contains only source code. To compile it yourself, follow the provided instructions. Alternatively, precompiled distributions are available from the Online Companion.
chapt3		
ncsahttp	NCSA httpd v1.4	http server software
cernhttp	CERN httpd v3.0	http server software
chapt5		
txt2html	txt2html.pl	A perl script that converts ASCII files into HTML documents.
rtftohtm	rtftohtml	A program that converts Rich Text Format documents into HTML.
wp2x		A program that converts WordPerfect documents to a large number of different formats, including HTML.
qt2www	qt2www.pl	A program that converts Quark Tags documents into HTML, matching Quark styles to HTML tags.
chapt6		
htmlchek	htmlchek	A program that checks the accuracy of HTML markup.
checker	Anchor Checker	A program that checks all of the links in an HTML document to ensure that they point to valid destinations.

	momspid	MOMspider	A Web-wandering robot that checks all of the documents on a Web site.
	weblint	Weblint	A program that checks HTML documents for style and validity.
chapt7			
	transgif	transgif.pl	A perl script that turns on trasparency in GIF images
	netpbm	The NetPBM Toolkit	A collection of utilities that translates images to and from over 50 different popular graphics formats.
	jpgtools	Independent JPEG Group JPEG Tools	Utilities for converting images to and from the popular JPEG format.
	xv	xv	A WYSIWYG graphic manipulation tool for X Windows.
chapt8			
	sox	Sox/Sound Tools	A sound processing tool for converting between numerous audio file formats and adding effects to sound files.
	mpegaud	MPEG/audio	An MPEG Layer II audio compressor that compresses CD-quality audio files to 1/10th their original size.
	xanim	Xanim	A multiformat animation viewer with a great X11 interface. (The CD-ROM contains only source code. To compile it yourself, follow the provided instructions. Alternatively, precompiled distributions are available from the Online Companion.)
	mpg2play	mpeg2play	An MPEG-1 and MPEG-2 movie playback utility.

Directory	Software	Description
chapt9		
aname		Sample code for adding a filter to freeWAIS
freewais	freeWAIS	A powerful search and indexing package that allows searching and indexing for any collection of documents.
chapt10		
fwais	fwais.pl	A CGI gateway, which gives WWW browsers easy access to databases built with freeWAIS.
gform	Generic Form Handler	Allows nonprogramers to create interactive forms in HTML and format the results.
chapt11		
cgi-exam		Example CGI scripts documented in Chapter 11.
uncgi		A tool for the CGI programmer that automatically parses the results of an HTML form, for easy access from any programming language.

Free voice technical support is limited to installation-related issues and is available for 30 days from the date you register your copy of the book. After the initial 30 days and for non-installation-related questions, please send all technical support questions via Internet e-mail to help@vmedia.com. Our technical support staff will research your question and respond promptly via e-mail.

Linux Hardware Compatibility HOWTO

Welcome to the Linux Hardware Compatibility HOWTO. This document lists most of the hardwares supported by Linux—now if only people would read this first before posting their questions on USENET.

Subsections titled "Others" list hardwares with alpha or beta drivers in varying degrees of usability or other drivers that aren't included in standard kernels. Also note that some drivers only exist in alpha kernels, so if you see something listed as supported but isn't in your version of the Linux kernel, upgrade.

The latest version of this document can be found on the usual sites with LDP docs, and on the Web at (http://roch0.eznet.net/~frac/hardware.html). Many thanks to Paul Erkkila and E-Znet for the account. No more wacky *.th links.

If you know of any Linux hardware (in)compatibilities not listed here please let me know. Just send mail or find me on IRC. Thanks.

From FRiC (Boy of Destiny), frac@ksc.au.ac.th; v6969, 14 April 1995. This document lists most of the hardwares supported by Linux and helps you locate any necessary drivers.

1.2. System Architectures

This document only deals with Linux for Intel platforms, for other platforms check the following:

- Linux/68k (http://www-users.informatik.rwth-aachen.de/~hn/linux68k.html)
- Linux/MIPS (http://www.waldorf-gmbh.de/linux-mips-faq.html)
- Linux/PowerPC (ftp://sunsite.unc.edu/pub/Linux/docs/ports/Linux-PowerPC-FAQ.gz)
- Linux for Acorn (http://www.ph.kcl.ac.uk/~amb/linux.html)
- MacLinux (http://www.ibg.uu.se/maclinux/)

2. Computers/Motherboards/BIOS

ISA, VLB, EISA, and PCI buses are all supported.

PS/2 and Microchannel (MCA) is not supported in the standard kernel. Alpha test PS/2 MCA kernels are available but not yet recommended for beginners or serious use.

- PS/2 MCA kernel (ftp://invaders.dcrl.nd.edu/pub/misc/)

3. Laptops

Some laptops have unusual video adapters or power management, it is not uncommon to be unable to use the power management features.

PCMCIA drivers currently support Databook TCIC/2, Intel i82365SL, Cirrus PD67xx, and Vadem VG-468 chipsets. (Read the PCMCIA HOWTO.)

- APM BIOS (ftp://ftp.aaug.org.au/pub/unix/linux/apm_bios.0.5.tar.gz)

- APM (ftp://tsx-11.mit.edu/pub/linux/packages/laptops/apm/)
- PCMCIA (ftp://cb-iris.stanford.edu/pub/pcmcia/)
- non-blinking cursor (ftp://sunsite.unc.edu/pub/Linux/kernel/patches/console/noblink-1.5.tar.gz)
- power savings (WD7600 chipset) (ftp://sunsite.unc.edu/pub/Linux/system/Misc/low-level/pwrm-1.0.tar.Z)

3.1. Linux on Laptops

- Compaq Contura Aero (http://domen.uninett.no/~hta/linux/aero-faq.html)
- IBM ThinkPad (http://peipa.essex.ac.uk/html/linux-thinkpad.html)
- IBM ThinkPad 755Cs (http://www.cica.fr/~basturk/linux/index.html)
- other general info (ftp://tsx-11.mit.edu/pub/linux/packages/laptops/)

4. CPU/FPU

Intel/AMD/Cyrix 386SX/DX/SL/DXL/SLC, 486SX/DX/SL/SX2/DX2/DX4, Pentium. Basically all 386 or better processors will work. Linux has built-in FPU emulation if you don't have a math coprocessor.

A few very early AMD 486DX's may hang in some special situations. All current chips should be okay, and getting a chip swap for old CPU's should not be a problem.

ULSI Math*Co series has a bug in the FSAVE and FRSTOR instructions that causes problems with all protected mode operating systems. Some older IIT and Cyrix chips may also have this problem.

There are problems with TLB flushing in UMC U5S chips. Fixed in newer kernels.

- enable cache on Cyrix processors (ftp://sunsite.unc.edu/pub/Linux/kernel/patches/CxPatch030.tar.z)
- Cyrix software cache control (ftp://sunsite.unc.edu/pub/Linux/kernel/patches/linux.cxpatch)

5. Video cards

Linux will work with all video cards in text mode, VGA cards not listed below probably will still work with mono VGA and/or standard VGA drivers.

If you're looking into buying a cheap video card to run X, keep in mind that accelerated cards (ATI Mach, ET4000/W32p, S3) are MUCH faster than unaccelerated or partially accelerated (Cirrus, WD) cards. S3 801 (ISA), S3 805 (VLB), ET4000/W32p, and ATI Graphics Wonder (Mach32) are good low-end accelerated cards.

32 bit color means 24 bit color aligned on 32 bit boundaries. Modes with 24 bit packed pixels are not supported, so cards that can display 24 bit color in other OS's may not able to do this in X. These cards include Mach32, Cirrus 542x, S3 801/805, ET4000, and others.

5.1. Diamond Video Cards

Early Diamond cards are not supported by XFree86, but there are ways of getting them to work. Most recent Diamond cards ARE supported by the current release of XFree86.

- Diamond support for XFree86 (http://www.diamondmm.com/linux.html)
- Diamond FAQ (for older cards) (ftp://sunsite.unc.edu/pub/Linux/X11/Diamond.FAQ)

5.2. SVGALIB

- VGA
- EGA

- ATI Mach32
- Cirrus 542x
- OAK OTI-037/67/77/87
- Trident TVGA8900/9000
- Tseng ET3000/ET4000/W32

5.3. XFree86 3.1.1, Accelerated

8 bpp (bits-per-pixel) unless noted.

- ATI Mach8
- ATI Mach32 (16 bpp) - does not work with all Mach32 cards
- ATI Mach64 (16/32 bpp)
- Cirrus Logic 5420, 542x/5430 (16 bpp), 5434 (16/32 bpp), 62x5
- IBM 8514/A
- IBM XGA, XGA-II
- IIT AGX-010/014/015/016
- Oak OTI-087
- S3 911, 924, 801, 805, 928, 864, 964, Trio32, Trio64
- See the table on page 554 for a long list of supported cards
- Tseng ET4000/W32/W32i/W32p
- Weitek P9000 (16/32 bpp)
- Diamond Viper VLB/PCI
- Orchid P9000
- Western Digital WD90C31/33

5.4. XFree86 3.1.1, Unaccelerated

- ATI VGA Wonder series
- Avance Logic AL2101/2228/2301/2302/2308/2401

- Chips & Technologies 65520/65530/65540/65545
- Cirrus Logic 6420/6440
- Compaq AVGA
- Genoa GVGA
- MCGA (320x200)
- MX MX68000/MX68010
- NCR 77C22, 77C22E, 77C22E+
- Oak OTI-067, OTI-077
- Trident TVGA8800, TVGA8900, TVGA9xxx (not very fast)
- Tseng ET3000, ET4000AX
- VGA (standard VGA, 4 bit, slow)
- Video 7 / Headland Technologies HT216-32
- Western Digital/Paradise PVGA1, WD90C00/10/11/24/30/31/33

5.5. Monochrome

- Hercules mono
- Hyundai HGC-1280
- Sigma LaserView PLUS
- VGA mono

5.6. Others

- EGA (ftp://ftp.funet.fi/pub/OS/Linux/BETA/Xega/)

5.7. Works in progress

- Compaq QVision
- Number Nine Imagine 128

No, I do not know when support for these cards will be finished, please don't ask me. If you want support for these cards now get Accelerated-X.

5.8. Commercial X servers

Commercial X servers provide support for cards not supported by XFree86, and might give better performances for cards that are supported by XFree86. Only cards not supported by XFree86 are listed here. Contact the vendors directly or check the Commercial HOWTO for more info.

5.8.1. Accelerated-X

- Compaq QVision 2000
- Matrox MGA-I, MGA-II
- Number Nine I-128

$199 from X Inside, Inc. <info@xinside.com>. Accel-X 1.1 is available right now for a promotional price of $99.50, with free upgrade to 1.2.

16 bit support for ATI Mach32, ATI Mach 64, Cirrus 542x/543x, IBM XGA, IIT AGX-014/015, Matrox MGA, #9 I-128, Oak OTI-077/087, S3 cards, ET4000, ET4000/W32 series, Weitek P9000, WD90C30/31.

32 bit support for ATI Mach64, Cirrus 5434, Matrox MGA, #9 I-128, S3-928/864/964, ET4000/W32p, Weitek P9000.

Accel-X 1.2 will support 24 bit packed pixel modes and have support for many more video cards.

5.8.2. Metro-X

$150 from Metro Link <sales@metrolink.com>. Metro-X 2.3 is now available for special introductory price of $99.00.

Metro-X has similar hardware support as Accel-X, however I don't have much more information as I can't seem to view the PostScript files they sent me. Mail them directly for more info.

6. Controllers (hard drive)

Linux will work with standard IDE, MFM and RLL controllers. When using MFM/RLL controllers it is important to use ext2fs and the bad block checking options when formatting the disk. Enhanced IDE (EIDE) interfaces are supported. With up to two IDE interfaces and up to four hard drives and/or CD-ROM drives. (1.1.76)

ESDI controllers that emulate the ST-506 (that is MFM/RLL/IDE) interface will also work. The bad block checking comment also applies to these controllers.

Generic 8 bit XT controllers also work.

7. Controllers (SCSI)

It is important to pick a SCSI controller carefully. Many cheap ISA SCSI controllers are designed to drive CD-ROMs rather than anything else. Such low end SCSI controllers are no better than IDE. See the SCSI HOWTO and look at UNIX performance figures before buying a SCSI card.

7.1. Supported

- AMI Fast Disk VLB/EISA (works with BusLogic drivers)
- Adaptec AVA-1505/1515 (ISA) (use 152x drivers)
- Adaptec AHA-1510/152x (ISA)
- Adaptec AHA-154x (ISA) (all models)
- Adaptec AHA-174x (EISA) (in enhanced mode)
- Adaptec AHA-274x (EISA) / 284x (VLB) (AIC-7770)
- Always IN2000
- BusLogic (all models)
- DPT Smartcache (EATA) (ISA/EISA)
- DTC 329x (EISA) (Adaptec 154x compatible)

- Future Domain TMC-16x0, TMC-3260 (PCI)
- Future Domain TMC-8xx, TMC-950
- NCR 53c7x0, 53c8x0 (PCI)
- Pro Audio Spectrum 16 SCSI (ISA)
- Qlogic /Control Concepts SCSI/IDE (FAS408) (ISA/VLB/PCMCIA) does not work with PCI (different chipset). PCMCIA cards must boot DOS to init card
- Seagate ST-01/ST-02 (ISA)
- SoundBlaster 16 SCSI-2 (Adaptec 152x) (ISA)
- Trantor T128/T128F/T228 (ISA)
- UltraStor 14F (ISA), 24F (EISA), 34F (VLB)
- Western Digital WD7000 SCSI

7.2. Others

- Adaptec ACB-40xx SCSI-MFM/RLL bridgeboard (ftp://sunsite.unc.edu/pub/Linux/kernel/patches/scsi/adaptec-40XX.tar.gz)
- Adaptec AHA-2940 (PCI) (AIC-7870) (ftp://remus.nrl.navy.mil/pub/Linux/)
- Acculogic ISApport / MV Premium 3D SCSI (NCR 53c406a) (ftp://sunsite.unc.edu/pub/Linux/kernel/patches/scsi/ncr53c406-0.10.patch.gz)
- Always AL-500 (ftp://sunsite.unc.edu/pub/Linux/kernel/patches/scsi/al500_0.1.tar.gz)
- Iomega PC2/2B (ftp://sunsite.unc.edu/pub/Linux/kernel/patches/scsi/iomega_pc2-1.1.x.tar.gz)
- New Media Bus Toaster PCMCIA (ftp://lamont.ldeo.columbia.edu/pub/linux/bus_toaster-1.5.tgz)
- Ricoh GSI-8 (ftp://tsx-11.mit.edu/pub/linux/ALPHA/scsi/gsi8.tar.gz)
- Trantor T130B (NCR 53c400) (ftp://sunsite.unc.edu/pub/Linux/kernel/patches/scsi/53c400.tar.gz)

7.3. Unsupported

- Parallel port SCSI adapters
- Non Adaptec compatible DTC boards (327x, 328x)

8. Controllers (I/O)

Any standard serial/parallel/joystick/IDE combo cards. Linux supports 8250, 16450, 16550, and 16550A UART's.

See National Semiconductor's "Application Note AN-493" by Martin S. Michael. Section 5.0 describes in detail the differences between the NS16550 and NS16550A. Briefly, the NS16550 had bugs in the FIFO circuits, but the NS16550A (and later) chips fixed those. However, there were very few NS16550's produced by National, long ago, so these should be very rare. And many of the "16550" parts in actual modern boards are from the many manufacturers of compatible parts, which may not use the National "A" suffix. Also, some multiport boards will use 16552 or 16554 or various other multiport or multifunction chips from National or other suppliers (generally in a dense package soldered to the board, not a 40 pin DIP). Mostly, don't worry about it unless you encounter a very old 40 pin DIP National "NS16550" (no A) chip loose or in an old board, in which case treat it as a 16450 (no FIFO) rather than a 16550A. - Zhahai Stewart <zstewart@hisys.com>

9. Controllers (multiport)

9.1. Supported

- AST FourPort and clones
- Accent Async-4
- Bell Technologies HUB6
- Boca BB-1004, 1008 (4, 8 port) - no DTR, DSR, and CD

- Boca BB-2016 (16 port)
- Boca IO/AT66 (6 port)
- Boca IO 2by4 (4S/2P) - works with modems, but uses 5 IRQ's
- Cyclades Cyclom-8Y/16Y (8, 16 port)
- PC-COMM 4-port
- STB 4-COM
- Twincom ACI/550
- Usenet Serial Board II

9.2. Others

- Comtrol RocketPort (8/16/32 port) (ftp://tsx-11.mit.edu/pub/linux/packages/comtrol/)
- DigiBoard COM/Xi contact Simon Park <si@wimpol.demon.co.uk>
- DigiBoard PC/Xe (ISA) and PC/Xi (EISA) (ftp://ftp.skypoint.com/pub/linux/digiboard/)
- Specialix SI0/XIO (modular, 4 to 32 ports) (ftp://sunsite.unc.edu/pub/Linux/kernel/patches/serial/sidrv0_5.taz)
- Stallion Technologies EasyIO / EasyConnection 8/32 (ftp://sunsite.unc.edu/pub/Linux/kernel/patches/serial/stallion-0.1.5.tar.gz)

10. Network Adapters

Ethernet adapters vary greatly in performance. In general the newer the design the better. Some very old cards like the 3C501 are only useful because they can be found in junk heaps for $5 a time. Be careful with clones, not all are good clones and bad clones often cause erratic lockups under Linux.

10.1. Supported

10.1.1. ISA

- 3Com 3C501 - "avoid like the plague"
- 3Com 3C503, 3C505, 3C507, 3C509 (ISA) / 3C579 (EISA)
- AMD LANCE (79C960) / PCnet-ISA/PCI (AT1500, HP J2405A, NE1500/NE2100)
- AT&T GIS WaveLAN
- Allied Telesis AT1700
- Cabletron E21xx
- DEC DEPCA and EtherWORKS
- HP PCLAN (27245 and 27xxx series)
- HP PCLAN PLUS (27247B and 27252A)
- Intel EtherExpress
- NE2000/NE1000 (be careful with clones)
- Racal-Interlan NI5210 (i82586 Ethernet chip)
- Racal-Interlan NI6510 (am7990 lance chip) - doesn't work with more than 16 megs RAM
- PureData PDUC8028, PDI8023
- SMC Ultra
- Schneider & Koch G16
- Western Digital WD80x3

10.1.2. EISA & Onboard Controllers

- Ansel Communications AC3200 EISA
- Apricot Xen-II
- Zenith Z-Note / IBM ThinkPad 300 built-in adapter

10.1.3. Pocket & Portable Adapters

- AT-Lan-Tec/RealTek parallel port adapter
- D-Link DE600/DE620 parallel port adapter

10.1.4. Slotless

- SLIP/CSLIP/PPP (serial port)
- PLIP (parallel port) - using "LapLink cable" or bi-directional cable

10.1.5. ARCnet

- Works with all ARCnet cards

10.2. Others

10.2.1. ISDN

- Diehl SCOM card (ftp://sunsite.unc.edu/pub/Linux/kernel/patches/network/isdndrv-0.1.1.tar.gz) only in asynchronous mode, not useful for some applications
- Teles ISDN car

10.2.2. Amateur Radio Cards

- Ottawa PI2
- Most generic 8530 based HDLC boards
- No support for the PMP/Baycom board

10.2.3. PCMCIA Cards

- 3Com 3C589
- Accton EN2212 EtherCard
- D-Link DE650
- IBM Credit Card Adapter
- IC-Card
- Kingston KNE-PCM/M
- LANEED Ethernet
- Linksys EthernetCard
- Network General "Sniffer"

- Novell NE4100
- Thomas-Conrad Ethernet
- Possibly more

10.2.4. Token Ring

- Token Ring (ftp://ftp.cs.kuleuven.ac.be/pub/unix/linux/)

10.3. Unsupported

- Xircom adapters are not supported.

11. Sound cards

11.1. Supported

- 6850 UART MIDI
- ATI Stereo F/X (SB compatible)
- Adlib
- ECHO-PSS (Orchid SW32, Cardinal DSP16, etc)
- Ensoniq SoundScape (boot DOS to init card)
- Gravis Ultrasound
- Gravis Ultrasound 16-bit sampling daughterboard
- Gravis Ultrasound MAX
- Logitech SoundMan Games (SBPro, 44kHz stereo support)
- Logitech SoundMan Wave (SBPro/MPU-401) (OPL4)
- Logitech SoundMan 16 (PAS-16 compatible)
- Microsoft Sound System (AD1848)
- MPU-401 MIDI
- Media Vision Premium 3D (Jazz16) (SBPro compatible)

- Media Vision Pro Sonic 16 (Jazz)
- Media Vision Pro Audio Spectrum 16
- SoundBlaster
- SoundBlaster Pro
- SoundBlaster 16/ASP/MCD/SCSI-2
- Sound Galaxy NX Pro
- ThunderBoard (SB compatible)
- WaveBlaster (and other SB16 daughterboards)

11.2. Others

- MPU-401 MIDI (intelligent mode) (ftp://sunsite.unc.edu/pub/Linux/kernel/sound/mpu401.0.11a.tar.gz)
- PC speaker / Parallel port DAC (ftp://ftp.informatik.hu-berlin.de/pub/os/linux/hu-sound/)

11.3. Unsupported

The ASP chip on SoundBlaster 16 series and AWE32 is not supported. AWE32's special features (MIDI, effects) are not supported. They will probably never be supported.

SoundBlaster 16 with DSP 4.11's have a hardware bug that causes hung/stuck notes when you use a WaveBlaster or other MIDI devices attached to it. There is no known fix.

12. Hard drives

All hard drives should work if the controller is supported.

(From the SCSI HOWTO) All direct access SCSI devices with a block size of 256, 512, or 1024 bytes should work. Other block sizes will not work. (Note that this can often be fixed by changing the block and/or sector sizes using the MODE SELECT SCSI command.)

Large IDE (EIDE) drives work fine with newer kernels. The boot partition must lie in the first 1024 cylinders due to PC BIOS limitations.

Some Conner CFP1060S drives may have problems with Linux and ext2fs. The symptoms are inode errors during e2fsck and corrupt file systems. Conner has released a bugfix for this problem, contact Conner at 1-800-4CONNER (US) or +44-1294-315333 (Europe). Have the microcode version (found on the drive label, 9WA1.6x) handy when you call.

Certain Micropolis drives have problems with Adaptec and BusLogic cards, contact the manufacturers for firmware upgrades if you suspect problems.

13. Tape drives

13.1. Supported

- SCSI tape drives (From the SCSI HOWTO) Drives using both fixed and variable length blocks smaller than the driver buffer length (set to 32k in the distribution sources) are supported. Virtually all drives should work. (Send mail if you know of any incompatible drives.)
- QIC-02
- QIC-117, QIC-40/80 drives (Ftape) (ftp://sunsite.unc.edu/pub/Linux/kernel/tapes) - Most tape drives using the floppy controller should work. Check the Ftape HOWTO for details. Colorado FC-10 is also supported.

13.2. Unsupported

- Emerald and Tecmar QIC-02 tape controller cards - Chris Ulrich <insom@math.ucr.edu>
- Drives that connect to the parallel port (eg: Colorado Trakker)

- Some high speed tape controllers (Colorado TC-15 / FC-20)
- Irwin AX250L/Accutrak 250 (not QIC-80)
- IBM Internal Tape Backup Unit (not QIC-80)
- COREtape Light

14. CD-ROM drives

14.1. Supported

- SCSI CD-ROM drives (From the CD-ROM HOWTO) Any SCSI CD-ROM drive with a block size of 512 or 2048 bytes should work under Linux; this includes the vast majority of CD-ROM drives on the market.
- Aztech CDA268, Orchid CDS-3110, Okano/Wearnes CDD-110
- EIDE (ATAPI) CD-ROM drives
- Matsushita/Panasonic, Kotobuki (SBPCD)
- Mitsumi
- Sony CDU31A/CDU33A
- Sony CDU-535/CDU-531

14.2. Others

- GoldStar R420 (ftp://ftp.gwdg.de/pub/linux/cdrom/drivers/goldstar/)
- LMS/Philips CM 205/225/202 (ftp://sunsite.unc.edu/pub/Linux/kernel/patches/cdrom/lmscd0.3d.tar.gz)
- LMS Philips CM 206 (ftp://sunsite.unc.edu/pub/Linux/kernel/patches/cdrom/cm206.0.22b.tar.gz)
- Mitsumi (ftp://ftp.gwdg.de/pub/linux/cdrom/drivers/mitsumi/)

- NEC CDR-35D (old) (ftp://sunsite.unc.edu/pub/Linux/kernel/patches/cdrom/linux-neccdr35d.patch)

14.3. Notes

PhotoCD (XA) is supported.

All CD-ROM drives should work similarly for reading data. There are various compatibility problems with audio CD playing utilities. (Especially with some NEC drives.) Some alpha drivers may not have audio support yet.

Early (single speed) NEC CD-ROM drives may have trouble with currently available SCSI controllers.

15. Removable drives

All SCSI drives should work if the controller is supported, including optical drives, WORM, CD-R, floptical, and others. Bernoulli and SyQuest drives work fine.

Linux supports both 512 and 1024 bytes/sector disks. There's a problem with msdos filesystems on 1024 bytes/sector disks on some recent kernels (fixed in 1.1.75).

16. Mice

16.1. Supported

- Microsoft serial mouse
- Mouse Systems serial mouse
- Logitech Mouseman serial mouse
- Logitech serial mouse
- ATI XL Inport busmouse
- C&T 82C710 (QuickPort) (Toshiba, TI Travelmate)

- Microsoft busmouse
- Logitech busmouse
- PS/2 (auxiliary device) mouse

16.2. Others

- Sejin J-mouse (ftp://sunsite.unc.edu/pub/Linux/kernel/patches/console/jmouse.1.1.70-jmouse.tar.gz)
- MultiMouse - use multiple mouse devices as single mouse (ftp://sunsite.unc.edu/pub/Linux/system/Misc/MultiMouse-1.0.tgz)

16.3. Notes

Newer Logitech mice (except the Mouseman) use the Microsoft protocol and all three buttons do work. Even though Microsoft's mice have only two buttons, the protocol allows three buttons.

The mouse port on the ATI Graphics Ultra and Ultra Pro use the Logitech busmouse protocol. (See the Busmouse HOWTO for details.)

17. Modems

All internal modems or external modems connected to the serial port.

A small number of modems come with DOS software that downloads the control program at runtime. These can normally be used by loading the program under DOS and doing a warm boot. Such modems are probably best avoided as you won't be able to use them with non PC hardware in the future.

PCMCIA modems should work with the PCMCIA drivers.

Fax modems need appropriated software to operate.

- Digicom Connection 96+/14.4+ - DSP code downloading program (ftp://sunsite.unc.edu/pub/Linux/system/Serial/smdl-linux.1.02.tar.gz)

- ZyXEL U-1496 series - ZyXEL 1.4, modem/fax/voice control program (ftp://sunsite.unc.edu/pub/Linux/system/Serial/ZyXEL-1.4.tar.gz)

18. Printers/Plotters

All printers and plotters connected to the parallel or serial port should work.

- HP LaserJet 4 series - free-lj4, printing modes control program (ftp://sunsite.unc.edu/pub/Linux/system/Printing/free-lj4-1.1p1.tar.gz)
- BiTronics parallel port interface (ftp://sunsite.unc.edu/pub/Linux/kernel/misc/bt-ALPHA-0.0.1.tar.gz)

18.1. GhostScript

Many Linux programs output PostScript files. Non-PostScript printers can emulate PostScript Level 2 using GhostScript.

- GhostScript (ftp://ftp.cs.wisc.edu/pub/ghost/aladdin/)

18.1.1. GhostScript supported printers

- Apple Imagewriter
- C. Itoh M8510
- Canon BubbleJet BJ10e, BJ200
- Canon LBP-8II, LIPS III
- DEC LA50/70/75/75plus
- DEC LN03, LJ250
- Epson 9 pin, 24 pin, LQ series, Stylus, AP3250
- HP 2563B
- HP DesignJet 650C
- HP DeskJet/Plus/500

- HP DeskJet 500C/520C/550C/1200C color
- HP LaserJet/Plus/II/III/4
- HP PaintJet/XL/XL300 color
- IBM Jetprinter color
- IBM Proprinter
- Imagen ImPress
- Mitsubishi CP50 color
- NEC P6/P6+/P60
- Okidata MicroLine 182
- Ricoh 4081
- SPARCprinter
- StarJet 48 inkjet printer
- Tektronix 4693d color 2/4/8 bit
- Tektronix 4695/4696 inkjet plotter
- Xerox XES printers (2700, 3700, 4045, etc.)

18.1.2. Others

- Canon BJC600 and Epson ESC/P color printers (ftp://petole.imag.fr/pub/postscript/)

19. Scanners

- A4 Tech AC 4096 (ftp://ftp.informatik.hu-berlin.de/pub/local/linux/ac4096.tgz)
- Fujitsu SCSI-2 scanners contact Dr. G.W. Wettstein <greg%wind.UUCP@plains.nodak.edu>
- Genius GS-B105G (ftp://tsx-11.mit.edu/pub/linux/ALPHA/scanner/gs105-0.0.1.tar.gz)
- Genius GeniScan GS4500 handheld scanner (ftp://tsx-11.mit.edu/pub/linux/ALPHA/scanner/gs4500-1.3.tar.gz)

- HP ScanJet, ScanJet Plus (ftp://ftp.ctrl-c.liu.se/unix/linux/wingel/)
- HP ScanJet II series SCSI (ftp://sunsite.unc.edu/pub/Linux/apps/graphics/hpscanpbm.c.gz)
- Logitech Scanman 32 / 256 (ftp://tsx-11.mit.edu/pub/linux/ALPHA/scanner/logiscan-0.0.2.tar.gz)
- Mustek M105 handheld scanner with GI1904 interface (ftp://tsx-11.mit.edu/pub/linux/ALPHA/scanner/scan-driver-0.1.8.tar.gz)

20. Other Hardwares

20.1. VESA Power Savings Protocol (DPMS) monitors

—

20.2. Joysticks

- Joysticks (ftp://sunsite.unc.edu/pub/Linux/kernel/patches/console/joystick-0.7.tgz)

20.3. Video Capture Boards

- FAST Screen Machine II (ftp://sunsite.unc.edu/pub/Linux/apps/video/ScreenMachineII_1.1.tgz)
- ProMovie Studio (ftp://sunsite.unc.edu/pub/Linux/apps/video/PMS-grabber.tgz)
- VideoBlaster, Rombo Media Pro+ (ftp://sunsite.unc.edu/pub/Linux/apps/video/vid_src.gz)
- WinVision video capture card (ftp://sunsite.unc.edu/pub/Linux/apps/video/fgrabber-1.0.tgz)

20.4. UPS

- Various UPS's are supported, read the UPS HOWTO

20.5. Miscellaneous

- Mattel Powerglove (ftp://sunsite.unc.edu/pub/Linux/apps/linux-powerglove.tgz)
- HP IEEE-488 (HP-IB) interface (ftp://beaver.chemie.fu-berlin.de/pub/linux/IEEE488/)

21. Related Sources of Information

- Cameron Spitzer's hardware FAQ archive (ftp://rahul.net/pub/cameron/PC-info/)
- Computer-related WWW/FTP/Newsgroup resources (http://www-bprc.mps.ohio-state.edu/cgi-bin/hpp/list.html)
- Computer Hardware and Software Vendor Phone Numbers (http://mtmis1.mis.semi.harris.com/comp_ph1.html)
- System Optimization Information (http://www.dfw.net/~sdw/)

22. Acknowledgments

Thanks to all the authors and contributors of other HOWTO's, many things here are shamelessly stolen from their works; to Zane Healy and Ed Carp, the original authors of this list; and to everyone else who sent in updates and feedbacks. Special thanks to Eric Boerner and lilo (the person, not the program) for the sanity checks. And thanks to Dan Quinlan for the original SGML conversion.

CHIPSET	RAMDAC	CLOCKCHIP	BPP	CARD
801/805	AT&T	20C490	16	Actix GE 32, Orchid Fahrenheit 1280+
801/805	AT&T	20C490	16	STB PowerGraph X.24
805	S3 GENDAC		16	Miro 10SD VLB/PCI, Spea Mirage VLB
805	SS2410	ICD2061A	8	Diamond Stealth 24 VLB
928	AT&T 20C490		16	Actix Ultra
928	Sierra SC15025	ICD2061A	32	ELSA Winner 1000 ISA/VLB/EISA
928	Bt485	ICD2061A	32	STB Pegasus VL
928	Bt485	SC11412	16	SPEA Mercury VLB
928	Bt485	ICD2061A	32	#9 GXE Level 10/11/12
928	Ti3020	ICD2061A	32	#9 GXE Level 14/16
864	AT&T 20C498	ICS2494	32	Miro 20SD (BIOS 1.x)
864	AT&T 20C498/ STG1700	ICD2061A/ ICS9161	32	ELSA Winner 1000 PRO VLB/ PCI, MIRO 20SD (BIOS 2.x), SPEA Mirage P64 DRAM (BIOS 4.x)
864	STG1700	ICD2061A	32?	Actix GE 64 VLB
864	AT&T 20C498 AT&T 21C498	ICS2595	16	SPEA Mirage P64 DRAM (BIOS 3.x)
864	S3 86C716 SDAC		32	ELSA Winner 1000 PRO, SPEA Mirage P64 DRAM (BIOS 4.x), Diamond Stealth 64 DRAM
864	ICS5342	ICS5342	32	Diamond Stealth 64 DRAM (some)
864	AT&T 20C490	ICD2061A	32	#9 GXE64
864	AT&T 20C498-13	ICD2061A	32	#9 GXE64 PCI
964	AT&T 20C505	ICD2061A	32	Miro Crystal 20SV PCI
964	Bt485	ICD2061A	32	Diamond Stealth 64
964	Bt9485	ICS9161A	32	SPEA Mercury 64
964	Ti3025	ICD2061A	8	ELSA Winner 2000 PRO PCI
964	Ti3025	Ti3025	32	#9 GXE64 Pro VLB/PCI, Miro Crystal 40SV
764	(Trio64)		32	SPEA Mirage P64 (BIOS 5.x), Diamond Stealth 64 DRAM, #9 GXE64 Trio64, STB PowerGraph 64

Table C-1: *S3 cards supported by XFree86 3.1.1.*

Installing Linux

Linux is a freely distributable implementation of UNIX for 80386 and 80486, and Pentium machines. It supports a wide range of software, including X Windows, Emacs, TCP/IP networking (including SLIP), the works. This document assumes that you have heard of and know about Linux, and just want to sit down and install it.

If you have never heard of Linux before, there are several sources of basic information about the system. One is the Linux Frequently Asked Questions list (FAQ), available from ftp://sunsite.unc.edu/pub/Linux/docs/FAQ. This document contains many common questions (and answers!) about Linux—it is a "must read" for new users.

In the directory /pub/Linux/docs on sunsite.unc.edu you'll find a number of other documents about Linux, including the Linux INFO-SHEET and META-FAQ, both of which you should read. Also take a look at the USENET newsgroups comp.os.linux.setup and comp.os.linux.answers.

Another source of online Linux documentation is the Linux HOWTO archive on ftp://sunsite.unc.edu/pub/Linux/docs/HOWTO. The file HOWTO-INDEX in that directory explains what Linux HOWTOs are available.

Based on The Linux Installation HOWTO by Matt Welsh, mdw@sunsite.unc.edu v3.3, 11 December 1994

The Linux Documentation Project is writing a set of manuals and books about Linux, all of which are freely distributable on the Net. The directory /pub/Linux/docs/LDP on sunsite.unc.edu contains the current set of LDP manuals.

The book *Linux Installation and Getting Started* is a complete guide to getting and installing Linux, as well as how to use the system once you've installed it. It contains a complete tutorial to using and running the system, and much more information than is contained here. This HOWTO is simply a condensation of some of the most important information in that book. You can get *Linux Installation and Getting Started* from ftp://sunsite.unc.edu/pub/Linux/docs/LDP/install-guide. The README file there describes how you can order a printed copy of the book (about 180 pages).

HTML versions of most of these documents are available at the Linux Documentation Project Homepage at http://sunsite.unc.edu/mdw/linux.html.

If you have questions or comments about this document, please feel free to e-mail Matt Welsh, at mdw@sunsite.unc.edu. I welcome any suggestions, criticism, or postcards. If you find a mistake with this document, please let me know so I can correct it in the next version. Thanks.

Hardware Requirements

What kind of system is needed to run Linux? This is a good question; the actual hardware requirements for the system change periodically. The Linux Hardware-HOWTO gives a (more or less) complete listing of hardware supported by Linux. The Linux INFO-SHEET provides another list. Here is the minimum recommended hardware.

Any ISA, EISA or VESA Local Bus 80386, 80486, or Pentium system will do. Currently, the MicroChannel (MCA) architecture (found on IBM PS/2 machines) is not supported. Many PCI bus systems are supported (see the Linux PCI HOWTO for details). Any CPU from the 386SX to the Pentium will work. You do not need a math coprocessor, although it is nice to have one. I don't recommend using a slower processor than a 486 DX for a Web

server. Also, you should seriously consider employing a machine with a PCI or Vesa Local Bus architecture; I recommend these faster buses, because most of the work that Internet servers do is IO.

You need at least 4 megabytes of memory to run Linux. Technically, Linux will run with only 2 megs, but most installations and software require 4. The more memory you have, the happier you'll be. I suggest 8 or 16 megabytes if you're planning to use X Windows. A Linux platform for a WWW server should have at least 16 megs, and more if you expect a lot of traffic or plan to use X Windows on the same machine.

Of course, you'll need a hard drive and an AT-standard drive controller. All MFM, RLL and IDE drives and controllers should work. Many SCSI drives and adaptors are supported as well; the Linux HARDWARE-HOWTO includes a complete list, and the SCSI-HOWTO contains more information on SCSI under Linux.

Free space on your hard drive is needed as well. The amount of space needed depends on how much software you plan to install. Most installations require somewhere in the ballpark of 40 to 80 megs. This includes space for the software, swap space (used as virtual RAM on your machine), and free space for users, and so on. Of course, if you plan to use your Linux box as your Web server platform, you'll need sufficient disk to hold the content you want to provide.

Linux will co-exist with other operating systems, such as MS-DOS, Microsoft Windows or OS/2, on your hard drive. (In fact you can even access MS-DOS files and run some MS-DOS programs from Linux.) In other words, when partitioning your drive for Linux, MS-DOS or OS/2 live on their own partitions, and Linux exists on its own. We'll go into more detail later.

You do NOT need to be running MS-DOS, OS/2 or any other operating system to use Linux. Linux is a completely different, stand-alone operating system and does not rely on other OS's for installation and use.

You also need a Hercules, CGA, EGA, VGA or Super VGA video card and monitor. In general, if your video card and monitor work under MS-DOS then it should work under Linux. However, if you wish to run X Windows, there are other restrictions on the supported video hardware. The Linux XFree86-HOWTO contains more information about running X and its requirements.

In all, the minimal setup for Linux is not much more than is required for most MS-DOS or MS Windows systems sold today. If you have a 386 or 486 with at least 4 megs of RAM, then you'll be happy running Linux as a personal workstation. Linux does not require huge amounts of diskspace, memory or processor speed. I (used to) run Linux on a 386/16 MHz (the slowest machine you can get) with 4 megs of RAM, and was quite happy. The more you want to do, the more memory (and faster processor) you'll need. In my experience a 486 with 16 megabytes of RAM running Linux outdoes several models of workstation.

Slackware & the Companion CD-ROM

There is no single, standard release of the Linux software—there are many such releases. Each release has its own documentation and installation instructions.

The one packaged on this Companion CD-ROM is the Slackware distribution maintained by Patrick J. Volkerding (volkerdi@mhd1.moorhead.msus.edu). It is one of the most popular distributions available; it is very up-to-date and includes a good amount of software including X Windows, TeX and others. The Slackware distribution consists of a number of "disk sets" (this term is a hold-over from when Slackware was mostly distributed on floppy disk instead of CD-ROM), each one containing a particular type of software (for example, the d disk set contains development tools such as the gcc compiler, and so forth). You can elect to install whatever disk sets you like, and can easily install new ones later.

Slackware Space Requirements

Unfortunately, Slackware does not maintain a complete list of diskspace requirements for each disk set. You need at least 7 megabytes to install just the A series of disks; a very rough estimate of the required diskspace would be 2 or 2.5 megabytes per disk.

The following disk sets are available:

a	The base system. Enough to get up and running and have elvis and comm programs available. Based around the 1.2.3 Linux kernel (4 disks).
ap	Various applications and add ons, such as the manual pages, groff, ispell (GNU and international versions), term, joe, jove, ghostscript, sc, bc, and the quota patches (5 disks).
d	Program development. GCC/G++/Objective C 2.6.3, make (GNU and BSD), byacc and GNU bison, flex, the 4.6.27 C libraries, gdb, kernel source for 1.2.3, SVGAlib, ncurses, clisp, f2c, p2c, m4, perl, rcs (9 disks).
e	GNU Emacs 19.28 (5 disks).
f	A collection of FAQs and other documentation. (2 disks).
i	Info pages for GNU software. Documentation for various programs readable by info or Emacs (2 disks).
iv	InterViews X11 interface libraries, includes files, and the doc (a word-processor) and idraw (draw program) apps (1 disk).
n	Networking. TCP/IP, UUCP, mailx, dip, deliver, elm, pine, smail, cnews, nn, tin, trn (4 disks).
oop	Object Oriented Programming. GNU Smalltalk 1.1.1, and STIX, the Smalltalk Interface to X (1 disk).
q	Kernel source and executable images with different hardware configurations—currently contains Linux 1.2.3 (9 disks).
T	The TeX and LaTeX2e text formatting and type setting systems (10 disks).
tcl	Interpreted languages and X11 toolkits based on TCL: TCL, Tk, TclX, blt, itcl (2 disks).
x	X Windows X11R6. The base XFree86 3.1.1 system, with X11R5 Compatibility libraries, libXpm, fvwm, and xlock added (14 disks).

xap X applications. X11 ghostscript, libgr13, seyon, workman, xfilemanager, GNU chess and xboard, xfm, ghostview, and various X games (3 disks).

xd X11 program development. X11 libraries, server linkkit, PEX support, and man pages for X programming (3 disks).

xv Xview 3.2 release 5. XView libraries, and the Open Look virtual and non-virtual window managers (3 disks).

y Games. The BSD games collection, Sasteroids, both the X11 and SVGA Linux versions of Doom, and Tetris for terminals (3 disks).

You have to install the "a" disk set; the rest are optional. I suggest at least installing the a, ap, and d sets, as well as the x set if you plan to run X Windows. To use your machine as an Internet server, you'll need the "n" disk-set, which includes standard programs for configuring TCP/IP.

The Boot Disk Image

You must boot your machine with Linux to install Slackware; the distribution includes several specially prepared boot disks for this purpose. These disks take the form of raw Linux disk images which you must write to a floppy to create the Slackware boot disk.

Since Linux includes device drivers for so much different hardware, a kernel that included all of them would take an incredible amount of memory. Also, such a boot image might not fit in on a single disk. Also, some hardware drivers conflict with each other in strange ways; it's easier to use a boot floppy image with only certain drivers enabled.

The first thing to do is find the disk image which is appropriate to the hardware on which you're installing Linux. In the top directory of the CD-ROM, there are two directories of boot disks: bootdsks.144 and bootdsks.12. If you have a 1.44 megabyte boot floppy (3.5"), look in the directory bootdsks.144. If you have a 1.2 megabyte boot floppy (5.25"), look in the directory bootdsks.12.

There is a README file in both of these directories describing the machine configuration for which each file in the directory should be used.

Since you're installing Slackware from a CD-ROM, you should choose from the following the boot disk image that supports your particular CD-ROM drive:

Filename	CD-ROM drive type
aztcd.gz	Aztech/Okano/Orchid/Wearnes CD-ROM drives.
cdu31a.gz	Sony CDU31/33a CD-ROM drives.
cdu535.gz	Sony CDU531/535 CD-ROM drives.
idecd.gz	IDE/ATAPI CD-ROM drives.
mitsumi.gz	Mitsumi CD-ROM drives.
sbpcd.gz	SoundBlaster-Pro/Panasonic CD-ROM drives.
scsi.gz	SCSI CD-ROM drives (on supported host adapaters).

All of these boot disks can install Linux on both SCSI and IDE hard-drives. Once you've selected the proper root disk image, copy it from the CD-ROM to your hard-drive.

The directory also contains boot images for installing Slackware from floppies, an MS-DOS partition, or from another machine on an ethernet network which is NFS-exporting it. All of these images support installing to IDE hard drives, and some support SCSI or 8-bit XT drive interfaces as well. Refer to the files README and WHICH.ONE in that directory for the details.

The Root Disk Image

In addition to boot disk, you'll need a root disk to install Slackware from the CD-ROM. The root disk provides basic tools that the Slackware setup program requires to install the system.

You'll find a selection of root disk images in two directories at the top directory of the Companion CD-ROM; look in rootdsks.144 or rootdsks.12 depending on the type of boot floppy drive you have.

If you have a 3.5" boot drive, choose one of the following files:

Filename	Description
color144.gz	The menu-based color installation disk for 1.44 meg drives. Most users should use this rootdisk.
umsds144.gz	A version of the color144 disk for installing with the UMSDOS filesystem, which allows you to install Linux onto a directory of an MS-DOS filesystem. This installation method is not discussed in detail here, but it will prevent you from having to repartition your drive. More on this later.
tty144.gz	The terminal-based installation disk for 1.44 meg drives. You should use color144.gz, but a few people have reported problems with it on their system. If color144.gz doesn't work for you, try tty144.gz instead. It is a bit dated and the installation procedure isn't identical, but it should work if color144.gz doesn't.

If you have a 5.25" boot drive, you have these choices instead:

Filename	Description
colrlite.gz	The menu-based color installation disk for 1.2 meg drives. Some things have been trimmed off of this disk to make it fit on a 1.2 meg floppy, but it should work if you only have a 1.2 meg drive.
umsds12.gz.	A version of the colrlite disk for installing with the UMSDOS filesystem. See the description of umsds144.gz, above.
tty12.gz	The terminal-based installation disk for 1.2 meg drives. Use this rootdisk if you have a 1.2 meg boot floppy and colrlite.gz doesn't work for you.

Inside both of the two rootdisk directories, you'll also find a directory named new-fdisk. You should use the images in this directory if you have a hard-drive larger than 2 GB.

Once you've selected the proper root disk image, copy it from the CD-ROM to your hard-drive.

Creating the Boot & Root Floppies

You must create floppies from the bootdisk and rootdisk images that you've chosen. This is where you need two MS-DOS programs that are included on your CD-ROM in the install directory:

- GZIP.EXE. This is an MS-DOS executable of the gzip compression program used to compress the boot and rootdisk files (the .gz extension on the filenames indicates this).
- RAWRITE.EXE. This is an MS-DOS program that will write the contents of a file (such as the boot and rootdisk images) directly to a floppy, without regard to format. You will use RAWRITE.EXE to create the boot and root floppies.

You only need RAWRITE.EXE and GZIP.EXE if you plan to create the boot and root floppies from an MS-DOS system. If you have access to a UNIX workstation with a floppy drive instead, you can create the floppies from there, using the dd command. See the man page for dd and ask your local UNIX gurus for assistance.

To create the boot and root floppies from an MS-DOS system:

1. Uncompress the bootdisk and rootdisk images using GZIP.EXE. For example, if you're using the scsi.gz bootdisk image, issue the MS-DOS command:

   ```
   C:\> GZIP -D SCSI.GZ
   ```

   This will uncompress bare.gz and leave you with the file bare.
2. Uncompress the rootdisk image. For example, if you are using the rootdisk color144.gz, issue the command:

   ```
   C:\> GZIP -D COLOR144.GZ
   ```

   This will uncompress the file and leave you with color144.
3. Make sure you have two high-density MS-DOS formatted floppies of the same type (that is, if your boot floppy drive is a 3.5" drive, both floppies must be high-density 3.5" disks.)

4. Use RAWRITE.EXE to write the boot and rootdisk images to the floppies. For example, if you're using the scsi.gz bootdisk, use the command:

```
C:\> RAWRITE
```

5. Answer the prompts for the name of the file to write (such as SCSI) and the floppy to write it to (such as A:). RAWRITE will copy the file, block-by-block, directly to the floppy.
6. Use RAWRITE for the root disk image (such as COLOR144).

When you're done, you'll have two floppies: one containing the boot disk, the other containing the root disk. Note that these two floppies will no longer be readable by MS-DOS (they are "Linux format" floppies, in some sense).

Be sure that you're using brand-new, error-free floppies. The floppies must have no bad blocks on them.

You don't need to be running MS-DOS in order to install Slackware. However, running MS-DOS makes it easier to create the boot and root floppies, and it makes it easier to install the software (as you can install directly from an MS-DOS partition on your system). If you are not running MS-DOS on your system, you can use someone else's MS-DOS system just to create the floppies, and install from there.

It is not necessary to use GZIP.EXE and RAWRITE.EXE under MS-DOS to create the boot and root floppies, either. You can use the gzip and dd commands on a UNIX system to do the same job. (For this, you will need a UNIX workstation with a floppy drive, of course.) For example, on a Sun workstation with the floppy drive on device /dev/rfd0, you can use the commands:

```
$ gunzip bare.gz
$ dd if=bare of=/dev/rfd0 obs=18k
```

You must provide the appropriate block size argument (the obs argument) on some workstations (e.g., Suns) or this will fail. If you have problems the man page for dd will be instructive.

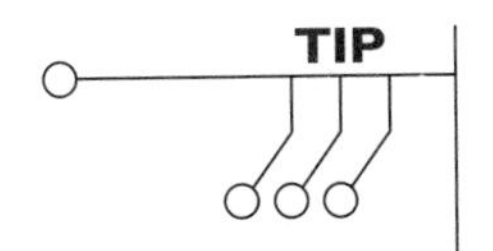

If you need gunzip to write the boot and root disks from a UNIX system, the portable source code is available here: ftp://prep.ai.mit.edu/pub/gnu/gzip.

Installing the Software

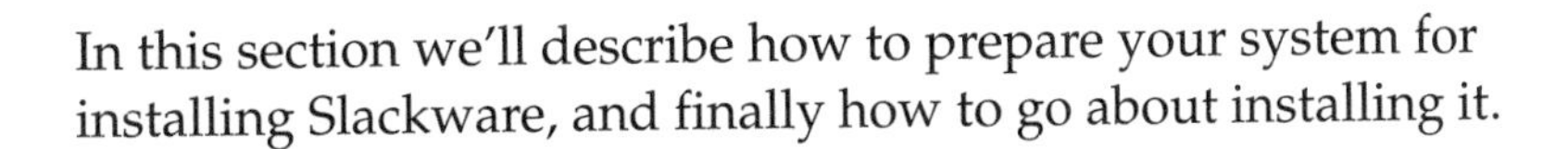

In this section we'll describe how to prepare your system for installing Slackware, and finally how to go about installing it.

Repartitioning

On most systems, the hard drive is already dedicated to partitions for MS-DOS, OS/2 and so on. You need to resize these partitions in order to make space for Linux.

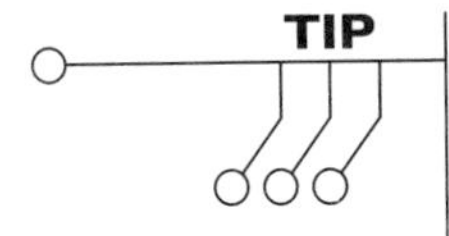

If you use one of the umsds root diskettes, you can install Slackware TO a directory on your MS-DOS partition. (This is different than installing FROM an MS-DOS partition.) Instead, you use the "UMSDOS filesystem", which allows you to treat a directory of your MS-DOS partition as a Linux filesystem. In this way, you don't have to repartition your drive.

I only suggest using this method if your drive has four partitions and repartitioning would be more trouble than it's worth. Or, if you want to try Slackware out before repartitioning, this is a good way to do so. But in most cases you should repartition, as described here. If you do plan to use UMSDOS, you are on your own—it is not documented in detail here. From now on, we assume that you are NOT using UMSDOS, and that you will be repartitioning.

A partition is just a section of the hard drive set aside for a particular operating system to use. If you only have MS-DOS installed, your hard drive probably has just one partition, entirely for MS-DOS. To use Linux, however, you'll need to repartition the drive, so that you have one partition for MS-DOS, and one (or more) for Linux.

Partitions come in three flavors: primary, extended and logical. Briefly, primary partitions are one of the four main partitions on your drive. However, if you wish to have more than four partitions per drive, you need to create an extended partition, which can contain many logical partitions. You don't store data directly on an extended partition—it is used only as a container for logical partitions. Data is stored only on either primary or logical partitions.

To put this another way, most people use only primary partitions. However, if you need more than four partitions on a drive, you create an extended partition. Logical partitions are then created on top of the extended partition, and there you have it—more than four partitions per drive.

Note that you can easily install Linux on the second drive on your system (known as D: to MS-DOS). You simply specify the appropriate device name when creating Linux partitions. This is described in detail below.

Back to repartitioning your drive: The problem with resizing partitions is that there is no way to do it (easily) without deleting the data on those partitions. Therefore, you will need to make a full backup of your system before repartitioning. In order to resize a partition, we simply delete the partition(s), and re-create them with smaller sizes.

Version 2.2.0 of Slackware comes with a non-destructive disk repartitioner available for MS-DOS, called FIPS. Look in the directory install/FIPS. With FIPS, a disk optimizer (such as Norton Speed Disk), and a little bit of luck, you should be able to resize MS-DOS partitions without destroying the data on them, and there is documentation on doing this in install/FIPS/FIPS.DOC. It's still suggested that you make a full backup before attempting to re-partition your drive.

If you're not using FIPS, however, the classic way to modify partitions is with the program FDISK. For example, let's say that you have an 80 meg hard drive, dedicated to MS-DOS. You'd like to split it in half—40 megs for MS-DOS and 40 megs for Linux. In order to do this, you run FDISK under MS-DOS, delete the 80 meg MS-DOS partition, and re-create a 40 meg MS-DOS partition in its place. You can then format the new partition and reinstall your

MS-DOS software from backups. 40 megabytes of the drive is left empty. Later, you create Linux partitions on the unused portion of the drive.

In short, you should do the following to resize MS-DOS partitions with FDISK:

1. Make a full backup of your system.
2. Create an MS-DOS bootable floppy, using a command such as

   ```
   C:\>FORMAT /S A:
   ```

3. Copy the files FDISK.EXE and FORMAT.COM to this floppy, as well as any other utilities that you need. (For example, utilities to recover your system from backup.)
4. Boot the MS-DOS system floppy.
5. Run FDISK, possibly specifying the drive to modify (such as C: or D:).
6. Use the FDISK menu options to delete the partitions which you wish to resize. This will destroy all data on the affected partitions.
7. Use the FDISK menu options to re-create those partitions, with smaller sizes.
8. Exit FDISK and re-format the new partitions with the FORMAT command.
9. Restore the original files from backup.

Note that MS-DOS FDISK will give you an option to create a "logical DOS drive." A logical DOS drive is just a logical partition on your hard drive. You can install Linux on a logical partition, but you don't want to create that logical partition with MS-DOS fdisk. So, if you're currently using a logical DOS drive, and want to install Linux in its place, you should delete the logical drive with MS-DOS FDISK, and (later) create a logical partition for Linux in its place.

The mechanism used to repartition for OS/2 and other operating systems is similar. See the documentation for those operating systems for details.

Creating Partitions for Linux

After repartitioning your drive, you need to create partitions for Linux. Before describing how to do that, we'll talk about partitions and filesystems under Linux.

Filesystems & swap space

Linux requires at least one partition, for the root filesystem, which will hold the Linux software itself.

You can think of a filesystem as a partition formatted for Linux. Filesystems are used to hold files. Every system must have a root filesystem, at least. However, many users prefer to use multiple filesystems—one for each major part of the directory tree. For example, you may wish to create a separate filesystem to hold all files under the /usr directory. (Note that on UNIX systems, forward slashes are used to delimit directories, not backslashes as with MS-DOS.) In this case you have both a root filesystem, and a /usr filesystem.

Each filesystem requires its own partition. Therefore, if you're using both root and /usr filesystems, you'll need to create two Linux partitions.

In addition, most users create a swap partition, which is used for virtual RAM. If you have, say, 4 megabytes of memory on your machine, and a 10-megabyte swap partition, as far as Linux is concerned you have 14 megabytes of virtual memory.

When using swap space, Linux moves unused pages of memory out to disk, allowing you to run more applications at once on your system. However, because swapping is often slow, it's no replacement for real physical RAM. But applications that require a great deal of memory (such as the X Window System) often rely on swap space if you don't have enough physical RAM.

Nearly all Linux users employ a swap partition. If you have 4 megabytes of RAM or less, a swap partition is required to install the software. It is strongly recommended that you have a swap partition anyway, unless you have a great amount of physical RAM.

For Web server platforms, it's best to have twice as much swap space as physical RAM.

The size of your swap partition depends on how much virtual memory you need. It's often suggested that you have at least 16 megabytes of virtual memory total. Therefore, if you have 8 megs of physical RAM, you might want to create an 8-megabyte swap partition. Note that swap partitions can be no larger than 128 megabytes in size. Therefore, if you need more than 128 megs of swap, you must create multiple swap partitions. You may have up to 16 swap partitions in all.

Booting the Installation Disk

The first step is to boot the Slackware bootdisk. Insert the boot disk in the appropriate drive and turn the machine on. After the system boots, you will see the message:

```
Welcome to the Slackware Linux 2.2.0 bootkernel disk!
```

in addition to a screen of instructions.

Here, you are given the opportunity to specify various hardware parameters, such as your SCSI controller IRQ and address, or drive geometry, before booting the Linux kernel. This is necessary in case Linux does not detect your SCSI controller or hard drive geometry, for example.

In particular, many BIOS-less SCSI controllers require you to specify the port address and IRQ at boot time. Likewise, IBM PS/1, ThinkPad, and ValuePoint machines do not store drive geometry in the CMOS, and you must specify it at boot time.

To try booting the kernel without any special parameters, just press Enter at the boot prompt.

Watch the messages as the system boots. If you have a SCSI controller, you should see a listing of the SCSI hosts detected. If you see the message:

```
SCSI: 0 hosts
```

then your SCSI controller was not detected, and you will have to use the following procedure.

Also, the system will display information on the drive partitions and devices detected. If any of this information is incorrect or missing, you will have to force hardware detection.

On the other hand, if all goes well and your hardware seems to be detected, you can skip to the following section, "Loading the Root Disk."

To force hardware detection, you must enter the appropriate parameters at the boot prompt, using the following syntax:

```
ramdisk parameters
```

There are a number of such parameters available; here are some of the most common:

- **hd=*cylinders,heads,sectors*** Specify the drive geometry. Required for systems such as the IBM PS/1, ValuePoint and ThinkPad. For example, if your drive has 683 cylinders, 16 heads and 32 sectors per track, enter:

  ```
  ramdisk hd=683,16,32
  ```

- **tmc8xx=*memaddr,irq*** Specify address and IRQ for BIOS-less Future Domain TMC-8xx SCSI controller. For example,

  ```
  ramdisk tmc8xx=0xca000,5
  ```

Note that the 0x prefix must be used for all values given in hex. This is true for all of the following options.

- **st0x=*memaddr,irq*** Specify address and IRQ for BIOS-less Seagate ST02 controller.
- **tmc8xx=*memaddr,irq*** Specify address and IRQ for BIOS-less Future Domain TMC-8xx controller.
- **t128=*memaddr,irq*** Specify address and IRQ for BIOS-less Trantor T128B controller.
- **ncr5380=*port,irq,dma*** Specify port, IRQ and DMA channel for generic NCR5380 controller.
- **aha152x=*port,irq,scsi_id,reconnect*** Specify port, IRQ and SCSI ID for BIOS-less AIC-6260 controllers. This includes Adaptec 1510, 152x and Soundblaster-SCSI controllers.

For each of these, you must enter "ramdisk" followed by the parameter that you wish to use.

If you have questions about these boot-time options, please read the Linux SCSI-HOWTO. The SCSI HOWTO explains Linux SCSI compatibility in much more detail.

Loading the Root Disk

Once you've booted the kernel, you'll be prompted to enter the Slackware root disk:

```
VFS: Insert ramdisk floppy and press ENTER
```

At this point you should remove the bootdisk from the drive and insert the rootdisk. Then press Enter to go on.

The rootdisk will be loaded into memory, and you should be presented with a login prompt. Login as "root".

```
You may now login as "root".
slackware login: root
#
```

After you have a root prompt, its time to create partitions for Linux. To do this, use the Linux version of the fdisk program:

```
# fdisk drive
```

where *drive* is the name of the drive that you wish to create Linux partitions on. Hard drive device names are:

/dev/hda First IDE drive
/dev/hdb Second IDE drive
/dev/sda First SCSI drive
/dev/sdb Second SCSI drive

For example, to create Linux partitions on the first SCSI drive in your system, use the command

```
# fdisk /dev/sda
```

If you use fdisk without an argument, it will assume /dev/hda.

To create Linux partitions on the second drive on your system, simply specify either /dev/hdb (for IDE drives) or /dev/sdb (for SCSI drives) when running fdisk.

Your Linux partitions don't all have to be on the same drive. You might want to create your root filesystem partition on /dev/hda and your swap partition on /dev/hdb, for example. To do so, just run fdisk once for each drive.

Using fdisk is simple. The command "p" displays your current partition table, "n" creates a new partition, and "d" deletes a partition.

To Linux, partitions are given a name based on the drive which they belong to. For example, the first partition on the drive /dev/hda is /dev/hda1, the second is /dev/hda2, and so on. If you have any logical partitions, they are numbered starting with /dev/hda5, /dev/hda6 and so on up.

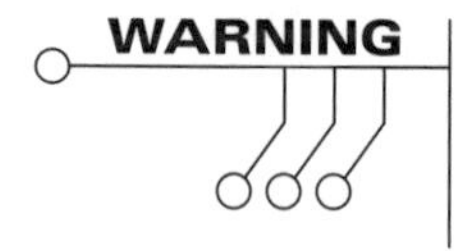

You should not create or delete partitions for operating systems other than Linux with Linux fdisk. That is, don't create or delete MS-DOS partitions with this version of fdisk; use MS-DOS's version of FDISK instead. If you try to create MS-DOS partitions with Linux fdisk, chances are MS-DOS will not recognize the partition and not boot correctly.

Here's an example of using fdisk. Here, we have a single MS-DOS partition using 61693 blocks on the drive, and the rest of the drive is free for Linux. (Under Linux, one block is 1024 bytes. Therefore, 61693 blocks is about 61 megabytes.) We will create two Linux partitions: one for swap, and one for the root filesystem.

First, we use the "p" command to display the current partition table. As you can see, /dev/hda1 (the first partition on /dev/hda) is a DOS partition of 61693 blocks.

```
Command (m for help): p
Disk /dev/hda: 16 heads, 38 sectors, 683 cylinders
Units = cylinders of 608 * 512 bytes
Device Boot Begin  Start   End Blocks  Id System
 /dev/hda1 * 1 1   203  61693  6 DOS 16-bit >=32M
Command (m for help):
```

Next, we use the "n" command to create a new partition. The Linux root partition will be 80 megs in size.

```
Command (m for help): n
Command action
  e  extended
  p  primary partition (1-4)
p
```

Here we're being asked if we want to create an extended or primary partition. In most cases you want to use primary partitions, unless you need more than four partitions on a drive. See the section "Repartitioning," above, for more information.

```
Partition number (1-4): 2
First cylinder (204-683): 204
Last cylinder or +size or +sizeM or +sizeK (204-683): +80M
```

The first cylinder should be the cylinder AFTER where the last partition left off. In this case, /dev/hda1 ended on cylinder 203, so we start the new partition at cylinder 204.

As you can see, if we use the notation "+80M", it specifies a partition of 80 megs in size. Likewise, the notation "+80K" would specify an 80 kilobyte partition, and "+80" would specify just an 80 byte partition.

Next, we create our 10 megabyte swap partition, /dev/hda3.

```
Command (m for help): n
Command action
  e  extended
  p  primary partition (1-4)
p
Partition number (1-4): 3
First cylinder (474-683): 474
Last cylinder or +size or +sizeM or +sizeK (474-683): +10M
```

Again, we display the contents of the partition table. Be sure to write down the information here, especially the size of each partition in blocks. You need this information later.

```
Command (m for help): p
Disk /dev/hda: 16 heads, 38 sectors, 683 cylinders
Units = cylinders of 608 * 512 bytes
Device Boot Begin  Start  End Blocks  Id System
 /dev/hda1 * 1 1   203  61693  6 DOS 16-bit >=32M
 /dev/hda2    204   204   473  82080  83 Linux native
 /dev/hda3    474   474   507  10336  83 Linux native
```

Note that the Linux swap partition (here, /dev/hda3) has type "Linux native". We need to change the type of the swap partition to "Linux swap" so that the installation program will recognize it as such. In order to do this, use the fdisk "t" command:

```
Command (m for help): t
Partition number (1-4): 3
Hex code (type L to list codes): 82
```

If you use "L" to list the type codes, you'll find that 82 is the type corresponding to Linux swap.

To quit fdisk and save the changes to the partition table, use the "w" command. To quit fdisk WITHOUT saving changes, use the "q" command.

After quitting fdisk, the system may tell you to reboot to make sure that the changes took effect. In general there is no reason to reboot after using fdisk—the version of fdisk on the Slackware distribution is smart enough to update the partitions without rebooting.

Preparing the Swap Space

If you have 4 megabytes of RAM (or less) in your machine, you need to create a swap partition (using fdisk) and enable it for use before installing the software. Here, we describe how to format and enable your swap partition(s).

If you have more than 4 megs of RAM, you need only create your partition(s)—it's not necessary to format and enable them before installing the software. In this case you can skip down to the section "Installing the Software."

If you get any "out of memory" errors during the installation procedure you should create a swap partition and enable it as described here.

To prepare the swap space for use, we use the mkswap command. It takes the form:

```
# mkswap -c partition size
```

where partition is the partition name, such as /dev/hda3, and size is the size of the partition in blocks.

For example, if you created the swap partition /dev/hda3 of size 10336 blocks, use the command

```
# mkswap -c /dev/hda3 10336
```

The -c option tells mkswap to check for bad blocks on the partition when preparing the swap space. If you see any "read_intr" error messages during the mkswap operation, this means that bad blocks were found (and flagged). So you can ignore these errors.

To enable swapping on the new device, use the command:

```
# swapon partition
```

For example, for our swap space on /dev/hda3, we use

```
# swapon /dev/hda3
```

We're now swapping with about 10 megabytes more virtual memory.

You should execute mkswap and swapon for each swap partition that you created.

Installing the Software

Installing the Slackware release is very simple; it's almost automatic. You use the setup command, which guides you through a series of menus which allow you to specify the means of installation, the partitions to use, and so forth. Almost everything is automatic.

Here, we're not going to document many of the specifics of using setup, because it changes from time to time. setup is very self-explanatory; it contains its own documentation. Just to give you an idea of what it's like, however, we'll describe what most installations are like using setup.

Before you begin, be sure that you have a high-density MS-DOS formatted floppy on hand. You will use this floppy to create a Linux boot diskette.

After running fdisk (and, perhaps, mkswap and swapon as described above), issue the command:

```
# setup
```

This will present you with a colourful menu with various options such as "Addswap" (to set up your swap space), "Source" (to specify the source of the software to install, such as CD-ROM, floppy or hard drive), "Target" (to specify where to install the software), and so on.

In general, you should go through the menu commands in the following order:

1. Addswap. If you created a swap partition (using fdisk), use the addswap menu option to tell the system about it. This option will present you with a list of possible swap partitions; just type in the name of the swap partition(s) that you wish to use (such as /dev/hda3). The system will then ask you if you want to format the swap partition, which you should do unless you already ran mkswap and swapon on it. That is, you should format the swap partition unless you already formatted and enabled it by hand as described in the previous section.
2. Source. This menu option lets you specify the source for the software to install. You can select several means of installation, such as from floppy or from hard drive. If you are installing from floppies, the system will ask you which floppy drive to use. If you are installing from hard drive, the system will ask you what partition the files are stored on, and what directory they are in.

If you are installing from CD-ROM, the setup program will ask you what type of CD-ROM drive is connected to your system; you should choose the one that goes with the driver on the bootdisk you selected. Once you've selected the appropriate drive type, setup will present you with several installation options. Options other than "slakware" are used with CD-ROM distributions that offer a "live" filesystem on the disk. This feature allows you to run some or all of your system from the CD-ROM, instead of installing it onto your hard drive. Read the Help file for more information.

3. Target. This menu item lets you specify what partition(s) to install the software on. The system will display a list of possible partitions. First you will be asked to enter the name of the root partition, such as /dev/hda2. You will be asked if you want to format the partition; unless you are installing on a partition previously formatted for Linux you should do so. You should use the Second Extended Filesystem (ext2fs) type for the partition.

You will also be given a chance to use additional partitions for different parts of the directory tree. For example, if you created a separate partition for the /usr filesystem, you should enter the name of that partition and the directory that it corresponds to (/usr) when asked.

4. Disksets. This option allows you to specify the disksets you wish to install. Use the arrow keys to scroll through the list; pressing the spacebar selects or deselects a set. Press Return when you're done selecting disk sets.

You may wish to only install a minimal system at this time. That's fine. Only the A diskset is required. After you have installed the software you may run setup to install other disksets.

5. Install. After setting up all of the parameters above, you're ready to install the software. First the system will ask you what type of prompting to use; you should use the "normal" prompting method (unless you're an expert and have modified the installation tagfiles in some way).

The system will simply go through each disk set and install the software. For each software package, a dialog box will be displayed describing the software. Software packages that are required will be installed automatically. For optional software packages you will be given the option of either installing or not installing the package. (If you don't wish to install a certain package now, you can always use setup on your system to install it later.)

While the software is installing, watch out for error messages that may be displayed. The most common error that you're likely to run into is "device full", which means that you have run out of space on your Linux partitions. Unfortunately, the Slackware installation procedure is not quite smart enough to detect this, and will attempt to continue installing the software regardless. If you get any kind of error messages during the installation procedure, you may wish to break out of the installation program (using Ctrl-C) to record them. The only solution for the "device full" problem is to re-create your Linux partitions with different sizes, or attempt to reinstall the software without several of the optional software packages.

After Installation

After installation is complete, and if all goes well, you will be given the option of creating a "standard boot disk", which you can use to boot your newly installed Linux system. For this you will need a blank, high-density MS-DOS formatted diskette of the type that you boot with on your system. Simply insert the disk when prompted and a boot diskette will be created.

You will also be given the chance to install LILO on your hard drive. LILO (which stands for LInux LOader) is a program that will allow you to boot Linux (as well as other operating systems, such as MS-DOS) from your hard drive. If you wish to do this, just select the appropriate menu option and follow the prompts.

If you are using OS/2's Boot Manager, the menu will include an option for configuring LILO for use with the Boot Manager, so that you can boot Linux from it.

Note that this automated LILO installation procedure is not foolproof; there are situations in which this can fail. Be sure that you have a way to boot MS-DOS, Linux and other operating systems from floppy before you attempt to install LILO. If the LILO installation fails you will be able to boot your system from floppy and correct the problem.

More information on configuring LILO is given below.

The post-installation procedure will also take you through several menu items allowing you to configure your system. This includes specifying your modem and mouse device, as well as your time zone. Just follow the menu options.

Booting Your New System

If everything went as planned, you should be able to boot your Linux boot floppy (not the Slackware installation floppy, but the floppy created after installing the software). Or, if you installed LILO, you should be able to boot from the hard drive. After booting, login as root. Congratulations! You have your very own Linux system.

If you are booting using LILO, try holding down shift or control during boot. This will present you with a boot prompt; press tab to see a list of options. In this way you can boot Linux, MS-DOS, or whatever directly from LILO.

After booting your system and logging in as root, one of the first things you should do is create an account for yourself. The adduser command may be used for this purpose. For example,

```
# adduser
Login to add (^C to quit): ebersol
Full Name: Norbert Ebersol
GID [100]: 100
UID [501]: 501
Home Directory [/home/ebersol]: /home/ebersol
Shell [/bin/bash]: /bin/bash
Password [ebersol]: new.password
Information for new user [ebersol]:
Home directory: [/home/ebersol] Shell: [/bin/bash]
Password: [new.password] UID: [502] GID:[100]
Is this correct? [y/n]: y
```

adduser will prompt you for various parameters, such as the username, full name, GID (group ID), UID (user ID), and so on. For the most part you can use the defaults. If you're unfamiliar with creating users on a UNIX system, I strongly suggest getting a book on UNIX systems administration. It will help you greatly in setting up and using your new system.

You can now login as the new user. You can use the keys Alt-F1 through Alt-F8 to switch between virtual consoles, which will allow you to login multiple times from the console. The passwd command can be used to set the passwords on your new accounts; you should set a password for root and any new users that you create.

Also, the hostname of your machine is set at boot time in the file /etc/rc.d/rc.M. You should edit this file (as root) to change the hostname of the machine. You should edit the lines in this file which run the commands hostname or hostname_notcp. (The default hostname is darkstar.) You may also wish to edit the domainname commands in this file, if you are on a TCP/IP network. (On most Slackware systems the hostname and domain name are set in the file /etc/HOSTNAME, so editing this file will probably suffice.)

Obviously, there are many more things to setup and configure. A good book on UNIX systems administration should help. (I suggest Essential Systems Administration from O'Reilly and Associates.) You will pick these things up as time goes by. You should read various other Linux HOWTOs, such as the NET-2-HOWTO and Printing-HOWTO, for information on other configuration tasks.

After that, the system is all yours... have fun!

Configuring LILO

LILO is a boot loader, which can be used to select either Linux, MS-DOS, or some other operating system at boot time. If you install LILO as the primary boot loader, it will handle the first-stage booting process for all operating systems on your drive. This works well if MS-DOS is the only other operating system that you have installed. However, you might be running OS/2, which has it's own Boot Manager. In this case, you want OS/2's Boot Manager to be the primary boot loader, and use LILO just to boot Linux (as the secondary boot loader).

The Slackware installation procedure allows you to install and configure LILO. However, this method doesn't seem to be smart enough to handle several peculiar situations. It might be easier in some cases to configure LILO by hand.

In order to set up LILO for your system, just edit the file /etc/lilo.conf. Below we present an example of a LILO configuration file, where the Linux root partition is on /dev/hda2, and MS-DOS is installed on /dev/hdb1 (on the second hard drive).

```
# Tell LILO to install itself as the primary boot loader on /dev/hda.
boot = /dev/hda
# The boot image to install; you probably shouldn't change this
install = /boot/boot.b
# Do some optimization. Doesn't work on all systems.
compact
```

```
# The stanza for booting Linux.
image = /vmlinuz # The kernel is in /vmlinuz
 label = linux # Give it the name "linux"
 root = /dev/hda2 # Use /dev/hda2 as the root filesystem
 vga = ask  # Prompt for VGA mode
 append = "aha152x=0x340,11,7,1"
# Add this to the boot options,
# for detecting the SCSI controller
# The stanza for booting MS-DOS
other = /dev/hdb1
# This is the MS-DOS partition
 label = msdos
# Give it the name "msdos"
 table = /dev/hdb
# The partition table for the second drive
```

Once you've edited the /etc/lilo.conf file, run /sbin/lilo as root. This will install LILO on your drive. Note that you must rerun /sbin/lilo anytime that you recompile your kernel (something that you don't need to worry about just now, but keep it in mind).

Note how we use the append option in /etc/lilo.conf to specify boot parameters as we did when booting the Slackware bootdisk.

You can now reboot your system from the hard drive. By default LILO will boot the operating system listed first in the configuration file, which in this case is Linux. In order to bring up a boot menu, to select another operating system, hold down shift or ctrl while the system boots; you should see a prompt such as

```
Boot:
```

Here, enter either the name of the operating system to boot (given by the label line in the configuration file; in this case, either linux or msdos), or press tab to get a list.

Now let's say that you want to use LILO as the secondary boot loader; if you want to boot Linux from OS/2's Boot Manager, for example. In order to boot a Linux partition from OS/2 Boot Manager, unfortunately, you must create the partition using OS/2's FDISK (not Linux's), and format the partition as FAT or HPFS, so that OS/2 knows about it.

In order to have LILO boot Linux from OS/2 Boot Manager, you only want to install LILO on your Linux root filesystem (in the above example, /dev/hda2). In this case, your LILO config file should look something like:

```
boot = /dev/hda2
install = /boot/boot.b
compact
image = /vmlinuz
label = linux
root = /dev/hda2
vga = ask
```

Note the change in the boot line. After running /sbin/lilo you should be able to add the Linux partition to Boot Manager. This mechanism should work for boot loaders used by other operating systems as well.

Miscellaneous

If you would like a more complete discussion of Linux installation (instead of the "quick" examples given here), read the book *Linux Installation and Getting Started*, from sunsite.unc.edu in /pub/Linux/docs/LDP. This book includes a complete discussion of how to obtain and install Linux, as well as a basic UNIX and systems administration tutorial for new users.

You can also buy *Running Linux*, an in-depth look at Linux use, programming, and system and network management.

Please e-mail me at mdw@sunsite.unc.edu if any part of this document is confusing or incorrect. I depend on feedback from readers in order to maintain this document! I also like to help answer questions about Linux installation, if you have any.
I'd like to thank Patrick Volkerding for his work on the Slackware distribution and assistance in preparing this document.
Best of luck with your new Linux system!
Cheers, mdw

The Linux XFree86 HOWTO

The X Window System is a large and powerful (and somewhat complex) graphics environment for UNIX systems. The original X Window System code was developed at MIT; commercial vendors have since made X the industry standard for UNIX platforms. Virtually every UNIX workstation in the world runs some variant of the X Window system.

A free port of the MIT X Window System version 11, release 6 (X11R6) for 80386/80486/Pentium UNIX systems has been developed by a team of programmers originally headed by David Wexelblat (dwex@XFree86.org). The release, known as XFree86, is available for System V/386, 386BSD, and other x86 UNIX implementations, including Linux. It includes all of the required binaries, support files, libraries, and tools.

In this document, we'll give a step-by-step description of how to install and configure XFree86 for Linux, but you will have to fill in some of the details yourself by reading the documentation released with XFree86 itself. (This documentation is discussed below.) However, using and customizing the X Window System is far beyond the scope of this document—for this purpose you should obtain one of the many good books on using the X Window System.

From Matt Welsh, mdw@sunsite.unc.edu, v3.0, 15 March 1995. This document describes how to obtain, install, and configure version 3.1.1 of the XFree86 version of the X Window System (X11R6) for Linux systems. It is a step-by-step guide to configuring XFree86 on your system.

2. Hardware Requirements

As of XFree86 version 3.1.1, released in February 1995, the following video chipsets are supported. The documentation included with your video adaptor should specify the chipset used. If you are in the market for a new video card, or are buying a new machine that comes with a video card, have the vendor find out exactly what the make, model, and chipset of the video card is. This may require the vendor to call technical support on your behalf; in general vendors will be happy to do this. Many PC hardware vendors will state that the video card is a "standard SVGA card" which "should work" on your system. Explain that your software (mention Linux and XFree86!) does not support all video chipsets and that you must have detailed information.

You can also determine your videocard chipset by running the SuperProbe program included with the XFree86 distribution. This is covered in more detail below.

The following standard SVGA chipsets are supported:

- Tseng ET3000, ET4000AX, ET4000/W32
- Western Digital/Paradise PVGA1
- Western Digital WD90C00, WD90C10, WD90C11, WD90C24, WD90C30, WD90C31, WD90C33
- Genoa GVGA
- Trident TVGA8800CS, TVGA8900B, TVGA8900C, TVGA8900CL, TVGA9000, TVGA9000i, TVGA9100B, TVGA9200CX, TVGA9320, TVGA9400CX, TVGA9420
- ATI 18800, 18800-1, 28800-2, 28800-4, 28800-5, 28800-6, 68800-3, 68800-6, 68800AX, 68800LX, 88800
- NCR 77C22, 77C22E, 77C22E+
- Cirrus Logic CLGD5420, CLGD5422, CLGD5424, CLGD5426, CLGD5428, CLGD5429, CLGD5430, CLGD5434, CLGD6205, CLGD6215, CLGD6225, CLGD6235, CLGD6420
- Compaq AVGA

- OAK OTI067, OTI077
- Avance Logic AL2101
- MX MX68000, MX680010
- Video 7/Headland Technologies HT216-32

The following SVGA chipsets with accelerated features are also supported:

- 8514/A (and true clones)
- ATI Mach8, Mach32
- Cirrus CLGD5420, CLGD5422, CLGD5424, CLGD5426, CLGD5428, CLGD5429, CLGD5430, CLGD5434, CLGD6205, CLGD6215, CLGD6225, CLGD6235
- S3 86C911, 86C924, 86C801, 86C805, 86C805i, 86C928, 86C864, 86C964
- Western Digital WD90C31, WD90C33
- Weitek P9000
- IIT AGX-014, AGX-015, AGX-016
- Tseng ET4000/W32, ET4000/W32i, ET4000/W32p

Video cards using these chipsets are supported on all bus types, including VLB and PCI.

All of the above are supported in both 256 color and monochrome modes, with the exception of the Avance Logic, MX and Video 7 chipsets, which are only supported in 256 color mode. If your video card has enough DRAM installed, many of the above chipsets are supported in 16 and 32 bits-per-pixel mode (specifically, some Mach32, P9000, S3 and Cirrus boards). The usual configuration is 8 bits per pixel (that is, 256 colors).

The monochrome server also supports generic VGA cards, the Hercules monochrome card, the Hyundai HGC1280, Sigma LaserView, and Apollo monochrome cards. On the Compaq AVGA, only 64k of video memory is supported for the monochrome server, and the GVGA has not been tested with more than 64k.

This list will undoubtedly expand as time passes. The release notes for the current version of XFree86 should contain the complete list of supported video chipsets.

One problem faced by the XFree86 developers is that some video card manufacturers use non-standard mechanisms for determining clock frequencies used to drive the card. Some of these manufacturers either don't release specifications describing how to program the card, or they require developers to sign a non-disclosure statement to obtain the information. This would obviously restrict the free distribution of the XFree86 software, something that the XFree86 development team is not willing to do. For a long time, this has been a problem with certain video cards manufactured by Diamond, but as of release 3.1 of XFree86, Diamond has started to work with the development team to release free drivers for these cards.

The suggested setup for XFree86 under Linux is a 486 machine with at least 8 megabytes of RAM, and a video card with a chipset listed above. For optimal performance, we suggest using an accelerated card, such as an S3-chipset card. You should check the documentation for XFree86 and verify that your particular card is supported before taking the plunge and purchasing expensive hardware. Benchmark ratings comparisons for various video cards under XFree86 are posted routinely to the USENET newsgroups comp.windows.x.i386unix and comp.os.linux.x.

As a side note, my personal Linux system is a 486DX2-66, 20 megabytes of RAM, and is equipped with a VLB S3-864 chipset card with 2 megabytes of DRAM. I have run X benchmarks on this machine as well as on Sun Sparc IPX workstations. The Linux system is roughly 7 times faster than the Sparc IPX (for the curious, XFree86-3.1 under Linux, with this video card, runs at around 171,000 xstones; the Sparc IPX at around 24,000). In general, XFree86 on a Linux system with an accelerated SVGA card will give you much greater performance than that found on commercial UNIX workstations (which usually employ simple framebuffers for graphics).

Your machine will need at least 4 megabytes of physical RAM, and 16 megabytes of virtual RAM (for example, 8 megs physical and 8 megs swap). Remember that the more physical RAM that you have, the less that the system will swap to and from disk when memory is low. Because swapping is inherently slow (disks are very slow compared to memory), having 8 megabytes of RAM or more is necessary to run XFree86 comfortably. A system with 4 megabytes of physical RAM could run much (up to 10 times) more slowly than one with 8 megs or more.

3. Installing XFree86

The Linux binary distribution of XFree86 can be found on a number of FTP sites. On sunsite.unc.edu, it is found in the directory /pub/Linux/X11. (As of the time of this writing, the current version is 3.1.1; newer versions are released periodically.)

It's quite likely that you obtained XFree86 as part of a Linux distribution, in which case downloading the software separately is not necessary.

If you are downloading XFree86 directly, this table lists the files in the XFree86-3.1 distribution.

One of the following servers is required:

- XF86-3.1.1-8514.tar.gz Server for 8514-based boards.
- XF86-3.1.1-AGX.tar.gz Server for AGX-based boards.
- XF86-3.1.1-Mach32.tar.gz Server for Mach32-based boards.
- XF86-3.1.1-Mach8.tar.gz Server for Mach8-based boards.
- XF86-3.1.1-Mono.tar.gz Server for monochrome video modes.
- XF86-3.1.1-P9000.tar.gz Server for P9000-based boards.
- XF86-3.1.1-S3.tar.gz Server for S3-based boards.
- XF86-3.1.1-SVGA.tar.gz Server for Super VGA-based boards.
- XF86-3.1.1-VGA16.tar.gz Server for VGA/EGA-based boards.
- XF86-3.1.1-W32.tar.gz Server for ET4000/W32-based boards.

All of the following files are required:

- XF86-3.1.1-bin.tar.gz The rest of the X11R6 binaries.
- XF86-3.1.1-cfg.tar.gz Config files for xdm, xinit and fs.

- XF86-3.1.1-doc.tar.gz Documentation and manpages.
- XF86-3.1.1-inc.tar.gz Include files.
- XF86-3.1.1-lib.tar.gz Shared X libraries and support files.
- XF86-3.1-fnt.tar.gz Basic fonts.

The following files are optional:

- XF86-3.1-ctrb.tar.gz Selected contrib programs.
- XF86-3.1-extra.tar.gz Extra XFree86 servers and binaries.
- XF86-3.1-lkit.tar.gz Server linkkit for customization.
- XF86-3.1-fnt75.tar.gz 75-dpi screen fonts.
- XF86-3.1-fnt100.tar.gz 100-dpi screen fonts.
- XF86-3.1-fntbig.tar.gz Large Kanji and other fonts.
- XF86-3.1-fntscl.tar.gz Scaled fonts (Speedo, Type1).
- XF86-3.1-man.tar.gz Manual pages.
- XF86-3.1-pex.tar.gz PEX binaries, includes and libraries.
- XF86-3.1-slib.tar.gz Static X libraries and support files.
- XF86-3.1-usrbin.tar.gz Daemons which reside in/usr/bin.
- XF86-3.1-xdmshdw.tar.gz Shadow password version of xdm.

The XFree86 directory should contain README files and installation notes for the current version.

All that is required to install XFree86 is to obtain the above files, create the directory /usr/X11R6 (as root), and unpack the files from /usr/X11R6 like this:

```
# mkdir /usr/X11R6
# cd /usr/X11R6
# gzip -dc XF86-3.1.1-bin.tar.gz | tar xfB -
```

Remember that these tar files are packed relative to /usr/X11R6, so it's important to unpack the files there.

After unpacking the files, you first need to link the file /usr/X11R6/bin/X to the server that you're using. For example, if you wish to use the SVGA color server, /usr/bin/X11/X should be linked to /usr/X11R6/bin/XF86_SVGA. If you wish to use the

monochrome server instead, relink this file to XF86_MONO with the command

```
# ln -sf /usr/X11R6/bin/XF86_MONO /usr/X11R6/bin/X
```

The same holds true if you are using one of the other servers.

If you aren't sure which server to use, or don't know your video card chipset, you can run the SuperProbe program found in /usr/X11R6/bin (included in the XF86-3.1-bin listed above). This program will attempt to determine your video chipset type and other information; write down its output for later reference.

You need to make sure that /usr/X11R6/bin is on your path. This can be done by editing your system default /etc/profile or /etc/csh.login (based on the shell that you, or other users on your system, use). Or you can simply add the directory to your personal path by modifying /etc/.bashrc or /etc/.cshrc, based on your shell.

You also need to make sure that /usr/X11R6/lib can be located by ld.so, the runtime linker. To do this, add the line

```
/usr/X11R6/lib
```

to the file /etc/ld.so.conf, and run /sbin/ldconfig, as root.

4. Configuring XFree86

Setting up XFree86 is not difficult in most cases. However, if you happen to be using hardware for which drivers are under development, or wish to obtain the best performance or resolution from an accelerated graphics card, configuring XFree86 can be somewhat time-consuming. In this section we will describe how to create and edit the XF86Config file, which configures the XFree86 server. In many cases it is best to start out with a "basic" XFree86 configuration, one which uses a low resolution, such as 640x480, which should be supported on all video cards and monitor types. Once you have XFree86 working at a lower, standard resolution, you can tweak the configuration to exploit the capabilities of your video hardware. The idea is that you want to know that XFree86 works at all on your system, and that something isn't wrong with your installation, before attempting the sometimes difficult task of setting up XFree86 for real use.

In addition to the information listed here, you should read the following documentation:

- The XFree86 documentation in /usr/X11R6/lib/X11/doc (contained within the XFree86-3.1-doc package). You should especially see the file README.Config, which is an XFree86 configuration tutorial.
- Several video chipsets have separate README files in the above directory (such as README.Cirrus and README.S3). Read one of these if applicable.
- The man page for XFree86.
- The man page for XF86Config.
- The man page for the particular server that you are using (such as XF86_SVGA or XF86_S3).

The main XFree86 configuration file is /usr/X11R6/lib/X11/XF86Config. This file contains information on your mouse, video card parameters, and so on. The file XF86Config.eg is provided with the XFree86 distribution as an example. Copy this file to XF86Config and edit it as a starting point.

The XF86Config man page explains the format of this file in detail. Read this man page now, if you have not done so already.

We are going to present a sample XF86Config file, piece by piece. This file may not look exactly like the sample file included in the XFree86 distribution, but the structure is the same.

Note that the XF86Config file format may change with each version of XFree86; this information is only valid for XFree86 version 3.1.1.

Also, you should not simply copy the configuration file listed here to your own system and attempt to use it. Attempting to use a configuration file which doesn't correspond to your hardware could drive the monitor at a frequency which is too high for it; there have been reports of monitors (especially fixed-frequency monitors) being damaged or destroyed by using an incorrectly configured XF86Config file. The bottom line is this: *Make absolutely sure that your XF86Config file corresponds to your hardware before you attempt to use it.*

Each section of the XF86Config file is surrounded by the pair of lines

```
Section "section-name"
EndSection
```

The first part of the XF86Config file is Files, which looks like this:

```
Section "Files"
  RgbPath    "/usr/X11R6/lib/X11/rgb"
  FontPath   "/usr/X11R6/lib/X11/fonts/misc/"
  FontPath   "/usr/X11R6/lib/X11/fonts/75dpi/"
EndSection
```

The RgbPath line sets the path to the X11R6 RGB color database, and each FontPath line sets the path to a directory containing X11 fonts. In general you shouldn't have to modify these lines; just be sure that there is a FontPath entry for each font type that you have installed (that is, for each directory in /usr/X11R6/lib/X11/fonts).

The next section is ServerFlags, which specifies several global flags for the server. In general this section is empty.

```
Section "ServerFlags"
 # Uncomment this to cause a core dump at the spot where a signal is
 # received.  This may leave the console in an unusable state, but may
 # provide a better stack trace in the core dump to aid in debugging
 #    NoTrapSignals
 # Uncomment this to disable the <Crtl><Alt><BS> server abort sequence
 #    DontZap
EndSection
```

Here, we have all lines within the section commented out.

The next section is Keyboard. This should be fairly intuitive.

```
Section "Keyboard"
  Protocol    "Standard"
  AutoRepeat  500 5
  ServerNumLock
EndSection
```

Other options are available as well—see the XF86Config file if you wish to modify the keyboard configuration. The above should work for most systems.

The next section is Pointer, which specifies parameters for the mouse device.

```
Section "Pointer"
 Protocol  "MouseSystems"
 Device  "/dev/mouse"
# Baudrate and SampleRate are only for some Logitech mice
#    BaudRate   9600
#    SampleRate 150
# Emulate3Buttons is an option for 2-button Microsoft mice
#    Emulate3Buttons
# ChordMiddle is an option for some 3-button Logitech mice
#    ChordMiddle
EndSection
```

The only options that you should concern yourself with now are Protocol and Device. Protocol specifies the mouse protocol that your mouse uses (not the make or brand of mouse). Valid types for Protocol (under Linux—there are other options available for other operating systems) are:

- BusMouse
- Logitech
- Microsoft
- MMSeries
- Mouseman
- MouseSystems
- PS/2
- MMHitTab

BusMouse should be used for the Logitech busmouse. Note that older Logitech mice should use Logitech, but newer Logitech mice use either Microsoft or Mouseman protocols. This is a case in which the protocol doesn't necessarily have anything to do with the make of the mouse.

Device specifies the device file where the mouse can be accessed. On most Linux systems, this is /dev/mouse. /dev/mouse is usually a link to the appropriate serial port (such as /dev/cua0) for serial mice, or to the appropriate busmouse device for busmice. At any rate, be sure that the device file listed in Device exists.

The next section is Monitor, which specifies the characteristics of your monitor. As with other sections in the XF86Config file, there may be more than one Monitor section. This is useful if you have multiple monitors connected to a system, or use the same XF86Config file under multiple hardware configurations. In general, though, you will need a single Monitor section.

```
Section "Monitor"
 Identifier  "CTX 5468 NI"
 #     These values are for a CTX 5468NI only! Don't attempt to use
 #     them with your monitor (unless you have this model)
 Bandwidth      60
 HorizSync      30-38,47-50
 VertRefresh  50-90
  # Modes: Name  dotclock  horiz  vert
  ModeLine "640x480"  25    640 664 760 800 480 491 493 525
  ModeLine "800x600"  36    800 824 896 1024 600 601 603 625
  ModeLine "1024x768" 65    1024 1088 1200 1328 768 783 789 818
 EndSection
```

The Identifier line is used to give an arbitrary name to the Monitor entry. This can be any string; you will use it to refer to the Monitor entry later in the XF86Config file.

HorizSync specifies the valid horizontal sync frequencies for your monitor, in kHz. If you have a multisync monitor, this can be a range of values (or several comma-separated ranges), as seen above. If you have a fixed-frequency monitor, this will be a list of discrete values, such as:

```
HorizSync      31.5, 35.2, 37.9, 35.5,      48.95
```

Your monitor manual should list these values in the technical specifications section. If you do not have this information available, you should either contact the manufacturer or vendor of your monitor to obtain it.

VertRefresh specifies the valid vertical refresh rates (or vertical synchronization frequencies) for your monitor, in Hz. Like HorizSync this can be a range or a list of discrete values; your monitor manual should list them.

HorizSync and VertRefresh are used only to double-check that the monitor resolutions that you specify are in valid ranges. This is to reduce the chance that you will damage your monitor by attempting to drive it at a frequency for which it was not designed.

The ModeLine directive is used to specify a single resolution mode for your monitor. The format of ModeLine is

```
ModeLine name clock horiz-values vert-values
```

name is an arbitrary string, which you will use to refer to the resolution mode later in the file. clock is the driving clock frequency, or "dot clock" associated with the resolution mode. A dot clock is usually specified in MHz, and is the rate at which the video card must send pixels to the monitor at this resolution. horiz-values and vert-values are four numbers each which specify when the electron gun of the monitor should fire, and when the horizontal and vertical sync pulses fire during a sweep.

How can you determine the ModeLine values for your monitor? The file VideoModes.doc, included with the XFree86 distribution, describes in detail how to determine these values for each resolution mode that your monitor supports. First of all, clock must correspond to one of the dot clock values that your video card can produce. Later in the XF86Config file you will specify these clocks; you can only use video modes which have a clock value supported by your video card.

There are two files included in the XFree86 distribution which may include ModeLine data for your monitor. These files are modeDB.txt and Monitors, both of which are found in /usr/X11R6/lib/X11/doc.

You should start with ModeLine values for the VESA standard monitor timings, which most monitors support. modeDB.txt includes timing values for VESA standard resolutions. In that file, you will see entries such as

```
# 640x480@60Hz Non-Interlaced mode
# Horizontal Sync = 31.5kHz
# Timing: H=(0.95us, 3.81us, 1.59us), V=(0.35ms, 0.064ms, 1.02ms)
#
# name      clock   horizontal timing   vertical timing flags
"640x480"   25.175  640 664 760 800     480 491 493 525
```

This is a VESA standard timing for a 640x480 video mode. It uses a dot clock of 25.175, which your video card must support to use this mode (more on this later). To include this entry in the XF86Config file, you'd use the line

```
ModeLine "640x480" 25.175 640 664 760 800 480 491 493 525
```

Note that the name argument to ModeLine (in this case "640x480") is an arbitrary string—the convention is to name the mode after the resolution, but name can technically be anything descriptive which describes the mode to you.

For each ModeLine used the server will check that the specifications for the mode fall within the range of values specified with Bandwidth, HorizSync and VertRefresh. If they do not, the server will complain when you attempt to start up X (more on this later). For one thing, the dot clock used by the mode should not be greater than the value used for Bandwidth. (However, in many cases it is safe to use modes with a slightly higher bandwidth than your monitor can support.)

If the VESA standard timings do not work for you (you'll know after trying to use them later) then the files modeDB.txt and Monitors include specific mode values for many monitor types. You can create ModeLine entries from the values found in those two files as well. Be sure to only use values for the specific model of monitor that you have. Note that many 14- and 15-inch monitors cannot support higher resolution modes, and often resolutions of 1024x768 at low dot clocks. This means that if you can't find high resolution modes for your monitor in these files, then your monitor probably does not support those resolution modes.

If you are completely at a loss, and can't find working ModeLine values for your monitor, you can follow the instructions in the VideoModes.doc file included in the XFree86 distribution to generate ModeLine values from the specifications listed in your monitor's manual. While your mileage will certainly vary when attempting to generate ModeLine values by hand, this is a good place to look if you can't find the values that you need. VideoModes.doc also describes the format of the ModeLine directive and other aspects of the XFree86 server in gory detail.

Lastly, if you do obtain ModeLine values which are almost, but not quite, right, then it may be possible to simply modify the values slightly to obtain the desired result. For example, if while running XFree86 the image on the monitor is shifted slightly, or seems to "roll", you can follow the instructions in the VideoModes.doc file to try to fix these values. Also, be sure to check the knobs and controls on the monitor itself! In many cases it is necessary to change the horizontal or vertical size of the display after starting up XFree86 in order for the image to be centered and be of the appropriate size. Having these controls on the front of the monitor can certainly make life easier.

You shouldn't use monitor timing values or ModeLine values for monitors other than the model that you own. If you attempt to drive the monitor at a frequency for which it was not designed, you can damage or even destroy it.

The next section of the XF86Config file is Device, which specifies parameters for your video card. Here is an example.

```
Section "Device"
   Identifier "#9 GXE 64"
   # Nothing yet; we fill in these values later.
EndSection
```

This section defines properties for a particular video card. Identifier is an arbitrary string describing the card; you will use this string to refer to the card later.

Initially, you don't need to include anything in the Device section, except for Identifier. This is because we will be using the X server itself to probe for the properties of the video card, and entering them into the Device section later. The XFree86 server is capable of probing for the video chipset, clocks, RAMDAC, and amount of video RAM on the board.

Before we do this, however, we need to finish writing the XF86Config file. The next section is Screen, which specifies the monitor/video card combination to use for a particular server.

```
Section "Screen"
  Driver        "Accel"
  Device        "#9 GXE 64"
  Monitor       "CTX 5468 NI"
```

```
Subsection "Display"
 Depth     16
 Modes     "1024x768" "800x600" "640x480"
 ViewPort  0 0
 Virtual   1024 768
 EndSubsection
EndSection
```

The Driver line specifies the X server that you will be using. The values for Driver are:

- Accel: For the XF86_S3, XF86_Mach32, XF86_Mach8, XF86_8514, XF86_P9000, XF86_AGX, and XF86_W32 servers;
- SVGA: For the XF86_SVGA server;
- VGA16: For the XF86_VGA16 server;
- VGA2: For the XF86_Mono server;
- Mono: For the non-VGA monochrome drivers in the XF86_Mono and XF86_VGA16 servers.

You should be sure that /usr/X11R6/bin/X is a symbolic link to the server that you are using. For example, if you have an S3 video card:

```
# ln -sf /usr/X11R6/bin/XF86_S3 /usr/X11R6/bin/X
```

The Device line specifies the Identifier of the Device section corresponding to the video card to use for this server. Above, we created a Device section with the line

```
Identifier "#9 GXE 64"
```

Therefore, we use “#9 GXE 64” on the Device line here.

Similarly, the Monitor line specifies the name of the Monitor section to be used with this server. Here, “CTX 5468 NI” is the Identifier used in the Monitor section described above.

Subsection “Display” defines several properties of the XFree86 server corresponding to your monitor/video card combination. The XF86Config file describes all of these options in detail; most of them are icing on the cake and not necessary to get the system working.

The options that you should know about are:

- **Depth.** Defines the number of color planes—the number of bits per pixel. Usually, Depth is set to 8. For the VGA16 server, you would use a depth of 4, and for the monochrome server a depth of 1. If you are using an accelerated video card with enough memory to support more bits per pixel, you can set Depth to 16, 24, or 32. If you have problems with depths higher than 8, set it back to 8 and attempt to debug the problem later.
- **Modes.** This is the list of video mode names that have been defined using the ModeLine directive in the Monitor section. In the above section, we used ModeLines named "1024x768", "800x600", and "640x480". Therefore, we use a Modes line of

```
Modes "1024x768" "800x600" "640x480"
```

  The first mode listed on this line will be the default when XFree86 starts up. After XFree86 is running, you can switch between the modes listed here using the keys ctrl-alt-numeric + and ctrl-alt-numeric -.

  It might be best, when initially configuring XFree86, to use lower resolution video modes, such as 640x480, which tend to work on most systems. Once you have the basic configuration working you can modify XF86Config to support higher resolutions.

- **Virtual.** Sets the virtual desktop size. XFree86 has the ability to use any additional memory on your video card to extend the size of your desktop. When you move the mouse pointer to the edge of the display, the desktop will scroll, bringing the additional space into view. Therefore, even if you are running at a lower video resolution such as 800x600, you can set Virtual to the total resolution which your video card can support (a 1-megabyte video card can support 1024x768 at a depth of 8 bits per pixel; a 2-megabyte card 1280x1024 at depth 8, or 1024x768 at depth 16). Of course, the entire area will not be visible at once, but it can still be used.

The Virtual feature is a nice way to utilize the memory of your video card, but it is rather limited. If you want to use a true virtual desktop, we suggest using fvwm, or a similar window manager, instead. fvwm allows you to have rather large virtual desktops (implemented by hiding windows, and so forth, instead of actually storing the entire desktop in video memory at once). See the man pages for fvwm for more details about this; most Linux systems use fvwm by default.

- **ViewPort.** If you are using the Virtual option described above, ViewPort sets the coordinates of the upper-left-hand corner of the virtual desktop when XFree86 starts up. Virtual 0 0 is often used; if this is unspecified then the desktop is centered on the virtual desktop display (which may be undesirable to you).

  Many other options for this section exist; see the XF86Config man page for a complete description. In practice these other options are not necessary to get XFree86 initially working.

5. Filling in Video Card Information

Your XF86Config file is now ready to go, with the exception of complete information on the video card. What we're going to do is use the X server to probe for the rest of this information, and fill it into XF86Config.

Instead of probing for this information with the X server, the XF86Config values for many cards are listed in the files modeDB.txt, AccelCards, and Devices. These files are all found in /usr/X11R6/lib/X11/doc. In addition, there are various README files for certain chipsets. You should look in these files for information on your video card, and use that information (the clock values, chipset type, and any options) in the XF86Config file. If any information is missing, you can probe for it as described here.

In these examples we will demonstrate configuration for a #9 GXE 64 video card, which uses the XF86_S3 chipset. This card happens to be the one which the author uses, but the discussion here applies to any video card.

The first thing to do is to determine the video chipset used on the card. Running SuperProbe (found in /usr/X11R6/bin) will tell you this information, but you need to know the chipset name as it is known to the X server.

To do this, run the command

```
$ X -showconfig
```

This will give the chipset names known to your X server. (The man pages for each X server list these as well.) For example, with the accelerated XF86_S3 server, we obtain:

```
XFree86 Version 3.1.1 / X Window System
(protocol Version 11, revision 0, vendor release 6000)
Operating System: Linux
Configured drivers:
S3: accelerated server for S3 graphics adaptors (Patchlevel 0)
mmio_928, s3_generic
```

The valid chipset names for this server are mmio_928 and s3_generic. The XF86_S3 man page describes these chipsets and which videocards use them. In the case of the #9 GXE 64 video card, mmio_928 is appropriate.

If you don't know which chipset to use, the X server can probe it for you. To do this, run the command

```
$ X -probeonly > /tmp/x.out 2>&1
```

if you use bash as your shell. If you use csh, try:

```
% X -probeonly &> /tmp/x.out
```

You should run this command while the system is unloaded, that is, while no other activity is occurring on the system. This command will also probe for your video card dot clocks (as seen below), and system load can throw off this calculation.

The output from the above (in /tmp/x.out should contain lines such as the following:

```
XFree86 Version 3.1 / X Window System
(protocol Version 11, revision 0, vendor release 6000)
Operating System: Linux
Configured drivers:
 S3: accelerated server for S3 graphics adaptors (Patchlevel 0)
 mmio_928, s3_generic
        ...
(—) S3: card type: 386/486 localbus
(—) S3: chipset:   864 rev. 0
(—) S3: chipset driver: mmio_928
```

Here, we see that the two valid chipsets for this server (in this case, XF86_S3) are mmio_928 and s3_generic. The server probed for and found a video card using the mmio_928 chipset.

In the Device section of the XF86Config file, add a Chipset line, containing the name of the chipset as determined above. For example,

```
Section "Device"
   # We already had    Identifier here...
   Identifier "#9 GXE 64"
   # Add this line:
   Chipset "mmio_928"
EndSection
```

Now we need to determine the driving clock frequencies used by the video card. A driving clock frequency, or dot clock, is simply a rate at which the video card can send pixels to the monitor. As we have seen, each monitor resolution has a dot clock associated with it. Now we need to determine which dot clocks are made available by the video card.

First you should look into the files (modeDB.txt, and so forth) mentioned above and see if your card's clocks are listed there. The dot clocks will usually be a list of 8 or 16 values, all of which are in MHz. For example, when looking at modeDB.txt we see an entry for the Cardinal ET4000 video board, which looks like this:

```
schip    ram    virtual   clocks   default-mode              flags
ET4000   1024   1024      768      25 28 38 36 40 45 32 0    "1024x768"
```

As we can see, the dot clocks for this card are 25, 28, 38, 36, 40, 45, 32, and 0 MHz.

In the Devices section of the XF86Config file, you should add a Clocks line containing the list of dot clocks for your card. For example, for the clocks above, we would add the line

```
Clocks 25 28 38 36 40 45        32 0
```

to the Devices section of the file, after Chipset. Note that the order of the clocks is important! Don't resort the list of clocks or remove duplicates.

If you cannot find the dot clocks associated with your card, the X server can probe for these as well. Using the X -probeonly command described above, the output should contain lines which look like the following:

```
(—) S3: clocks: 25.18 28.32 38.02 36.15 40.33 45.32 32.00 00.00
```

We could then add a Clocks line containing all of these values, as printed. You can use more than one Clocks line in XF86Config should all of the values (sometimes there are more than 8 clock values printed) not fit onto one line. Again, be sure to keep the list of clocks in order as they are printed.

Be sure that there is no Clocks line (or that it is commented out) in the Devices section of the file when using X -probeonly to probe for the clocks. If there is a Clocks line present, the server will not probe for the clocks—it will use the values given in XF86Config.

Note that some accelerated video boards use a programmable clock chip. (See the XF86_Accel man page for details; this generally applies to S3, AGX, and XGA-2 boards.) This chip essentially allows the X server to tell the card which dot clocks to use. If this is the case, then you may not find a list of dot clocks for the card in any of the above files. Or, the list of dot clocks printed when using X -probeonly will only contain one or two discrete clock values, with the rest being duplicates or zero.

For boards which use a programmable clock chip, you would use a ClockChip line, instead of a Clocks line, in your XF86Config file. ClockChip gives the name of the clock chip as used by the video card; the man pages for each server describe what these are. For example, in the file README.S3, we see that several S3-864 video cards use an "ICD2061A" clock chip, and that we should use the line

```
ClockChip "icd2061a"
```

instead of Clocks in the XF86Config file. As with Clocks, this line should go in the Devices section, after Chipset.

Similarly, some accelerated cards require you to specify the RAMDAC chip type in the XF86Config file, using a Ramdac line. The XF86_Accel man page describes this option. Usually, the X server will correctly probe for the RAMDAC.

Some video card types require you to specify several options in the Devices section of XF86Config. These options will be described in the man page for your server, as well as in the various files (such as README.cirrus or README.S3. These options are enabled using the Option line. For example, the #9 GXE 64 card requires two options:

```
Option "number_nine"
Option "dac_8_bit"
```

Usually, the X server will work without these options, but they are necessary to obtain the best performance. There are too many such options to list here, and they each depend on the particular video card being used. If you must use one of these options, fear not—the X server man pages and various files in /usr/X11R6/lib/X11/doc will tell you what they are.

So, when you're finished, you should end up with a Devices section which looks something like this:

```
Section "Device"
  # Device      section for the #9 GXE 64 only!
  Identifier "#9 GXE 64"
  Chipset "mmio_928"
  ClockChip "icd2061a"
  Option "number_nine"
  Option "dac_8_bit"
EndSection
```

Most video cards will require a Clocks line, instead of ClockChip, as described above. The above Device entry is only valid for a particular video card, the #9 GXE 64. It is given here only as an example.

There are other options that you can include in the Devices entry. Check the X server man pages for the gritty details, but the above should suffice for most systems.

6. Running XFree86

With your XF86Config file configured, you're ready to fire up the X server and give it a spin. First, be sure that /usr/X11R6/bin is on your path.

The command to start up XFree86 is

```
$ startx
```

This is a front-end to xinit (in case you're used to using xinit on other UNIX systems).

This command will start the X server and run the commands found in the file .xinitrc in your home directory. .xinitrc is just a shell script containing X clients to run. If this file does not exist, the system default /usr/X11R6/lib/X11/xinit/xinitrc will be used.

A standard .xinitrc file looks like this:

```
#!/bin/sh
xterm -fn 7x13bold -geometry 80x32+10+50      &
xterm -fn 9x15bold -geometry 80x34+30-10      &
oclock -geometry        70x70-7+7 &
xsetroot          -solid midnightblue &
exec twm
```

This script will start up two xterm clients, an oclock, and set the root window (background) color to midnightblue. It will then start up twm, the window manager. Note that twm is executed with the shell's exec statement; this causes the xinit process to be replaced with twm. Once the twm process exits, the X server will shut down. You can cause twm to exit by using the root menus: depress mouse button 1 on the desktop background—this will display a pop up menu which will allow you to Exit Twm.

Be sure that the last command in .xinitrc is started with exec, and that it is not placed into the background (no ampersand on the end of the line). Otherwise the X server will shut down as soon as it has started the clients in the .xinitrc file.

Alternately, you can exit X by pressing ctrl-alt-backspace in combination. This will kill the X server directly, exiting the window system.

The above is a very, very simple desktop configuration. Many wonderful programs and configurations are available with a bit of work on your .xiitrc file. For example, the fvwm window manager will provide a virual desktop, and you can customize colors, fonts, window sizes and postions, and so forth to your heart's content. Although the X Window System might appear to be simplistic at first, it is extremely powerful once you customize it for yourself.

If you are new to the X Window System environment, we strongly suggest picking up a book such as *The X Window System: A User's Guide*. Using and configuring X is far too in-depth to cover here. See the man pages for xterm, oclock, and twm for clues on getting started.

7. Running Into Trouble

Often, something will not be quite right when you initially fire up the X server. This is almost always caused by a problem in your XF86Config file. Usually, the monitor timing values are off, or the video card dot clocks set incorrectly. If your display seems to roll, or the edges are fuzzy, this is a clear indication that the monitor timing values or dot clocks are wrong. Also be sure that you are correctly specifying your video card chipset, as well as other options for the Device section of XF86Config. Be absolutely certain that you are using the right X server and that /usr/X11R6/bin/X is a symbolic link to this server.

If all else fails, try to start X "bare"; that is, use a command such as:

```
$ X > /tmp/x.out 2>&1
```

You can then kill the X server (using the ctrl-alt-backspace key combination) and examine the contents of /tmp/x.out. The X server will report any warnings or errors—for example, if your video card doesn't have a dot clock corresponding to a mode supported by your monitor.

The file VideoModes.doc included in the XFree86 distribution contains many hints for tweaking the values in your XF86Config file.

Remember that you can use ctrl-alt-numeric + and ctrl-alt-numeric to switch between the video modes listed on the Modes line of the Screen section of XF86Config. If the highest resolution mode doesn't look right, try switching to lower resolutions. This will let you know, at least, that those parts of your X configuration are working correctly.

Also, check the vertical and horizontal size/hold knobs on your monitor. In many cases it is necessary to adjust these when starting up X. For example, if the display seems to be shifted slightly to one side, you can usually correct this using the monitor controls.

The USENET newsgroup comp.windows.x.i386unix is devoted to discussions about XFree86, as is comp.os.linux.x. It might be a good idea to watch that newsgroup for postings relating to your video configuration—you might run across someone with the same problems as your own.

8. Copyright

This document is Copyright (c)1995 by Matt Welsh. This work may be reproduced and distributed in whole or in part, in either printed or electronic form, subject to the following conditions:

1. The copyright notice and this license notice must be preserved complete on all complete or partial copies.
2. Any translation or derivative work must be approved by the author in writing before distribution.
3. If you distribute the Work in part, instructions for obtaining a complete version (in printed or electonic form) must be included, and a means for obtaining a complete version provided.
4. Small portions may be reproduced as illustrations for reviews or quotes in other works without this permission notice if proper citation is given.

Exceptions to these rules may be granted for academic purposes, write to the author of the Work, and ask. These restrictions are here to protect the authors, not to restrict you as educators and learners.

APPENDIX F

Legacy Technologies: FTP & Gopher

Contrary to the impression one receives from the popular media, the Internet *did* exist before Tim Berners-Lee invented the World Wide Web. In fact, the first glimpse of the Internet's potential and utility came in 1991 with the development of Gopher.

Gopher

Gopher was the immediate predecessor of the Web in popularity and ease of use. It was developed at the University of Minnesota as a way of integrating their Campus-Wide Information System. In the Gopher data model, network resources are presented as a simple text menu. A menu entry is a short string of text, representing either the name of the resource or a short description of its content. The resources that Gopher menu presents can be either local to the server that's presenting the menu, or across the network.

The Gopher Protocol

The Gopher protocol is very simple; it was designed to be extremely lightweight so that even low-end microcomputers could be used as servers. Like HTTP, Gopher uses a file typing system that allows clients to execute helper applications for file types that they can't display. Also like HTTP, Gopher requires a new connection for every transaction. A sample Gopher session might go like this:

1. The client connects to a Gopher server A and requests a menu.
2. The server sends a list of menu items and their associated file types.
3. The user selects a menu item which is a link to an image file on Gopher server B.
4. The client connects to Gopher server B and requests the image file.
5. The server transmits the image file.
6. The client executes a helper application to display the image, if the client's computer supports graphics.

As you can see, this is very similar to the communication between an HTTP server and client. There are a few important differences though, that differentiate HTTP and Gopher:

- Gopher was not designed as a hypertextual system. There is no way (before the World Wide Web created the Gopher URL) to embed any sort of hyperlink inside of a Gopher document.
- Although any sort of data object may reside on a Gopher server, there is no way to integrate these objects into a single document or presentation.
- Although Gopher includes a file typing system, it uses a closed and unscalable design. The Web's use of MIME typing solves this problem.

- Although Gopher provides a simple interface to multiple sources of information, it's not flexible enough to provide a platform for interactive applications in the same way that the Web does.

Considerations & Commentary

As you can see, the Web includes all the functionality provided by Gopher; in fact, almost all Web browsers can access Gopher servers with ease. Yet, there is no service that Gopher provides that one can not as easily provide with the Web. With the success of Lynx, a text-mode browser for UNIX, MS-DOS, and VMS, there is no set of users for which there is a Gopher client but no WWW client. For these reasons, we strongly recommend not starting any new information service based on Gopher.

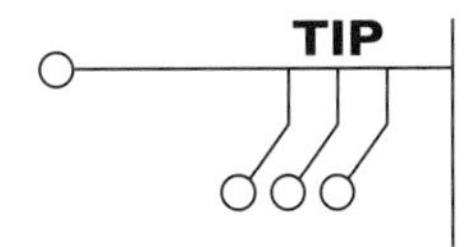

In our opinion, the University of Minnesota's decision to capitalize on business' use of their (previously free) server software contributed to Gopher's decline as an important Internet protocol. There is a complex symbiotic relationship between free and commercial software in the fledgling business of Internet information services, and it's very difficult to predict what business models will be successful.

In both the short and long run, starting a new Gopher server is a waste of time and resources. Gopher was a vital step in making information services accessible on the Internet, but in our opinion, its day is done. The time that you might spend maintaining your Gopher server for the few remaining users of that declining technology would be better spent taking full advantage of all the Web has to offer. Furthermore, once you begin to support a service like Gopher, it's difficult to stop; you have a tacit commitment to those few who use it. So be smart, don't start.

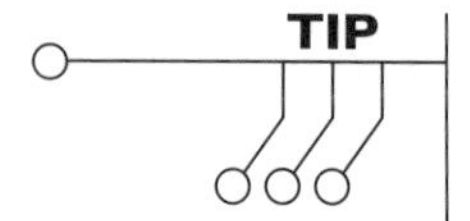

If you already have a Gopher server, don't despair. You need to gradually transfer your document and user base to the Web. Read the suggestions and documentation provided with GN, a WWW server that also acts as a Gopher server. There's a somewhat longer review of GN and its features in Chapter 3, "Setting Up the Server." You can read about it for yourself at: http://hopf.math.nwu.edu:70/.

Anonymous FTP

Although the development of easy-to-use services like Gopher and the World Wide Web made the Internet a household world, hundreds of thousands of people used anonymous FTP to trade software and information over the Net for many years before the Web was even a glimmer in Tim's eye.

Introduction to FTP

FTP stands for File Transfer Protocol, and it is one of oldest protocols used on the Internet. At one time, FTP was the secret to all information transfer on the Net; hosts even traded e-mail with FTP. Although the FTP protocol has some things in common with HTTP, it's much more complex; the FTP standard defines almost forty commands.

If the FTP server is enabled on your system, users with valid accounts there can connect and transfer files to and from the machine. The FTP daemon authenticates the user by asking for their normal login password; users may only retrieve files for which their UID has read permission and may only upload files into directories for which their UID has write permission.

In addition to this generally useful capability, the FTP server also allows the system administrator to create an *anonymous FTP* archive. Anonymous FTP allows any user to log into FTP with the standard *ftp* or *anonymous* usernames; although it's customary to type one's e-mail address when prompted for a password, this isn't usually required by most servers.

When an anonymous FTP user logs in to the FTP server, the server gives them access to a special, secured directory from which they may download files. The secure area is separated from the rest of the filesystem with UNIX system call chroot(). This system call designates some directory as a virtual root directory for the invoking process. For that process, the specified directory looks like the system root directory: /. Once the FTP server invokes chroot() it can not access any data or executables above the virtual root directory. You can build a publicly available archive within this directory with some assurance that files outside of the FTP directory hierarchy is safe and secure from anonymous FTP users.

Despite the soaring popularity of HTTP and the Web in general, FTP is still a very important protocol on the Net. In fact, more bytes and packets are transferred with FTP then with any other protocol (but the difference between FTP and HTTP shrinks every day). Still, FTP offers few advantages over the Web in information distribution. It's main lead is in its traditional use for transferring software packages for several reasons:

- Inertia. There are thousands of anonymous FTP archives which contain millions of software packages for computers of every description. Transforming these sites into World Wide Web sites would require an incredible amount of labor from archive administrators, who are usually volunteers.
- Uploads. Currently the Web offers no convenient way for a user to upload a file to an archive. This will change in HTML v3.0 (see Chapter 13, "Future Directions").
- Tools. Over the years, archive administrators have developed many tools, such as mirror and Archie that make administering an FTP archive fairly easy. Largely, these tools have yet to be developed for the Web.
- In addition, many people prefer to use FTP to transfer software, although FTP is no more efficient for this purpose than HTTP. If your site hosts many software packages, you should offer them by anonymous FTP, as well as on your Web site.

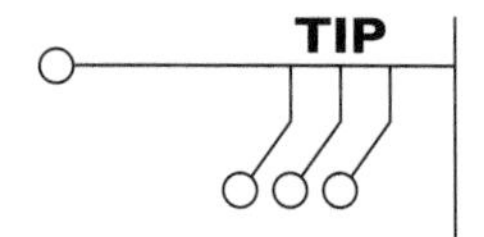

You can watch the main protocols fight it out for bandwidth on the NSFnet Internet backbone at the NSFnet statistics page: http://www.cc.gatech.edu/gvu/stats/NSF/merit.html.

Configuring Anonymous FTP

It's fairly easy to add anonymous FTP to your system, but there are a few considerations which you must take into account to secure your anonymous FTP server.

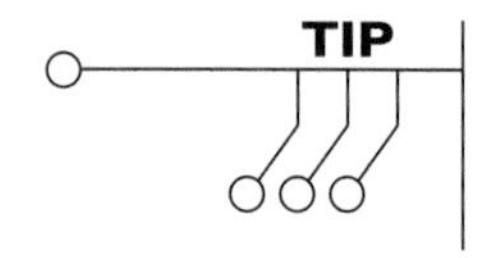

Before you start running an anonymous FTP server, you should make sure that the version of the FTP daemon you're running has no known security problems. You can find information about known security problems in various FTP daemons in these CERT advisories:

- *ftp://ftp.cert.org/pub/cert_advisories/CA-93:06.wuarchive.ftpd.vulnerability*
- *ftp://ftp.cert.org/pub/cert_advisories/CA-92:09.AIX.anonymous.ftp.vulnerability*
- *ftp://ftp.cert.org/pub/cert_advisories/CA-88:01.ftpd.hole*

You should also read CERT's tips on anonymous FTP and security; it's available at ftp://ftp.cert.org/pub/tech_tips/anonymous_ftp.

The FTP User

The first step to configuring your system for anonymous FTP is to make sure that the ftp account exists. If it doesn't, create the account, with an entry in /etc/passwd (unless you're using shadow passwords or NIS, in which case, you should consult your manual) like this:

```
ftp:*:2332:55:Anonymous FTP:/public/ftp:
```

Note that this account entry differs from the average UNIX /etc/passwd record. The asterisk (*) in the password field disables non-FTP logins for programs that authenticate by password, and the empty shell field prevents logins by trusted hosts (see Chapter 4, "System Security"). These two measures ensure that the ftp user will only be used by the FTP server.

The FTP Directory

As explained earlier in the section, the security of anonymous FTP largely depends on the chroot() system call, which cuts off anonymous users from files you don't want them to access. You need to create a directory that will be the home directory of the ftp user, and the top directory for the anonymous FTP archive. In the example /etc/passwd entry this directory is /public/ftp.

You should put some thought into selecting the proper filesystem for this directory in order to make sure you'll have sufficient disk space for your FTP archive. Since the chroot() call cuts off all connections between the archive directory and directories outside of it, it can be difficult to add additional disk space to an archive.

In general, the only way to do so is to mount additional filesystems under the FTP directory. You can't merely symbolically link directories from other filesystems into your FTP archive directory; after the chroot() call is executed, the server will be unable to access the resources above the archive's top directory.

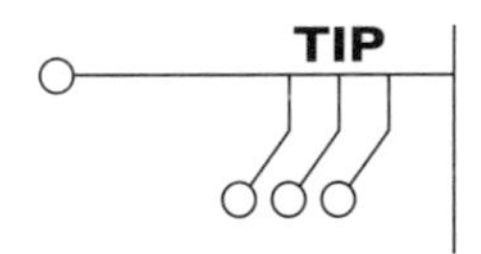

You may want to share data between your Web server and anonymous FTP. If you do, remember that all files that you wish available by anonymous FTP must actually be beneath the ftp home directory—symbolic links to files above this are "cut off" from their targets by the chroot() call. So, any data that you wish to share between the two servers must reside in the FTP hierarchy. You can access directories within the hierarchy through HTTP by symbolically linking them into Web server directories or by mapping them to specific URLs with the Alias directive (see Chapter 3, "Setting Up the Server").

Depending on the operating system, there are other solutions. Some modern UNIX's support the concept of a *loopback* filesystem, which mounts a directory, rather than a device, from one filesystem to another. If your OS allows this, you can loopback mount additional space into your archive directory. Alternatively, many recent OS's will allow you to combine multiple partitions on different disks into a single *meta-disk*, to which you can add additional space as needed.

Although these options provide a solution for some operating systems, both of them can make your site more difficult to administer if not used wisely. It's better to start your FTP archive on a file system with sufficient space from the beginning.

Once you've found a good location, create the FTP directory. This directory must be owned by root, and a group to which the ftp user does not belong.

```
# mkdir /public/ftp
# chown root /public/ftp
# chgrp bin /public/ftp
# chmod 755 /public/ftp
```

Next, you'll need to create the directories that go within the FTP directory: bin, etc and pub. Each of these has a specific purpose in the FTP hierarchy:

- bin The home of auxiliary programs that the server runs on your behalf.
- etc Location of the tables that ftpd and its support programs need.
- pub All publicly available files in the archive go inside this directory.

All of these directories should be owned by root, with a group other than the one that ftp belongs to. When you're done, the directories should look something like this:

```
drwxr-xr-x 7    root bin 512   Apr 5    15:17 ./
drwxr-xr-x 25   root bin 512   Jul 13   11:30 ../
drwxr-x--x 2    root bin 512   Aug 28   15:43 bin/
drwxr-xr-x 2    root bin 512   Jun 22   16:23 etc/
drwxr-xr-x 10   root bin 512   Jan 14   10:54 pub/
```

These directories re-create a basic operating environment for the chroot()'ed FTP server. For security's sake, you should note that

- All directories are owned by root.
- All directories have a different group than the ftp user.
- None of the directories are world-writable.
- The bin directory is only executable (searchable) by the world.

In general, no files or directories inside the anonymous FTP area should be owned by the user ftp. Anonymous FTP users can manipulate files with this ownership.

Binaries & Libraries

The FTP server needs a copy of the ls command in order to generate a directory listing. Make a copy of the system ls command for the FTP directory:

```
# cp /bin/ls /public/ftp/bin
# chown root /public/ftp/bin/ls
# chgrp bin /public/ftp/bin/ls
# chmod 111 /public/ftp/bin/ls
```

These commands also ensure that the copy has the proper ownership, and can't be read or written by anyone. If the binaries on your system are statically linked, you can go on to the next section.

If you're on a system which uses dynamic linking, such as SunOS, Solaris or Linux, you'll also need to make copies of the dynamic libraries that ls needs in order to run, because the server won't have access to the system copies of these libraries after it calls chroot().

You can figure out which libraries you need for ls by using the ldd command:

```
$ ldd /bin/ls
```

This command prints a list of the dynamic libraries upon which a binary is dependent. In addition, most dynamic linking systems require a copy of ld.so, the linking shared library.

Once you've found the necessary libraries, you need to create directories for them within the FTP directory, such as ~ftp/lib and ~ftp/usr/lib for example. Follow the rules given for the other directories above.

Most versions of UNIX that use dynamic libraries require the special /dev/zero device to link. You should create a private FTP copy of this file. To do so, you'll need to know the major and minor number for the zero device. To find out, get a long listing for /dev/zero:

```
# ls -l /dev/zero
crw-r--r-- 1 root  bin  1, 5 Nov 30 1993 /dev/zero
```

The comma-separated numbers before the modification date are the major and minor numbers respectively. Make the directory ~ftp/dev and create a new zero device like this:

```
# mknod /public/ftp/dev/zero c 1 5
```

Replace 1 and 5 with the appropriate numbers for your OS. Once you've created the file, make sure that the device and the directory it's in are both owned by root and are not world-writable.

Consult the ftpd manual page for an exhaustive list of device files and shared libraries required for anonymous FTP on your system.

passwd & group

You need to make a mock-up copy of the passwd and group files to put inside ~ftp/etc. These files aren't needed for authentication, but to allow ls to print the owner and group information in directory listings. *Do not* put a copy of your system's actual password and group files there. This would allow intruders to access your system's password information (see Chapter 4, "System Security," for more information about password security and password cracking).

Your mock-up copy of /etc/passwd should contain entries for root and ftp, both with an asterisk (*) in the password field. You may also include entries for any users who are maintaining files within the FTP area. This isn't necessary, but it allows directory listings to display file ownership by name, rather than by UID. You should replace the encrypted password in these entries with an asterisk as well.

For the mock-up copy of /etc/group, you need only include entries for groups which appear in the FTP archive. For example, the bin group that we used above should be there. For group entries, delete the group's membership information and be sure there is an asterisk in the encrypted password field.

Be sure that the ~ftp/etc/passwd and ~ftp/etc/group files are owned by root and are not world-writable.

Running the Server

On all present-day UNIX systems, the FTP server is run from inetd (you can find a full description of inetd in Chapter 4, "System Security"). Unless you've disabled it, the FTP server is almost certainly already configured to run in /etc/inetd.conf, but you should at least check over the entry.

For proper operation, there should be two FTP-related entries in /etc/services (or in the NIS server's services map if you use NIS):

```
ftp-data    20/tcp
ftp         21/tcp
```

Make sure that both of these are defined.

In /etc/inetd.conf, you should find an entry for FTP similar to this one:

```
ftp stream tcp nowait root /usr/sbin/in.ftpd ftpd
```

On your system, /usr/sbin/in.ftpd will be replaced by the actual location of the FTP daemon. There are several options you can use with ftpd, by adding them at the end of its inetd.conf entry:

- -d Send debugging information to syslogd, the logging daemon (see Chapter 4, "System Security," for more information about syslogd)
- -l Log all FTP sessions to syslogd. This is very verbose.
- -t Sets a time-out (in seconds)—the amount of time an FTP client may remain idle before the server automatically disconnects. The default is 15 minutes (900 seconds).

Once you've configured the FTP entry in /etc/inetd.conf as you want it, you need to send a *hangup* signal to inetd, which forces it to re-read its configuration file. On a System-5 based system, use the following commands:

```
# ps -ef | grep inetd
root    125     1     80    00:01:10   ?       3:04   /usr/sbin/inetd -s
root    1998    1978  12    09:47:38   pts/11  0:00   grep inetd
# kill -HUP 125
```

On a BSD based system, use these instead:

```
# ps aux | grep inetd
root   48      0.0  0.1   72    76    con S  Apr 18  0:05  /usr/sbin/inetd
root   19219   0.0  0.4   157   256   ppa S  10:27   0:00  grep inetd
# kill -HUP 48
```

Once you've configured inetd, anonymous FTP should be ready.

Testing the Server

Once you think you've correctly configured anonymous FTP, you should test the server next. To test the server, connect and login as ftp or anonymous:

```
ftp localhost
220 ftp.shoop.com FTP server ready.
Name (localhost:jem): ftp
331 Guest login ok, send ident as password.
Password:
230 Guest login ok, access restrictions apply.
ftp> dir
200 PORT command successful.
150 Opening ASCII mode data connection for /bin/ls.
total 12
drwxr-xr-x 9    root  bin   512 Feb 26    18:25 .
drwxr-xr-x 9    root  bin   512 Feb 26    18:25 ..
drwxr-x--x 2    root  bin   512 Jan 23    19:30 bin
dr-xr-xr-x 2    root  bin   512 May 26    1994 dev
dr-xr-xr-x 2    root  bin   512 May 26    1994 etc
drwxr-xr-x 17   root  bin   512 Feb 13    00:37 pub
drw-r-xr-x 3    root  bin   512 Feb 7     15:53 usr
226 Transfer complete.
399 bytes received in 0.12 seconds (3 Kbytes/s)
ftp> cd ..
250 CWD command successful.
ftp> pwd
257 "/" is current directory.
ftp>
```

This example illustrates a successful test of our anonymous FTP server. We successfully get a directory listing, which shows that the server works and that we've correctly installed ls and all the necessary shared libraries. Next we check to make sure that the chroot() was successful and that anonymous users can't change directories above the FTP root directory; again, all is fine. The next step is to add some content to the archive and to try transferring them.

That's an example of a successful test. An unsuccessful test might look like this:

```
$ ftp localhost
ftp: connect: Connection refused
ftp>
```

The "Connection refused" message means that there's no server process listening for connections on the FTP port. This indicates that inetd is misconfigured. This is a list of things to check, if FTP isn't accepting connections:

- Make sure that there is an ftp entry in /etc/services.
- If you use NIS, make sure that the services map has been pushed.
- Check that you've given the correct path to the ftp daemon in /etc/inetd.conf.
- Verify that the ftp entry in /etc/passwd is correct.
- If you use NIS, make sure the passwd map has been pushed.

References

Apple Computer, Inc. "Quicktime Continuum," http://quicktime.apple.com/.

Bahneman, Liem. "tkHTML—tcl/tk HTML Editor Information," http://www.infosystems.com/tkHTML/tkHTML.html.

Behlendorf, Brian and Mark Pesce. "Virtual Reality Modeling Language (VRML) Forum," http://vrml.wired.com.

Boutell, Thomas. "Portable Network Graphics Specification," http://sunsite.unc.edu/boutell/png.html.

Bowers, Neil. "Weblint" home page, http://www.khoros.unm.edu/staff/neilb/weblint.html.

Bunn, Jean. "MBONE (Multicast Backbone)," http://www.unige.ch/seinf/mbone.html.

Bush, Vannevar. "As We May Think," *The Atlantic Monthly* (July) 1945.

Center for Innovative Computer Applications. "CICA Graphics 3D Object File Formats," http://www.cica.indiana.edu/graphics/3D.objects.html.

Chen, Raymond. "WP 5.1 to HTML converter (version 2.3)," ftp://journal.biology.carleton.ca/pub/software/wp2x.html.

Cheswick, William R. and Steven M. Bellovin. *Firewalls and Internet Security: Repelling the Wily Hacker*, Reading, MA: Addison-Wesley, 1994.

Churchyard, Henry. "htmlchek HTML syntax and cross-reference checker version 4.1," http://uts.cc.utexas.edu/~churchh/htmlchekprog.html.

CU-SeeMe Development Team. "The CU-SeeMe Project," http://cu-seeme.cornell.edu.

Curry, David A. *UNIX System Security*, Reading, MA: Addison-Wesley, 1992.

CyberCash, Inc. "CyberCash" home page, http://www.cybercash.com/index.html.

Digicash bv. "Digicash" home page, Amsterdam, The Netherlands, http://www.digicash.com/index.html.

Garfinkel, Simson and Gene Spafford. *Practical Unix Security*, Sebastopol: O'Reilly & Associates, 1991.

Golub, Seth. "Text to HTML Converter," http://www.cs.wustl.edu/~seth/txt2html/index.html.

Fielding, Roy T. "IETF—Hypertext Transfer Protocol (HTTP) Working Group," http://www.ics.uci.edu/pub/ietf/http/index.html.

———. "Maintaining Distributed Hypertext Infostructures: Welcome to MOMspider's Web," *Computer Networks and ISDM Systems* 27(2), November 1994.

Filippini, Luigi. "MPEG Moving Pictures Expert Group FAQ," http://www.crs4.it/~luigi/MPEG/.

First Virtual Holdings, Inc. "First Virtual: General Information," http://www.fv.com/info/index.html.

Franks, John. "WN—A Server for the HTTP," http://hopf.math.nwu.edu/.

Geometry Center (UMN). "The WebOOGL" home page, http://www.geom.umn.edu/software/weboogl/welcome.html.

Gibbs, Simon. "Index to Multimedia Information Sources," http://viswiz.gmd.de/MultimediaInfo/.

Goldman, Jonny. "fwais.pl," http://waisqvarsa.er.usgs.gov/public/fwais.pl.

Grimm, Steven. "Un-CGI version 1.3," http://www.hyperion.com/~koreth/uncgi.html.

Hector, Chris. "rtftohtml User's Guide," http://ftp.cray.com/src/WWWstuff/RTF/Users_Guide_ToC.html.

HomeCom Communications. "Pointers to Pointers," http://www.homecom.com/global/pointers.html.

HTTP Working Group, Internet Engineering Task Force. "Hypertext Transfer Protocol—HTTP/1.0," http://www.w3.org/hypertext/WWW/Protocols/HTTP1.0/draft-ieft-http-spec.html.

Hylton, Jeremy. "Quark to HTML," http://the-tech.mit.edu/~jeremy/qt2www.html.

Internet Security Systems. "Security FAQ," http://iss.net:80/~iss/faq.html.

Internet Town Hall. "Radio on the Internet," http://town.hall.org/radio/index.html.

Kumar, Vinay. "MBONE Information Web," http://www.eit.com/techinfo/mbone/mbone.html.

Lane, Tom. "JPEG image compression FAQ Part I," ftp://rtfm.mit.edu/pub/usenet-by-group/comp.graphics/JPEG_image_compression_FAQ%2C_part_1_2.

Lee, Brian Patrick. "Inlined Images FAQ 8.1b," http://www.uwtc.washington.edu/Computing/WWW/InlinedImagesFAQ0.8.1b.html.

Luotonen, Ari, Henrik Frystyk and Tim Berners-Lee. "CERN HTTP Server Status," http://www.w3.org/hypertext/WWW/Daemon/Status.html.

Lynch, Patrick J. "Yale C/AIM WWW Style Manual," http://info.ed.yale.edu/caim/StyleManual_Top.HTML.

Macedonia, Michael R. and Donald P. Brutzman. "MBONE Provides Audio and Video Across the Internet," ftp://taurus.cs.nps.navy.mil/pub/mbmg/mbone.html.

Mosedale, Dan. "Dan's Quick and Dirty Guide to Getting Connected to the MBONE," http://www.eit.com:80/techinfo/mbone/how-to-join.html.

Mueller, Frank. "IP Videoconferencing over IP for Linux," http://www.hrz.uni-giessen.de/~l018/nig.html.

Mumpower, Eric. "Transparent Colors in GIF89a," http://www.mit.edu:8001/people/nocturne/transparent.html.

Nemeth, Evi, Garth Snyder, Scott Seebass and Trent R. Hein. *Unix System Administration Handbook*, Englewood Cliffs: Prentice Hall, 1995.

Netscape Communications Corporation. "How to Create High-Impact Documents," http://www.netscape.com/home/services_docs/impact_docs/creating-high-impact-docs.html.

———. "Netscape Navigator Extensions to HTML," http://www.netscape.com/home/services_docs/html-extensions.html.

———. "Tables in Netscape 1.1," http://home.netscape.com/assist/net_sites/tables.html.

Pesce, Mark. "VRML*Tech: The Virtual Reality Modeling Language Technical Forum," http://www.eit.com/vrml/.

Raggett, Dave. "Hypertext Markup Language Specification Version 3.0," http://www.hpl.hp.co.uk/people/dsr/html3/CoverPage.html.

Raggett, Dave, Lie W. Hakon, Henrik Frystyk, and Phill Hallam-Baker. "Welcome to Arena," http://www.w3.org/hypertext/WWW/Arena/index.html.

Reckhard, Tobias. "alt.binaries.sounds.mods FAQ," http://www.cis.ohio-state.edu/hypertext/faq/usenet/mod-faq/top.html.

Rettinger, Leigh Anne. "Desktop Videoconferencing Products," http://www2.ncsu.edu/eos/service/ece/project/succeed_info/dtvc_survey/products.html.

Saunders, Tony. "Plexus HTTP," http://www.bsdi.com/server/doc/plexus.html.

———. "Why Validate Your HTML," http://www.earth.com/bad-style/why-validate.html.

Sattler, Michael. "CU-SeeMe Reflector FAQ," http://www.indstate.edu/msattler/sci-tech/comp/CU-SeeMe/faq-reflectors.html.

Silicon Graphics, Inc. "WebSpace" home page, http://www.sgi.com/Products/WebFORCE/WebSpace/.

SingNet WWW Team. "OneWorld/Singnet WWW & HTML Developer's Jumpstation - ver 2.0," http://oneworld.wa.com/htmldev/devpage/dev-page.html.

Software Development Group, National Center for Supercomputing Applications. "A Beginner's Guide to HTML," http://www.ncsa.uiuc.edu/demoweb/html-primer.html.

———. "The Common Gateway Interface," http://hoohoo.ncsa.uiuc.edu/cgi/overview.html.

———. "HTML Quick Reference," http://www.ncsa.uiuc.edu/General/Internet/WWW/HTMLQuickRef.html.

———. "Mailcap Files," http://www.ncsa.uiuc.edu/SDG/Software/Mosaic/Docs/mailcap.html.

———. "Mosaic for X version 2.0 Fill-Out Form Support," http://www.ncsa.uiuc.edu/SDG/Software/Mosaic/Docs/fill-out-forms/overview.html.

———. "NCSA httpd Overview," http://hoohoo.ncsa.uiuc.edu/docs/.

———. "NCSA Imagemap Tutorial," http://hoohoo.ncsa.uiuc.edu/docs/tutorials/imagemapping.html.

———. "NCSA Mosaic(tm) Tables Tutorial," http://www.ncsa.uiuc.edu/SDG/Software/Mosaic/Tables/tutorial.html.

———. "Status Codes in HTTP," http://www.w3.org/hypertext/WWW/Protocols/HTTP/HTRESP.html.

Spero, Simon. "HTTP-NG Architectural Overview," http://www.w3.org/hypertext/WWW/Protocols/HTTP-NG/http-ng-arch.html.

Sun Microsystems Inc. "HotJava" home page, http://java.sun.com/.

Tranter, Jeff. "The Linux Sound HOWTO," http://sunsite.unc.edu/mdw/HOWTO/Sound-HOWTO.html.

Trusted Information Systems. "Firewall Papers," http://ftp.tis.com/Home/NetworkSecurity/Firewalls/Firewalls.html.

van Hoesel, Franz. "The Expo Story," http://rugmd4.chem.rug.nl/hoesel/expo/expo.story.html.

van Rossum, Guido. "The CWI Audio File Formats Guide," http://cuiwww.unige.ch/OSG/AudioFormats/.

Welsh, Matt and Lar Kaufman. *Running Linux*, Sebastopol: O'Reilly & Associates, 1995.

Withagen, Heini. "The MIDI" home page, http://www.eeb.ele.tue.nl/midi/index.html.

WXYC. "WXYC," http://sunsite.unc.edu/wxyc.

Xie, George G. H. "Anchor Checker," http://www.ugrad.cs.ubc.ca/spider/q7f192/branch/checker.html.

Yahoo. "Yahoo—Computers:Multimedia:MBONE," http://www.yahoo.com/Computers/Multimedia/MBONE/

Index

A

B

C

D

E

F

G

H

I

J

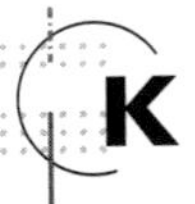

K

L

M

N

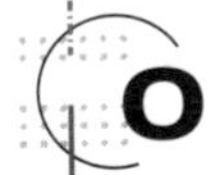

O

P

Q

R

S

T

U

V

W

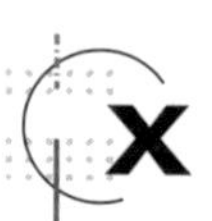

Colophon

The Web Server Book was produced on a Power Mac 8100/80. Page proofs were printed on a Hewlett Packard LaserJet 4M Plus.

PageMaker 5.0 was used for all layout. Body copy is Palatino, heads are Bembo.

Internet Resources

PLUG INTO THE NET!

Internet E-Mail Quick Tour

$14.00, 152 pages, illustrated

Whether it's the Internet or an online service, most people use their connections primarily for electronic messaging. This all-in-one guide to getting it right includes tips on software, security, style and Netiquette. Also included: how to obtain an e-mail account, useful addresses, interesting mailing lists and more!

Internet Virtual Worlds Quick Tour

$14.00, 224 pages, illustrated

Learn to locate and master real-time interactive communication forums and games by participating in the virtual worlds of MUD (Multi-User Dimension) and MOO (MUD Object-Oriented). *Internet Virtual Worlds Quick Tour* introduces users to the basic functions by defining different categories (individual, interactive and both) and detailing standard protocols. Also revealed is the insider's lexicon of these mysterious cyberworlds.

Internet Chat Quick Tour

$14.00, 200 pages, illustrated

The first eyewitness reports of the USSR's demise came not from radio but the Internet! Discover how worldwide chat networks are changing the way we communicate, with live help forums, discussion groups, performing arts and more. An inside look at chat software includes sources, how-to's and tips on locating chat servers.

Looking Good with QuarkXPress
With CD-ROM!
For Versions through 3.3
Annotated Color Gallery
The Designer's Companion for Mac & Windows
Joe Grossmann
LOOKING GOOD IN PRINT
A Guide to Basic Design for Desktop Publishing
How to Produce Attractive, Effective Newsletters Advertisements Brochures Manuals Correspondence
third edition
Roger C. Parker
The VISUAL GUIDE To
VISUAL BASIC 4.0 FOR WINDOWS
The Illustrated, Plain-English Encyclopedia to the Windows Programming Language
NEW! WITH DISK!
Through Version 4.0
Richard Mansfield
VENTANA PRESS